RICHMOND F.C.

"THE TIGERS"

A PROUD HISTORY OF A GREAT CLUB

AS TOLD BY THOSE WHO MADE IT HAPPEN

Tigers of the 1960s learn their new club song.
Clockwise from top left: Neville Crowe, Kevin Smith,
Mike Perry, John Ronaldson, Dick Clay, Owen Madigan.

RICHMOND F.C.

"THE TIGERS"

A PROUD HISTORY OF A GREAT CLUB

AS TOLD BY THOSE WHO MADE IT HAPPEN

UPDATED AND REVISED EDITION

INTERVIEWS BY RHETT BARTLETT

HISTORICAL ESSAYS BY TREVOR RUDDELL

slattery MEDIA GROUP

visit *slatterymedia.com*

The Slattery Media Group
Level 39 / 385 Bourke Street
Melbourne VIC 3000
Visit slatterymedia.com

First published by GSP Books, 2007
Second edition 2012
Third edition 2019

Other Images: AFL Photos, Richmond Football Club Museum, Richmond Football Club, Rhett Bartlett, Roland Weeks, MCC Museum, Michael Roberts, Brian Davie, Jan Richmond, Barry Richardson, Matthew Richardson.

FRONT COVER Roger Dean, captain of Richmond's 1969 Premiership team, wore the lace up guernsey on occasions.
BACK COVER Richmond greats: (L-R) Jack Titus, Jack Dyer, Kevin Bartlett and Francis Bourke, Dustin Martin and Trent Cotchin.

Group Publisher: Geoff Slattery
Art Director: Kate Slattery
2007 edition designed by Andrew Hutchison, updated in 2018 by Kate Slattery
Authors: Rhett Bartlett (interviews) and Trevor Ruddell (historical essays)
Statistics: Col Hutchinson and Cameron Sinclair
VFA Player list: Rhett Bartlett

A catalogue record for this book is available from the National Library of Australia

Printed in China by Everbest Printing Investment Ltd.

Eat 'em alive, Tigers

Richmond had won its first premiership and we were celebrating. There he stood, a crayfish in each hand, ruckman Barney Herbert, rampant, on the pedestal of Richmond Mayor G.G.Bennett's statue with a background relief of the Richmond Town Hall.

Barney was yelling: 'What did we do to them?!'

'Eat em Alive!!' roared the mob, and Barney waved the crays again and again.

VIC THORP, PREMIERSHIP PLAYER, 1920-21

Dustin Martin's 2017 season was a once-in-a-lifetime performance. He became the first player to win the Brownlow Medal and Norm Smith Medal in the same season. Added to that was his second Jack Dyer Medal, the AFLPA's MVP, and a host of media awards; and, of course, a Premiership Medallion!

RICHMOND F.C.

"THE TIGERS"

FEATURES

PLAYERS & OFFICIALS

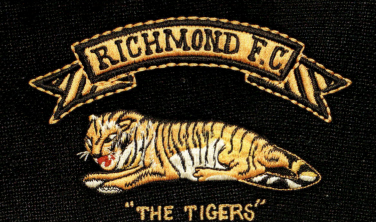

INTRODUCTION

A REMARKABLE JOURNEY

BY RHETT BARTLETT

It has been 18 years since my journey begun. With an analogue dictaphone (now since retired) in hand and my car full of petrol (the car since retired, too) I drove off on September 30, 2000, to conduct my first interview.

Joe Murdoch looked confused. The then 92-year-old, who had played in two Richmond premierships in the 1930s, was perhaps expecting someone much older. But he got me who, at 21 years of age, had travelled up to Castlemaine, Old Joe had agreed to have all facets of his Richmond career recorded. More importantly, about certain events of his football life that still resonated, most notably the Gordon Coventry incident. And that's how this book began.

By 2007, with the first print of this book I had recorded some 65 interviews. By 2019, it has grown to more than 120. The idea was born from Lawrence S. Ritter's remarkable baseball publication *The Glory of their Times*. Ritter travelled the breadth of America in the 1960s, speaking to old baseballers, some of whose careers dated back to the 1880s. What he collected and recorded was immeasurable. And it had me thinking about the history of Richmond F.C., and how the first-hand accounts of many players before the 1960s were gone or at least fading out of reach of the supporters.

Some interviewees lasted 30 minutes; others, like Sid Dockendorff, went six hours across three sessions. The last interview ended with a powerful lamp shining on my face so the ailing Sid could make out who he was speaking to.

He was, after all, 94 at the time.

The interviews were conducted in family rooms and dining rooms, on balconies and couches; in Traralgon, Castlemaine, St Kilda, Woodend and Carlton; in weight rooms, cafés, at businesses, over the phone and at the football club museum. Once the interviews were completed, the participant's answers were collaborated to create their oral history. Only slight editing was required to ensure that relevant topics and opinion were coupled together.

Across 18 years of interviews, many memories stay in my mind.

The 'Gentle Giant', Roy Wright, driving up from Duck Arm in Gippsland in the smallest car imaginable, and dropping by my father's house for the interview on his way to see his dying friend Doug Heywood. They would pass away within four days of each other in mid-2002.

Or heading to Castlemaine, losing my way, and asking directions at the local petrol station. The attendant didn't know the whereabouts of the street I was looking for. "Joe Murdoch?" I asked. He simply pointed north: "Drive two more blocks and turn right at the roundabout."

Bob Wiggins finally agreed to be interviewed after numerous requests over the course of a year; he then explained to me before the interview that he had cancer, and was dying. His last words to me as I left will remain with me forever, "Thank you for making me forget about the worries in my life." He lost his battle six months later.

Jack Malcomson, who penned the Richmond theme song, hummed and played the trumpet part in his rendition of Tigerland. Polly Perkins sang for me the ditties he would sing for the players some 60 years earlier. And Jack Watson emotionally recalled the last time he saw Bill Morris alive.

Interviewing Neville Crowe at the club had a personal feel for both of us. He talked of the drama of the dismissal of Kevin Bartlett, as coach. The appearance of us both in the Richmond administration building raised a few eyebrows.

I learnt many things from this journey. Everyone has a Jack Dyer story, for instance. And each person in some way has been saddened by football as much as enlivened by it, even if it is simply mourning the

Roy Wright, a favourite interviewee, proudly displays his medals – including two Brownlows.

passing of their career, or teammates they cherished in a special bond. Finally, I have found that football makes it easier for generations to talk to each other.

Unfortunately, some former players passed away before I could interview them. Mike Patterson, Geoff Strang, Terry Smith, Denis Collins, Brian "Whale" Roberts and Peter Welsh all left this world far too early.

Thankfully, I was able to record the memories of Des Rowe, Roy Wright, Sid Dockendorff, Joe Murdoch, George McHutchison, Maurie O'Connell, Len Ablett, Arthur Barr-Kemp, Frank Bourke Snr, Allan Cooke, Polly Perkins, Frank Hughes Jnr, Max Oppy, Frank Drum, Ray Stokes, Jack Turner, "Bull" Richardson, Bill Roach, Kevin Betson, Jack Watson, Neville Crowe, Tom Hafey, Bill Barrot, Bill Williams and Maurice Rioli before they passed away.

A publication of this size is made up of the generosity of the sum of those who are in it. And below is a list of those who were very generous in supplying time to ensure this book reached the standard I had envisioned.

I am grateful for the support of publisher Geoff Slattery, for his decision that there was value in the interviews I had done, and that the transcript of the Des Rowe chapter was strong enough to warrant a book. As well, the contribution of all the editors for their knowledge, advice and understanding for a budding author was immeasurable.

With more than 120,000 words transcribed, the onus of checking facts and grammar fell to several people – my thanks goes out to Ron Reiffel, Bill Meaklim and Kevan Carroll.

The Richmond Football Club Museum, especially curator Roland Weeks, was most supportive in allowing the inclusion of its material. Equally, the club's Historical Group, provided unlimited assistance and was the place to turn to for my endless questions.

Trevor Ruddell and the staff at the MCC provided many illuminating chapters and photographs for the book. Trevor, a fellow historical group member, wrote the excellent "era-setting" chapters in this book – his contribution is therefore significant in helping the book come together.

The AFL, in particular Col Hutchison, assisted with statistical data. And at News Limited, the help of Vicki Ritchie and her staff was also appreciated.

As well, to my close friends, work colleagues, my former English teacher Dan Hartley, former Richmond VFA player Alexander Salton and those who have offered support and advice, I am forever thankful.

Of course, to every player who allowed me to invade their privacy for a few hours, and their respective wives and families for providing endless conversation and cups of tea, thank you.

A publication of more than 18 years required the love of my dear parents, Kevin and Denise Bartlett, and my sisters Sharna, Cara and Breanna.

My passion for football history is as strong as ever. I will continue to interview former players about their memories of Tigerland. Our history must not be lost.

RHETT BARTLETT, DECEMBER 2018

Place of his own

Jack "Skinny" Titus, seen preparing a placekick, owns a unique slice of Tiger history. The all-time leading Richmond goalkicker was the first Richmond player to kick a century in a season; he compiled 970 goals, and set a then-record of 202 consecutive games, between 1926-43.

A true Tiger

Kevin O'Neill, a member of the famous Bolger-Sheahan-O'Neill backline of the 1930s, clears from defence against the Saints in Round 1, 1936 (Richmond won by one point). O'Neill played in the 1932 and '34 premierships sides, and two losing Grand Finals. His father, Ed, played for Richmond in 1900, when the club was still in the VFA.

7

Enduring memory

Richmond full-back Ron Durham kicks out, round 15, 1947. Club icon Tommy Hafey recalls that, at 12 years of age, he watched the graceful Tiger defender play in the 1943 Grand Final: "Ron Durham for Richmond, oh, a star! ... each one of his kicks were big drop kicks going right to the wing nearly every time."

Captain's last call

Jack Dyer is chaired from Punt Rd after his last game: round 19, 1949. He kicked six goals that day against Geelong, but the Tigers missed the finals.

A thirst slaked

The sweet taste of success. Watched by Francis Bourke (left) and Bill Brown, Richmond captain Fred Swift celebrates the 1967 premiership as the Tigers end a 24-year drought. It was Swift's last game of VFL football.

Holy grail

The Tigers of 1980 celebrate their premiership thrashing of Collingwood. From left: Michael Roach, Stephen Mount, Geoff Raines,Dale Weightman, Francis Bourke, Mick Malthouse, Emmett Dunne, Greg Strachan, Daryl Freame, Bryan Wood (obscured), Robert Wiley.

At Last!

After what seemed an eternity, the Tigers dominated the 2017 final series, culminating in a thrashing of Adelaide in the Grand Final. It was the club's first Grand Final appearance since 1982, and first flag since 1980, and was the culmination of a plan put in place by the Board at the start of the decade. The Tigers won 16.12 (108) to Adelaide 8.12 (60).

Pictured are:

BACK: Dan Butler, David Astbury, Alex Rance, Jack Riewoldt, Nick Vlastuin, Kamdyn Macintosh, Toby Nankervis.

MIDDLE: Dylan Grimes, Dustin Martin (Norm Smith Medallist), Shaun Grigg, Kane Lambert, Jacob Townsend, Shane Edwards, Jack Graham, Trent Cotchin (c), Jason Castagna.

FRONT: Daniel Rioli, Dion Prestia, Nathan Broad, Brandon Ellis, Josh Caddy, Bachar Houli.

Herald Sun
ORORA
AFL
Jeep

1885-1907

A CLUB IS BORN

The Richmond FC experienced humble beginnings as a struggling VFA club. But by the turn of the century, its success on the ground – and inner city location – made it an attractive acquisition for the VFL.

The Richmond Football Club need not look far to gaze upon its place of origin. Across Punt Road, in fact, lies the Royal Hotel, where on the evening of February 20, 1885, the club was born.

Its first secretary, Jimmy Charles – a former North Melbourne footballer and a local small businessman – would later recall that it was founded to enable the Richmond Cricket Club to increase its revenue and secure its tenure of the Richmond Cricket Ground. The cricketers were desperate to have senior football played on the ground, and they threw their support behind the formation of a football club after discussions with Melbourne Football Club dissolved in January, 1885.

Club colours were determined the following week. They were to be, "all blue, with a yellow and black sash; cap with yellow and black stripe running from front to back."

The famous yellow and black colours were taken directly from the RCC, which had used them since the mid-1870s.

In 1887, Richmond adopted a yellow and black vertically striped uniform. Still, it seems that the colours were more important than the orientation of the stripes, and motley Richmond teams wore a variety of horizontally and vertically striped outfits through to 1909. The following year the club changed to a black guernsey with a yellow band across the chest; it was not until 1914 that the famous black jumper with a yellow sash was adopted.

Richmond's first game was against Cremorne on Saturday, April 25, 1885. Despite a handicap of three players, it won two goals to nil. A week later they played their first VFA game against Williamston at the Gardens Reserve, Williamstown, losing one goal to nil, and seven days later at Punt Road, against University, William Wells kicked Richmond's first goal in VFA competition.

A membership ticket, Richmond F.C. season 1885.

Richmond won the match three goals to one to secure an historic first victory. (Wells would father Charlie "Chinger" Wells, who played five games for Richmond in 1912, and grandfather Billy "Jumbo" Wells, who played 23 games for the Tigers in 1936 and 1937.)

George "Geordie" Smith captained Richmond in 1885 and '88. Geordie had played with an earlier Richmond Football Club in the 1870s and, after a stint at East Melbourne, he joined the crack Carlton team in 1877, where he rose to vice-captain the Blues in 1884. He was a natural leader and a favourite of Richmond supporters.

Smith's lieutenant in 1885 was Tom Graham. In 1886, Graham was elected captain but the stint will be short-lived – officials at Richmond took offence at his behaviour during an away game against South Ballarat in June. Graham, with teammates Jack Taylor and Dave Elder, were asked to resign from the club for one season owing to their antics (some reports hint at intoxication, others at foul language) and three other players, who refused to play without them, Harry Layton, Alf Searle and Paddy Purcell, were expelled from the club. Elder and Purcell played for Richmond in 1887 but Graham, Layton and Taylor shifted their allegiances to Port Melbourne.

Thus the events of 1886 may have spawned Richmond's first great rivalry. Matches between Port and Richmond were often characterised by ill-feeling, yet the three prodigal sons would come home. Layton and Graham returned as players in 1890; Graham even captained the club in 1891, while Taylor was employed as trainer from 1896 to 1899.

Richmond's most successful season during the 19th century was 1888. The club defeated the reigning premier Carlton during the year but its most memorable victory was against the mighty South Melbourne team at Punt Road. On June 30, it defeated South six goals to two, and it would be fondly recalled well past the turn of the century. At the end of the 1888 season the club was ranked fifth and provided the VFA's leading goalkicker, South Australian recruit Billy Brown.

The early part of the new century was a winning period for Richmond, with the club winning the VFA premiership in 1902 and 1905, and were runners-up in 1901, 1903 and 1904.
Back Row: Charlie Taylor (trainer), Dick Knell, Edward Leach, Ernie Rudduck, Tom Williams, Harry Rigby, George Bownas, Bill Lang, Walter Sykes, Joe Watson (trainer).
Middle Row: Herb Whittaker (trainer), Ernest McDonald, William Carkeek, Bert Lithgow, Alec Edmond, Jack Hutchinson, Jack Smith.
Front Row: Arthur Cleghorn, Charlie Williams, Charlie Ricketts, Jack Megson, Archie McNair (treasurer), George Beachcroft (secretary).

It augured well for a bright future, but success was fleeting. From 1889-96 Richmond finished eighth twice, 11th twice, and 12th four times. The club's poor performances were matched by poor attendances and membership numbers.

The economic depression of the 1890s strangled the eastern seaboard and Richmond found it hard to maintain its list or recruit talented local juniors. Its adherence to amateurism placed it at a distinct disadvantage against less scrupulous clubs that had touted openly for players since the 1880s – such as Port and South. Closer to home, Melbourne and Essendon, who would become two of the dominant clubs of the early 1890s, played at grounds within sight of Punt Road and enticed some footballers who lived in Richmond to play for them with offers of work.

Even when the club tried similar tactics to recruit Dinny McKay from South Melbourne, the club was clumsy. Richmond City Councillor, George Charman, promised to secure relief work for McKay if he played in 1891. An unemployed McKay accepted the offer, but the scheme was uncovered in 1892 when it was learned that McKay lived in South Melbourne and was ineligible for the Richmond City Council's relief work. This did not contravene the rules

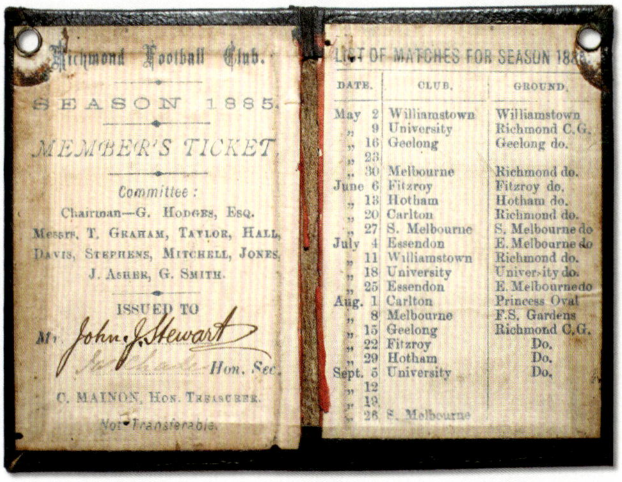

Richmond Football Club.

SEASON 1885.

MEMBER'S TICKET.

Committee:

Chairman—G. Hodges, Esq.
Messrs. T. Graham, Taylor, Hall, Davis, Stephens, Mitchell, Jones, J. Asher, G. Smith.

ISSUED TO
Mr John J. Stewart

Hon. Sec.

C. Mainon, Hon. Treasurer.

Not Transferable.

LIST OF MATCHES FOR SEASON 188

DATE.	CLUB.	GROUND.
May 2	Williamstown	Williamstown
(May) 9	University	Richmond C.G.
(May) 16	Geelong	Geelong do.
(May) 23		
(May) 30	Melbourne	Richmond do.
June 6	Fitzroy	Fitzroy do.
(June) 13	Hotham	Hotham do.
(June) 20	Carlton	Richmond do.
(June) 27	S. Melbourne	S. Melbourne do
July 4	Essendon	E. Melbourne do
(July) 11	Williamstown	Richmond do.
(July) 18	University	University do.
(July) 25	Essendon	E. Melbourne do
Aug. 1	Carlton	Princess Oval
(Aug.) 8	Melbourne	F.S. Gardens
(Aug.) 15	Geelong	Richmond C.G.
(Aug.) 22	Fitzroy	Do.
(Aug.) 29	Hotham	Do.
Sept. 5	University	Do.
(Sept.) 12		
(Sept.) 19		
(Sept.) 26	S. Melbourne	

A membership card from Richmond's first season in the VFA, 1885, listed matches against some of today's recognisable teams, and some long-forgotten ones – Hotham became North Melbourne, Williamstown has remained a VFA club, and University would join Richmond in the VFL in 1908.

of the VFA but it was embarrassing; McKay returned to South in 1893.

In October, 1896, the most influential clubs in the VFA decided to secede and form a new football association, the Victorian Football League (VFL). Unfortunately, the year was one of the worst in Richmond history. It won just three matches, lost the other 15 in succession, and shared the wooden spoon with another defiantly amateur club, Carlton. Richmond was also pulled up twice for having too many men on the field, and on one occasion a couple of Richmond players left the field before the close of play.

Again, Richmond's on-field performance was reflected in its balance sheet. The attendances at Punt Road were supposedly so poor that the opposition's share was exceeded by the postage required send it to them.

Despite the split, the VFA clubs decided to continue with their own competition, yet Richmond continued to struggle. Its pitiful 1896 membership of 233 slumped to just 81 in 1897, the lowest in club history.

Richmond again finished last in 1897 and struggled in the VFA until 1900, when it finished third. However, the first years of the new century would prove to be the club's first golden era. It won the 1902 and 1905 VFA premierships, was runner-up in 1901, 1903 and 1904, and third in 1900, 1906, and 1907.

It could very easily have been three premierships had it not forfeited the 1904 Grand Final against North Melbourne – the club was unwilling to play under a particular umpire, who the VFA then duly appointed. (It was not the first premiership controversy. In 1902, Charles "Fishy" Taylor was disqualified for life for match-fixing in the week leading to the last game. Richmond, however, won the match, and with it the club's first premiership. Richmond and Taylor would protest his innocence for decades.)

George Peckham-Beachcroft, took over as Hon. Secretary in 1900 and only relinquished the job in 1906 after he was injured in a railway accident. Peckham-Beachcroft built a Richmond team that utilised bulk to physically dominate their opponents on the small VFA grounds. So small was the Punt Road oval that after it entered the VFL its ground was nicknamed the "saucer". Some of these grounds were poorly policed, and fixtures against Port Melbourne and North Melbourne often ended in crowd violence.

Alec Edmond, a local Richmond lad and son of a former vice-president, captained the yellow and blacks from 1901-1907. Although the team used a number of bulky players, such as the famous heavyweight boxer Bill Lang (a.k.a. Lan Franchi), it also had players of real class. Richmond's premiership ruckman George "Mallee" Johnson joined Carlton, and rover Charlie Ricketts went to South Melbourne; both achieved great fame in the VFL. However, not all players departed. Charlie Backhouse was probably as good a centre player as any in the League and he was often the target of opposition roughs. Jack Hutchinson, who joined Richmond

Richmond and Footscray do battle in a Victorian Football Association match at the Punt Road Oval, June 18, 1904. The Tigers of the day drew substantial crowds, making them an attractive new member of the VFL four years later.

in 1904, was the greatest VFA forward of the era, and probably Richmond's greatest since Billy Brown. In 1907, his last year at the club, Hutchinson booted an Australian record 67 goals in a season.

By 1905, Richmond accounted for one third of the Association's gate takings and was drawing VFL-sized crowds to the enlarged terraces of the Punt Road Oval. It was the dominant economic force in the VFA, and enjoyed a good relationship with League clubs – Richmond regularly programmed a number of pre-season trial games against them, but in 1907 the VFA banned its clubs from meeting VFL teams. Richmond received an exemption to play one last game against Geelong – which it won.

The Yellow and Blacks had a strong team, they were now financially sound, and they had a centrally-located ground. They were an ideal candidate to join the VFL but all they needed was an opportunity. Throughout 1907, officials Andrew Manzie, Jack Fayle and Hector Milne secretly courted VFL club delegates for admission to the League. They found strong allies in Beachcroft, who was now secretary of the Melbourne Football Club, and Collingwood's Ern Copeland. Late that year, after University was admitted to the League vfor the 1908 season, the club was free to act overtly.

With one spot available, Richmond fended off three rival bids from Brighton, the Ballarat Football League, and a combined North Melbourne / West Melbourne submission to gain admittance to the VFL as its 10th club. TREVOR RUDDELL

An early embodiment of the Richmond Football Club won the 1872 Junior Challenge Cup, defeating the Collingwood, East Melbourne and Southern clubs. The trophy was presented to the family of captain, Fred Hyde, who died late that season in a "gymnastic accident"; it was donated to the club in September, 1953, and resides at the RFC museum.

Local kids form the bulk of the crowd behind the goals at a Victorian Football Association match at the Punt Road Oval in 1904. The Tigers played in the horizontal stripes (yellow and black) seen in the image. Punt Road was developed as an oval by the Richmond Cricket Club from 1860, and it has been the home ground of the Tigers since the club's formation in 1885.
(PIC: COURTESY OF RICHMOND FOOTBALL CLUB)

FROM 1855

TIGERLAND

The Punt Road Oval Story

Trevor Ruddell is a lifelong Richmond fan, the deputy librarian at the Melbourne Cricket Club and historian. He has traced the history of the famous Punt Road oval as it grew from a paddock through the VFL years to a modern training ground for the Tigers.

Before the establishment of a settlement at Melbourne—from 1835—Yarra Park (including the Richmond Cricket Ground) was a small part of the Kulin-speaking Wurundjeri-willam estate. Yarra Park was a location where Kulin people would assemble periodically for ceremony, sport and business—such as arranging marriages and settling disputes. The area west of Punt Road between Wellington Parade and the Yarra River was formally designated the Government Paddock in 1837, but it was also called Police Paddock and Richmond Paddock from the 1840s to the 1870s.

On 18 November 1855 the Richmond Cricket Club (RCC) obtained permissive occupancy of a section of parkland across from the Royal Hotel on Punt Road. There, it began improving the site and by late October 1856 it had been cleared and fenced. During the winter of 1860 the Richmond Cricket Ground (RCG) was levelled and re-sewn, a wooden fence replacing the iron railing, and the refreshment area was enlarged. Cricket club member and Royal Hotel proprietor Gideon Elliot also erected a "shelter from the sun" at the ground. On 29 September 1860, in *Bell's Life in Victoria*, a correspondent wrote that it was "now in better order than at any previous period since the formation of the club". However, it would not be until October 1865 that the RCC's first true pavilion was constructed. This weatherboard building would stand on the western wing for 70 years.

Elliot was one of a number of cricketers who formed the inaugural Richmond Football Club on 25 April 1860. *Bell's Life in Victoria* reported on 18 August that a match between Melbourne and Richmond would commence at two o'clock that afternoon on the "R.C.C. ground". However, throughout the 1860s until the late 1870s most important football matches in Melbourne were played in parkland.

On 21 June 1879 the junior club East Melbourne leased the ground for two guineas for the day. Football has had an uninterrupted presence at the Punt Road Oval ever since. In 1880 East Melbourne declared itself a senior club, and although the RCG hosted a moderate number of its games against junior teams, the ground only saw East face senior opposition twice in its two years as an RCG tenant. Hotham defeated East five goals to nil in 1880, and four goals to one in 1881. For a few years thereafter, the ground was a junior football venue and was the headquarters of Anglo-Australian football (soccer).

In April 1884 the RCC and the Melbourne Football Club discussed the possibility of a Melbourne tenancy at the RCG. Melbourne's ground, in the parkland beside the MCG, was unsatisfactory. Negotiations with the RCC apparently fell through, but Melbourne did play at least one game against a junior team at the RCG in 1884. By the end of April the RCC had agreed to let its ground to the Anglo-Australians again.

The RCC was instrumental in facilitating the creation of the current Richmond Football Club to alleviate its debts, which in September 1884 stood at £140/5/5/. In 1909 committeeman Jimmy Charles would recall that, "I, being one of a committee, with the others, being responsible to the bank for the amount, thought that the only way out of it was to start a senior football club, which we thought in time might relieve us of our burden."

A senior football club, by increasing the ground's patronage, proved to be a financial and membership boon for the cricketers. The RCC would be very accommodating: it granted free use of their pavilion for committee meetings and was willing to negotiate the extension of the football season into September. Still the RCC was forced to make improvements to the ground in order to accommodate the new football club. Richmond's 1885 home attendances, ranging from 1,000 to 3,000, were modest compared to those of the established clubs of the 1880s, but larger than had been seen at the ground previously. To cater for

A group of men in various outfits gather at the Richmond Cricket Ground in the 1880s, reportedly for Richmond training. The range of guernseys and hats was typical of the era. (Pic: courtesy of Richmond Football Club)

the spectators, ticket booths, a kiosk and a urinal were constructed by June. Trouble with barrackers invading the playing space brought about the construction of a line of seats bordering the western side of the ground in July 1885.

Major works took place at the RCG during September and October 1886. The playing field was extended over the bicycle rink and seats encircled the ground. Another dressing room and a curator's room were added to the pavilion, with a shower/bath in each. A scoring/press box was also constructed. For the RCC members a skittle alley was established inside the pavilion and a second asphalt tennis court was installed south of the building. However, few other architectural structures were added to the RCG over the next decade.

At the close of the 1896 football season, eight clubs left the Victorian Football Association (VFA) and established the Victorian Football League (VFL). This coincided with the first attempt to relocate Richmond Football Club from the Punt Road Oval. The RCG was just outside Richmond's civic boundary and many City of Richmond councillors wanted to base the club at a more central location—the council's own Richmond City Reserve. Like a similar proposal to move the club to the City Reserve in 1909, it would come to nought.

Richmond remained in the VFA, which was now regarded as a second-rate senior competition. The diminutive size of the ground, nicknamed the "Saucer", and its lack of spectator amenities told against its inclusion to the VFL. However, in the early 1900s, as Richmond teams began to dominate the VFA, spectators flooded to their games and the banks of the outer were raised in response.

In September 1903 the football club considered erecting a dedicated grandstand at the ground but decided to hold it over until the club is admitted to the VFL. In July 1904 it discussed purchasing a pavilion for the Ladies Reserve, and in 1905 its secretary George Beachcroft made inquiries into acquiring the grandstand at the nearby Friendly Societies Gardens. On 16 January 1906 the Melbourne Cricket Club offered its now redundant Smokers' Pavilion to the RCC for free. It was erected north of the pavilion in time for the beginning of the football season. It remained at the ground until 1917 when it was sold by the RCC for £35/10/0.

By then a new RCC grandstand had been built. Richmond entered the VFL in 1908 and as early as 1910 football club secretary Andrew Manzie proposed the erection of a brick grandstand on the western side of the ground and the demolition of the present buildings. He also proposed a high brick wall along Punt Road to increase the size of the embankment and allow the enlargement of the play field. In June 1913 the RCC received permission to increase the size of their ground to the north-west. Soon a grandstand, designed by Thomas Watts & Son would be erected there. It was paid for through the sale of indentures. Work on it began in early 1914 and the foundation stone was formally laid on May 2. The new 1,200 capacity grandstand was officially opened on Saturday 6 June by former Prime Minister and federal Labor Party leader Andrew Fisher. The grandstand was extended southward in 1927 with the addition of the D. P. Chessell Wing. In 1998 it was renamed the Jack Dyer Stand.

In the 1920s the football club was outgrowing the Punt Road Oval's facilities. Before the start of the 1925 season the ground's capacity was enlarged, in line with the recent agreement between the football and the cricket club. Embankments were raised, a new press box was erected, the cricket club's reserve was terraced, and a portion of the old 1865 pavilion was pulled down. The old weatherboard and tin pavilion was feeling its age. In 1920 its verandah, which was being used as a perch by supporters collapsed under their weight during a match against Collingwood, and in August 1926 a portion was burnt. It was finally burnt to the ground on the morning of 13 July 1935.

Growing attendances and the demands of the VFL forced improvements to the Punt Road Oval throughout the 1930s. In 1932 the playing arena was extended by 11 yards, the tennis court was removed, and the goalposts were re-orientated. The plans even provided space for another grandstand—although it would not be constructed for some time. However, these changes were not enough and in 1935 the Richmond Football Club courted Melbourne Carnivals Pty. Ltd., the manager of Olympic Park. In response the RCC proposed a number of ground improvements that were conditional upon the football club's continued tenancy. They included a new grandstand for cricket club members, a concrete fence on the railway side, new lavatories and a ramp for spectators over the conveniences on the north side, and the removal of the Punt Road turnstiles to the north side. Negotiations between the clubs continued until mid-February 1936, when the football club's Board accepted the VFL's decision that the RCG, though currently unsuitable for League football, will be made so by the proposed improvements by the RCC.

The following year the capacity of the area behind the northern goal was increased with the erection of a concrete wall from the turnstiles to Punt Road, and a new scoreboard and bar were also built. The long proposed grandstand, named the Ernest H. King Stand, was operational in time for the first round of 1938, although it was formally opened two weeks later on May 27. Punt Road's tenure as Richmond's home ground would not be seriously threatened until the 1960s.

In the 1960s the football club's administration was troubled by the proposed widening of Punt Road (a project that did not commence until 1989) and the impact it may have on the ground's capacity. Negotiations between the football club, the RCC, the Melbourne Cricket Club and the Melbourne Cricket Ground Trust began in 1964, with the object of transferring the club's home matches to the MCG, from 1965. The MCG regarded as the home of football, was Australia's largest stadium and located just a couple of hundred metres from the Punt Road Oval. The Melbourne Football Club even played home matches at Punt Road when the MCG was being used as a military camp during World War II. The larger capacity of the MCG and the comfortable spectator facilities that it provided were noted in the Richmond Football Club's 1965 annual report. Richmond's home attendances increased from 174,540 at Punt Road in 1964, to 321,237 in 1965 at the MCG.

"Growing attendances and the demands of the VFL forced improvements to the Punt Road Oval throughout the 1930s'"

The Punt Road Oval has continued to host football matches, although it is no longer an elite football venue. But it has remained the club's primary training base and administrative address. It is also the spiritual home of the club. In 1980 the Richmond Cricket and Football Club Social Club was established in a re-purposed Ernest H. King Stand, while disused facilities were removed and the arena was beautified. Punt Road's training and administrative facilities at the ground have been regularly upgraded since 2000, aided by funds raised through the Jack Dyer Foundation (est.1996).

In 2004 a new administration office, encompassing a boardroom and a swimming pool, was built between the Jack Dyer Stand and the Social Club building. Less than six years later the Social Club was demolished for the construction of the David Mandie Building, where the Korin Gamadgji Institute is headquartered. In 2011 Punt Road became a year-round football training venue. The ground was levelled (it previously sloped towards the southern goal) and enlarged. The cricket pitch was also removed and the RCC was relocated to Central Reserve, Glen Waverley. The cricket club that established Punt Road now trades as the Monash Tigers.

TREVOR RUDDELL

The day they packed Punt Road

Richmond vs Carlton, Punt Road,
Round nine, 1949. Crowd: 46,000
Carlton 14.15 (99) d Richmond 12.12 (84)

"It was on the King's Birthday. They were around the boundary and they pushed the fence over. It took me nearly 30 minutes to get from the turnstiles into the rooms, I couldn't get through the crowd, they were just jam-packed. A huge day, huge atmosphere." HAVEL ROWE

"The fence in the forward pocket got pushed over by the force of the crowd while the match was on. I was there with a mate of mine, I took my own football so we could have a kick at half-time and I've got this football between me and a bloke in front of me. We were about 10 yards back from the fence and the crowd was just surging.

I had the football stuck up my belly and I'm thinking I'm not going to let it go, I just had enough room to hang onto my footy and then the fence gave away, and that created a bit more breathing space. The fat part of the fence got flattened and if I remember rightly we still stayed where we were. They took some of the people and put them in the Cricket Stand. It was a terrible feeling that you couldn't move, just going back and forwards with the crowd." JACK WATSON

"They broke the fence down and they sat inside the fence. We still ran into them. The police came out and they sort of circled the ground." DES ROWE

W.A. 'Bill' Maybury

Bill 'Dad' Maybury served on the committee of the RFC for more than 30 years; he was secretary in 1896 and from 1917-1923. Maybury's playing career in local football was ended by a knee injury, so he dedicated his sporting interest to administration for the Tigers. He was made a life member in 1912.

Excerpt from *The Richmond Guardian* July 26, 1913

Mr W. A. Maybury was a barracker for Richmond before they had knickerbockers. That was when the old senior club used to play out in Yarra Park – or Richmond Paddock, as it was then called. The uniform of the players in those days consisted of a navy blue guernsey with long white flannel trousers, and a blue and white striped cap. Players of other clubs all aired a similar attire, the only distinguishing mark being different colored caps.

Things were mixed in those days. Players had to hold their caps as well as their temper. Melbourne had red caps, Collingwood magenta and black, Albert Park red and white, Barwon black and white. One umpire was sufficient then, and he was also the timekeeper.

When the present senior Richmond club was formed (1885) he was a paying supporter, the following year he joined as a member, and he has held on ever since. He has held almost every office in connection with the club, except that of president.

Bill Maybury, a significant figure in early RFC history.

When Mr. "Jimmy" Eastman, hon. secretary, retired, Maybury was, with Mr. Dave Chessell, elected joint hon. secretary and delegate to the Football Association, but illness and his family compelled him to relinquish the offices. For a time he was absent from active management, but continued to follow the team in rain or shine, and when six years ago (1907) he again offered his services for committee, the members gladly embraced the opportunity and returned him at the top of the poll. He was the only one of the old committee to hold his seat when the Reform Committee put up their great fight two years ago (1911), and they did not oppose him. There is no more unassuming, better liked, straight-forward personality in the club, and the members continue to show their appreciation by repeatedly awarding him more votes than any other candidate at the annual elections. He has been with the club in its bad as well as its best times. He remembers when the club was down to 89 members. He would like to have the names of those loyalists now and organise a grand reunion. Others also would cheer the fellows who kept the flag flying.

He has had many proud moments on the Punt Road ground. One of the proudest was when he carried his first son, Percy, as a baby in arms to show his friends. Years after there was another big heartbeat when Percy stepped out on the field as one of the Richmond team (round 2, 1910).

Maybury has a fund of reminiscences. When he first attended a football match a lady spectator was as rare as at a prize fight. Now a bigger rarity would be a game without them.

He often chuckles when he remembers incidents that came under his notice when he acted as auditor. But the yarn breaks off before it ends. No power on earth would make him break a confidence.

Though of the old school he is for the present. Asked to express his opinion, he says "Old teams would not live with the present teams. The days of little marks were the days of splendid individual opportunities.

Occasions brought forth the men who shone as individuals greater perhaps than the champions of to-day, but the combination of crack teams to-day would knock the splendid individual champions of old into the proverbial cocked hat."

And most people with any extensive connection with the game will agree with the opinion.

The core of the early V.F.L. Tigers celebrate 10 years' service in 1919. From back left: Barney Herbert (later RFC president); Vic Thorp, a 263-game veteran; 14-year ruckman Hugh James. Seated: Percy Maybury, captain-coach in 1917; and brilliant centreman Sid Reeves.

Football Then and Now
Excerpt from The Richmond Guardian, May 7, 1921. By WA Maybury

It's a long way back to the 1870s when, as a youngster in knickerbockers, I first barracked for the old Richmond that used to play out in Yarra Park (then called Richmond Paddock) alongside Wellington Parade, near where the Jolimont Station is now.

The uniform then worn was trousers – white for preference, like cricketing pants – a heavy blue guernsey such as sailors wear, and a blue cap with one white stripe running from front to back.

It was all in, "Rafferty's Rules," for football in those days, and intervals for "stoush" amongst the players were fairly frequent. There was no Sword of Damocles hanging over them in the shape of a tribunal to be hauled before to answer any charge of striking, or attempting to strike, laid by the umpire. In fact, I am doubtful if there were an umpire.

If there were, he was not very much in evidence, as each player was a law unto himself. Get the ball when possible and kick it anywhere and anyhow, so long as it was in the direction of the opponent's goal. It will be very hard to understand that in playing around trees and dodging roots and stumps the "Irish Punt" was the favorite method of propulsion.

A badge noting season 1903, when RFC finished runner-up in the VFA.

There was no "ball up" in those brave days of old. Get the ball and hold it until it was taken or torn away from you; if you could do nothing else, lay on it until help arrived. It was common to see a heap of players, 20 or more strong, in the centre of the ground on top of one another, squirming and struggling to get the ball from the player underneath, and relays from the back and forward lines rushing into the fray trying to disentangle their own side from the opposition by pulling men from the human pyramid.

No-hold was barred – catch as catch can, by arms, legs, neck, or head, whichever was nearest. After a man was sorted out he took a breather for a space, then he would go back 10 or 15 yards and take a running jump, landing right on top of the heap, and then start pulling out in his turn, until finally the ball would get out somehow and the game go on again.

When the spectators crowded on to the playing space too much the play would be stopped and the players on both sides line up and, with clasped hands forming a long line, charge the crowd to get them back to the invisible boundary line. This

Action from the Richmond-Footscray VFA match of 1904. The game was drawn.

action sometimes led to "arguments" by indignant fathers or big brothers whose young sons or brothers had been bowled over in the wild rush to safety from the charging athletes, and "blood noses" and "fancy colored faces" were no unusual results of these little diversions.

After peace had been restored, off they went again. There was no quarter-time then. I think they used to change ends after each goal was kicked, and so on until the time-keeper said it was time. There was no bell to ring or whistle to blow, and play often went on for a good while after time was up; perhaps a goal would be kicked, and then disputes arose, in a close finish, as to who really did win, some of which are not settled to this day.

Goals only counted, not behinds. After the finish the players dressed in the open under their favorite tree, no bath, no rub, no hot shower, no anything, and went their ways, each looking forward to the next match as eagerly and enthusiastically as the players of today are looking to the opening of the coming season. Such was football as I saw it in those days.

Everything was rough and ready and solid, especially the grand old trees that a man was sometimes hurled against by a none to gentle opponent. Still, they enjoyed it, and I am sure those who played football in those days who are still with us look back with many pleasant memories of football as played in the 1870s.

The next Richmond in the field was a junior team with whom I played a few games until 'footballer's knee' settled my chances of becoming a champion. Some critics were unkind enough to say after my first game that I ought not have forsaken my position as onlooker if the team wanted to win matches, but, then, truthful people are often unkind.

This Richmond's colors were blue and white hooped jersey and stockings, blue knicks. The ground, the Botanical Reserve, the site of the old Lonsdale cricket ground, where can be seen at the present day the outlines of the old circle that enclosed the pitch. This is an historical ground, as I think every local footballer, senior and junior, has at one time or another played on it.

This Richmond faded out in 1883, like most junior clubs of those days, and in 1884, Mr J. Charles, RFC's first secretary, founded the present club, and secured admission to the Victorian Football Association, and Richmond made its debut as a fully fledged senior club.

From the outset, our progress, though slow, was steady and sure. The top-notches, after giving us some holy hidings, began to get some nasty jars from us, especially on our own ground, and found we had to be very seriously considered when we were meeting them at Richmond. The long-expected arrived at last, when we defeated the mighty "South" by four goals in June, 1888, and Richmond went "dippy" over the win. South Melbourne had an undefeated run until they met us that season, and they did not get over the shock for some time.

This performance made our name for us, and although we were often thrashed unmercifully on visiting grounds, we were very seldom used now by the leading teams as a "try out" for their recruits when they had to play on our Richmond ground.

Almost invariably they played their best available team against us, and were indeed happy when they were over that "doubtful" fixture on the RFC ground. After the breakaway of the eight clubs who seceded from the Association to form the League, only five clubs, of whom Richmond was one, were left in the Association. Three junior clubs were invited to join up with the five who were left, and thus the present VFA was kept in full working order.

Richmond at once took a leading position in the reorganised Association, which they held until, with the University Club, they were invited to join the League in 1908.

Our career since linking up with the League has been one of steady progress, and although at the start we had to take many gruelling defeats by the stronger clubs, we never lost hope, but came up smiling again and again, beaten but never dismayed, until, after judicious building up of the team, we are now holding the proud position of premiers of the Victorian Football League.

Richmond has placed many fine teams in the field in the past, but for thorough efficiency in every part of the field, and consistency of performances, our team of 1920 was in my opinion, undoubtedly the very best that has ever wore the "yellow and black" of the redoubtable "Tigers" who have made the name of Richmond famous throughout the football world of Australia.

Ed's Note: the first Richmond F.C. Maybury refers to was that of 1871-1876; the second, 1882-83; and the third, 1885 to present.
The famous "South" game he refers to was the 1888 game at the Richmond Cricket Ground.
Maybury's son, Percy, played 128 games and kicked 61 goals for Richmond between 1910 to 1919; he was captain-coach in 1917. Percy served on the committee from 1927 to 1933.

Hector N. Milne

A Tiger player during the Victorian Football Association era, Milne's contribution to the club spanned three decades – a distinguished turn-of-the-century playing career, committeeman, vice-president, delegate to the Association and, in turn, the Victorian Football League.

Hector Milne played 24 games for Richmond in 1899 and 1900, and in his first season topped Richmond's goalkicking with 16. He was very familiar with all major personalities at the club throughout the first quarter of the 20th century.

The article he penned below was first published in *The Richmond Guardian, February 16, 1924*. While he made several factual errors – and did not play senior football with Richmond in 1905 as implied – when it is considered that it is based on 25-year-old memories, the account is surprisingly accurate and detailed.

Now that the football season is drawing on apace, I am egotistical enough to assume that the foregoing reminiscences of the RFC will prove of interest to the majority of the large membership of the club. My first contact with the old club was in the late 1890s. At that time I was a slim youth, playing with the old Lennox F.C. Having made a bit of a reputation as a goal-getter, I was corralled one evening by the late Bob Guthrie (then hon. secretary) and the late Jimmy Parker, and there and then I verbally signed on as a full-blown Association footballer with the RFC.

On the following Saturday I was selected to play against North Melbourne. I accordingly presented myself at the Richmond dressing room, with my bag containing a pair of boots and knicks. The late Chris Bahen (who played from 1893-1902) gave me a pair of stockings and a guernsey somewhat the worse for wear, and these proved to be my issue for the whole season.

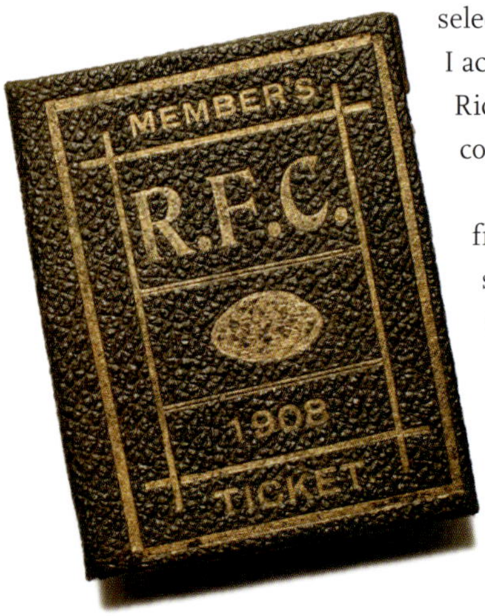

In the room with me at the time, stripping for action, were Arch McNair (1900-04), Barlow Carkeek (1899-1900, 1902, 1905-07), Ern Rudd (1988-1904), Punch Elder (1888, 1890-99), Fishy Taylor, (1894-96, '98-1902), the four Watson brothers (Tom (1897-1901, '03), Joe (1898-99), Dave (1898-1902), and Bill(1898)), Alec Edmonds (1900-05, '07), Charley (1892-1905) and George Backhouse (1897-1901), Tom (1898-1900) and Hughie Williams (1892-94, 1898-99), Phil McGuire (1898-99), Dan Donnelly (1899), and others well known to the older generations in Richmond.

In this match I managed to secure one goal. A gentleman on the opposing side took umbrage at me scoring my first goal at a difficult angle, and promptly showed his displeasure by knocking me half-silly with a healthy blow on the ear. Hughie Williams, who happened to be near at the time, immediately upheld the dignity of the Municipality of Richmond by whipping in a heavy uppercut which connected forcibly with the chin of the attacker. This action was such that the 'ranks of Tuscany could scarce forbear to cheer'.

Needless to relate, the aggressive gentleman on the opposing side lost much of his enthusiastic interest in subsequent events. My next match was against Brunswick at Brunswick. We had with us about a couple of hundred supporters. Some difference nowdays. I managed to secure three goals in this game, which set the seal on me as a permanent member of the team. This match was remarkable for the number of free fights that took place amongst the supporters of the two teams. One enthusiastic Richmond supporter went so far as to say that 201 supporters accompanied the team to Brunswick, and that there were exactly 201 fights. I fear that this estimate was grossly exaggerated.

One of the most exciting matches I ever played was in the following season when George Beachcroft was honourary secretary. We were playing

The motion that the Richmond Club be admitted was then put and carried unanimously

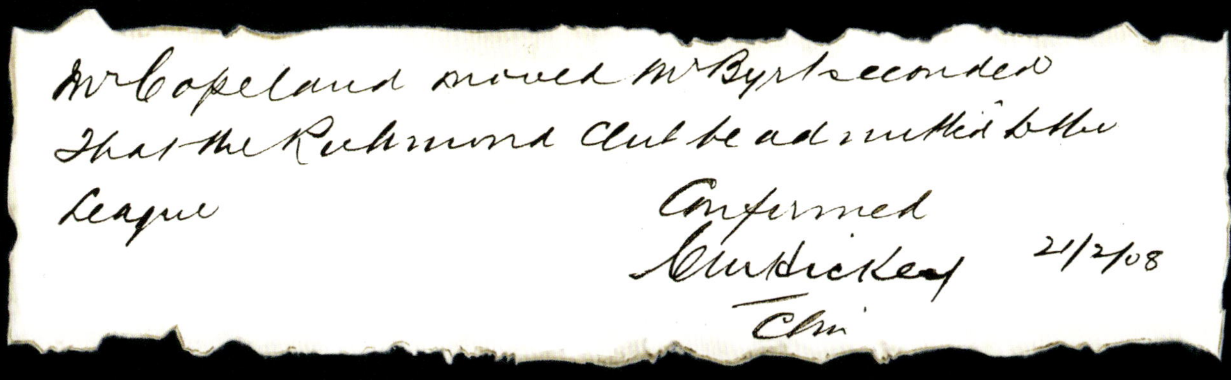
Mr Copeland moved Mr Byrt seconded That the Richmond Club be admitted to the League

Confirmed
Hickey 21/2/08
Chm

The 1900 Richmond team in which Milne made his VFA debut. Eight years later, the official VFL minutes confirm that the "Richmond Club be admitted to the league".

Port at Port Melbourne. A yelling horde of wild-eyed Port supporters were encroaching on the playing arena just near the end of the match. With five minutes to go, Port were leading by four points, and the ball was in the vicinity of their goals. Suddenly Charley Backhouse received the ball from Alec Edmonds and stab-kicked it on to me. It was fully 70 yards out and the time nearly gone. Chris Bahen made me place it instead of trying a forlorn drop-kick.

"One enthusiastic Richmond supporter went so far as to say that 201 supporters accompanied the team to Brunswick, and that there were exactly 201 fights."

I took a run at the ball with both eyes closed and kicked. The next instant Chris Bahen cried out, 'Run for your life, Hec!' The ball had gone through, the bell had rung, and the roaring mob was swarming on the ground after us. We got to the dressing room in record time, and cooled our heels till about 7pm, when a great majority of the barrackers had departed.

A couple of years after I had a little difference of opinion with George Beachcroft, and accordingly I transferred to North Melbourne. (When we played Richmond), Alec Edmonds was making a swing at the ball, but got me on the eye instead. I bore the mark for a week or so; poor Alec was reported for striking me.

I gave evidence that it was an accident, but the committee of the association thought otherwise, and Alec went out for a month.

This was the match when 'Son' Noonan (captain of North) called his team off the ground in the third quarter because of the umpire's alleged unfairness to North. The match went to Richmond by default.

My last match was played against Richmond on the Richmond ground. I again met with misfortune. Mallee Johnson accidentally kicked me in the ribs, and down I went. Mallee was the first to help me in, and I was finished for the day. The next season I transferred back to my old comrades and wrote "finis" to my career at the end of 1905.

After this I was returned on the committee and appointed a co-delegate with Jack Fayle to the Victorian Football Association. During the whole of the 1907 season Jack Fayle, Andrew Manzie, and myself worked night and day with certain delegates of the League in regard to the admission of Richmond to the League.

Not a solitary soul in Richmond (outside the three mentioned) knew what was going on in regard to the promotion of the club. At last, word was given to me by a certain high in the League that the majority was for Richmond's inclusion, and to forward our application at once. We did so, and were admitted in 1908.

In regards to the merits and demerits of the long serving office-bearers of the club, I would unhesitatingly place the late Geo. Bennett, M.L.A., as the most popular and hard-working president that the Richmond Club has possessed. He was always available when wanted, and was the means of placing a lot of players in work. Old Billy Malone (with his familiar bottle of sherry for "the boys" at half-time) was one of the best club men in Richmond's history. To my mind as regards treasurership, I am confident that Archie McNair will be hard to beat. Being of canny Scots descent, he wanted to know the ins and outs of every penny

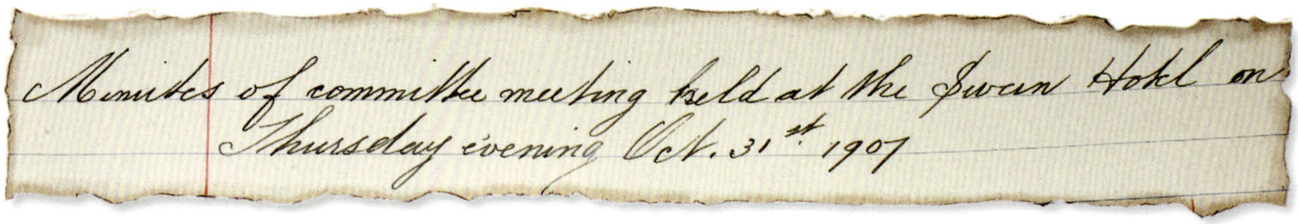

Minutes of committee meeting held at the Swan Hotel on Thursday evening Oct. 31st 1907

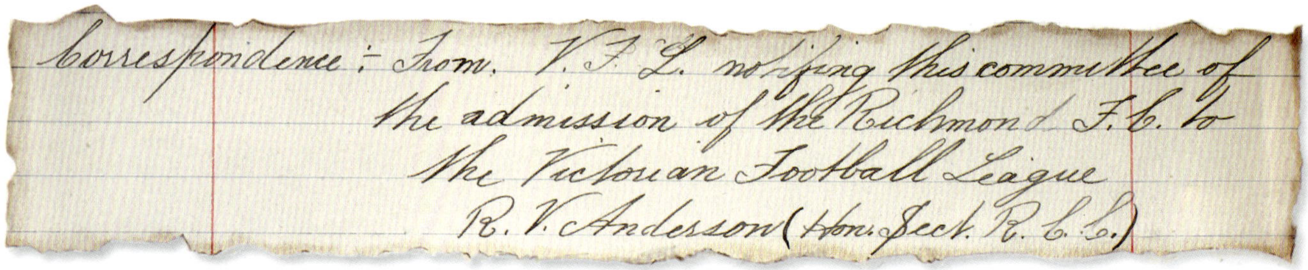

Correspondence :- From. V.F.L. notifying this committee of the admission of the Richmond F.C. to the Victorian Football League
R. V. Anderson (Hon. Sect. R.F.C.)

The Tigers become a League entity. Club minutes from October 31, 1907: Correspondence from V.F.L. notifying this committee of the admission of the Richmond F.C. to the Victorian Football League.

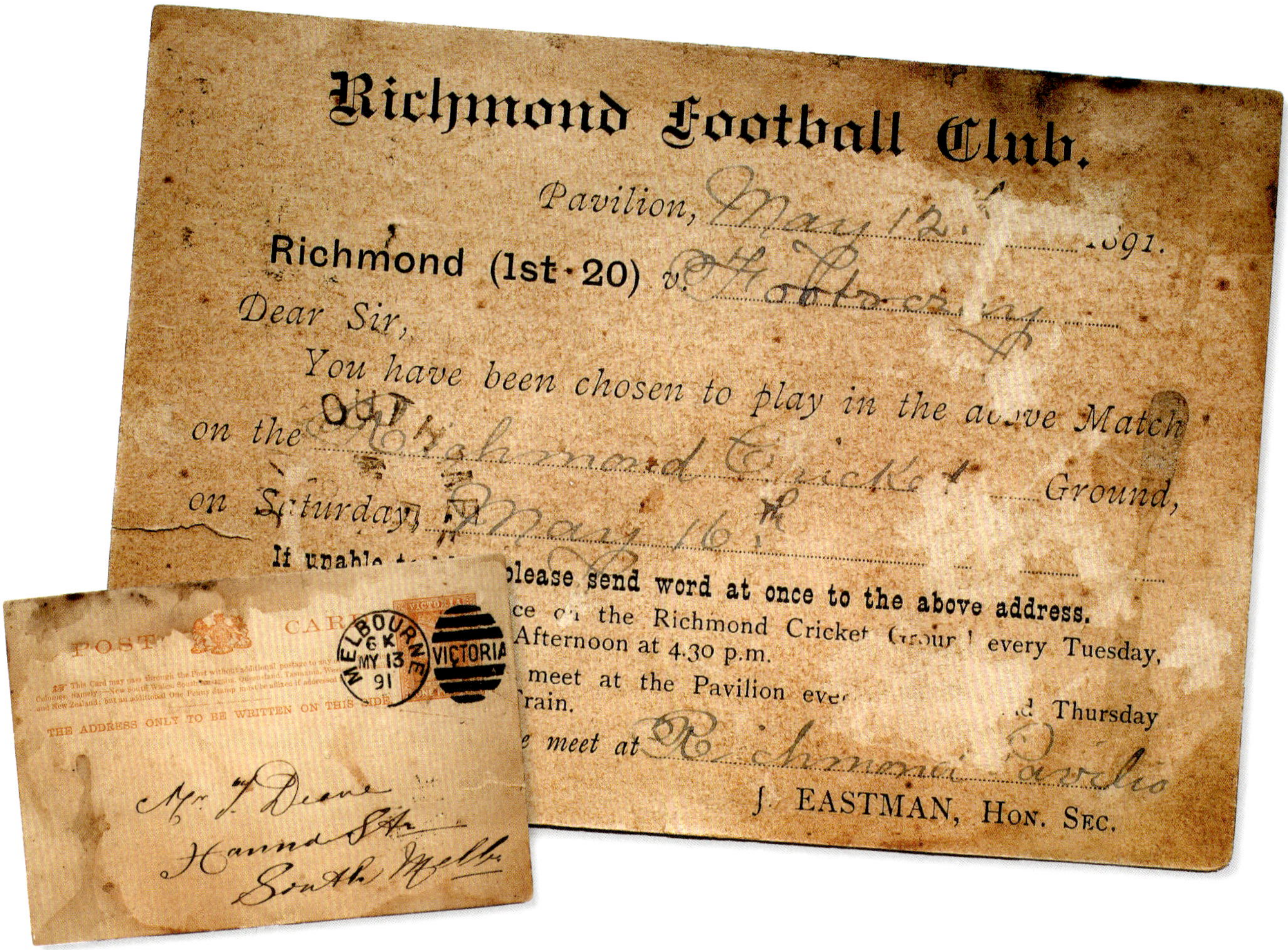

Tom Deane played with Richmond from 1890 to 1895. Players of the time were informed of their selection by postcard. This card refers to Deane's selection for the game against Footscray on May 16, 1891.

that was spent. I would bracket Jack Archer with McNair in regard to the saving of every penny where possible. As far as an outstanding delegate for the club is concerned, it is universally admitted that Jack Fayle did wonders for his club.

His work on the Association and League on behalf of Richmond was brilliant in the extreme. His forced retirement from the committee by the nominees of the reform party some years ago (1912) proved to be a distinct loss to Richmond and the League. It is a matter of congratulation that Jack Fayle may be seen again in the position that he filled so ably for many years.

George Beachcroft has been the most brilliant secretary of the club. He took the club in hand when it was floundering in the slough of despond, and before long had guided it to its first premiership. His work for Richmond was magnificent, and the mane of George R. R. Beachcroft will be entwined with the honors of the club as long as it exists.

Andrew Manzie ran George very close, and was a most popular secretary. It must be borne in mind that these two men were secretaries when there was no district scheme, and they had to battle all the time for players. Nowdays, the job of a League club secretary is practically a sinecure as compared to the days when Beachy and Manzie held the reins. Jack Stewart and Billy Bicknell were two of the greatest club men in Richmond, and their work cannot be overestimated.

In the field of play I would place Alec Edmonds as the greatest captain and half-back player, Jack Hutchinson as the most brilliant forward, and Charley Backhouse as the champion centre player. Barlow Carkeek as the absolute champion all-round player that ever joined up.

Hugh James and Jimmy Parker as the best followers, Vic Thorp as best full-back and Charley Ricketts as the one and only rover. As regards to wingmen, I think that Jimmy Shore still holds the palm.

In the past, Richmond have made serious mistakes when rejecting prospective players. A case in point: Arthur Cleghorn was rejected by the then-committee because he was too small. He was snapped up by Essendon and became a champion.

Another case was that of my brother, "Boxer" (Herbert) Milne. He was told to go back to the juniors for another season. Fitzroy snapped him in the height of his prime, and as is well known, "Boxer" became the champion follower of Victoria a season or so after.

1908-1927

THE TIGER AWAKENS

After a disappointing opening decade in the Victorian Football League, the Richmond Football Club came alive after WWI ... and a memorable catchphrase was coined.

Richmond's early performances in the VFL were mediocre, and a rapid turnover of players occurred as the VFA stalwarts bowed out. Their places were filled by young recruits who would form the backbone of future Richmond teams.

Men such as Ted Ohlson, Billy Burns, Barney Herbert, Hughie James, Vic Thorp and Percy Maybury had joined the club by 1910. Others, such as Billy Schmidt and Clarrie Hall, who played their first games for Richmond in 1907, came of age in the League.

The club was led by Collingwood identities Dick Condon (playing-coach in 1908 and 1909) and Charlie Pannam, who joined Richmond midway through 1907. The Magpie pair were unsuccessful; Pannam left at the end of 1908 and Condon a year later. It was the pre-World War I generation of recruits that would form the nucleus of the club in its early League years and would be the first to earn the sobriquet "Tigers".

"Quiz", the sports writer in the *Richmond Guardian*, began to regularly use the nickname "Tigers" to describe Richmond in 1910. Soon writers for other magazines such as *The Sport* would also use it, though spasmodically. The name, after all, was informal.

It first appeared in an official Richmond publication in the 1916 Annual Report. However, it was in 1920 that it officially became the club's moniker, and a tiger's head was embossed on Richmond membership tickets.

The early years were difficult, and were not helped by a political battle surrounding professionalism. In February, 1911, the League discussed a scheme to permit open professionalism but limit payments to players. The club supported this in principle but argued for a higher payment, yet one of Richmond's delegates, Jack Archer, opposed the scheme in its

The 1920 premiership team, plus the Cubs, later travelled to Hobart on an end-of-season trip (left to right): Back Row: Tom Delaney, Dave Stewart, B Schultz, W Lyle, V Fayle, Bill Burns, Abe Aarons, H Hartley, P Smyth. Fourth Row: W Baker, T Wright, Joe Watson, Vic Thorp, Frank Huggard, Frank Harley, Frank Hughes, Jimmy Smith, J Cook. Third Row: Norm McIntosh, Wilfred Stott, George Ogilvie, George Parkinson, Barney Herbert, George Weatherill, Paddy Abbott, Ernest Taylor, William Thomas. Second Row: George Bayliss, Robert Carew, Stan Morris, Max Hislop (VC), E Weymouth, Bill Maybury (Sec), Dan Minogue (Capt), Clarrie Hall, P Tuck, Arthur Bettles, Donald Don. Front Row: James Karthaus, Reg Heade, Bill James.

Vic Thorp marks against St Kilda in the early 1920s. The Richmond player to the left is 1921 premiership player Norm "Snowy" McIntosh; behind Thorp and a St Kilda opponent is Ernest Taylor, a two-time premiership back pocket.

entirety. Archer, labeled a traitor by other committee members, decided to create a Reform Party to run against the committee at the 1911 Annual Meeting.

The incumbent committee gained the support of the players and trainers, and won the election easily. But the Reform Party was reconstituted for the 1912 election. They called for players to be paid according to merit rather than a standard one pound per-game. This year the Reform Party had the players' support. Richmond's secretary, Andrew Manzie, may have seen the writing on the wall – he was appointed Melbourne secretary 10 days before the vote. Of the incumbents, all but Bill Maybury, who was on both tickets, lost their place on the committee.

In 1913, the Richmond Cricket Club obtained permission to increase the size of the Punt Road Oval to the north-west, and a design for a grandstand was prepared by Thomas Watts & Son. Although the ground had a pavilion since 1865, and a ladies stand (the old Smokers' Pavilion from the MCG) since 1906, it was the first grandstand at the ground. It accommodated 1,200 people and was opened on June 6, 1914.

From 1920 on, the Tiger motif started to appear on membership tickets.

Twenty-two days later, the Archduke Francis Ferdinand of Austria was assassinated in Sarajevo – this event was the catalyst for WWI, which in turn would hamper the cricket club's ability to pay off the stand.

There was controversy as to whether football should continue during war. In 1916, only four VFL clubs (Carlton, Collingwood, Fitzroy, and Richmond) decided to play. Richmond justified its position by raising money for patriotic funds at games, and noted that a number of Richmond players had enlisted in the AIF – some gave their lives. Bill Nolan's death in France shocked the club and received substantial local press. Other ex-Richmond players to die in Europe include Alexander Salton, Patrick "Toots" O'Loughlin, Arthur Harrison and Les Lee. On the home front, Richmond in 1916 was aided by four uncleared Geelong players. Some commentators were outraged that players the quality of Alec Eason, Harry Marsham, Percy Martini and James Kearney were paid 15 shillings per game for traveling expenses, and labeled Richmond the "Gee-Riches". The club played in its first VFL final that year by default; there were just four clubs competing.

In 1919, Hughie James returned from Europe a hero, sporting a Military Cross, and he soon resumed his football

Dan Minogue's 1920 arrival as captain-coach helped transform the Tigers. Here he reaches for a mark against Fitzroy in round 4, 1924, at Punt Road. Behind him is Gordon Hislop, to the left is Gerald Beare and George Rudolph watches on from the rear.

career with Richmond. Dan Minogue, a Collingwood champion who had become close friends with James during WWI, sought a clearance to play with Richmond, but it was refused. It was Richmond's most successful season to date – the club reached the Grand Final but lost to Collingwood.

By 1920, the team had developed an in-house system of signals and calls that allowed it to act as a cohesive unit. It bewildered opponents. Minogue had arrived (his photo had been placed in a cupboard and faced the wall at Collingwood); he used the system to captain-coach Richmond to its first VFL pennant. The Tigers defeated Collingwood in the 1920 Grand Final, 7.10 (52) to 5.5 (35).

The match was fought possibly as much off the ground as on it. Three days before the Grand Final the VFL acted on a protest from Carlton and debarred Richmond's George Ogilvie from playing because he was tied to Essendon. George Bayliss, who was the first Richmond player to top the league goalkicking with 63, was also left out through injury.

He was replaced in the side by debutant Billy James. James played well, and kicked Richmond's seventh goal, but it was his last and only game of VFL football – he was injured in a shooting accident during the off-season.

Many of the symbols associated with the club were present by 1921. Two years earlier, Richmond's iconic guernsey design, a yellow sash over the left shoulder (rather than the right as had been the case since 1914) was worn for the first time. In 1920, Richmond officially adopted the Tiger moniker, and – as noted in Vic Thorp's memoirs – during the celebrations after Richmond's first premiership Barney Herbert did his best to popularise the "Eat 'em Alive, Tigers" motto.

In 1921, the club received its first tiger skin to celebrate its Grand Final victory against Carlton. The match was close, and Max Hislop possibly saved it in the dying moments when he spoiled Carlton forward Alec Duncan. Richmond won 5.6 (36) to 4.8 (32). Yet the years following the second premiership were dogged by misfortune. In 1924, Richmond made the finals, but the structure of the finals series was bizarre; it consisted of a round-robin series of games between the top four teams. The Tigers won their first game, lost their second and defeated Essendon by 20 points in the last game. However, Richmond was required to beat the Dons by 39 points to win the premiership, therefore Essendon claimed the premiership by percentage.

This was Thorp's and Hall's last game, but the old champions were soon to be replaced by new ones like Jack Titus, Percy Bentley, Allan Geddes, and Basil McCormack.

Minogue resigned after 1925 and was replaced as coach by another pre-WWI Richmond player, Frank 'Checker' Hughes. Hughes was a member of the 1920 and 1921 premiership sides and cut his teeth coaching the Richmond Junior League Football Club, later to become the Tigers' Second XVIII, and colloquially known as the Cubs.

TREVOR RUDDELL

Vic 'Flipper' Thorp

1910-25

Fast and aggressive, Vic Thorp was arguably Richmond's first VFL champion. He was a premiership player of 1920 and '21 and 14 times a Victorian player. Thorp was elevated as the club's sixth Immortal in 2015. Here, in an 1938 extract from his memoirs – printed in *The Sporting Globe* – Thorp reflects on life as a Tiger.

Born
Oct 25, 1890

Died
Oct 1, 1941

Played
Richmond
1910-1925
263 games,
7 goals

My story is the story of the Tigers. It begins back in the days when we played for a hatful of coppers, and often not that. But they were days just as dear to memory as these days of prosperity.

I began in 1910. The peculiar part of it was I wasn't keen to join Richmond. I was set to play for St Kilda. In fact, the negotiations were almost complete when Andrew Manzie, the Richmond secretary, came out to see me at Toorak on the morning of the match. He stressed the point that I was a Richmond lad and should play there. I had previously played with Beverley, who were really the Richmond second eighteen in those days.

Earlier still I had been captain of cricket and football at the Yarra Park State School. Strange how things happen. Richmond were very small fry those days. Nobody seemed to be interested in whether we won or lost. Week after week we went out and were trimmed. One day something went wrong and we won. Ruckman Barney Herbert went home full of joy at our luck, but his wife thought he was tight and wouldn't believe him. "I won't believe it till I see it in *The Herald*," she said.

I remember the first time I ran out in the Tiger stripes. I had on new boots, socks, guernsey, pants, a brand-new player with a brand-new kit. It was against South at South (round 1, 1910). As I threaded my way through the crowd to the ground I heard someone ask 'Who's the dark chap?' 'That's Thorp, a new man, wonder how he'll shape?' 'Won't matter much,' was the reply of the disillusioned one.

I was stationed at centre half-back. Opposed to me was a well-known South Melbourne champion. The first time we flew for the ball together he gave me a rabbit killer on the back of the neck and I was out on my feet for some time. My play that day won the following comment: *Thorp did fairly well but was not up to expectations. Thorp was just another dud in a dud team.*

With a touch of pride, I confess to a record. When I folded away my uniform I had played for 16 years with the Tigers. In nine seasons I had seldom missed a match. [Ed's Note: between 1917- 1925 Thorp missed only three matches and finished his career tally on 263 games.]

I was 35 when I gave it away and I felt l still had a year or two of football in me. I went out when I felt I was just at my top and that any further football would find me slipping back a shade or two.

You know, people who follow football can be very unkind to the champion of yesterday. You like the winners and the man who is slipping is forgotten. One little incident connected with the Richmond team made me determined that I would go out of the game whilst still pulling my weight in the eighteen.

One of the finest forwards I have seen and certainly the most delightful kick football produced during my time was the late George Bayliss. He was a pretty player to watch. He moved gracefully and was chock-full of good football. He headed the list of goalkickers in the League (1920, 63 goals) and was presented with a gold watch and chain. George was cheered to the echo, and carried off the ground shoulder high.

Two years later occurred one of the worst things I have to associate with you, Richmond barrackers. You hooted and jeered at Bayliss when as a very sick man; he was still battling for you and not meeting with the same success. I have never seen a man run through the gate wearing your colors that was not doing his best for you. So I plead to you to honour every man who wears your uniform.

Vic Thorp (5) flies for the ball during a Round 7, 1924 match at the MCG against Melbourne. Number 13 for Richmond is Frank Huggard.

Few people realise that behind the Thorp of the Tiger lair was the brain and co-operation of my fellow players, which allowed me to do spectacular things with every degree of safety. There was a simple code of signals between us that brought elaborate results.

When Norman Clark came to Richmond as coach (1919) he was insistent that surprise, backed by solidarity, was the greatest factor in winning football matches. I could see from the first time he ran on the ground to supervise our training that he was not satisfied with the methods of Victor Thorp as full-back.

'Vic, you are not nearly as good as you could be,' he told me one night. 'You haven't the dash you should have, and anyone who knows football can see a mile off what you are going to do with the ball.'

He said that if I did as he told me he would make me the best full-back in the game. I said I was willing to learn anything he could teach me. There and then began one of the finest lessons any full-back, or any player for that matter, ever received.

He started to drive the ball a yard short in front of me, kicking it to me from the centre of the ground. Then it got two yards short and three yards until he had me reaching out and taking balls that previously I had been content to gather on the first bounce.

This increased my pace and judgement and anticipation, which are the main things a full-back must have.

The next step in this education was instruction in swinging the ball when kicking. I soon learned how to drive a ball to a pack and then swing it across the side where our big fellows were.

Tiger rover Doug Hayes collects the ball as Thorp trails him into the goalsquare during their round 1, 1923 meeting against the Demons.

We developed a system of signals. I knew Barney Herbert or Hughie James would be standing innocently on the edge of a pack when one or the other would move his right hand or his left hand. Barney would wave a left hand and start to run across to the left with the pack chasing him. Hughie would stand where he was. I would run as if to drive the kick-off to Barney and swing it across to Hughie. If I held the ball in my left hand the left hand back pocket would immediately, when I went to kick, block the full-forward. Over the line I would go with the wing man giving me a lead.

The first time I tried the little kick and run technique for which I became noted was at St Kilda. Coach Clark pointed out that I was not making enough use of my pace. He convinced me that a full-back can be as tricky as a full-forward. It was prearranged that with the assistance of my back pocket men I would just tap the ball over the goal base and bolt. The first time I tried it, the field was so amazed and I got well up to the centre and found George Bayliss (1914-23, 89 games, 217 goals), our centre half-forward, with a long kick. We got the goal and naturally the move was a sensation.

On the 1920 premiership, Richmond's first VFL triumph

The bell! – I'd had an ear cocked for that first note – and this was a premiership. Something turned over in my stomach. I felt as if I was going to be ill. The crowd became a mass of blurred faces. I fumbled my way forward to the dressing room. What was the premiership anyway? I remember asking myself as I pushed my way through the crowds to the Richmond dressing room. Strange the way things affect you. Here was something I had been fighting for since 1910: a premiership. I did not know what it was, or whether I wanted it.

Richmond had won its first premiership and we were celebrating. There he stood, a crayfish in each hand, Barney Herbert, rampant, on the pedestal of G.G.Bennett's (former Mayor of Richmond and Richmond FC President) statue with a background relief of the Richmond Town Hall. Barney was yelling: 'What did we do to them?!'

'*Eat em Alive!!*' roared the mob, and Barney waved the crays again and again.

I know one thing: the players of my day were brought up on very hardy times. In those early days at Richmond, if you got a hard crack you picked yourself up off the ground, if you could, shook your head and went on with it. The use of a hot shower in a visitors' room was unheard of in our time. In some dressing rooms there weren't even showers. We were rubbed down on hard plain – very plain – boards. There were no covers and cushions like today. And dressing gowns for players! We were lucky to get uniforms in our early days.

Richmond have always followed a fixed course in meeting a Grand Final. Lunch at somewhere just after 11; a good beef steak. Afterwards, early to the ground and, as a golden rule, every man to lie flat on his back in relaxation for some time, before the time came for final preparations, rubbing, togging, etc. The team plan should not be left 'til the last moment. A team should be ready, waiting for the bounce of the ball. There's no good purpose served by a coach getting up and yelling at his charges like a native witchdoctor to intoxicate them to a state of hysteria. Every man's part in the big game should have been explained to him earlier in the week. On the day a coach should have a cheery word for his charges. He might even discuss briefly their part in the game, but games are not won by stump oratory. Better a team calmly determined than a team intoxicated by battle talk.

The strange thing about my football career was the way I was always forced to do the thing I liked to do least. Just as I wanted to badly play with St Kilda and finally ended up with the Tigers, so I hated the idea of playing full-back.

"I was willing to learn anything he could teach me. Norman there and then began one of the finest lessons any full-back, or any player for that matter, ever received."

The greatest forward I was ever asked to mind was Dick Lee of Collingwood. There was always something subtle about Lee, just like that ... lean over on to me ... nothing that the umpire could have detected, but definitely sufficient pressure to over balance me.

Any full-back hoping to stop Dick Lee had to be shrewd as a monkey. The only way to stall him was shoulder to shoulder. There are times when he left me standing, as he left every other full-back in the game, for he seldom did the same thing twice. It was when he ran towards the boundary line that he was most dangerous. He would streak across goal to what looked like an improbable position. However, to the full-back's amazement the ball would be passed to Dick Lee, who would mark it just inside the boundary line.

He would go back and place the ball and from a very short run drive it through. The best forwards of the day: Lee, Gordon Coventry, George Bayliss, Lloyd Hagger, Jimmy Freake, Jack Moriarty and Ted Johnson.

In a match against New South Wales (1925) occurred one of the most comical incidents I have seen. George Rudolph, a regular outlaw to football convention, stood at one end of the ground with a cigarette whilst the game was in progress. The ball was kicked to him. He took a one-handed mark, holding the precious cigarette in the other. Then turning sharply he collided with the umpire and knocked him cold.

There stood George – cigarette in one hand and the ball in the other – looking down at the prostrate umpire.

Pivoting on his heel, George kicked the ball through the goals, put the cigarette in his mouth and then stooped down and picked up the umpire.

I would rank the players of my experience as follows: Roy Cazaly (Sth Melbourne), Ivor Warne-Smith (Melb), Syd Coventry (Collingwood), Colin Watson (St Kilda), Hughie James (Richmond). Roy Cazaly was a drifter. His balance was perfect. He drifted out of trouble with a swaying body that you missed by inches as you dived at him.

It's us against them

Minutes before the 1920 Grand Final, Richmond president Jack Archer implored the players to defend their club's honour. An extract from his speech follows.

'Players, I am not going to tell you how to play the game, your captain will do that, nor am I going to make a 'froggy' speech such as you were deluged with last year, which sickened you to death.

You know how to play the game. The fact that you have been selected to play in the Grand Final before one of the largest crowds ever present at a football match in Australia proves that. The eyes of Richmond and the whole of the football world are upon you today, so go out and win.

The Collingwood Club we used to hold up as a pattern for sportsmanship. Yes, they were good sports at social gatherings after the matches they won, but the scene changed at Collingwood this year when we beat them, and we're going to beat them again to-day.

At Collingwood I was admiring their beautiful room and its appointments, and I noticed a nice souvenir sent by Danny Minogue to the club while away in France fighting for his country. At that time all clubs wanted to boost their representation at the war.

While I was admiring the souvenir, the secretary of Collingwood advised me that they had a fine photo of Minogue which used to adorn their walls but was now relegated to obscurity with its face to the wall on the top shelf of a cupboard. Is that sportsmanship?

I've come to the conclusion that it is all self, self, self, with the League clubs, and the Richmond club from now on is going to be the same. We're pleased to know that Les Hughes will be playing today, and we sympathise with him in his sad bereavement. He is one of the finest and manliest men playing the game. We have several players like him. I will mention just one: Dave Moffatt, who is the most maligned player in the game. I have never yet seen Moffatt do a dirty action on the field. I have been with officials of other clubs and they've criticised Moffatt and I've challenged them to prove a cowardly or dirty action by Moffatt.

Jack Archer helped inspire the Tigers to their first flag.

Though just a lightweight, the athletic Jack Titus was a stunning goalkicker for most of his 18 seasons.

Until Michael Roach achieved the feat in 1980, Jack Titus was the sole Richmond century goalkicker, kicking exactly 100 goals in 1940. He led the club goalkicking 11 times, and his remarkable tally of 970 career goals places him sixth on the all-time VFL/AFL list, headed only by Tony Lockett, Gordon Coventry, Jason Dunstall, Doug Wade and Gary Ablett. Titus – that's his right boot, pictured – played in the 1932 and 1934 premierships, won the best and fairest in 1929 and 1941 and represented Victoria 14 times.

Jack 'Skinny' Titus

Jack 'Skinny' Titus is a giant among the goalkicking greats. The first Richmond player to kick a century in a season (1940, 100 goals), his durability was extraordinary – he set a League record of 202 consecutive games, which stood until 1996.

1926-43

I was born in what some city folk are pleased to call 'the bush', at Maldon. Later I went to Castlemaine Technical School. When about 14, I played centre half-forward in the school football team, and our captain was Perc Bentley. But if I, in my innocence, thought I was a footballer in those days, I had a rude shock coming in the not distant future.

I went to live in Richmond and at once became a Tiger barracker, never thinking that before long I'd actually be playing in my dream team. That day of days for me when I first played with the Richmond first 18 was early in 1926, the season after Bentley became a Tiger. It was against South at Richmond (Rd 12). I was stationed at half-forward (and) on the wing. I could not have been a terrific success because I was dropped for the next game. I was bought back after missing three matches and played on the half-back wing.

Richmond actually dropped me twice in my first years with them. Each time I just managed to escape back into the side by the skin of my teeth. At the time I was one of the leanest figures you ever saw – just a wisp of 10-stone humanity (Titus was just 175cm and 65kg), and I was actually tried out as a defender! Barrackers, in that kindly way they have, promptly nicknamed me 'Skinny'.

In 1927 I had to swallow a bitter pill. I got a terrible drubbing on the Melbourne ground (his only game of the year). It was the blackest day of my career. Frail and thin, I was as helpless as a babe in that back pocket against such huskies as (Hughie) Dunbar, (Ivor) Warne-Smith and (Charles) Streeter in turn. Down to the seconds I went with a thud. Then came more misfortune. I dislocated a cartilage against St Kilda seconds and was eight weeks in hospital. I had plenty of time to reflect that the path to honour and glory in League football was hard and thorny.

I'm afraid Richmond were a bit dubious about sending me an invitation to train in 1928. A doctor said that I'd never be able to play football again unless I had a cartilage operation. Anyway, I received word to train and for a time was in and out of the side. Evidently despairing of me as a defender, they began to play me at half-forward and wing. That was the turning point of my football fortunes. Richmond had a trip to Mildura that season. There I got my first taste of goals, kicking seven from full-forward (July 21, Richmond 16.10.106 to Mildura 5.16.46).

After we returned, Jack Baggott broke a finger, so they put me at full-forward against Melbourne. Bill Tymms, the opposing full-back, was too good for me this day. In the last quarter my captain shifted me to centre half-forward up against the great centre half-back Bert Chadwick.

In the last quarter they put Warne-Smith on to me. What pleased me most, however, was that Richmond won. The crowd who gave me the bird earlier in the game were sports enough to give me encouraging cheers at the finish. How thankful I am to them! That season set me firmly on my feet in the goal-kicking business. The next Saturday I got nine goals against Essendon, five the following Saturday and another six against Carlton in the semi-final. You must remember that teammates deliver the ball to the forward and are a big factor in his goals. On the field I try to get in front of my man or give him the slip. Any accuracy I get in kicking comes naturally rather than from assiduous practice.

[Ed's Note: Titus has long been incorrectly credited with 204 consecutive games; upon revision, the actual tally is 202.]

Born
Mar 3, 1908

Died
Apr 19, 1978

Played
Richmond
1926-43
294 games,
970 goals

Arthur 'Joe' Murdoch

1927-36

A Richmond Hall of Fame member, Joe Murdoch played in six Grand Finals in seven years. His career was most notable for an incident with Collingwood's Gordon Coventry – he was accused of punching boils on Coventry's back to antagonise him, and both men were suspended.

Born
Oct 30, 1908

Died
Dec 26, 2002

Played
Richmond
1927-1936
180 games,
6 goals

Interviewed
Sept 30, 2000

I played my early football with Brighton Street State School. Then I started with the Church of Christ around 15 or 16 years of age. Every church used to play and I had to go to church once a month to be eligible to play. I came from Church of Christ as a forward and (Richmond) played me on the backline until, one day against Collingwood, Percy Bentley got the idea to play me full-forward and I kicked three goals against Jack Regan (round 15, 1934). I was leading poor Regan up to the centre half-forward to get the ball and I was kicking a goal from centre half-forward over the fence into Brunton Avenue.

That was a day and a half because my wife lost her blooming purse with all my week's wages in it. They took up a collection afterwards, about the only collection they ever took up, and they got enough, but the tram conductor found the purse in the Kew depot and got the money back to her on the same day. So what they gave to me I think I gave to one of the Richmond Dispensaries.

You got a uniform and boots every year. I say we had only one guernsey, and all you'd do is hang it on a nail on the wall. You had to look after it yourself, if you lost it, you'd have to get another from property steward Charlie Callander, and he'd give nothing away! If you wanted an ankle bandaged, you'd have to get on your hands and knees, he wouldn't give anything away, old Charlie. And they were all superstitious. Charlie said: 'I've only got one guernsey left, Joe,' and I said, 'What's the number?' and he said, 'It's number 13.' I said: 'Oh, that'll do me.' They couldn't get rid of it. I played about three matches with the reserves, or the Cubs as they called them, and I got picked to go to North Melbourne (round 5, 1927). I got a terrible surprise to be picked in the team and I'll never forget that match, because I was only 18. I got out there and I see the crowd all around the ground, and I'm

running around like a stunned mullet. Next thing, I get a big whack over the back of the head. It was big George Rudolph, he nearly knocked me over. He said to me, 'Now forget the crowd and bloody play football.' Percy Bentley was centre half-back then and I played centre and I played against Fred Metcalf, a big fireman from North Melbourne.

(Before the 1927 Grand Final) it rained all Friday and it rained all Saturday and the Melbourne Cricket Ground was underwater ... and they played! I was first emergency. They had no 19th man or anything then. Tom O'Halloran was picked and a quarter of an hour before he turned up old 'Checker' Hughes came to me and said, 'You better get stripped to go out.'

So I got stripped and in walks Tom with about 10 minutes to go, so I didn't play. Richmond scored one goal. That was the start of Collingwood's 1927 to 1930 victories. I played in Grand Finals in 1928 and 1929, plus in 1931, when Geelong was premier.

The moment: Murdoch grapples with Coventry. Dick Harris restrains Murdoch, while Kevin O'Neill comes in from the left to assist.

It took us six years to win it and that was one of the proudest moments in my life when I played in the bloody year we won the 1932 Grand Final. We beat Carlton ... it was just another game, you got nothing for it. We were all together and we went around to all the theatres on the Saturday night after the Grand Final.

You never sang after a game or anything like that, you just played the game and off you went. If they had a social on at the club you might go to the club for a dance. I used to get away from the ground as quickly as I could.

There were 75,000 (at the 1933 Grand Final) and that was one of the record crowds at the time at the MCG. In 1933 we had Billy Schmidt, who gave the worst ever coach's speech before going out to play a Grand Final: 'If you can't win it, make a game of it.' God strike me, that was his speech.

I always gave back what they gave me. Umpire Bill Blackburn, when he bounced the ball, he used to throw his hands up in the air. As he did that there were whacks and things going on all over the ground – waiting for this bloke to throw his head up. There was the day (revered Carlton tough man) Tommy Downs came up to Tiger wingman Alan Geddes. He shook hands with him before the game and he said to Alan, 'You going to be all in or you going to play football?' Alan said, 'You please yourself, but what do you want to do?' 'Well, we will play football.' As soon as the ball was bounced, Geddes was flat on the ground.

Well! What Tommy Downs took after that was amazing.

The Tigers mark their 1934 premiership: "May you continue in the colours."

Murdoch and Gordon Coventry were suspended for striking each other in round 13, 1936. Coventry unsuccessfully claimed he had boils on his neck, and that Murdoch deliberately punched them. He received eight weeks and missed playing in a premiership; Murdoch was outed for four weeks, returned for round 18, then retired.

Don't bring Coventry up. It was most disappointing when I got rubbed out. It was at the end of my career, in 1936. It's worried me all my life. I've put up with it all my life. The boundary umpire had seen this melee, you see there was (Jack) 'Cracker' Knight and Harry Collier, and they were all in it. I was centre half-back and Gordon Coventry came running down the ground after he got hit in the goalsquare. I didn't hit him. He ran from full-forward and I was going back to my position at centre half-forward and he came rushing down the ground. I turned around and looked at him, spun him around and sat him on the ground. Nobody saw the boils. He shouldn't have been playing if he had boils.

Of course, that's when old John Wren had the old 'Carringbush'. You ever read *Power without Glory*? There's a lot of truth in that. Still, that's all gone by now. So Mr. John Wren came down on the Sunday morning and there was Harry Dyke and Jack Smith, the secretary of Richmond. They'd all come to see me, and they said, 'Will you come with us this morning, we want to go over to Studley Park Road.' I said, 'What for?' They said, 'Oh, we'll tell you when you get there.'

So we went over to Studley Park Rd and there's John Wren's place! I walked in there, and I don't remember if it was old John Wren or his son, but they offered me £50 pound if I go up and plead guilty. That was a lot of money. But I said, 'No, no.' I told them where to go and what to do. I was really crook on them. So, no, I didn't plead guilty at the tribunal, no fear I didn't.

They knew bloody well I was right. Of course, you had to defend yourself in those days. I said 'He never hit me, I never hit him.' But he got eight weeks (and missed the 1936 Grand Final) and I got four. I don't know why – for not hitting him? I didn't know if he (Coventry) was there at the tribunal or not. I never spoke to him. Never spoke to any Collingwood player. Still don't.

"I didn't know if Coventry was there at the tribunal or not. I never spoke to him. Never spoke to any Collingwood player. Still don't."

Worst injury I had was a broken jaw, that was at South Melbourne. I think it was Laurie Nash that did it. Anyhow, they put me down in the forward pocket and there was Brighton Diggins. He finished me off. I didn't even know my jaw was broken. I went out to tea that night and I was just about done, I didn't know until Monday morning when the doctor came down. I've also had broken ribs and a broken nose. I was playing against Geelong and big Bill Kuhlken had one of those new canvas guernseys on. I went to grab him and it knocked my finger right back. I looked down and my knuckle was sticking right out. I yelled out to old Ernie Saunders, the head trainer at the time, and he came out and had a look at it, got it and pulled it back into place. He put some old sticky plaster around it and I played with that for four years afterwards.

Bob Pratt was a bloody good footballer. I can see Pratt now, getting a mark, kicking it from centre half-forward on the MCG for a goal. Roy Cazaly, he was good, a left-footer who played in the ruck. Haydn Bunton was all right, Nathan Buckley reminds me of him – he's a fringe player, waiting for the man to give him the ball and run around. 'Kick it to me, Kick it to me.' I was playing full-back against Fitzroy one day. The full-forward was got a mark 30 yards out in front of goal, and Bunton's yelling 'Kick it to me!' I said, 'Don't you kick that ball to him, have a shot at goal.' He had a shot for goal. I said to Bunton, 'If he had kicked it to you, I would have knocked you right over.' Old Dickie Lee was a great place-kicker. He was a great forward.

In the Richmond side they were all pretty good. There was a famous backline: O'Neill, Sheahan, Bolger, Baggott, Murdoch and McCormack. Then there was Judkins, Zschech, Geddes. They were picked every week. If Maurie Sheahan got hurt I went full-back and Gordon Strang came and played centre half-forward.

They all say to me, 'Did you play with Jack Dyer?' I reply, 'No. He played with me.' He was only a kid when I started.

Murdoch's 1934 premiership medallion and his pocket watch for winning RFC's most improved player award in 1929.

Man against Machine

There were no bigger VFL rivals than Richmond and Collingwood in the late '20s and early '30s. In second quarter action from the memorable 1930 semi-final, Martin Bolger (21) evades the grasp of diving Magpie great Gordon Coventry and the oncoming Harry Collier. Watching on are Richmond teammates Maurie Sheahan (left) and Kevin O'Neill – a rare image of the famed Tiger trio together. The Collingwood 'Machine' won by three points, and went on to win the premiership.

Sid Dockendorff

A man who lived through every Richmond flag, Sid Dockendorff enjoyed brief success with the Tigers before choosing to cover the game on radio. Deeply modest, he attended Jack Dyer's funeral in 2003, at age 93, by catching public transport from his Parkdale home.

1932-33

Born
May 6, 1908

Died
Aug 9, 2005

Played
Richmond
1932-33
13 games,
5 goals

Footscray
1935-37
17 games,
15 goals

Interviewed
Dec 12, 2000;
Mar 6, 2001;
Aug 26, 2001

I was born four days after Richmond's first ever VFL game, which makes us nearly twins. I was a kid from the country, born in Wangaratta. There were 11 in the family. My mother died aged 37, when I was seven, and my father died aged 59, when I was 19. My mother's family had a big property up at Hansonville and the home now is in fact National Trust. On my father's side, there were four boys and my grandfather came from America.

Ned Kelly, the bushranger, used to work for my grandfather. My grandfather used to have a lot of sawmills around the Wangaratta area. Ned Kelly worked as a teenager, cutting down trees. And my father went to school with Stu Hart, from the Kelly Gang, in Wangaratta. My father was with an auctioneering firm and a flour mill. He used to travel around the Riverina selling flour and wheat.

In the war time I knew Jim Kelly, the youngest of the Kelly family; I was at his funeral. I helped fill up his grave in Glenrowan. My father's brother, Bob Dockendorff, he was in the Station Master's Office when they brought Ned Kelly in after they shot him. He knew Ned Kelly very well, they almost grew up together.

At about 12 years old I was sent to St Pat's College in Ballarat. I was a boarder out there with (teammate) Maurie Sheahan and (Geelong legend) Reg Hickey. When I left school I went to Melbourne for a job and went to Middle Park and played for the Catholic Young Men's Society (CYMS). Austin Robertson, he was a good footballer for South Melbourne and a famous runner, he and I played in the same team. They were depression days, there was a lot of unemployment everywhere in the 1930s, which changed things a lot.

I was fortunate never to be out of work. I spent many years at Marchants at Richmond, in York Street.

I came to Richmond in 1930, but I couldn't stay there as I was tied residentially to South Melbourne. Stan Judkins and I boarded together at the same house in Punt Road, the year he won the Brownlow Medal (1930). In those days there were no first, second or third votes, there was only one, and he got four votes and won. There were about three or four tied but he got it because he played fewer games than the other fellows did (Judkins played only 12 games that season).

The funny part about Stan Judkins was that his second name was Lucas and mine was Christopher so we'd call each other by our second names on the field. I would call him 'Lucas' and he used to call me 'Chris'. Everyone would say, 'What are you bloody talking about!?'

I believe the training was harder than games themselves. It was non-stop. You went for about an hour and a half and there was no let up at all. That's where you got physically fit and if you turned your back, 'Checker' Hughes would abuse you, he'd make you lead for the next ball. Today they just go around handballing to each other.

Trying out for League football was a major trial in those days. It was the biggest shock I've ever had. On a Saturday in March, 1930, they had about 100 people training. It was hard to get a bloody kick because the Richmond players would be kicking to each other. We even had practice matches to delete the numbers, and I was still there.

There used to be a priest called Father Tehan, who came from Rochester, the same place as Basil McCormack (1925-36, 199 games, 1 goal). And my name was in the paper one day, that I was training at Richmond. I ran into him at Scott's Hotel in Melbourne, and he must have read the paper because he said, 'Do you know Basil McCormack?

The 1933 Tigers. Back row, left to right: Jack Baggot, Joe Murdoch, Jack Titus, Doug Strang, Tom O'Halloran, Maurie Sheahan, Jack Dyer, Gordon Strang. Middle row: Eric Zschech, Kevin O'Neill, Maurie Hunter, Basil McCormack, Percy Bentley, Alan Geddes, Martin Bolger, Ray Martin. Front row: Stan Judkins, Jack McConchie, Sid Dockendorff.

This ball was mounted after Doug Strang, pictured in the team shot above, kicked a club record 14.2 against North Melbourne in Round 2, 1931 – his second game of League football.

Sid Dockendorff played in Richmond's great era of the thirties, and was privileged to play in the same side as the famous Strang brothers. Few footballing pedigrees have produced talent the equal of Albury's Strang family. Doug (right) and Gordon figuring prominently in the Tigers' success of the early 1930s, and Doug's son Geoff playing in two premierships of the late 1960s. William Strang – father of Gordon and Doug – played 69 games for South Melbourne from 1904-07 (and in a brief 1913 return).

If not, make yourself known to Basil.' So at the next night down at training I made myself known. 'Oh! Well, get out next to me,' he said. And every time he got the ball, he kicked it to me. So it comes down to the deadline, there's about 40 of us left trying to make the final list with the current players and Basil, the vice-captain, said, 'They tell me you've got a big chance of making the list, but I've got to give you the works.'

We were told to come down on Sunday morning and they'd name the list.

The two Strangs (Gordon and Doug), Kevin O'Neill and I made the list. But I had to give my guernsey back because South Melbourne wouldn't give me a clearance. So I had to play with Sandringham for two years.

When I got to Richmond in 1932, 'Checker' Hughes was coach. He was very technical and very successful both at Richmond and later Melbourne. Bill Schmidt coached in 1933. He came from the bush at Warracknabeal. He was only there for 12 months, then Percy Bentley took over as playing coach. In 1932 (round 10) against Collingwood, at Collingwood, there were three of us as emergencies, and somebody was taken ill and they had to pick a player to take his place. So I got picked in my first game. You had to take your gear with you as emergency, just in case. It was a fairly wet day and I played in the forward pocket. I hardly got a kick and Collingwood beat us.

When we won the premiership in 1932 we headed for Jack Smith, the secretary's, place. He lived down around the end of Burnley Street and we had a celebration down there. During the night (Carlton forward) 'Soapy' Vallance turned up. He and Maurie Sheahan were great mates but Allan Geddes wouldn't have a bar of him and we had to try and separate them a couple of times during the night.

In 1933 I got hurt pretty bad in an accident against Collingwood. (Albert) Leeter Collier caught me in the back accidentally flying for a mark. I didn't know how bad it was at the time but I was bleeding internally. But there was a famous doctor, Dr Roy Park, a former Australian cricketer, and he put injections in and I played in the second semi-final against South Melbourne. They beat us, so we had to play Geelong in the preliminary final.

However, a couple of days later I went down for treatment to Roy's place in South Melbourne and I collapsed in the carpark and they rushed me to hospital. I knew my days were finished.

In 1934, I got talked into broadcasting football with 3UZ. A fellow named Jack Gurry was the full-time sports broadcaster and he invited me to a test case in

"We're tossing the coin and Percy has his arm around me. I win the toss and he tells HIS players to kick with the wind. I said 'I won the toss!' and he just had this grin, ear to ear."

Bourke Street. So they gave me a book and the three chaps were up in the balcony and they said, 'Turn to page so and so, clause so and so, and read that.' So I read that. It went on two or three times, and the next thing was 'Broadcast a match, visualise a match.'

Anyway, I got the job broadcasting and we had Richmond and St Kilda games. They made a little staircase, about 10 feet high, down the railway end of Punt Road.

Only three of us could fit – the mechanic, Jack Gurry and I. It had cover over the top but nothing around the side. We used to climb up a ladder to get there and one time somebody pinched the ladder and we had to slide down the pole to get to the ground.

The Argus had a map of the ground in the shape of a clock and you had to mention the fact that the ball's at 'such and such o'clock'. One day I said 'The ball is at such and such a time' and somebody yelled 'You're a bloody liar Dockendorff, it's not.' It went all over the air. On Friday nights we used to go in for a half-an-hour show. The more letters you got for the abuse, the better the station liked it.

In 1935, Sandringham was in the Association and the doctor said I was fit to play again and they offered me five pounds a week to be playing-coach. So I went down to Sandringham and I finished up halfway through the season; I couldn't cope because of my work. So I retired. Then, John McCarthy, who was at Footscray at that stage came to me and said, 'Are you interested in playing League Football again?' So I went out to Footscray and captained them in 1937. I was an old man and they were only kids. Syd Coventry was coach. The second match we played Richmond at Punt Road and Percy Bentley was captain-coach.

It was fairly windy and we're tossing the coin and he has his arm around me. I win the toss and he tells HIS players to kick with the wind. I said 'I won the toss!' and he just had this grin, ear to ear.

Ron Todd, what a player! We were playing Collingwood at Collingwood and it was his first game in League football. So on the Saturday I am going out to the ground and on Flinders St. Station here's Ron Todd, all on his own. So we went out to the ground together, and he played wing and half-forward and kicked four goals in his first game.

Haydn Bunton should have won four Brownlow Medals, not three. Bunton could go on forever, he never stopped running. This bloke was an all-rounder who played all over the ground. He never walked, he trotted all the time. He had three jobs at one time. He was captain-coach, which took in £7 a week, he worked at a retail firm and got £7 a week and got £7 a week to write for *The Herald*. We used to call him the 'Three Sevens'. That's a lot of money then – £21 a week. He also won three Sandover Medals in Western Australia.

The biggest compliment I ever got in football was when I was at Footscray and we were playing Fitzroy. Syd Coventry said to me 'I've got a job for you today, wherever Bunton goes you go.' He didn't get a Brownlow Medal vote and neither did I, but I chased him all over the ground all day long and got knocked up.

Dockendorff contemporary, 1930 Brownlow Medallist Stan Judkins.

Frank 'Checker' Hughes

Having played 87 games for the club, 'Checker' Hughes coached the Tigers to the 1932 premiership, having lost the Grand Final in four of the previous five seasons. His son, Frank Jnr (who played three games for the Tigers) recalls his father's career.

1914-15
1919-23

Frank Hughes Jnr

Born
Feb 9, 1921

Died
Apr 1, 2008

Played
Richmond
1944, 3 games
Melbourne
1945, 8 games

Interviewed
2003

Frank 'Checker' Hughes Snr

Born
Feb 26, 1894

Died
Jan 23, 1978

Played
Richmond
1914-15, 1919-23
87 games,
51 goals

Dad was a Freemason and he was elected Chairman of the Freemasons Club yet he was only a Master Mason. That was like a Private in the army, the lowest rank to ever be the chairman of the club. He was something of a philosopher. He had the ability to sum up a player, starting with, 'Now, son ...!' He could severely reprimand them and be really hostile towards them but they would accept it and they'd respond – in most cases.

After a match he might go to town on a player for his performance on the day and perhaps dress him down; at the finish of it he would say, 'Well go on, better have a drink,' and they'd go and have a drink together. That was it. He had his say and it was up to the player to say, 'He doesn't know what he's talking about,' or, 'I had better take notice of the coach.' They were the alternatives.

He was quite a good scholar, dux of Collingwood State School. So he had the intelligence and the ability to learn. He was quite a good speech maker. He'd raise his voice at the right time and do the same lowering it. It didn't matter what the subject was. He didn't have any written notes.

He did it comfortably. Jack Dyer himself would say, 'When Checker Hughes had given a speech, he was so forceful, so emphatic that you'd go out on the ground with the hairs on your arm standing up.'

Coach Checker Hughes, third from right, enjoys the Tigers' trip to Brisbane aboard *The Canberra* for an exhibition match in 1930.

Dad was working down at the wharf and then in the Victoria Railways. He had to travel from Brunswick sometimes twice a day for a pick-up and it was a bit expensive, so he bought a bike – he used to bike it down and back maybe twice a day. The Great Depression came along, so you can imagine how things were; they were pretty tight at that time.

He was playing with Richmond before the First World War and then had a break because of the war. He was very keen to play with Collingwood after the war and they showed a bit of interest in him. But at some stage Dad was supposed to have done Military Training; he got detention for not turning up. When he was in detention Collingwood didn't bother with him, but Richmond turned up and brought a football down and said, 'You had better have a bit of practice while you're here.'

So when he came out he was free to play. Richmond contacted him and he signed up. The president of Collingwood came around on his horse one day and said 'Well, now what about you coming over to Collingwood?' Dad replied, 'Oh. I'm sorry, I've signed with Richmond.' He said, 'You bloody fool ... giddyup!' and away he went. And that's how he got to be at Richmond, and played in the 1920 and 1921 premierships.

Between 1924 and 1926 he went to Tasmania. A very good friend of his, a chap by the name of Johnny Bain, who was a golf professional

“Checker” Hughes, flanked by two of his finest players of the era, Percy Bentley (left) and Allan Geddes.

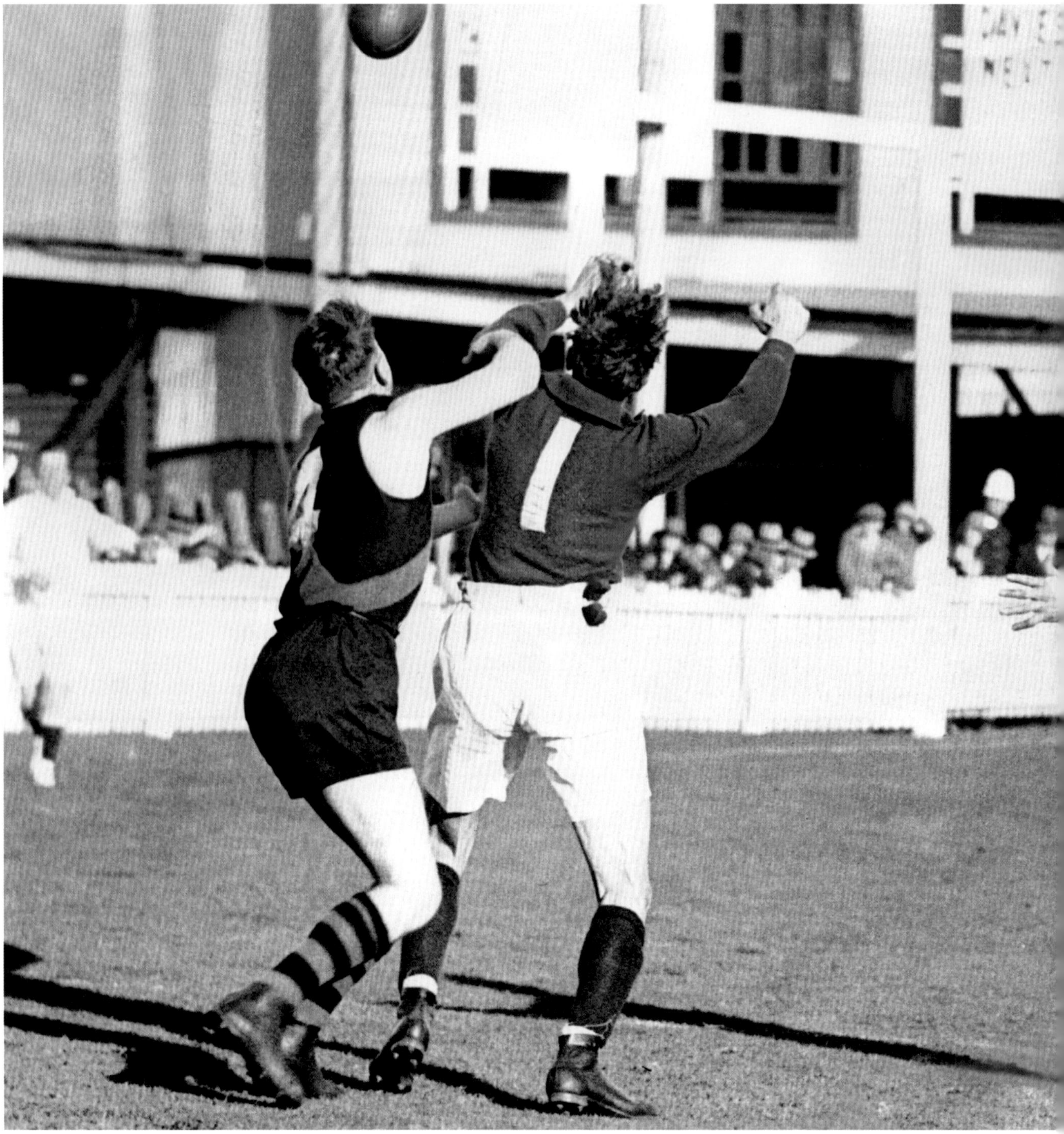

The Tigers played Carlton in an exhibition match in Brisbane in 1930. Carlton's Horrie Clover, is spoiled by Maurie Sheahan, while Don Harris looks on.

in Tassie. He said 'There's a coaching job going over here; captain-coach', so he went there and the best he could do there was to get runner-up with Ulverstone.

We lived in Tasmania. As a matter of fact, over there he owned a billiard room and when he came back to Melbourne he had a billiard room in Bridge Road, near the corner of Burnley Street, opposite the Royal Oak Hotel.

From there, he went into a hotel – he took over from the Strang brothers.

Percy Page, who was secretary at Richmond, invited him back. He said, 'C'mon over, I think there could be a coaching job over here.' So he came over in 1926. We took up residence in Burnley and he got the job and did pretty well.

He used to sit on a bench when coaching, no shelter whatsoever, just a hard wooden bench. You'd put something over your head that was waterproof. It wasn't easy. I would sit at the end of the bench because he would have the 19th man alongside him,

the chairman of selectors, and (property steward) Charlie Callander. I used to walk out on the ground with dad at three-quarter time. He loved football. Nothing would please him more than to refer to a footballer as one of 'his football sons'.

The nickname 'Checker' came from his youth. He had a friend living in Lincoln Street in North Richmond. And this mate had pigeons and he had a younger sister, and whenever dad called around to pick him up, she would see dad and she would come up to him and say 'Checker!' Of course, he used to lift her up to see the 'Checker' pigeons and that was how he got his name. It seems logical to me. When she wanted to see the pigeons she'd say 'Checker'.

A year or two before they got the premiership in 1932, Percy Page went over as secretary of Melbourne Football Club. He was talking to dad, he said 'Well you know, are you going to continue on at Richmond?' Dad said, 'Yes I would, but they can't get me a job.'

And Perc said to him, 'Well, I've got a printing business' – which he did have in Queen Street – 'and you can come as a sales rep if you come over and coach.' So he talked to Richmond about it and they said, 'Well, sorry, we can't get you a job.' So that's how he came to go to Melbourne. You had to have a job. He'd been at Richmond coaching from 1927 to 1932; he had no income other than being paid for football. I think that had Richmond been able to provide that opportunity for him he would have remained there, but he went on to at Melbourne. There's a photo of him when he first went to coach Melbourne ... (he's) in the centre of the ground and he still wore his Richmond jumper.

"Dad christened Melbourne the Demons. They had been called the Fuchias ... He said, 'You're not Fuchias, you're Demons, red-blooded Demons!' And it stuck."

You're talking about leaving after a premiership. He coached Richmond to a premiership and retired, went to Melbourne and got three premierships (1939-41), then retired, came back in 1945 ... in 1948 they won a premiership and he retired and never coached again. On three separate occasions he coached teams in the VFL, won premierships and retired.

Dad christened Melbourne the Demons. They had been called the Fuschias, because of the blue and red colours. He said, 'You're not Fuchias, you're Demons, red-blooded Demons!' And it stuck.

He and Percy Page set themselves a target of three years for a premiership. It was six years before they got the premiership. Dad went over there in 1933 and they won their first premiership in 1939. With the nucleus of players they had at Melbourne at that time, had there been no war they would have won more than three on end – it would not have been an exaggeration to say five or six in a row. They were that good.

1928-1949

PERC, 'CHECKER' & JACK

Three colourful characters defined Richmond football through the '30s and '40s, none moreso than a local kid called Jack Dyer. Embarking on his career from 1931, he came to embody the Tiger spirit.

Football at Richmond in the late 1920s and early 1930s was booming, and the Punt Road Oval was redeveloped to cater for the growing attendances. In 1927, the Chessell Wing was added to the 1914 grandstand but most work on the ground took place in the 1930s.

In 1932, the reserve was expanded to the southwest and the tennis court was removed. By 1934, crowds of more than 35,000 were squeezing into the tiny arena and a new grandstand was proposed in 1936. It was opened two years later and christened the Ernest H. King Stand. The stand would be transformed into the Richmond Football Club Social Club building after the Tigers began playing matches at the MCG.

In 1931, Richmond had three sensational recruits: Gordon and Doug Strang from Albury, and a local lad named Jack Dyer. Although the Strang brothers debuted in round 1, all would have cause to remember the Round 2 game against North Melbourne – it was in this match that Dyer, as 19th man, made his debut; he was not called upon, and spent the afternoon watching Richmond kick a League record 30.19 (199) to North's 4.7 (31). Doug Strang kicked 14 goals, a Richmond record, while Jack Titus chipped in with a handy eight himself. Strang would finish the season with 68 goals, breaking Jack Hutchinson's club record of VFA days.

Bill Cosgrove, on the right, adorned his WWII fighters with the famous 'Eat-Em-Alive!'

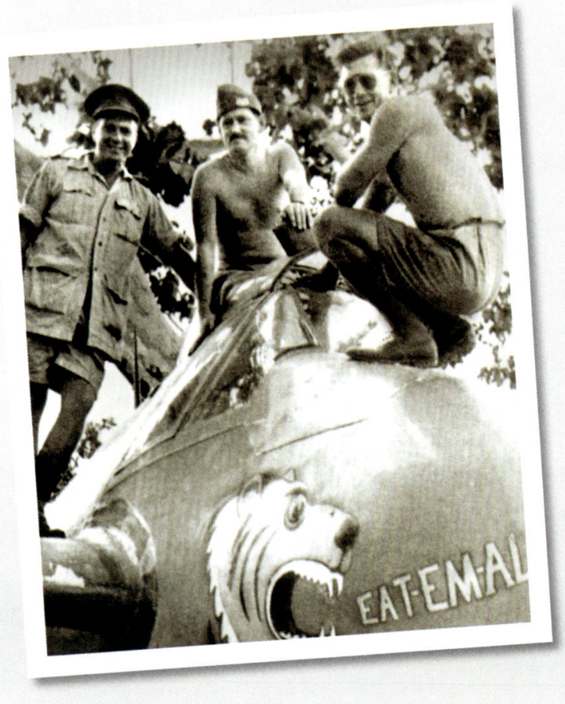

Checker Hughes was at Richmond's helm and coached the Tigers to the 1931 Grand Final, only to be defeated by Geelong. It was the first Grand Final played under the Page-McIntyre finals system, a finals format that the VFL would use until 1974.

The system's sponsor was Richmond's secretary Percy Page; he had played with the Cubs and was its secretary in 1922 and 1923. With Jack Archer, he led a Reform Party and replaced Bill Maybury as secretary in 1924. Page was a brilliant recruiter and he scoured the bush for its most promising talent – the team he built played in four Grand Finals before he resigned at the end of 1931.

As well as the aforementioned Strang brothers and Dyer, players the calibre of Percy Bentley, Allan Geddes, Titus, the "Three Musketeers" (as the Tigers' resolute defenders Basil McCormack, Kevin O'Neill and Martin Bolger were collectively labelled for their off-field antics) and full-back Maurie Sheahan were at their prime. The Tigers lost the 1927, 1928, 1929, and 1931 Grand Finals before winning the 1932 flag against Carlton. In this era it was also pitted against South Melbourne's famous "foreign legion" team that had so many Western Australian players that it was dubbed the "Swans". That was Bentley's first year as captain, and Hughes's last as coach (in 1933, Hughes was appointed to coach Melbourne by its new secretary, Percy Page.) In 1933, Richmond made the Grand Final under coach Billy Schmidt, but it was defeated by South. A year later Bentley took the reins as captain-coach and he marked his first coaching season with a premiership win over the Swans.

The era spawned Richmond's greatest character in "Captain Blood", Jack Dyer. Dyer was a tough footballer, hated by opposition supporters but loved by the Tiger faithful. In 1940, some of the committee believed that Bentley should stand aside as coach for Dyer; it resulted in

some board members losing their seats. A few older players sided with Bentley, and as a result Maurie Fleming and Harry Dyke were elected secretary and president respectively. Dyke would serve as President until 1957; Fleming would be secretary until 1954, and president from 1958 to 1963.

Bentley was appointed coach in 1940 yet his future was clearly limited. Richmond lost the Grand Final to Melbourne – the game was Bentley's last for Richmond after 16 years and 263 games for Richmond. He left to coach Carlton in a bitter split. Dyer became captain-coach, and initially found success: the club made the Grand Final in 1942 and 1944, and won the 1943 premiership against Fitzroy. But Richmond would not play in another Grand Final until 1967.

The Tigers provided a number of servicemen during the war, including Bill Cosgrove, who served in the RAAF and would name his planes after Jack Dyer – he even had a tiger's head with the club's slogan, "Eat 'em Alive", painted on their fuselage. Cosgrove played three games in 1940 before he left for the war. In 1943, he was killed in action.

In the years after the war Richmond's performance was mediocre. The club often hovered on the edge of the finals. It qualified in 1947, but was bundled out in the first week. However, there were moments of individual glory. In 1948, Bill Morris became the second Tiger to win the Brownlow Medal (Stan Judkins being the first, back in 1930).

Dyer's last game was Richmond's last of the 1940s.

TREVOR RUDDELL

Percy Bentley's ascension to captain-coach in 1934 helped continue a Richmond tradition of success, but six years later he departed in bitter circumstances when the board sided with Jack Dyer. Bentley had been a club hero: he is pictured below being chaired from the ground after winning the 1932 Grand Final, at 25 the youngest League premiership captain to that point.

Jack Dyer

They named the grandstand after him. Likewise, the best and fairest medal. The captain of the day wears his number 17, his portraits dominate the walls at Punt Road and his statue stands proudly at the door. At Tigerland, Jack Dyer is everywhere, always.

1931-49

Born
Nov 15, 1913

Died
Aug 23, 2003

Played
Richmond
1931-49
312 games,
443 goals

Captain-coach
1941-49

Coach
1950-52

In death as much as life, no other figure has so singularly represented the Richmond Football Club as Jack Dyer. He was a towering figure as player and coach, the Captain Blood mythology secured long before he played his 312th and final game. His nickname came from an Errol Flynn buccaneer movie, and indeed Dyer played his football with a swashbuckling air. He projected a ruthlessness on the field, and his captaincy and coaching tenures were marked by a fixation on the game being played by men. "No beg pardons", as it were.

In his book, *Captain Blood* (co-authored with Brian Hansen), Dyer expanded upon the origins of his nickname:

'While Errol Flynn was butchering film extras as 'Captain Blood' in 1935, I was being accused of even more brutal carnage on the football fields. Scribes at the time claimed I was littering the fields with as many broken and bloodied bodies as Flynn was in his films. So when John Ludlow, the foremost football writer of the time, dubbed me 'Captain Blood', the name stuck.'

Yet time exposed the Dyer paradox, and we got to know him away from the on-field bluster. In life after football, Jack (that's all you needed, just "Jack") engineered a successful media career on the strength of his larger than life persona, and enhanced by a perennial twinkle in his eye. His malapropisms were always funny, always forgiven. Before our eyes, he had turned into a lovable rogue.

World of Sport. Three Wise Men. The Captain and the Major. Dyer was a ubiquitous media presence at a time when we took no offence to that, and as the generations ticked by we perhaps lost our grasp of his significance as a player. Well, consider this: the first Tiger to play 300 games; a five-time winner of the best and fairest award (an honour that now bears his name); captain-coach of a premiership team (1943); two-time captain of Victoria; and, as his body aged and failed him, he moved forward to twice lead the club goalkicking.

Dyer's legacy is each week extant when the Tigers emerge from the rooms. His No. 17 jumper has permanently been awarded to the captain of the day, a Punt Road tradition of which he would surely approve. At his funeral, Kevin Bartlett and Bob Davis read the eulogies. From Bartlett's came the defining line of the service: "We are gathered here, in the heart of Richmond, to reminisce about the heart of the Richmond Football Club".

Memories of Dyer

VIC THORP

Two-time premiership defender.

Dyer is the type of player who mows down the opposition. He offers protection to his teammates as well as protecting himself. You don't maul Dyer twice. Dyer is a caveman, but that doesn't mean that he is unfair. I have never seen Dyer guilty of an offence warranting an inquiry. He will knock opponents flat. He will tear through a pack fending off his opponents with his arms but he has never to my personal knowledge ever kicked, hit or elbowed an opponent.

Dyer sets himself and tears through a pack with his shoulders and hips fearlessly turning aside opposition. There is no beg pardons about Dyer's football, but he is fair. I have seen more instances of a player trying to knock Dyer than the reverse.

Dyer has one great weakness in an otherwise flawless game – he will try to run with the ball. A big fellow should save himself all the travel he can. I think if you were looking for the greatest footballer today you would finally select Dyer.

Jack Dyer leads out a collection of Tiger talent: from the rear, Bert Edwards, Jack Scott, Robert Bawden and Dick Harris… premiership players all.

If you were seeking a key position man around whom to build a team, you would still select Dyer.

George McHutchison

Long-time Richmond statistician

Perc Bentley, he made Jack Dyer. He used to protect Jack at the bounces and then he went to Carlton (1941) and Jack Dyer was never really as good. In the early days, Jack was a 'greaser' at the Yellow Cabs. He would arrive down in training covered in grease. And at that time there used to be a mid-week competition between the Yellow Cabs, Victoria Market, Fire Brigade and the Police and he was playing in that. He hit somebody and got reported, and (long-time RFC president) Barney Herbert, the policeman, got him off.

"Perc Bentley, he used to protect Jack at the bounces and then he went to Carlton and Jack was never really as good." GEORGE McHUTCHISON

Frank Hughes Jnr.

Played three games for Richmond in 1944. His father, Frank ("Checker") Hughes Snr, was Dyer's first coach.

Dad was coaching Richmond when Jack arrived. Jack was playing with St Ignatius Old Boys and they used to play of a Sunday down on the reserve and everyone was saying to Dad, 'What a good player this Jack Dyer was.' So he said, 'I'll go down and see this fellow and see what he is like.'

Rather than be with all these fellows that were pushing Jack up a bit, Dad walked away around to the other side of the ground and got on his own to make up his own mind. And at half-time, when he went back to the rooms, these fellows were there and they said 'Well, what do you think about Jack?'

And he said 'I don't know about Jack Dyer but that bloke wearing the number 13 is ...?'

'That's it! *That's him!*' they yelled.

So that was the introduction Dad had to Jack Dyer. He didn't know who Jack Dyer was; it's as simple as that. He was probably thinking to himself 'Where is this Jack Dyer?'

Jack came down to a Pie Night to give us a talk and he was explaining about 'co-operation.' That was the theme. He said, 'When I first started to play football, we were playing a match against Geelong one day and there were two brothers playing, the Metherell brothers (Len and Jack). They were tough men and I was in ruck with Fritz Heifner and the two Metherell brothers were the opposing ruckmen. So they bounced the ball and one of them came over and flattened me, and away went the ball and, ultimately, a goal. It came back to the centre and they bounced the ball and I went down again.

And I got up and I said to Fritz, 'Fritz I'm not frightened, I can take them. But if I get downed again I don't think I'll be able to get up. So when the umpire bounces the ball next time I'll step across in front of the umpire.' So they bounced the ball and I stepped across in front of the umpire, and Fritz went *bang! bang!* and down went the Metherells!'

And then Jack said: 'Now *that's* co-operation.'

Alan Maple

Played 3 games with Dyer in 1937

I always had to oppose him when I was training if there was a game on. I reckon I am the one guy who knew what made Jack Dyer such a champion. You know what it was?

His ability to be able to be standing flat-footed in one second and within three strides he could cut you in half. That's if you were silly enough to be standing there.

Len Ablett

Played his 70 games with Dyer as first a teammate, then as captain-coach

I remember one game in particular at Toorak Park (St Kilda's home ground during WW2). Jack and I were in the ruck at the time and he said to me at half-time, 'I want you to keep an eye on Jack 'Cracker' Knight, he has been trying to get you all that second quarter. I've got my eyes on him, watching him. He hasn't got quite close enough but if he does he will hurt you.'

I said, 'Thanks very much for the warning, take note, you're my caretaker from now on,' and he said, 'Well, you go for the knock and I'll make sure he doesn't hit you.' So the ball is bounced in the centre and I went for the knock and I hadn't hit the ground when I hear, '*Ohhhh!*' – you could hear it from the other side of the street.

And I stopped and I said to Jack ,'Whatever happened to him?' and he said, 'I think he must have had a heart attack, Len.'

'Cracker' was in the fire brigade and on the next Sunday morning he came over to me and he said, 'I'll get even with him,' and I said, 'Jack, just a little word of advice. Be thankful for small mercies. If you tried to get him he is certain to end your football career. The best thing you can do is forget all about it.'

A famous Dyer moment – he tangles with St Kilda's Tom Meehan.

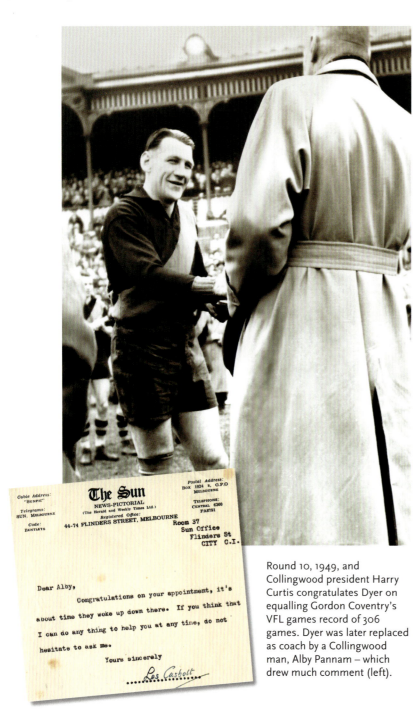

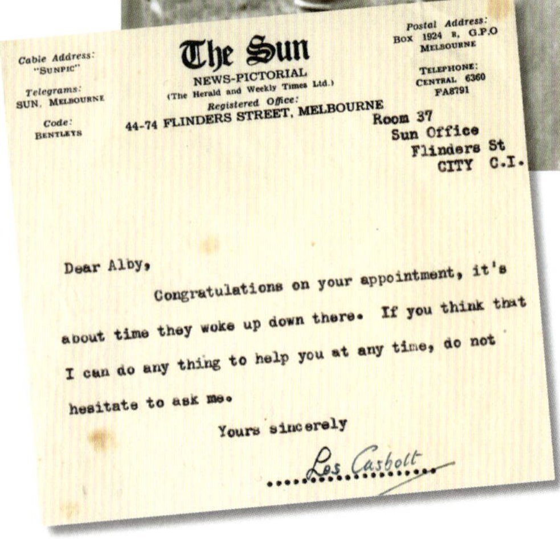

The Sun
NEWS-PICTORIAL
(The Herald and Weekly Times Ltd.)
Registered Office:
44-74 FLINDERS STREET, MELBOURNE

Cable Address: "SUNPIC"
Telegrams: SUN, MELBOURNE
Code: BENTLEYS

Postal Address: Box 1924 R, G.P.O MELBOURNE
Telephone: Central 6360 FA8791

Room 37
Sun Office
Flinders St
CITY C.I.

Dear Alby,

Congratulations on your appointment, it's about time they woke up down there. If you think that I can do any thing to help you at any time, do not hesitate to ask me.

Yours sincerely

Les Casbolt

Round 10, 1949, and Collingwood president Harry Curtis congratulates Dyer on equalling Gordon Coventry's VFL games record of 306 games. Dyer was later replaced as coach by a Collingwood man, Alby Pannam – which drew much comment (left).

They put a blanket over him on the ground and that's when that famous myth where Ray Dunn supposedly came up to Jack at half-time and said, 'It's not looking too good Jack, but I might be able to get you off on manslaughter.'

William "Polly" Perkins

Perkins was a teammate for the final decade of Dyer's playing career.

He had a trick. He had a training table and an oil bottle on it and he'd and give us an inspirational speech. He would turn around and go *bang!!* and knock the bottle off the table and yell *'Are you listening!!??'* It would frighten the hell out of some of us.

Jack was always concerned with players getting booked. But I got reported for doing something that Dyer should have got reported for. One day down at Footscray, I was playing on Ambrose Palmer, who was a boxer, and Dyer had a go at him and so did Jack Crane (1937-42, 102 games, 25 goals). Now, during the game, just before half-time, Ted Ellis – who was playing centre for Footscray – took a mark and turned around and Dyer ran right through him, fractured his nose and knocked him out. The umpire came in and said 'Perkins reported for pushing Ellis in the back!' and I said 'I knocked him with my shoulders'.

So Frank O'Brien, the barrister, went up with us and I said, 'Listen, I ran through him with a shoulder,' and I got off. It was the only time I was reported. We were playing down at Geelong and I was playing full-back on Lindsay White. I came in at half-time and Lindsay had kicked three goals and Dyer got on the bench and said, 'Listen Perkins, you and (Leo) Merrett, you think you're out on Corio Bay fishing! Pay attention and get on with the game!' It was the one time Jack did his lolly.

Frank Howard

Played a single game in 1943, then war interrupted his career. Added seven more games in 1948.

(I played) the day Dyer flattened Frank Hanna from Melbourne. We had a pretty small side in that day and Wally Lock, who was the Melbourne half-back and sometimes full-back, he clocked Ron Evans, and Uncle Jack decided it was time to show the flag. Right in front of the Melbourne members, Hanna turned out of the pack and Jack had lined him up from about 20 yards away and went through him like a bloody bulldozer, broke his collarbone and knocked him unconscious.

Frank Bourke Snr.

In a career cruelled by injury, Bourke Snr. played 16 games under captain-coach Dyer between 1943-47.

Maurie Fleming made Dyer, in that Dyer was the first fully professional footballer we had in Melbourne. After he got away from the police force, he had that little shop and he didn't do anything except play football. But Maurie got Jack a job writing for the paper and Maurie built Jack.

I played with Jack and I never saw Jack do anything untoward. Jack didn't kick people, but they changed the rules for him, you had to now fend off with an open hand. But he was a very honest player and a good player.

He could dish it out and he played for the ball and if you got in the road, then bad luck. Jack was an old fashioned coach: 'Big kick boys, straight down the centre.' That was the way to play in those days. He was a colourful man, Jack.

Arthur Kemp
1943 premiership teammate.
Jack had a talk to me and told me what his requirements were, what I was supposed to do and how I was supposed to ensure – and this was with everybody – that your ankles were strapped. If you rolled your ankle you were going to be in deep trouble because that was your fault, so you had to have your ankle strapped before you went out.

He talked about self-defence. Not aggression, but self-defence. That if you got hurt, that was also your fault because you weren't protecting yourself. And then proceeded to talk to me about the elbows and the knees and how you protected yourself, (how) it's far better for the other bloke to get hurt than you, because it's better for the team.

When I was picked to play in the first match he told me what we were going to do and how we were going to do it. He took the centre of the ground, up and down, and acted as a sort of kick behind the play, as they talk about these days. I ran the boundaries and did the tap-ins from the boundaries. He was captain and coach and he wasn't going to wear himself out when he could be more valuable for the whole game by conserving his strength, whereas me, (being) younger, I could run longer and be happy about it.

I don't remember any real team plan as such. You were expected to do your job, the positions that you played were such that if you did your job and the next bloke did his job you won the match. But there was no specific ways.

This is what Dyer said to me: 'You go for your marks, and I'll be behind you.' Because in running around the ground he didn't have to be first there ... if I could be first there or second there and had a chance to take the mark he would protect my back as best he could, so it gave me confidence, of course.

He used it to make sure that the man might not get up and wouldn't therefore be a factor in the game ... he was physical, very physical. I remember a game at the MCG, playing Melbourne and a fellow named (Frank) Hanna was playing for Melbourne. It was one of these skyscrapers going up in the air and he was standing waiting for it. So Dyer just ran straight through him, and the bloke got a broken collarbone. I remember another game where we played North Melbourne. Les Foote was captain-coach at that stage and I think arguably as good as Teddy Whitten in his day. He was going for the ball with four or five in the run and Dyer just uppercut him. Put their best man out of the game.

Dyer the tough man became the lovable rogue at the end of the World of Sport football panel. From left, Dyer, Bruce Andrew, Bob Davis, Neil Roberts, Kevin Coghlan and Lou Richards.

Dyer (17) in full flight. Teammate George Smeaton (24) flies alongside the Tiger legend.

BOB WIGGINS
Six seasons as a teammate.
I always thought Jack was a wonderful leader but I don't think he was a coach. I have often said that I was taught nothing by Jack, apart from what Jack wanted which was to use brawn, which wasn't my nature. I think maybe that's what kept me out of the game. I wasn't that type of player. Jack's coaching was nothing really to me. You don't like to run an icon down, but all of Jack's coaching and training was circuit work and a sprint across the ground. There was no change in routine.

When Jack wasn't there and Alby took the seniors he had great pleasure in running the guts out of everybody because he reckons we were all under-trained. Which we were. With Pannam in the seconds they were all fully fit and he had great delight in having you hang over the fence throwing your guts up. Pannam was trying to show Dyer up for his lack of coaching and training.

The last one he would take in would be Bill Wilson. He would have him down at the bottom end goals just running in and out of the goals, dodging the posts. Just to get that weave. He would also show him how to kick the goalpost as he went past, like kicking an ankle. Pannam's coaching was such that you had to be on the move otherwise you never got the ball. Jack's tactics at three-quarter time on most days was, 'All up to the backline to save the game.' That didn't breed any confidence in the side I didn't think.

I'll say this about Jack, many a game Jack would be on the forward line and we would be in trouble and he'd walk up to the centre of the ground and just stand there and you'll be battling your guts out on the backline and just by him doing that it would lift the side. His influence as a leader was far better than what he was a coach.

He was a magnificent specimen of a man. As a kid, being tall and rather big for my age, you imagine yourself to be a superman and if you stood beside Dyer in the shower you went so much down in significance. Here is this fellow with a big barrel chest and muscles on muscles. He didn't know his own strength really.

I saw him mark a torpedo going end-on once, by just putting his hand out while he was running full pace across goal and it stayed there, end on. I thought it was one of the most wonderful things I have ever seen. A great club man, would do anything for the club. I would see him come in black and blue from neck to ankle, bandaged up like an old war horse.

His influence on the game was starting to wane towards the end. He couldn't have gone any longer. That was his limit. He was slowing down and he stayed in that forward pocket.

KEVIN BARNEWALL
Played four games in 1945
I don't think Jack coached much at all. He was getting on a bit when I was there. Jack's idea, as he often said to me on the first few weeks I was there: 'If the club has signed you up, you must have enough skill. All I have to teach is how to protect yourself. Football is 90 per cent protection.'

I reckon I could run backwards and beat Jack at that stage. Although he did play on for years later. Somehow he used to get down and take marks at full-forward and kick the goals. I used to be amazed at how in the hell he did, because at training and that he was the last one you would pick. He could hold them out and take that mark with that big one hand. You'd be on your hands and knees on the mud and you hear Jack saying 'Go for it Barney! I am here, I will look after you, I will protect you.'

"Jack's tactic at three-quarter time on most days was 'All up to the backline to save the game.' That didn't breed confidence in the side." BOB WIGGINS

DES ROWE
Captained Richmond for six years (1952-57), and later coached the Tigers. Interviewed 45 days before Dyer's 2003 death, Rowe passed away in May, 2007.
There was a bit of friction in the club, because Alby (Pannam) was a typical small man, he was a Collingwood type of man. Dyer was a typical big man and Dyer wasn't too keen to go to a bloody small man. As a matter of fact, Jack didn't come near the ground for two years.

Oh, I think Jack had had enough. He'd been coach for about 11 years and I think he had enough. He had a hotel at that stage and then he had a milk bar which wasn't that far from the hotel I bought, and he and I were very close friends to the end, although I didn't see that much of him because he was so ill. I got on very well with Dyer over the years but I also got on all right (with Alby). I was in a hotel at the time and he was the sort of fellow that used to come to training and the first thing he would do is walk up to you and just smell your breath. He felt that you may have been drinking. He wasn't the most trustworthy bloke, put it that way.

(Jack) was tough but he wasn't as tough as Oppy, for instance. Max Oppy was as tough as you could make them. Jack had a lot of natural strength and you couldn't help but look up to him. He was terrific, Jack, and if he had a fault, (it was that) he wasn't as brutal as everybody thought he was. His fault as a coach was that he was a bit easy on fellows who took advantage of him. You know, they didn't train as hard as they should. In those days you could get away with blue murder, fellows like Don Fraser and Bill Morris, terrific footballers but they didn't make enough sacrifices. One was centre-half forward, the other was a ruckman. Neither of them devoted enough time or thought to their football. They were natural footballers.

Jack Watson

Watson played 18 games in the late 1940s.

I was only 18 and playing half-forward flank. If you were on half-forward flank, the first thing Dyer would tell you even before you ran out was 'Keep out, keep out!' (But) if you keep out, you're out of the game and you don't get a game next week. So you come in, try and do something and if you mess it up you're a goner. If you move yourself into centre half-forward, or down to the forward line to try to kick a goal, unless you got a goal or made a success of it you'd get a roasting. You should never have been in there. But if you didn't put yourself in a game you wouldn't get a game next week. That was Dyer's style of play.

One game against Geelong at Richmond, I was centre half-forward and the ball was coming around the wing but I led over towards the race and took the pass on my chest. Dyer was playing full-forward, and evidently he made a lead too, which I didn't see, and he pulled up. If he had have kept going he would have knocked me through the race, he was going that fast.

And he said, 'All right, all right, you've got it.' I always remember him saying, 'Don't kick it until I get back to the goalsquare.' Well, while Jack was running back to the goalsquare, which took about 10 minutes, Bill Morris was standing in the goalsquare one out and he's pointing up to the stick as if to say 'Get it down here and kick it up.'

So I let fly with a torpedo and it went through, it was a goal. Bill Morris gave me a bit of a clap and said, 'Well done!' At quarter-time, Dyer walked up to me and said, 'Next time I tell you to wait 'til I get back, you wait!' Nothing about the goal!

That was the difference between the two coaches. Alby Pannam (1953-55) would pat you on the back and say well done. Dyer wouldn't because you didn't do what he told you. As a matter of fact, I think it did come to a conflict later on in years, with a couple of the senior players, when Alby was coaching (after replacing Dyer), complaining about his method.

That would be because his style of training and teaching were not what they were used to under Dyer for so many years, and it caused a bit of a conflict between Pannam and the players. That's why he didn't last long at Richmond.

"Two knees are gone, two thighs are gone, his right hand is bandaged up, he's got ulcers, but where is he? In the grandstand? No. On the bloody ground." BILL WILLIAMS

The famous Dyer kneebrace. He wore a variety of support on both knees throughout his career, and could barely kick 30 yards by the time of his retirement.

Bill Williams

Coached by Dyer during his brief league career of nine games.

I was playing quite good football at Spotswood and they found out about me. One day I was studying for an exam at 18 and there was a knock at the door. My sister answered and said, 'I think Jack Dyer's at the door, you better come up and have a look. He's in the front room with (Richmond secretary) Maurie Fleming.' I thought they were having a joke and fair dinkum my jaw nearly hit the ground. Here's big Jack standing up there with Maurie Fleming.

He said, 'My name's Jack Dyer, we know who you are.' I said, 'I know who you are.' Jack said, 'We'd like you to come and try out. We'll have a chat to your dad then come over to my milk bar in Richmond.' I couldn't get there quick enough to sign up. I went over to sign up on a table in his milk bar and he said 'We'll give you a blazer for signing up.'

One day were playing South Melbourne at Richmond and Dyer used to play in the forward line mainly in those days. He had his two knees bandaged, he had his two thighs bandaged, he had his right hand bandaged and he had his ulcer.

I remember Jack got up on the stool to give his talk. He used to take powder for his ulcer and he got quite vocal this particular day, and the powder was coming out of his mouth. It looked like he was frothing at the mouth. Noel Ross, the centre half-forward said to me, 'Have a look at Dyer, he will kill some bastard today. I've never seen him this wild.'

I was playing on the half-forward flank against (South Melbourne's) Len Crane and Jack came leading out. They passed the ball a bit low and Jack missed it. He followed up, got about 40 yards out and he got a free kick. I thought, 'He can't kick this distance.'

That's why he was playing full-forward, he only used to kick maybe 30 yards. So I led up the ground and he kicked it to me and I got the ball 20 yards out and kicked a goal. As Jack walked past me he said, 'Thanks, Bill.'

That's all he said. *Thanks for not making a fool of me*, because of his legs. That's the type of man he was: two knees are gone, two thighs are gone, his right hand is bandaged up, he's got ulcers, but where is he? In the grandstand? No. On the bloody ground.

Tom Allen

Allen (22 games, 1949-52) made his debut against North Melbourne in Round 14, 1949, kicking a remarkable 11 behinds, as the Tigers scored 8.24 to North's 17.11. He played all his footy under Dyer as captain-coach, then coach.

I'll always remember my first game, the day I kicked 11 behinds against North Melbourne. I was playing half-forward flank. That was the year (1949) North was in the preliminary final, they were a good side. If we won we could go into the four. North had great defenders like Reg 'Dodger' Ryan and Pat Kelly. I took the tram to Punt Road by myself and then walked to the ground. The only way the supporters used to twig you were a player was the kit bag. Anyone walking in with one of those kit bags, the supporters would say, 'Oh, you're playing!' It was a dead giveaway.

Dyer leads Leo Merrett out, round 1, 1946. Richmond won by 4 points in front of 31,000 people at Brunswick St.

I walked into the rooms, no one said anything, and they couldn't get me a jumper. There used to be a bloke there called Wally Seitz, and they had cleared him to Yarraville and they said, 'You better wear his.' The bloody thing hung down below my shorts and the armpits came right down; it was a huge jumper.

Then Dyer gave his speech and I just ran out with the rest of them. No-one had told me what to do, and as I ran on the field Dyer ran over to me and said, 'Don't worry son, I'll look after you.' And the ball got bounced, it went our way and Dyer came out from forward pocket and marked it. Of course, I was moving in that direction and I was in the goalsquare by myself and, being a good bloke, he gave me a little 15-yard kick. And I always remember this – it was a sunny day, the ball was brand new and it was sparkling and it was one of those loopy drop kicks, and I could see it coming and I could see (feared Kangaroos defender) Pat Kelly coming! And it was a bloody dead heat. So here I am, lying on the ground, and there's Dyer and Mopsy (Fraser) and they are ironing blokes out left, right and centre. Their blokes are going down, and I'm thinking to myself 'I'm not going to get up,' and they're saying, 'If you touch this kid again, we will bloody well kill the lot of you.' And I never got touched again.

Havel Rowe

The first two years of his career were played with Dyer as captain-coach, then he was coached by Dyer until the end of the 1952 season.

Father and son combinations Alan and Doug Hayes, John and Jack Dyer, and Paddy and Dan Guinane.

Jack's ability was putting you out on the field. The pre-match talk was just *'Eat 'em alive!'* It was great. In 1948 and 1949 I played with Jack. He slowed up as he had a crook knee and he used to stay within 25 and 30 metres of the goal and he had this drop punt which he developed.

He was the first one I have ever seen use a drop punt. And he didn't miss many goals.

I'll never forget his last match.

We played Geelong at Richmond and he kicked six goals for the day. Dyer was in the police force, and he got the ball in the forward pocket and there were five Geelong players cornering him – he put up his big mitt like a policeman and they all stopped and he just kicked a goal from the boundary. He had that presence.

It was just incredible.

Peter Sherman

War interrupted Sherman's career, and he played just two games under Dyer in 1947.

During training in 1947, Jack took me aside. He said, 'Peter, you've got everything, but you're too much of a gentleman. You have to be prepared to walk over your best mate to get to the ball.' Jack, when he was stripped, he had big shoulders and came down to a very narrow waist, and he had strong legs and a big chest. And that was his strength.

Tom Allen

Allen played his first season in Dyer's last, and was coached by Dyer for his 23-game career.

We played at Richmond one day, and Bill Morris was after a Brownlow, I reckon. Because he used to go and pick players up who were knocked down. And before the game one day Dyer said to Morris, 'If you bloody well pick blokes up today I will bloody well knock you out myself. You don't do that!'

Anyhow, it was down at the grandstand end and Dyer had this bloke lined up and the bloke dodged and poor old Billy was on the other side and *whack!*, bloody Billy went down. So after the smelling salts he said to me, 'Careful Tom, that Dyer is bloody fair dinkum. He bloody knocks you out. He told me! He told me! He's fair dinkum. Do what he tells you.'

Jack was tough, harder than anyone, had terrific body strength. His body was like a bloody brick wall. He was strong, but his body was hard and that's when he used to hit blokes.

Allan Cooke

A long-standing Tiger official after his 116-game playing career finished.

I actually played in Jack's last game as a player, it was at the Richmond ground. They were kicking it all backwards to him to get him some kicks (Dyer kicked six goals). He was all bandaged up like a broken down racehorse.

Dyer didn't leave, Dyer got the sack. Jack took it very bitterly. In fact, they all tell you how good Jack was back at the club. But Jack really never ever got back to the club properly after that. He never came back as a Dyer guy. It really hurt him deep down.

It was time for a change, really. Jack would have been there for ever. I think it was Harry Dyke who had to go down to his hotel and tell him he was getting the sack.

Frank Ryan

Coached by Dyer in his first two years.

One of Dyer's faults was that he didn't train you hard enough. People used to bludge. I played under Dyer for two seasons and the rest of it was under Pannam. You know when he coached, (Pannam) was Collingwood. One Sunday morning he came down with his Collingwood blazer on!

I was 18 when I went to Richmond and Jack Dyer was coach for two years. He was a hero, of course. I'd always dream about him. He was a legend. You couldn't think past him.

My feeling was I couldn't believe that they got rid of Dyer. But he hadn't moved with the game. He was still back in the 1930s and 1940s. I was in Findlay's Gymnasium when I heard the news, it was in the paper at the gymnasium room. He was quite bitter, because he was replaced by a Collingwood man.

KEVIN BETSON
Coached by Dyer during his 42 games in the early 1950s
Dyer used to tell you that when he was there he used to say, 'Right, if there is going to be a brawl – all in it. They can't report the lot of us.' You had to be in it, because if you didn't your mates wouldn't think too good of you. You had to be in it whether you wanted to be in it or not.

RON REIFFEL
A brief playing career has been followed by many years of service for the past players' association.
I could run okay, I was pretty fast. I won school sports sprints and I used to love that because Jack Dyer used to come and present the trophies at the Richmond Cricket Ground.

I can remember Dyer saying to me one day after training – he was standing in the race talking to (journalist) Alf Brown and he had a football under his arm – and just as I got to the race he shoved his arm and flattened me and he said, 'Hang on, I want to see you.' So I stood over on the side and he came over and he grabbed the football and he gave it to me and said, 'There you are, son, take this home, practise your kicking over the summer. Your old man (Lou Reiffel played for Melb. and Sth Melb. in the 1930s) was one of the best kicks in the league when he played and you can't kick over a bloody jam tin. We were going to play you on the wing but we were frightened you would kill all our forwards with your floating punt kicks.'

We used to haunt him at his milk bar. Once you had been to see him play, you were easily converted to Richmond. We used to go to the pictures, either the National in Bridge Road or the Globe down near Swan St, or St Ignatius had a picture theatre, so I used to like going to the Globe or St Ignatius because at intervals you could whip over to Jack's milk bar to see if Jack was there of a Saturday night.

You'd want to see Jack, and quite often his mother-in-law would be there. Sometimes we would say to her 'Could you get Jack's scrapbooks?' and she would put them up on the counter. We'd all sit up and flip through the scrapbooks. Sometimes we never went back to the pictures.

Dyer was a one off. He was inspiring. When (Melbourne) played in 1936 at Richmond they hadn't beaten them in 10 years at Punt Road. Dyer got injured, but he didn't go off, he was holding his arm and couldn't use it and (Demons coach) Checker Hughes said at half-time, 'We got the big cat, he's hurt, we can go on with this.' And they did.

As a child, I started selling lollies, Minties and Hoadley Crumble Bars, down at Richmond with my tray. You'd walk around the inside of the oval and sell back over the fence to the people in the first few rows. I can remember selling lollies there one day; we were playing Footscray and you could hear the players and the thunder of the feet. And I was around near the Social Club building where the race is and Dyer was coming towards the Brunton Avenue end. This Footscray player was coming the other way and they both went to pick up the ball. As Dyer scooped it up with one hand he tucked his shoulder in and hit this bloke and the fellow went up in the air as though he was hit by a bull.

I could see all this dust flying out. The bloke was lying out flat on the ground and Dyer was running around bouncing the ball. It happened within six metres of where I was standing. I could hear the whack when they hit. I can still see Number 17 running away from me. It was really frightening, hearing the crash. He was something special, Dyer.

"Dyer got injured, he was holding his arm and couldn't use it. (Demons coach) Checker Hughes said at half-time, 'We got the big cat, he's hurt, we can go on with this.'" RON REIFFEL

RAY JORDON
A longtime coach of Richmond thirds, Jordon once used Dyer's eye to judge new arrival Kevin Bartlett.
Graeme (Richmond) and I said to Jack Dyer, 'Geez, we've got a really good player here.' Jack said, 'I'll come down and see him.' We were playing a curtain-raiser in the finals so Jack came down and the ball was bounced and there was a flurry of players, next thing we see, Kevin Bartlett is on the ground. So they run out, got a stretcher, dragged him off and went up the race. Jack said to Graeme, 'Is that the guy?' Graeme said, 'Yeah' and Jack said, 'What a waste of the bloody Saturday for me now,' and then he went in and saw Kevin Bartlett.

I saw old Jack play with his knee bandages; he got 35 yards out from goal and never made the distance. He was gone in those days. My old man (Clarrie, who played 15 games with Dyer in the 1930s) told me he was fantastic, how quick he was.

KEVIN BARTLETT
The man who broke Dyer's club games record, Bartlett also won five best and fairest awards.
In 1965 I was in my first year of League football, and was training with Mick Erwin. Mick had come

Dyer keeps local kids happy in his renowned milk bar.

across to Richmond from Collingwood. This night Jack came down to training.

I think it was a bit of publicity for the club – Graeme Richmond was very big in those days on getting Richmond into the papers as many times as they possibly could. Being close to the *Herald Sun* building, it was quite easy for reporters and photographers to shoot down to Punt Road and take photographs and get stories.

Jack came out dressed in a Richmond jumper, shorts and boots. He took us out there on a training night and explained how he held the drop punt – he was credited with inventing the drop punt – and how it was the most accurate of all kicks, particularly from 25 metres out.

Jack spent probably 40 minutes with us, we had a few kicks and then photographers came around and took a few photographs. It was a one-off. It was a thrill for myself and Mick that Jack Dyer took the trouble to come down. To be honest the drop punt wasn't really used a lot; at that stage I probably didn't go around doing drop punts, so Jack opened our eyes in that maybe we should be using it.

Jack Dyer Jnr

Played three games for the Tigers in 1960.

Dad never forced me to play football. I just wasn't interested in sport or football, which is wrong, but that's the way it was. Dad had a bit of a problem with me, wanting me to play sport. So there you go. He never ever pushed me to play any sort of sport. In hindsight, I wish he had, because maybe I would have been better. From the time I could remember, as a kid everyone would come up to you and say, 'Oh, you're going to play football like your father,' and it used to drive me up the wall. I was that shy I used to say anything. Once I got into it and I got to know these guys at East St Kilda YCW, it sort of came easier then. Actually, Dad came and coached the team I played for. The first year I played I think we lost the first nine games of that season and Dad came along and took over as coach and we just missed out on the four. The next (season) we won the premiership and also the year after that. If I wasn't getting a kick he would pull me off the ground. He wouldn't muck around.

Royce Hart

A champion of the 1960s and 70s, Hart saw Dyer as the great character of the club.

Jack used to drive a little Corona and he rolled it; he wasn't the best driver, Jack. And he put a big dent in the roof. There was a panelbeater down the road called Noel Stevens and he said it would cost Jack two or three hundred dollars to take the dent out. And Dyer said, 'Is there a cheaper way of doing it?' and Noel said 'Yeah, we can put some putty type stuff in it and put some canvas over the top.' Jack said 'I'll take that option.' So he's got this Corona with a big dent in the roof filled up with putty!

Ian Wilson

Richmond Football Club president 1973-85, Wilson often used Dyer to help recruit young prospects.

He helped us get Neil Balme at the airport. Collingwood sent somebody over there who we had never heard of. Neil Balme sees Jack Dyer and we sign him. When he first met me, he said to me and Graeme (Richmond), 'I hope you two public school poofters don't fuck up my football club.'

In 1974, I went down to *World of Sport* and because I was the premiership president I was going to be interviewed. Afterwards, you go and have a couple of beers in the side room and I said, 'Jack, we've won back-to-back premierships,' and I remember him saying, 'Yeah, you have done all right the pair of youse.' In 1980, the same thing. I was at *World of Sport* and Jack walked over to me and kissed me and said, 'I can die happy ... beating Collingwood in a Grand Final.'

In 1996, Jack Dyer was one of 12 inductees in the Australian Football Hall of Fame to be elevated to Legend status. It's a role that could have applied equally to his happy-go-lucky commentary on radio and TV, a role that made him one of the favourites of all football fans, no matter which club they followed.

Polly Perkins drives through an opponent in a 1948 match.

William 'Polly' Perkins

English-born Perkins arrived in Australia at the age of one, his family settling in Noble Park. A member of the 1943 premiership team, he figured in the Tigers' best three players in the winning Grand Final.

1940-49

Being born in England there was a song over there many, many years (ago), and the song was 'Pretty Polly Perkins from Paddington Green'. (Tigers secretary) Maurie Fleming gave Hector DeLacy, the *Sporting Globe* editor, a story about Pretty Polly Perkins from Paddington Green and it stuck ever since then. So there was a Polly about before Polly Farmer.

People say things are tough now – they don't even know what toughness is, the things we went through. You wouldn't be having a bottle or sandwiches and you wouldn't be having ham and you wouldn't be having cake for morning tea. Saturday morning mum would buy a couple of saveloys and a piece of bread, that was all there was for lunchtime on Saturday.

I played for Noble Park when I was 16 in an open competition, playing in the Dandenong district competition against Ferntree Gully, Boronia, Emerald and Pakenham. That's how I got signed by Richmond. About four big gentleman walked down our homemade footpath in Noble Park where I lived ... A big Buick car driven by Perc Bentley, with Maurie Fleming, Jack Smith and Lou Roberts.

My mother said, 'What have you been doing, Billy? There are four policemen at the front door.' She thought I was in trouble. They'd come to sign me up with a form four. I had won the best player in the Grand Final for Noble Park, that's why they probably signed me up. So they signed me on the kitchen table.

In 1938, I went to Richmond, played in four practice matches, didn't make it, so came back and played at Noble Park again. Practice games were hard to play in those days; we played against some second XVIII players. I played full-back and half-back flank and I played some of the practice games on the ball. I was disappointed, I suppose I might have been expecting a bit too much of myself.

I finished up making the list and I stayed down until 1950.

My first impression when I went to Richmond to start training was that I was amazed at the size of these footballers. I barracked for Collingwood because I liked the Coventry brothers, Syd and Gordon. I had a cigar box filled with autographs. The Coventry brothers were my idols.

(Richmond) got me a job at Mintern Products, making yard equipment. I worked there for three years before it burnt down. Bill Mintern was on the committee and his father owned the company. I then went to work at a roller company with Bill, who was personnel manager; we had Bill Morris, Ian Hull, Jack Scott, Jack Broadstock, Charlie Priestley and Leo Merrett all in that area.

It might have been a stunt by Maurie Fleming because all those that worked in that industry were protected from going in the army, because you weren't allowed to leave under any conditions when you were manufacturing things for the army.

We made dies for bullets for the army for the munitions factory. And permanent magnets, which I was mainly interested in, for doing walkie talkies and ships. And wire for winding coils for loud speakers.

Maurie Fleming said to me, 'I have never seen a lad kick a ball as far as you could.' When I played full-back for Richmond, I used to kick torpedo punts that would go for miles. They'd say, 'Go back and kick the drop kick, Polly'.

Born
Feb 10, 1920

Died
May 30, 2009

Played
Richmond
1940-49
148 games

Interviewed
Jul 2, 2001

I'd say, 'No, I'm kicking a torpedo, it goes further'. I kicked a ball against Melbourne at Punt Road and they measured it at 83 yards (75m) – it landed in the middle, with a wet ball too. I was a very solid player. I believed in playing the ball and if the man was there I would take him, too.

I met Jack Dyer in 1938. Jack wasn't tough, he was hard. I hate the word tough. I got invited to his wedding when I was 19. My wife came as my girlfriend. Percy Bentley was coach then, and a thorough gentleman and a very great person in my book, but there was a lot of animosity between him and Jack. Jack was going to go to Yarraville to play and coach, and that's when he stayed at Richmond, and Bentley went to Carlton (in 1940). He never came back.

Percy coached me first in 1939, then Jack in 1940, right on to 1950. 'Checker' Hughes would coach us on Tuesday and Thursday morning, for some of the players who worked shift work.

The real solid players at Richmond were Jack Dyer, Dick Harris, Martin Bolger and Kevin O'Neill.

Kevin O'Neill smothers Geelong forward George Moloney during the 1933 preliminary final. Perkins rated O'Neill among the very best during his time at Tigerland.

"Percy Bentley was coach then, and a thorough gentleman and a very great person in my book, but there was a lot of animosity between him and Jack Dyer."

But the real hard players would be Les Jones, Arthur Kemp and Dick Chergwin. Dyer, Harris, Merrett, Titus, Morris and Wright were always the best players and if you got in the first six players then you were a very good player. I did that on quite a few occasions so I was a fair player.

I was among the best three players (in the Tigers' 1943 Grand Final win). It was a great game. There was a lot of pressure all the time. I always thought we could beat Essendon because we had the edge in the backline and Dyer was playing very well on the ball. We had a couple of good rovers, including Dick Harris and Leo Merrett on one wing and Bert Edwards on another.

It was a very evenly balanced side. We only won it by five points and it was a very even day. I had a pretty good day from the half-back flank ... I kicked the ball to Jack Broadstock and he passed to Harris, and Harris went through and got a goal. That was the climax of my game.

Before there was 'Oh, We're From Tigerland', the players used to sing a song called 'With My Hat on One Side'. *'With my hat on one side... what have I here ... is in my knicky knacky noo ... My nose right, my eye ...'* And we used to sing those after the game or in social chatters.

But we didn't sing the songs like they sing now, around the group. When we won we probably go and have a shower and have one dozen bottles of beer between eighteen of us; Richmond Beer too it was. There wasn't much about, then we'd probably go and get another dozen from somewhere else – sly grog – and have a drink.

I later forged a career in the media, joined 3AW in 1956 and stayed there for 29 years doing football commentary. I worked with the gentlemen of radio: Norman Banks, Bill Jacobs and Harry Lister and Doug Heywood.

FAYR
ATS

Max Oppy showed complete commitment to the Tigers, playing through injury for much of his career.

William 'Max' Oppy

1942-54

Just 175cm, Max Oppy can perhaps best be summed up with the following words (his own): "I probably wasn't afraid and I didn't care if he was big or little. If he was in my sights, as far as I was concerned he was fair game." Four times he represented Victoria.

I was born in Maryborough. In the olden days everybody was named after their fathers and grandfathers and it became a bit confusing as to who was 'William' – they didn't use the juniors. My father was a tailor but he died when I was 12. In 1939, I left Maryborough and came down to do an apprenticeship in tool-making because most of that time was during the war years. After that I did a couple of courses in heat treatment of metal and I had a business for 30 years.

I just played footy like all kids. When I first came down I boarded and I was living on apprentice wages and didn't even get enough to pay board so I had to get subsidised from home. I used to ride my bike from Kew to Carnegie.

There was the 'Carnegie Sons of Soldiers', they played in the Oakleigh Junior League, and the only reason I played there was that the boy I worked with in the apprenticeship, he was the only kid I knew in Melbourne. At that time I was an on-baller, but wasn't very good at it.

The next year I went to Kew, I was still only 16, playing in the sub-district open competition and that's where I played my early football and started to play cricket there as well. I also played a bit of tennis and golf.

I barracked for Essendon, like all the family. Being related to Dick Reynolds (Oppy's cousin), what else! I never saw a League game up until I played; it's crazy, isn't it? I suppose like everybody else, it wasn't important to me. Not being a city person you really haven't any allegiance to a footy team like you did at that time in Melbourne.

I liked to play football but League football was far from my mind. No one got a bigger shock than me when Richmond asked me to go down and train with them. I was bound to Richmond anyway.

Ray Martin took me down to Richmond, he was recruiting for them. He didn't know me through playing – he was the coach of Kew and, being virtually Richmond thirds you got an association with the club. He may have said to me, 'Next season we will get you down and have a training run at Richmond,' but it wasn't until I read it in the paper that I'd knew I had made the supplementary list.

See, I was on nightshift because the war was on, the basic wage was £3/17/6 and you were getting three quid when you played. If you didn't play you didn't get the three pound, you got virtually the training fees, which were half price.

In 1942, there were full training sessions from the start of the season, then you played in the practice games, then the final lists were brought out a fortnight before the first game. Then you'd know whether you were going somewhere else or going home. After the training list you had to be signed by Maurie Fleming, Jack Dyer or old Pat Kennelly. So they travelled up to Maryborough and my mother was glad to get rid of me, I wasn't exactly the best kid on the block. In my first year I only played nine games, I was 17. You just live in your own little world and think, 'Geez, what is going on?' I think being from the country, it didn't matter so much.

You weren't in awe of all of them; you were living in a little world of your own, just doing your best and pinching the ball because a lot of the blokes wouldn't kick it to you. If you were going for the list or playing for a game on the training track half the bastards wouldn't kick it to you. You had to earn the respect of the others before they kick it to you.

Being the youngest of three boys and being in the country you had to fight for your bloody block. I thought I was a ball

Born
Oct 14, 1924

Died
Nov 25, 2008

Played
Richmond
1942-54
185 games,
29 goals

Interviewed
Aug 8, 2004

Oppy (centre, sitting) and Ron Durham during the three-quarter time break, Melbourne vs Richmond, 1947.

player. I probably wasn't afraid and I didn't care if he was big or little. If he was in my sights as far as I was concerned he was fair game. If I bounced off or got the worst of it that was bad luck. There's an old saying – it's not getting knocked down that hurts, it's getting up.

I reckon George Smeaton (1935-46, 149 games, 36 goals) was tougher than Dyer, and that's pretty tough I tell you. He was rock solid, good balance, great to be alongside. I've seen George Smeaton getting injections in his toe, and his toe was bloody awful, they'd just wrap it up and George would say 'She'd be right.' He was tough as shit.

I was only reported three times, I was innocent. I think they were only stupid little things. I always said that I did nothing stupid or nothing in anger. Oh, I copped a few, don't worry about that. We played Melbourne one day and Fred Fanning had kicked six goals up to half-time.

There was George Smeaton and Charlie Priestley and myself, and George worked out what we were going to do. He said to Priestley: 'You take him from one side, I'll take him from the back, and Max, you run underneath him.' Well, the ball came down and up Fanning goes and they've whacked him. I've gone underneath him and unfortunately the big bastard landed on top of me. He didn't kick another goal.

Des Rowe was 15 and I was 16 and we got dressed alongside each other. That's where we formed our friendship. He didn't make the list, he went away and played with Coburg and then he came back in 1946. When he came back we still got together again and we finished up partners at the Vaucluse Hotel in Swan Street.

I had a knee injury. I ruptured the cruciate ligament, and two or three pieces of cartilage from my ribs. I got concussed a couple of times, and a bloke kicked me and I hit him in the head and broke my thumb. I only played six games in two seasons due to injuries. I broke my wrist and I used to play with that in plaster.

The umpires would come in prior to the match and inspect everyone and it would be wrapped in bandages. As soon as the umpire went we'd put the bloody plaster on and wrap it up.

I think my first full game was against South Melbourne (round 7, 1942). I had the best view on the ground – all I saw was that bloody ball fly over my head all day. The *Sporting Globe* said *'Oppy, Richmond's new rover, needs a doctor to keep up with the play.'* That's how much in awe I was. I didn't know what I was doing. It was a learning experience, I knew that. At that time Richmond were fairly strong and I was told I would get six games straight, didn't matter what happened, but after three games they dropped me.

To break into premiership sides wasn't all that easy – I was actually lucky. There was no doubt that I was improving as they year went on and that is why I got that big job in the '43 Grand Final, looking after Dick Reynolds.

I was 18 when I took on Reynolds. If they wanted anyone out I got the job anyway. It didn't matter where Dick Reynolds went, my job was to keep him out of the play, because at that time he was the match-winning rover and probably the best rover of the League at that time. That was my job, to blanket him and keep him out of the game. Dick got about six stitches in his eyes but that was all right, he snuck into my fist. I did what I was supposed to do, put him out of the game and still play a bit of football. If they kept kicking the ball to him it became a contest, if you're close and in front and you're mauling him a bit, he just didn't like it.

That was one of the jobs I was able to do – tag people. I used to study them and didn't even give them room to spit. I was given a job by Dyer to tag Lou Richards and Des Fothergill and put them out of the game. Lou got best on the ground one week and they clapped him off the ground and the next week they booed him. In the finish, Lou wouldn't come back to the back pocket at all. Put it this way, I was disciplined. They talk about taggers or whatever today; virtually that was my job for the day.

I was always hoping to win in 1944 but couldn't see it (the Tigers lost to Fitzroy by 15 points in the Grand Final). You've got to have players. We thought we were a pretty good side in 1944, but we were beaten in the Grand Final and then we went downhill. Probably because Jack Dyer was getting towards the end of his career. On the day of the 1944 Grand Final we were a bit weakened. One of our main players, Jack Broadstock, got reported the week before, and that upset the side a bit. He was a great player. They talk about ball handlers like Baldock and the others, Broady would have killed them! He was the only bloke I've ever seen who could run and bounce the ball one hand while he was playing. It was like a yo-yo.

Jack Dyer would lift the game on his own, he could go in the ruck, next minute he'd be centre half-forward and centre half-back. Jack was a great player, there's no doubt about that. Above all he was a leader. Me being so close to Jack, he used to put me up first and every now and then if he wanted to have a go at somebody, he would have a go at me first. It meant if he had a go at me he could say anything he liked to the other players. I used to stop lacing up my boots and I'd be looking up and I'd be, 'Shit, he couldn't be talking about me.'

"That was my job, to blanket Dick Reynolds and keep him out of the game. Dick got about six stitches in his eyes but that was all right, he snuck into my fist."

I thought I just about had enough and I wanted to go out when I wanted to go, not when they said you've had enough. There was no incentive to play on, not like now. Life membership of the League, we didn't have that luxury. Having played 13 years it was getting a bit of a grind anyway. Thinking back on it I got a better send off on my final day at Richmond against Collingwood, last game of the season, than probably Jack Dyer did. The supporters gave me a send-off more so than the club. I was chaired off the ground – it brought tears to my eyes.

I was asked to coach; I was really only caretaker coach. They just asked me would I coach because they didn't have anyone. They sacked Alby Pannam and approached me and asked me if I would coach. Pannam was a tough little bloke himself. He could take a bit of punishment. He wasn't an easybeat and he liked to get the best out of the players and was pretty hard on them, but he didn't have the players.

Training was just a normal two or three days a week. It was pretty hard to get under the ball when you've got big blokes like Roy Wright. One day I found out he was at the club, but he wasn't out on the field, so I went looking and there he was out in his car eating snowballs.

He used to complain to the president (Harry Dyke) that I was training him too hard. One for all and all for one, everybody's got to do the routine whether they like it or not.

Arthur Kemp

Although he only played 34 games, Arthur Kemp was a member of the 1943 premiership team, and was voted best player of the 1943 finals. He played as Arthur Kemp, but changed his surname to Barr-Kemp 10 years later; this still causes confusion in some history books.

1943-46

Born
Sept 6, 1921

Died
Sept 25, 2003

Played
Richmond
1943-1946
34 games,
4 goals

Interviewed
Sept 27, 2001

My original full name was Arthur Lionel Kemp. Very well-known people in Fitzroy named the Barrs were uncles of my mother. One was Mayor of Fitzroy, the other was President of the Cricket Club at Fitzroy and the Bowls Club ... and they had no kids and so they asked my mother if I would mind tacking Barr onto my name. They were particularly good to my mother, she was a widow [Ed's note – his father died of diabetes when Arthur was 13 months old] and they financed her into a home. I would have been very churlish to refuse, it wasn't going to hurt me; it was going to be a bloody nuisance but it wasn't going to hurt me. And especially when I had very curly hair and all I was known as was 'Curly Kemp' throughout my life and in the army and wherever else, so people that I'd run into with this new name would think there was something wrong with me. Anyhow, that's the way it came about and I was very happy to do it. They died happy, still childless, but happy, the old boys.

I used to play about six feet, half an inch (184cm) and my weight was around 12 stone seven (79kg). I was never any heavier, I was always fairly light. But I used to be 13 and half and six-one and a half (85kg and 187cm) in the newspapers. Looking through a book this morning, I was looking at the sizes and weights and thinking, 'What the hell!' It's the same with Collingwood. Collingwood were renowned for their six-footers, and none of them were.

If you look at the photos I was about the third tallest. But if you talk to (Robert) Bawden he was about six-feet one-and-a-half, he looked down on me and always said, 'You're too short for a ruckman.' He was a forward pocket and second ruck because of his height. I played first ruck to Dyer because he was the main man and I was the younger man, expected to do a lot more leg work. So the fact that I wasn't quite as tall as Bawden ... they had Bawden as a backup in the second ruck with his height. Which is sensible, a taller man coming in as a second. So I acted in those days in what you call now a ruck-rover. I didn't know it, they hadn't invented it!

I actually barracked for Carlton in a sense. I lived in Brunswick and we used to go to Carlton to watch the practice matches. There used to be some terrific footballers like Vallence and Shea, and we used to watch them and really enjoy the skills that they had, but I wasn't terribly deeply involved at that stage. It wasn't until I got to Tech that I started football; I was certainly not an early developer.

We were pretty fortunate because we ran a house trade dairy. The man that ran the milk rounds, the dairy bloke, delivered to our house and we had a dairy built with ice chests in it. We had cans in it and a counter and people used to call and ask for their milk and cream. My mother was a war widow by that time, they managed to get her a pension. We paid 30 shillings a week rent and we made 30 shillings out the dairy.

My junior football was with Brunswick Sons of Soldiers. They were the Brunswick Returned Soldiers and they formed a junior sports club and Sons of Soldiers played there. Over the Brunswick Baths they had rooms and they had billiard tables up there. We played (teams such as) Williamstown, Port Melbourne, Coburg. The only team we could beat was Coburg. We only won two games in the two years that I was there. You didn't want to go to Port Melbourne or Williamstown because you knew you were in for a bloody fist-belting.

Due to World War II and metal shortage, the 1943 premiership players received their commemorative plaques on Dec 16, 1948. Here, Jack Dyer receives his from club president Harry Dyke at the Melbourne Town Hall.

About '39, when the war broke out, I first played with Brunswick Firsts and I was developing into a pretty good ruckman in my opinion. Jack Chessel was our secretary at Brunswick and Jack became secretary at Melbourne, and Jack wanted me. In a sense it was a good move (not to go) because Melbourne had the Cordners and all these big blokes and it would have been pretty hard to get a go anyhow. Jack at that time had just got the job as secretary and was of course looking at recruiting.

I signed a form four with Richmond before the war. Richmond took it to the League when Melbourne wanted me and the League said, 'Well, that's it.' They didn't require form fours after that because the war was on and you were a free agent but I had already signed it.

So I went to Richmond. Not that it worried me terribly because I was going to play football. If you were going to get paid for playing football, what more did you want? I just signed it, they went away happy and that's it.

As a football club, you knew you were going to another dimension. I was getting towards 21. But outside of the tiger skin, it was like every other football club. It smelt and looked the same.

I used to change (in the ruck) with Jack Scott in the back pocket. Bill Morris wasn't there in 1943, he was away in service, but when he came back I used to still be back pocket and second man to Bill. They had me playing block for Bill. I used to make sure Bill could get to the ball, keep their ruckman away without giving free kicks away. Shield him around the boundaries and run in so I ran across people so it gives him a free go at the ball, which he was capable of doing but it just meant he didn't get knocked about.

Football is what Hafey says: it's a simple game. You get the ball and you kick it. We did a lot of running, a lot of kicking at training. You thought you were fit, but compared to today's footballers we are probably only half. When you look at the running they do today and the skills today we were really amateurs, and that's all there is too it. Not using amateur in a derogative term in that sense, but we weren't professional. We were only doing it for fun and a few bob. Training was interesting; Tuesday and Thursday, a few hours. I had no means of transport so I used to go by tram into the city and then tram out and walk down Punt Road. Even on Saturdays I used to walk down with the people who were going to the football.

When I was picked in the first game to play against Fitzroy, that was quite a thrill. You thought to yourself, 'You've got your name in the paper that you're going to play for Richmond ... everyone is reading it'. They didn't tell me, I had to read it in the paper. First game of the year. They just put the teams in and I read my name. 'Oh gosh, I got a game. Marvellous.'

"We did a lot of running, a lot of kicking at training. You thought you were fit, but compared to today's footballers we are probably only half as fit."

When we played at Fitzroy, one of the first things Dyer said to me was, 'You'll be playing in the back pocket. Now there is a bloke down there in the other forward line by the name of (Keith) Stackpole. If you happen to be knocked over or fall over,' he said, 'roll over on your face, 'cause he won't have any thoughts of running the full length of you with his boots'. Not that it happened, but he was just letting me know that people around weren't too fussy on how they played football.

I think that the atmosphere at Richmond was the main thing. There was more feeling of something better. You thought to yourself, 'This is a better quality of people, I've got to try harder. I can't play any better than my best but I've got to get to my best.' Brunswick was very different money for starters because you had very few people. If you got anything up to 1000 spectators you were lucky.

The 1943 premiership plaque of Bill Morris– he was absent on national service that season, but was still honoured by the club.

Dick Harris used to spend most of his practice time kicking goals. He used to get as close to the boundary as he could get and practise kicking goals. He was really terrific. And so when it came to a game day he didn't care where he was, it didn't faze him because he knew he could kick it. He'd been playing for a lot of years when I got there and he was a very experienced footballer, as was Bawden.

They were blokes that you knew you could depend on and, of course, it made a difference to your own outlook. You felt if I could get the ball up there these blokes could do something with it.

When I got over the line, I was a different bloke to what I was outside. I knew that. I had lots of aggression playing football. But only because if I didn't, again you'd be challenged. You had to show that you were prepared to mix it, or go under – they'd run over you. The blokes knew that Bawden was quite aggressive; he was gangly in a sense but he was good with the arms and shoulders.

Robert Bawden was tough. We were playing Essendon and (Elton) "Duffy" Plumber was in the back pocket. As the ball was thrown in, Duffy Plumber was in the pack and the next minute he was on the ground with his eyes rolled back in his head. I thought he was dead. I thought he had killed him. Bawden had uppercut him.

My first final was the 1943 second semi-final against Essendon. They just outplayed us in the true sense. But we weren't that far away; as a football match it wasn't a hiding. We (then) had to come out against Fitzroy. We knew Fitzroy had some lovely footballers but they were suspect under pressure. So the plan was, when the ball was bounced the pressure went straight on and those blokes were expected to have to pick themselves up off the ground. So they never got back in the game.

In the Grand Final against Essendon, Tom Reynolds kicked seven goals and he was always a good little goalkicker. Dick Harris kicked seven goals and he was being minded by Duffy Plumber. Duffy was a noted ball-chaser, a back pocket and a good one. But Harris used to drift down the ground far enough to the half-forward line for Duffy to get anxious, and he'd start chasing kicks.

Dickie would wander back to the goals and stand back waiting for the ball to come back, and he kicked seven goals. But I reckon Dyer won the game for us. He came off the ground with bruises where they'd be hanging on to his body, and clutching him through the jumper, trying to hold him down. I reckon it was as much his premiership as anybody's.

I played very well in the other two (finals). But the Grand Final seemed to be a bigger occasion and I couldn't get into the feel of the game, and I wasn't very happy. It was a bigger occasion and I didn't react as well.

I got too excited too early. But I won the Best Player of the Series Trophy. I didn't expect it, I didn't expect anything. On any given day, Jack Broadstock was the best footballer on the field. He was a magnificent runner, fast and a lovely kick and sure ball-handler.

Unfulfilled

Tiger full-back Jack Crane flies between two Saints during the first semi-final, 1939. Crane was yet another player denied a premiership by the war; he played 102 games for the Tigers between 1937-42, then enlisted and headed to war 12 months before Richmond won the 1943 flag. He played two seasons for North Melbourne after his 1945 return to League football. Veteran teammate Martin Bolger is pictured, right, during the last match of his memorable 185-game career – St Kilda won by 30 points, and Bolger announced his retirement.

Frank Bourke Snr

He was quite simply a sensation. Des Rowe called him a 'wonderful player'. His son, Francis Bourke, played for Richmond, as did his grandson, David. In his first seven games, Frank Bourke kicked 33 goals, but his career was ended prematurely by a knee injury.

1943-47

I was born Numurkah, which is next door to Nathalia (where Bourke grew up and played football). They are mortal enemies in football and all things ... the rivalry between Numurkah and Nathalia is so intense I remember once, a long time ago, Numurkah beat us by 10 points at the football, but we had 25 points of rain more the next week, so we beat the bastards in the rain anyway. That's what happens between neighbouring clubs.

In my time, you played cricket and football, and if you were a bit of a sissy you played tennis, and when you got old you played golf. I think I was a better cricketer than a footballer, only because I am built more like a cricketer. If I had my time over again I would have played baseball. I always aspired to play for Nathalia. My father played for Nathalia. We are lucky that father, son and grandfather played at one club. [Ed's note: there are 10 instances of this in the VFL/AFL, though only two combinations, the Richards/Pannam (850 at Collingwood) and Rankin/O'Donnell (481 at Geelong) families, have bettered the Bourke's single-club tally of 401 games].

I don't think my father ever saw me play League football ... he was the best of the lot of us. He could jump 6' 3" (190cm) high; he won a hurdles event at Stawell in 1909, was a successful farmer, started from nothing. He was a very good athlete, so much so that Bob MacCaskill (Tiger centreman of the '20s who later coached North Melbourne and Hawthorn) named my father the best player he ever saw.

I came down to the Melbourne with my father and saw Collingwood play Richmond in the 1929 Grand Final. My father barracked for Richmond and, prior to the Grand Final, Collingwood came out when the seconds game was on and walked around the boundary. They had oily shoulders and great bloody bruises. I'd never seen that before! Richmond were runners-up four out of five years and Checker Hughes said to me it was the most frustrating period of his life. Checker got a military declaration, did you know that?

But he couldn't get a job and he used to pull his hat down over his eyes when he went to pick up the dole. It was a humbling experience; he was an old digger and didn't have a job. He had a distinctive face with wrinkles on it.

I lived in Richmond and had a telephone and they were hard to get. So when I was leaving to go to the country, Checker said, 'Can I have your telephone? I'll pay your telephone bill if you transfer your telephone to my house.' So my telephone number was Checker Hughes' silent number for many years. Checker didn't laugh. He saw me not long before he died. I had the pub, the Vine, in Richmond and he lived at Checker Mansion, which he built in East Melbourne; he came down to the pub and sat over there in the open bar to pay his respects to me and just to say g'day.

I barracked for Collingwood. (Jack) Regan and (Gordon) Coventry were my heroes at that time. I said to Jack Regan, walking off the ground, 'Jack, you were my hero.' He said, 'That's nice of you to say that, Frank. When I was a kid, (Carlton forward) Horrie Clover was my hero and he played his last game against me (the 1931 first semi-final).' And I played against Jack Regan in his last season (1946).

When I played on Jack he was blacker than a crow and whiter than a fairy. He had his black hair done, and on his jumper his black was black, his stripes were white, his boots were black and his socks were black. It really was magnificent to come down and play against him. He was a good-looking man as well. Jack suited me because he tried to mark with me. In fact, if you don't mind me boasting, I kicked

Born
Feb 3, 1922

Died
Dec 27, 2011

Played
Richmond
1943-1947
16 games,
48 goals

Interviewed
Jul 6, 2001

Athletic and determined, Frank Bourke displays his prowess on his non-preferred left foot, a rarity of the time. Round 1, 1946, and Bourke kicked six.

After playing in the 1943 premiership, Ron Durham returned to work on his family's Bacchus Marsh orchard, and played just 10 games in the following two years. On a day trip designed to lure him back, teammates including Leo Maguire (far left), Bill Morris (second from left) and Polly Perkins – up the ladder – helped with the picking. Durham came back in 1947-48, then retired.

twice Collingwood's score by myself at Victoria Park (round 5, 1946). I kicked 7.5 and they kicked 2.18.

(Richmond secretary) Percy Page came up to see a fellow in a country Grand Final. We were playing Berrigan. As it transpired, the player he had come up to see was playing on me and he changed his mind and interviewed me – I only found out about that afterwards. So he came to see my mother, and my mother thought he was a wonderful man and so that's how I came to go to Richmond. I trained with Melbourne in 1939, and nearly went to Melbourne. But then war came on and things changed. And if I can quote Percy Page, 'Football is an entrée to society.'

Bourke played his first game at Brunswick St oval. It was at Fitzroy's home ground. I went with Maurie Fleming and we were standing outside the ground and the great Ron Todd came past.

Maurie spoke to him on his way down to play with Williamstown. Todd was a hero of mine; he would be close to if not as good as Coleman. Charlie Callander was property steward, and Charlie gave me a slurp of whisky to settle the nerves. When I ran out I was so dry in the mouth from this whisky I was out of breath. Fred Hughson was captain-coach of Fitzroy and I played against him later that day. And I was wondering why I was always tripping and I realised that Fred Hughson would tap your heels, it was a very clever thing to do. The umpire didn't see it and I didn't.

I remember my first goal. I know I picked it up in the forward pocket and ran around the front of goal, which was a natural thing to do, to kick with the left foot but I was a natural right-footer. There wasn't many in my time that could kick both feet.

The next thing I know I am called up to win the war for Australia. I wanted to go to the Air Force but my mother did not want to sign the papers and she probably saved me life, because everyone else got killed. Still, when I was training to be a pilot, I was in Benalla and we had a football side. They were just kids, mainly training pilots, but after the war they nearly all played League football. Our captain was Ian Johnson, Australian Cricket captain, and he played in the centre. Geelong didn't play League football at this time, so there was a gap (bye) in the season and he challenged Richmond on the week off during the war. So we came down on the train and came back that night.

We were five points up going into three-quarter time. And I played against the great (Tiger

Frank Bourke Snr (right) looks on as Jack Dyer gets physical.

full-back) Ron Durham and Maurie Fleming told us afterwards, 'We couldn't have a scratch team coming down beating us.' So Jack Dyer came out and went in the ruck in the last quarter. And they won. I remember Dyer doing this big punch out from the ruck in the last quarter that set Richmond alight. He was a great leader that way. Durham was a nice bloke. He would just play each week and go back home to Bacchus Marsh. Sadly he died young (at 41), he was electrocuted.

I went to England with the war for a couple of years and I didn't play football for five or six years, so when I was 24 I was making a comeback. I wasn't very experienced. When I went to England, Maurie Fleming sent me pictures of Richmond's winning Grand Final, that's how much he had me in his sights. I remember my father wrote to me in 1944 saying, 'Richmond were beaten in the Grand Final, but not a big man's day.' After that I ran out of war and came home.

In 1946, I wanted to kick 100 goals. I was averaging five goals a game. At that time I can tell you the players who had kicked 100 goals: there was Bill Mohr at St Kilda, Gordon Coventry, Bob Pratt, Ron Todd and Jack Titus, and I wanted to be the sixth player to do it. I was going well enough to do it.

And then I did my knee against South Melbourne in Round 9. I remember thinking to myself, 'I better get up high here, and get right over his back,' and that's when I did my knee. At first I thought I would be all right and I tried to play later with knee bands. Then I had an operation on my knee and that was a success.

"I remember my father wrote to me in 1944 saying, 'Richmond were beaten in the Grand Final, but not a big man's day.' After that I ran out of war and came home."

But I never found that same form again for one reason or another. It seems to be a pattern, that a promising player's second season is often flat. Mine was no exception. It was disappointing. I had high hopes. But I guess you make other arrangements, don't you? If I had not done that, what would have I been doing?

I've had a great life. You can't live to be 80 years old and not have some disappointments.

Richmond didn't give me the sack, so much as a conditional clearance; it's still conditional now... if I go back to League football I would play with Richmond!

Bob Wiggins

Wiggins grew up in difficult times, but the Tigers' success proved a tonic for a kid with promising talent. From childhood memories of Percy Bentley at Punt Road, to being asked to toughen up by Jack Dyer, his story resonates with the tie between a club and its suburb.

1944-51

Born
Nov 8, 1925

Died
Aug 29, 2002

Played
Richmond
1944-51
68 games,
2 goals

Interviewed
Feb 9, 2002

My father was a foreman carpenter and my mother was a housewife. We lived in Richmond. We originally came from Hawthorn and during the depression we lost our house because my father was out of work. We moved to Bennett St, Richmond. My father used to get footballs for me from Hawthorn. Apparently he knew someone from Hawthorn and often gave me a football used from Saturday. It was a big thing because you never had enough money to buy footballs.

Behind us was a laneway and the other side of the lane was Leslie St, and Joe Murdoch lived there. As a kid I'd go down the laneway and his jumper, Number 13, would be there on the line of the house on the Monday morning drying. You could see it through the fence from the back lane. Jack Smith, the secretary, lived in Leslie St and Maurie Hunter lived further down in Richmond and used to ride his bike around, delivering his groceries from the wire basket on the front.

I went to St James School in North Richmond and the nuns wouldn't allow us to play sport. As a matter of fact we had cinders from the furnaces on the ground. It was a terrible place to play any sport. Maurie Hunter came and saw the parish priest and asked if he could take the seventh and eighth grade for football; we used to pick up a side between the two on a Wednesday afternoon for an hour. He would umpire. That was really the start of our football career. And it was a great rebellion against the nuns, this act of playing sport.

In those days, my father bought his work boots home and we bought some leather stops up at Johnson's, the hardware place in Bridge Rd, and hammered the stops in. And they were the football boots for the day. We all got a flogging on the Monday when we went back to school because none of us did our homework; we were locked out of the school. We got six of the very best of the cane on each hand because the head teacher didn't want us to play football.

From there, I went to St Joseph's Technical College in Abbottsford. Brother Hanley was the sports master. I asked Maurie Hunter if I could wear his jumper – Number 20, which he gave to me. I grew six feet tall, because I had a real Richmond player's jumper on and by that time I had a pair of football boots because my father was back at work, working at Caulfield Grammar. Some of the buildings at Caulfield Grammar in Glen Eira Rd were built by my father.

Maurie suggested we play a game against St Ignatius. I was nominated to go and see if we could play a game against St Ignatius so I fronted up and found out where the sportsmaster was; while I was talking to the Brother I referred to him as 'yes Sister, no Sister,' nervous as. Finally he said to me, 'I must say to you I am a Brother, not a Sister.' I felt about that big. But we played them and I think they kicked about 24 goals to one point.

I barracked for Richmond, of course. I used to go down to their matches as a kid and carry a member's bag in. You'd stand outside the gate and they wouldn't let you in the through the gate on your own, so you'd see a member come along with his membership ticket and his bag and you'd ask him could you carry his bag. And so you went through the turnstile and got in for free. Once you got in the gate you gave him his bag back and off you'd go. Perc Bentley and Skinny Titus used to intrigue

me. With Skinny he used to hook the ball. He'd always go out and hook it around, never run straight with the ball. When the ball was coming down on one wing, Skinny would drift down to the opposite wing and then lead into the centre, which was an open space. So he was always within kicking distance and in a reasonable arc. That impressed me as a kid. Bentley would drop down to the behind post, and be doing up his boot and the ball would come around the grandstand wing and I used to notice that Bentley was always in a position to be doing up his boot, then all of a sudden he would lead out into the pocket. It was just a ruse. He'd get at least one goal a week doing that. He was a very accurate, straight-on kick.

We used to go out at three-quarter time and listen to the speeches. In those days you were allowed onto the ground and we would all run out and gather around. Perc Bentley was coach in those days. I used to go down and watch the seconds and Dan Guinane was coaching. Jack Smith and two committee members, they made arrangements to see my father to see if I could go to Richmond – I was rapt as billy-o. But my father said to me, 'Forget it, you're not going there.' Because in his days playing with clubs there was a lot of beer, and young people got into the grog and he didn't want me to do the same thing. Consequently, he did not want me to go into a club where there were older people and get involved with grog.

At the end of that year, 1939, my father died. At St Joseph's we played curtain-raisers to Collingwood home games and there was a competition between the schools. We were playing off in the Grand Final and my father died that morning, which meant that I didn't play in the game, of course, and which left just my mother and myself. We didn't have much money. Then the next year they came and saw my mother and said they would put me on the supplementary list, which was 10 shillings. To her it was big, because I was going to school. So she allowed me to go down there. That was my introduction to Richmond as a 15-year-old kid. My mother died 18 months after my father died, and before I played my first game. I was then living with my Aunty out at Hawthorn.

Richmond sent me out to Kew, Ray Martin was the coach out there. I came back and played with the seconds, plus with the local catholic team on Sunday, which was good because you'd get an injury on the Saturday and run it out on the Sunday.

Richmond's Maurie Hunter leaves the ground after his last game, the final round of 1933. Hunter later gave his jumper to – and had a strong influence on – a young Bob Wiggins.

My first game was against North Melbourne in round 13, 1944 at Nth Melbourne. I knew by the Thursday night on the radio. I can tell you there was many a tear. George Smeaton played on the half-back flank and he was great, because he would yell and let you know what was happening. We came down to the last couple of minutes and North were in attack and the ball came in high.

I was out in front and I could hear the pack coming and I thought, 'Well, what do I do?' and I gambled and jumped backwards and the pack bought me forward and I took the ball and kicked it away.

The siren went. We won by five points. And Dyer words were, 'Just as well you marked because if you have missed that you would never have got another game at Richmond.'

In the whole time I was at Richmond I was never offered a glass of beer. I think it was one of the great things about the club. (Roy) Wright, Billy Wilson, Ray and Jervis Stokes, Fred Burge and I drank our lemonade. I was still only a kid really and the likes of (George) Smeaton, Polly (Perkins) and those senior players used to look after you, which was great – they were your idols as a kid and here they are protecting you.

One time we were playing Fitzroy and Don Fraser, who was a brilliant footballer but was having a really bad day. Every time he went to the ball he would stumble or do something wrong. And Dyer went crook at me, and said, 'Try to bring Fraser into the game, give him a short pass and make sure he gets it. Give him a bit of confidence.' So I said to Don, 'Well, the second kickout, regardless of what you do and where you go, drop in short and I will give it to you.' So this particular time he led and I gave him the ball and hit him right on the chest and it bounced out, and (Bruce) Calverley came from the wing picked the ball up and kicked a goal.

And I screamed out, 'It's the last bloody kick I will give you.' So what happened then was he led one way and I would kick the opposite way. That was the only time I went against what was really told to me.

Jack Dyer said one time I was too much of a gentleman. I suppose he meant there wasn't enough killer streak. At one stage there Jack was trying to instill in me how you come in close and you rip one into their belly. I think it was the only time I ever answered Jack back and I said, 'Well, I have never had it done to me, and I don't think I would ever do it to anybody else.'

Blow me down if it didn't happen to me. It was at Carlton and it was done by Ron Savage. He was playing on the half-forward flank and Ken Hands was full-forward and we led out – I was just beside him and I took the mark on my chest.

And Ken Hands was trying to wrestle the ball off me and I turned around and copped this one from Savage. It was the first and only time I have ever got one.

In Wiggins' first year at Punt Road, 1944, the Tigers sought back-to-back premierships. But Fitzroy – Lions captain Fred Hughson here shakes Jack Dyer's hand before one of four meetings that year – denied the Tigers by 15 points in the Grand Final.

Grounded

In round 5, 1951, Jack O'Rourke soared over Jack Hamilton to take this stunning mark. Problem was, umpire Bill Barbour judged it a push, and awarded Hamilton a free kick.

O'Rourke ran into Barbour at the train station after the game. "He said 'I made a blue by not awarding the mark. I should have paid it,'" O'Rourke recalls.

"Jack was sky high," Barbour remembers.

"He knocked Jack Hamilton flying, but put his hands on his shoulder and pressed himself up.

I took it off him; there was hell of a screaming.

It was in the rules in those days. In reality it would have been better to turn a blind eye to it."

The heartbeat of Richmond in the 1950s poses for Victorian honours. Players Ray Poulter, Des Rowe and Roy Wright are joined by club and state treasurer Bill Quinn (back left), club president and state selector Harry Dyke (back right)and club and state property steward Charlie Callander (front).

1950-1965

WE'RE FROM TIGERLAND

The club struggled to win through the 1950s and early '60s, yet the emergence of a lumbering, gentle giant, a change of playing venue to the MCG and the adoption of a new club song injected life into the Tiger story.

Jack Dyer continued to coach the Tigers after his 1949 retirement as a player, but he lacked success. In 1953, he was replaced by an old rival, former Collingwood captain Alby Pannam, who had achieved great success with the Cubs.

Pannam captain-coached Richmond's Second XVIII to the 1946 premiership in his first season and to second place in 1947 and 1948. He was a hard taskmaster and would train his players at a level unheard of under Dyer. Unfortunately, however, his success with Richmond's seconds was not repeated at the senior level.

Pannam was replaced by Max Oppy in 1956; in turn, Oppy was 12 months later replaced by Alan McDonald. The club's on-field performance was poor, and in 1960 it 'claimed' its first wooden spoon since the end of the First World War. The following year former captain Des Rowe took over as coach. The club did not compete in the finals until 1967, although under Rowe and captain Ron Branton the Tigers won the 1962 night premiership, a post-season competition for clubs that did not qualify for the finals.

As poor as the Tigers results were, they had some very talented players in their ranks. The retirement of Dyer in 1949 and Brownlow Medallist Bill Morris in 1951 allowed for another ruckman to shine. Shaded by the established rucks of the 1940s, Roy Wright played 21 games for Richmond in the four years after his debut in 1946. Yet he would win two Brownlows, in 1952 and 1954, and retire in 1959 with 195 games to his credit. Wright also captained the Tigers in his last two years, but this responsibility fell on the broad shoulders of defender Des Rowe from 1952 until 1957.

The Second XVIII were Richmond's success story of the 1950s. The Cubs won the 1954 and 1955 premierships, and were third in 1953 and 1956. They were virtually another club, with its own budget, committee, and training staff. It even had its own awards, and a separate list of life members. However, this independence was eroded in 1959. That year the Cubs played curtain-raisers to senior matches at Punt Road, rather than on the ground of the away club.

When this was extended to the entire VFL Second XVIII competition in 1960, there seemed little reason to maintain a separate committee. So immediately prior to the 1960 season the Cubs were absorbed into the senior body as Richmond's reserve XVIII and their committee was replaced with a reserves manager.

If one excludes Wright's individual achievements, the 1950s was a grim period, but there was light at the end of the tunnel. In 1964, Len Smith (who had coached Fitzroy from 1958-62) took over as head coach and restructured the team and its mode of play. Out went the old kick-and-mark game; in its place, Smith encouraged players to play on. Misfortune struck on the eve of the 1964 season – Smith suffered a heart attack. Former champions Dick Harris and Jack Titus stood in as coach while Smith was ill; he returned to coach the first four games of 1965 before ongoing ill-health forced him to stand down again.

Not only was Richmond's game being restructured in the mid 1960s, the club was outgrowing its rough, antiquated home ground. In the 1960s inner-city traffic was becoming heavier and a Punt Road widening scheme was considered. If it proceeded it could severely reduce the capacity of the Punt Road Oval, and therefore the earning ability of the Tigers' traditional home ground.

In the pre-season of 1965 the Richmond Football Club negotiated a tenancy agreement with the Melbourne Cricket Club for use of the MCG when the Melbourne Football Club was playing away. This relocation, plus the recruitment of swift, long-kicking youngsters and the play-on style introduced by Smith, would allow Richmond to achieve its most successful era.

During this period two important cultural items were added at Richmond. In 1953, Ray Dunn donated a new tiger skin to the club. A decade later, local cabaret artist Jack Malcolmson had heard that the Tigers lacked a memorable club song. The club had used songs, plenty of them – the first was written in 1888 – but most failed to catch on.

So Malcolmson penned the lyrics to new one, with the great opening line, "We're from Tigerland". Jack presented the new song to Richmond's coach Des Rowe, who allowed him to sing it to the players before a match. It caught on immediately, and would be heard many times in the decade to follow.

TREVOR RUDDELL

Des Rowe

Des Rowe grew up in the shadow of his father, Percy, one of the Magpie's tough men of the 1920s. Rowe captained the Tigers for six seasons, won two best and fairest awards, captained Victoria and coached Richmond during the dark days of the early 1960s.

1946-57

Born
Nov 19, 1925

Died
May 12, 2007

Played
Richmond
1946-57
175 games,
24 goals

Interviewed
Jul 10, 2003

I was an only child and dad and I were close. He coached me in my junior football from the age of 16 or 17, but he never interfered at all. He said I had a different style from him. He was a very good footballer, a ruckman, but he was a hard footballer, much harder than I was, whereas I had a lot more pace than dad and was more of a ball player. And he realised very early in my football life that I wasn't a knock 'em down merchant. He let me learn my own style of football but, against that, he always helped me if I was in trouble thinking about football. Dad came from Rutherglen and he didn't support anybody, but when Collingwood chased him he decided it was a case of wherever he got a game. Dad was there nine years. He played in the first two of Collingwood's run of four premierships in the twenties. He coached Fitzroy in 1935, he coached Carlton in 1937 and he was captain-coach of Northcote from 1929-1933.

Richmond knew they had me because I was residentially bound and in consequence they didn't have to spend a lot of time with me ... there was no father-and-son rule in those days. Maurie Fleming lived on my doorstep, really. A lovely, delightful man, and a very capable secretary. He treated us – Ray Poulter, Roy Wright, Ray Stokes and myself – as though we were his kids. We were all about the same age. But he didn't offer me a cracker; they didn't in those days.

They didn't have to offer me any money. Dyer came and saw me, because he was still coach. When they were first interested I was 16, but I didn't go to Richmond until I was 19. So I had one year at Coburg [Ed's Note: coached by his father.] And then it took me the best part of a full season to become a regular player. It was the best thing that ever happened to me to go to Richmond. I did better being at Richmond – with Collingwood in those days you were only a cog in the machine.

Oh, there were expectations at Richmond but not as much as there would have been at Collingwood. And what's more, if you didn't show the ability that was expected of you, I think Collingwood would have given me away pretty smartly. They (Richmond) persevered with me for the first year, I reckon because I was the son of Percy Rowe and I had started to show a bit of ability by that stage.

I purely went there to train and to see whether I had enough ability. It was 1942 and a chap by the name of Max Oppy, one of my closest friends to this day, was introduced to me and he took me out on the ground and looked after me. He says he still does. He was in the seniors and he was only 16. Maurie Fleming said to Max, who was 12 months older than me, 'You take Dessie out for a run' and Max took a bit of a liking to me. When I came back to Richmond in 1946 he grabbed hold of me again and we started a friendship. I went and played with Fairfield and then one year with Coburg and when I came back to Richmond in 1946 Max was there and he looked after me again.

First year I played five games. I struggled to hold my place, I was playing as a half-forward flanker. I wasn't good enough. No other reason. But then I got picked and we went down to Geelong – they were a good side. We went down there in private cars. I went down there with Maurie Fleming, he had a two-seater Chevrolet. I sat in the dickie seat and Bill Perkins might have sat with me. It was only 45 miles (72kms) but it was a long day. It wasn't very far if you won and we did that day.

Tiger skipper Des Rowe leads his men out in 1955, the year he won his second club best and fairest.

I got picked on the half-forward flank. I was playing reasonably well and Dyer switched me about halfway through the third quarter to half-back flank. Every time the ball came down I got it and kicked it back into play and I finished up playing very well. Consequently, the following week they picked me on the half-back flank, and that's where I started to make a name for myself. From then on I never got dropped again in my whole career. I gradually became a recognised player.

I was a natural ball player because I had certain abilities – I was a pretty fast runner and good ball handler and a good ground player. I wasn't a great mark. But you played on your strengths, everybody does. It sounds as though you're skiting but you've got to have those abilities to get where you got. If you get into state sides you soon realise that you got those natural abilities.

"Morris was a great palmer of the ball, he had a terrific leap and Roy Wright learnt from Bill to palm the ball well. Roy had bad judgement ... people never knew that."

Roy Wright, Ray Poulter and I started the same year. Roy and I were very close right through our football career. But I think Roy was too nice, he wasn't a ruckman in the old tradition, but he was a good player. If anything, he never used his strength as much as he should have. I finished two years before him, he played 14 years.

(Reserves coach) Alby Pannam was a little fellow and little men don't make great coaches. If you look over the history of football there are very few small men who have developed into coaches. Except Charlie Sutton, he had a premiership and he played football as a big man anyway because he was a strong little fellow. Max (Oppy) was small but he was a much bigger, stronger fellow. I played the majority of that first year (1946) in the seconds and we won the premiership.

Although I was getting a game at Richmond I didn't think I was getting much of a go. Collingwood had contacted dad and asked would I come and have a run; they knew I wasn't very happy. That was bought about by the fact that they (Richmond) wanted me to play a certain style of football, like my dad. I had played in the Northern Districts Under 21s, run by the Coburg Football Club, and I won the best and fairest in the competition in two years, so that's why Richmond wouldn't consider clearing me. I was a pretty good junior footballer without being a champion.

I went before the selection committee and said to Maurie Fleming, 'Collingwood invited me down to have a run ... I don't reckon I am getting a go here.' And he said, 'You're not going,' and then said, 'I have to talk to Jack (Dyer).' Jack said, 'No bloody way, you haven't given us enough time.' Needless to say I didn't get a clearance to Collingwood. Only about a week or so later I got back in the senior side. Once I got in on a permanent basis, I never got dropped again.

I remember Frank Bourke very well, he was a wonderful player. But he was very lightly built. He was about six-feet-three (188cm), fairly thin and Frank had a different build altogether from Francis. Francis was a solidly built boy, this fellow was pretty lightly built and I think to his detriment – he wasn't strong. He was a very accurate kick and he never got a great deal of distance away from goals. He was always close enough to be able to kick it.

But he injured himself (in 1946) and virtually never played again. We also had a chap by the name of Ron Durham, who won his best and fairest and a premiership in his first year. We were stiff at Richmond, because we lost Ron Durham, who was probably the best full-back in the game, and Frank Bourke at the other.

We had just a side. It was around about that period that all the League sides started to get better, because it was after the war and football improved considerably in one to two years. We weren't a good side. We had some good players – Bill Morris, Leo Merrett – but we had some pretty ordinary ones, too.

When I was at my best we had about six players who would have got into any League side, but then your other 12 fell by the wayside. And I sometimes think back to some of the footballers who were getting a game ... God, it was pretty ordinary. And yet I finished in 1963 as coach and within four years they were premiers.

John Coleman was magnificent. He would have gone to Richmond; he was very sweet with Jack Dyer; he had a run with us. Essendon got word that he was very close to coming to us and they got to work on him and offered him this and offered him that. We all knew he was pretty good, but not as good as he turned out to be. I played on John about

Rowe celebrates a Round 18 win over Fitzroy in 1963. It was just his fifth win of the season, and his last game as coach. From left: Barry Cameron, Dick Grimmond, John Northey, Rowe, Mike Patterson (rear), Neville Crowe, John Caulfield and Paddy Guinane.

three times in my career. One day we played on him at Richmond, I was playing centre half-forward and the message come out for me to go onto Coleman. I thought, 'Oh, shit,' and I went down. He said, 'G'day, Des, how are you?' And I said, 'Not bad' and he said, 'How's business?' We were both publicans, you see. We talked business for the last quarter and a bit! Coleman was strong, he was a beautiful mark, and he was quick. He didn't have anything wrong with him.

I played on Ron Barassi one day in 1953 when Norm Smith was coaching. They couldn't find a place for Barassi, truthfully. And when they picked the side on Thursday night they had Barassi playing at centre half-forward and I was centre half-back. I played on him and I never gave him one touch. He will tell you this himself.

Norm Smith said to me as I went up the race, 'Thanks very much Des, I will never play Barassi in a key position again.' And he never ever played centre half-forward again. They put him as a ruck-rover the following week and he never looked back. True story.

Coaches in those days got about £9 a week. I had the Vaucluse Hotel and of my £9 I used to tip back nearly the whole lot after a game – used to take back a couple of bottles of beer. If we went on a trip, because I was getting nine pounds a week, I used to spend pretty freely.

So from my coaching career I got very little out of it, virtually nothing out of it.

In Round 16, 1961, we failed to kick a goal against St Kilda, a feat which has not been matched since. It was frightful. We had a bloody awful side and we just played poorly. St Kilda wasn't a bad side, but the stand couldn't have swallowed me up quick enough. I think we kicked a hell of a lot of points (12.19 to 0.8) but it was one of the days I like to forget. It was a windy day and it was such an unheard of thing for a side not to kick a goal.

I then went on the committee when I finished coaching. I went on as a selector for three years, just going to the football and watching them play and giving an opinion on the side the following Saturday. It's the most unenviable job because, once again, it comes back to the fact that if you haven't got a good side you take a certain amount of the blame.

I had a wonderful career. Everything you could do as a footballer I was fortunate enough to do. That in itself was great.

Bill Morris

Bill Morris was Richmond's flawed genius. The 1948 Brownlow Medallist succeeded Jack Dyer in the ruck, but was the antithesis of Dyer's bullocking, ruthless style, preferring a gentlemanly approach to the game. Tragically, Morris committed suicide at 39.

1942
1944-51

Born
Apr 24, 1921

Died
May 25, 1960

Played
1942, 44-51
140 games
98 goals

Jack Watson

Teammate

I saw Bill at the Caulfield races, a week before he died. Sometime during the afternoon I was walking through the betting ring and I happened to look over on my right under the stand, and here's Bill Morris leaning up against the post. I thought, 'Gee, he doesn't look too bright.' He looked like he lost all of his money; he had that sort of look, like he had done his last lot on the favourite.

So I went over and said 'How you going Bill?' And he said, 'Oh, Watto, not bad, things aren't going as well as they should.' And I said 'What, financially or health-wise, Bill ?'

'Bit of both,' he said. 'Got me worries. We will get over it though, we will come good.' He said a few more words, said he was on his own, and then we parted. And he's bloody dead a week later. I just thought he's down in the dumps, he's lost his money, he's having a bad day. And then you found out in his mind it must have been more serious.

Unfortunately, he was a bloke who had never many friends. It might sound silly, a bloke who won a Brownlow Medal and was a champion, but outside of football I don't think he had many friends. That's why he'd probably go to the races. He might have had people he met at the races ... You go to a betting ring, you've got blokes standing all around and I think he wanted company.

I don't think he knew how good he was as a footballer. Champion footballers have got that air about them, like that air of confidence and arrogant. He never had it. He was so quiet. He had the knack of palming the ball out. Bill would stand back and as the ball was in the air he would start to float in from the side and he had a terrific leap. He had this terrific understanding with Billy Wilson, who was his number one rover. He was beautiful to watch.

Bob Wiggins

Teammate

Bill was a nice fellow, quiet, sincere. Unfortunately he was in with the wrong crowd who were all mostly gamblers, like Ron Clegg, (Alan) Ruthven and Don Fraser. His personality was completely different. He used to sort of go bush and he had a milk bar in Swan St and his wife would be down the back – he would be up the front of the shop and he would get a phone call to say 'We are going to the races.' Bill would go to the till and clean the till out, so I am told. He would be missing for a couple of days. Which I thought was a terrible shame. It was a terrible shock with what transpired. Everybody was in shock.

He was a lovely clean mark, and read the ball well and palmed the ball out beautifully. He was not a vigorous player, a very gentlemanly gamely player.

Allan Cooke

Teammate

Morris was just an out and out champion. He was such a good reader of the play, a beautiful mark, a very clever player as far as handball and tapping the ball out of the ruck. It was a tragedy, but if you knew Bill, he used to knock himself around. On and off the field you never would meet a nicer guy.

Arthur Kemp

Teammate

Bill was a willowy type of player, not a big body player. Not like the John Nicholls type, no bulk, he was a bit like myself in terms of build. But I had bigger bones and (was) more able to go at the player if I had to. Bill was more of a ball man, straight at the ball player, and a very good spring.

Billy would ruck all day. If you were changing with Billy you were wasting your time. You wouldn't get a go.

Always the gracious gentleman, Bill Morris still managed to dominate a tough era of League football.

A gangly, awkward youth,
Roy Wright blossomed
into a dominant force in
the Richmond ruck.

Roy Wright

A late developer, Wright became a Tiger legend, the only player to have won two Brownlow Medals at Richmond and a loyal servant through a 15-year career. The "Gentle Giant" won four best and fairest awards and played for Victoria 18 times.

1946-59

I had osteomyelitis as a child, which is a decay of the marrow of the bone. Every time I'd stand, my legs would just blow up like footballs and then they just put me in splints. They did a lot of treatment, blood tests and skin tests and all these sort of things you know, but eventually one day, out of the blue, it cleared. I was about eight when that happened and then at the age of 10 I got rheumatic fever, which put me down for a couple of years.

I wasn't allowed to play football or any sport because I had a little murmur in the heart. Then one day in 1944, halfway through the season, North Kew F.C. were short of players and they said, 'Oh well, you'll have to help us out.' I wasn't supposed to be playing football. Anyway, they whacked a jumper on me, I had big long pants and those golf shoes that had the rubber soles and they put me full-back. Dad and mum didn't know, but when they found out they absolutely went ape. They were worried because I still had this heart murmur you see.

What motivated me was, I used to sit there in this wheelchair and I'd see these kids playing football and sports. Colin Austen, who played for Hawthorn and then later came to Richmond, used to wheel me around and I used to say to Colin, 'One of these days I'm going to be doing what these kids are doing.' I wasn't going to try and do it any better but I just wanted to prove I could do it. I think that was the motivating factor that went right through my whole career that I still had to prove that I was as good as the next fella on the football field.

In 1945 I won the best and fairest in the East Suburban League and then was invited to Richmond. I lived in North Kew ... in those days a street divided territories and North Kew, for some obscure reason, was Richmond rather than Hawthorn. The first practice matches I played for Richmond were in 1946 and then they said, 'Don't ring us, we will ring you'.

But Hawthorn was interested so I trained with them for a few months. They used to take me to Grangos Café, which was up at the railway bridge, after training and give me something to eat, then drive me back home to North Kew. They obviously wanted me. Richmond must have heard about it because all of a sudden they said, 'Hey, get back here!' Collingwood was also interested and they offered me a new pair of boots and all that sort of jazz.

When I finally went down to Richmond at the age of 17, of course I had heard of Jack Dyer, so I knew to meet Jack was going to be terrific but I had no sport heroes at that stage. I think Maurie Fleming said to me at one stage, 'You'll meet Jack Dyer,' which was great, because Jack was a huge magnet, a big name. Meeting Jack was a big thrill. To go to training with Jack Dyer and Bill Morris was just huge, to play in a practice match was just out of this earth and you think, 'God, just one League game!' Then you get hungry because you want to play 10.

Anyway, the 1946 season started and I played three games with North Kew in the seniors. Richmond called me up and said, 'We want you to come up and play with the seconds.'

So I played a few games and then I was pulled into the firsts. On the Thursday training night, Maurie Fleming, who was just the prince of secretaries and was always looking after me, came up to me and said, 'You'll be in the seniors on Saturday, so watch the paper.'

My first game was against St Kilda at the old beautiful ground at the corner of Fitzroy St

Born
Feb 23, 1929

Died
Jul 30, 2002

Played
Richmond
1946-59
195 games,
127 goals

Interviewed
Feb 21, 2001

Wright, Bill Williams, Allan Cooke and Kevin Webb enjoy a club trip to Perth to play Western Australia in 1949.

and St Kilda Road. Jack Dyer got reported over me, which he never forgave me for. There were two fellas, Ernie McIntyre and Reg Garvin, who had muscles on muscles.

And Reg would go *bang!* and hit me behind the ear and say, 'Gee, you're doing a good job, son.' I thought, 'How long is this going to go on?!' Anyway, the ball was in the centre and it was a muddy day, young Jack McMurray was the umpire – he bounced the ball and Dyer positioned himself and went *bang!*, and broke Garvin's nose, then *bang!* smashed Ernie McIntryre up.

Dyer then said to me, 'Get down to full-forward'. So I got down to full-forward and who do you think is waiting for me down there? Keith Miller! Test cricketer! Mad as a snake, he was, on the footy field. Anyway I've led out and *bang!* he's knocked me over, tiptoed straight over me and kept running. So next minute Jack's come down and he's put himself in the forward pocket and he said, 'Next time you lead, keep running.' I said, 'Don't worry about that.'

I nearly ended up in Fitzroy Street I ran that far! Next minute, *boof!* I look around and there's poor Keith out flat. Of course, he and Jack were the tightest of mates, you know, and he's laid him out. When he came to, Jack said, 'Now leave the kid alone.' Anyway, Jack was up on a charge after the game. He got off it. It was a great baptism into football, I can tell you that.

The first year I played something like three games in the seconds, 10 in the seniors and then I played 12 games in the next five years. So there was no sort of saying 'Well, you're going to be a great player,' or any sort of that rubbish. From there on I played a few games up until the start of 1951, which was the turning point in my whole career. I suddenly thought, 'Hey, I'm a chance', because Bill Morris left the club at the end of 1951 and I became the number one ruckman. The responsibility was on me.

I had trucks at this stage, carting bricks for the Clifton Brick Company. I had two trucks and my dad was in one and we used to do three loads a day, 1750 bricks, hand on-hand off, none of this palettes and lifting them off. But I was very soft on the field. I was big, 15 stone (95kg), but you know, I'd get whacked ... I'd always bruise because I'd never been knocked around as a kid. That's why I was big in the arms and the chest and everything because it was all this strong working side, but the first couple of years I was soft as butter.

I then worked for Myer in the carpet department and then I went to Ron Charman, a big carpet warehouse in Flinders Lane and worked there cutting carpets and lino.

When I started we got 15 bob for each training night and 30 bob for playing Saturday, which made your three pounds. We didn't train like they do now, however. Because of your job you were there around about half-past four, and you had to get your boss to let you off, too. We had to run a lap at the start, then we'd have end-to-end kicks and we'd run a few sprints and a couple of laps to finish and we're in.

Maybe even a couple of throw-ins, about four or five on a Thursday night with me and Cookie (Allan Cooke) or Neville Crowe, and then it was like, 'Yeah, terrific, right we know where we are going ... the rover will get over there and we'll hit it over there.' Oh, it was very scientific.

We were a reasonable side in 1947 and I played in the first semi-final against Fitzroy, where they donkey-whipped us. That's the only final I played in. From there on we were basically unsuccessful really, just never made the four, until I finished. The old players carried us into the finals in 1947 but then they all started to drop out and of course new youngsters kept coming in who didn't have experience.

We just didn't have that nucleus of top players. I think we all knew our limitations, we knew that there was that one bigger step that we had to go, but in our own minds didn't think we had enough talent in the side to make that one step up. We often used to talk about our lack of success.

I think they hung onto their old great players like Jack Titus and Dick Harris those extra two years without thinking, 'Listen, we're going to have to replace them, then we'll get kids and bring them up through the ranks so that when they go we've got replacements who've got a bit of experience.' They just didn't do it. It was lack of planning in a lot of ways really.

In 1949, I saw John Coleman's first League game at Essendon. He kicked 12 goals. We had him under wraps, you know, and Doug Bigelow of Essendon got him and he was a bloody sensation. He just came out and he would jump over their heads from standing starts; he led like a gazelle. He was just sensational. For a fellow that's come straight into League football, he just blew me away. I'm glad I didn't have to mind him.

We're playing Essendon, Mopsy Fraser was full-back on Coleman and Dyer said to me: 'The moment they come towards you, or see Coleman lead, I want you to go from the back pocket and run straight in front of him to stop the run of him. Mopsy will be coming in over the back of him.' Which was a great plan, other than the fact that Coleman from a standing start would go up, lean over me and mark the ball.

Well this went on about two or three times and I said, 'Stuff this, I'm not going to run out in front of him anymore ... he just made people look so foolish. So I tried to get in front and prop back on him. Of course he'd have to go back on his heels, but from a standing start he'd get up over you and say, 'Thanks very much!'

> "I was big in the arms and chest and everything because it was all this strong working side,but the first couple of years playing I was soft as butter."

At the end of 1951, I tied with Des Rowe for the best and fairest and Jack Dyer had me off the list. I was staggered. He was going to swap me for Harvey Stevens, who was at Collingwood, because he was a big tough strong sort of player and Jack thought he'd rather have him than me. Secretary Maurie Fleming was a very wonderful man to me – he had faith in me where a lot of others didn't. He said to Jack that he would clear me to the club of my choice and then would resign immediately. That was the only reason I stayed at Richmond.

Of course, next year I won the Brownlow Medal, then more best and fairests, then another Brownlow Medal and also represented Victoria 18 times, so Jack made a big mistake I think. Jack was an inspirational player but I didn't agree with the way he played the game. I used to say to Jack, 'I can't play your caper, you can't play mine.' If I can't beat them with ability I don't want to beat them. We did not agree at all on the way we played football, to knock someone out because you're bigger and stronger just didn't sort of rub with me.

If you couldn't beat them with ability, they're just too good. You've got to learn from them and try and beat them next time.

But if you didn't learn why he beat you, you shouldn't have been playing football.

Because I'm 16-stone-4 (102kg) and I run through someone 13-stone (82kg) and knock him out of the game, does that prove I've got ability? Well, it doesn't to me.

The challenge to me was to beat them with ability. Interestingly, that's how Lou Richards gave me my nickname. The fact I played 16-stone-4 and I didn't crash through fellows and knock them out of the ground or that sort of jazz, he just said, 'He's a gentle giant.'

Dyer certainly was tough and inspirational, which lifted a lot of players, but it just didn't sort of gel with me. But that's just different people's opinion. Jack and I never saw eye-to-eye on that.

"At the end of 1951, I tied with Des Rowe for the best and fairest and Jack Dyer had me off the list. I was staggered. He was going to swap me for Harvey Stevens at Collingwood."

You want to know how I knew that I had won the Brownlow? Well, in 1952 I fell out of the tree, no-one had even tipped me. Bill Hutchison and I tied on 21 votes each and I won on a countback. So (*Herald* journalist) Alf Brown found me at home in North Kew and he came in and said, 'You've won the Brownlow Medal.' I said, 'Oh, fair dinkum ... oh, oh that's good.' I had no idea I had won until Alf Brown knocked on the front door.

I got the medal in February of 1953 at the annual meeting of the Richmond Football Club. It just came in a little white plastic box, no ribbon, none of that caper, and Like McBrien just pinned it on my lapel at the Richmond Town Hall.

It was much the same in 1954. My grandmother was crook, so my mum and all of us moved up to her place, which was two streets up in North Kew. On the night we were up at her place and the phone rang and I picked it up: 'Hello?'

'It's (club president) Harry Dyke, Roy.'

'Oh, yes Harry?'

He said, 'You're that far in front you'd have to fall over to lose the Brownlow, you've got a second one.' 'Oh, that's terrific Harry, thanks.'

So that's how I found out. I got 29 votes that year and Neil Mann got 19 and I was that far in front I couldn't be beaten. Later on I think they all converged on my grandmother's house. It's amazing how they found out where you were. It was incredible. In 1954, I was again at the annual meeting, that same little white box, no ribbon, though it did have a little bit of plush lining. Later that year they got me to walk out from the members during a final. I met the Governor General and then waved to the crowd and walked straight back to the members, all in my footy gear.

I suppose playing at Punt Road was no harder than anywhere else but the ground was a quagmire. In the wet weather it was just a total bog to be honest. I remember Dyer used to say, 'We are kicking to the Punt Road end, that's where the tide flows.' There was just water! Bloody incredible.

St Kilda and South Melbourne were the two best grounds because they'd topdress them with sand. Just beautiful to play on. The old Geelong ground wasn't a bad ground, actually. We got on particularly well with Geelong because their trainers and our trainers used to take it in turns to put on pies and sandwiches. We'd go to Geelong and we would stay overnight and go out to Clifton Springs and play the Geelong boys in nine holes of golf on the Sunday morning after the game.

No one knows this, but (Fitzroy follower) Alan Gale and I had a book. He kept his book and I kept my book. And we'd meet once a week and we'd sit down and go through the fellow that we'd played on last week. But sometimes they'd come up with a new move on you and unless the fellow had played him beforehand, you'd all of a sudden have a big surprise because you were playing on your old theories.

So we used to work out these little theories on players. I used to say to him, 'Nicholls, he's a left-hander. Don't ever fall for his right-hand caper because he'd use his left and he'd go '*bang*'.

Alan Morrow, not a big fellow, but he had a huge spring, and he always tried to sit on you, so once you felt him, you'd move away and he had to slip off.

I would say to Alan Gale, 'I played against John Gill, now Gilly comes in, he lets you get in front of him, because he's such a big man, then come in from the side and use the left hand.' He'd never palm Gilly, he'd go *bang* with his fist. So I said, 'You've got to get on his left-hand side and as you go up you've got to put your arm up to block his arm coming up and then you can use your own left arm.'

I used to put Dennis Cordner in my book, who I thought was sensational, just a great player. I never ever did very well against him at all.

Alby Pannam replaced Jack as coach. That was a bitter pill that stuck in Jack's throat all his life

because Alby was Collingwood, who were always great rivals.

However, our biggest foe in those years was Carlton because, again, Percy Bentley got shafted for Jack to take the coaching job (in 1941), so that created the ill will between the two clubs. Percy cut all ties, he was a very hurt man. He had a petrol station on the corner of Sydney Rd and Brunswick St and I used to see him quite a lot; he was still very hurt and disappointed. It really affected him for a long time.

I did my knee in the ninth game of 1959 against South Melbourne and that's when I knew I was gone. I can tell you the blade of grass now. It was on the Richmond Stand side, the Cricket Stand, going towards Brunton Avenue, and I steamed down and I was bouncing the ball and there was no-one between me and the goal.

I was about 40 yards out and I thought, 'I've got to make a certainty of this,' so I kept running and bouncing the ball. Out the corner of my eye I saw (165cm Swans rover) Brian McGowan come in and I thought, 'Oh hell, I can't hit him,' so I propped and tried to baulk him and he's gone straight over my bloody leg. My knee jammed, locked. I tried to come back. I even wore an American knee brace in those days, which was a great big thing. In those days, when you did a cartilage, you were 'See you, pal.' So that was it.

The best player I ever saw was Ian Stewart. Doug Heywood and I did television and we were doing a St Kilda game. Every time the full-back would kick out he'd kick it to Stewart. Doug and I were saying, 'Bloody hell! Poor Stewart.' So when we went in after the game, Doug said to the coach, 'Every time the full-back kicks out, he kicks to Stewart. Why?'

And the coach replied, 'Because he is the best mark I've got in my side.'

Ian could outmark ruckmen, he could run backwards into packs, he could hit you lace in, lace out. He fascinated me. He was just a brilliant player.

I loved football. It was the competitiveness of football, being able to match your strength and your skills against opponents, that to me was the most beautiful part of the game.

You had the opportunity to express your own ability in your own way, your strength and your skills and competitiveness. Football gave me a sense of purpose in life.

Wright was a Victorian stalwart, playing 18 times for the Big V, including this 1954 clash with South Australia at the MCG. The other Victorian player is Bill Hutchison, with whom Wright shared the 1952 Brownlow Medal.

Havel Rowe

1948-57

While the Tigers struggled throughout the 1950s, one of their bright lights was Havel Rowe. No relation to his captain of the time, Des, Havel could play wing, centre or half-forward and he won a best and fairest in 1953. Rowe was inducted into the Hall of Fame in 2015.

Born
May 8, 1928

Played
Richmond
1948-57
123 games,
43 goals

Interviewed
Apr 24, 2004

Havel is my middle name. I'm Stewart Havel Rowe. My uncle's name was Stewart and we spent a lot of time together so my grandmother decided she would call me by my middle name. My great, great grandfather's name was Havel, I think it is a Czechoslovakian name actually.

We barracked for Melbourne as a family. My cousin, Don Hooper, during the war was a ruckman. I grew up knowing Melbourne. My idols were Melbourne players in those days like Norm Smith and Jack Mueller. Mueller was my favorite. Actually, he struck me in the seconds one year he was playing and just about finished. I was just an up-and-comer. He flattened me twice – I tried to avoid him in his tackle and he hit me in the solar plexus and dropped me like a log. Blow me down if it didn't happen another 20 minutes later, he did the same thing. I used to think I was pretty good avoiding other players with blind turns but I will never forget that.

I was playing with Ormond Amateurs and had two years there. Jack Dyer and Maurie Fleming came over to a pie night one time and convinced me to go to Richmond. I admired Jack, he was a terrific bloke, great approach, very friendly. I lived in Caulfield at the time, it was a Melbourne area. I just moved from the country and I had about six weeks to make up my mind or else I was a Melbourne player, because you had to live in the area for 12 months. So I made up my mind and decided I would go to Richmond. I went down and trained with them at the end of that year when I finished with the Amateurs in 1947. (Rowe won the best and fairest in the A Grade Amateurs that year.)

I would have paid to play, there was no incentive needed. You used to get a free pair of boots occasionally. They gave me the Number 3 jumper, which was good. Incidentally, that number has only been worn by six players since I took over in 1948. Roger Dean took it over from me, then John Pitura, Paul Feltham, Dale Weightman and Duncan Kellaway. Brett Deledio has since assumed the honour.

I was 19 when I played my first game. I was studying accounting and did the exam on the Friday night before the match. It was a two-hour exam and I finished it in an hour and then I was home ready for the match the next day. I played on the wing and played against Chris Lambert out at Essendon. I played pretty well. Dyer was full-forward and he came steaming out for a pass and I came running around the boundary bouncing the ball and I hit him on the chest with a stab pass. I came in at half-time and he said, 'Next time put the lace out, will you please'.

Which I hadn't heard before, but which was quite funny. When I came off, Bill Morris, who was the star ruckman and won his Brownlow that year, gave me a big hug for doing well.

When (Alby) Pannam was coach he said, 'I want you to run anywhere you want to go.' He was the first person who tried to do something different. Alby is the only one who tried to even teach me a few tricks of the trade.

A very nimble mind and a real thinker. He would do tricks most players wouldn't even think about, like baulking the bloke on the mark and going the other way, or run towards you and pass to someone over there. I used to like to talk to Alby because he had a lot of thoughts about football. But he wasn't as good a speaker as Jack.

Havel Rowe was an in-and-under player who failed to get the recognition of his more illustrious teammates.

Kicking for goal I used a flat punt. Since I was a kid I was kicking a football and I always taught myself to kick left foot. I could kick either foot. In fact, Dyer used to go crook at me because I used to turn on my left foot more than I did on my right. It was a good way to lose an opponent. Dyer was mainly into the fitness side. Bill Morris didn't train because he rucked four quarters each week. I finished up only training one night a week the last three years I played because I bought a business. I had a hardware business in Malvern. Basically it was after dark so I used to run, kick the ball and try to find it.

"Morris was a great palmer of the ball, he had a terrific leap and Roy Wright learnt from Bill to palm the ball well. Roy had bad judgement ... people never knew that."

Maurie Fleming helped me go into business. The year after I won the best and fairest (Rowe won in 1953) I decided to go into business and so I bought this hardware business and I was running short of funds to the amount of £500, which in those days was huge money. Anyway, I went to training this night before the start of the season and I'm trying to nut out how I'm going to get this money. Maurie Fleming was talking to a fellow up near the changerooms, and I came out of the showers. This fellow left and I walked up to Maurie and I said, 'Maurie you can't lend me £500 can you?'

He pulled this bundle of notes out of his pocket and he handed the money to me! And he said, 'You saw that fellow give me those, didn't you?' And I said, 'No Maurie, I didn't actually, I only saw you talking to him.' And there was exactly £500 there – the fellow had repaid a debt. Maurie gave me that £500 which I put in the bank and paid off over the year. It was incredible, wasn't it? He was a very capable bloke, very impressive as an administrator and a speaker and I think he helped Jack Dyer with language and taught Roy Wright how to speak in public. I used to pick Wright up and bring him to training. There was Max Currie as well. Wright and Currie were vying for a ruck position and Bill Morris was the star, of course.

I think Roy learned a lot from Morris. Morris was a great palmer of the ball, he had a terrific leap and Roy learnt from Bill to palm the ball well. Roy used to tell me he had bad judgment going for the mark so he used to go up with the pack so he knew when to jump. He was a good mark but didn't have that judgment on his own; people never knew that.

We were nearly successful. We ran fifth four times. We had a terrific backline, Des Rowe and Don Fraser, Allan Cations and Bob Wiggins. Col Austen came over from Hawthorn and he was on the half-back flank. He was a Brownlow Medallist and a very solid player. At a practice match I'll never forget, Col put a hand on me when I was trying to avoid him bouncing the ball running past him. He just put one hand on my hip and pulled me up. I will never forget it, he had a huge grip; he was strong.

When (Max) Oppy was coach he went through all the players and he said I was good ball handler. My friends used to reckon it was a fluke that my foot passes would hit players on the chest. I played against Ted Whitten one time and he got three votes in one paper and I got three votes in another. He was standing on shoulders taking marks, but I got so many more kicks than he did. But people look for that spectacular side of people that I didn't have. I wasn't a high mark but I reckon I was a solid mark.

They reckon I was the only one who handballed in my day. Actually, Dyer mentioned later he thought I was before my time because I used to think about what was going on. When I was on the half-forward flank, Geoff Spring was often on the wing and he had terrific pace; he used to come running past and I would flip him the pass. It was just a pattern of play. It was man-to-man and it was quick-paced.

For my best and fairest I got an armchair. It was given by a sponsor. The year I won the best and fairest I didn't get a vote in the Brownlow. Bill Hutchison won the Brownlow in 1953 and he got votes in the last match but I reckon I was the best player on the ground. That happened to me a couple of times. I played against Jack Clarke in the centre and he got three votes in the paper and I reckon I beat him. That was my game, I was more an under-the-pack player, rather than spectacular. It was the first year I was really in the centre for the whole year and that's why I went to the club in the first place.

Peter Bennett was playing full-forward with St Kilda and I was playing in the centre at Richmond. The ball was kicked to him and I ran the way the ball was kicked and I tried to knock the ball out of his hand and I hit him on the jaw. I felt it go, I knew I broke his jaw. Harry Beitzel was the umpire at the time – I ran past him and I turned around and came back to have a look at Peter, because I knew I broke his jaw, and Max Oppy and Des Rowe were there and Max grabbed me around my shoulders

Two key men in Havel Rowe's life: Jack Dyer (left) and long-time club secretary Maurie Fleming.

and I said, 'I've broken his jaw, I've broken his jaw and Max said, 'Pity it hadn't been his fucking neck.'

Someone said, 'Report him.' Beitzel said it was an accident and left it at that. And that's the way we were umpired in those days.

We got spat on by our opponent's supporters a couple of times. Carlton was pretty bad. The Carlton ground was awkward too, it was a strange shape, one pocket bigger than the other. Punt Road was too small for me, I used to like a bigger ground. I loved the MCG. Hawthorn was a funny little ground with the little wing area where the people used to stand between the wing and railway line. One instant there, Ken Roberts (1947-51, 58 games) got hit in the head with an umbrella when he bent down to pick up the ball. Some old woman whacked him on the head, he was so close to the crowd.

We always put Don Fraser on John Coleman. Fraser was our talent and our strength. Fearless. In fact, Des (Rowe) used to say 'If you hear Don coming, let him go for the ball.' He would run through anything. One day out at Essendon, Coleman kicked one goal to three-quarter time and Don was playing the game of his life and Coleman came out and kicked five in the last quarter.

Another time at the Richmond ground, Coleman needed six goals for his hundred and Don let him get them.

That's a fact. I was there that day. Not many people actually knew about it. He got them early. There was no fire in Fraser that day, he would run after him but there was no attempt to spoil him. Fraser got a bit fair dinkum after that.

We were never taught anything, it was just natural ability. I just thought it was a great experience and it has helped to make my life. People say to me, 'You played football,' and I say, 'Yeah, many years ago.' It's because of my name. If my name had been Bill Rowe, they probably wouldn't have remembered, but they always remember 'Havel'. You were taught to play for the jumper in those days.

Even now when I see the team run out sometimes I get a lump in my throat.

Bill Williams

His career lasted only nine games, but Bill Williams still made a significant mark on the sporting world – he is the last Richmond player to win the prestigious Stawell Gift, having won the 1956 running of the race.

1948-49

Born
Jun 22, 1929

Died
July 7, 2016

Played
Richmond
1948-49
9 games
3 goals

Interviewed
Oct 12, 2003

The Tigers' commemorative badge from the 1949 tour of Western Australia.

I was a 15-year-old spectator at the 1944 Grand Final. I saw Fitzroy win the seconds and the firsts. That was a great game. There's a fellow called Bernie Waldron, who used to play in the centre, and they put him on half-back flank.

A couple of years later, Jack Dyer was in the shower and he was telling us that he told Bernie, 'Keep everyone in check there and tell 'em what to do.' Apparently Dyer came down there (to the backline) during the game and Bernie said, 'What the hell are you doing here, Jack? You gave me the job to look after the backline, so piss off.' He told Dyer, the coach, where to go.

I played in the cricket finals with Williamstown in 1948 and Richmond contacted me and said the practice games are starting. I said I can't come over, I am playing cricket. So we won the Grand Final, and on the following Saturday I just grabbed my boots and went over and they said, 'You're going to play full-forward in the first practice game.'

I kicked four goals in the first half and they took me off and put me in the practice match of the seniors for the second half. I remember I was playing in Leo Merrett's side; the captain of the other side was Bill Morris.

I played in maybe a couple more practice games and I finished up making the senior list. And that was the headline in the paper *'Two schoolboys make the list.'* I was 18.

I used to go by myself (to Punt Road) and stand in front of the cricket club rooms on the wing and I often thought to myself, 'I'll wonder if I will ever be out there one day.'

The first time I made the seniors, when I was running out I looked over into the other side of the fence to the space where I used to stand and I looked up to the heavens and said, 'Thank God I'm on this side of the fence.'

Bill Morris was top of the tree. I used to wear number 5 in the seconds because I idolised the man so much. He being a left-footer and I was a left-footer. He used to palm the ball, he never used to hit it ... They used to call him 'Paleface'. He was a pasty-looking fella but he could ruck all day, he never used to come off the ball. I don't think I ever saw him kick with his right foot. Morris was my hero.

When I got to the seniors, I initially got number four, then number 12, Jack Titus's number. I ended up with 34. I never wore 4 and I never wore 12, but I was in the Football Record as 4 and 12.

I played two games at the end of the season, and you had to play three games before they gave you a jumper, then the jumper was yours. So the next year I played the first game and I said to Charlie Callander, 'This is my third game, Charlie, I get to keep my jumper.'

'No you don't, Danny,' he said – he used to call me Danny as he said I was like Danny Kaye – 'You have to play three in the one year. That's the rules.'

Anyhow the next game I played and the third game was North at North. I'm all set to go and I've got no jumper and everyone else has got theirs, and I said, 'Charlie, where's my jumper?' I looked around and here's Jack Dyer with the jumper and he said, 'Here you go, Bill, here's your jumper. It's yours now, you've earned it. Congratulations.' And I looked at Charlie and he gave me a little wink.

I felt as though I let Richmond down a bit. I was torn between being a runner and being a footballer. I knew that I would make more money out of winning the Stawell Gift than I would out of playing football. My trainer used to say, 'Don't play football.'

Then I had a collision at Richmond with a recruit while we were doing circle work at training. He knocked me out – I don't remember anything,

and weeks later they told me Jack Dyer carried me off the ground.

In 1947 Alby Pannam was ill with the flu and Jack Titus was on the selection committee. The first we knew about it, Titus (who had been retired since 1943) was down at the ground; we (the reserves) were playing North Melbourne and Jack said, 'I'm the captain-coach today and I'm playing full-forward.' So he was ready to go, and he gets up on the rubbing down table and gave us this great speech. 'Righto, boys, out we go!' and he jumped off the table and ran out and we said, 'Jack! Jack! Don't go yet!' and he said, 'I'm going, get out of my way', and we said, 'Jack, for God sakes, put your shorts on.' Then he called Stan Wilson and me over and said, 'When I signal to the right, I'm actually going left.' So he kicked six up to half-time and he said, 'Right, now when I signal to the right, they will go to the left, well I'll go to the right.' He kicked 12.

Essendon and Richmond combined to form a team to play a Western Australia team. Dick Reynolds was captain-coach. I played half-forward flank and Reynolds played centre half-forward and he said to me: 'Go about your game as you want to play it.' I kicked three goals ... Reynolds kicked three and he came to me at the end of the game and said 'You really kicked five, because you gave me two.' When the paper came out the following morning I got the best player. After the game, Dick said 'If ever you're not happy here, come to Essendon.' I should have, but I went to Williamstown.

In 1956 I was running like an old cab horse. But I was fit, I was sound. So we went to Stawell that year, we backed ourselves from 100-1 to 5-2 on favourite. Biggest betting plunge in the history of the race up to that stage. When I finished I thought I'd won, but a bloke called McDonald went to Alan Gooden and congratulated him. I turned to the nearest person and asked, 'Who won?' He said, 'You did, look at the flag.'

They have a gantry, and they've got all the flags up there on rollers. When they go through they pull the ropes and your colour floats in the breeze. I had never seen it in the six years I have been running here, I never looked up that high.

And it was the most pleasant sight to ever see in your life, to see your colour floating in the breeze. I was on cloud nine, I could have run back to Melbourne I reckon.

Bill Williams fends off his West Australian opponent during a 1949 Richmond v W.A. exhibition game in Perth. Teammate Kevin Webb has the ball.

Allan Cooke

1949-58

Allan Cooke enjoyed a long association with the club, beginning with his recruitment from Mitcham, and continuing through a lengthy stint as chairman of selectors. Cooke also played a key role in appointing Richmond coaches in the '70s and '80s and was recognised for his lasting contribution to when inducted into the Hall of Fame in 2006.

Born
April 9, 1930

Died
May 12, 2010

Played
Richmond
1949-58
116 games,
54 goals

Interviewed
July 19, 2000

Dad was a mad keen footballer, he played a few games with North Melbourne. I didn't barrack for North – they tried very hard to get me to go to North and dad tried to persuade me. They were up chasing me and interviewing me, but you'll remember a chap name Charlie Pannam (Jnr), he used to play with Collingwood. He had a grocer store in Vermont and I used to do the paper round for him in the morning and work in the shop a little bit, just for pocket money. Charlie's brother, Alby, went on to coach the seconds at Richmond, and Charlie said to me: 'Alby wants you to come down and have a run with the Tigers.' I said, 'You have to be joking.' So Charlie took me to a picnic with Richmond and introduced me to Maurie Fleming and Alby. I went down there not dreaming I would go any further than that.

I was only 15 and they had the under 19s down at Richmond, and they used to play the curtain-raisers to the League then. Vin Dyer, Jack's brother, was coaching the under 19s. So I left Mitcham and played with the Richmond under 19s and won the best and fairest, and the next year progressed to the seconds – Alby was coaching – and went on from there to the firsts, which Jack Dyer was coaching.

We'd been over to Western Australia on a footy trip; the carnival was on in Victoria, and we went over and played Subiaco and combined Western Australia sides. I played pretty well in those games, and the state players were over there too, like Bill Morris and Bill Wilson. When we came back I was emergency for the seniors and I went into the rooms and Maurie Fleming said, 'Get your gear on, you're playing.' I said, 'How come?' He said, 'I'll tell you later, just get your gear on.' Morris hadn't turned up. Obviously he had gone out the night before over in Western Australia and didn't make the plane.

Tom Allen and I would have quite a few bets on when the side was going well. We would bet on the Saturday and Jack Titus would put our bets on for us, because we knew we would get paid. We played Collingwood one day at Collingwood and Morris came around and said, 'We are all putting in two pound each, we are going to win this game today.' He said, 'You're changing with me in the forward pocket. You won't get much of a run, but if you can kick us three goals we are going to win this game and win the money.'

Jack Collins was a great player for Footscray and we were playing out at Footscray and Jack had a bit of a go at Mopsy Fraser. I distinctly remember hearing Mopsy saying, 'It will keep.' The season went on and Mopsy was up in all of the awards, he was having a marvellous year. We were playing Footscray at Richmond – he came out in the first 10 minutes and *whack!!*, he's flattened Collins, and got rubbed out. He got square, but mucked up his awards.

(As chairman of selectors), number one, you're working very closely with the coach. I knew what style of play he wanted. I knew exactly what type of player he wanted to fit into the side. I had a firm belief that I would never make judgment on a player unless I saw him play. In all my seven years as chairman of selectors I never missed one seconds game. I was there every Saturday morning at 9am, I saw the whole game through, then the firsts. That was my whole day, watching football. If a player came to me during the week saying 'Why wasn't I getting a game?' I would honestly answer him with my opinion. That's my belief and I stuck by it, that's why I was there for that long.

In those days you used to bring a player down from the country and play him in the seconds for two or three games to get a permit.

After a respectable playing career in the '50s, Allan Cooke contributed in critical off-field roles until well into the 1980s.

Michael Green, Francis Bourke and Cooke ponder the Tiger lineup.

Graeme Richmond would ring me up: 'Cocko,' he would call me, 'we are sending a player down from Mildura on Saturday, get him in the seconds, see how he looks.' Some of the ones they'd bring down, after the game, which Graeme wouldn't see, he'd asked 'How'd they go?' I would say 'Oh, Jesus, Graeme, where did you get this guy from!'

Billy Barrot was a champion, but around 1970 Tommy Hafey and I could see that time was running out for him. We tried to advise him that it was time to capitalise on it, go out and get a good coaching job. But Billy wouldn't hear of it. And out of the blue, Schwabby (secretary Alan Schwab) rang me up and said, 'Would you think about swapping Barrot for Stewart?' and I said, 'You have to got to be bloody joking, you couldn't pull that.' He said, 'You have a yarn with Tommy and get back to me.'

Tommy was a real stickler for his boys, he didn't like to part with his boys. 'I don't know about that,' he said, 'I like Billy. Anyway, you couldn't pull that.' I said, 'Will you be in favour if we do?' He said, 'Oh yeah, sure. Stewart's still got some football left in him.' And I said, 'Okay, you're happy to leave it with me if Schwabby can pull this. I don't think he can either.' So I rang Schwabby and I said, 'Look, I talked to Tommy, we reckon there might be a deal if you could pull it off.' He said, 'Meet me down at the Junction Hotel, 5 o'clock.'

So down we go and Drakey (Ian Drake) is down there from St Kilda. There's Drakey, Schwabby and I. He said, 'Okay, here's Barrot's clearance, here's Stewart's clearance. We'll get Barrot, you'll get Stewart. Deal done.' We go back and Ray Dunn gave us the biggest spray of all time. At the annual meeting he got up and slated us: 'You irresponsible pair of blokes!' Of course, Ray was like that, he put on a bold front for the supporters, but deep down he would back us, know we are right.

Stewart won the Brownlow in his first year with us (1971). Then the next year during summer training I said to Tommy, 'Where's Stewart?' and he said, 'Hasn't turned up yet,' so I went to chase him up. Time was running out. Anyhow, he finished up coming three weeks before the first game.

And I was coming to pick the first side against Essendon, at Essendon, and I said to Tommy, 'I'm not prepared to play Stewart. He hasn't done the right thing by the club. We are setting an example to the young boys. They are busting their guts. They've been training for three and four months.

I reckon we have to set an example here, I don't think we should play him.'

Anyhow, he went along with it, and we left him out the side. And there was hell to play in the paper the next morning. He abused the selectors! So I get a phone call on the Friday night from Ian Wilson, the president. He said, 'Stewart rang me, he wants to play in the seconds tomorrow.' I said, 'Well that's fine. That's what it's there for. So send him there.'

Col Saddington was coach of the seconds. Stewart walked in and didn't speak to anyone and got changed. He didn't say anything to me. I usually go out on the ground at quarter-time, and I said to Col, 'As soon as Stewie goes down on his haunches, he's buggered.'

And just before quarter-time, he is down on his haunches and Col came back and said, 'Stewie wants to come off.' I said, 'Send the runner out and tell Stewie he is staying on.'

Well, by half-time he is really down on his haunches and he came in and came over and I said, 'Listen, this is what you're down here for, you're going back on.' Well by three-quarter time he has really cracked it. 'I am buggered,' he said. 'You're making a fool of me. You've proved your point. You're right.'

I said to him, 'If you don't apologise and retract your statements in the press, for what you said, you will never play for Richmond again. It will be you or me, and I know who it will be.'

Well, Alf Brown wrote the story in *The Herald*. The headline was *'Ian Stewart apologises to Selectors'*. And we have been best of mates ever since.

Everyone says Richmond got rid of Tommy Hafey. Richmond did not get rid of Tommy, he was appointed coach for 1977. But Tommy rang me up and he said he thought his voice was running out, he thought his time was up, time he'd move on. I tried to talk him out of it. And then he announced his retirement. So I sat with him at the football at the finals, him and Maureen and myself. We just discussed the football and I asked him what he was doing.

And he said, 'I've had three or four really good coaching offers.' He told me one was Melbourne, one was Carlton, one was Collingwood. I said, 'You take the best offer you can get. Wherever you go you're going to do the same job.' He said, 'I think Melbourne is too close to home, I don't want go. It's too close to Richmond.' He rang back and said, 'Oh Jesus, Collingwood has come up with a fantastic offer,' and I said, 'Go for it!'

Barry Richardson (coach, 1977-78) took over from Tommy. He used to come into the selection committee on Thursday night and put his feet up on the table. He was such a laidback bloke. He said, 'We will work a few things out as we go along, that will do.'

Mike Patterson was a great theory man. We weren't getting anywhere with Patto. At the time when Patterson was coach (1984), he was a very lowly-paid coach, he didn't cost the club anything.

Tony Jewell (1979-81, 86-87) was a very good tactician, but wild, bloody wild. I had the job of interviewing the coaches, and out of all the coaches he had the best qualifications for allround situations. So I recommended him to the board that he be coach. I still remember them saying 'By geez, Allan, you're responsible, you better hold him down.' We went to Waverley one day, and Ian Wilson used to walk around the boundary with all his hierarchy, like Lindsay Thompson (former Victorian Premier, 1981-82), and bought them into the room at Waverley.

Tony came out of the coach's box and said, 'Get out of the bloody way, Wilson, get your bloody crew out of here.'

Next week I got a letter to the board from Lindsay Thompson: 'Can't put up with this bloke.'

Allan Jeans is a lovely bloke, I know him very well, but in the interview he was just so laid back. I like a bloke full of enthusiasm, full of go in him. He did get the job a couple of years later (1992) and they weren't going too good (Richmond finished 13th).

I went down to training and he said, 'Come and have a yarn.' So I went in the coaching room and he said, 'Jesus, what have I stuck my neck into here?' And I said, 'Just have a look at those players up there,' – he had the big list of players on the board – 'you tell me who on that list who would get a game at Hawthorn.'

He said, 'Oh, I never looked at it that way ... Dale Weightman perhaps.' And I said, 'Dale would, but he's not getting any younger. There's not another player up there ... Matty Knights?'

Jeans said, 'Matty Knights won't run through a brick wall for you,' and I said, 'Of course, Matty Knights won't run through a brick wall for you,' meaning that he's not that sort of player.

Next Saturday I am in the rooms and he comes out with: 'One of the well-known identities around this club said that none of you bloody players will get a game in the top sides, and he's bloody right!'

Les Flintoff

1950-52

If you played with Richmond in the early sixties, there if a reasonable chance you were recruited by former Tiger player Les Flintoff. It was Flintoff's responsibility to recruit those players who would build the most successful team in the club's history.

I came down to Richmond in 1950. I was recruited from Warburton by Maurie Fleming. I had a run with Melbourne under Allan la Fontaine, then went across to play in the Richmond senior practice match on the same day.

I played in the first game in the reserves and then I played in the seniors on Vic Chanter from Fitzroy, a tough full-back. In fact, he kept Ray Poulter goalless for a half, so Dyer threw me on to him and would you believe I had six set shots for goal in the last quarter and kicked one goal, five behinds. But at 5-feet-10 (178cm), and kicking one goal five, Dyer soon relegated me to the backline from 1950 to 1952. It was only a handful of games. I ended up in the country, coaching Ganmain.

But then in 1963-64 I returned to Richmond on the senior committee after Graeme Richmond and Ray Dunn phoned me up and said they wanted me to join them. I thought about it for a while, then I thought I might as well because I could get a nice cushy job being Chairman of Selectors, which was an easy sort of a job. But Graeme Richmond, he said, 'No Les, that's a job for a 'yes man', and we want the man in that position to always be agreeing with the coach's selection.

GR said, 'We've got a big job (for you) to do. We haven't won a premiership since 1943 and we've got a big job to do in recruiting, development and promotion ahead of us, and that's what I want you to head up.' So I had three caps to wear.

Every Saturday and Sunday I was away recruiting somewhere in Victoria, South Australia, Tasmania and even Western Australia. So it was only occasionally did I get to see the Tigers play at any time. I was away seeking out players and recruiting them and rounding them up and bringing them into the office. I can recall saying to Graeme in 1966, halfway through the season: 'I think we are ready to roll, I think we will go!' He said, 'No, no, 1967 will be our year.'

I'd say (to prospects), 'We'd like you very much to come join us at Tigerland. But to make sure you come to us when you come down from the country we have a registration form called a form four, which means you're not entitled to play for any team except the Tigers. If you come on in the last five minutes as a 19th man, you would have cemented your name in Tigerland history, because you were then a Tiger.' For the ones who didn't come down, the form four held them for two years, then expired. That's how we got Dick Clay. His term had expired from North Melbourne and then he became a Richmond player.

Zoning came in our first premiership year, 1967, around about September. It came overnight. Bang. It took the fun out of bargaining. We'd say we can get this guy for a television set, (or a) suit so we used to take television sets into the mums and dads as an inducement to sign. Or a little bag of low denomination money. We had to compete with the other clubs.

GR said, 'I've seen (Peter Hudson) play but I don't think he is much good.' So I went down to North Hobart and I (later) said, 'GR, this guy is good. He's kicked three or four in the first half, he's got a belt across the mouth, he's picked himself up and kicked another three. He kicks them from well out and he kicks them off the ground and in the goalsquare and he's cunning as a rat.'

Other players I had been in contact regularly with, prior to zoning coming in were Barry Round, Bernie Quinlan and Darrel Baldock. They were all on the fishing line, ready to be pulled in, but zoning came in and that killed us. I reckon we would have

Born
Oct 5, 1930

Played
Richmond
1950-52
16 games,
4 goals

Interviewed
Apr 21, 2002

Les Flintoff with a prize catch, ruckman Brian Roberts. "We finally nailed him ... then presented him with the biggest jumper we could find at Tigerland."

Flintoff and Tom Hafey made a formidable combination of recruiting and coaching.

got two or three of them, because I was in regular contact with Hudson and Round. Barry Round I used to see every fortnight as I went through Gippsland travelling. Anyhow, you can't win them all.

I had some great battles with Ron Cook, secretary of Hawthorn, and Ian Drake of St Kilda. We'd go away to some game and you'd run into them and they'd say 'Which one you looking at, which one you after?' But you wouldn't say. Bert Deacon of Carlton said to me: 'I'm worried about the number of recruits you are signing and only leaving us the has-beens.'

GR always liked the recruits to be bought back to the office and get them signed up, because it had a more official atmosphere and a little bit more credibility. You couldn't do that sometimes, when you've got two other clubs buzzing around the player. You had to be able to sign him up then and there. Another fellow we missed was Stan Alves.

I took GR down to see Alves and he said, 'No Les, he's too bloody small.' You know how Alves ended up, so we missed out on that. It was healthy disagreement. I recall Graeme and I met Alves and offered him a suit, shirt, tie and boots and he bounced back and he said, 'Sorry, I can get two suits, two shirts and two sets of shoes at Melbourne.' So GR said, 'Oh well, we wish you luck.'

When I went to recruit Mike Hammond in Maryborough, there were three club cars outside his house. So you've got to sign him up on the spot just to get him. Brian Sarre, he was an All-Australian full-back from Western Australia and he just moved into a house and all he had was a fridge and a couple of chairs, so I signed him up on the fridge. He didn't come over. Some of the other players got signed in cars, outside, in their own home. Craig McKellar I signed in South Australia and his mother and father suddenly cracked a bottle of Johnny Walker Black Whisky, and of course I didn't drink. They were having a celebratory drink and I had a cup of tea.

The only person paid on a salary was the secretary, Graeme Richmond. As it's shown in 1967 Annual Report, our recruiting expense was $3892. Then the recruiting expenses for the 1969 premiership year jumped to $6800. It doubled. But we introduced the squad and the clinic and that was all included.

We were well rewarded by the Tiger premierships. We were well rewarded from the fact that we got acknowledged from GR that we had done a power of work. This is what the love of the game is. The passion. The Tiger passion.

We had good guidelines: we wanted physical power, physical pace, physical kicking ability, otherwise the guy's got to be smart and fast. We used to border on different things and invariably from time to time we would look at their parents to see if they were big-boned people or short people. It gave you an idea of how this boy was going to grow and also gave you an idea of their temperament.

We made many trips to Albury and Wodonga to get Barry Richardson. But what a recruit, he's done well in football and business.

The first meeting with Francis Bourke? I wasn't too impressed as I met him on the farm in Numurkah. His father, Frank, called him up from the dairy shed, and it was pouring rain and he had this big black raincoat and hat and long big gumboots and he didn't look too impressive as a footballer. But what a great recruit and what a footballer. One of the best.

John Northey, from Mortlake, turned out a great footballer and coach. GR asked me after we signed him to phone up Geelong Football Club just to tell them not to bother to go down and see Northey on the weekend as we had already signed him. John Perry and Geoff Strang were recruited from the Albury area. At the same time I noticed this guy who could also kick the ball a mile so I signed him up as well, and that was Kevin Smith. Boy, he could belt the ball. I thought, 'Where did this guy come from?'

Graham Burgin was a great player. When I visited him and his parents in Mitcham, his parents said he was going to have a run at Hawthorn. So I said to them both, 'Well that's okay, as long as he signs this form four.' So I signed him up, and I said, 'He can have a run now at Hawthorn.' Dick Clay, we pinched this great recruit off North Melbourne.

Neil Busse? I made many trips to Benalla and I said, 'How do you spell your name, son? I'll just sign you up now. B-U-S-Y?' and he said, 'No, B-U-S-S-E.' He ended up as the AFL Tribunal Chairman.'

Rex Hunt, high-marking, big left-foot kick and he's done very well for himself. Brian Roberts, this big guy I chased in Western Australia and South Australia, and finally nailed him in Victoria. Then I presented him with the biggest jumper we could find at Tigerland.

Royce Hart, the Tasmanian Tiger. What a recruit and footballer! When Royce first came to Richmond I must have said to him, 'If you keep playing like you are now, one day you will end up captain and you'll play in premierships with the Tigers and you'll play at least 10 years.' One day he came up to me and he said, 'Do you remember what you said to me 10 years ago? Well, today's the day.'

Eric Moore and Darryl Beale, we pinched them from Essendon. But when you go and see them play in the practice game you don't know who they are because you don't have a *Record*. So I had to ask someone. I went up and asked Harry Hunter, the chairman of selectors at Essendon – he didn't know me – and I said to him 'They're two good players, where do they come from?' And he said, 'Oh, that's Eric Moore and the other bloke's Darryl Beale.'

'Oh, Eric Moore. Where from, Harry?' And he told me Coleraine. Security was pretty slack in those days.

Noel Carter came from Tasmania after numerous trips. Brian Pilcher was another recruit I picked up from down there.

This was an interesting one, Keith Smythe. GR said, 'Now I want you go and recruit this guy on Saturday,' I said, 'Where?' And he said, 'In the centre of the Essendon Football Ground, he will be playing the practice game there.

"Barry Round, Bernie Quinlan and Darrel Baldock ... they were all on the fishing line, ready to be pulled in, but zoning came in and that killed us."

'All I want you to do is sit down beside him at three-quarter time and try and sign him up, you might get a biff in the ear but don't worry about it.'

So at three-quarter time I sat down beside him and talked to him and, before I could sign him up, John Coleman, who was coach then, saw me and came straight for me.

So I said to Smythe, 'I will catch up with you later, where will you be?' And he said, 'I'm going to have a run with Hawthorn.' We finally got him in the end.

When I retired, in 1973, I found it very hard to listen to the crowd roar at the MCG. I was across the road at Olympic Park athletics helping my daughter (Olympic gold medal-winning hurdler Debbie Flintoff-King).

The crowd would roar while I was stuck over in the athletic track. Debbie would be saying, 'Come on, dad, concentrate on me.' She was training for (and won) the gold medal and winning the gold medal is the next best thing to winning a VFL premiership.

Ron Reiffel

Though he played only a handful of games, Ron Reiffel recalls a colourful era at Tigerland. He has remained involved with the Former Players & Officials Association since 1963, and only recently retired as curator of the club museum.

1951-52

Born
Mar 15, 1932

Died
Dec 30, 2018

Played
1951-52
6 games

Interviewed
Nov 25, 2006

There is a bit of a story to my name. When my wife and I went to England my passport had run out, and the first time I got a passport you could take an extract but the second time we had to get a full birth certificate. So when I got the birth certificate back I was named Donald as my first name. I was supposed to be Ronald, I don't know whether my dad told them the wrong name when they wrote it out. When I went there they said, that's not you. So I had to change my name ... and this was only 10 years ago.

My mum always called me Ronald because she was a Ronald Coleman fan, he was the idol of the matinees in those days. She was Florence and my dad was Lou (Melbourne 1936-39, Sth Melbourne 1939-41). He had quite an elaborate system of names, he was Guy Louis Lindsay Reiffel and everyone called him Lou, or 'Pop'. Some of those 'Wells' cartoons used to say he was only as big as a pop gun. But it's strange. In one of those cartoons, I read where it says 'Reiffel – he is only the size of the pistol' and that is the nickname of my son Paul. Sometimes (Bill) Morris or (Don) Fraser, a few of the older blokes, used to call me 'Son of Pop', or 'Young Pop' or 'Popper'.

We came from Ballarat in 1936 as dad was recruited by Melbourne. He was approached by Geelong and Richmond but he picked Melbourne because only (Percy) Beames was roving and they had a position, whereas Richmond had (Ray) Martin and (Dick) Harris and he didn't think he would get a game with them. He then played at South for a while.

Melbourne put us in a house in Richmond, in Highett St, and got him a job with the wool firm Lambricks. Johnny Lewis was working with them too, the ex-North Melbourne and Melbourne player. Melbourne used to get their players jobs. Dad had a job, and in those days, in the middle 1930s, that was pretty important. When we lived in Ballarat we didn't have a traditional team we followed. But when I went to school at St Ignatius I wore my Melbourne jumper one day to school. I only wore it once. Never again, they drove me mad. It was around that time I think I changed to Richmond.

My dad was very friendly with George Smeaton, Jack Cotter and Jack Scott. George used to come to our place quite a bit and he used to tell all his tales and I used to love just listening to them. My dad's friends were real Richmond fans and they used to tell me about (George) Rudolph and (Allan) Geddes, in the late 1920s. One of them, Jack Hickey, a great Richmond fan, he had a canvas-top car and we would go to the matches sometimes in it.

Dad only played probably 30-40 games, but he averaged about two goals a game for a rover, which wasn't too bad (35 games, 73 goals at Melb; 29 games, 45 goals at Sth Melb). He kicked five a couple times against Richmond, eight against Collingwood at Victoria Park. He was only five-six (168cm) and nine-stone-six (60kg). He was getting hurt a lot; he got cleaned up once in the finals and Melbourne were looking for someone a bit stronger. Albert Rodda and (Ron) Barassi Snr were stronger built people. So he went to South for a couple of years and he won their goalkicking in 1940.

I do remember in 1944 or 1945, Richmond United used to play on the Richmond Reserve, behind the Tech. They said to him 'Would you come and play for us?' as he had been retired a few years. By that time I was about 12 or 13, and I went over to watch him play one day and he played in the centre and I think he kicked 12 goals this day. The Metropolitan

Troubled Tiger star Don "Mopsy" Fraser. "He was a Damon Runyon character you know. One day he had plenty and other day not," recalls Ron Reiffel.

League wasn't bad, he was kicking them from the centre. I was staggered. They were coming like missiles and I was standing up the Church Street end goals. And he kicked about six or seven in the second game.

(Former Richmond captain) Maurie Hunter coached us as a kid when I was playing in the YCW but I don't remember him saying much other than 'don't forget your raffle tickets'. When you're a kid you lose track of all perspective. I knew Maurie Hunter, I used to see him playing tennis but I didn't really respect him as a sportsman. I can remember he had this big knee bandage on. We got into the Grand Final one year and he said, 'We are going to have a pie night down at my place.' All the team went and I was staggered. As I walked into the house here was all these photos of Maurie with Richmond and Victoria. I just thought he was an average bloke who used to come up on his push bike, and it changed my opinion straight away.

"When I went to school at St Ignatius in Richmond I wore my Melbourne jumper to school for football. I only wore it once. They drove me mad. I changed to Richmond."

I wore Number 6. (AFL statistician) Col Hutchinson said to me, 'You're one of the few blokes who played the same number of games as your number.' I wanted to play cricket for Richmond. When I was asked to go down to Richmond, I wasn't home and I thought they had asked me to come down and get ready for cricket training. It was halfway through 1950. Mal Wishart came the second time and said, 'We want you to play in the seconds on Saturday.' We went into Harrison House to register as a player, because I was playing with the YCW under 18s, church football.

So that night we went on the train to Harrison House, and I played on the Saturday with the seconds. I trained only the one night under (Alby) Pannam, the Thursday night, and played in the seconds on the Saturday. I had just turned 18.

We played out at Footscray, the Western Oval and it was a beautiful sunny day, the only trouble was there was a hurricane blowing down one end. I played on the wing. They bounced the ball and someone booted it out and I took a mark and went back to kick it. It wasn't a very good kick, I think it went 20 metres and blew out of bounds. I thought, 'I have made a fool of myself.'

But they said, 'Come down next week for training,' and I played the next week at North Melbourne. The thing that struck me when I started was that the seconds and the firsts were different clubs. The seniors trained and played at one end of the ground and the seconds trained and went into other rooms. You virtually were separate. It was a strange setup, that sort of surprised me.

The seconds had their own president, secretary, social committee, did their own annual reports, they were two separate clubs. And that stayed like that until much later, when Ray Dunn changed the structure in 1960 because they tried to take over.

I played in a few games in the under 19s the same year and they played the curtain-raisers to the seniors. It was great atmosphere after half-time, the ground would be full, people would get there early to get a spot. But when you played for the seconds there would only be your mother or your girlfriend.

Mum used to come, she was more keen than my dad. He was one of those fathers who never really wanted to intrude, which was unfortunate because being the only child I could handle the ball and run but my kicking was very ordinary and he never really worked on me. Mopsy (Fraser) was probably one of the senior players who helped me a bit because he knew an uncle of mine, so when I got a little bit closer to them he really tried to help me.

In 1950, I played in the thirds and seconds, I was really a cricket fan and I played in the finals for the cricket team and our Grand Final finished the week before the footy season started. In 1951, as soon as the cricket finished I went down to training and Pannam said, 'Where have you been?' and I said 'I've been playing cricket.' He said, 'Well, you'll be back in the thirds then,' because I hadn't played in a practice game or trained.

So I played the first game of the year in the thirds, then I went into the seconds and later in the year I went into the firsts. I think I came third in the best and fairest for the seconds, two years running, and they gave me a smoker's stand each time, and I never smoked in my life. I think it was from the Richmond furnishing company down in Swan St. They were the people who gave the club the original tiger skin in 1921.

When I did get picked in the firsts we were playing at Hawthorn and I got on the bus and went out to Glenferrie Oval. I had been with Richmond half of 1950, and all of 1951 until the last three or four games when I got picked, and I can remember

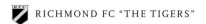

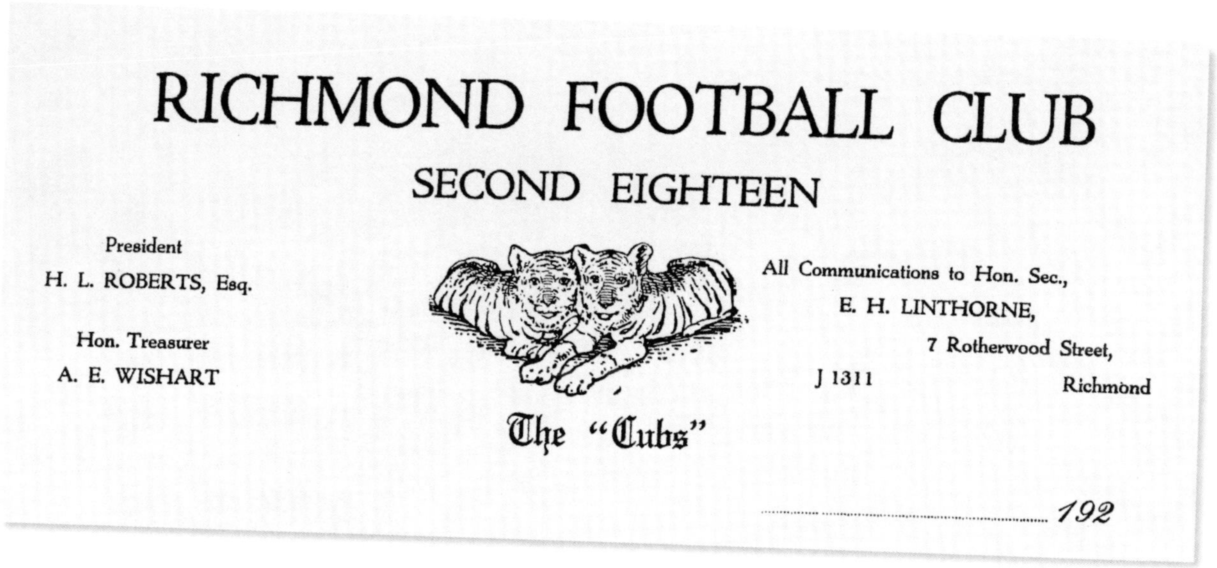
RICHMOND FOOTBALL CLUB

SECOND EIGHTEEN

President
H. L. ROBERTS, Esq.

Hon. Treasurer
A. E. WISHART

The "Cubs"

All Communications to Hon. Sec.,
E. H. LINTHORNE,
7 Rotherwood Street,
Richmond
J 1311

.... 192

Charlie Callander taking me around saying 'This is Geoff Spring, this is Bill Wilson, this is Bill Morris...' I had been at the club a year-and-a-half and had never met them! That's the way it worked.

I was a reserve and I'm sitting next to Dyer and Pat Kennelly, chairman of selectors. Ken Albiston was the other reserve in the dugout. I saw this policeman walking around the boundary line and he had this little kid with him, and he was lost. As the policeman was bringing him around the ground, hoping somebody will see who he is and claim him, and it was my mate's brother's son. I was sitting there in the middle of the game, and what do I do? Do I say I know him? Do I say to Jack, 'Excuse me, Jack, I have to go and try and see if I can find this bloke?' I didn't know what to do so I just sat there and the policeman kept on walking by.

Don Fraser was my idol as a kid. I just thought he was a tremendous player. Dyer was the best player I ever saw down at Richmond and there was a group of players that are very hard to split like Bartlett, Bourke and Hart.

Fraser wasn't a champion but he was a real character. I can remember playing practice games with him ... I'd be in the back pocket and Mopsy would be full-back and he'd say to me 'I'll catch them and you kick them, when I get it you start running.' He was a beautiful mark over the pack and then he'd boot it out and I'd start running, every time.

The last game in 1952, Coleman had to kick six goals to kick 100 goals for the year and he kicked them by half-time. Dyer said that the committee said Fraser took a dive and they told him he wasn't welcome back at the club. [Ed's Note: Fraser left to coach Port Melbourne in 1953.]

The Tigers ran their reserves – The Cubs – as a separate club until 1960.

We played Ovens and Murray up at Corowa – the club wasn't going interstate that year – so the players decided to have a weekend away. A lot of the senior players had gone up on the Thursday and they were staying up there. They went up there and there was no Mopsy. Dyer met us at the race. The people who were going with Dyer and Fraser were meeting after the game and Dyer said, 'We have a problem, I can't find Mopsy.'

I said, 'We've got a real problem, he's our treasurer.'

We had put in through the year to pay for all the things. Dyer found him and brought him up later. When Mopsy got up there, all the money was gone, he had done it on the horses. He was a Damon Runyon character you know. One day he had plenty and other day not.

I was told one day before training he couldn't get the money in the calico bag before training (there was so much of it), and the next week he was going around saying 'Could you lend me 10 shillings?' He was told not to come to the club again. Not that that worried him, he used to come down to the former players' night.

I was at Richmond from 1950 until 1953. And I went back in 1963 on the committee of the past players' association and have been there ever since. We used to talk about the history of the club. Bill Meaklim was the instigator in forming the historical group in 1993. Bob Phillips was the board member who helped us get it going. And in 1996 the museum opened. [Ed's Note: Reiffel was curator of the museum from its inception through to his retirement at Easter, 2007.]

Brian Davie

An orthopedic surgeon in later life, Brian Davie represented Richmond 89 times before choosing medical studies over football. From 1967-80 he turned his hand to assisting Richmond players with injuries, an era which bridged five premierships.

1953-59

Born
Aug 31, 1934

Played
1953-59
89 games,
36 goals

Interviewed
Jun 6, 2006

My father was a school teacher, he taught at Melbourne Grammar where I went to school. He played football for Tasmania and he played cricket for Victoria and Tasmania. He was born in Hobart and came over to Melbourne and was captain of Prahran (he is in their Hall of Fame). He had a big sporting background. He never told me who he barracked for, but when I played for Richmond he became a keen Richmond supporter.

During the war I played a bit, and my father had access to a football because he was a school teacher. Anyway, dad brought a football home and we used to kick it in the street.

When I was a little boy I barracked for Melbourne. In fact, I saw Jack Mueller play a lot of times. I went to the 1948 Grand Final with my brothers and saw Melbourne win; I remember vividly we went along expecting to get in, and the fence broke down so we all rushed in and got a spot. We ended up sitting on the steps on the outer. It was a draw. They played again next week and Melbourne won easily. Jack was a fantastic player and a wonderful mark and he impressed me at that age.

I only played while I was at Melbourne University. I played full-forward and kicked quite a few goals there. There weren't too many of us around at the time. I know Don Cordner from Melbourne was a doctor. But as far as I know I could be the only medical practitioner who ever played for Richmond [Ed's Note: Dr David Henry played in 1976]. I was zoned to Richmond. At the start of University I was 18 and I trained with the University Blues and Blacks and, frankly, I didn't like it very much. Maurie Fleming was a very persuasive secretary of the Richmond Football Club and he got me to come down and train, and I was hooked on the Tigers. I have very high regards for Maurie, during his lifetime he raised thousands of dollars for the Prince Henry's Hospital, just in his own capacity.

I was 18 in 1953 and Jack Dyer had been sacked. Jack wasn't to be seen. The new coach was Alby Pannam, who was his arch-nemesis from Collingwood. I never saw much of Jack Dyer when I was at Richmond, because he felt a bit subdued and not happy. He only returned when Graeme Richmond got him back in the 1960s. I would say he was not seen much from the early 1950s to the early 1960s.

I can tell you a story about Alby Pannam. I knew that he was a real goalsneak for Collingwood, he kicked goals out the back of his head. I wasn't kicking the ball too well and I said to him, 'What am I doing wrong Alby, is it the run up? What's going on?' An expression came over his face and he pondered for a while and said, 'I don't know what you're doing wrong. Just kick it.' You know it wasn't a profound response because that's how he kicked goals. He had no knowledge or plan about it.

In those days the coaching was negligible. He thought if you got on the league ground you were a good footballer and didn't need any coaching; he was quite incorrect in that way. So you got very few instructions when you went on the ground.

Col Austen was the coach of the seconds and he came up to me and said, 'I think you went all right today and think you will have a chance (of senior football).' You just read it in the paper, no-one ever told you, and so I found out I was full-forward for Richmond.

I played one game in the seconds against Melbourne. Jack O'Rourke was the full-forward at

As Brian Davie receives heat lamp treatment, the club noticeboard gets its priorities right.

Brian Davie (35) flies for a mark against the Cats. Far right is Jim Deane (11), Magarey Medallist of 1953, who arrived from South Australia the following year with a huge reputation; Deane managed only 33 games before returning to Adelaide. No. 30 (left) is John Ritchie.

Richmond and Jack suddenly disappeared – he was never really seen (at the club) again – he went to the Lady Bay Hotel in Warnambool and somehow they decided I was going to be his replacement.

So I played full-forward in the second round of 1953, against Fitzroy. I was very lucky, I kicked four goals but we didn't win the game. I stayed (at full-forward) for 11 games and got progressively worse. It didn't help that Richmond lost the first 10 games I played there. So I went to the half-back line and played there most of the time. I did kick 35 goals but I was a failure at full-forward. I was only just six feet (183cm) and there were some tremendous players at that time. I played on Herb Henderson, Footscray full-back, and Fred Goldsmith, the South Melbourne Brownlow Medallist.

I played on quite a few good players, John Brady, Ron Clegg, Murray Weideman, Owen Abrahams and Brian Dixon. One day I came onto the ground as 19th man. I was always a bit slow to get going at the start of the season and they sent me down onto Neil Mann, great Collingwood stalwart, and I walked down to him and he said, 'What's your name, sonny?' I said, 'Brian Davie, and what's yours?' And that annoyed him. You've got to have a bit of go in you.

The only thing I am famous for is ending Charlie Sutton's career. We were playing at the Richmond ground against Footscray, and Charlie was changing on the half-forward flank, and he was getting stuck into one of our players. The ball came down and I just took off and ran at the ball as fast as I could. As he came in from the side I hit him on the shoulder and broke his collarbone.

I kept going and all the Footscray team kept chasing me and I got to the centre of the ground and they jumped on me and I got a free kick. And Charlie went off the ground.

The best players at time were Roy Wright, Bill Wilson, Geoff Spring, Allan Cooke and Ray Poulter. Roy Wright used to call me 'Brizza' and I don't know why. And 'Doc', he would call me too. Geoff Spring was a very good goalkicker; he played on the wing but ran everywhere. Roy Wright was the best and Des Rowe was the second best. Des had very sure hands and had a strong body and often would get people out the way. He never ran straight ahead when he got the ball, he always ran off to the side and when the opposition came to get him he then changed direction. Often he would clear the ball in dashes where he would bounce the ball, and that was something that wasn't done very much in that time. He'd run 20 yards and kick it 50 yards.

I was a straight ahead player. When I look back on it I was so frightened about doing anything wrong I just got the ball and kicked it, or I would run hard and kick the ball as far as I could on the backline. We didn't handball very much, there wasn't a lot of finesse, so I was a direct sort of player. I used to go in as hard as I could. If I got it, I thought, 'I'm not going to get crunched by someone I am going to get rid of it.'

In the early days, you had to go to lectures at 9am. I'd go in on the train to the city and up on the tram. Sometimes you had free time during the day and you'd go to the medical library and study there. Training was Tuesday and Thursday and I'd get down there at 4.30 and train and then play on the Saturday.

I didn't really make a lot of friends and it's probably because I was very concerned about studying. I had to leave shortly after the game. At that stage I was always trying to keep up with the lectures and didn't have any time to fraternise with the players.

I regret that, but that was the way it was.

In total, I had a broken nose once and a fractured scaphoid in the wrist and a few hamstring tears. Dr. Grogan, the club doctor at the time, was fairly matter-of-fact but he was quite a character. He was said to give injections to people through their coats ... I remember when my nose was out, he just pushed it back and said, 'You'll be right.' My wife saw it and went, 'No, not for me', and took me to the hospital.

I captained Richmond three times and we won each time. The best players, (Billy) Wilson and (Roy) Wright, were of course in the state side. I got very obsessed with the game and became very different to what I normally am. I became more aggressive.I wanted to do what I could to win the game. I played in the Victorian side in 1957 and that was my best year.

Then, frankly, I slowly got worse. I was in charge of the Medical and Surgical ward and I just couldn't keep up. Maurice Ewing was the professional surgeon at Melbourne University and I was his resident-to-be. And so I had to cease. It was the right time – I was 25 when I retired.

I later met Graeme Richmond on the train coming into the hospital. We had become friends at school when he was at Geelong Grammar and I was at Melbourne Grammar. We used to play sport against each other.

I went overseas and came back in 1967 and he looked me up and said he wanted me to come on the Richmond committee. So I was on the selection committee for one year in 1967. That was a funny situation because Tom Hafey was there – Tom liked his own way and he always said to kick long. Jack Titus and I couldn't understand why it wasn't a good idea to throw in a few small kicks from time to time.

But Tom was very successful and maybe we were wrong, and we kept arguing all the time. Eventually they dismissed me from the selection committee at the end of 1967.

"I said to Kevin Sheedy, 'There are two alternatives: standard treatment for 12 weeks, or you can see how you get on without the plaster.' And he didn't have any treatment at all."

I operated on Royce Hart's knee the first time. Royce had a cartilage injury, but I don't think he was happy with the way I treated him as he has had several other operations since.

Maybe there was more to the Royce injury than what was apparent. He did it again and had other operations. It was an open operation, it wasn't arthroscopic, you had to make a cut there. And I treated him for a fractured wrist. Don Scott had pushed him into the boundary line and broke his wrist.

Kevin Sheedy, I remember, had a fractured scaphoid in the wrist and I said to Kevin, 'There are two alternatives: standard treatment for 12 weeks, or you can see how you get on without the plaster.' And he didn't have any treatment at all. He's probably got a sore wrist by now.

Graeme Richmond would ring me and say, 'Billy Barrot's no good, we need him for Saturday.' I know Billy very well and he was a bit of a worry. I operated on Barry Richardson two or three times. He always seemed to get back to play, but he certainly had a strange gait at the time.

And I operated on Francis Bourke's knee and he returned successfully. He did better than his father ... Frank Bourke could have been a better player but he did his knee.

I was the Chief Orthopedic Surgeon at the Prince Henry's Hospital and the Monash Medical Centre, and I felt I should no longer be involved in Richmond. You can't stay there forever. I felt I was just as keen on their success but better to move on (in 1980). It was the most wonderful experience of my life and I really enjoyed my time at Richmond.

Tom Hafey (The Player)

Before the coaching legend was born, Tommy Hafey was an honest, nuggety back pocket player for Richmond in the 1950s. Recruited from East Malvern, he played six seasons for the Tigers before recognising his true calling, and he headed to a country coaching job.

1953-58

I can remember the Tigers' 1943 premiership. My dad took me, it was up at Carlton and it was standing room. I can remember different things in it, the two full-backs, Cec Ruddell for Essendon and Ron Durham for Richmond; oh, a star! They were such beautiful kicks and each one of their kicks were big drop kicks going right to the wing nearly every time. Durham played not many games compared to a lot of people; he wore number 1, and came from Bacchus Marsh. He got electrocuted. I remember reading it in the paper, many years ago; he was very young when he died.

I barracked for Collingwood as a youngster. My father had a very best mate barrack for Hawthorn. So in 1942 and 1943 I think we saw Hawthorn, it was only a tram stop away. That's how you went, you'd catch a train or tram going to the footy. I would have seen probably every game they played at Hawthorn but then we would go to Richmond or Collingwood to see their teams as well.

My father barracked for the Magpies even though we lived in Richmond. When we were growing up we went to Canberra at the end of the depression, there was very little work, and my father being a printer was working one week in every four with two little boys. So in about 1936 or 1937 we went up to Canberra and lived there for six years.

We came back and lived in East Malvern, which was Richmond's area, even though we probably lived in six houses in Richmond before we went up to Canberra. I played down at East Malvern in the Caulfield Oakleigh District League, which was an ordinary competition and we were a very ordinary team. Then I went to the Tigers in 1953.

Everybody thought they were going to play League football. But as you got a little bit into your local football you realised that to play at a higher level was a very difficult thing, so therefore you'd probably be more interested in your own local team and your teammates, things like that. If I was to ask 10 youngsters at the schools I go to, 'What are you going to do?' they'd answer, 'I'm going to play football, I'm going to play football, I'm going to play football.' 10 in a row! And I think, 'Well, half your luck.'

I was in Richmond's area and somebody must have said, 'There's a player at East Malvern' and I was invited to come down and train by Maurie Fleming. No other club could show interest, you were zoned to your metropolitan zoned club. I was thrilled. I didn't think I'd make it, I thought if I played reserves that was a big step from playing senior football out in the suburbs. If you ever saw anybody who actually played in one of the reserves teams, you'd talk about him, because he had stepped up and was now a little bit elite. If anybody made the firsts, well that was big. If you'd seen somebody in the street and he was a Melbourne footballer or a South Melbourne footballer, it was like seeing royalty or a film star.

I played practice matches between our own players at Punt Road. They probably had three practice matches at a weekend. On a Saturday they started at 10 o'clock, 12 o'clock and two o'clock. But they would then put a list up naming who they were going to keep. If you read your name on the board then you were still needed to come down for training.

There were 150-odd players running around the training track so obviously at times some would be overlooked. Then it was a matter of elimination. If you were in the main practice match you got a big chance of making the final list. I suppose they must have thought what they'd seen was worth another look. I played in the centre out at East Malvern and

Born
Aug 5, 1931

Died
May 12, 2014

Played
Richmond
1953-58
67 games,
10 goals

Interviewed
Aug 2, 2004;
Apr 1, 2007

Fresh-faced and enthusiastic, Tommy Hafey played during the club's battling 1950s.

because of my size, five-seven-and-a-half (171cm), was going to be a rover or half-forward.

I was an apprentice at Carnegie and I remember saying to the boss would it be all right if I left early to go to training. And he was a little bit wary, so I gave him my notice instead. So I went out and worked in Footscray in the printing trade. I could work right through lunchtime, which I did, and get away at 4pm, so I could catch the train in. Training would probably start at 5pm.

"You'd do a lap and you'd just start kick-to-kick. The coach would bring you in and talk a little while, then you'd do circle work. That was training in those days."

The under 19s used to be the curtain-raiser to the firsts. The reserves played at the away ground. So my first game, Richmond played Melbourne at Punt Road and we played across the car park at the MCG. It was Ron Barassi's first game also, but he was 18 and I was probably 20 at the time. I thought I played pretty ordinary and I got dropped the following week. Col Austen was a very good reserves playing coach, so therefore he was a cut above the other players in the team. He probably would have been early 30s at that stage and as you know he won the 1949 Brownlow Medal at Hawthorn, retrospectively. And he played at Richmond for quite some time.

For many, the perception of Alby Pannam (pictured, left, with Maurie Fleming) as a "Collingwood man" could not be shaken at Punt Road.

You'd do a lap to start training and you'd just start kick-to-kick, the coach would then bring you in and talk a little while, then you'd do circle work, then he would bring us in a couple of times, and then do circle work again. Alby Pannam was terrific in my opinion, I really loved him. Very fit and very enthusiastic, I was a real fan. As a player I was just a solid trier, probably height and pace was a disadvantage.

I was in the senior team probably sixth match of the year. People said, 'Tommy will be sitting down in his black dressing gown at four o'clock in the morning waiting for the game to start.' I was on the bench against Collingwood at Victoria Park and I came on in the third quarter. I don't know who I replaced but I picked up the ball, and *bang* ... goal! I was 25 metres out from goal, and luckily I was facing that way.

All the time I was at Richmond we never looked like making finals. We didn't have a strong team, compared to others. I always knew we would be going along to watch Melbourne play Collingwood (in the finals) or Essendon or teams like that.

We had some really good players; Roy Wright was probably the best player in the competition, along with Bob Rose.

We had Kevin Dillon on the half-back line, who was strong and very dashing. Billy Wilson was the rover in the state team, Ray Poulter was a big strong man at centre half-forward, a beautiful goalkicker. Ron Branton was a terrific player, he came down the same time as me, but he played from the word go and when he was captain he won three consecutive best and fairests (1960-62).

I thought we messed around too much with the ball. I used to think Melbourne's style was just so much above everybody else's. I can remember being in the back pocket and having different views on what things should have been done, like kicking the ball quicker and more direct. It is so elementary. We were too intent on kicking the ball to a player on the lead all the time.

I know when I left in 1958 the single match payment was £10, but I think it might have gone up gradually. If you look at it, 18 games, plus two finals which we never played, the most anybody would get would be £200 because there was a Coulter Law – nobody got paid anymore than anybody else. You weren't allowed to break the Coulter Law.

If anybody got paid extra, it would be a couple of pound under the table. Sometimes they would give players money to sign them up and that was against the law; usually fellas in the country because they weren't zoned.

Polly Farmer was West Australian, now he would have got a sign-on fee, maybe about £1000. But that's why a lot of players left to play in the country at a very young age. Bob Rose was probably the best player in the VFL, he won four Copeland Trophies by the time he was 26.

He was captain and coach of Wangaratta when he was 27. I said to him once, 'Why did you play at Wangaratta Rovers?' I knew what he was going to say: 'Because I got £800.' Four times as much!

I can remember some little groups talking about the coach and I couldn't understand that because I put him on such a pedestal. I was probably very coachable because I just believed what the coach said was gospel. But I was really in shock when I knew that some of the players down at Richmond in my playing time didn't do the right thing by the rest of the team.

It was really disappointing when I heard them, and even people around the club, committeemen and workers, criticise someone, let's say Alby Pannam, because he was a former Collingwood person. I would never have done that.

When I played at East Malvern players would go into the pictures on a Friday night at 8 p.m. and they'd come out at 11 o'clock, because there was always two shows and an interval. And we would be playing on the Saturday and I felt that was too late to go to bed.

So we'd go up the shop where they all used to hang out, which was a milk bar and hamburger shop, then they'd go across to the pictures across the road. Well, I'd be there until they all went to the pictures and I'd turn and run home and get to bed early because I had football tomorrow. That was me.

Not that I am saying they were told what they should be doing and shouldn't be doing, but that's the way they went. But I just thought you had to go to bed and have an early night because you got the game tomorrow.

I had read in the paper that I had been dropped off the list at the start of the next season (1959). They hadn't told me. I trained in all the practice matches and I played 14 of the 18 games the previous year and I just thought I would be in the back pocket at the start of the season.

One of few images of Hafey from his six seasons as a player at Punt Road.

So in 1959 I played with Richmond Amateurs, which was a Sub A competition. They called them Amateurs but they weren't, they were very highly paid – I got £10 a week playing there, same as what I was getting if I was playing in Richmond seniors.

It was a very rough competition. They had Montague, Carlton Royals, Carlton Stars, Kensington, Richmond, North West and a Footscray team. There was a lot of betting on the game, and a lot of teams that had a lot of former VFL players or Association players, and we ended up winning the premiership.

In fact, then I played one game with East Malvern, the Grand Final, and we won that as well. So I won two premierships in the one year. I felt a bit embarrassed to play there after being a League player the previous year and put somebody out who'd been playing all the year.

Maurie Fleming

A tireless worker for the Tigers, Fleming was secretary of RFC from 1940-54, and later became the club's first paid president from 1958-63. In 1956, the gentlemanly Fleming penned the following article about running a football club; it appeared in *The Sporting Globe Football Book.*

Born
1902

Died
Oct 6, 1980

It costs about £200 a week to place a League side in the field, what with payments to players, provident fund allotment, trainers' wages, honoraria, and purchase of gear etc.

The work of 50 people, ranging from committeemen, coach, trainers and masseurs to property stewards working at high pressure, is necessary to fit a new player for his first League game. It costs perhaps £100 to get him onto the field by the time fares, accommodation, gear, training, necessities, have been provided.

Behind every successful football team is an army of honorary workers who give long hours of private time. Their work is entirely unrecognised by the huge crowd whose roar greets the successful team.

The work goes on for nearly 12 months of the year, and a League secretary is often on the job 18-20 hours of the day.

Consider the set-up of a typical League club. There's a general committee – president, secretary, treasurer, six vice-presidents, six committeemen, all of whom are elected at the annual meeting. Additional are cricket club and second eighteen representatives, plus three players' representatives elected by the players and trainers of the previous season.

RICHMOND FOOTBALL CLUB
Testimonial Dinner
TO
J. M. FLEMING, ESQ., M.B.E.
at
TUDOR COURT, 141 KOOYONG ROAD,
CAULFIELD.
March 25. 1964.

A coach is appointed who, with the selection committee, immediately reviews the previous season's training lists, first and second eighteens. Recruits are considered. Their decision made, the secretary has to write letters to them all, inviting them to train. The secretary has to make arrangement for travel, and board for country recruits. Introductions are very necessary and the president and secretary, in addition to general duties, must become hosts to these young players.

The selectors appoint a head trainer and the training staff. The general committee appoints the medical officer, masseur, timekeeper, boot-studders, property stewards, transport officer, door stewards, and chiropodist. Each begins his preparation for the opening of the season.

Coincidental with these preparations, the finance committee makes arrangements for the handling and sale of 8000 membership tickets. Its duty also is to be paymaster to the coach, players, trainers, boot-studders etc. It undertakes the handling of the various insurances, players', fidelity, burglary, transit and fire.

The secretary and the property steward set about procuring supplies. Guernseys (match and practice), knickers, (white and black), medical supplies, eucalyptus, anklets, knee bandages, thigh supports, shin guards, boots and stockings are only a few of the things needed.

The boot-studders are also busy on the boots of old players and recruits. Where necessary for the certainties, orders are issued for boots to be made to measure. This is vitally necessary. Your star player, on many occasions, has one foot smaller or wider than the other, perhaps has a corn or a bunion, and his boots must be correctly made or perhaps a vital game can be lost. On the Thursday evenings during the season, boots are cleaned and studded to suit the ground conditions of each Saturday.

All this, and not a game has been played as yet. News of possible recruits pours in. Each has to be followed up; if not, a Haydn Bunton might be missed.

Fleming, right, with long-time club benefactor Ben Alexander (from Alexander's Men's Wear store in Swan Street, Richmond).

Few realise the amount of correspondence received each year. During the early part of the season, more than 100 letters are received weekly, ranging from appeals, requests for photos, autographs, footballs, guernseys, donations, advice on how to place the team, and tremendous fan mail for the popular players, most of which are answered through the secretary.

Mor than 4000 outward letters were sent by my club last year. Is it any wonder that a number of the committees have seen fit to provide for full-time secretaries?

The football work becomes almost the full-time work of a secretary, to the detriment of the ordinary vocation of the official.

To give just one instance. When a player is injured, he is in the constant care of the secretary, who might be called out at any hour to provide immediate medical care for the injury that has deteriorated since the player left the club rooms. He might need hospitalisation. He might need special attention. The secretary must provide it, no matter what the hour.

A prolific letter writer, Fleming sought out Edgar Bateman by post in 1941: "Jack Dyer has asked where you had got to. He missed you at training." Bateman had headed off to war; he survived, but never played for the Tigers.

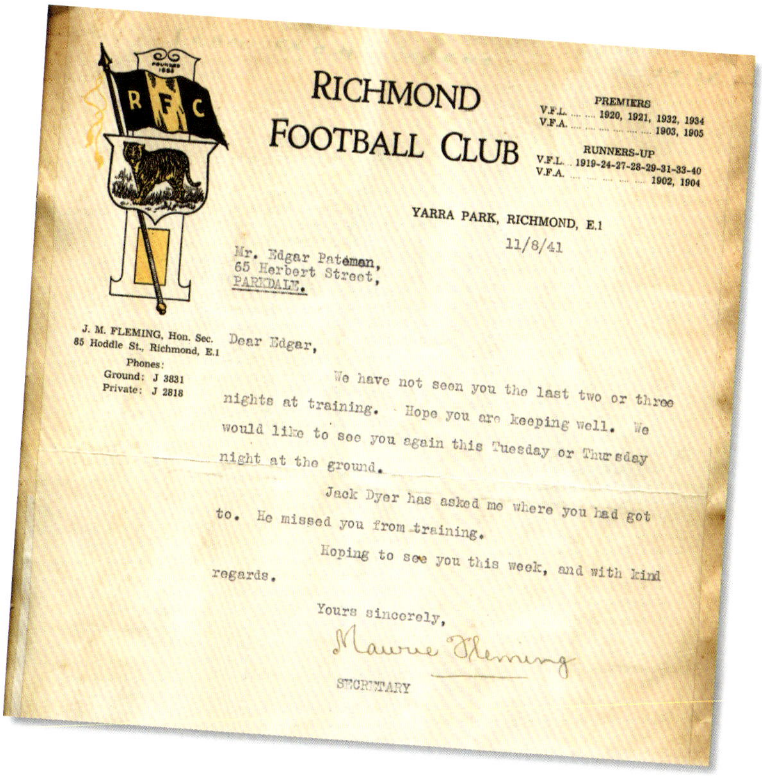

RICHMOND FOOTBALL CLUB

PREMIERS
V.F.L. 1920, 1921, 1932, 1934
V.F.A. 1903, 1905

RUNNERS-UP
V.F.L. .. 1919-24-27-28-29-31-33-40
V.F.A. 1902, 1904

YARRA PARK, RICHMOND, E.1

J. M. FLEMING, Hon. Sec.
85 Hoddle St., Richmond, E.1
Phones:
Ground: J 3831
Private: J 2818

11/8/41

Mr. Edgar Pateman,
65 Herbert Street,
PARKDALE.

Dear Edgar,

We have not seen you the last two or three nights at training. Hope you are keeping well. We would like to see you again this Tuesday or Thursday night at the ground.

Jack Dyer has asked me where you had got to. He missed you from training.

Hoping to see you this week, and with kind regards.

Yours sincerely,

Maurie Fleming

SECRETARY

Neville Crowe toiled for a decade at Tigerland, only for fate to deal him a cruel hand at career's end.

Neville Crowe

He played for a decade and dedicated years of service to the board, and as president, and steered the club back from disaster during the Save Our Skins campaign. Yet Neville Crowe is perhaps best remembered for missing the 1967 Grand Final through suspension.

1957-67

I can't remember never having a football in my hands. I had a bunch of guys, including Stuart Maxfield's dad, Brian, and we used to go down to Chadstone Park. Once I found a way to get out of Sunday school we were there all day and we'd go home when it was dark. We just kicked the footy and pretended we were, in my case, Bill Morris, and Brian was a Bob Rose fan. Strangely enough, later on I gave football away to play tennis. I was a reasonable sort of tennis player, I didn't want to damage my hand so I finished up playing soccer, but the only position they gave me was the only one that can touch the bloody ball – there I was, the goalkeeper, trying to save goals.

During my time at Melbourne High School I didn't kick a football. I know in Year 3 or 4 I was five-nine (175cm) and nine-stone-seven (68kg) and all of a sudden I got to six-four (192cm) and 12 or 13 stone (approx. 80kg). My first real hitout was when I went to play with the Ormond Amateurs in the under 19s. I didn't even own a pair of football boots; I went down there and trained in a pair of desert boots. We won every game of the year, apart from the one that matters, the Grand Final. I was working in the State Savings Bank at the time and they were in the A Grade Amateurs. We were coached by George Coates, a famous centreman at Fitzroy, and when I was training there I was invited down (to Richmond) by Maurie Fleming and Roy Wright. They came out to see me, I was playing down at the beach where our oval was. I asked George, 'Should I go down and start training with Richmond?' and he said 'Go down there and do the pre-season, it will do you the world of good.' Lo and behold, I was picked in the first game!

I was a Richmond barracker by the time I arrived on the planet. My brother, John, who was nine years older than me and used me as a punching bag, threatened if ever I didn't barrack for Richmond he would kill me. And he nearly did, about seven times I reckon, but nothing to do with football. He was a maniac. John used to bring me to all the games. I used to perch on the fence down the Jolimont End, on a little steel thing with barbed wire all over it, and I used to yell out 'Carn the Tigers!' in my squeaky little boy soprano.

And John used to get me in the rooms, which was just mind-boggling stuff, with Ray Poulter, Jack Dyer, Don Fraser, Des Rowe, Roy Wright, so it was just a genuine thrill to have been part of that Richmond culture since day one. Kids used to love getting in the rooms and they got plenty of pats on the head from those players; it was just sensational.

I just loved watching Bill Morris, he was so graceful. He had that sort of Royce Hart "hang in the air" thing, and he was only relatively small. Six-one (185cm) and a left-foot kick. I was actually staggered at the grace with which he did everything. He was just a fluent sort of guy. You just couldn't see how he could do the things he could do. His palming was just magnificent to Billy Wilson. I just loved that connection between ruckman and rover. I just idolised him. He wore number five, so when I got here and I was handed number five it was a joyous thing.

In those days there were zones, and I was zoned about 200 metres in from Dandenong Road, so I was in Richmond's territory. It was just a wonderful thing to grow up and come down here (Richmond) and I know when I first came down I used to call Roy Wright, Mr. Wright. I just thought it was the thing you did. He got me out of that habit pretty quickly. Roy was an early mentor. When I first came down here the player who took an active interest in me was certainly Roy, which was terrific, because he was in locker number two and I was in locker

Born
Jun 1, 1937

Died
Sept 2, 2016

Played
Richmond
1957-1967
150 games,
84 goals

Interviewed
Mar 13, 2007

number five. I didn't own a car, and Roy used to drive me home – he was just a great delight to talk with on a constant basis and a very, very good mentor in terms of teaching me more about the game and what it was all about, giving me some life lessons as well, I guess.

Roy was a big fella but he was only 6'2" and a half (189cm), therefore I was a couple of inches taller than him. One thing he told me right from the start was, 'You've got to be in front, but don't be in front while the ball is being thrown in from the boundary. If you time everything right you can arrive as the ball hits your hand, that's when you need to be in front so you can direct the ball wherever you want to.'

And he was a great proponent of telling me to be able to use both hands in ruck duels. Interestingly, I passed that bit of advice onto Mike Green and he said it was some of the best advice he ever had.

"I learnt more in one season with Len Smith than I learnt with anyone else I ever worked with. He showed us such a lot in a scientific manner for those days."

No one told me I had been selected (for my first game). I was just tuning into 3UZ or 3KZ and I heard I was in the seniors. I did cartwheels around the dining room at home, I had not really thought about it. It never occurred to me that I would be going out there. You feel a bit intimidated – you're playing against guys who have been around a long while. Each week passed and I kept playing well in the practice games, and it was only my second or third season of actual competitive footy.

Roy was the first ruckman, but I played stationary in the forward pocket and was lucky enough to kick a goal with my first kick in AFL footy. My cousin took a photograph of it with his box brownie camera. I was down in the forward pocket down near the pub, Havel Rowe got the ball from the centre and broke down the wing and I just lead out and he hit me on the chest with it. I was about 30-40 metres out on a very slight angle. The old flat punt struggled its way through.

I played a bit of full-forward when I was at state school. But I came down as a ruckman. At one stage they tried to teach me full-forward, I think I kicked 1.7 in the first half against Verdun Howell and they decided maybe I wasn't a full-forward after all.

Tom Hafey was fantastic, he was just one of those guys who befriended me quickly and helped me enormously. My little rover mate was Ted Langridge. He was a very useful fellow to have around. He used to dong blokes and I didn't – he didn't mind letting fly here and there. He always reckoned I was too soft, and maybe he was right. But I only knew one thing and that was getting the ball. If they kept whacking me in the head while I was doing that, and I didn't whack them back, well he thought it was best to whack them back. That wasn't in my nature.

I learnt more in one season with Len Smith than I learnt with anyone else I ever worked with. He was just a mastermind! Part of the deal was to move on quickly and get the handball away, so I'd have Langridge running alongside me, asking for the ball all the time. Whenever I got it he was there. Later on, when Alan Richardson came along, 'Bull' was just a magnificent ruck-rover, and he had an unbelievable and uncanny ability to get to where I could hit it.

Len Smith came and really took on with a vengeance that handball was the way to get the ball moving. He showed us such a lot in a scientific manner for those days ... what a ball can do when it's in transition from being kicked, how quickly a man can get from player A to player B while the ball is in the air. You never thought about it, that someone could run 50 yards while the ball was being kicked in the air. Smithy said, 'Just keep handballing it. Every time you get it, whenever there is a chance, run on, play on and handball, because we've got some great players up the ground'.

My two major opponents were Polly Farmer and John Nicholls. I absolutely loved playing against them. I'd set myself up (for) the week that I was going out to play Farmer or Nicholls. I just looked forward to it immensely. I had a very good record against them, which was terrific – I could probably out-spring (Polly) and I think that helped me enormously. But then I'll have someone like Elkin Reilly from South Melbourne come out and dust me up. It's a great mental and physical war at the end of the day.

I remember going out to Footscray to play against Gary Dempsey and he had a little rover called George Bissett. They were calling out numbers, like 'Number 10!' And I'd be thinking 'What's going on here?' I couldn't work it out. Then I was talking with the rovers and one of them said 'They are calling on a clockface.' Plus, straight up and down

Always a popular figure, Crowe was an outgoing, inspired figure as president.

the ground was North and South, across was East and West. Bloody Dempsey gave me a real hiding there one day.

Geoff Leek at Essendon gave me the biggest thrashing I ever had on the field early on in my career. I've had the pleasure in telling him later he was one of the toughest opponents I've had.

Crowe is best known for the John Nicholls incident in the 1967 second semi-final – he was suspended for striking and missed playing in the Grand Final, but maintains to this day Nicholls was faking.

When I got rubbed out and I didn't play in the Grand Final, that was shattering. I was physically sick directly after the game when I was in the showers. I was one of the last guys in the showers, and I remember sitting there with my head down, thinking 'What is this all this about?' I was obviously very highly strung and nervous. I actually collapsed in the showers, and someone came into the showers and found me there laying on the ground, blubbering like a bloody fool.

The interesting thing is I've never blamed John Nicholls for what happened on the ground, that was professional. He attempted to get the ball back after I received the free kick; he wrestled me and put me in the bear hug and Peter Sheales the umpire whistled the 15-metre penalty. But while the wrestle was on, and you can actually see him rip a right into my stomach and I've just sort of stepped back and thrown an open hand that has missed him ... and over he has gone.

Now all of that, up until then, is professional. But then he let me down at the tribunal and lost his memory. There is a touch of bitterness attached to that. The reason was simple; he wouldn't want me around if we played them in the Grand Final.

Before the tribunal we did all the things that we used to do. We went out to have a bit of dinner – he got a free dinner out of it as well, the whacker. Bill Tymms was my delegate and he just said 'What are you prepared to do?' and John said 'It all depends on the questions they ask.'

John Nicholls reacts, while a disbelieving Crowe looks on. Crowe was suspended for the "strike" – he missed the 1967 Grand Final, and never played again. Looking on are teammate Francis Bourke and Carlton's Cliff Stewart.

But when they asked him in the tribunal, Alf Bowden – a Carlton man, incidentally – was Chairman of the Tribunal, 'What are your recollections of the incident, Mr Nicholls?' And he said, 'I have no recollections of the incident.'

And I went, 'Fuck. Shit.'

And he said, 'Could that be as a result of the blow that Mr Crowe struck you?' And he just shrugged his shoulders. And I felt the blood drain out of my face! I thought, I am a shot duck here. And, sure enough, the boundary umpire who came from the wrong direction and saw the wrong thing, put two and two together and got five, and I got four weeks. That was the end of that.

It's an intimidating experience to go up to the tribunal. It was scary. All these sombre-looking people hanging around ... of course, I was incredibly nervous.

I just couldn't believe when the verdict was handed down. I just couldn't believe it. I couldn't say anything, I just walked out and that was the end of me. I wish you could have had a legal appeal and taken it to the next step back then.

I am a great believer that it doesn't matter what happens to you, it's how you choose to react to it that really counts. In many people's eyes I retired too early, I was only 30, but that was my last game of football.

I still had plenty of footy in me but I went off in a new direction in terms of business. I hold no grudge against Nicholls, though I joke about it a lot. I get asked the question a lot, it's great to say 'The big prick, if I get another chance I'd run over him with a truck.'

I was very dirty on it at that stage, but I still wanted to take part in Grand Final week, so I did all the training with the guys. I just wanted to do whatever I could.

There was even a bit of a movement taking place that maybe I could be the official runner on the day, but I wasn't allowed on the ground, so they took that away. I couldn't get out on the ground until after the siren. I think I was just up in the rows of seats with the wives and kids. I reckon it took two or three weeks to just get it out of my system, and get on with it from there.

I was reduced to tears at the Grand Final after-party. I remember driving home in the car and I was done then, I was a shot duck. It just knocked me around from that point forward. I cried myself to sleep that night.

As club president, Crowe played a key role in the sacking of coach Kevin Bartlett after season 1991.

I will certainly tell people the way I saw it. The first thing I always say is, there is no way known that a board of 12 people is going to make a decision on not re-employing the coach unless we get all the information from the 'factory floor'. And the feedback we were getting at board level, through the football department, was Kevin wasn't doing the job as well as we would have liked.

Now, that put us in a quandary. The information that they gave us was that it probably wasn't going to get better. So when the board has all that information then they will make that decision. The board itself doesn't make that decision, if you know what I mean.

They aren't saying 'Oh, KB can't coach.' Would we have done anything differently? The answer is yes, we would have, Kevin made it pretty hard for us. He wouldn't answer our phone calls; we wanted to bring him down, as had been done with other clubs and their coaches, we wanted him to come down and meet with the board or the appropriate people at board level.

We wanted to explain our reasons why we weren't going ahead with his contract, but he didn't offer us that opportunity. To the point that (general manager) Cameron Schwab and I had to go out and knock on the door one day. Now, it leaves us in an invidious position – we want to do it right, but if the man won't come down and talk to us across the table, then we have a problem.

It was the hardest thing I have done in my life. And Cameron was with us and I said, 'Cameron, we have got to make sure that we understand that we can't let the possibility of some massive resistance of what we are about to do stand in the way of what we believe is right. Now, what we believe is right, could be wrong. But we have to trust the people who were the executives who deal with this on the daily basis.' It was always an awkward one. If there was a better way to do it, we couldn't find it at that moment. At that moment in time we were in a position where we had to make our next move.

He invited us in to sit down, which I thought was a nice thing to do. Then when we tried to explain, it obviously wasn't going to go anywhere, he asked us to leave and we did. We had to do what we believe was the correct and proper thing for the football club. A lot of other people have said the board did the wrong thing. Well, we had a lot of debate about it and I wanted to be sure on the day that everyone was coming down the same track. If two or three were saying, 'I don't think we should be doing this,' then we might to have delayed the decision. But everyone said 'We are with you all the way.'

"Nicholls let me down at the tribunal ... There is a touch of bitterness attached to that. The reason is he woudn't want me around if we played in the Grand Final."

Ian Wilson has asked me for years to come to the premiership reunion. I have always said 'No, I can't do that, because I am not a premiership player.' There is a gap there that I can't transverse. I am not a legitimate premiership player. I don't care what the players say: 'You deserve the right to be with us.' But he kept at me, and then Big Red (Mike Perry) stuck his head in and said, 'You had better come or I'll smash you.'

I was a little bit intimidated by the atmosphere, that I didn't really belong. I didn't know the format of the evening, and certainly when Kevin Bartlett got up and started going around telling little stories about each player I thought 'Shit, what is going on here?'

But he was very, very gracious. I went over to thank him for his kind words and we shook hands ... it was just a nice thing for him to do. I did have a quick window of opportunity to say thank you. If he was fair dinkum, that's terrific; if he wasn't, at least now I can feel comfortable going along to join in with those blokes.

I understood his anger, and I understand the way he feels about it. Maybe there are two stories, and maybe in the middle the real truth lies. My commitment at that stage was to do what we believed as a group of people was right. If it proved we were wrong, maybe the (Allan) Jeans move was wrong, you can argue that as well. It was pretty radical to jump in the car and go there.

He might have shot us.

Royce Hart soars in the 1967 Grand Final, a defining moment in a contest that re-ignited the Tigers as a VFL force.

1966-1980

EATING THEM ALIVE

When Richmond stepped out for the 1967 semi-final against Carlton, it was the club's first final since 1947. Few could have predicted the decade and a half that followed, the most successful era in team history.

It is impossible to talk of Richmond's rise in the late 1960s without referring to Graeme Richmond. "GR" was the club's secretary from 1962 to 1968, and an official until 1983. His association with the Tigers began with the thirds in 1952, which he captained, winning the best and fairest award.

He never played senior football but he would become an excellent talent spotter and recruiter, choosing the likes of Richmond's most successful coach, Tommy Hafey, in 1966 – the Tigers would win four premierships under him – and Royce Hart, centre-half forward in the Team of the Century.

Richmond, nicknamed "The Godfather", knew what he wanted (ie; premierships) and was ruthless in his pursuit of his goal. He also had a fiery temper, and was at the centre of a wild brawl between Essendon and Richmond players at Windy Hill in 1974 as the players left the ground for half-time. A team of tall, fast, long-kicking players was recruited. It was a style of play suited to the large and open MCG. The amount of talent injected into a club to support its stalwarts such as Neville Crowe, Mike Patterson, Roger Dean, Fred Swift, Paddy Guinane and Bill Barrot was incredible.

Between the beginning of the 1965 season and Richmond's 1967 Grand Final triumph, Kevin Bartlett, Barry Richardson, Dick Clay, Michael Green, Francis Bourke, Kevin Sheedy and Royce Hart made their senior debut. The 1967 Grand Final was a tense affair, but Richmond was victorious by 14 points and in the last quarter Hart took one of the great marks of Grand Final history (opposite page).

Richmond defeated Carlton in the 1969 Grand Final; in 1972, the Blues gained revenge in the highest scoring Grand Final in history ... Carlton 28.9 (177) defeated Richmond 22.18 (150). The Tigers' score would have won any previous Grand Final.

The next year the teams met again in a brutal Grand Final but the result was reversed. Carlton ruckman John Nicholls was felled by Laurie Fowler three minutes in, and in a violent second quarter Carlton's full-back Geoff Southby was concussed and unable to see out the game. Richmond won by 20 points. That day the Tigers won the seniors, reserves, under 19s and under 17s premierships, the first club to do so.

Success permeated the club. During the late 1960s and 1970s the reserves won four premierships while the under 19s won seven. The under 19s were not the only Richmond team claiming back-to-back flags; he seniors followed up their 1973 premiership with a win over North Melbourne in 1974. Ageing greats were replaced by new champions. In the early 1970s, Neil Balme, David Cloke and Bryan Wood made their debuts, though Richmond was not just after young players – in 1971, St. Kilda exchanged centres with Richmond. The Tigers received dual Brownlow Medallist Ian Stewart for Billy Barrot. Yet the instability that ruthlessness engenders had its pitfalls. In 1976, Richmond finished seventh. Hafey had led Richmond to four premierships, but he felt he lacked the support of the board, and was replaced by Barry Richardson for the 1977 season. Richardson led the club into one finals series before he was replaced by Tony Jewell after 1978. The club was still able to recruit players of outstanding talent; Geoff Raines (1976), Michael Roach and Mark Lee (1977) and Dale Weightman (1978); in 1980 the Tigers won their fifth premiership in 14 years, defeating Collingwood by a record 81 points.

When the Tigers failed to make the finals in 1981, Jewell was replaced by the recently-retired Francis Bourke. In his first year at the club he took the Tigers to the 1982 Grand Final against Carlton – Richmond was favourite, having dominated the Blues two weeks earlier in the second semi-final, but it surrendered a half-time lead and lost by three goals.

The following year Richmond failed to reach the finals and Bourke was sacked. The club would not play in another final for 13 years. As well as Bourke's departure as coach, 1983 also saw the retirement of Kevin Bartlett, who played a League record 403 games. Graeme Richmond bowed out from the club in an official capacity when he resigned as vice-president in the same year. An era was over.

TREVOR RUDDELL

Roger Dean

Having worked up to the seniors from the fourths, Dean was one of the finest defenders of his generation, and he captained the 1969 Richmond premiership. He exemplified versatility when positional flexibility was rare, and remains a revered figure at Punt Road.

1957-73

Born
Apr 30, 1940

Played
Richmond
1957-73
245 games, 204 goals

Interviewed
August 10, 2006

I was a very timid person. I can always remember when I first started playing for Richmond, I was 17, and Mum wrote to my uncle in Broken Hill and said 'Roger's playing for Richmond' and he wrote back 'Which Richmond? Under 16s or under 17s?' And Mum wrote back: 'No, *Richmond*!' He still couldn't get it. It wasn't until we sent him a clipping of my name in the paper. He could never imagine me playing football because I was too shy and too timid. And maybe that's what bought it out in me, because I was so shy and timid I felt that maybe I had to prove something, that I could be just as tough as anybody else. What people would think of me on the field is not the person who I am off the field.

I lived in Richmond. Was born in Richmond, and always barracked for Richmond. When I was 15 and 16 I played in the fourths; when I was 17 I was in the thirds. But when I was in the fourths I used to go to the (senior) football match after I played and I would be watching Roy Wright, Des Rowe, Ron Branton and Teddy Landridge. They were my idols, especially Roy Wright. Anyway, the year after, when I was 17, I went from nine games in the thirds, eight in the seconds and the last game in the seniors. All of a sudden, from being a 16-year-old boy the year before, who was very shy and timid, to be playing alongside these players who were my idols – it was hard to believe I was there.

I can even remember Roy Wright, he was a little bit like my father to me. He gave me a lot of confidence and would always say 'You're doing well son, keep it going.' He was always encouraging me. I always remember the first time he said to me: 'You're coming all right, keep going.' Well I couldn't get home fast enough to tell my mum and dad that Roy Wright had spoken to me. It sounds corny, but when all your life you run out on the football field to get autographs from the players you idolised, it's from another world!

Bob Dummett was also really good with me. Bobby, who I was very frightened of when I started, seemed a very stern sort of a person, always seemed to be crook on everybody, or crook on the world. But for some reason he took a bit of a liking to me. Maybe because I was timid and shy, maybe he thought I wasn't too outlandish and too outspoken. When you're young and shy and timid you need these sort of people around you to give you that little bit of confidence. Ron Branton was very encouraging, he was a good captain. There was another chap, John Jenkins, he was a big old softie. I played with him a bit in the seconds and he was really encouraging.

My father was a labourer in the Bryant and May match factory. He was evidently a very good player in his time. I was told when he was only 16 they wanted him to play for Camberwell. Even when I just started playing for Richmond I would go up to see Dad at the match factory, and every now and then one of the chaps would say 'You'll never be as good as your father.'

He was invited down to Richmond but never got there because he had a job in the war years; if you played and got injured you never had a job. Dad was a very tough person and he would have been a tough person on the field.

I would have only been nine, and I used to go to Punt Road to collect beer bottles. Me and my mate were paying our bikes off, so we'd take our trolley, used to go at three-quarter time, get in for nothing, get the bottles, take them back home, dump them

HERE'S ALWAYS ROOM FOR ANOTHER—
"TIGER"

Tough yet amiable, Roger Dean was a driving force behind the club's 1960s revival.

and then go back when the game was over and get another load before the gates closed. That was our introduction to League football, selling the bottles and paying off my bike. I was there the day Jack Dyer played his last game. Probably in those days when you're young, all that mattered was whether you won or lost, I didn't really know much about football. I always fantasized, playing football by myself with the old rolled-up paper football, kicking it around in the laneway.

I was only 14 when I finished Tech School, and I didn't play football for six months. It was my brother, he was only a year older, who got me back into football. He said 'Why aren't you playing football?' and I said 'I don't know anybody', and he said 'I know somebody who plays down in the Richmond Scouts'.

Richmond Scouts was a junior side around Richmond and I've got a feeling we played down on the corner of Punt Road and Swan Street. It would have been halfway through the season before I played for Richmond Scouts, and from there I got an invitation to come down to the fourths a year later.

Square-jawed and rugged, Dean became a favourite of the Tiger fans as he led the club back from mediocrity.

We matured a little bit earlier than some of the players now. See, I was working from the time I was 14. I was digging roads and I was a plumber. Everything was galvanized iron, screw-in pipes, everything was hard work in those days, and your body got a lot tougher because the work was just so hard. Wherever you went you walked, or rode a bike, nobody had cars. So if you went somewhere you just ran, you got there quicker. I think I developed quicker than most. Mum had solid legs like I've got. And maybe the fact having those solids legs was a way of giving me a bit more strength to be more stable on the ground. I was strong by the time I got to 17 and by 18; I almost had a man's body and could survive.

In my first game I was 19th man and I got on five or six minutes before the end of the game; someone got injured and I got put on. It was on the Melbourne ground, of all places, against Melbourne. I just ran out and didn't know what I was doing. The next minute someone kicked the ball and it's landed on my chest. I was about 50 yards out and I messed up the punt kick and it's gone straight to Bob Dummett, 20 yards out, but looked like a fantastic pass. He kicked a goal.

In the first six minutes I know I had five kicks. I don't think Dad was there, he was a bit frightened I was going to do something stupid, and didn't want to be there to see it. From then on it took me a while to make the grade.

I'll tell you a story and you'll think it seems hard to believe. I was always 19th man and I couldn't quite get in there, and I thought I was playing well enough. I had been there two years and about halfway through the next year Dick Harris, who was coach at the time, came up to me and said 'Look, I am pushing for you, but I don't know what they have got against you. Every week I go there and say you should be playing, and I don't know why they won't pick you. Because you're playing well enough in the seconds.'

And I said 'Well, why wouldn't I be chosen?' and he said, 'The only thing I can think of is that you're not the right religion.' I said 'What do you mean?' And he said 'Because you're not a catholic.'

Over those years certain clubs were certain denominations, and I wasn't a catholic. And he said 'That's the only thing I know why you can't get a game.' And I said 'What will I do?' and he said 'You either change your religion or leave the club.' So I went to Fitzroy on a training night, and met (coach) Len Smith and told him who

I was. He knew me and I asked if I was able to get a clearance would I have any chance of getting a game. And he said 'I'm pretty sure if you came here I would fit you in somewhere.' But he said 'You have to get a clearance first.'

So I went back to Bill Tymms, who was secretary of the time, and I said 'I've been to Fitzroy and they said they would love to have me there. Here, I can't get a game', and he said, 'No, they won't clear you.' Anyway, come Thursday night again, just to keep me happy I'm 19th man again and we are heading down to Geelong. Anyway, Alan McDonald was coach then and Alan came up and said 'You're in today, Roger,' and I said 'Oh, I'm 19th man?' and he said 'No, you'll be playing today.'

I've often looked back and thought what might have been. I actually played really well. I kicked three or four goals and they used to have the *Herald* 'Best and Fairest' in those days and I think I might have got two votes. That kept me in the side the week after. We went down to South Melbourne and I'm pretty sure I got best on the ground and that was basically the start of my career.

I probably was never ever out of the side until the last three or four games of my career in 1973. Often I look back and think what would have happened to me if I hadn't put in two good games. It's a frightening thing when you look back – anybody can put in a couple of bad ones at any point of time in their career but I was lucky to put two good ones in, and that was it.

I said to (Len Smith, then coaching Richmond) 'Len, you remember me coming over one night?' He said 'We made a mistake not pushing to get you.' I said, 'I asked to get a clearance but they wouldn't give it to me.' He said, 'Oh well, how it has turned out is probably good for you, you're still with your club, which is what you always wanted to be.' Len was a lovely bloke, a gentleman of all gentleman.

Me, Tony Jewell, Ricky McLean and St Francis Bourke had a little bit of white line fever. Francis was probably similar to myself in some way, we probably hated the thought of getting beaten. Even

"I was working from the age of 14, digging roads ... your body got a lot tougher because the work was so hard. I almost had a man's body and could survive."

His own toughest critic, Dean drove himself hard during his 245-game career.

in the early stages, when we were second last or last, it could be the last game of the year and we could be 15 goals down and I still wanted to get another kick. It was pride. I never ever wanted to be beaten; even if we were beaten I still wanted to get another kick.

Someone said at a function I was at one day, 'It must be fantastic playing around Royce Hart, Francis Bourke and Kevin Sheedy, and must give you a lot of inspiration playing alongside them.' I said no. I've always felt if you need someone else to give you inspiration to play there's something wrong with you. It should be just your own pride. Every time I went onto the field I wanted to be best on the ground. I didn't care about anybody else, I couldn't control them. I wanted to be best on the ground because I didn't want to be beaten. If I could play well that meant it could help the side anyway.

I felt I went at the ball hard, but there were times when I thought 'Gee, maybe I shouldn't have done that,' hitting somebody who probably didn't deserve to be hit. But I suppose it was part of when you're young, growing up, you're told that you've got to be

Dean leads the Tigers out. Quietly spoken off the field, he became an aggressive personality once he crossed the white line.

tough. You don't really understand what tough is. Tough is going for the ball at all costs at all times, and then somewhere along the lines it gets a bit blurred.

I played it very hard. I copped a lot of knocks too, along the way. When I look back on my career and some of the things I might have done, I feel a bit of ashamed of myself now. I think it was the mentality in those days, you were just taught that you had to be tough, so you did things that in some cases probably weren't that tough.

I hate talking about myself, but to be honest I feel my marking was one of my best attributes. I am not tall, I am just on the five-nine (175cm) mark and for my size I felt I was a very good strong mark and I could get off the ground quite high. I took a mark out at the Melbourne Cricket Ground against Hawthorn, and Kevin Bartlett and Mike Green both said it was the best mark they ever saw. So this day I had a perfect run at the ball and I actually stood on top of this chap's shoulder, and I jumped down the other side and I always remember I then quickly kicked it across to Billy Barrot just up past the centreline, who took half a dozen steps and banged it into goal. The runner came out and said 'Tommy said you should have punched it'.

First and foremost I felt I was a team man. I know my dad at times used to say to me 'You've got to do things for yourself every now and again. If you get the ball kick it yourself.' When we first started playing, they only counted the kicks you got. You could have eight or nine kicks and 18 handballs but they'd say 'Gee, he had a very ordinary day, he only had eight kicks,' and they'd forget about the 18 handballs. Dad used to say 'You're stupid, they don't count the handballs, just kick the ball when you get it.' It was always in me, when someone was there to handball to, I always handballed. Kevin Bartlett once said to me, 'I always tried to get close to you when you went in to get the ball, because I always knew the handball was coming out.' It was in me, I always felt I had to play a team game, and that's what it is, a team game.

I played probably nearly every position on the ground. I played full-forward and full-back. Actually I used to always love the half-forward flank. A funny thing happened, in the old days if you got too slow for the half-forward flank they shifted you down to the back pocket and from there it was gone. Anyway, Tommy and Graeme Richmond came to me one day, and said 'We are going to have to shift you to the back pocket, we just feel you've slowed down a little bit, and you'll be suited to the back pocket, you'll just go straight ahead.'

I played about four years in the back pocket and Tommy came to me one day and he said 'Look, you're getting a bit slow for the back pocket. I think you're going to have to shift to the half-forward flank. I haven't worked it out yet, but you're too slow for the back pocket.'

I did enjoy the back pocket, I felt I achieved something there, you've done something that maybe you think you couldn't have done. I was talking to Dick Clay once and I said to him 'Dick, I reckon you were a better full-back than a wingman' and he said 'Glad you said that. I've always thought the same thing, it was something I achieved, nobody thought I could do. I know when I went there they probably said 'He's going to be too loose because he was a wingman and he's not going to keep on his man.' And I felt I really played well and did well at full-back.'

"Kevin Bartlett always used to say, 'I always tried to get close to you when you went in to get the ball, because I always knew the handball was coming out'."

I played on players like Baldock. I was probably an inch smaller but had the mobility on him. I got a lot of different of jobs. The half-back flank might be out for the day so they'd shift me to half-back flank for a couple of games. I played centre a lot, when Billy Barrot wasn't playing I'd fill in for Billy. I played in three decades (50s, 60s, 70s). It sounds great; it's true, you can't dispute it.

My first game as captain was against Collingwood. It must have been halfway through the game, and there's a chap called Gary Wallis ... we were playing the ball and it moved out of reach, maybe 10 or 15 yards away. I went to go towards the ball and Gary grabbed me from behind, and I threw my arm back and connected with him in the solar plexus, and down to the ground he's gone. I meant to hit him though. I really wanted to get rid of him.

And the worst place of all I could have done it was in the front of the Collingwood grandstand.

They've all booed. The umpire turned around and saw him on the ground and I can still remember him coming over and saying 'I'm reporting you for hitting Wallis,' and I can always remember saying 'What do you mean? I never hit him.' I knew this umpire never saw me, because I was watching the umpire before I threw my hand back. I said 'I don't know how he got there, I didn't hit him.' Anyhow, he still reported me. When I got up to the tribunal it convinced me he didn't know, he said that I took two steps towards Wallis and gave him a right rip to the stomach. In the evidence I said to him, 'He grabbed me from behind and I threw my arms back just to get rid of him but I didn't realise I had hit him so hard.'

But they suspended me on the evidence the umpire had given, which was completely wrong – he made the story up. I ended up going crook at this umpire. I got four weeks just for a backhander. I was so wild with what he said that we were on our way out and I called him a liar. I went up to him and I said 'You're a liar, I don't care what they say, I'm not saying I didn't hit him, but you didn't see it and you made up a story. You're just an out and out liar, you should be ashamed of yourself.'

He never said anything to me and just walked away. I was so wild. I think I was respected enough. I would never abuse a player for doing something wrong, I just say 'You should have done this,' or 'You should have done that,' and most times they say, 'Yeah I know.' But that's all you could do as captain in those days, all you could do was play well yourself and any little thing you pick up that

"I was only a plumber, I achieved something in my life ... I was very lucky to be actually born with an ability to play football for some reason."

Tommy may not see on the field. Like 'You should have handpassed that,' or 'You should have put your body there to block somebody.'

I must admit, I've had players come up to me – which I really get a kick out of – and said to me, 'I never played many games but we always appreciated the fact that you came up and talked to us like we were one of the other players.' It's something I think that you should be proud of that you are willing to give somebody else the time of day.

Dean introduced Prince Charles and Princess Anne to the team during the Round 1 match against Fitzroy at the MCG in 1971.

I was a bit flustered. I thought, 'I hope I remember all the players' names.' They don't look real somehow. I don't believe I am talking to royalty; I've got to go around and introduce this chap. It was done at half-time, I used to play in a favourite old jumper and it had gone a navy blue, not black, and they made me change into a brand new jumper so I'd look decent to introduce them all around. I knew I would be doing it beforehand. He seemed nice enough, he didn't say much, just being

The Ron Barassi incident Round 17, 1963

I was a very volatile person on the field and we'd been at each other all day. And there came a time where I tackled him from the front and somehow, I don't know how, I slipped in front of him, and here I am on my knees and he is looking down at me, and it was just a reaction – he gave me a quick punch.

It was because I was below he just thought 'Bugger, I'll give him a whack.' Since then, he says I was acting, which is all rubbish, but I think he has now convinced himself he didn't do it. There was an article he wrote which I was really a bit hurt about, because he almost insinuated that when we went to the tribunal I didn't give him any help whatsoever and that hurt a bit.

What used to happen in those days was that Melbourne came across and picked me up at training. We went for tea, we discussed what we were going to do and say to try and get out of it, which we did do, and he never got out of it.

We made up some story to try and get him off, but it didn't work. And they drove me back to the club, and when I hopped out of the car they said 'Thanks very much Roger for helping us out.' Years later he doesn't remember things like that.

I'll tell you a funny thing that happened, that he probably won't admit to, but when he did get suspended, he walked into the room where they held us in and he's picked up a chair and smashed it right across the room right into the other wall. I thought 'Gee, if they had seen him do that he would have got another two weeks, too.'

Celebrating a win in the '60s: from left, Graham Burgin, Mike Perry, Basil McCormack, Geoff Strang, Martin Bolger, Roger Dean. McCormack and Bolger were committeemen of the era.

courteous to the players, 'Enjoying the game?' and 'It's a very hard game, isn't it'. It probably bored him to snores. It was pretty formal.

Roy Wright was someone I really admired. As far as being an idol, Roy Wright would have to be well and truly above anybody else.

People who I played with? Kevin Bartlett. I've never seen a player who played so many consistent games, game after game. There were players down there at times, like Paul Sproule, and Kevin used to rove most of the times but a few odd times that he was out I can remember Paul Sproule getting something like 18 or 19 kicks and two or three handpasses and they'd say, 'Gee, Sprouley played well, he might be pushing Kevin.' And I used to think, how could they possibly say that? Kevin would get 25 kicks minimum. I can hardly ever remember him not getting any less. And one bloke starts getting 19 kicks and they start to talk about Kevin might have competition!

He was a great player. There are lots of other good players but they might play two good ones, three ordinary ones and one bad one. I can look through all of his career and I can hardly remember him playing a bad one.

He got kick after kick, running all day. He lasted so long because he was a one-grab player, he never fumbled a ball. Going into a pack and he would pluck the ball as though it just came up into his hands and keep on going. You've only got to make a little bit of a fumble and they've got you. That's why they never caught him. I can remember Bobby Skilton running down the ground one day yelling out to him to kick the damn thing because he was getting further and further away.

Football has been good as far as recognition (and) pride come into it. These days they go into it very scientifically, but in my time it was just an honour and as far as I was concerned to have done something! I was only a plumber, I achieved something in life.

I was very lucky to be actually born with an ability to play football for some reason. I still love people coming up and talking to me and to be recognised. Something I feel proud about, it sounds like you're being big-headed, but it's great.

Tom Hafey (The Coach)

Tom Hafey coached football teams the way he lives his life: with total commitment, complete honesty and a philosophy of keeping things simple. It resulted in four premierships, ownership of the most successful era in the club's history and coaching honours of the RFC Team of the Century.

Coached
Richmond
1966-76
248 matches
173 wins
73 losses
2 draws
4 premierships

Also
Collingwood, 1977-82

Geelong, 1983-85

Sydney, 1986-88

Career coaching record
522 games
336 wins
182 losses
4 draws

Died
May 12, 2014

Everybody wanted to coach. When they're getting £10 to play League football, they go up the bush and get £40 as a playing coach. The clubs never stopped them because they probably felt they were denying them the chance to make a big dollar – they fought like crazy to keep them, but in the end they would go.

I went to Shepparton for £800 in 1960. You got your jobs out of the paper and it was in the classified section of the *Sporting Globe*. There'd be three or four pages of advertisements after the Grand Final had been played. So I wrote letters away to Shepparton and Ganmain, although I didn't put how much I wanted because I didn't know how to ask for a price. Shepparton came back; others never even rang me or spoke to me.

Shepparton President Jack Edwards, who would have bought and sold every AFL administrator that I have ever met in my life, by a mile, came down. He was demented about country football, mad about the Shepparton Football Club. Left no stone unturned. I loved that man. He came down on Sunday to my milk bar and I saw him sitting out the front. I didn't have a clue who he was and on Sundays there are not too many cars going up and down. But he's just sitting, looking, and the shop was jampacked because we had one of those shops where the youth used to come in. And so he came in and leant on the counter down the end and told me who he was. He made arrangements for me and my beautiful wife to go to Shepparton the next week. So I was playing coach at Shepparton for six years in the early '60s and we won three premierships in a row.

There was a lot of speculation that I wouldn't come back to Richmond. We were settled into Shepparton, had a nice house, little children, good job. But really I suppose the opportunity to coach League football was there. So Ray Dunn, Graeme Richmond and Ron Carson all came up to see me. Graeme Richmond then said we will pay you the same as you were getting up at Shepparton: $1600. Decimal currency had just started. That's what I got for the year, not each week!

The most money I ever got at Richmond was $8000, the same as the players were getting. So in 11 years it went from $1600 to $3000 to $5000 to $8000, which from what I understood was what the four leading players got; Royce Hart, Kevin Sheedy, Kevin Bartlett and Francis Bourke. I never got a cent from anybody with all the premierships we won. I tell you what I did get: two suits from Reg Varley for winning one of the premierships. I thought I was walking on water at that stage. As far as bonuses, it never entered my head. It wasn't something that I even expected.

When I came back, we had gone from Punt Road to the MCG for a start. I thought it was a better environment, a bigger ground and I know when I went to Shepparton I followed Norm Smith's style of coaching, which was kicking the ball long and not stuffing around. It is so basic. We had a stack of teams who used to root around with the ball. Honestly, like South Melbourne, Fitzroy, Footscray, Geelong, Melbourne and St Kilda, they used to do that all the time, the same stuff.

And we trained hard. We were criticised for training hard, but we kept on winning. And the people who criticised us were the ones who were probably sitting in the grandstand watching us run around with the cup. You'd get a lot of people in the media who really wouldn't understand what you were at, but who cares; people can say what they

Close friends Tommy Hafey and Kevin Bartlett chat in the MCG Richmond rooms. Both men were elevated to Immortal status in the Richmond Hall of Fame on the same night in 2003.

like. I would never ever talk back or try and make excuses for myself. What the heck, they've got the last word. Then you don't keep on coming back and coming back. Just crap.

We would start training six weeks after the Grand Final down at the Richmond ground. We would let the players go to their own gyms if they wanted because the weights we had down there weren't really adequate. But not only that, I felt going away to somewhere else might have been better. So they could go to the Oasis, Finley's, the Golden Bowl (gymnasium) down in Camberwell, and if anybody lived in Frankston they could go and work in the gym down there, anywhere they like, to get away from the place.

"We were criticised for training hard, but we kept winning. The people who criticised were the ones who were probably in the grandstand watching us run around with the cup."

But then we would have a period over at Christmas, maybe a fortnight, where they didn't do anything, but they had to run 100 miles during January. Training started the first week in February, so they were expected to have done that, on an honour system. Bill Boromeo, who ran as a pro himself at stages, would take people like Kevin Bartlett, Daryl Cumming and quite a few of the boys who ran pro, and even those who didn't run pro. We trained Monday, Wednesday and Friday in the early part before the practice matches came along.

I can tell you what the first week was in nearly every year. We trained on the first Monday of February, and they would do a time trial around the Tan. I don't think we would even do a slow jog, we might just only jog across to the tan and then do a time trial around it.

On the Wednesday night we did 10 by 440s against the clock. And the third night we did 20 by 220s. You might have read sometimes where people have said we have done that on the one night. That was never ever the case! And my memory has never been clouded with alcohol. I've actually thought sometimes when I've read these things I wish I had thought of that at the time.

We were never on the ground after seven o'clock. At seven o'clock we would finish and then the boys would often do things themselves. That was the great part about Richmond, because you would get, say, Francis Bourke and Bryan Wood belting the ball at each from about 10 metres apart. We called it 'Bashball'. And there might be Kevin Sheedy with Mervyn Keane or somebody like Billy Brown with Kevin Bartlett having shots at goals. So a lot of times they weren't expected to be out there, but a lot of them would stay out doing things they wanted to do.

I remember my first match as coach quite well. Barassi was coaching Carlton and we were leading right at the end, and the siren doesn't work! And the trooper's horse has got to go out, and they tried to ring the bell but nobody could hear it properly to let the umpire know. I thought, this is another Carlton ploy. It was a bit strange, but we did win the game.

You've got to win the premiership; there is not much good winning just a lot of games. Don't mess up on opportunities. In 1966 we were actually on top of the ladder three weeks before the finals, and we lost two games in a row and we missed the finals by two premiership points. We lost four games for the year. So we were in with a big chance but we never made the finals. We had a lot of young players in our team so that experience of the previous year in 1966 might have been good. But (1967) was the first time the Tigers had made the finals for 20 years. And they hadn't won a premiership since 1943. I often smile now when people say they are too young to win the premiership. I felt reasonably confident.

Fred Swift was captain. We played him during the course of the year on the ball, we didn't play him full-back; he used to beat most of the full-forwards, but the better ones were too big for him, too quick for him. And we struggled at full-back for quite some time. We knew that we just struggled with the people we put there because of their deficiencies, like not strong enough, tall enough, or experienced enough. But we weren't having success there.

Instead of dropping our captain, which we probably could have done at that stage because he was at half-forward flank and it's not his position really, we put him back to full-back with about three games to go, and it was an amazing success. I thought if we dropped our captain it could have a reflection on the rest of the players. But we didn't have to.

I've got so many memories of the 1967 Grand Final. People often asked of the premierships I have been connected with, I surprise them, because I say the premierships at Shepparton were equally as important to me. Because I see how many people have worked so hard during the year and seen how many people cried in the room after we won the premiership, just with the emotion of the whole thing. Each one was special. I don't know if every coach feels this way.

I can remember before the game talking to the players in the room. There were only the 20 players, the runner and the coach. Nobody else was there, never ever was. And we were talking about different players that we had to be aware of.

I remember saying to Billy Barrot, looking right into his face in front of all the players, 'What's going to happen when they put Denis Marshall on you, how do you feel about that?' Because he usually played on a boy called Wayne Closter, who was a very good player, but Billy used to beat him. After 10 minutes they used to take Wayne Closter out of the centre and put in Denis Marshall, who had actually done very well on Billy.

Billy didn't say anything for a long time, he just was thinking. I then remember Michael Patterson breaking the silence saying 'He can't wait to get at him!' and everybody practically at once said '*Yeahh!*' And that's what happened; Billy was nearly best man on the ground. He probably played better when Denis Marshall went on him than what he had played on Wayne Closter.

I remember Polly Farmer having cramp at a vital time. And I often used to think about that because a racehorse hangs under pressure, a pacer gallops under pressure, and obviously cramping could be something like being under pressure.

I remember Michael Patterson doing such a good job because he had to replace Neville Crowe in the first ruck. I remember the goals that big John Ronaldson kicked and I remember us giving away a couple of silly free kicks, and Kevin Bartlett kicking that very vital goal right at the end of the game, which more or less sealed the whole thing. And of course we all remember Fred Swift taking that mark behind the goal, in front of the goal, on the line, whatever. When I coached Geelong somebody mentioned that mark every day for the entire three years I lived down there.

In the other Grand Finals we won, the premierships, it was expected. 'We've only done what we have set out to do, don't get excited, don't make a fool or yourself.' That's what I thought when we were sitting in the box.

And the other people in the box congratulated me and shook hands and you could see the smile and the love that they had. By the time I got down to the ground I was a raving lunatic! I didn't want to be that way. I'd often seen people do things and I think 'What a poser.' I tried not to, but honestly something just gets into you.

I felt that in 1968 probably we were too slow on the backline. A player or two being hurt and the players we replaced them with just didn't have the initial acceleration, which is something we prided ourselves on, playing off the backline – playing on very quickly either by handball or running around the man on the mark. But we didn't have anybody who could do that.

That was one of the reasons, but also we might have got ahead of ourselves as well. I think that we probably felt 'We will do all right once the finals come along.' But we never got there. (Richmond finished fifth, a game out of the finals.)

My father had died during the course of the 1969 year. I think he died on the Saturday morning when we were playing Essendon. And there were some terrible articles in the paper about sacking Tommy Hafey. The day my father was buried they had big headlines on the backpage '*Hafey for Sack*', or something like that, written by Greg Hobbs. I was really disappointed in that sort of stuff.

But the players rallied for me. They were never going to toss the towel in; they just were going to give it their best shot. So that was a really very important

Short in stature, Hafey was a giant at Punt Road for more than a decade.

one because it gave me a tremendous amount of satisfaction, particularly the way the papers had been screaming for me. And I had heard players make mention of that. The players really rallied.

Incidentally, I was the meat in the political sandwich between Ray Dunn and Graeme Richmond. They were at loggerheads; they had been great mates before and all of a sudden they weren't. Graeme was so supportive of me and I just felt Ray Dunn probably could have been feeding the stuff to the media. I just got on with life; you can't do much about that. I suppose my father, who had been such a big influence on me, probably would have expected me to continue as normal.

I was probably closer to players than most coaches get. A lot of people think that's not a good idea, but I can remember when I was about to leave Shepparton to coach Richmond, our old president Jack Edwards said to me, 'Tommy, a word of advice. No, a word of warning. You spend too much time with the players and not enough with the administrators and board, you've got to remember they put you in the job, they keep you in the job.' I said, 'Jack, if I've got to suck up to people to keep my job, I'd rather not have my job.' If you're having success they can't get rid of you. My job is with the players, that's what I always felt.

In 1969 we just struggled into the finals. We had to win it from fourth position. Not too many clubs had ever done that. And every game in the last six or eight was a semi-final – if we lost one we were out. We had lost five games in six during the year.

I'm not quite certain the reason why, but that can happen particularly when you've got leading players out. Things just don't go your way. Maybe we were expecting so much.

The start of the finals that particular year, we were playing Geelong in the first semi-final and they were favourites to beat us. And I got Percy Cerutty to come in and speak to the players. I didn't have a clue what he was going to be speaking about. Nobody ever used to get into the room outside the 20 players and the runner, but I've got Percy in the room, and I didn't know what he was going to say. I could see when the door opened and there were different people looking in and they could see Percy there – you see the look on their faces, they weren't pleased somebody else was allowed in the room. Percy was very eccentric, and a fiery sort of character. And it was really quite amazing because he spoke to the players about Tom Hafey. He talked about my passion and my love for the players and my love of the football club, and things I had to go through for the course of the year. It was really amazing, he really knocked me over, I nearly had a tear in my eye.

It was different from what I thought he was going to talk about. It was a lesson.

We beat Geelong by 118 pts. They kicked five goals in the last quarter to go from two to seven goals to make their score respectable. Two weeks later we played Collingwood and we beat them convincingly and we just had so much momentum going into the Grand Final.

We had players who rose to the occasion. Ian Owen played on the half-back line and he played so well. He played on Ken Newlands in the first game, he played on Ian Graham the second game and he played on Brent Croswell the third game. Ian never lowered his colours, and they hardly kicked a goal on him. Earlier in the season we were playing Carlton, the best side in the competition, and we were at Princes Park and getting beaten when we put Billy Barrot to full-forward. And he kicked eight goals on Wes Lofts. He had eight kicks. It doesn't matter where he got the ball, it was just going for the goal. He just dominated. *Dominated!* And that set us up to put him in another position, or take him into full-forward, which we did in the Grand Final, and he kicked three goals on Lofts.

In the Grand Final, I remember Eric Moore taking a mark and getting crunched. We were two goals down just before three-quarter time and he kicked the goal. We had 73 kicks in that last quarter, the most kicks any side had during the course of the entire year in a quarter. Carlton had 36 kicks in the most important quarter! That's the least number of kicks that any side had had for the entire season. I think there were seven players for Carlton who never got a kick in the last quarter. If you can remember Rex Hunt and Graeme Bond both kicked goals in the last quarter after coming off the bench. We just dominated.

In 1971 we were the best side in the competition, but we really struggled a bit on the backline. We probably really made up ground because we were so good around the field, kicked the ball long and direct and we had a good forward line. We got beaten in the preliminary final, which rained. It was one thing we couldn't handle at that stage, which we came to be very good at later. Carl Ditterich was a dominating player, and when it rained it just suited St Kilda right down to the ground.

Losing the 1972 Grand Final was probably the thing that made me be positive in my life. It was so shattering to be the best team in the competition and only have to front up to win the Grand Final and it didn't work out that way. We dominated during the year. We killed them. I felt so low. I could see how people can do stupid things in depression. I was not going to see people who I had to see in my job, because I knew they were just going to talk about football. I was in a real down. Five weeks later, when I was driving home – I was in the car by myself going past the Elwood Football Ground – I was thinking to myself 'Poor old me, poor old me ...' then I said out loud 'I've got to snap out of this. I can't help what's happened. It's over. It's finished. It's done! I can't do a damn thing about it. It should have been, but it wasn't. I can't do a thing about '72 but by living hell I can do something about '73!'

I said this aloud! I can remember it, nearly word for word. And I say 1973 started then, and we were only in the first week of November.

We always felt we needed players. We talk about our team being such a great team but back then we could see a stack of weaknesses. The fact that I have pushed them up and feted them so much, people probably think they must have been a super team. Michael Green used to do well in the finals but Michael dropped out that year in 1972. I remember saying to him, 'I hope it's not a case where we will be needing you and you're sitting in the grandstand.'

Well, that's exactly what happened.

We played Ray Boyanich in the back pocket. Ray wasn't a back pocket player but we had nobody else to play the position and he had six goals kicked on him. We played Rex Hunt at centre half-back on Robert Walls; now Rex wasn't a centre half-back, really.

He finished up playing all right the following year in the back pocket on John Nicholls. Craig McKellar used to run out and punch the ball toward our goal. I never saw a fellow punch the ball so far. It was just unreal. We had such momentum, but we were probably still weak on the backline. That was probably our weakness – we always felt that.

So 1973 comes along and the Blues have gone ahead of us – they had to play us in the Grand Final. We've had the meeting, we've had the video, we've had the brunch and the coach gets up and usually talks for about 30 minutes, and if the players feel they've got something to offer please feel free. But after five minutes I thought 'It's not much good hanging onto them. They are ready,' and I remember clapping my hands: 'Over to the ground, not much good holding off.' I can remember the faces of the players, they were like men on a mission. Not a player said a word. It wasn't a game – they brutalised Carlton in every way.

Injured star Barry Richardson, Hafey and Kevin Bartlett celebrate the 1973 premiership.

It was just one of those things. When we got back to our function at the Richmond ground after we'd been out for dinner, Paul Sproule said to me 'You had the easiest day of your life today. There was no way known that mob were going to get anywhere near us.' I thought, that's exactly how I felt, even before the game.

In 1974 it was fantastic as it was back-to-back. And sides had not been winning back-to-back for a long time (Melbourne, 1959-60). I can remember that one also very well because there was a lot of controversy after some of the remarks people made after Keith Greig won the Brownlow Medal. As a result a lot of the people were against us. There had been a lot of controversy when Kevin Bartlett didn't win the Brownlow, as he won 13 out of 15 awards that year. When he didn't win the Brownlow we had a high official get up and say 'This is an absolute joke.' Which is sad, because Keith Greig is such a champion and such a beautiful person, I felt embarrassed.

I thought the Grand Final crowd was going to be so against us it could sway the umpires. So I can hear Harry Beitzel saying, 'It might not be a bad idea after the teams line up if you have a couple of players go over and congratulate Keith Greig.' And quite a few players did that. I just felt it was a little tactic that might have helped us in some way.

We made a big mistake in as much we cleared three players after the 1974 season, in particular Brian Roberts (1971-75, 77 games, 34 goals). The other two players couldn't quite get a game with our team. Francis Jackson (1973-74, 6 games) played 100 games at South Melbourne, but he couldn't quite get into our team as we had a couple of good players playing in that position. Graeme Teasdale, who we didn't give many opportunities (six games), played on the forward line, and everybody realises what a great ruckman he became. [Ed's Note: Teasdale won the 1977 Brownlow Medal while at the Swans; the three Tigers were controversially traded for South's John Pitura].

Losing Brian Roberts was a massive disappointment. I reckon five minutes after we swapped Brian Roberts all of a sudden we were thinking 'He was everybody's friend, we laughed with him, we laughed at him, and he was a butt of a lot of jokes and he put the jokes on other people.' It was a real downer. In John Pitura's case, he was a star down in South Melbourne. Unfortunately, he never really got into it to that extent at Richmond. Maybe he felt the weight of the world on his shoulders because there had been so much controversy over it.

The Windy Hill brawl (in May, 1974) was quite amazing. I had a ringside view of the whole thing. Mal Brown (1974, 14 games, 25 goals) got reported for striking. At half-time I was sitting in the coaches boxes inside the rooms and I saw, when he was coming off the ground, little John Cassin fly at him. I've got no doubt John was the one who started the whole thing.

And then all hell broke loose. I remember people trying to break it up and getting king-hit, and that's how the 'Whale' (Brian Roberts) got his jaw broken; he was king-hit him from the side. I remember Graeme Richmond hitting the fellow on the ground. It was a strange one.

When I left Richmond after season 1976, I was disappointed with a few people down there. I'd been appointed for my 12th year and I wasn't comfortable with it. A fortnight later I thought, 'I just don't want to be here,' which was very strange. People think I got the sack but I had already given them notice.

I thought I would go to Western Australia or South Australia, because I didn't think I could coach against the Tigers. Harry Kernahan rang up, he was general manager at Glenelg, and Stephen Kernahan's dad. He said 'Tommy, the best club in Australia hasn't got a coach, the best coach in Australia hasn't got a job.' But I thought, 'I'd have to up stumps and go.'

Collingwood spoke to me, they were on the bottom of the ladder and I just felt that Collingwood shouldn't be there. I felt that they would probably be a bit embarrassed and keen to improve where they were. So that's where I went. I felt that I'm more suited to the Collingwoods and the Richmonds and the Fitzroys and Footscrays. But there would be some clubs that really wouldn't be Tommy Hafey.

Over the years I have had approaches by 12 clubs. And whenever I've been contracted to another club I've never even thought of it. I always feel the coach has got to be the most enthusiastic person in the place. First there, last to leave. No excuses.

Every day's a great day; if you don't believe me, try missing one. I say that all the time now. So many people have got a grouch on the world, got a terrible attitude. I just think you're dead for a long time, why don't you enjoy what you're doing?

When I come to think of my life, I never had a job I didn't like. And that just comes about because you like people and like working. You've got to be busy, busy, busy, busy, like every job I have ever had. I did leave the printing trade from time to time, I was a brickie's labourer, it was a great job, and when I delivered papers I loved it. I delivered papers for five years, even when I was starting work I would still go in and deliver papers before I went to work, it was a great job.

I delivered green groceries, because you used to ride the push bike on a Saturday morning and you'd have the banana box between the handlebars. You've got to do things to make dollars. I sold the papers after school from time to time. But I always did two out of the three paper rounds from around when I was 11 or 12 to the time I was a second year apprentice (16 or 17).

Extract from a letter Tom Hafey wrote to Bruce Tschirpig:

During his coaching career, Tom Hafey would regularly write to players, including this letter to Bruce Tschirpig at the end of the 1971 season.

Every player must analyse his 1971 season honestly and thoroughly and do everything in his power to be better value to the side this year. You no doubt would be pleased to have played eight games in your first League season and also in a couple of games you showed that you could really make it by playing quite well, but overall much thought must go into your game as on other occasions you were disappointing with lack of real desire notably missing. Of course this could have come about because of your knee injury and after your successful operation this could be your year but you must realize this is a very important business you are now involved in, with no place for sentiment, and only a real professional outlook can bring out the best in you. You must set certain aims or targets this year and let nothing stand in your way in order to accomplish them. Your number one aim must surely be to be selected in our first match against Collingwood and then to hold your position for the year. To be the most enthusiastic on the training track, not wasting one second of daylight practicing weaknesses and working at your game all the time you are out there, maybe it would be of benefit to you to train an extra night or do a weight circuit after training in the gym. You must get tougher and more desperate in the game, see the ball and go madly after it, not giving up until you have won it and then breaking away to get your kick. Make aims for each match which is a means of mentally preparing yourself, examples once again are, to receive four handpasses as well as giving four, to play on four times, to smother your opponent's kick four times, to be in front of your opponent every time you contest the ball, there are many many more but you must never be satisfied with your game, make each game better than the previous one by learning from it, working out why and how to get more touches of the ball. You must know exactly what is required of you in a match, what your position demands and how to play it, how your teammates around you play and what they are likely to do at different times, when and how you can back them up. As a rover, ruck-rover or centreman it is important that you know every team-mates weaknesses, strengths and habits so sum them all up and get to know them better, it will pay in the long run.

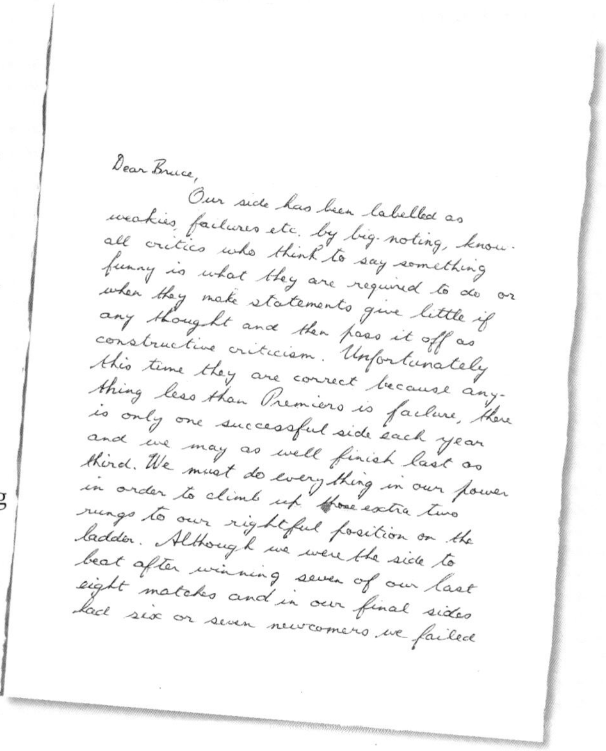
Dear Bruce,

Our side has been labelled as weakies, failures etc. by big-noting, know-all critics who think to say something funny is what they are required to do or when they make statements give little if any thought and then pass it off as constructive criticism. Unfortunately this time they are correct because anything less than Premiers is failure, there is only one successful side each year and we may as well finish last as third. We must do everything in our power in order to climb up those extra two rungs to our rightful position on the ladder. Although we were the side to beat after winning seven of our last eight matches and in our final sides had six or seven newcomers we failed

Reproduced courtesy of Bruce Tschirpig.

I had a milk bar in Bridge Road, Richmond. Loved the milk bar, even though we worked 12-14 hours a day, seven days a week.

It was great; I met a lot of lovely people, made a lot of friends. I think being very family is a big help, you've got a beautiful loving family and very close, I think that's lovely.

You only get out what you put in. You learn so much about football. Look, there's no race, colour, creed in a football or netball club.

There's no rule for the rich or rule for the poor in a football or netball club. It doesn't matter what school you went to, what car you drive, or how big the house you live in is, when you get down to the ground everybody is an equal.

The camaraderie, the respect, and the getting to know the life disciplines, whether you're youngster, older folk, parents, grandparents, there's history and tradition that comes from football clubs that is so special and I don't think people understand that.

I've just finished reading Polly Farmer's book. He said, even though he was a boy from an orphanage, and he loved the orphanage: 'When I got down to the football club, it was like the home I never had'. Isn't that a lovely way of putting it.

Jack Malcomson

You won't find his name as having played for Richmond. But Jack Malcomson's contribution at Tigerland is immeasurable. As a cabaret singer in 1960s he was asked to write the Richmond song, and he produced what is widely acknowledged in football circles as the best club theme.

I used to do lots of cabaret shows and I used to wear a top hat, tie and tails. I was a tap-dancer. My whole act was voice impression; Louis Armstrong, Johnny Ray, George Formby and impressions of a trombone and a bass. As I got older I was under an agent and he was booking acts for the different clubs and so I did pleasant Sunday mornings for Richmond in 1962. It was 10 shillings to get in the door, all the beer you could drink, and all the pies you could eat and it was fantastic. You could imagine what they could charge for this nowadays.

After I finished I'd go get in a corner with the Committeemen and Alf Barnett was one of them. We'd chit-chat about different things, the players, yesterday's game, or next week's game. So it was this pleasant Sunday morning, and after I had been on Alf said to me, 'God, it was embarrassing'.

And I said, 'What was embarrassing?'

He said 'We went away on this trip and other teams got up and sang their songs in front of all these people and Richmond got up and by the time they all ummed and ahhed they soon started singing *Barefoot Days*, and I was absolutely disgusted.'

"Then I thought and thought and suddenly 'We're from Tiger ... YELLOW AND BLACK!' and I thought 'That's it!' It's funny how something like that clicked."

I said, 'I can't believe Richmond doesn't have a theme song. I've written a few songs, would you like me to write one, a theme song?' And he said, 'Well that would be terrific, but a bouncy one!' 'Well, naturally it will be bouncy, I can promise you.'

I'd never in my wildest dreams thought about writing a theme song.

Born
Apr 4, 1922

Died
Sept 22, 2009

The next week I was going to open a cabaret in King Island, so I wrote *Tigerland* while I was there. I went through quite a few songs and then, overnight, sitting in my motel room, I went over a few again and cut them all down from at least 20 until I was left with the tune *'Row, Row, Row'* and four others.

Coming back in the plane I started to sing again, quietly of course to myself, and I started cutting this one out and that one and suddenly I was left with (singing) 'Da da da. Da-da-da-da-da-da-da Da da da. And I thought 'Yes! That's it!'

I scratched out a line here and there, put another line in and scratched out a word here and there but it all started to fall into place.

When I first started it was 'We're from Richmond Land'. I thought that sounded terrible so I thought, well they're Tigers, so that's where they are, in Tigerland down at Punt Road. With the line 'Like the Tigers of Old' I was thinking of Alan Geddes, Roy Wright and Jack Dyer.

I loved Alan Geddes. I consider one of the greatest moments in football seeing Jack Dyer kick his drop punts, while everyone kicked torpedos and flat punts all over the place. He wasn't as ruthless as people say; he just played the game hard. If you were in his way and he wanted to go through, he went through.

I started writing the lyrics and rhyming them as best as I could. When I got to that end bit – ' We're from Tigerland' – I thought, 'Oh, God, that's terrible, it's flat just like the other songs.' Then I thought and thought and suddenly 'We're from Tiger ... *YELLOW AND BLACK!*' and I thought 'That's it!' It's funny how something like that clicked.

So I sung it through again. Oh, I was loving it! I could imagine everyone yelling out '*YELLOW AND*

A cabaret singer, Jack Malcomson made his most memorable mark by producing one of the game's great theme songs.

BLACK!'. So when I got home I said to my daughter, Dawn, 'I've written a song, if I get a big foolscap will you write all these words down for me?'

So she put the bit of paper on the floor and wrote it, and I said 'When you come to the end, 'Oh we're from Tiger...', put a stroke and write 'YELLOW and BLACK', then, 'We're from Tigerland!'

I rolled the paper up and went down to Richmond and went into the rooms and said to Alf, 'Look, I've written a song, do you think I could sing it to the boys?' So off he went and came back and said 'Yeah, Des Rowe said okay, you can sing it to the players if you want too.'

So I went into the rooms, and the backs were sitting in their big lounge chairs, and the forwards were over there and the rucks, and they were all sitting around and Des was about to give his pre-match talk.

He said, 'Fellows, we've got here Jack, he's written a song for the club and he wants to know if you like to adopt it'.

So I unwrapped it and he took one side and I took the other side so the boys could see it and I sang: 'We're from Tigerland' and you could see them bouncing a little bit and when I got to the end: 'We're from Tiger, Yellow and Black! We're from Tigerland' they all stood up and went 'Yeah!' All these footballers just stood up out of the chairs and sofas and yelled out.

I rolled up the song and said 'Thanks very much fellows, good luck.' I then said to Des Rowe 'Will I leave it with you?' and he said 'No, give it to the committee, it sounds great.'

So I gave it to Alf Barnett and I said, 'The boys loved it, so do what you can with it. It's entirely up to you.' I never said draw up a contract and if it's any good I'd like royalties, or anything like that.

No matter how old I'm getting and no matter how my memory is going, I shall never forget the day of seeing those boys listen to me sing and then as one – and I mean one – all stand up and roar like a tiger. It really proved the song struck a note.

The next week I sang it when I did my show. 'I'm going to sing my Tiger song,' I said, and I just sang it and no-one joined in because they didn't know it. Then I started to see little fliers that were being passed out to the crowd. The next thing I'm starting to hear it at the ground and it sent a ripple down the spine.

When I am on my way to that big football ground in the sky I'll know that I have left something behind. It's something for my four children, two daughters-in-law, two sons-in-law, my ten granddaughters, my great grandchild and, of course, the most wonderful women ever, my good wife Eileen.

I felt good that here was something that I did accomplish that not only made the club happy but probably made thousands happy. There is no other theme song that reverberates across an oval like that one does. It gives me a hell of a thrill to know something I did in my life had an effect on thousands of people. I'd like to be noticed. I'd like someone to come up and say 'Jack Malcomson, you're the guy who wrote the theme song.'

When it's all said and done, I've been very lucky and I've had a big bonus, the Richmond theme song. I'm very fortunate.

Paddy Guinane flexing his muscles in a Dyer-esque pose. A youthful Kevin Bartlett in support.

Paddy Guinane

The popular, muscular Paddy Guinane was an imposing figure up forward in his 11 years at Richmond. He played centre half-forward in the Tigers' 1967 premiership team and was later chairman of selectors.

1958-68

My father, Dan, played with Richmond for eight seasons (1934-39, 1942-43, 102 games). And we lived in Richmond for the first 30 years of my life. I used to be around the footy club all the time as a kid kicking the football, and I knew quite a few people there, like old Charlie Callander. My second uncle, Jack Smith, was also a treasurer of the Richmond Football Club.

Growing up as a kid in Richmond I was mates with Jack Dyer's son, Jack, and daughter Jill. I was often in their house in Docker Street. In the Dyer household, Jack's wife, Sybil, would call young Jack, Jackie – to differentiate the father and son.

Dad wasn't keen on the promotion of Dyer's 'Captain Blood' image. I remember my father and I were watching *World Of Sport* one day in the early 1960s, and Jack came on and Lou Richards was talking with him about how many opponents' bones Dyer had broken in his career. I remember my father muttered to himself, but just loud enough for us to hear. I remember thinking, 'Gee, it sounds like my Dad is a bit crook on Jack', so I asked him, 'Did you had a blue with Jack?' and he said, 'No not at all. I'll tell you what I'm crook on – all we hear about is this swashbuckling vigorous image. I played with Jack for 10 years and you wouldn't find a better footballer. He was the fastest big man in the League, a magnificent mark, a beautiful kick. He had all the skills, but you don't hear about that.'

In my early days I lived in Edinburgh Street and then we went to Neptune Street and our last address was Coppin Street. The family got bigger, I was the first of six kids and we just kept moving. We used to joke that Dad couldn't pay the rent, so we would have to go to another house.

I remember footballers like Don Fraser and Bill Morris coming to our place. Morris had a milk bar in Swan Street and Dyer himself had the Tiger milk bar in Church Street. You sort of migrated to these places because they were run by ex- or current footballers.

Tom Hafey opened a milk bar in Bridge Road opposite the National Theatre. He had a jukebox in there and all the larrikins – and me – just lived in the place. He would have big aluminum canisters which contained pineapple crush, which he made himself and he would just ladle it out into big, tall glasses and we used to love it. He would have made a fortune out of it.

Richmond was a great social club. My mother knew Sybil Dyer exceptionally well and George Smeaton's (Richmond 1935-42, 44-46, 149 games) wife Myrtle. She remembers the wives pushing their prams up Bridge Road, or shopping together or going to someone's house for a cigarette and a cup of tea. My mother was a better storyteller than my father, she had a bit of Irish in her and she had a great ability to exaggerate.

Jack Dyer was something else. He was a rock star to my mother. Jack's mother lived about 200 metres from our place. We'd often see Jack walking down Edinburgh Street into Fraser Street in his suit, carrying his Gladstone bag, off to see his mother. Often he'd stop at our front gate and talk to us. He was like an uncle really.

My father didn't talk much about his football career. He didn't have a scrapbook. I remember that he took me out to Richmond vs Carlton at Princes Park one afternoon and we ran into Laurie Nash. Dyer often said that Nash was the greatest player he had ever seen. Nash was working in the media

Born
Jan 31, 1939

Played
Richmond
1958-1968
146 games
216 goals

Interviewed
Sept 27, 2011

at the time and my father introduced me to him and Laurie said to me, 'Did you ever see your father play son? By geez he was a good player.' And I said 'Is that a fact?' and Nash said, 'Oh he was good. I always had a lot of trouble with him.' And then would jokingly add, 'You know, one day he kept me down to just eight goals'.

My father's funeral, in 1992, was at St Ignatius Church, at the top of Church Street. One of the stories told was by Father (Monsignor) Gerald Cudmore, who was a mad Richmond supporter. He remembered being at Carlton one day with my father and some mates, watching a game I was playing in. They were in the outer, standing in the terraces and there was a Richmond supporter about half-a-dozen steps down from them and right through the game he was giving me buggery.

"'Did you ever see your father play son? By geez he was a good player.' And I said 'Is that a fact?' and Nash said, 'Oh he was good. I always had a lot of trouble with him.'"

'You're bloody useless Guinane, get off the ground!'. One of the men, named 'Bull' Eddie, turned to Dan and said, 'this is getting on my goat, if you don't go down and shut him up, I will.' Dan initially said, 'Oh just let him go'. However, I was involved in a bit of the play after that and this bloke started again. So my father starts to push his way through the crowd, getting closer to the supporter, ready to shut him up and he was about one step from him when the supporter yelled out, 'And further more Guinane, you'll never be half as good as your old man'. Well my father simply turned around, walked back to his mates and said, 'that bloke's not a bad guy.'

I can honestly say my father never told me he was at my games. But I've often heard from several former players, 'Oh,I had a drink with your father the other day at the MCG during your match'. He was always there, but he never once gave me feedback or even acknowledged he had watched me play. The only question he ever asked me, was one night when we were sitting at the tea table and he said, 'Now answer honestly here, you've been playing for the Tigers now for five years. Is there anything you have learnt about playing or improving your performance from any of the coaches you have had. Have they coached you to be a better player?'. I told him 'I can't honestly say anyone has pulled me aside to give me words of advice to improve my game.' He already knew the answer before he asked the question. He was quite right. It never happened until Len Smith came to the club in 1964.

My father came down from Bungaree at the tail end of the Depression, in 1933. He once told me people played football in that time to stay alive. You wouldn't believe it, would you? He had never been to the city in his life, until he came to Richmond. He had lived on a spud farm in Bungaree and was 21 years old. So he caught the train at Ballarat all the way to Spencer Street railway station and there was nobody from the club to meet him when he arrived. He had no idea how to get to Richmond. So he had to ask someone on the corner who pointed the way. With his suitcase beside him, he walked all the way to the Richmond Town Hall. That was his first day as a Richmond player. He made his debut in round 1, 1934, and played six games in his first season.

When I was about five years old, my father had a job as a tram driver based out at the Hawthorn depot. As we were growing up, he always seemed to have a second job somewhere, whether it was pulling beer in a hotel, or running a milk round. My brother and I used to go with him on a Friday night down to the dairy, saddle up the milk cart and the horse. The milk round took around three hours. We thought it was great fun.

I played with St Ignatius YCW in the Under 16s and then the Under 18s. Strangely our guernseys were Essendon colours. Jack Dyer had a hotel down in Chapel Street, and Jack Jr went to school around South Yarra so he was playing with St Kilda YCW and there were times in Under 18s competition when I was playing against him. And at the time Jack Sr was on the Richmond committee and he said to me after one of my games, 'Now listen here young Danny (a name Dyer would call me, because of my father), you better get down to Tigerland and have a kick with the Under 19s'.

I didn't go, because of my lack of confidence and I thought he was being ridiculous. And besides, I was going to Richmond games each week, barracking, watching all these champions – and he wanted me to play alongside them! In the end I think Dyer thought I was hanging out for money, which wasn't the case.

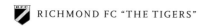

Paddy Guinane (top) and Neville Crowe in the 1967 Moomba Parade. The win (bottom): Fred Swift on the *Footy Week* front page.

So one night Jack came down to our house in Edinburgh Street and spoke to my parents. He said, 'If you sign this form, we will give you 50 pounds.' It just sounded ridiculous. People would have *paid* 50 pounds to sign the form. So I said, 'That's very kind and generous of you Jack' and so I signed. By the way, I never ever got the 50 pounds. Richmond still owes me that!

I was 28 years of age when I played in the 1967 premiership. I'm now the oldest-living Richmond premiership player. Fred Swift, our captain that day (Swift died in 1983) was about seven months older, and Roger Dean was about 15 months younger than me. At the early stages of my career, we were always at the bottom of the table, and 'won' the wooden spoon in 1960. We were pretty hopeless. We obviously didn't have the talent. When I followed Richmond as a teenager, they had a fair side. In the early 1950s the Tigers had top players like Roy Wright (two Brownlow Medals), Bill Morris, Des Rowe, Jack O'Rourke, Billy Wilson, Ray Poulter and Don 'Mopsy' Fraser.

My father coached 'Mopsy' Fraser in the early 1940s in the Richmond Seconds. He was a fabulous footballer – when he played well, he was brilliant. Mopsy used to come to our place. Off the field he was very likeable.

Any kid growing up in Richmond in the 1950s, never really considered Richmond to be premiership

Paddy Guinane's father Dan had many jobs in the '40s and '50s, including as a hotelier, a milkman and a tram driver, as this excerpt from *The Argus* shows.

RICHMOND FOOTBALLER'S ESCAPE

Leaping from a tram an instant before a motor-car wrecked the cabin, "Danny" Guinane, half-back of the Richmond football team, had a fortunate escape from serious injury in Church street, Richmond, last night. Guinane was driving the tram.

Two persons were injured in the collision. The driver of the car, L. C. Pullar, of Maude street, North Balwyn, was admitted to St. Vincent's Hospital suffering from head injuries and shock. Mrs. Charlotte Hogan, 52, of Powderham road, Caulfield, who was a passenger in the tram, was treated for shock.

As the car, which was travelling in the opposite direction, approached the tram Guinane realised that a collision was inevitable. He jammed on the brakes, and as the tram stopped he jumped to the roadway.

An instant later the car crashed into the front of the tram and shattered the cabin.

material. There was never really a thought that one day they would win the flag. That was for the other sides in the competition.

When the day came in 1967, it was like the realisation of the impossible dream. I played pretty average in the 1967 Grand Final. I don't think there was one game I ever played for Richmond when I wasn't a little on edge. My nerves were that I wouldn't live up to the expectations that were put on me to perform.

For winning the 1967 Grand Final we got the normal payment of $25. If you played 20 games in a season, you would have earned perhaps $500 for the year, and that was taxed. I remember getting a cheque at year's end for $397. Back then you didn't play football for money, you played for the honour and glory.

I remember the game where Richmond failed to kick a goal. It was against St Kilda, round 16, 1961. It was a genuine winter's day, cold, but no rain and no wind. Des Rowe, our coach, really appealed to us at three-quarter time, 'for God's sake get a goal on the board'. The score at the last break was 12.15 to 0.5. I can recall that with only five minutes to go, I was down in the forward pocket and this beautiful kick sailed in. It was going to land right in the middle of the goal square and I got this beautiful run at it, and took off. I could see my name written all over the ball. I was about to grab it in a pack and the next minute I got poleaxed. I got up, looked around and I saw it was my teammate Michael Patterson who had knocked us both down. I said to him, 'What the hell are you doing, I nearly had that ball in my hand.' And he said, 'Nah, you wouldn't have kicked it from that distance anyhow'. Keep in mind all this happened about five metres out from goal. That's the only incident in the whole game I can remember. *(The final score was 12.19 to 0.8.)*

My closest friend, since I was 15 years of age, was Graeme Richmond (GR). The first year I knew Graeme he was attempting to play with Moorabbin in the VFA. He was playing in the centre, but had very bad knees and he finished up having the four cartilages in his knees removed.

I first met Graeme in Tom Hafey's milk bar, while I was playing at the jukebox and drinking a pineapple crush. He called in one night. He was driving a white MG sports car and had a big mop of blond hair. Tommy introduced me to him. With his great knowledge of the history of Richmond, Graeme said, 'You're not Dan's son are you?' and I said, 'Yes that's my father'. He seemed to take a bit of an interest in me from that point on. At that stage Graeme was working at the Gas and Fuel Corporation.

A few years later when I was at Richmond, GR was managing the Melbourne Health Studios in the city. He was the first to say to me, 'Listen Cocko, you have got to get in here and build up your body'. I was only 12 stone (76kg). I just took to the weights under his guidance, three nights a week. I ended up playing at 16-and-a-half stone (104kg); it was all due to weights.

GR coached the Fourths and then the Thirds. He had a very good relationship with Maurie Fleming, the secretary. Graeme offered to recruit young boys to come into the Under 17s and Under 19s. We had our own metropolitan zones, but outside of those zones it was a free for all – there were no country zones then.

GR wanted to take a League footballer with him into the households as it gave him a bit more presence for his recruiting. He had a way about him, the way he spoke to people, he had a lovely choice of words. He'd win the mum over, then the dad. He was so sincere, he never ever sounded corny.

Many times he said to me, 'at this stage we have no player on the list you could call a genuine rover'. So we chased every young kid playing in the country, trying to find the right rover. What he didn't realise was that while we were chasing these kids around the country, we had Kevin Bartlett playing in the Fourths, then the Thirds, then the Seconds. All the miles driven and the money spent trying to find the best rover in the business and here he was, right on our doorstep!

GR was frustrated and disappointed that when he was coaching the Fourths and the Thirds, he was promoting very good players up to the Seconds but they were being handled by people who couldn't develop them or nurture them the way he wanted. In late 1962 GR took over as Secretary. His first move was to chase a coach who could help the club move up the ladder. He drove Len Smith mad. Len said to me, 'I was sick of saying no to Graeme and he wouldn't accept it. Three times he came at me with a different argument, so to get rid of him I said yes'. When Len came to the club (1964) all of us suddenly understood all the *team* elements of football and what it took to make a great side. He had all those beautiful rules that he made us learn – it was like being in school.

I saw a lot of people getting brown paper bags full of pound notes. Graeme had a beautiful way of doing it. I remember signing Peter Hogan (Richmond 1963-66, 40 games). He was the star young rover of country football and it looked like he was going to sign with Essendon. John Coleman, who was coaching Essendon, said to Graeme 'you are wasting your time, he is a certainty to come to Essendon, we took him to Hawaii last year on a holiday.' Well that conversation made Graeme more and more determined.

"If you played 20 games in a season, you would have earned perhaps $500 for the year, and that was taxed."

I went down to Portland with GR four or five times, trying to secure Peter Hogan. The last time we went GR had a paper bag full of two pound, five pound and ten pound notes. And GR said to Peter's father, 'you look at the Richmond line up, we haven't got a rover, there is a position there calling out for your son. The opening and opportunity is here, staring us in the face.' GR added: 'I just can't convey any more thoughts to you as to why Peter should sign with us but I'm just hoping...' and as he was talking he stood up, lifted the paper bag up from the bottom as high as he could and shook the bag and all these notes fluttered down to the carpet. Peter's father had never seen money like that in his life. Tears started to well in his eyes. He grabbed young Peter, turned to us and said, 'can you excuse us for a minute', and they went into a bedroom and closed the door.

In the 1980 premiership year, Paddy Guinane (right) was assistant coach to Tony Jewell (left).

GR turned to me and said, 'I'd better get out the Form Four. He's ready to sign.' They came back out, GR had the form out and Peter Hogan signed then and there on the spot. The drama of it. GR was a brilliant operator.

Graeme was a pessimist at times. I remember he said, 'You know we've got a good list of players, our Seconds are always extremely strong, but if we lose most of those senior players for one or two weeks, we can replace them with someone who would do a satisfactory job. But the only player we cannot replace is Kevin Bartlett. He is irreplaceable.' It was a great tribute to KB.

My first impressions of KB was that he was like lightning. I haven't seen a faster runner on the footy ground. When he was going flat out, he reminded me of Black Caviar. Always in cruise control. He always seemed to have another gear that he didn't want to use. I remember one day we were playing Hawthorn at Glenferrie Oval. It was a tiny ground shaped like a sardine tin. I was at centre half-forward and the ball went out towards the railway line and I was running flat out and it was my ball and I was just about to pick it up and KB cruises past me yelling, 'Just shepherd for me will you', and I thought, what a cheeky bugger!

After my playing career was over I did a number of jobs for the club. In the mid-1970s it was recruiting and in 1980 I was assistant coach to Tony Jewell and was also assistant to Francis Bourke when he was coach.

After the 1980 Grand Final we went to the Southern Cross Hotel. Tony Jewell said to me, 'Listen, I'm hanging around with you all night tonight. I don't want to have a drink. I want to remember everything about tonight from now until I go to bed. It's a night I don't want to forget.'

I was on the ground when Francis Bourke was conducting Mick Malthouse's fitness test. It was pitiful what happened. After training finished and we were walking off, Francis called Mick over because Mick had trained perfectly and Francis wanted to test Mick himself. He didn't get another player to do it. Francis' style of playing was that of a ferocious tackler. Well he did all that, he tackled Mick, brought him down and this went on for five to 10 minutes and it appeared to me that Francis was going to keep doing this until Mick broke down. I was a bit upset, I felt like saying to Francis, 'hey listen, you've done enough mate, let him go.' I remember Francis grabbing Mick's arm at the wrist and pulling it as though he was trying to pull it out of the shoulder socket. I've never spoken to Francis personally about it. In a game that lasted 100 minutes no player would have been tackled like Francis had tackled Mick. My opinion is that Mick's absence from the 1982 Grand Final side was the reason why we did not win that day.

Mick had a lot of shit in him, he was a nasty bloke on the ground. He was our back-pocket man, and resting Carlton rovers who would head down to the forward pocket were terrified of him. He'd do anything to you, whack you, tap you, fall on you with his knees, but he could play football. For him to be out of the side would have been a breath of fresh air for Carlton.

Also in 1982, Brian Taylor was left out of the Grand Final team. I wasn't on the coaching panel at that stage. I'd been given a job by Graeme Richmond to look after Francis, during his coaching time. I was at a lot of the meetings, but never had any voting rights on who was to play and who wasn't. Right up until the last minute, Brian was talked up in the press as being in the side. I would have had him in. He had a lot of shit in him and he played that way. He was very aggressive. But it was a day-to-day thing leading up to Grand Final Day. He had missed rounds 14 to 19, and hadn't played since round 22. In the last week he trained and had come off a very nasty knee injury. Day by day we were conferring with the medical staff whether he could play 100 minutes. When it came to the final training night on the Thursday we had the medicos in and it was almost unanimous among them that he would break down. They felt his knee was too unstable.

In the end, even though we lost the 1982 Grand Final, leaving Brian out was correct decision. Around two weeks after the Grand Final, the Commonwealth Games were in Brisbane. Richmond and Carlton were invited to put on an Exhibition Match during the Games. I can clearly recall I was in the coach's box that day. Brian played full-forward and it wasn't five minutes into the game, when he led out, leapt up for a chest mark and as he landed, his knee crumpled under him.

Coach Francis Bourke puts Mick Malthouse through the now infamous fitness test before the 1982 Grand Final.

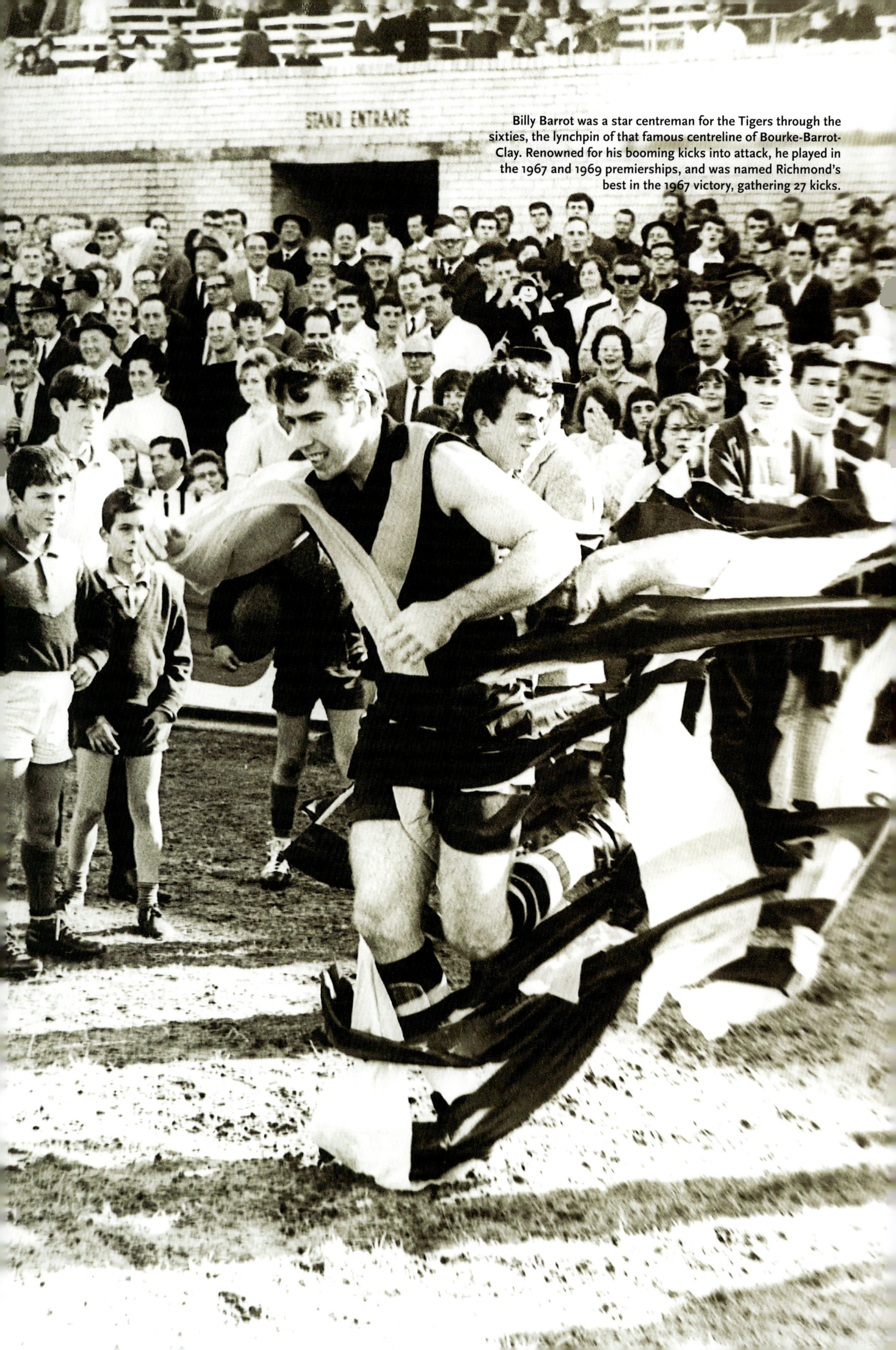

Billy Barrot was a star centreman for the Tigers through the sixties, the lynchpin of that famous centreline of Bourke-Barrot-Clay. Renowned for his booming kicks into attack, he played in the 1967 and 1969 premierships, and was named Richmond's best in the 1967 victory, gathering 27 kicks.

William 'Billy' Barrot

One of the most colourful figures from the Tigers' success of the late '60s-early '70s, and the fulcrum in the storied Bourke-Barrot-Clay centreline, Barrot was an 11-time state representative, best and fairest winner and two-time premiership player.

1961-70

Ron Barassi was my childhood hero because he was Melbourne's captain. They were a top side and had a lot of good players. I liked his strength and enthusiasm. He wasn't a great kick, he was a good handballer, and he'd run, run, run all day. I played for the Victorian schoolboys when we went to Tasmania.

Maurie Fleming wanted me to go to Richmond. I was promised a suit and £50. It was before Richmond had the territory where I lived, in Ashwood. Hawthorn had chased me and Alan Mudge, who was Secretary of Oakleigh Football Club, wanted me to go to Oakleigh, and he also took me down to Hawthorn.

Then I could have played for Collingwood seconds, they chased me. But Maurie Fleming kept sending nice letters to my parents.

A gentleman, plus.

I was quite slim when I went to Richmond. I was 11-and-a-half stone (72kg). The next year I built up to 12-and-a-half (79kg) with just weights and bodybuilding. I went to Terry Bennett's gym. He was a Mr. Victoria, or a Mr. Australia. I trained in his gym for quite a number of years. When I did sprint running for one year I didn't play well because I lost too much weight and I couldn't absorb the punishment.

At the football club they had barbells and dumbbells, and some weights. I used to do some weights before and after training, 15 minutes before, 20 minutes after. I was able to bench press 300 pound (135kg).

One night I wore out four players – I did 800 situps non-stop with a small strong medicine ball, where you put your feet in the cleats. I had blisters ... I couldn't sit down for four days. I could do 30 chin ups, crucifix-style behind my neck.

I hadn't played against men before I went to Richmond. I played against Alan Hayes in a practice game and did quite well. They promised to put me on the supplementary list, then I played against Fred Swift. I was only 16. Running down the race before the game, because it was dog-eat-dog to get a game, he said 'I am going to kick your such-and-such head off, right across the grandstand.' So I kept running all day and beat him, and after the game he shook my hand and said 'Well done, son.' So I got on the senior list at 16.

My first game was in 1961. I had turned 17, it was at the end of the year and I played on John Devine against Geelong. I think I kicked three goals that day at half-forward flank. Richmond were down at the bottom in those days. They had some great players who could mark and kick like Ron Branton, Ted Langridge, Neville Crowe, Fred Swift and Alan Hayes. There were, individually, super players. It was all about keenness and success. They tried hard in their own certain ways. We didn't have a *style* of football until Len Smith came along and taught them football. Naturally, the players were trying to be successful and not knowing how to be successful. It was just a battling football club.

I just took each week to try and win and be successful and didn't think of the future at all. I didn't know where the club was going, didn't know where I was going, but I know when I went through the years, my thoughts changed and I educated myself to be smarter, stronger, quicker, with more endurance. So I gradually got myself away and trained twice a day, and trained and trained.

I had been told many times in the past that I might have been 25 years ahead of my time. I never sort of looked

Born
May 6, 1944

Died
Nov 29, 2016

Played
Richmond, 1961-70
120 games, 91 goals

St Kilda, 1971
2 games, 4 goals

Carlton, 1971
12 games, 10 goals

Interviewed
May 2007

Billy Barrot flew over Roger Dean (3), and Fitzroy's Noel Zunneberg, in Round 1, 1970, but failed to hold the mark. The match was attended by Queen Elizabeth II, who unfurled the club's 1969 premiership flag.

at it that way. All I wanted to do was play against the best and beat the best. Some days I played terrible and some days I over-trained, which made me play terrible. So I had to accept all the publicity that went with it, good and bad. It was very draining.

Publicity can be good and bad. I think I was manipulated and used many times over. I did write for *The Herald*, every Monday night. When I read the articles it was nothing like I had said. It was just twisted around to sell newspapers and Bill Barrot was the scapegoat. I had too much publicity when I look back now and it wasn't all good. It can cause resentment amongst the players. I was a bit disillusioned ... Lou Richards said many times, 'You should have a manager, Bill.'

My heart stopped at Torquay one year when I was about 23 or 24. I had been at the gym all summer, (was) about 14-and-a-half stone (92kg) of massive muscle. I had massive pains, I fell on my face, couldn't get my breath and I said to Tommy Hafey, 'I don't feel well, coach, could I finish?' He said okay. So I played a practice match next day for a half and that's all. I was frightened to train hard for the next three or four months. I didn't go to the doctors, I didn't tell anyone.

The most important games we won. If we did lose when I was playing, we might have lost to the bottom side now and then, but in the most important games we did win. All I did was try my hardest; whether it worked out how it should have, I couldn't do anything about it. I know I'd play sometimes and kick a couple of goals and I'd jokingly say 'Thanks mate' to the man upstairs and he said 'No worries Bugsy, kick a few more.' And I did.

Before the finals and top games, my shadow was my opponent. Mentally he was chasing me all the time on the training track a month before the finals, so I got myself up that someone was chasing me all the time. It was just the way I was. I had a fear to be beaten. The fear drove me on to win.

The fear actually was my nervous fear within me. I couldn't afford to be beaten and no-one was going to beat me even if I had to die for the cause. I had to survive whatever was thrown at me. That's the way I looked at it. It was fear that drove me to success, not so much the love of being successful.

I couldn't handball left hand that well. I could kick left foot okay, 60 yards. I wasn't allowed to take a mark in a pack, I had to stay down. I sort of tried to cover my weakness on the training track. If I had any weaknesses I would work on them but I couldn't see I had too many. They could go at me and hurt me but I'd still bounce back. I was never frightened. Never. I never showed any fear. The only fear was within me to be beaten by them. If I got kicked in the face, pain, I would still keep going through the pain barrier. I practised drop kicks a lot on the run, night after night, so it was just a natural thing. I practised down at Ashwood High School running and kicking flatout drop kicks every Monday and Wednesday nights.

(Barrot was best afield in the 1967 premiership) Statistically I had twice as many kicks than any other Richmond player that day. My feet never hit the ground that day. Adrenalin high plus! Which I have been told by doctors was higher than cocaine and heroin and all the other drugs. I felt no pain. I couldn't hear the crowd. Everything was mapped out, concentration-plus. I was high as a kite on adrenalin.

I don't know why players need drugs, because I didn't need any drugs – I was just mad to win. I was mad before games. I just wanted to win. And really it knocked me down for two or three games after. It took me two or three days to recover after a lot of the top games because of the mental energies I used up.

In Dick Clay's first game against Ted Whitten at the MCG (1966) I took five paces out of the centre and kicked to the north end of the ground a torpedo punt about five or 10 minutes into the third quarter and it hit the fence on the full for a goal. When I look back at some of my kicking I couldn't believe I kicked the ball that far. I have to scratch my head and say 'How did that go so far and accurate?'

Tom Hafey used to try and drag me off the ground and I wouldn't go off. That happened at Essendon one day. Barry Stanton wouldn't give the correct messages and I sent messages back with Barry Stanton lots of times. I never did what I was told. I wouldn't get a game today if I was playing. If I had followed Tommy Hafey's instructions all the time, we wouldn't have won top games. I did what I thought was best. Tommy mightn't have liked it but I don't care. I had to do what I thought was best for Richmond Football Club and Tommy understands that now.

Len Smith thought I was an Owen Abrahams (a fleet-footed half-forward from Fitzroy), that kind of player. (Smith sent Barrot to a half-forward flank at the start of a practice match at Hamilton). So I stood there with my hands folded in the first quarter, and the ball went between my feet and I wouldn't move.

Bill Brown said 'Help me, Bugsy, help me,' and I said 'Get the ball yourself, Browny.'

At quarter-time Len Smith called us in and said 'One bloke's not trying', so I took off my jumper and threw it at him and Wilf Dickeson (1965-66, 23 games) said 'Bill ... Bill ...Bill!!"

I wasn't allowed to train for a week. And they had to have a vote, all the players had to put one hand across their eyes and put their hand up to vote whether I should stay or not at the club. Michael Patterson walked out on the meeting, he told me. He didn't believe in what was happening. **See, I was just as determined to do that as I was to win.** I didn't like defeat. I am not stubborn, I am very determined and I often stood there debating my own rights. I'll put it this way: if Tommy Hafey said to all the players 'Jump off the cliff!' and they all did, I would stand on the cliff arguing with Tommy Hafey and say 'Coach, you jump and I might consider.'

I was very heavy on asking questions and the reasons why and what for. And people didn't like that. I am not a yes man to anybody, never have been. **Len Smith was a good teacher of football.** Tommy took over and had a similar style but got us a hundred times fitter. Tommy was a lot closer to the players than Len Smith. Len never showered with the players at all. He always showered at the other end of the rooms. He never got close to the players like Tommy did. There was quite a fair bit between Tommy and Len. Len would stay aloof from us, he was a good teacher but we weren't as fit.

> "They could hurt me but I'd still bounce back. I was never frightened of them. Never. I never showed any fear. The only fear was within me to be beaten by them."

Tommy was keen, he was one of the boys, and just as fit. I was still a hard man to coach, ask Tommy, because I had thoughts of my own. 'Why did I have to do this? And why do you want me to do this? Tell me why you want to do it first.' That was just me. I queried and questioned. I tried to do most things he asked me to do and I did play for him, I suppose, more than the Richmond Football Club and more than Bill Barrot actually. A discipline disciple of the game. That's what I call him. I liked to be like him.

I didn't like football crowds because they threw cans, and spat at you and flicked lit cigarettes at you going up the race. I could see the animal in the human being when you played football, in the crowd and how they'd react and act. I always tried to be a gentleman, which we were told to do. We were always warned by the football club: behave yourself. I never got into trouble away from the football club.

I used up too much energy and then I'd hit the bottom of the wave. I'd have to level out and restore my batteries. I think that happens to all of us, we all ride high on waves and lower waves. I'd have to do it even today. It's like the tortoise and the hare. I can go like the hare but I need that rest to recharge. I can go light speed then all of a sudden stop.

In those days, I never had peace of mind after football because there was always the next season to go on with. I was never relaxed and never fulfilled the things I would like to have fulfilled.

I always wanted to be good, dressed properly, neat and tidy and football was part of my make

Always an impressive physical specimen, Billy Barrot believes his preparation for football was 25 years ahead of its time.

up. My mother tells me I always wanted to be a perfectionist. I suppose that has been my downfall at times, trying to be a perfectionist.

The game I played at Carlton that day (in 1969), Tommy shifted me to full-forward to get Richmond in the game. I think Tommy shifted me there about half-way through the second quarter and I kicked eight goals against Wes Lofts – that was a very important game for the football club to win.

I was a bit of a lair. It was elation more than lairising. You got the ball and you got the chance to do something with it. You do things you don't realise you do until you watch yourself and say 'I didn't do that, did I?'

One day, Ken Fletcher's boot and stops got caught in my jaw. It just opened up like that. You could have put three fingers in there. So Dr Vern Vivian said 'You're going to hospital' and I said 'I'm not going to hospital, fix it up.' So he put five or six stitches there and then three or four stitches there, without anaesthetic.

Trainer Sid McCrae, the club doctor, and Charlie Callander held me down. It really did hurt. I was on the ground, lying down on the boundary line and they stitched me up without anesthetic. I was screaming in pain. I kept playing and got nearly best on ground that day. I played in shock.

After the game I said 'Come on Vern, let's go back and re-do it.' He said 'No Bill, we are going up there to have two or three scotches first.' So we went up stairs and had a couple of scotches and he put 11 stitches in there and five in there.

"One day Ken Fletcher's stops got caught in my jaw. I said, 'I'm not going to hospital, fix it up'. So they put stitches in there without anaesthetic. I was screaming in pain."

Graeme (Richmond) was for me for quite a few years and he was against me for quite a few years. Now that could have been because of a power struggle between him and Ray Dunn but I got beaten by one vote to leave the club (in a committee vote). 13 people voted, 6-7. I got beaten by one vote to get the sack and (president) Ray Dunn told me himself. Ray Dunn told me 'I tried to hold you.' But I think there was more under the water than I actually knew about and I was the scapegoat of the power struggle between two strong men of the football club.

I think the articles in the paper got me into trouble because I was representing the club when I was writing for the paper. They had a meeting one night and they had all been over at Graeme Richmond's Vaucluse Hotel. I said 'All of you had been over at the Vaucluse,' and they didn't know what to say.

Ray Dunn didn't know what was going on. They knew I knew – they all went as red as a beetroot. Then Ian Stewart was on the phone to me a lot, ringing me saying 'Go to St Kilda, Bill, come to St Kilda. I want to come to Richmond.'

I spoke to Collingwood and spoke to Norm Smith from South Melbourne, and I went and trained at South Melbourne one morning. John Kennedy at Hawthorn rang me up quite a few times. Perth football clubs were ringing me up and I thought 'What's going on here, who's giving these clubs all the information?' It was coming from inside the football club.

It broke my heart to leave the club. I wasn't the player I used to be after that. Looking back now, it was the best thing that happened to me because I learnt so much about life elsewhere, but not for my football career – it was no good. But for life itself it was an excellent learning curve.

I must admit I learnt a different style of football when I was at Carlton with Barassi in 1971. I played 12 games for Carlton, and I kicked six goals from the centre one day. Barassi was surprised I could change my style of football to handball and short passes. I did play against Richmond when I played for Carlton. But I had a calcification in the thigh

from a bad knock; I played against Ian Stewart and I played poorly.

None of the Richmond boys had a go at me that day. I disappointed myself, as I had a knock on the thigh a week before and I was debating whether to play or not. They said 'Don't play' and I shouldn't have. So it was my own mistake. I thought it would have been weak of me if I didn't play. The only thing I would have liked to have achieved was to have stayed at Richmond and play in the other premierships. That's the disappointing part.

I had a cholesterol blockage in my main artery (at the 2003 Richmond Legends game). I must have handled the ball a few times, but I don't remember the game much. I felt crook in the showers, Dick Clay and I came off at half-time. Tommy wanted to drag me off before and I wouldn't come off. Typical of the past! I went in the showers and asked Dick Clay to get the soap for me, I felt giddy,

I went out to the trainers and said 'Look, I'm not feeling well' so they laid me down and they found Marshy (David Marsh, the club doctor). There was a (car) accident outside the ground with an ambulance. I was lucky it was there and Marshy got the ambulance. My heart stopped five times between Richmond and Epworth, 30 seconds at the time. I woke up at 9.30 that night, there was about 25 people in the room. They put a stent in my heart, that was it. I was exercising within three or four weeks.

My football epitaph? Win at all costs. I was exuberant, enthusiastic, had stamina and strength. Never gave in. Killed to win. And too determined for my own good.

Shortly after their controversial trade, Stewart and Barrot sport their new colours.

A young Kevin Bartlett poses at Punt Road in the mid-'60s.

Kevin Bartlett (The Player)

Club games record holder, five-time best and fairest, five-time premiership player, Norm Smith Medallist, four times leading goalkicker, captaincy among 20 state appearances ... Brownlow Medal aside, there is nothing Kevin Bartlett did not achieve on the football field.

1965-83

I was at the 1954 Grand Final. I was going on seven-and-a-half years old. My mum and grandparents came from Footscray and my godparents came from Yarraville. My mother was a Bulldogs supporter.

Every time we went to the MCG we always sat right in the middle of the ground in the Southern Stand, Bay 9. I can remember seeing Charlie Sutton lead the team out with a big bandage on his thighs. Herb Henderson was my favourite player. I can remember my mum crying and my godparents were so happy and my dad was with us. Somehow that night we finished at the Footscray Town Hall, it was all floodlit and they introduced the players, there were a lot of people there. I think we went in an old Nash motorcar. I would have had my Footscray gear on with number 25 on the back, the socks and Bulldog beanie.

I went to Hawksburn State School because I originally lived in South Yarra, at 285 Malvern Road, where the housing commission flats are today. There were shopfronts leading all the way up from Commercial Road at the corner of Chapel Street, all the way up to Williams Road, and we used to live behind a boot-making shop when I was a kid. I was about 200 yards from Hawskburn State School. When I finished Grade 6 we had to go to Technical School, which was Prahran Tech, and that was when we shifted to Richmond. From Year 7 I used to catch the Number 77 tram from Swan St and that used to take me down to Chapel St., over the Yarra River all the way to High Street. And that's where the school was.

We lived at 189 Lennox St Richmond. It was a big boarding house and it was fairly dilapidated and run down. It was a very old, big, double-storey house, but back then it had a staircase and lots of people living in different rooms. We only had one room as such, we thought it was a reasonably sized room, there was a little kitchenette off it and there was a tiny little room off that as well. For a while my dad built a wooden wall three-quarters of the way across the room and I would sleep on one side and my parents on the other. In the other little room we had a little kitchen table. Then we moved that around. I moved into the little room, big enough really to get a single bed in and the tables and chairs went on the other side of the partition. There were community toilets, washrooms and bathrooms. An old lady owned it. She used to come around and knock every Thursday and ask for the rent and mum would give her the money. In the backyard you didn't have grass, just gravel, and there were five or six bungalows and there were community kitchens.

I never sold newspapers myself but I helped people sell newspapers. Every night after school you would come home, see your mum and then you would just go straight across to a park and play there until six o'clock. Kids would just meet there. Sometimes I had a football. We used to play a lot of paper football where you make it out of paper and rubber bands and you could kick it a fair way. Even in the schoolyards you played most of the times with a paper footy.

You'd just sort of get there and all of a sudden you would start up a match. Goalposts were two trees at one end and you would throw your jumper down at the other end.

Kevin Sheedy lived in Prahran, opposite the old Australian Jam Company, and he would come down to Princess Park with his brother Pat. Again, he was just one of the

Born
March 6, 1947

Played
1965-83
403 games,
778 goals

Interviewed
Jan 2, 2005,
Feb 11, 2007

kids you would meet down in the park. He used to sell newspapers near the jam factory where the Morning Star (hotel) was, and the Prince of Wales hotel, and I had friends who used to sell on the corner of Commercial Road and Chapel St. I used to stand on the corners with them and help them sell a few papers.

"I raced home and said to mum and dad, 'I'm in, I'm playing in the seniors.' 'Who said?' 'Len Smith.' Mum wouldn't believe me, she said, 'You must have got it wrong'."

I was 14 at the time and had been playing with Try Boys Society, which was a youth club in South Yarra just up from the school that I went to, Hawksburn State School. I also went to Prahran Tech, and while there I heard that Richmond had an under 17 team, so I thought I would go down to the club and ask about playing. It must have been early February and I just walked to the club, down Rowena Parade, straight into Yarra Park where the club is and knocked on the door. Bill Boromeo answered the door. And I just said I wanted to play for the under 17s. It was quite miraculous that Bill Boromeo was coach of the under 17s and he was training some boys from the under 19s.

Bill was a fitness person and did pro running, and he was down there doing a bit of weight work. He invited me in, and as a result gave me a few weights to lift for 20 minutes and told me the actual training for the under 17s wasn't starting until five weeks later. (He) gave me the date and day to come down and train on those nights, Monday and Wednesday. He used to do the pre-season training, in those days a lot of players didn't do it. He would train down behind the Richmond Town Hall on the Reserve there – he would train down there Monday, Wednesdays and Fridays.

Collingwood, Hawthorn (and) Melbourne had under 17s. I can remember one of the games against Collingwood in Clifton Hill, Graeme 'Jerker' Jenkin was playing and he was the biggest man I had ever seen in my life. I think we played Hawthorn at Box Hill. We certainly played our games at Punt Road on Saturday mornings. I think we used to kick off at 12 o'clock. I've got a feeling when we played at Richmond the under 19s would play directly after us. Graeme Richmond was the coach of the under 19s in 1962. I had a good year.

I actually won the best and fairest and the goalkicking for the under 17s. They had an end of season night, it was held at Café Kanis on Bridge Road, Bill organised it and Des Rowe and Ron

Tiger speedsters Graeme Bond and Bartlett during summer sprint training, under the eye of pro running (and RFC fitness) coach, Bill Boromeo.

Branton were there and presented the trophies to us. Michael Green came down and played in the under 19s from Assumption College. He has been a life-long friend.

I won the best and fairest the next year, under 19s. Graeme Richmond was no longer the coach, he left to take over as club secretary. Maurie Fleming was the president and Ray Jordon was bought in to coach the under 19s. I still could have played in the under 17s. I can remember Graeme Richmond coming to me as the secretary and said, 'There are great opportunities at this club, we are looking for rovers, so train hard and be conscientious.' Hence I started playing in the under 19s in 1963. We actually had the count at the club rooms. (Jordon) had a book and wrote down best players – it was like a count. He was quite loud and forceful and quite a taskmaster. I can remember his bellowing voice coming across the ground. I can't specifically remember him swearing at the players. He used to go crook at the umpire a fair bit. He was good in terms of being a teaching figure.

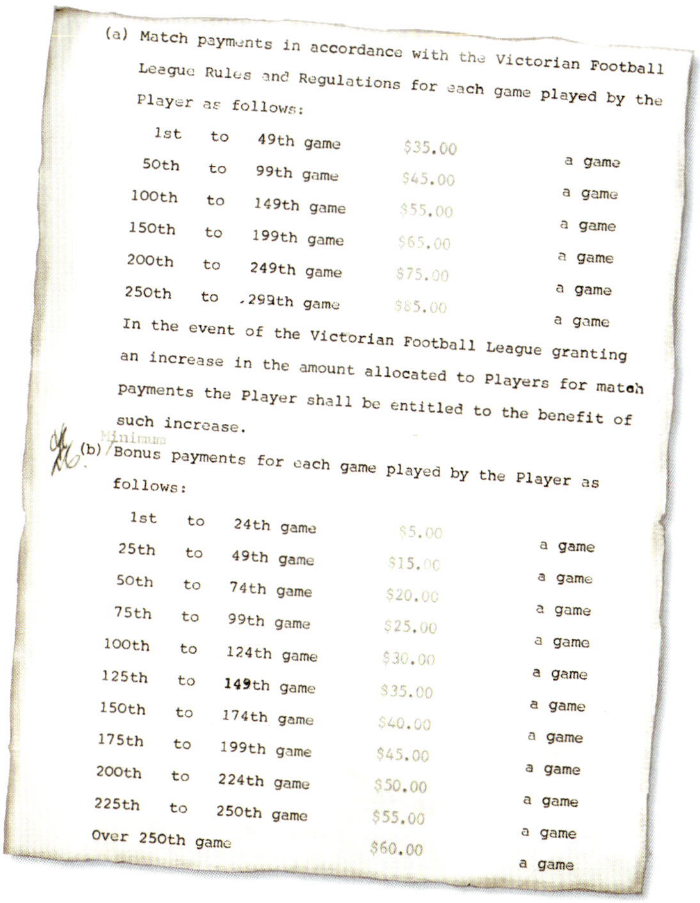
(a) Match payments in accordance with the Victorian Football League Rules and Regulations for each game played by the Player as follows:

1st	to	49th game	$35.00	a game
50th	to	99th game	$45.00	a game
100th	to	149th game	$55.00	a game
150th	to	199th game	$65.00	a game
200th	to	249th game	$75.00	a game
250th	to	299th game	$85.00	a game

In the event of the Victorian Football League granting an increase in the amount allocated to Players for match payments the Player shall be entitled to the benefit of such increase.

(b) Minimum Bonus payments for each game played by the Player as follows:

1st	to	24th game	$5.00	a game
25th	to	49th game	$15.00	a game
50th	to	74th game	$20.00	a game
75th	to	99th game	$25.00	a game
100th	to	124th game	$30.00	a game
125th	to	149th game	$35.00	a game
150th	to	174th game	$40.00	a game
175th	to	199th game	$45.00	a game
200th	to	224th game	$50.00	a game
225th	to	250th game	$55.00	a game
Over 250th game			$60.00	a game

An excerpt from Bartlett's 1972 contract; on top of a $5000 bonus – making him one of the club's four highest-paid players – were match payments and bonuses tied into an individual player's experience.

We made the finals that year. I didn't play as a rover in the under 19s, I played in the centre. We were against Geelong at the MCG. The very first bounce of the ball wasn't such a great bounce – I moved backwards with the ball and then someone came in from the side and collected me and knocked me to the ground. I was in a great deal of pain. I lasted three seconds. I couldn't stand up, I was in a lot of pain in my right hip. They came out and got me to my feet and carried me down to the forward pocket but I couldn't stand up or put weight on my leg, it was so painful. So they carried me from the field and I was inside laying on the trestle table and they had to get the ambulance.

And it was the very first time I met Jack Dyer. I was laying there in this room waiting for the ambulance to come and I looked up and there was Jack Dyer. I knew who he was because I used to watch *World of Sport*. He asked me how I was going and I said I was a bit sore. He just gave me a few words of encouragement like 'You will be okay,' and 'You'll get over this quickly.' Here was the famous Jack Dyer, who didn't know Kevin Bartlett from a bar of soap. What a fantastic thing it was for him to come into the rooms and speak to someone he didn't know – I have always had great admiration for Jack starting from that particular day.

It was interesting, I was lying in Prince Henry's Hospital and an hour later they wheeled in Frank Dimattina. Frank had been concussed and there was Frankie groaning beside me. The centreman and the first rover both finished up in the Prince Henry's Hospital. They thought I had broken my pelvis but they took X-rays and there was a shadow on my right hip. I had to come back and see the specialist in a few days and I was still very sore. Consequently they said I had a cyst embedded in my hip. I could have been born with it, they suspected, but it had to be removed. It left me with a very nasty gash that is 30 centimetres long and quite gaping around the back, from my kidneys to the front of my thigh; the scar is still very visible. I didn't get out of bed for two weeks.

Tommy Hafey has told me he had come down from Shepparton to watch all the finals in 1963. He often mentions to me he thought he would have a look at this young Kevin Bartlett play in the under 19s but he was off the ground in the first seconds. So that was probably the first time that Tommy saw me, albeit briefly.

1964 was very much rehabilitation for me. I was very tender and I was very numb in my hip, back and groin area, and I know I had to go back to the hospital in May for a final check up and X-ray.

(In) 1965, I played in some of the reserve-type practice matches. They played a lot of the recruits in the first practice game and I was playing in these games. I played in the first couple of early games and I must have done well – I was coming home from work and I was sitting on the tram reading the paper; on the back page it started off by saying '*Tiger young recruit could be shock selection*' and I started reading this thinking, 'Who could this be?' and then it read: *Under 19s player Kevin Bartlett is going to be rushed into the last practice game*, and I got quite a shock.

So I went home and said to mum, 'Look at this,' and she said, 'Well, there's a telegram here.' We didn't have the telephone at this time. It said, 'You have been selected to play in the main practice game on the MCG , please bring your boots ...' On that day I got my bag and wandered across to the MCG and found my way to the rooms. Charlie Callander was there and handed me a pair of socks. I played quite well and kicked three goals in the practice game, playing as a second rover to Peter Hogan or Frank Dimattina.

"The facilities were terrible. How half of us never finished up with diphtheria, glandular fever and every other disease known to man completely puzzles me."

They named the side for Richmond's first game for the season, which was Richmond's very first game at the MCG, since they (just) made the move. I was selected to play in the reserves as first rover against Melbourne. I played okay, it was a very wet day and Richmond nearly pulled off a big upset. The next week was against Collingwood out at Collingwood. My opponent was Mickey Bone. Again I did okay because on the Thursday night before the next game – round 3 versus St Kilda – Len Smith was the coach, and I was running around training with the senior squad.

He called me over and said, 'Now this week you will be 19th man.' When he told me my initial reaction must have been one of unhappiness or disappointed, because Len said to me, 'Aren't you happy?' and I said to him, 'I thought I probably played okay in the first two games and therefore I thought I would get another game.' He realised I thought he was talking about me being 19th man for the reserves and he said, 'No, no, you're 19th man for the seniors. You're in the firsts.'

I just couldn't believe it. So he congratulated me and I just went off training, but I didn't know many people in the senior side. Here I was running around calling for the ball in circle work and not being able to tell anyone. I got dressed after training, raced home ... and ran inside and said to mum and dad, 'I'm in, I'm playing in the seniors.' They said, 'You're in the firsts? Who said?' I said, 'Len Smith' and my mum wouldn't believe me, she said, 'You must have got it wrong.' So we just waited until nine o'clock for *League Teams* on 3DB. On came Ron Casey and Lou Richards and Allan Nash and they read out the sides; 19th and 20th were Kevin Bartlett and Trevor Gowers. And that's how it all started back in 1965.

At half-time I can remember Len Smith saying to me, 'just be patient you will get on' but I came on not long before three-quarter time. Sadly, my very first game was Len Smith's last game as coach, because Len had a heart attack the following Monday. I was at work when I heard it. Len didn't coach Richmond again ... by the time we got to training it had been announced that Jack Titus, just a board member – he wasn't even coach of the reserves – would be coach.

Jack was in his late fifties. I always remember the first night of training under him. Here I am in my first year as a player and I've played one game of senior football and this man, decked out in a Richmond jumper, black shorts, Richmond socks and football boots, trotted down the race in the full garb and took training. He was an old-style coach, a bit of fire and brimstone.

He was very much a loved figure and we actually played pretty darn well. I can recall they'd have a long stool and he would jump up on the stool in the room and walk up and down the stool and players would sit down in front as he gave that last rousing speech. The only time I saw Jack Titus not wear a bow tie was when he took training.

The facilities were terrible. How half of us never finished up with diphtheria, glandular fever and every other disease known to man completely puzzles me. You would come in off the track after a hard training session; it was genuinely always very muddy.

You'd come off and Charlie Callander would have a big pot of soup there and four or five cups. On cold nights the blokes would dip their cup into the soup and drink that soup down and they would put that cup down and the next bloke would pick up the cup and whack that into the bowl as well. There were no ladles. There were a couple of old baths; the tiles

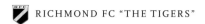

Kevin Bartlett emerges from the race for game number 400, the first player to that milestone. He finished on 403.

around the bath were off or cracked, the showers were terrible in the main training area. There used to be an old heater there that used to heat up the shower, and Charlie had to stoke up the heater to get it going.

1967 was certainly a big year for me, because I had just turned 20, we won the premiership and I won the best and fairest at the club. In 1968 I was a very warm favourite to win the Brownlow Medal, which I didn't – Bob Skilton won that year. In 1969, I was four votes away. In 1970, I was runner-up in the best and fairest. In 1973 and 1974 I won best and fairests. 1974 was an extraordinary year, there were 12 or 13 major awards and I think won every one of them but one.

There was a motorcar from *World of Sport*, and a caravan, trips and money. I was an extra hot favourite to win the Brownlow but Keith Greig won.

1977 was a very good year, I won the best and fairest, I came second in the Brownlow Medal. I thought 1978 was a good year – I played a lot as a ruck-rover in 1978, and I came second in the best and fairest. In 1980 I moved to the half-forward flank; from a small forward's perspective I would say that was a very good year. [Ed's Note – Bartlett kicked 84 goals in 1980].

When Tommy Hafey left in 1976 (to coach Collingwood) that was a very strange time for me. I remember speaking to Tommy and I just couldn't believe he had decided not to coach the Tigers. He had been reappointed but my understanding at the time was that Tommy felt he did not have the support of the committee. Most of all didn't have the support of Graeme Richmond. And he felt that was untenable without their support and there was no point continuing. I can remember he rang me at home and told me he was quitting as coach. I just couldn't believe it.

I think I said, 'That's silly, you don't have to, we want you to stay as coach.' But he left at the end of 1976 and Barry Richardson was appointed as coach. I felt very, very empty. Because in the time Tommy had been coach (1966-1976), they were happy days; I just assumed I would play my whole career under Tom. I never thought for one moment that anyone else would come and coach. We had shared those four flags together.

Barry Richardson called me into his office one day and asked me, 'Is there a problem?' I was not training well and my demeanor was not happy or excited, and I didn't know whether or not I wanted to be at the club. I said, 'I am going to do my best but I feel a bit flat with Tommy not being here.'

In fact, I won the best and fairest that year, and the following year under Barry I came second. Then Barry unfortunately got the sack, not an unusual trait at Tigerland as it turned out, and Tony Jewell took over as coach and I was appointed captain.

In 1979, I was playing as a rover but the club must have felt I wasn't giving them the on-ball drive that they required. No-one ever spoke to me about it, although I was the captain. Out of the blue, I was named on the half-forward flank. That was fairly significant considering I had been roving for 15 years. In those days it was called the 'graveyard' because you were stuck out there on the flank and lacked the freedom of roving.

We were playing Essendon out at Waverley Park and I was walking into the ground after being named on the flank when I was met by Channel 10's Rob Astbury, then the game's biggest reporter. Rob was the biggest story-breaker in football. He came up to me as I was going through the turnstiles and he said, 'I've been told today is your last game for Richmond.'

It completely shocked me and I said, 'I don't know what you are talking about.' Where he got the information from I have no idea, but he had the ear of a lot of people at the club so I assumed someone gave him a tip-off. As it turned out I am pretty certain we lost the game but I kicked four goals and was named one of the side's better players.

At the end of the season, with Rob's words ringing in my ears and knowing a bit of the machinations of the football club over the years, I decided to resign from the captaincy and ask for a clearance. There was something brewing and I thought maybe I should take the signs. If I still loved to still play, which I did, maybe I could play a few more years somewhere else.

I had a number of clubs speak to me. My first thought was if I am going to leave I am going to play under Tommy. That would have been the way for me to finish my career. And I spoke to Tommy and Ron Richards, who was the chairman of selectors at Collingwood. We talked a number of times, but Tommy felt that it would be wrong for me to leave because he felt my name was synonymous with the Tigers. He said he would love me to come and play but didn't want to be responsible for taking me from Richmond. But at that stage I was still a bit gung-ho to leave. I spoke to Essendon and in fact I signed a letter of agreement that I would play for the Bombers. I told Tommy about that and he again thought it was the wrong thing to do. So he swayed me to initiate a truce through Michael Green, my great friend and solicitor. Michael went to the club and instigated my return. So I went back.

In the book: Nash takes Bartlett's number as Nankervis assesses the damage.

KB reported ... once

Umpire Neville Nash tells his story

When Kevin Bartlett struck Bruce Nankervis (round 8, 1982) I had no option but to take his number. When it happened I had no hesitation in blowing the whistle and telling him I was reporting him. They were grappling with each other at the time and then I just saw Kevin throw his right fist out and make contact with Bruce's face.

The game stopped. There was a bit of a delay because I know David Cloke was fairly close to the incident and he was quite distressed, saying 'You can't report him, you can't report him!' Bruce was a little bit distressed. He had a bit of a whack down his nose and a bit of blood, so the game stopped a little bit while I did what I had to do and then I moved on. It was a reasonable contact and I think Bruce ended up with five or six stitches.

I didn't do pre-season really for 1980, it was interrupted, I was training by myself. So it was an interesting year, I went in with limited preparation but with things ringing in my ear from 1979 I was absolutely desperate to prove everyone wrong and that I could still play at the highest level. Absolutely desperate. By the time we got through to the finals series of 1980 it just happened to be that the first game of the finals series was the day that I broke the League record, held by John Rantall –it was my 337th game and it was against Carlton,a great club, with great players.

The cheer squad made a huge banner. It was before the days of banner size restrictions and I felt 10 feet tall when I broke through on this special day. It turned out to be a fairytale day – the late Terry Smith set me up early with a pass along the boundary line from which I kicked a goal. By quarter-time I had booted three and then all hell broke loose. Tony Jewell and Peter Jones swapped blows as we went to our huddles, two coaches boxing on was unheard of. I felt focused and was not interested in the stoush. I had kicked four goals by half-time and kicked a couple of goals in the third quarter and finished with six for the game. Richmond won. It was highly satisfying for me to prove to people and myself that I was still able to play well in a final. I was 33 years of age.

Ron Barassi presents Bartlett with the 1980 Norm Smith Medal.

Whenever you report someone you just say 'I am reporting you for striking, do you understand?' I know that Kevin made a comment along the lines of 'It's partly your fault!' At the tribunal he basically apologised for saying that. He had been saying he was tagged and hung onto by Bruce and this was the only chance of trying to break the hold because he wanted to go where the football was. This was about 20 metres away from the play. It was just his way of releasing the tag.

I know when I pulled up outside VFL House in Jolimont there were quite a number of Richmond people out the front. It was a bit daunting walking to the front door and walking through them. No-one did anything untoward, they just made a bit of a noise and waved banners around, but I did notice there were a couple of policeman there. Interestingly, Jack Gaffney was chairman and the other two were Allan Nash, my uncle, and Brian Bourke.

Kevin said he made contact but it wasn't intentional. During me answering one of the questions I was sitting fairly close to the three members of the tribunal and Brian Bourke was closest to me. While I was answering a question he said under his breath, 'He's an ornament to the game,' referring to Kevin. I thought then, 'Okay, he is going to get found not guilty, but that's not my problem.'

Bruce never even came into the tribunal room. It was unusual. He was there in the next room but was never called in as a witness. I never saw Bruce. So we all gave our versions of the event and then we went outside and it was only a short period of time and we came back. Not guilty.

When we finished Kevin and I shook hands and we went upstairs. We had a laugh about it all and I said 'I've got to walk to my car now and all those people are out the front' and Kevin said 'I'll drive you.' So we went downstairs and Kevin drove me to my car.

Then we came to the second semi-final against Geelong, and they were a crack side. I can remember in the first quarter that I collided with Jim Jess, we just cracked heads together and we both went down, fortunately no damage. Just after that incident I ran onto a loose ball and kicked a goal. It gave me a surge and I felt I was running on top of the ground. The adrenalin was pumping. We went into the game without some stars. David Cloke and Barry Rowlings had ankle and knee problems, and early on we lost Paul Sarah with a broken cheekbone and Bruce Tempany broke an ankle. Plus we had lost Graeme Landy, who was suspended after knocking out Ken Sheldon the week before.

Our captain, Bruce Monteath, who was a very good player, had battled injury all season, came off the bench and gave me a brilliant tap-on as I ran past, which resulted in a goal.

The quarter again had started on a high. Four goals at half-time became six at three-quarter time, thanks to some unselfish blocking by Daryl Freame. I finished with eight.

"I had a big gum tree in the middle of the block with a fork in it, and I went out there on Friday evening and I played that 1980 Grand Final in the backyard."

I'll always remember Francis Bourke and me hugging each other at the end of the game. We were delirious to think we were going to play in another Grand Final together. We had already played in four premierships and we were both coming to the ends of our careers. Two old-timers had played alongside each other in this campaign. Another premiership was now a reality. Because I had kicked 14 goals against Carlton and Geelong, I remember a clairvoyant gave a media interview, predicting I was coming up for a bad game and my biorhythms were down. As a result, there was no way I could play well in the Grand Final. He said to the effect, 'Don't expect anything from Bartlett.' I had never ever heard of biorhythms, so it was all a giggle to me.

I used to love to visualise playing. The night before the Grand Final I went out into the backyard where I could kick the ball 40 metres. I had a big gum tree in the middle of the block with a fork in it, and I went out there on Friday evening and I played that Grand Final in the backyard. It was probably just a way of reinforcing to myself that I could actually play well on that day. I think the sports science gurus today call it 'imagery', a powerful motivating technique.

I snapped goals, I threw the ball on the ground and picked it up as though I was roving off the packs. I took set shots. I just visualized scoring goals and being involved in passages of play. I would have done that for an hour, because I wanted to so badly to play well in that Grand Final. It was in the back of my mind I had played well in the qualifying final and second semi-final and it would be disappointing to not play well in the Grand Final.

It may sound strange, but some of the things I visualized the night before happened in the Grand Final. Taking the ball off the pack, running into goals, shooting from angles, taking marks, they all took place. It turned out to be a great day for the club and for myself. I was able to kick seven goals in the Grand Final against Collingwood and experience this enormous thrill. Francis showed everyone how great he was for he lined up at full-back. We had now played in five premierships together, winning Grand Finals in three different decades. It was a mighty thrill.

As the siren sounded, while I felt exhilarated, I felt on the other hand so disappointed for Tommy, who had been my inspiration and the biggest influence on my career, and my best friend. It was surreal. In all my premiership wins I had celebrated with Tom, we had run our laps of honour together. Here I was on this day, winning the Grand Final, and Tommy was not the coach. Tony Jewell did a fantastic job and got the best out of every player at the club, and was a great support to me. But to see Tommy as coach in the losing side was very strange for me. I can remember going across there and talking to him and Peter, his brother, who was the Magpie runner. It was hard to know what to say, because I knew how hard Tommy would have taken the loss. It was difficult.

I think there have been so many great players that have played for the Tigers over the years. If you go back in time, obviously Jack Titus was a fabulous player, Jack Dyer was a fabulous player and Dick Harris was a fabulous player. I never saw them play but you read about their exploits in what they did in finals and what they did for the Richmond Football Club. Of those that I played with, Royce Hart and Francis Bourke were fabulous players. I am quite happy to fall in behind Francis Bourke, Royce Hart and Bill Barrot.

Bartlett's performance during the 1980 finals series, capped by seven goals against Collingwood in the Grand Final, marked him as a player for the ages.

INTERNATIONAL
HARVESTER

With a twist of his left knee, Barry Richardson's career all but ended on this day, round 1, 1973, when Ken Fletcher (Dustin's dad) attempted to spoil a mark.

Barry Richardson

Barry Richardson became one of Richmond's great full-backs, playing in three premiership teams, despite struggling with restricted movement, as a result of a knee injury in round 3, 1965.

1965-74

My nickname 'Bones' was given to me by Raymond Clarence 'Slug' Jordan. Early on in my career I did my knee and 'Slug' was coach of the Thirds and I was sitting there kind of feeling sorry for myself and 'Slug' in his usual sympathetic tone came over to me and said 'Jesus Christ, you must have chalky bones'. So it stuck.

In fact my nickname used to be 'Chalky Bones'. But as I became a physiotherapist the nickname degenerated into 'Bones'. Actually Ray Jordan still calls me 'Chalky'. If I was in Times Square in the middle of the night and someone yelled out 'Chalky', it could only be one person.

'Slug' had a philosophy that you needed to be hard enough to get past him to be able to play at a higher level. If you couldn't get past his abrasiveness, chances are you were going to be too soft to play League football. Rightly or wrongly, that was pretty much his philosophy. He would be hard on blokes, but then soften them by saying 'but you did this well'. He was pretty clever and a very fine thinker of the game.

I was coached by Len Smith in my first two senior games in 1965. I was 19. I played against Melbourne and Collingwood and then I was dropped. I played my first two senior games straight out of school at about 11-and-a-half stone wringing wet, at full-forward. Then I got dropped and played around four games in the Reserves and did my knee.

So I missed the rest of 1965 with the cruciate ligament injury. In those days no one knew how to operate on it. I found I could run to a marking contest and jump off my left leg and if I moved to the right I was fine. But if I jumped off my left leg and moved to the left I would simply crash into the pack. So I basically taught myself to jump off my other leg and only turn one way and changed myself from being a jumping player to a running player.

I came back the following year in 1966, and only played three senior games but was lucky enough to play in the Reserves premiership side. Our coach was John Nix, a very good coach for his time. We had a lot of young blokes who came through that team – Royce Hart, Michael Green, Graham Burgin, John Perry. The Grand Final was relatively close with Royce Hart, the golden boy, kicking the winning goal. I think I topped the Reserves goalkicking that year.

By the end of 1966 I had learnt how to cope with my bad knee. I played my entire career with no cruciate in one knee. But because I was a physio I knew how to get around it. I was always strengthening it, always riding bikes. It was my take-off leg, so I became a gangly ruck-rover in 1967 and then in 1968 I went to full-back which meant I could run in straight lines. I learnt to jump off my other leg and land back on that leg, which means now I have a stuffed ankle on that leg.

I used to run up and down Glenferrie Road, where I was boarding, jumping up and touching the milk bar signs that hung overhead. That was the way to teach myself to jump off the other leg. Milk bar signs were always lower than the other signs on the street so I could always touch them. It was just a way of learning to co-ordinate. Whenever I drive down Glenferrie Road these days, I have flashbacks to that memory.

Born
Jan 22, 1946

Played
Richmond
1965-1974
125 games
134 goals

Richmond coach
1976
(acting coach)
1978

Interviewed
Mar 13, 2012

Barry Richardson and champion Hawthorn full-forward Peter Hudson in a tangle during one of their many memorable clashes. Richardson is one of two League players to keep Hudson goalless.

If I have one regret in my sporting life, it is that I achieved only 80 per cent of what I could have, with a sound knee. I went from being a leaping high jumper to someone who could never really jump again. I sometimes catch myself thinking – 'what if?'.

I was boarding, and down the road from me lived the Dimattinas. Frankie Dimattina was probably my best friend at Richmond as I had been at school with him at St Pat's Ballarat. I thought I had died and gone to heaven, because Mrs Dimattina was the best cook in the world, so I spent most of my life up there because the lady I was staying with was a Pommie who couldn't cook at all.

Len Smith suffered a heart attack early in 1965. Jack ('Skinny') Titus took over and then Tom Hafey arrived. I remember Titus well, he was a bit of a character. On the first night he became coach (he was 57 at the time), he walked out to take training and he had the high shorts on, the Richmond guernsey, the socks and the boots. He didn't always wear his teeth either. The word was that for his pre-game speeches you shouldn't sit in the front row, because you would most likely get spat on.

When Len was ill he was still a bit of a mentor around the place. I remember one day we were playing against Geelong at the MCG (round 7,

1967) – probably the match the Tigers started to come of age. The scores were level at half-time and it was a fantastic game. I was playing centre half-forward, Royce Hart was full forward. At half-time I was lying down on the bench and Len came up to me and said, 'Now son, I really want you to enjoy this game. This is a terrific game.' No one had said anything like that to me before. They would normally say 'Let's go out there and kill 'em'. But this stuck with me. I did what he said and kicked two goals in the third quarter (and we kicked eight goals to one). It was an unusual father-like figure thing to say. But that's what he was – a bit of a philosopher on the game. Way back then he was coaching the person, as well as the player.

I had never heard of Tommy Hafey before he came to coach Richmond. He arrived in 1966, but he wasn't good for me in that year as I was still trying to come to terms with my knee problem. John Nix, the Reserves coach, had a very strong influence over me. He trusted me and was a bit more like Len Smith in the way he approached the players. The Reserves role then was to help blokes get up to play senior football, so John was more of a teaching coach.

In the pre-season of 1967 we went down to Percy Cerutty's place at Portsea. This was hard but good in a way because it gave me the confidence knowing that if I could get through that I could get through anything. As that year wore on I played games at centre half-forward but I ended up in the finals playing on the half-forward flank and ruck-rover. If I was fully fit and could choose only one position it would be centre half-forward.

I had played centre half-forward and full-forward at St Pat's. I made their Team of the Century and was probably spoken about in the same breath as another past pupil, John James (the 1961 Brownlow medallist from Carlton). I captained the combined Ballarat Public School side in Year 11. So I was the number one draft pick of my time!

The Number 17 guernsey was very important to me. When I was recruited by Richmond, Jack Dyer came up to the family farm in Wodonga with Graeme Richmond and Des Rowe. I remember Jack came into the house and said 'What beautiful scones you make, Mrs Richardson'. At that stage I was being wooed by everyone. Melbourne had come up previously to see me, and along with Richmond, they both offered me the same amount of money, which was fees and books for university. When I was boarding at St Pat's, the Brothers wouldn't let recruiting people come into the school, they could watch from afar, but weren't allowed to talk to me. So they would therefore drive me mad in the school holidays on the farm.

> "So when Dyer left after visiting I remember he leaned on our front gate and said: 'Listen son, if you come to Richmond, you can have my Number 17.'"

If I ever saw someone come up the track, I'd piss off up the hill and shoot rabbits. But Richmond had an in – a friend of my father was an old Richmond player called Jack Eames (14 games, 1946). So when Dyer left after visiting I remember he leaned on our front gate and said: 'Listen son, if you come to Richmond, you can have my Number 17.' So that was part of the deal. I signed up during the school year of 1964. In fact I played one night game at the old South Melbourne ground, but hardly touched the ball. I remember I took a mark and kicked it out of bounds.

I think this is an example of how cerebral I was with the game. In 1969, Peter Hudson kicked 16 goals against Melbourne (on Robert 'Tassie' Johnson), two weeks before I was to play on him. Every goal Hudson kicked was shown on the news that night. What I noticed was that most of those goals were of him running into an open goal. They would leave Hudson in the forward line all by himself and then kick the ball to the one-on-one contest, but usually over his head. He would use his big arse to push you out and run back into an open goal. I thought I'm going to at least eliminate that one, so he might only kick eight against us. When I played on him in round 7, 1969, I stood around 15 metres behind him. Every time he turned around I just pretended to look around with folded arms and showing a total lack of interest. So the Hawks kept kicking the ball over his head and I kept taking chest marks. It worried him, he told me later, because every other full-back had stood next to him. The next time we played he stood on the goal line.

It was actually a great day for me. Not only did I hold Peter Hudson goalless, but it was the day I became engaged to my future wife Judy.

In 1973 Richmond won the Grand Final and I missed out on that game because of a knee injury. I played only one game for the year, round one against Essendon, and injured my knee. And I have to tell you something, I don't know what is worse – playing in a losing Grand Final (like in 1972), or not playing in a winning Grand Final (like in 1973). I reckon the latter is worse, because you have this mixed emotion, and – I'll be brutally honest here – you almost hope that your team loses because you know how bad you are going to feel not being part of it.

"You and I Lingy are part of a very exclusive club. We played in three premierships and one losing Grand Final. Our last kick in our career was a goal in a Grand Final."

I sat on the bench with the staff in the 1973 Grand Final. The emotion you see from me in the photograph with KB and Tom Hafey is not elation. I think it's more of me crying. Because the feeling is that you are sort of part of it, but sort of not.

The five minutes after a winning Grand Final is, in the words of Vince Lombardi, 'as good as man ever feels'. He's not wrong. It's a wonderful feeling of elation and relief. So when I missed out on those emotions in 1973, the next day I went 'Bugger this, I'm going to have one more shot'. So I went and had an operation, which I found out later removed my cruciate.

I made a comeback in 1974, played in the Reserves, then Mal Brown did me a favour by throwing the ball at an umpire and getting suspended for four matches. I came into the side for the second last game of the year (round 21) against South Melbourne and I kicked three goals. It was my first senior games in almost two years. Then I kicked four goals in the last game against Footscray.

In the two finals, both against North Melbourne, I kicked bags of five goals. The 1974 Grand Final was my last game for Richmond. I was really lucky, because what I didn't want to do was have my last football thought being part of a losing Grand Final.

The last kick in my career was a goal. I wrote a letter to Cameron Ling, who I knew from my Geelong days and it said, 'You and I Lingy are part of a very exclusive club. We played in three premierships and one losing Grand Final. Our last kick in our career was a goal in a Grand Final.'

I actually intended to play on in 1975. I played in a practice game in Broken Hill against Port Adelaide early in the 1975 season and the following week did my right knee again and thought 'maybe it is time to give it up'. I was gone.

I worked for Channel 7 in 1975 and in 1976 I was Richmond Reserves coach. The powers that be saw me as being a potential coach. Sometimes, people see in you what you don't see in yourself.

I started thinking about coaching when I was 27. In the first game of 1973, after doing a huge pre-season to make up for being pissed off that Carlton beat us for the 1972 flag, I did my other knee, my left knee, in the first quarter. Ken Fletcher, Dustin's dad, jumped into me as I took a mark. He was running with the flight of the ball and I just relaxed and he jumped on my shoulder and I twisted my knee. It turned out I was really busy at work, so I basically thought that's it, I've probably had it. Then I had an offer to coach Ormond College in 1974 – it was only a four-game season – and I thought I would do that. So I coached them and that gave me a taste of what coaching could be.

I was always a deep thinker about the game. I went to the United States with Tom Hafey at the start of 1976. We visited the San Francisco 49ers and a college gridiron team. We actually spent some time with a sports psychologist, Thomas Tutko, so that gave me more of a cerebral approach to handling players in the game. I had a very inquiring mind. I was doing kickout drills before any other coaches were doing them.

I remember writing a plan and the plan was something that Allan Jeans was credited with years later. When we have the ball what do we do? When they have the ball what do we do? And when neither side has the ball what do we do? The frustration of that was, as I look back now, I was only 29 when appointed Richmond's senior coach in 1977 and I never had enough time to implement what I wanted to do. We were only training Tuesday and Thursday afternoons after work.

The stark reality is that I was ahead of my time, but we never had the time to implement the drills to

A youthful Barry Richardson snaps for goal in his early days as a forward.

reproduce in a game. Even so we did all right. We finished 4th in my first year, and 7th in the second year before getting the sack.

If you go back to 1974, our forward line was David Cloke (6 feet, 5 inches) on a half-forward flank, Royce Hart at centre half-forward who marked everything that came his way, Neil Balme in the forward pocket changing with Michael Green (both 6 feet, 5 inches) and me 6 feet, 4 inches at full-forward. So sure, kicking it long into the forward line worked because one of us was likely to mark it. By 1976 Richmond finished 7th, which is really why Tom Hafey got the sack which was unfair but that's the way it was. He would switch to Collingwood from 1977.

"I think my coaching career hung on that kick."

1977 was probably a year where older players were just hanging on. I was a new coach, with a new voice. It was a different dynamic. Neil Balme was at the height of his powers in that year. Michael Roach was in his first year. I played him on the wing that year. He was too skinny to play full-forward. Royce was now slowly finishing his career and Michael Green had retired. Geoff McMillan was playing and had ability, David Cloke was a bit more mature, Robert McGhie was past it, and we recruited Alan Noonan from Essendon, but he unfortunately wasn't good enough for us. By the time my second year of coaching came around, we were into a total transitionary period. I had given Mark Lee, Dale Weightman, Bruce Tempany and Greg Strachan their first games.

In 1977 we played Collingwood in round four at the MCG. It was Anzac Day and it was Hafey's first game coaching against Richmond. It was new coach vs old coach. We got smashed before 92,000. Peter Moore just murdered us. In the press conference afterwards the journalists were all poised to say that the young coach wasn't up to it, so they started the press conference with 'What do you think about that performance, Barry? And I said 'I thought it was the Quintessence of Athletic Atrocity' and then walked out. I had read that quote somewhere before, so I just plagiarised it. I thought it was a pretty smart comment but on the Monday morning, Tom Prior writing for *The Sun*, wrote, 'No wonder Richmond is going nowhere, their new coach is too intellectual'.

In 1978 with two games to go we were sixth. We were seven goals ahead at half-time against Collingwood at the MCG. We ended up getting beaten by 14 points and drifted out of contention. It is funny how things stick in your mind. I can remember during the third quarter Neil Balme centreing the ball to Francis Bourke who marked about 25 metres out straight in front. We were four goals up by this stage, so if Francis kicks a goal we go five goals up. He misses, the ball goes from full-back to Len Thompson in the forward line and he scores and now we are only three goals up. I think my coaching career hung on that kick.

I had never really seen myself as a career coach but I would have liked to complete four seasons at Richmond. I didn't have a contract. I was coaching year by year until I got tapped on the shoulder by Ian Wilson, who had been sent by Graeme Richmond.

Because of the 'old ruthless Richmond' stuff, I thought it was on the cards that they wouldn't give me another year, considering we didn't make the finals. They had no concept of what it meant that I had played all these new kids.

When I took over as coach there was a feeling that Graeme Richmond had far too much power. He didn't have an official role at the club, that's the frightening thing about it. Graeme and I had great respect for each other, but for some reason Graeme felt he had to prove his toughness by nailing blokes he liked the best.

So when I took over as coach of Richmond, I wrote Graeme a letter. 'Dear Graeme, thanks for everything you have done, but butt out. I'm my own man and I'll do it my way.' From that time on, I reckon I only had to not perform and I was going to be sacked. Graeme was always hovering, like a guillotine. It was just the way he was.

I think coaching makes a man of you. I later went on to coach again in the Old Xavs, which was very satisfying. Coaching in the Amateurs is pretty pure. You've got these blokes who aren't full-time footballers, they are intelligent and you have their respect. It was a very satisfying way to finish my coaching.

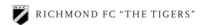

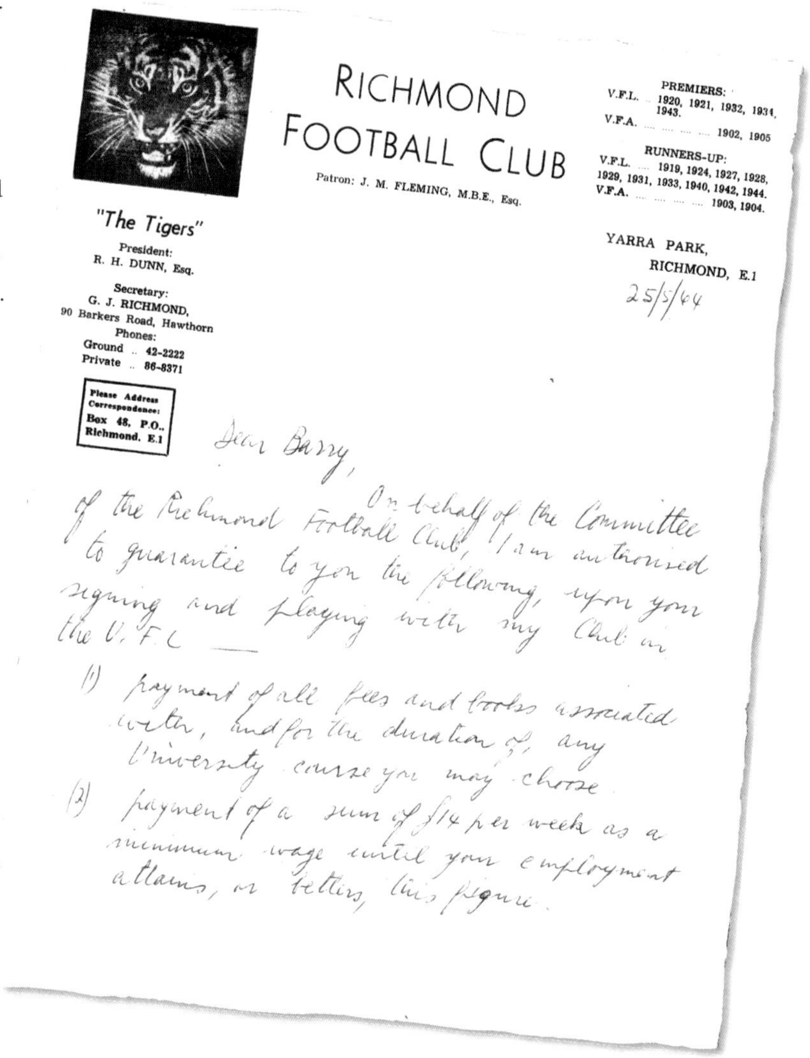

"The Tigers"

President:
R. H. DUNN, Esq.

Secretary:
G. J. RICHMOND,
90 Barkers Road, Hawthorn
Phones:
Ground .. 42-2222
Private .. 86-8371

Please Address Correspondence:
Box 48, P.O.,
Richmond, E.1

RICHMOND FOOTBALL CLUB

Patron: J. M. FLEMING, M.B.E., Esq.

PREMIERS:
V.F.L. ... 1920, 1921, 1932, 1934, 1943.
V.F.A. ... 1902, 1905

RUNNERS-UP:
V.F.L. ... 1919, 1924, 1927, 1928, 1929, 1931, 1933, 1940, 1942, 1944.
V.F.A. ... 1903, 1904.

YARRA PARK,
RICHMOND, E.1

25/5/64

Dear Barry,

On behalf of the Committee of the Richmond Football Club, I am authorised to guarantee to you the following, upon your signing and playing with my Club in the V.F.L —

(1) payment of all fees and books associated with, and for the duration of, any University course you may choose

(2) payment of a sum of £14 per week as a minimum wage until your employment attains, or betters, this figure.

The letter to Barry Richardson outlining the "rewards" of his signing on to play for the Tigers.

I've conveniently forgotten that I was President of Richmond. However long it was, it was too long. I replaced Ian Wilson in 1985. I was asked to be President and to be honest I reckon my ego took over. Richmond was going badly at the time, yet it was only a couple of years since the 1982 Grand Final. The club seemed to be in disarray. I was approached by Bill Durham and a couple of other people, and it seemed like a good idea at the time. I went into it thinking that I could probably change the club, but I should have gotten out after a week.

I hired Paul Sproule as coach. He had been highly successful in Tasmania, winning three premierships in three years at Sandy Bay, was a physical education graduate and I thought he had been a wonderful player. We signed him on the same arrangement that I had been signed on, but I gave him two years on a handshake agreement. I left it to the board to produce a contract. I later found out that they never gave him one to sign. But Paul said 'thats all right, I trust you Barry'. He coached Richmond for only the one year.

At the end of 1985, I went away and had a holiday for one week in Surfers Paradise and when I came back the powers that be had decided to sack Paul and appoint Tony Jewell as coach. It had been their agenda all along. They wanted to appoint Jewell in the first place, but I gave my vote to Paul, because St Kilda under Tony Jewell had finished last in 1983 and 1984. So I came back to the meeting and said 'If that is a case, and you've sacked Paul Sproule, then I'm resigning as President, because a handshake for me is more binding than a formal contract'.

"Graeme and I had great respect for each other, but for some reason Graeme felt he had to prove his toughness by nailing blokes he liked the best."

I don't think I was the right person to be President. I wasn't good with politics, I was good at being straight. That doesn't work. It was a year I could have done without. It was a year in which I didn't achieve anything. It was unfulfilled, unsuccessful and unrewarding. Having said that, Alan Bond came along in 1987 and wasn't that good at it. The club had the idea to bring in a high flyer – John Elliot was at Carlton, Geoffrey Edelston was at the Swans – they wanted that style of bloke.

I've been blessed. Football's been part of a parallel life for me – physio and family were first. I've had some great experiences. I worked in assistant roles on the match commitee with Ron Barassi for four years, David Parkin for two years, Neil Balme for two years, Mark Thompson for three years, as well as working for Peter Rhode. I coached the State Amateurs for four years and Old Xavs. It's been a really interesting parallel career.

What we did was fantastic. If I was reflective and egotistical, I think maybe I never quite achieved what I could have achieved in the game. Though, I'd like Richmond fans to remember me as a good big game player.

Respected on and off the field, Michael Green has been and remains an outstanding servant of the club.

Michael Green

High-marking and reliable, Michael Green was Richmond's top ruckman before retiring, aged 24, in 1972, to pursue a law career. He was lured back to star in the 1973 and 1974 premiership teams before retiring again at 27.

1966-71,
1973-75

I played in four premierships. I did not play in any losing Grand Finals. That's a very good strike rate.

In the 1967 premiership I sat on the bench. I was 19th man and never made it on the field. I was picked in the side for the second semi-final against Carlton. On the morning of the match I woke up with a very sore left shoulder. I couldn't lift it. We had the Under 19s playing that morning and the club doctor Vern Vivian was at the ground so I went to him and pulled out of the side.

You will remember Neville Crowe got rubbed out after the second semi. He had missed John Nicholls with a slap but still got suspended. That's a terrible injustice in Crowe's football life. Kevin Shinners was named emergency for the Grand Final side. So with those players out, John Ronaldson and myself came into the team and the club decided to start Ronaldson on the field and put me on the bench.

I've always assumed they chose Ronaldson ahead of me because I spent all of 1967 playing as a permanent back pocket. Ronaldson spent that year as a ruckman and forward-pocket player. They probably felt they would get more value out of him. History proved their decision correct because he kicked three telling goals.

With the game always close, I just assumed Tommy Hafey thought there was nowhere to use me so I stayed on the bench. In hindsight I can understand his decision.

When the siren went for the 1967 premiership, I didn't feel part of the victory. If you see any photos from the match, I am running around the ground with my tracksuit on. I never took it off. I reckon deep down it might have been a contributing factor to me playing well in the 1969 premiership year.

In the room after the game, chairman of selectors Bob Dickinson said, 'Bad luck Michael, the way things worked out we just couldn't put you on'. I didn't break down completely when he said that, but I did cry. I didn't feel a part of it.

I feel a part of it now, however. I played in other premierships with the same blokes and they are all my friends. I'm happy to have that premiership medals they gave us. I'm happy to be known as someone who has played in four premierships. I've got some friends, outside of football circles, who are prepared to give me a jab and tell me that I didn't actually play in one of my four!

My memories of the 1967 are of Royce Hart's great mark, and Fred Swift's mark over the goal line. I've got a general memory of 'Bugsy' Barrot bursting out of the centre with great dropkicks. And, of course, Ronaldson's drop-kick goal from the pocket. He told me once his only thought with that kick was to get it up in the square quickly for Paddy Guinane to contest the mark.

I can't remember most of my football career. It's not that I have a bad memory, it's just there are so many things in my footy career I cannot recall. Not long ago I was watching the 1973 Grand Final and Ian Stewart grabbed the ball out of the centre and I suddenly had a flash in my mind – 'I'm going to mark this'. Yet without that video prompt I couldn't remember it. Something deep in the back of my memory was obviously triggered. I saw another game against Carlton replayed on Foxtel. They beat us and the commentators said 'Richmond's forward line was

Born
May 14, 1948

Played
Richmond
1966-71,
1973-75,
146 games
83 goals

Interviewed
May 1, 2012

no good today, apart from Michael Green who kicked three goals'. I couldn't remember the match. I couldn't remember any of the goals. Nothing.

However, I can remember Laurie Fowler's bump on John Nicholls in the 1973 Grand Final. I was in the forward pocket next to Neil Balme and we looked at each other and just smiled. I remember thinking to myself, 'Gee, wasn't that good!'

I had a very good year in 1969. I played consistently well for the whole year. That was also my last year at university. The following year, Rita and I got married (on January 1, 1970) and I started as an articled clerk on 18 January. Football became third in my priorities behind married life and my career as a solicitor. I assumed that's why I never had a year again as consistent as I did in 1969.

One bloke who was a big help in 1969 was Mike Bowden. At boundary throw ins, Mike would compete in the ruck contest, and commit the opponent, so that I would come over unopposed and get the last shot. This idea had been suggested to us by Roy Wright. Roy and Neville Crowe were the two people I would get advice from about ruck play.

Old Jack Dyer was never around the club at that stage. But I did get to see Jack not long before he passed away. There was some legal issue involving him, and a barrister rang me in my office and said 'I have someone here you would know'. So I went upstairs and there was Jack. I sat beside him and we had a chat. He remembered me and spoke about the past. It was a really nice little moment.

I wasn't a great player. That's not humility, that's the truth. Great players were Francis Bourke and KB, who came to play week in, week out. I played well when the chips were down. I had a well-founded reputation for not being the most reliable person when it was a horrible day or it was a nothing day.

As you get older, and the longer you get away from playing, the better you become in people's minds. I say to my wife, 'they don't remember how many shocking games I played'. But I do.

"I've never met a Richmond supporter I didn't like" – Michael Green with his fans.

What made me a good ruckman? Someone said to me once that my greatest ability was to read the play and I think there was a fair bit in that. But I had to be switched on. I never had a motivation problem in big games, but in other games I did, because I had other priorities in life. Big games were important for me. I guess it was my ego, in that I didn't want to embarrass myself in important games in front of so many people.

Footy wasn't your job back then. Everyone had other jobs and mine was as a lawyer. My first priority was to be successful as a lawyer because that was what would support my family – it wasn't going to be football.

I retired at the end of 1971 when I was 23. I was struggling to maintain the priorities between work, football, and family. It was an easy decision because I had put in a poor second half of 1971.

In July 1971, my son Christopher was born. Also during that year I was approached by Graeme John (not the footballer) to join him in partnership as a self-employed lawyer. It was during the year that I decided it would be my last. The footy club was understanding of my situation – they always allowed me to cut corners at training for study purposes. They didn't try to talk me out of retirement.

In 1972, after retiring, I became a writer for *The Sporting Globe*. Ian McDonald, the leading writer, rang and asked me to write for *The Globe*.

I rang match reports through from the press box. They always had an experienced journalist with you in the press box. For me it was Graham Minihan, who had played 77 games for St Kilda. He came to all the games with me and taught me the craft.

I was asked to come back and play for Richmond 24 hours after the 1972 Grand Final loss. I had watched that Grand Final as a spectator. At 5pm on the Sunday, Rita and I were at home in Mentone and the phone rang and it was Graeme Richmond. He said 'what are you going to do next year?', and I told him I would train over summer and see how it goes. And that was it. Graeme offered me an additional $1000, which I assume came out of his own pocket.

I was so disappointed we had been beaten. My ego took over a bit as well, because I thought 'I could have done that, and I could kicked that'.

Michael Green takes a mark: 'Someone said to me once that my greatest ability was to read the play and I think there was a fair bit in that.'

In 1973 and 1974 I still struggled with balance. Family life, my legal practice and my football were all whirling together and so at the end of 1974 I retired again. I remember Paul Sproule saying to me 'Come on mate, we might be able to win the premiership again next year. This is becoming really special'. And I told him, 'it is too much, I can't keep doing it'.

So I retired again. Halfway through 1975 I was watching a game at North Melbourne that Richmond should have won and we got rolled (round 8), and the club rang me again and the next week I was playing. Tommy Hafey lived near me and would have seen me running in the mornings, so he knew I was still fit enough. It seems like I was always on call!

So I played against Carlton the following week. I kicked two goals on Geoff Southby. I always thought he was the best full-back I had seen.

I was involved in a famous moment during the 1974 Grand Final. Kevin Sheedy handballed over the man on the mark to me and I kicked a goal. How I ended in the goal square all by myself I still don't know.

I realised the pass was on. If Sheeds got it to me then it would be a certain goal; but I didn't know if he knew. So I'm watching Sheeds run in and all of a

Michael Green, the chairman of selectors, with coach Kevin Bartlett (right) during the 1991 season.

sudden he gets to a point where he should kick and he continues. He knows the handpass is on, and I know it is coming. I did think to myself that I would look a complete fool if I drop this. You will see in the footage that I don't take the handball in my hands, instead I let it come into my chest.

In 1974 the only way I felt we could lose was if North Melbourne played above themselves. We were a far better side. My worry about them playing above themselves was reasonable. Apart from Richmond supporters, everyone else was barracking for North to win their first premiership. I worried that the crowd would carry them over the line.

Sports psychologists say the great elation of victory lasts about 10 minutes. After that you start to go down and the emptiness starts to kick in and you think to yourself 'is this all it was about? We've lived this for the last 12 months, is this all it was for?'

During that 10 minutes, running a lap of the ground is great fun for Tiger supporters. I always knew where Rita sat and I always made eye contact with her and waved. In fact, in the 1969 Grand Final, after Graeme Bond kicked a vital goal in the last quarter, I ran back to the centre for the ball up and I looked to where I knew Rita was sitting and I waved to her and Dick Clay yelled out 'Don't do that Greeny, we haven't won yet' and I said 'yes we have'.

I was Reserves coach to Francis Bourke in 1982 and 1983. I can remember Michael Malthouse's fitness test before the 1982 Grand Final. I remember we were walking towards the race at Punt Road and then Bourkey put him through the test, bumping him. I've always thought what Francis did was a fair and reasonable thing to do before a Grand Final – any game in fact.

There's been controversy about whether the fitness test was too hard and whether a sound player might have finished up with an injured shoulder. Yes, it was a hard test, yes it was a tough test but that's what fitness tests are meant to be. I don't remember it being anything more than what it would have been in a game.

I also became Chairman of Selectors during Kevin Bartlett's time as coach. That experience was difficult because we weren't a talented side and the club was in financial trouble. For what it's worth I believe Kevin coached the team as well as they could be coached. We won games we never should have won. We beat Geelong down at Geelong in 1990, with Tim Powell playing the game of his life off the half-back flank gathering 29 possessions and getting three Brownlow votes. He 'cheated' outrageously – he didn't pick up his man! He was zoning off before zoning off was invented. Then there was the 'Mother's Day Massacre' when Jeff Hogg kicked 10 goals against Collingwood in round 8, 1991.

"We haven't done enough since 1980 for our fantastic supporters ... I think we should build a monument to Richmond fans."

It got to a stage where we had to beg people for money. We were no different from people who beg for money in the streets. We were like homeless people. We had to literally rattle tins in front of people to pay off our debts.

When I played, coming up through the Under 19s and Reserves, certain supporters 'claim' you. They put an ownership on you. They see you as a young player and they must think that 'he will be a good player' and they adopt you as theirs. I had one of those, a guy called Barry Page, who had a banner made up that read 'Mike Green 37', and he would hang it over the fence at every game. Barry was such a lovely guy. He died a few years ago and I didn't even know. I was so disappointed, because I wasn't aware he had died. I would certainly have gone to his funeral. Barry was a gentle man. Every time Rita had a baby, the first lot of flowers that arrived in the hospital came from Barry Page.

How would I like to be remembered? I'd like to be remembered as a Richmond person. My grandparents lived in Richmond, my father was born and raised in Richmond. I started in the Under 17s at the club under Bill Boromeo, then played under Ray 'Slug' Jordan and was involved with Tom Hafey, Barry Richardson, Francis Bourke and KB.

I have never met a Richmond supporter I didn't like. I reckon we have the best supporters in the League.

We haven't done enough since 1980 for our fantastic supporters. The Tigers win two games in a row and we get 70,000 the next week at the MCG. I think we should build a monument to Richmond fans.

Derek Peardon

Derek Peardon is the first Indigenous Australian to represent the Tigers, making his debut as a teenager in 1968.

1968-70

Born
24 September, 1950

Played
1968-70
20 games
1 goal

Interviewed
June 2018

I am a child of the Stolen Generation. I went to a boys' home when I was seven and was there until I was 15. My sister Annette and I were dropped off by the authorities on a September night. She and I were taken from our mum on Flinders Island because of neglect. Annette was left in the car and she went straight to the girls' home. Our mum got three months' hard labour for neglecting Annette and me. It took me years to find out all about this.

For a little boy from Cape Barren Island I will never forget it. I was crying and calling my sister Annette, who was 9, 'Mum!' 'Mum!' 'Mum!' I remember getting some pyjamas in a locker room and there were nearly 50 boys there at the time and I was that scared I wet my pyjamas. I was never ever a bedwetter, but it scared me going from Cape Barren to all of a sudden a place with 50 boys.

I've just about got over it now. I did have a talk to the ABC a while ago and I broke down and I had to stop for five minutes, but I've found out about my life and everything.

In 2006 Paul Lennon, the Premier of Tasmania acknowledged the Stolen Generation. There was a payment, and Annette made a lovely speech thanking the Government for acknowledging the Stolen Generation. I was by her side.

I can remember being on Cape Barren Island, about 5 years of age, and I had this little rubber football. Day in day out, I'd be on my own and I used to kick this football into a pine tree. I went back there in 2012 and that pine tree was still there. I can't kick much now, I've had 6 operations on one knee.

I can remember living on Flinders Island and Cape Barren Island, but I always call myself a Cape Barren Islander. I thought I was born there, but I was actually born at Whitemark on Flinders Island. I got all the paperwork from the Government some years ago as I tried to find out a bit about myself. They only tell you what they want to tell you I guess.

A few people have mentioned I'm a very strong-minded person. I never have thought of myself that way.

I started off playing with Youngtown Primary School in Launceston. I played my first games there, then I went to Kings Meadows High School just down the road. I never played every week—if you misbehaved you weren't allowed to play.

I was the first Indigenous player to play for Richmond. I think I might have been the first Tasmanian Indigenous player to play in the VFL.

In 1964 they picked out the best players from tryouts from the north, north-west and Hobart for a Tasmanian team. I was picked to play for Tasmania and we went to Western Australia for the Under 15 championships and I came equal Best and Fairest in the Carnival with a little rover from Western Australia, I'll never forget his name – Max Ford.

That's when clubs got onto me. Geelong, Carlton, St Kilda and Richmond flew over and had a talk with me. I got to play with Richmond because of St Kilda. I was only 14 when me and the Superintendent of the boys' home were guests of St Kilda at the Moorabbin Oval. That's where I met Ian Stewart, Darrel Baldock, and Berkley Cox who was playing on a half-back flank for Carlton that day.[1]

1 This was round 11, 1965

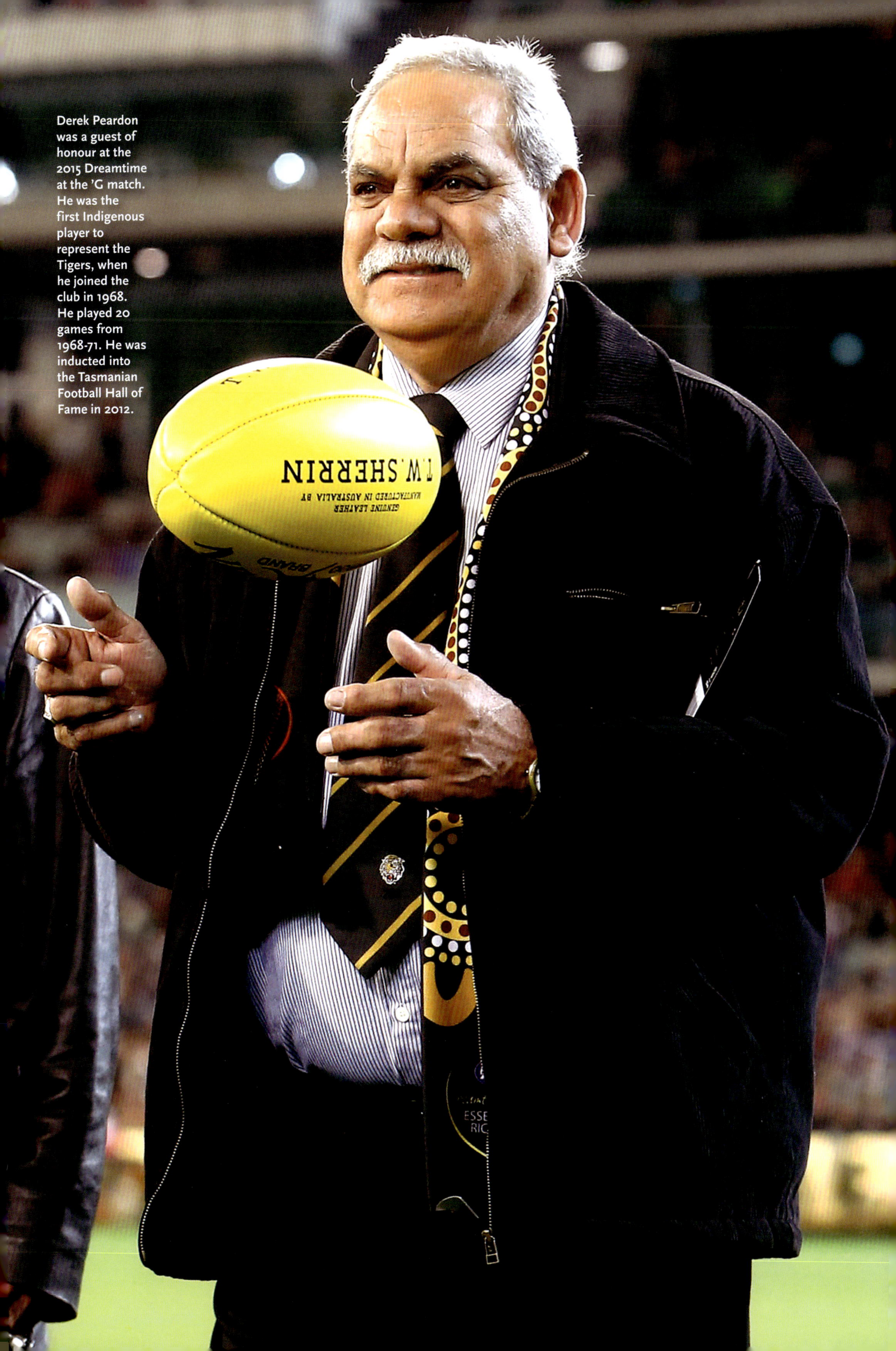

Derek Peardon was a guest of honour at the 2015 Dreamtime at the 'G match. He was the first Indigenous player to represent the Tigers, when he joined the club in 1968. He played 20 games from 1968-71. He was inducted into the Tasmanian Football Hall of Fame in 2012.

Derek Peardon's last game in Richmond colours was in the 1971 Reserves Premiership team. He returned to Tasmania where he played in Premierships for City South (Launceston) in 1972 and 1974.

We were up in our motel room and the phone rang and the superintendent said it was the Richmond Football Club asking if he could bring the boy down for a training run Sunday morning. They picked us up and that's how I played for Richmond.

They had snuck us out behind St Kilda's back. I wasn't even 15! I had a bit of a run with the Seniors at Punt Road on the Sunday morning. I can remember going down to the club rooms and having a small training session with all these great big senior players.

The board and coterie at the home thought the best place for me to be was the Richmond Football Club. They only told me a fortnight before I went to Melbourne. I flew into Melbourne on January 13, 1966. That date is in the files I got from the Government.

I was housed at 15 Goodwood Street, Richmond. We stayed with Keith Cleaver and his wife Elsie.

"I ran professionally for one year and won the Maryborough Gift at 6/1. I won about 600 dollars"

Keith was was a Phys Ed teacher and a trainer at Richmond. Other boys from the country stayed there as well: Paul Morrison, Daryl Cumming and Wilf Dickeson.

Our Under 19s coach was Ray Jordon. I'll never forget one day, we were playing in the U19s at Victoria Park against Collingwood and just on half time I went up to take a mark from behind and it come to the ground and they kicked a goal and put them a point or two in front. Jordon came out and called me a black this, and a black everything. That fired me up. I think I was the best on the ground after that. He came and thanked me afterwards, but I just think it was the wrong way to go about it. I've hated him ever since.

I came third and fourth in the Gardiner Medal (under 19s) and the Morrish Medal (Reserves) respectively. I was set for a career and injuries got me. It just wasn't meant to be.

I played U19s, Reserves and Seniors in the one year. My first game was one of the last games of the year (round 20, 1968) at the MCG against Melbourne. I was only 17. I came on in the last 10 minutes. it was my only game for that season.

It took me two seasons before I kicked my first and only goal. It was at the MCG, against Geelong. I flew down form the wing and Eric Moore, who was playing half-forward flank, marked and handballed to me and I kicked a goal on the run and I ran back to the centre and I remember a Geelong player said, 'black bastard'. It fired me up a bit.

They're might have been just the odd abuse from the crowd, but I can't remember that as much as a few from the players. A couple of players would call you black this, and black that. I used to concentrate on the game. Inside me it used to fire me up more when I heard that. It used to make you go that little bit harder. It was motivation.

I played throughout my career on the half-back flank. I couldn't get a game in the centre because you had Francis Bourke on one wing, Dick Clay on the other and Bill Barrot in the middle. That was the Victorian centreline! I had no hope even if I was best on ground every week in the Reserves. I played Under 13s premiership, Under 19s premiership, Reserves premiership and I was part of Richmond's 1969 premiership season (he played seven senior games in 1969). I'm in the team photo bottom right hand side.

Tom Hafey was a pretty hard man. I got on all right with him, but I was never that close. He was a hard taskmaster. He expected 100 percent every time you went out to train. He used to go on the pre-season runs and beat most of us. I know Kevin Bartlett and I used to come last in the long distance, we weren't built for running long distance. For sprint work we used to be up the front. We were built for speed.

I ran as an amateur for a season with St Stephen Harriers. They had their club rooms at the Punt Road Oval. Then I ran professionally for one year and thought I'd try to have a run at Stawell. The club wouldn't let me run at Stawell because the football season started at Easter time.

Bill Boromeo used to train me, Graeme Bond and Kevin Bartlett at Punt Road.

We went up to have a go at Maryborough on a New Year's Day. I won the Maryborough Gift at 6-1 with the bookies, winning about 600 dollars. Graeme Bond and I represented Richmond two years in a row for the Footballers' race which they have now on Grand Final Day. I won that two years in a row.

We ran at the Botanical Gardens, and a lot of 400s at Gosch's Paddock. Kevin, Graeme Bond and myself were guests of Percy Cerutty down at Portsea and we stayed for the weekend and ate his special food. He was a great man. I'll never forget he loaned me a book and signed it. We went up the famous sand dune and we thought we were fairly fit. You go up there about 8 times and that was it, but Herb Elliott I think he held the record 65 times non-stop.

Then everything went haywire with my football. I did my back. I missed nine games, played a couple in the reserves then back in the Seniors again the following season and then I did my knee and played only three senior games in 1971 but did play in the reserves Premiership side of 1971 against Essendon. I was on the wing and had a run on the ball. After that I just hopped on a plane and went back home, I was sick of Melbourne to be honest.

I've only been back to Melbourne once since. It was in 2015 for the Essendon and Richmond Dreamtime Game. That was the first time in 43 years I'd been back.

I was very nervous. It was very emotional and they gave me a yellow ball and I had to give it to one of the little kids as I was walking back off the ground. I autographed it and all the kids were jumping up and down and yelled out and put their hands out and there was a little boy just behind them and he was just looking at me as if to say can I have this ball and I gave it to him. He never said boo. And all these kids in front of him were yelling and screaming.

Actually, walking off someone yelled out 'Hello Derek,' and it was Neil Balme's brother Ian. I hadn't seen him for 43 years! It was very emotional. I was very nervous. I got through it. It was a good night. I stuck with Kevin Sheedy a fair bit but I hardly met any of my former players to be honest with you.

The supporters love their club. They're magnificent.

I still follow Richmond. I will never change.

Derek Peardon twice won the City-South (Launceston) best and fairest award and, in 1980 was named in City-South's Team of the Century.

Royce Hart

1967-77

Centre-half forward in the Richmond Team of the Century, Hart overcame knee problems to be one of the VFL's dominant forwards for a decade. He was a key member of the four "Hafey era" premierships, won best and fairest awards in 1969 and 1972, captained club and state, and was elevated to a Richmond Immortal in the Hall of Fame in 2008.

Born
Feb 10, 1948

Played
1967-1977
187 games,
369 goals

Interviewed
April 2007

I got six white shirts and a grey suit to sign with Richmond. The reason was that I was working in the bank and mum said I didn't have enough clothes. That's what Graeme Richmond said he would offer me if I came over. So I signed the form four and posted it back.

They got them from a little tailor shop on Lennox St (Richmond) run by a gentleman called Hersche. It's just over the road from the London Tavern, going up the hill on the left-hand side. He made them for me. I didn't get them until I got over there, and I went and got measured for them. Had to wear them every day for the job as I was a teller in the Commonwealth Bank.

We were playing in front of 100,000 people by the end of the 1966 reserves Grand Final. It was a good preparation for the 1967 Grand Final. I kicked the last goal (in '66). The ball came in quickly, as our style of play demanded it at that particular time, and I just led out and marked it. I can remember Barry Teague coming up to me at that stage; I was 50 or 60 metres out, and he said 'We are a point down, for Christ's sake kick a point!'

So I kicked a torpedo punt and it went straight through the middle. The siren went about 30 seconds after the bounce back in the centre.

The players would have breakfast at Punt Road and we'd go across to the MCG and some would say, 'What if I make a fool of myself in front of 100,000 people?' I used to think the other way; if you thought you could

A triumphant Royce Hart emerges from the crowd after receiving the 1973 premiership cup.

RICHMOND FOOTBALL CLUB

Patron: J. M. FLEMING, M.B.E., Esq.

PREMIERS:
V.F.L. .. 1920, 1921, 1932, 1934, 1943.
V.F.A. .... 1902, 1905.

RUNNERS-UP:
V.F.L. .... 1919, 1924, 1927, 1928, 1929, 1931, 1933, 1940, 1942, 1944.
V.F.A. .... 1903, 1904.

YARRA PARK,
RICHMOND, E.1

"The Tigers"

President:
R. H. DUNN, Esq.

Secretary:
G. J. RICHMOND,
90 Barkers Road, Hawthorn

Phones:
Ground .. 42-2222
Private .. 86-8371

Please Address Correspondence:
Box 48, P.O.,
Richmond, E.1

24/6/65.

Mr. Royce Hart,
Hobart, Tas..

Dear Royce,

In reply to your letter of the 20th., which I was very pleased to receive and to note your real interest in our approach.

We shall be very pleased to purchase a suit for you, as well as six shirts and a pair of shoes, in order to start you in your job over here. Besides reimbursing you for your accountancy studies annually as you pass each stage, which we have already agreed to do, we shall pay you a minimum of £2-10-0 per week during the football season. Should you be selected in the Reserves or First Teams, you will, of course, be paid in the normal way.

Your accommodation will be in Richmond or close by and you will pay either £5-10-0 or £6 per week board.

Naturally, all your expenses allied with you coming to us to commence work, which would have to be by January 20th. at the latest, will be paid by us.

This letter can be taken as an official agreement, binding on us.

Looking forward to seeing you in October and very best wishes for continued success with your football. Kindest regards to Mum and Dad.

Yours sincerely,

Graeme Richmond

(Graeme Richmond)

The letter of offer from Graeme Richmond that secured Hart's services for six shirts and a suit.

play football okay, they could see how well you could play. That was a good stage to perform on.

None of us had played in a final before that year in 1967. In the leadup the biggest doubt about Richmond was that we had no finals experience. We didn't even have one player. Grand Final day it was 28 degrees and the ground was rock hard. The centre wicket and the practice wicket were like concrete. And from half-time on I had blisters on my feet. I was stuffed, I was really tired.

(Hart's most famous mark came late in the Grand Final) It was at the 20-minute mark of the last quarter, over Peter Walker. The ball came out from the backline about a minute before that, and Peter Walker got control of the ball. It went down to the other end of the ground and then we got it back and kicked a point. I couldn't mark the ball (from the kickout) because it was going over my head; Peter Walker was next door, so I just jumped on him.

I used to high jump at school in Tasmania and I had a record which lasted 30 or 40 years; I used to practice high jumping a lot and I reckon that did help. It was the most publicised mark I ever took, I don't know if it was the best one.

But at that time of the game I suppose it was important to the side. After that I just got up and kicked it down to Paddy Guinane who dropped the ball in the goal square.

I flew in to play (from interstate) on Saturdays in 1969 having completed minimal training. I was in the army in Sydney and I had one or two training sessions when I was on leave. I trained in the army with John Scarlett, Matthew Scarlett's father. All we did was have a couple of kicks for half and hour in the park near the army barracks. And we used to fly backwards and forwards from Sydney to Melbourne each week. I was only there for the first three or four weeks of the season, then I got transferred to Adelaide.

I was in Woodside, about 60 kilometres out of Adelaide in the hills, and I used to come down to Glenelg and train under Neil Kerley one night a week. I would come across to Richmond on Friday night, stay at my girlfriend's place, play on the Saturday and go back on Sunday afternoon. I ended up winning the Best and Fairest for Richmond that year and we won the Grand Final.

"We played Geelong in the 1969 first semi-final and won by 20 goals. That was the game when we decided we were good enough to win the premiership."

A junior high jump champion, Hart used his exceptional leap to arrive at packs late ... and simply go over them.

We had to win our last six games in 1969 to get into the four, and we played Carlton at Princes Park and Bill Barrot kicked eight goals. Later we played Geelong in the first semi-final and we won by 20 goals. That was probably the game when we decided we were good enough to win the premiership, as Geelong were a pretty fierce side at that time.

I think I struggled a bit in the 1969 Grand Final. This might sound strange, but I had problems. See, we had to march in Adelaide with army boots which had heels on them, then I would come across to Melbourne and we would put these football boots on with no heels.

And I got shin soreness really badly. I was under contract to Adidas and I got them to put a heel in my boots – they all have them now.

We were pretty basic with our gameplan. One thing about our gameplan, we always had confidence that it was built for big games on the MCG and I think that was the reason why we won four premierships in eight years.

I was captain in 1972 (the losing Grand Final versus Carlton) and that was the biggest disappointment about that particular period. I think that the players were that desperate to try and redeem themselves in 1973. I thought I wouldn't want a record of being the captain of the side and getting in the Grand Final and losing two in a row.

"Half-time came and we were six or seven goals down. Graeme Richmond said to Tommy Hafey: 'You had better bring Royce on'."

In 1973 I had a torn cartilage and I built it up through gym work so I could play in the finals. And the doctor said for the preliminary final against Collingwood that I should sit on the bench and see how it goes.

So half-time came and we were six or seven goals down and we got into the room and there was me, Graeme Richmond and Tommy Hafey. Graeme said to Tommy: 'You had better bring Royce on.' And Tom said, 'If you bring him on now you won't have him for the Grand Final.' Graeme said: 'We won't get to the fucking Grand Final if he doesn't come on.' So I came on and got a couple of kicks and we won the game. I kicked a couple of important goals and I think that restored a bit of confidence. I played reasonably well in the Grand Final, I had over 20 possessions. I got the cup off Sir Rohan Delacombe, who was the patron of Richmond at that time.

We had to go up in the cricket stand, walk up through the crowd, and he was just sitting up there and he just gave us the cup and we walked back through the crowd.

Opposite page: Royce Hart and teammate Barry Richardson during the Tigers' golden era.

I can remember after the 1974 Grand Final being really tired. I was stuffed. Then I went across to Punt Road and went into the Committee Room and there was Jim Ahern, who was the VRC Chairman of Stewards, a fanatical Richmond supporter, and he had come down to celebrate the win. We sat down for half and hour before anyone else got back, just talking about the game.

The fact is, I was short (187cm) for a key position player, and they'd always drop a ruckman back at centre-half back. More often than not I was shorter than my direct opponent, so I used to stand off, basing it on the high-jump theory, and I'd run and let them judge where the ball was going and I'd jump in front of them.

If it was the high jump you don't stand at the bar and jump over, you go back and run in and jump high. I could jump a bit higher going across the front.

I took Mal Brown to the football the day of the Windy Hill brawl. I picked him up and took him out to Windy Hill. On the way out in the car he said to me 'Where is a good place to have a fight on this ground?' and I said, 'Not in front of the Essendon stand, they will all go mad!'

I wasn't playing that day. I was in the stands. When Brown was going up the race (after the fight) someone threw a can of beer at him; he caught it and I said, 'What you going to do with that?' He said, 'You wait and see.'

So the bloke is still standing outside and it must have been three or four minutes later, then Mal opens the door and hits the bloke over the head with the can of beer! I can also remember Graeme Richmond going through the air like Superman, he was very angry.

Ron Carson came down from the country in Victoria and set up a garage in Swan Street. He didn't know what colours Richmond were, but decided he should get involved in the local football club so he presented himself and down the track he became the treasurer of Richmond. He also ran a garage. We all got our cars fixed there, but whether they truly got fixed we don't know.

It was a really interesting place because the players used to go there for a drink and a bit of socialising in one of the back streets of Richmond. Tom Hafey backed it because he knew where the players were.

Today you have footballers going to nightclubs and getting in all sorts of trouble in the early hours of the morning. We just had this garage in Richmond and we won four premierships while we were meeting there. There would be someone there nearly every night.

It was just a get together. We all used to meet, and that was where I first socialised with Jack Dyer. He walked in with Brian Hansen, his ghost writer for *The Truth* newspaper.

Francis Bourke displayed utter determination to win the football at all costs. He was inducted into the Richmond Hall of Fame in 2002, and elevated to Immortal status in 2005.

Francis Bourke

1967-81

Francis Bourke is the middle link in three generations of RFC football, for whom he achieved almost everything. Yet an agonising loss as Tiger coach in the 1982 Grand Final haunts him today. In 2005, Bourke was named the club's fourth 'Immortal'.

The Bourkes are an institution in Nathalia. Old Michael Bourke, the great grandfather, actually selected land west of Nathalia in the 1880s. He applied to the government to be allocated a piece of land. He then had to clear it, build fences, build his house, cultivate and start a farm. And he had 18 children, some of whom died, and out of that came my grandfather and my great uncle, who then became the two patriarchs of the Bourkes.

My grandfather was Francis William Bourke, my father is F.M. Bourke and I'm F.W. Bourke. So I was always called Francis, because it was old Frank and young Frank. It was nice I suppose in some respect that you passed on the name from one generation to the next, but not very practical.

I can remember my first footy and my first set of football boots. They weren't really football boots, they were my school boots with leather soles that my father tacked in the knock-in stops, which were prevalent in those days. We were playing an interschool game against Numurkah State School and on the day that we played the match, my father sent me off to school with these knock-in stops in my normal boots and I was able to wear my best shoes to school. So I came home and my father ripped the stops out and the next day I went back to school in my old normal boots again.

I was diagnosed with a symptom called aortic stenosis. It was, broadly speaking, the slight narrowing of the aorta. It was picked up as a murmur by our doctor at Nathalia, who at the time was quite concerned. He said I shouldn't do anything that was physically heavy, and that included playing sport, until they had time to examine it and monitor it. Here I was feeling plenty normal and all of a sudden some bloke says, 'I don't think he should play sport'.

My mother said, 'That's it, you're not playing sport.' After a while she bought me down to Melbourne to see one of the leading heart people in Melbourne. He said, 'I don't think there are any problems and I can't see why you can't lead a normal life.' So I went for it. All the time I felt it was a waste of time. I have never felt any side effects. It was something the media picked up through my father's association with Jack Dyer and Brian Hansen, and of course they loved it. It became a bit of embarrassment for me. I think it has been exaggerated.

If I was growing up in these times I would have probably been shunted across to the Murray Bushrangers. They train at Shepparton one night of a week, which is three-quarters of an hour drive from Nathalia, and the other night in Wangaratta, which is an hour-and-a-quarter drive. I found it very hard playing for Nathalia because I was a boy playing against men and I was playing key position, full-forward, centre half-forward and I was 17, 18 and 19 years old. That in a way helped my development; I didn't get things my own way and I didn't dominate the competition at all. These were rough and tough times with rough and tough men.

My father was a mentor but he never came and watched me because he didn't like watching football. He saw very few games I played, even right through to the League level. I think it was to do with getting too worked up, he didn't want to make a spectacle of himself, or didn't want to become critical, those sort of issues. And I think they're issues I grapple with when I go to the footy, too, because of my profile.

He used to hear things anecdotally and so we used to talk about things like that. Lots of things we talked about

Born
Apr 2, 1947

Played
Richmond
1967-1981
300 games,
71 goals

Interviewed
Jan 18, 2006

I still remember, and still think he was right what he told me. A lot of things he told me, not only about football or cricket, I still tell my kids. As I got older and we were working on the farm together, I played football on the Saturdays, he'd milk the cows, he'd play golf on Sundays and I'd milk the cows.

He kicked 46 goals in the first seven or eight games for Richmond and led the goalkicking in 1946 by 11 or 12 goals. I did enjoy looking at his scrapbooks, which I learnt all this from – he never told me this. He'd talk mainly about the personalities, and Jack Dyer was a huge part of his experience at Richmond ... he's really not one to talk about himself at all.

"Roger Dean was tough by any definition. For Roger it was win at all costs and it was his own costs, too. There are other tough players around, but Roger was so impressive."

I wrote to Roy Wright as a kid and he sent me back a photo of himself, autographed, which I thought was fantastic. Looking back I am even more appreciative because of my own life and how it has evolved, I can understand the trouble he went to. I was in primary school when that was happening. I suppose Roy Wright was the man for me.

Graeme Richmond saw me play for Assumption College, that started it. Graeme carted Jack Dyer around basically as the foot in the door man. But I always barracked for Richmond because of my father – I didn't need much talking or encouragement to come to Richmond.

The country wasn't zoned in those days, so you could go where you like, but you had to sign a Form Four and that expired after two years. Then you had to sign again. In my case I didn't want to play anywhere else but Richmond. But I wasn't highly sought after, as Dick Clay and other people were. It was only basically Graeme signing a hundred to get one that saw me at Richmond.

My mother wouldn't let me go until I was 20. So I signed as an 18-year-old in 1964, and I didn't go until I was 20. I think my father could foresee a bit of a problem with the farm because I was home working on the farm, but he was certainly happy for me to try my luck and I don't think he thought I would make it either. Basically it was a 'have a look around, have a go, see how you go and then, when all that's over, come back'. Not that I ever left, really. It was only in the fourth year at Richmond that I stopped working on the farm, because I was coming back and forward to play. By that time I was an established player and played in two premiership sides. It was only after that I came to Melbourne to live. I never thought I'd make it really. So I played a couple of games with Richmond on permit in 1965 and 1966, then came to Richmond full-time in 1967. I never saw Richmond play until I actually played for Richmond.

I can remember at Assumption, as I grew older, having a photo inside my locker of Richmond's Ian Hayden taking a strong mark in front of Bernie Massey, who was full-back for Melbourne. I met him in the rooms one day and I said, 'I used to have a photo of you in my locker at school,' and he said, 'Isn't that funny, some of my kids have got your photo on the wall at our place.' Graeme Richmond said Hayden was a very good player and they would have liked to have played him at centre half-back but his knees packed up.

The first year I stayed at the Glensborrow Hotel on Wellington Parade. On Friday I went over and worked at the footy ground as assistant curator to Peter Mead. Graeme gave me that job; the first job was that there were asphalt terraces right around the outer and there were weeds starting to grow up, like cape weed. So it was my job to start off and pick all those weeds starting from the end of the big old stand, right around to the outer to where the terraces finished at the Cricket Club members. It took most of the year to do it because I was on there one day a week. I can remember looking at the ground on TV one day, because Neville Crowe did an advertisement, and in the background you could see the terrace half clean of weeds one way and completely overrun with weeds on the other way. I was the only one who appreciated the background.

The next year Graeme gave me a car, he told me club president Ray Dunn paid for it. It was a green Holden 1964 EH with a white top, it was fantastic. Instead of coming on the bus on Thursday and going home on the bus Sunday night, I'd drive home after the game and drive down on Thursday for training and stay in Melbourne on the Friday. The next year Graeme had me working at a hotel one day a week.

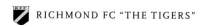

I can remember Rex Hunt buying a car and Michael Patterson pinched his keys while he was out training. This was a brand new one he bought. First night, he drove it down to the club, out he went to training and while he was out there, Patto got the keys out of the bag that Charlie Callandar had valuables in, opened up the car and drove it around further behind the Cricket Club. So Rex came out and it was gone. Of course, everyone was in on the know and Rex was very upset – they didn't have the heart to string it out much longer.

I suppose the player I admired most was Roger Dean. He had such an impact as a player. I was aware growing up that Roger was a bit of a cheeky sort of a player, and that Ron Barassi got rubbed out for belting him in the last game of the year and missed the finals. When I got to Richmond I saw just how good he was. In my first year he played back pocket and I also saw how small he was. But Roger could mark with the big blokes, he was strong for his size.

As a back pocket player his racket was cutting across the lead of the full-forward and taking his run. I can remember in 1967 he took a spectacular mark just jumping on someone's back. But he's only 5'8" (173cm) and genuinely tough. Now, he was tough by any definition. In the 1969 Grand Final, Roger was running down the ground bouncing the ball, heading towards our goal, and Kevin Hall, who is 6'3" (191cm) and about 14 stone (90kg), was coming at him, And Roger got his kick away so late that Hall was always going to collide with him so that we got a penalty kick down the ground – wow, that's real tough.

And he continued on longer than the others of that era. Paddy Guinane had retired after 1968, Fred Swift had gone after 1967, 'Patto' went to coach Norwood in 1970, 'Bull' Richardson had gone to South Melbourne, Crowe retired, but Roger was actually still a good player. Captain of 1969, he played until 1972 and went out captain of Richmond's seconds premiership team.

He got full marks from me for doing that, so this just added to all the reasons why I like Roger and admire him. For Roger it was 'win at all costs' and it was his own costs too.

I was determined. I think I had good understanding and instinct for the game. I thought I was quite stylish but when I looked at the TV I realised I wasn't quite as stylish as I thought. I was motivated, it was important to me to play and play well. I think I had more weaknesses than people realised and I tried to keep pretty quiet. And I think if people had known the weaknesses I had they might have been surprised, like a battle for confidence, battle for self-belief, battle for motivation. They're all things that vary from one minute to the next, one week to the next and one year to the next. I think they were issues I had to never take for granted.

Bourke's attack on the ball ensured he is remembered as one of the club's most fearless players.

I never regarded myself as a particularly gifted player. I just couldn't believe my luck that the ball came to me when it did. As I got older and slower I really had to minimise the opportunities for exploitations in those parts of the game that I had deficiencies in and maximise my strengths.

My best season individually was 1970, when I played on the wing. I won the best and fairest. It was my first year living in Melbourne, playing and training. But I think I had more valuable seasons for Richmond as I was moved to the backline and started to play on players who were more important and integral to the opposition's prospects of winning the game. On the wing I had a physical advantage over a lot of players I suppose. From an individual point of view that was my best year. But, as I said, I think I had more important roles to play in subsequent years.

Bourke is famous for playing with a broken leg, though he now admits the story is a myth.

I've kept it a secret. Don't tell my kids. I always told them when I broke my leg at Glenferrie (that) I actually broke it on the Thursday night before the game and played on the Saturday with it, just to enhance the myth. I broke the fibula bone in my left leg, which was not a weight-bearing bone, but that was sufficiently serious to have me come off the ground. At the time I didn't know it was broken, I just knew I heard this crack as I slipped to dodge an on-coming Hawthorn player.

I had the ball and as I put my foot out to go that way, my foot slipped and I heard this crack, fell over and basically tried to see if it would come good and it didn't. It happened at the swimming pool end of Glenferrie Oval and our rooms were behind the goals at the other end, so I just walked off the ground. At the time it was sore; only later, when it cooled down, I knew I couldn't walk anymore. I was given some kudos for being tough, walking off the ground with a broken leg.

Technically it was, but the reality was it was just sore. I was able to walk, so I did, but I knew I couldn't play any more. I spent six weeks in plaster ... it probably took a couple of years before the soreness went. Some people say that was the start of me not being as quick. I'm not sure about that – my knee injury had more to do with that. See, I was only 22 when this happened. I think I played my best football at 24, 25 and 26 years of age.

The Bourke-Barrot-Clay centreline never got beaten. Ever. It was always Barrot-Bourke-Clay, first, second and third best on ground. It was only a matter of who came first, second, or third and we just steamrolled the opposition week after week, year in, year out. And all that has been really perpetuated by Tom Hafey. And so it suited the club and marketing. All in all, I would have played about 100 games on the wing, but the times we actually played together on the line is substantially less. I think the actual figure is 31 times we were picked. When I told Tom Hafey that he said, 'Well, shoot the bloke who found that out.'

The bloodied eye picture that helped cement the Bourke legend at Punt Road.

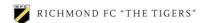

The 'bloodied eye' picture is, once again, a bit of a situation that looked worse than what it was. I got a cut when teammate Greg Strachan and I collided at Arden Street. He got me a beauty but we were both going different directions at the ball and were expecting each other to give way and I came off second best. It was a nuisance while it bled, and I couldn't see properly. It was crimson and, with colour TV, all the embellishments and heroics have been attached.

My first game as coach was against Fitzroy at VFL Park Waverley, which we won. Robert Walls was coaching and he had just introduced the huddles at the kick out. I think we led most of the day and I can remember Kevin Bartlett saying to me after the game how difficult it was to counter (the huddle) as a player. I didn't worry about it, perhaps I should have. I think huddles are great but until someone keeps a stat as to how many goals it costs, as against how many goals it produces, I'll then assess whether it is worth the bloody trouble. I just reckon it has cost Richmond more goals over the years than what it has ever created.

Two Grand Final losses stick with Bourke: 1972 as player, 1982 as coach.

They were different, but both devastating. Of the two, the 1982 loss was the more difficult for me personally because I felt so responsible. There were issues that came up; you think, well, maybe if I did it this way or that way, when you're responsible for a whole group of people. In 1972, I was responsible for myself and accountable for the team with my own performance.

Whereas in 1982 I was accountable and responsible to the whole Richmond club, its supporters and the committee. It was a much bigger cross to bear, I suppose, and one that I really have never got over ... At the time, and subsequently, it's a period of intense disappointment for me. The 1972 situation was nullified to a larger extent by 1973-74, we got immediate pain relief. Which is why 1982 was the most disappointing part of my football life.

I read where Bartlett said one of the reasons he retired was because the training had become tougher, and it had. I made it tougher and my advisers made it tougher. And I think in Kevin's case, I should have given him preferential treatment; this is in hindsight. I think that was a mistake on my part. Whether he could have gone on I don't know. I've got a huge respect for his determination and will. He certainly was still quick and certainly was therefore a threat. I think he was finding it harder to come up each week, as you do when you grow older.

At 37, maybe he could have. He might have been encouraged to go another year if I had been a bit easier on him, in particular in terms of his training regime. But he had decided to retire before the 1983 season had finished anyway.

Bourke's approach to coaching mirrored that of his playing: complete commitment. Brian Taylor looks on.

I wouldn't have lost anything for being a 299-game player, just the same as Wayne Campbell for retiring on 297. No-one thinks any less of him as a player. One of the reasons that he retired was that he saw himself as being behind Kevin Bartlett, Jack Dyer and myself, which was a very nice thing to say, but I said to him, 'It's not too late to change your mind here, because this is only a bunch of numbers, you shouldn't retire because of that.'

I'm glad I got to 300. I couldn't have played one more game because I would have been in the seconds. I'd run my race. I had made up my mind that I was going to play for Richmond for as long as I absolutely could. But I elected to retire before I played in the seconds. I just knew I wouldn't have got back because I wasn't good enough anymore to play. I think I was born lucky, and in the right place at the right time.

Blair Campbell

It is rare that one player can be credited with introducing a new skill into football. But Blair Campbell did just that when, in 1966, he popularised the 'banana' kick, named by Campbell as the 'boomerang'. In a brief career, it became known as his trademark.

1966,'68

Born
Aug 20, 1946

Played
1966, '68
8 games,
12 goals

Melbourne
1969
12 games,
23 goals

Interviewed
Sep 23, 2005

Four generations of my family have played football. Starting with dad's grandfather Jack, then dad himself (Colin), then my two brothers, Allan and Christopher, and me. Then my own children, five boys, Tim, Luke, Steven, Nathaniel and Nicholas. And I'm glad they all played because it's a magnificent game. Dad played A Grade Amateurs for Collegians after leaving school, where he kicked 32 goals in a game for Trinity Grammar First XVIII. He had this remarkable finish to his career which could only happen back then. In 1946, he played for St Kilda seconds. In 1947, he played for Camberwell in the VFA and in 1948 he went back to Collegians in the Amateurs. So he went from League to Association to Amateur football in the last three seasons. I said to him, 'What number were you for St Kilda, dad?' and he said, 'We just used to pick our jumper up off the pile in the room.'

Geelong was my first team, probably because they were so good through the early '50s. The great footballers, Bernie Smith, Bob Davis, Fred Flanagan and Peter Pianto, they were a classic side and I've always been attracted to the skilful side of footy. Bob Davis is as good as he facetiously says he was. He was the Laurie Nash of his time. He'd grab the ball on the wing, start running down the field, bounce, bounce, bounce, and drop kick it into the square for a goal. That's how he'd play, fast as lightning and 14 stone (88kg). There was a guy called Noel Rayson, he was a left-footed half-forward flanker who played at full forward, he was the sort of player I would have liked to have been.

I was zoned to Richmond, which was an unfashionable side and was having a very low period. You wouldn't have picked Richmond by choice. Graeme Richmond wrote me a letter at one stage, saying 'Come play in the under 17s', but I was playing at Melbourne High School under 17s. I played in Ray Jordon's under 15 side in 1961, and in 1963 I had gone to East Malvern and was playing in the Federal League. That was the start of knee trouble for me. At some stage during that year Ray came to watch a couple of games; I trained at Richmond myself in the under 19s at the end of 1963, and started playing in 1964.

(Tommy Hafey) was the fittest person there, yet there were no weights at all. That's amazing, isn't it, when you think of Tom Hafey, physically strong. And you would think he would be very enthusiastic about weight training, but there was none. It was hard training. I wouldn't call it gruelling, however it might have been by the standards of the time.

For older players like Michael Patterson and Fred Swift, it must have been gruelling for them, because when we were doing the single file, Indian-style, around the Richmond ground in the mud and blood and the beer, they'd be sitting in the coach's box. And that's not an apocryphal story, it's true. I can remember seeing Swifty and probably Michael Patterson sitting there waiting until it was done. They would have played most of their footy in the era where training was not as intense.

Dad and I were listening in the time-honoured fashion to the footy sides on the radio, that's how I heard I had been selected. After I kicked seven goals in round 15 for the reserves I thought I would be a big chance to get a game, and I didn't. Funnily enough, I played another game and I thought it was an ordinary game and I was picked 19th man (in the seniors). In fact, I was a bit disappointed because 19th man could mean just watching.

My earliest memory of the game was running out after half-time when for some reason I replaced

Blair Campbell kicks the winning goal after the first siren, in his first game of League football. It was also his birthday. John Ronaldson looks on.

Peter Hogan. Even now I can remember running out and my feet not really touching the ground. I went to the forward pocket and in the back pocket was Herbie Matthews, a good player, and his dad had won the 1940 Brownlow. So I'm thinking, 'How am I ever going to get a kick?' That's the status that League football had.

This gigantic pack of players flew for the ball, with (Paul) Harrison from South Melbourne right in the middle, and he was a very good high mark, and the whole pack collapsed in front of me. All of a sudden the ball was just there, so I picked it up like in training and that was my first kick. I used a boomerang pass to Paddy Guinane. He was on an angle and, knowing Paddy, I don't reckon he would have kicked it.

"They had that peculiar game on World of Sport called touch football. It was really good fun, but that's when (my knee) went properly. I missed the whole season."

I then roved with Kevin Bartlett and had plenty of time on the ball, too. Michael Green was full-back on Austin Robertson and held him to six goals, which was a pretty good effort. I remember feeling comfortable and getting a few kicks, except for that early moment when I thought I would never touch the ball. I remember trying to baulk around Bob Skilton and getting caught holding the ball. And I remember one very embarrassing moment when I've grabbed the ball on the half-back line and I've attempted to pass it to a centreline player for Richmond, and I just missed the mark and a South Melbourne guy screamed down the ground and kicked a goal.

Jack Dyer was commentating that day and the first shot I had for goal was down in the St Kilda end; I would have been about 30 or 40 yards out and I got a free kick on the angle and I've gone for a boomerang kick, instead of kicking a torpedo or drop punt. So I've run out and hooked it back and missed my first shot to the right. Someone said to me later, 'Jack Dyer called that 'a helicopter punt'.' You know how Jack had that extraordinary way of words, and he came up with that expression already.

I knew the game was close and I knew the game was getting towards the end. I reckon it was Bill Barrot who came screaming out of the centre and attempted a drop kick and miskicked it. I took the mark overhead, standing by myself, 25 yards out, dead in front. The siren must have sounded but I didn't hear it. Isn't that strange? You know sometimes how you hear on replays of games where the umpire didn't hear the siren – I did not hear the siren at all. I knew it was over because I think people were starting to run out.

This will show you the era it was, I've gone for the torpedo. The sun's just coming down over the grandstand at South Melbourne and I'm trying to shield my eyes to kick. So when I did kick it, it was a very poor kick and just cleared the hands of the ruckmen in the goals and went through. So it was given a goal. But Matthews was on the mark and Skilton was there and there was some sort of protest about it being touched. I wasn't particularly aware of that, nor did that particular protest last long, people weren't yelling or cursing. I reckon they did touch it – it was such a poor kick and Skilton was there. I would say that Skilton was an honest man.

I just loved playing my first game of League football and the fact that I kicked the goal after the siren was all a bit surreal. There were three things that made it not quite as spectacular. One, the South Melbourne players were claiming it was touched. Two, it was a shocking kick. Three, I didn't hear the siren.

I called it the 'boomerang kick' because of its flight through the air. It was started by (Saints star forward) Bill Young. Dad loved Bill Young and so did the St Kilda crowd; the grandstand would rock when he went near the ball down at the Junction Oval. He didn't get it very often but they knew when he did he'd kick a goal. He was the sort of player that appealed to me – very skilful, fair and a magnificent kick.

I was just a young boy in the crowd watching him run out and snap the ball back over his left shoulder and I'm thinking, 'He is doing something radically different there. It's not the normal way people snap for goal, he is holding the ball really in the opposite direction to normal.'

And I watched him kick a few goals like that and started to experiment with it myself. Funnily enough, he played five years as a very successful player and everyone acknowledged him as a brilliant kick for goal, snap and torpedo, but no-one seemed to notice that he did anything different when he was snapping goals around corners or from a deliberate shot. Why didn't his teammates notice it? Why didn't the press notice it? Why didn't his opponents notice it and copy it?

People just called him a 'freak kick for goal'. So when he retired in 1961, the kick went with it.

"Tommy was the fittest person there ..." Hafey (centre) puts (from left) Neville Crowe, Mike Patterson, Alan Richardson and Frank Dimattina through their paces at the Caulfield racecourse.

The kick disappeared altogether until I started using it at Richmond and for some reason people started to notice it. I'm not sure why. A few people from other clubs even used to start copying it when I used it. St Kilda players were saying to me 'We are kicking it in the rooms', it was a novelty kick.

I reckon a football historian put it accurately when he said I 'popularised' it. I think that's a good word. Even though not too many people were using it after I finished.

The secret is you have to be a good kick of the football for a start. And it's the angle it hits the boot that's important – to me it's held at a 45-degree angle across your body. It is a very good kick for keeping the ball in play when you're running tight to the boundary, and of course it makes impossible goals look easy.

One of my bitter regrets would be that I didn't get a chance to play in the 1967 (premiership) season. I'd got into the firsts at the end of 1966 and played well, yet funnily enough, even at the end of 1966, I couldn't even kick on my right foot. The knee was dodgy then. I played cricket for St Kilda that summer and I was batting at Prahran one day in the seconds and I noticed something clicking in the leg. The next day, they had that peculiar game on *World of Sport* called touch football. It was really good fun, but that's when it went properly. Eventually I had the cartilage out of the right knee and missed the whole season and coached the Little League.

Half-way through the 1968 season I semi-seriously asked for a clearance to Melbourne and at the end of the year I got it. I would have preferred to stay. They were very good, Richmond, and I knew they were going to keep being very good and I thought it wouldn't be that easy to get a game regularly. Melbourne had been a great club and were struggling. I thought I would be a better chance of playing regular senior football there.

I was only playing in the seconds and probably thought I should have been doing better, and I didn't go to training so I was dropped for the Monday seconds game as a one-week discipline. It was around that time I looked for a clearance to Melbourne.

I should have gone to training but three nights were enough for me. I played against Richmond once and I only played that one season at Melbourne (1969) and then the knees gave way and I never played League football again.

Neil Balme

Neil Balme has had a career in football like no other. He played for Subiaco before joining the Tigers in 1970, and ended his playing career in 1982, while a playing-coach with Norwood in the SANFL. He coached Norwood to the 1984 Premiership, was later coach of Woodville-West Torrens, then Melbourne, before embarking on a management role—firstly at Collingwood, then Geelong, then Collingwood again. He returned to Tigerland as Football Manager in 2017.

1970-79
2017-

Born
15 January 1966

Played
Richmond
1970-79
159 games
229 goals
Premierships
1973-74

Interviewed
May 2018

What does a Football Manager do? (laughing) If you win he takes the credit, and if you lose he finds someone to blame. The way footy has developed these days you are across all of the areas of footy—how are the coaches going, do the doctors need support, have we got enough people on matchday, what are the recruiters doing, what's the List Management strategy, are we reporting back to the Board. It's actually all-encompassing.

There's not a lot of specific hard work to do, it's more oversight. Even now the contracting of players is done by the List Manager. In the old Football Manager days, I would have done that. Alan Schwab did all of that in my playing days. He was GM of Footy plus Footy Manager plus CEO really. He was outstanding, so much energy. Graeme Richmond was just pulling the strings. One of the great things about Schwabby was that he would offer you something before you asked. It's not necessarily a negotiation tool, but seeing where all your people are, where they fit, trying to make them feel as though they are important and belong. One example is you don't wait for someone to come knock on your door and say *I need some more money*.

That's what we try to do these days. There are some adversarial parts of negotiating a contract but you've got to make that as little as possible. The reality is the Salary Cap pot is what it is, is what it is, is what it is. You can't do much about it so you've got to go to all of your players and say you need to fit in here somewhere, and someone has to make a decision on where you fit and we will try to do it openly and give you every chance to understand where you are so you can make a choice—do I want to be in this or not. That's a bit of an extension to the way Schwabby did it.

I think I am pretty good at the human side of things, understanding how people fit and making them understand where they belong and making them feel valued. Because all we've got in football is people. It's just a bunch of people pulling together. If you're not pulling together you're not going to win. If you are pulling together you've got a much better chance. That's what I try and do more than anything else.

I coached in Adelaide for a long time and coached a bit here. So I've been pretty involved, but I've always had the ability to be relatively normal at home which is sometimes not easy to do. It's a consuming business, but you've got to be able to be the dad, the husband, the normal bloke, the neighbour.

I spoke to Richmond a few times in the 1980s (to potentially coach). We did go a little mad when you think about it, which did put me off a little. Tommy Hafey had been such a wonderful coach and we decided to change him—was that a good idea? "Bones" (Barry Richardson) comes in for a couple of years and we think *oh that's no good*, though I thought he did a pretty good job. Then TJ (Tony Jewell) comes in and we win a flag and one year he doesn't and he's out! Then Bourkey (Francis Bourke) is in.

They did go mad. I did talk to them a couple of times about the possibility of coaching but I didn't

Neil Balme dashes onto the MCG for the Round 9 match against Collingwood at the MCG, leading Gareth Andrews. Balme kicked 3.3 in that match, and was a significant performer in the 1973-74 Premierships. He returned to Richmond in 2017 as the club's General Manager–Football.

think it was for me at that stage. I did say to them 'Who appointed him, him, him and him' and they said 'Oh we did' and I asked 'Who sacked him, him, him and him' and they said 'Oh we did'. I said, 'well why do you think I'm going to be any different from them?' I think it was probably the right thing to do.

BALME REFLECTS ON SOME OF THE "VIGOROUS" MOMENTS IN HIS CAREER:

I've grown with the game over 50 years. To see what is okay now and what was relatively okay then, I think *oh god that doesn't look all that good*. But I think back to what my mindset was, I never played angry. It was just this is the stuff we have to do to be any good and this is my part to play.

Off the field I've never been in a fight—that's not my nature. I was never angry, it was just shit you had to do. I look back and I think *how do you manage to justify that type of behaviour*, but the times were a bit different.

"The 2017 Premiership was an emotional experience. I was very very happy"

I often hear Leigh Matthews say 'that was then this was now'. If you talk to Leigh he's not a nasty person at all but as a player very aggressive and very confrontational because that's kind of the way we had to play in those days.

Getting away with it isn't an excuse but that's relatively accepted—if they do it you do it. It certainly wasn't personal and again in my case there was no anger and I thought no nastiness, but there probably was seemed to be by the opposition. That was part of the intimidation factor. It is a little bit hard to rationalise.

One of my kids, Will, loves his footy but he hadn't seen me play. Because I finished relatively early, and one of the other kids gave him the 'Sensational Seventies' DVD for Christmas. He's 6 or 7 years old watching it and he goes 'Dad is that you!' he couldn't' believe it. The only good side effect was he did what he was told—for a little while—as he wasn't too sure how I was going to respond.

I don't suppose the old Carlton players I run into are in love with me, but I get on well with them. Even Geoff Southby and that's a famous incident (in the 1973 Grand Final, Balme ko'd Southby with a whack that may have cost him eight matches in this era) where you look at it and say *that's pretty ugly*. David McKay and I worked on radio with and got on really well.

I remember running into John Elliott when I was doing some work on the radio a few years ago. He said off-air, 'You wouldn't have done what you did if Big Nick (John Nicholls) was still on his feet'. (Nicholls had been concussed earlier in the match). I was a little taken aback by it and then I said, 'I feel a bit better about now because you are still worried about it and it was 25 years ago," which is a little unkind by me, but they probably still think about it.

I'm kind of a Richmond guy deep down. When you play for the club that's where you kind of belong, but because I've worked in footy for such a long time I'd never really allowed myself to have had the realistic dream of going back to Richmond. Obviously I've always warmed to them and I'm pretty good mates with Dan Richardson, so I was close enough anyway. But it was a really opportune thing as it turned out and the best thing that ever happened to me really.

I always look on the positive side. I thought Richmond was okay, but I had no thought that we were as good as we were though. You always talk positively and we weren't too bad but I think the reality of the last four or five games of 2016 is they made a conscious decision to play a couple of kids which made the results worse than they were.

It's been miraculous really. Again, I'm in the right place at the right time. I know we all make our contributions and we're not underestimating our contributions, but I remember the final against Geelong and in the last quarter I had a tear in my eye. I didn't realise we were that good. We played so powerfully. We are going somewhere here. It was marvellous.

I'm just an observer in the coach's box. The coaches do all the work. Obviously I see things and every now and then I feel like saying something but what I've done is I now take a notebook and write down notes and don't say anything. It's just my view of things and later on I'll talk to (Head of Coaching) Tim Livingstone, or (coach) Damien Hardwick and

I'll say 'what are we trying to do with this, its looks like we are on the right track, or wrong track. I'll get some feedback from that; that's my only real contribution.

The 2017 Premiership was a marvellous emotional experience. I was very very happy, we were fantastic, unbelievable. So much pride.

I've watched the game lots of time. The camera caught me smiling when Dan Butler kicked that banana goal. I said, 'he going to go the banana here', that amused me. It was all over by then.

There's never too much (football critiquing) because we know we have to promote the game. But if you want to take it seriously there's a hell of a lot too much. I don't take it seriously, I don't think most people do. You take people's words seriously but you don't live and die by all the stuff. You watch those footy shows and they're talking about which player should go to which club and I understand why they have to do that but it's relatively meaningless. They don't really know what is going on.

I don't like all the talk about players leaving clubs. I'm a bit old-fashioned with this. It's disrespectful to the player and the club, and they may leave, and the rules have been set up so they can and possibly will, but I just don't like that part of it.

All the stuff in 2017 we and poor old Dusty had to put up with was horrible. I can see why it happened, you have to deal with it and you have to accept it and treat it objectively and rationally. I thought we did it pretty well, and I thought Dusty kept playing well during the whole thing. But it was just every day there was something else to deal with. [The conversation we had was] Let's get this in perspective. We respect your right to pursue, but just make sure you are getting the most out of your 2017. Just concentrate on the footy, try not to worry too much about that, it will all work itself out, it will all be done respectfully and decently, we don't have to fight about it. And Dusty always had that kind of attitude and that's why he had such a good year. You've got to get the other people on board, because the coach can't be then coming to me saying "I wish to hell he would sign" (which Damien never said). He always said, "No, we have to treat it respectfully."

Neil Balme shares the victory in the 2017 Grand Final with coach Damien Hardwick and president Peggy O'Neal. It was the third time he has enjoyed a Tiger flag, after kicking two goals in the 1973 and 1974 Premiership wins.

Tim Livingstone is really Damien's right-hand man. Tim does all the organisation around the coaches, but I'm Damien's...what would I be? I'm his 'Robin'. I'm kind of the conduit between the other side of the club and the coaches. I'm there for all those people. The coach has got to be on edge, he's got to be driving for stuff, but he does need the leveller at times.

I'm intelligent enough and humble enough to realise where I fit in it. Poor old Adelaide guys had to fly over and endure the whole parade where there's 150,000 mad Richmond people and just a few of theirs. It can't have helped their mindset. They were a fantastic team over the year and had a lot of pressure on them on Grand Final day, like there was with us. But we tended to enjoy it.

I was part of the Richmond family some time ago. Then I came back to the family and we get that dream—miracle—outcome. It's a good feeling and people do come up and say, 'thanks for helping'.

Ray 'Slug' Jordon

No coach in the history of the Richmond Football Club has been as successful as Ray Jordon. His 10 years as under 19s coach yielded five premierships, including four in succession, and he developed a factory of talent for the senior grades.

Born
Feb 17, 1937

Died
Aug 13, 2012

Interviewed
Oct, 2007

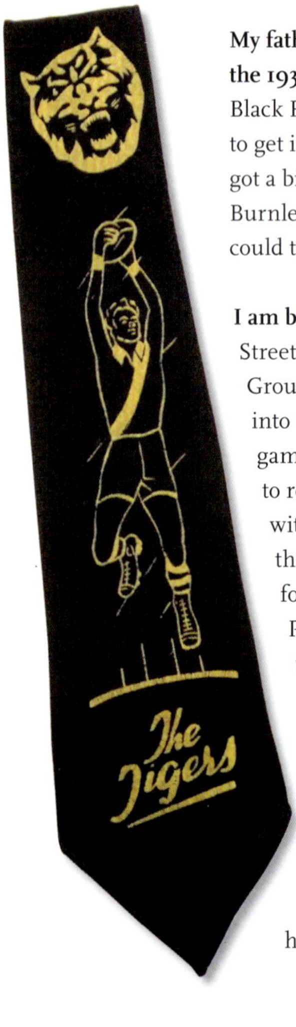

My nickname came from my National Service days. They gave you what should have been blank cartridges, which opened out and blew out cardboard. Harry Herbert, who was full-back at Geelong at the time, came past and I blew one at his feet. Dirt went everywhere. Harry shit himself and I took off and he turned around and fired at me.

Instead of it coming out as blank cardboard it came out as what they call a 'slug', and hit me in the back. It was defective ammunition. Blood went everywhere but I was okay.

My father Clarrie played 15 games for Richmond in the 1930s. He used to ride a bike from Richmond to Black Rock to work on the roads; he couldn't afford to get injured so he gave up playing. Then things got a bit easier and he went back to coaching at Burnley. He was an all-round cricketer, golfer, he could turn his hand to anything.

I am born and bred in Tigerland. In Bennett Street. I used to go past the Richmond Football Ground and I loved football but I was really into cricket. I used to think, not that I'd play a game of League football but that I just wanted to represent Richmond on the Cricket Ground with those black and yellow caps. I used to think that would be fantastic. I played cricket for Richmond Citizens. You know Gosch's Paddock? [Ed's Note: now Collingwood's training ground] Well, that was all cricket grounds and I used to play there with Ted Langridge, who played football for Richmond.

Graeme Richmond told me, 'I'm going to be secretary of the Richmond Football Club.' He rang me up after the election and he said, 'I want you to come and coach the under 19s.' It was a good out for me because I didn't know whether to play football again, so I went down there.

We used to play these kids in the thirds (under 19s) to have a look at them; they weren't in our area. We won our last six or seven pretty easily with Rex Hunt at full-forward, Royce Hart at centre half-forward, Daryl Cumming and Graeme Bond.

I got caught in 1966. South Melbourne found out we played an illegal player called Frankie Loughran, who played down at Sale. In those days you had to get a permit for the kid to come up and play, and Graeme thought that was too much worry. We used to bring a kid up, then we assessed him: 'Looks good, tall, quick enough, kicks the ball well.' Rather than have him train we used to play him and we used to play guys under different names.

It happened with Noel Judkins and Frank Dimattina. We came to the last game that year and were playing Fitzroy at Brunswick St Oval. Graeme said, 'We are going to have a look at Dimattina in September, on the fast big ground, in the finals.' And he was a game short – you had to play three under 19s games to play in the finals. Frank was playing against St Pat's Ballarat that day. You had to put names on the list and I said to Noel Judkins, 'You're not playing today, we've got Dimattina in.' We changed his name; Judkins got the drift.

But we didn't know Judkins knew the umpire, and the umpire came in after the game and said to Judkins, 'I was going to give you three votes but I couldn't find your name.' Judkins said 'I'll tell you about it later.' When it came to the Morrish Medal count (for the VFL under 19s best and fairest), Dimattina got three votes in the last game and Judkins got beaten by one for the Morrish Medal. He blames me to this day.

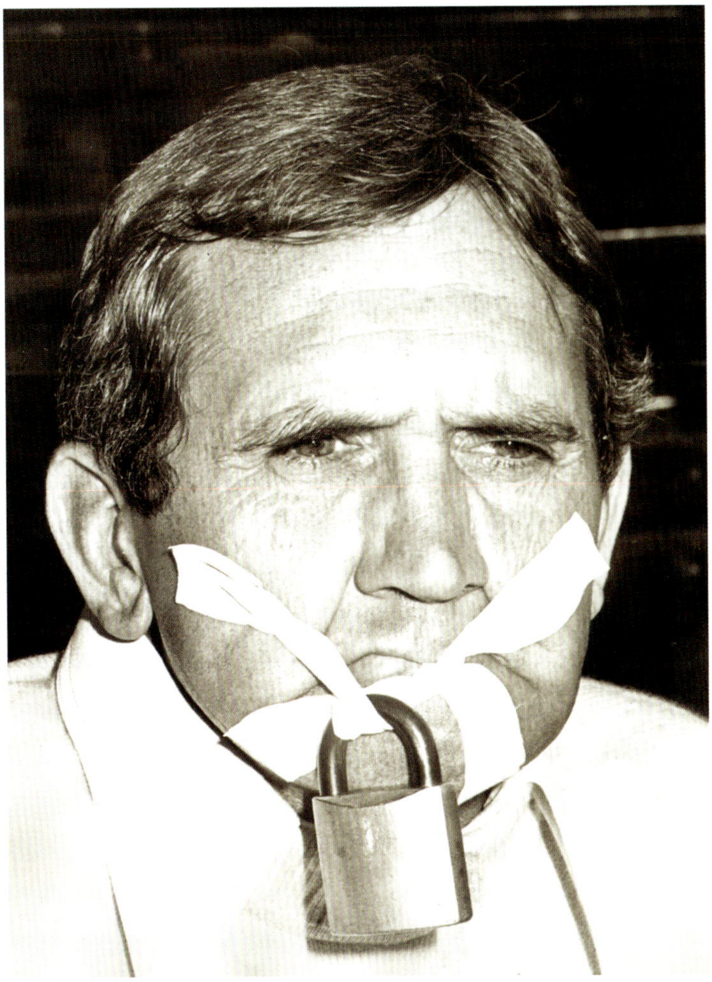

Ray Jordon's language was colorful enough to earn him a reputation.

I was bought up in football and cricket and when you play those at a certain level you had to be disciplined. We won the flag in '67, '68, '69 and '70. One day we left the captain out because his hair was too long. He didn't want to get a haircut. So I said, 'If you don't get your hair cut, I'm not going to play you.' I dropped him – that sparked up a few people. My style wouldn't be accepted today because they have sanitised the game so much. That's a sign of the times.

I went over and saw Norm Smith at Pascoe Vale, after we had won the second premiership; he gave me a couple of hours. All I wanted to know was whether I was on the right track and he verified it: 'Don't change now.'

We won the third flag and I went to see him before the fourth and he reassured me again, which was always comforting. His favourite saying was, 'Jesus, kid, you look like bloody Tarzan, you're playing like bloody Jane.'

"I must admit that swearing was right up there with me. There is no doubt about that ...I probably used it where other people wouldn't use it."

I used to say that when you won, the beer tasted like champagne; when you lost it tasted like kerosene. I also must admit that swearing was right up there with me. There is no doubt about that ... I probably used it where other people wouldn't use it.

I used to say, 'Don't worry about how I say it, worry about what I am saying.'

When I came back from South Africa (Jordon was reserve Australian wicketkeeper for the 1970 tour) Channel 9 was starting up with the Ted Whitten panel and they approached me to be a panel member. I said, 'You'll have to see my manager, accountant Ray Dunn.' He got me an enormous contract – they were doing Friday night shows, and Saturdays I would call a senior game. They had to put a newsreader with me to call the game because it would take away from the raspiness of my voice.

I had a year of that, but I missed the coaching and the involvement of players. And Graeme came and asked, 'Do you reckon you could come back?' So I went back in 1972.

In 1973 the Essex Heights Football Club unofficially became the Richmond 'fourths'. I came up with the idea. I used to go out and see some kids and we had no idea how to get them so Ray Dunn and Graeme approached Essex Heights and said they would be sponsored by the Richmond Football Club. We used to channel all these really good kids in, even though they weren't in our area.

Some were from interstate or the country and we had a red hot side. I used to go down and see them play; I knew where they were from but everyone thought they were local players, because they were coming through Essex Heights.

Emmett Dunne was 17 years old and he just had fantastic character about him. So I made him captain. He couldn't run backwards – he had no balance and strength in his legs – so instead of running forwards for his laps, I used to make him run backwards to improve his strength, therefore he was able to double back. He had a brain that was far ahead of his body.

The Tigers won the premiership from the firsts to the fourths in 1973. You know where the celebration was? Graeme was a miserable man, (it was) over at the Olympic Park dog track on trestle tables with white paper.

Small in stature but tireless in his commitment to the club, Richmond suffered no fools.

Graeme Richmond

Determined, ruthless and dogmatic, no administrative figure so fired the Richmond revival of the 1960s as club secretary Graeme Richmond. A junior player of modest talent, he made his mark in the game by the force of his willpower, tremendous work ethic, a lack of respect for authority and pure, simple rat cunning.

Ian Wilson
Committeeman and president

Graeme came from the Bellarine Peninsula. I can remember this kid with this massive curly blonde hair, aged 10, and he loved football. We found out we both barracked for Richmond and there weren't many people from Geelong Grammar School who barracked for Richmond. So we would talk about Richmond but, of course, they were hopeless in those days. He was just a desperado about all sport but he died wondering about synchronized swimming and why it was an Olympic sport.

He never called me Octa, he used to call me 'Boss' or 'Chief' or 'The Big Fella'. We had a great relationship because we both trusted each other, in completely everything. People running other clubs couldn't work it out. We were both fiery individuals when we were young but when we had our differences of opinion we had it out one to one, never at a committee table or anywhere where people would see us. He was hard-hitting and had a very squeaky voice for such a tough fellow. He didn't have a great speaking voice but he had a great power behind it.

Graeme never drank, except with me. Never had a drink in his hotel, he didn't like people seeing him drink, but he didn't drink much anyway. Ron Carson's garage was a great, warm meeting place. We spent too much time there. I don't think Tommy was overly happy but he would go in there and have a cup of tea. He gave the eulogy at Ron Carson's funeral. Ron was a close friend of mine too. There was a rule they couldn't drink after Monday night. I'd make a point of not going there after Monday night because I didn't want to be compromised. Most of the blokes didn't abuse it too much.

The most massive difference we had was that Harry Beitzel picked the Galahs to go to Ireland in 1967 and Graeme said, 'This is great,' and I said, 'Yeah, but what about the insurance arrangements?' because I was a bit more commercial than Graeme.

I said, 'We have the most valuable assets in the Richmond Football Club in 23 years, there's Billy Barrot, Kevin Bartlett, Royce Hart and Paddy Guinane. Get stuffed, we are not going to send the most valuable assets when they aren't insured.'

He said, 'You've had to go overseas a couple of times on business; half these poor buggers won't get past St Kilda pier.' Because back in 1967 it was a big deal to go overseas. I said, 'Listen, we have got to be responsible to run this club and we have got to be insured.' Eventually Ray Dunn stepped in and said, 'I want you to compromise.' So anyway I eventually compromised – the players went – and it was really the biggest row we ever had.

It sounds mad, doesn't it?

Graeme had connections all over the countryside. If there was someone best on ground at Corowa he would know about it on Saturday night; if (the player) was that good he would be up there on Sunday with Ron Carson and sometimes me and sometimes Jack Dyer.

He was just brilliant at that. He had this coterie of people all around and in Tasmania, like Harry Jenkins, who found Royce Hart. We were both single-minded people; if he wanted someone he would do anything possible to get him.

It's a true story that Graeme watched Peter Hudson twice and didn't think he could play. I mean, we did make mistakes. And Graeme said, 'The two games I saw him play over there were ordinary.'

There is a super story. Harry Jenkins rang up and said, 'We've got this fellow, played a sensational game on Saturday, we have got to get him.' I couldn't go, Alan Schwab the secretary couldn't go, so Graeme said, 'I'll go across.' So GR and Harry

Born
Jan 27, 1934

Died
Sep 15, 1991

went to see this player and knocked on the door and Graeme says 'Hello, Graeme Richmond, Richmond Football Club. That's right, we are the boys in the Black and Yellow guernsey and I tell you what we have heard about your son: we think he can play, we'd love to talk to him. By the way, lovely hydrangeas you've got there. Now, can we see your son?'

So Graeme goes out there and says 'G'day, Graeme Richmond, Richmond Football Club. That's right, we are the boys in the Black and Yellow guernsey and we play on the big MCG, and I tell you what, we have heard about you and we think you can play.

We'd like to see you in the Black and Yellow guernsey on the big MCG with 100,000 people there, playing in a Grand Final in the Tigers' colours. What do you think about that?'

And the player said, 'Mr. Richmond, I signed a form four with Noel Brady of South Melbourne last night.' So Graeme turns around and says, 'Jesus, Harry, what are you doing!!??'

Anyway, Graeme gets his composure back and says 'Well, you've signed with Noel Brady of South Melbourne last night. Well I'll tell you what, when you play your first game, I hope you break your fucking leg.' True story.

Francis Bourke Jnr

Club captain, best and fairest, coach

My father and Graeme Richmond are two of the most gifted people I have ever met. Graeme had a very good sense of humour but it was a different sense of humour. Graeme was very political and very gifted politically. He also was very ambitious and very relentless; he was a 'no stone unturned' person.

And he had an amazing ability to be able to cope with lots of different issues at one time.

Frank (Snr) is a very gifted orator as well because he is able to intertwine his humour but is a very deep thinker. Graeme was a very gifted orator in the traditional fashion. Frank wasn't ambitious at all, Graeme was. They were very different, but nevertheless very talented people.

Les Flintoff

Recruiter

(President) Ray Dunn and Graeme never got on too well. They were great people in their right jobs, but they used to fight like hell. Graeme resigned as the treasurer of the club, Schwabby was then secretary.

And he walked out on the Annual Dinner we had and resigned, and pandemonium broke out.

Though he rarely drank, Richmond – pictured here working with Francis Bourke – made his living running pubs.

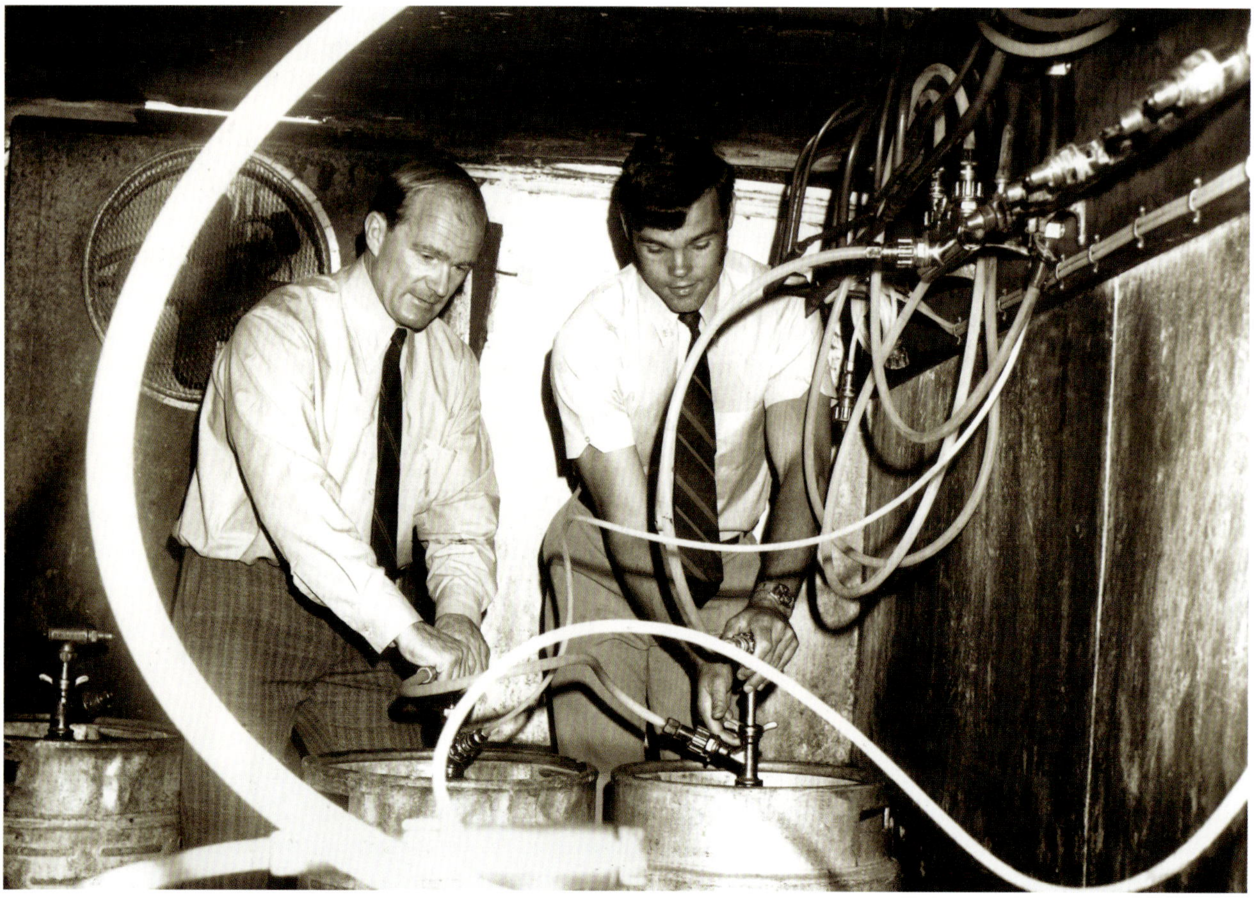

For the simple reason that three of us were going in on the one card, Graeme Richmond, myself and Ron McDonald, called the 'young breed'. And Graeme and Ray were great administrators but used to fight like hell because of their difference of opinions. The night we went to the election we had to smooth everything down.

RAY JORDON
Thirds coach, recruiter
We used to go around to areas that weren't even touched, like Eltham. We'd walk in the dark in the winter and Graeme would go in and he would suss out who was in charge of the family, the mother or the father. Now, if it was the mother he'd say 'By God, you've got lovely chrysanthemums,' and I thought how did he know there were chrysanthemums in the garden – I couldn't see anything.' And Graeme would hold this conversation with her and the kid and the father would be over there and Graeme wouldn't say a word to the kid or father. I would be sitting there and every time he paused for a break I'd say to the father, 'How you going? ... What you do for work?' and the father would get halfway through telling me and Graeme would chime in again and take over.

And the kid is still sitting there and at the end Graeme would say, 'Now listen Cocko, we heard you can play and we'd like you to come down to Tigerland.'

That was his approach. Graeme used to say to me, 'Now we've got to do this quick, Richmond have been down too long and we've got to do it quick. We don't want to be six or seven years to try and get in the finals.'

TOMMY HAFEY
Coach
Richmond by name. Richmond by nature. He was such a demented Richmond person. He was terrific for the club because of the amount of work he did bringing players to the club. I can remember when I was coaching Shepparton and he came up to see me, he was on his way up to Cohuna to see the Farrant brothers. I said, 'I'd like to be able to pinpoint players in Richmond's area, what should I look for, and he said, 'Look, you sign 10 to get one. As long as they are quick and they've got some talent. It's your opinion, and we'll send other people up there to see them play.'

I just thought he was never going to be too tired to go see someone. He would be out on a weekend. He never had days off because he worked

Richmond oversaw the most successful era in club history.

so tirelessly for the football club. I remember he came back from Mildura and I rang him and he'd already gone to Bairnsdale to see a player. That was on a Sunday. He was terrific at our club and very passionate about the Tigers.

ALLAN COOKE
Chairman of selectors
Graeme would ring me up on a Saturday night. I'd been all day at the football, had a couple of drinks with the players, arrived home and the phone would ring. It's Graeme.

'Well, you better look at the side next week. What about this one, and that one and this one,' and I would say 'Now listen Graeme, we've got a bit of a problem, we can only play 20 blokes. And we are going to make the decision.'

And he said, 'Oh well, that's your decision. And you're going to make it.' I said, 'You ring me back with your 20 players tomorrow.' He never rang back.

GEORGE MCHUTCHISON
Statistician
I knew Graeme very well. Tough man. I was working in the pubs for Graeme. I would do all his books at his pubs. At one stage I was doing the balances for five pubs. You'd get a balance from Graeme, say $30,000, and it would be $10 out and he would say, 'See if you can find that.'

When he knew he was doing a speech, instead of an impromptu one, he would go to all the research in the world to get the right quote and stir you from your toes.'

Jan Richmond

Jan Richmond has been an integral part of the Richmond story; she was the strength behind Graeme Richmond, the legendary powerbroker and club secretary in its most productive years.

I was born in Adelaide. My parents lived there and that's where I grew up.

Graeme was born in 1934 and his father was a farmer, and he was born in Geelong. His father was a Geelong supporter and young Graeme wrote to Jack Dyer and Jack wrote back.

Because of Graeme's surname he decided to follow Richmond. Ian Wilson and he went to school together at Geelong Grammar—they were nine when they met. Graeme was in the First XVIII football and First XI cricket teams at school.

Graeme and I met in 1965 in Melbourne. My parents were friendly with neighbours Merle and Bill Wilson, a Richmond player who finished his career playing in Adelaide. I came from Adelaide to stay with Merle and Bill in Melbourne for a holiday and Bill picked me up from the airport and said, 'I haven't got time to take you home as I'm having lunch with Graeme Richmond'. I had never heard of him, but apparently Graeme wanted Bill to come on the Richmond committee, because Graeme was secretary at the time. And that's how we met.

I barracked for Glenelg, "The Tigers". The first experience I have about going to the football was going with Merle and Bill Wilson[1]. It was very easy to barrack for Richmond when I moved to Melbourne in the middle of 1965.

Graeme and I didn't actually live together for another 15 years. Graeme was a bachelor, he was Secretary of the Football club which took up all his time, and because in those days there was no zoning, he was always in the car going somewhere. He didn't stop—he was an absolute workaholic. His goal was to get everybody around him—those on the field and off—to win a Premiership.

Graeme's father had gone off to war. His mother had passed away, so Graeme was brought up by his aunt and grandmother. Graeme didn't have his father for seven years when he was little. That's quite an important time not to have your father. My kids had the same experience because Graeme died when they were quite young too.

Graeme used to have great conversations with Denise Bartlett, Kevin Bartlett's wife. They often used to talk on the phone about the footy. She was the only woman really that Graeme spoke to about the football, the game and the play. He didn't speak to me about it. I didn't know the first thing about who should play where.

I used to go every week to the football and take our kids to the Berry Street creche.

Kerry Bourke (Francis's wife) started that. There was a real explosion of children of players in those years, so Kerry marched up to Graeme, because she was not backwards in coming forwards and said: 'we've got to do something about all these kids'. Graeme would really rather we all stay home and get the dinner ready for when the boys came home. He was a dinosaur really. Kerry would have none of that. She said, 'no we've got to have some where to leave our children, because we are all going to come to the football'.

Graeme leased pubs and he started off with the Vaucluse Hotel. He didn't drink, didn't smoke. He was a fitness fanatic and that's why it was so ironic that he ended up with bowel cancer. He ate health foods before anybody knew about health foods.

1 Bill Wilson died in 1969, aged 44, in Manila.

He exercised every morning on the bedroom floor. He did push-ups and sit-ups, the same as Tommy Hafey, and used to have the kids on his back. I've got photos of him and he was like a bodybuilder. He died with a body like that, he never wasted away. Tommy and Graeme were very close, despite things that have been said and written.

Graeme got Tommy Hafey to Richmond. When I first was going to the footy with Graeme, Len Smith was the coach. And I remember Len getting very sick and us going to the hospital to see him and Graeme then went up to Shepparton and talked to Tommy and Maureen. He knew them because they had lived in Richmond and had the milk bar up in Bridge Road, and Paddy Guinane and Graeme used to go there all the time.

Graeme was brought up in an old-fashioned way he had very good manners. That struck a chord with people's parents. He just knew what to say to parents to get them to let their kids come to the city, to come to Richmond, to be boarded out in somebody's house, and he would promise them he would look after them. He had his own house and he had players living there with him.

He signed up everybody. I went with him a lot of times—all that driving around.

I went down to Tassie with him to get Michael Roach[2], and we used to go and talk with Royce Hart—as much as you could ever talk with him.

Graeme was the master recruiter. Dick Clay was signed to North Melbourne and Graeme poached him. There was a form signed, it was like a promise and Graeme thought, bugger that we will just hide him until that runs out and get his assurance that he's going to sign up with Richmond. Poor Dick was only a kid, he had no front teeth when I first met him. We snatched him and hid him at Graeme's house in Barkers Road.

It always grates on me when people call Graeme ruthless. I suppose he might have appeared ruthless if you were on the end of it. Francis Bourke said this once, 'Graeme had great powers of persuasion'. He never did anything when he was on the committee without talking it over with other people. If he was able to persuade them to his way of thinking, well fine. And he could, that's what he could do.

2 Michael Roach played 200 games exactly from 1977-1989.

Jan Richmond was the strength behind the legendary club power broker, Graeme Richmond. She said of her husband's negotiating skills: "If he was able to persuade them to his way of thinking, well fine. And he could, that's what he could do."

And people like Ron Carson[3] and Ian Wilson[4] and Les Flintoff[5] and the people on the committee, they agreed with him. But Graeme was the one who had to deliver the message and he never shied away from it. Everything he did was, he felt, in the club's best interest. When he was Secretary that's what he was paid to do. But later on, he was never paid for anything. He never took any money for anything and everything he did was on a voluntary basis.

When he was appointed Secretary his salary was 5 pounds a week. He answered the phone, he wrote the letters, he paid everybody, that was his job. He did everything. Unlock the door. Lock the door.

When it came time for players to move on, of course they'd be angry and upset at him. He didn't put up with anyone being 'a naughty boy', as he used to say. He used to say, 'If you are going to be a naughty boy you can go be a naughty boy somewhere else. But not at Richmond'.

The Sunday after a Grand Final we would call Chop-o Sunday. All the committee would meet

3 Ron Carson was Treasurer of Richmond Football Club from 1966-1968, 1970 and again in 1981-1984.

4 Ian Wilson was President of Richmond Football Club from 1974-1985

5 Les Flintoff was on the committee from 1964-1972. He had played for Richmond from 1950-1952.

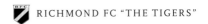

"Graeme gave his blood for the bloody club"

at Julia and Ian Wilson's house in Armadale and they'd go through all the players and decide who performed, who hadn't, who had to go, who they'd get, including the coaching staff and everybody else—from the bootstudder to you name it.

Julia Wilson and I used to hide in her kitchen during that time. She and I were always in fear and trepidation about who would be going because their wives were our friends. It was horrible. It was horrible. And Graeme didn't like it either.

At the end of his life he said, '*My biggest regret is the friends that I've probably lost over football'.* And I thought how sad that is, that he felt that way. Somebody went to the club once and said, 'Graeme Richmond ruined the club'. I was so hurt over that and horrified that anyone would say that. He gave his blood for the bloody club.

When Tommy went, Maureen Hafey and I decided we would never let that interfere in our friendship[6]. And you know we never have. We said that because there was so much written in the press about Graeme and Tommy, sworn enemies and all that. That was bullshit. That wasn't right. I'm sure Tommy was upset and cross because Graeme didn't support him in the end but it wasn't right that they were enemies.

The day Graeme died, in September 1991, Tommy was the last person to see him. Maureen rang me and said, 'We have to see Graeme'. And they came in and sat by his bed and they were holding each other's hand. It was the saddest thing. Of course, that sort of thing doesn't get written up.

He made no secret that he had cancer. There is film of him saying that he hadn't had a good diagnosis. But he lasted for six years. He just wouldn't lie down. He was the bravest person.

He went to work right up until a week before he died. And he went to the football. He was on the selection committee for the Victorian team, with Ted Whitten. He went to all the interstate games **that were played.** He went to Richmond every week and he worked at the pub and they had a pub with a 24-hour licence if you don't mind. There were discos and it was a nightmare honestly. That's how our life was really. It was hard.

Graeme was very well-read. He was like Kevin Bartlett, he never had to make notes. If he lived longer he would have had a very lucrative career at public speaking. It would not have surprised me if he had gone into politics.

Graeme got Alan Schwab to Richmond. Alan Schwab was assistant secretary at St Kilda[7]. That's when I first met Alan and Annette, at a secretaries' dinner at The Australia Hotel. He was just a boy. I lived with Annette's mother which was an absolute co-incidence, so we had that sort of connection as well.

Graeme really liked Alan. He felt that in his succession planning, I suppose, he wanted somebody to carry on with the same sort of views about things that he had. Graeme wanted to move into hotels after a couple of years, and also he was bloody worn out with all this driving. He ran into a herd of cows one night, and killed one. He was lucky he didn't get hurt himself. There was no seat belt law in those days. He could have gone to sleep. He was exhausted all the time.

So many people try to impersonate Graeme. Some people have taken it on permanently, Sheedy does it, Francis does it. He did have a very unusual way of speaking.

He didn't say, 'Listen Cocko' as much as people say he said it. It's quite an old-fashioned war time term. Don't forget Graeme used to pick peas and dig potatoes on a farm.

I have never let him die in my children's minds. We talk about him and of course the boys go to the football every week.

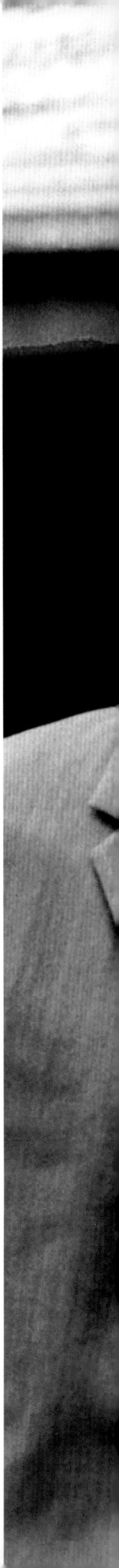

6 Tom Hafey's tenure at Richmond ended on Sept 20, 1976. He had coached RIchmond since 1966, winning four premierships.

7 Alan Schwab was secretary of Richmond from 1968-1976, and treasurer from 1972-1976.

Alan Schwab (right) and Tom Hafey were drivers of change at Richmond through the club's golden years. Jan Richmond noted that Graeme Richmond anointed Schwab as his successor. "Graeme got Alan to Richmond," she said. "He wanted somebody to carry on with the same sort of views about things that he had." Schwab later moved to the VFL as its Administration manager when the Commission was set up in 1984.

Verdun Howell

The St Kilda champion premiership player coached the Richmond Reserves from 1969 to 1971. Verdun Howell coached one senior game, in 1971, as a fill-in for Tom Hafey, who was required to coach Victoria.

Born
Jun 16, 1936

Richmond coach
1971
1 game

Interviewed
Aug 2009

Alan Schwab was the assistant secretary at St Kilda when I was in my final years of playing there (1958-68). He then transferred to Richmond where he became the Secretary. John Nix was in charge of the Richmond Reserves in 1969 and for business reasons he had to give up the job part way through the season. So Alan Schwab and the club approached me to see if I could do the job, and I was quite happy to accept it. I had been retired for around 18 months.

Richmond and St Kilda were a bit like chalk and cheese. Richmond was a powerful club because of the way Alan Schwab got everyone together. They recruited extremely well whereas St Kilda had quite a few opportunities, but never became a real powerhouse.

Alan and I were very close great friends. He was a very popular young fellow down at St Kilda and I used to go on recruiting trips with him and we built our friendship from these journeys. He often told the story of this one player he liked down Chelsea way. I couldn't get away from work to go and have a look at the player in question. So I spoke to Alan one day, and I said, 'Did you get a chance to have a look at that kid you keep mentioning?' and he said,'Yeah, but he has a bit too much weight and is a bit slow.' It turned out he was talking about Leigh Matthews.

I have very great memories of my time at Richmond. Firstly I had three years as Richmond Reserves coach (1969-71). We won the 1971 Grand Final against Essendon and we were beaten a year earlier in the 1970 Grand Final by Melbourne – by two points. Although to this day I believe we actually should have won that game. The ball went down the ground and Neil Balme was playing at full-forward and one of our guys had a long shot at goal and put us four points in front and the score went up on the board. But the umpire ran down the ground and took the ball off us because he felt Neil had shepherded the guy in the goal square. So Melbourne kicked out from defence and the siren went. We went from four-point winners to two-point losers!

Tom Hafey was coaching Victoria in 1971 and that was the reason Richmond wanted me to look after their senior team for one week. I was on the

selection committee anyway so I knew plenty of time in advance that I was going to coach, so I took Thursday-night training.

Then in round 16, 1971, I coached Richmond in my only game as senior coach. In fact, I actually coached two games of football that day. We always played our curtain raisers at 12 o'clock, so I coached the Richmond Reserves until three-quarter time.

Allan Cooke then took over the last quarter as coach, while I went to look after the seniors for the rest of the day. Cooke didn't have to do much – the Reserves had a quite good win.

The senior team was going pretty well up until the day I coached them. They had lost only five games up to that round. Richmond was a real power at the time. I had no real specific plans to carry out because the opinion was that our ability would carry us through. We just thought we had a team on paper that would win. In the end, we got thrashed by 35 points by Footscray at Footscray. Tommy returned the following week and Richmond won its next six, before losing to St Kilda in the preliminary final!

I remember the media interviewed Billy Brown after the game. They said, 'Oh, you missed Tom Hafey', and he said, 'Verdun told us what to do, we just didn't do it'.

It was just one of those days that everything they did was wrong. Ian Stewart played in the centre and he came up to me after the game and said, 'I couldn't get near the ball', and I said, 'You weren't the only one, there were 17 others who couldn't get near the ball.'

Verdun Howell (left), pictured with Brent Crosswell and Paul Sproule (right), coached Richmond for one senior game. Here they attend Tasmania's Hall of Fame gala dinner at Wrest Point Casino, Hobart, in 2007.

Ian Stewart

The deeply private Stewart lives quietly in country Victoria, away from the glory which followed his football career. A man who played in two premierships, won three Brownlow Medals and best and fairest awards at two clubs, he is a Legend of the AFL Hall of Fame.

1971-75

Born
Jul 30, 1943

Played
Richmond
1971-75
78 games,
55 goals

St Kilda
1963-70
127 games,
25 goals

Interviewed
Nov 26, 2006

My real name is not Stewart, it's Cervi. My mother married an Italian, she had a baby, they separated when I was two. After a while, it was convenient to go back to my mother's maiden name, which was Stewart. At the time we lived in Queenstown, a mining town in Tasmania, and you can imagine 60 years ago what the miners, the Anglo-Saxons, thought of the wogs. So it was safer and probably easier for her to go back to Stewart. But as I reached the twilight of my life I am now prepared to own up to a lot of these little things.

My father left when I was two and I never saw him again. Well, I did see him again, when I was 27. His brothers arranged a barbecue and I met him then briefly for 10 seconds. He shook my hand and moved on. He wasn't interested ... I never saw him again. I don't regret that. The legacy of a lot of those things is that you are on your own and you lack confidence. I didn't deliberately keep to myself, it was just the way you were. Don't forget that was the way you were bought up, on your own, by yourself.

The interesting thing and the good thing is a lot of sportsmen gain their confidence and their self-esteem out of achieving things ... Seriously, up until I was 50 I found it difficult to go into public places (and) sit down and talk. Now, I live with it.

Once you got out on the field you got your confidence. That was your theatre. If you played badly, you were so upset that you turned it around very quickly.

Your bad patches lasted less because you needed to get back your confidence and the only way was to start playing well again.

You couldn't go through a three or four week bad trot thinking 'I'll be right next week or the week after.' Or, 'Bugger this, I better get going.' It was your life. It was your air, your oxygen.

I don't think I have ever said anything about this, but I helped orchestrate (the 1970 trade to St Kilda for Billy Barrot). I encouraged the president of St Kilda, Graham Huggins, and let it be known that Billy Barrot might be available. I wasn't getting on well with the coach, Allan Jeans, at the time. The president got very keen on Barrot and started talking to him, because Richmond were at that stage getting sick of Billy and wanted to move him on. I went to WA on the pretext of coaching. St Kilda then said 'Stewart's going to coach out in Western Australia' ... subconsciously they were saying 'We are going to lose him.' So the people who ran St Kilda were conditioned into thinking they were going to lose Stewart. They got pretty enthusiastic about chasing Barrot.

They hooked into Billy Barrot because at that stage it sounded like a coup and at the last second my name was thrown up. So it was a ploy that I developed. Everything worked out perfectly. Perfectly. Except for Billy. It was a big deal really, because Billy was an integral part of Richmond's premierships and it looked as though he'd almost run his race at Richmond. The same could be said of me at St Kilda, even though I was only 27. When you looked back on it, there was a case for both of us, but at the time nobody knew. It was big, huge.

I had a couple of ordinary years at St Kilda. Success came to me fairly quickly in League football at St Kilda (but) people were saying I was finished, or maybe near it. I had a lot to prove. But it's like I used that as a reason to motivate myself. But it really shouldn't be the reason to motivate you ... you use every little thing to help but really the best

When he arrived in 1971, Ian Stewart's talent clearly stood out in an already successful team.

motivation comes from within yourself. That was the amazing thing at Richmond, Tommy didn't fill your head with 'Do this or do that.' He wanted to run, run to the next line, get to the pack so you create numbers, kick it long and do things like that. I trained every day for a year with (running coach) John Toleman. I went to his place and we ran every day, every single day, Christmas Day even.

The reason I am grateful to Richmond is the way I was accepted by them. It was a very, very supportive, friendly, caring group of people and I go as far to say that the group of people who were at Richmond through that time are some of the finest people I have ever come in contact with, at any capacity. I'm talking about Francis Bourke, Michael Green, Alan Schwab, Graeme Richmond, Ian Wilson, Charlie Callander, Dusty O'Brien and the trainers.

"I wasn't finished, actually. I slipped, I wasn't finished. I could have played another 50 games, easily, but I lost the desire. I was on the way down ... and gave it away."

Stamina was my weakness. It still happens. I don't know what it's called, but there's a power strength where you can lift one weight, but you can't do it three or four times. And there's a thing where you can jump very high just once. But I lacked the stamina to be able to do these things. My running leap was good.

One power lift was good, but all of a sudden I fell away pretty quickly – my best was quite good, however. I was a left-footer, I could mark all right, read the ball well. If I had fear, which I did, I tried to overcome it. I was a reasonable kick and I always tried to be the team player – first, second and third.

The first time I played against St Kilda I remember the barrage I got from the St Kilda players and the many hits. Allan Jeans told them to 'Go and kill Stewart,' the blokes have told me since. I was crook on St Kilda blokes who went for me and hit me for years after that.

The Windy Hill brawl was a nasty, vicious game. Mal Brown was in it, he had a lot to do with it. He was a rumbler. He was sort of an agitator, he agitated everybody.

I was right there in the middle of it but I didn't throw any punches. I endeared myself to Graeme Richmond for life then, by saying that I was very close to Graeme and I never saw Graeme lift his arms or legs or anything.

As far as I was concerned Graeme didn't touch anybody. Well, as you know there is footage of Graeme punching! See, I had won three Brownlows at the time and that had a little bit of weight and Graeme never forgot that. As you know he's a good friend and a bad enemy. A bond developed and he became a life-long friend.

Winning a best and fairest wasn't a shock at Richmond. I trained like buggery to get it. That was the way I played. That was my ambition and goal. That's the epitome of success within the club. The Brownlow has a lot of issues about luck, the position you play, which foot you kick with, whether another player might have been mouthing off to the umpire so he was disregarded, all those contributing things. The best and fairest is the be-all-and-end-all. In one other year I came second to Kevin Bartlett, he passed me in the last game or two and the finals, as he had a better final series than me.

I retired in 1974 for three or four games, and Des Tuddenham signed a petition to get to me to play. I don't know why because he was at another club. Many people signed it, so I played. But I had lost the urge to play. I was involved in business and I was enjoying business and enjoying life other than football.

I wasn't finished, actually. I slipped, I wasn't finished. I could have played another 50 games, easily, but I lost the desire. I was on the way down. I played four or five more games and gave it away.

I thought, I can't be bothered training, I can't be bothered doing anything and the side was a pretty good side. One of the reasons that I lost interest was I was getting injuries then, and when I didn't play through injuries, the side would win by more. So I said they don't need me. And when they don't need you, it affected your confidence and self-esteem.

In 1972, after I won the Brownlow, I had hamstring injuries before and during the season and they (Richmond) said I wasn't right to play and that I wasn't fit enough. They had a lot of emphasis on fitness. And I disagreed with them and I had a verbal blue with the Chairman of Selectors, Allan Cooke. So I lasted half a game at Essendon and I came off exhausted in the reserves. I didn't play any practice games either but I was exhausted after about 10 minutes out there and I realised they were right. They were right and I was wrong. I have apologised to Cooke since, many times. Next week I was in the seniors.

It's safe to say I should never have been picked in the 1972 Grand Final. It was ridiculous. I tore a hamstring on the Thursday night. They thought I could get away with it. I sat on the bench then came on and the first time I went for the ball I realised I was no value for them. It was a bad move.

So many people thought in those days that a half-fit so-and-so could do all right. Now, I'd suggest that would be Graeme Richmond's thinking, not Tommy's. Graeme would say, 'If he's not right we could put him in the forward pocket and he'd be able to snare a couple.'

I would say that centre would be nearly the easiest position to play, or the best position. I would hate to be a centre half-forward or a half-forward flanker permanently. I wouldn't mind being at full-forward, sitting in front of goals all day. I became a better kick after a while. I could kick in the general field but was not as good for goal. When I went to Richmond, Tommy's game was different; you had to kick more goals.

Funny, I built up not a resentment, but a mini dislike for my opponents and a heavy dislike of the suburbs where they lived. As an example, I would never drive through Collingwood, Essendon and Hawthorn, I'd go around the areas, because it was tribal. I know you might say '70s wasn't that tribal, but it was in my mind and it motivated me. I never went into their areas, only on the day I played. I'd never go down the main street of Collingwood. That's what motivated me, all that psychology you'd be using on your subconscious.

And then I've found out since what a lovely suburb Essendon is. I didn't know Maribyrnong and all those places existed. I drive through Collingwood now and I love it.

Royce Hart was an out-and-out champion – tremendous mark, tremendous courage and tremendous kick. Royce may not agree with this, but he wasn't too good on his right side and I don't think he read the ball as well as people think he did. How do I come to say that? Some of Royce's marks came at the last second; what does that suggest to you? A better reader may have already been in the position. He took some spectacular marks in the last second. I thought sometimes when I turned out of the pack he wasn't there, wasn't in my vision. But Darrel Baldock would have been there. You'd twist and turn and you wouldn't look for him because he was just there.

Securing a third Brownlow Medal after crossing to Richmond also secured the Stewart legend.

Football meant salvation. It meant an opportunity to rise, it gave you a chance. It taught me to be a team player, taught me to make sacrifices, taught me to be unselfish.

It is a wonderful thing, football. Wonderful, wonderful character builder, and that's at all levels of football. It's a wonderful, magnificent game. It gave me an opportunity to rise, gave me an opportunity to live, an opportunity to have a good life. If you rely on football to help you in business, you are greatly mistaken. I'm not a networker, so I have never, ever, ever tried to tie the two, football and business.

But if you rely on people who help you, you will miss the boat. No matter what they say, if you rely on people you fall over very quickly.

The Man Eater

The most iconic of Richmond symbols, the Tiger skin was an almost compulsory accessory for any newcomer's photo taken at Punt Rd. The actual tiger was known as the Kemasek Man Eater ... 'bagged' by Colonel A. Locke in Malaya in 1951 (note the bullet hole, opposite page), it had killed and eaten at least 12 people in the six months before its death. These days, in a state of advanced decay, it makes only rare public appearances (such as on Jack Dyer's coffin for his 2003 funeral).

Ian Wilson

In partnership with Graeme Richmond, "Octa" Wilson helped create the indomitable spirit that typified a glorious era of Tiger success. First a committeeman, and later president, he came to represent the defiant "us against them" stand that set Richmond apart during a run of five premierships in 14 seasons.

Born
May 11, 1934

President
1973-85

Interviewed
May 1, 2005

I am William Ian Wilson. My father was William Wilson, he was called Bill Wilson and I have always been Ian. There was a Billy Wilson who was on the committee with me, an outstanding rover. He was probably the best rover Richmond had before Kevin Bartlett came along. He and Roy Wright and Bill Morris were in the state squad together. He died tragically overseas of some mystery illness. He didn't drink or smoke.

When I was at Geelong Grammar, a boarding school, I was a little fat kid aged 10, I used to eat a lot. And we did Latin, and 'Octo' is 'eight' in Latin. Some smart bastard said 'Octa Belly, Triple Bum', meaning 'eight bellies and a triple bum'. Little boys are lazy so it reduced itself in one day to just 'Octa Belly', because it was too hard to say 'Octa Belly Triple Bum', and after a week it just became 'Octa.' That name has just stuck. It's a pathetic reason, but that's it.

My father took me, aged seven, to the the 1943 Grand Final. The war was on. It was at Carlton, and Richmond was playing Essendon and Jack Dyer ran onto the field first. Maybe if Dick Reynolds had run on first I might have barracked for Essendon. I was in awe of Jack Dyer. The only real things I remember about that game were Jack Dyer and Max Oppy.

From that day onwards I became a Richmond supporter. My dad barracked for Melbourne. But he became Richmond when I became president. He was J. Wilson, trucking business, furniture movers.

I used to scull, in rowing – I was actually state sculling champion three years in succession. I used to come across to Punt Road after the rowing and one game we were playing I was standing in front of the old stand. Graeme Richmond said, 'Oh, good to see you mate, why don't you come down and meet the president?' Graeme and I went to school together so we were good mates. So we went down to the little baby office and there was Charlie Priestley, Ron Garraway, Martin Bolger and Ray Dunn. I met Ray and apparently when I left the room he said to these other fellows, 'That fellow will be the next president of Richmond.'

Within months I got on the committee and I was given the job of being reserve grade manager, which I was for two years from 1967. Then GR approached me and said, 'We want you to give away that job and come on the executive and become a vice-president.' I said, 'I am loving what I am doing now', and he just made it clear that that wasn't going to happen. 'You're doing this or you're not doing anything.' So I became vice-president on the executive committee in 1969.

Ray Dunn died in 1971 and a very nice fellow called Al Boord took over as president – he had been finance chairman for years. But he was old and for most of the 1973 season he went to Queensland, leaving Graeme and I to run the club. But it suited everybody. And of course we won the premiership and he came back for the finals, then went to Queensland again. I was actually president, really, for the 1973 Grand Final.

While Graeme was keen for me to become president I just felt I could do whatever I could do as vice-president while (Al) was away. Anyway, he stayed for a year and I took over at the end of 1973.

Graeme didn't abide fools, which is a weakness in a football club. He didn't handle small talk very much. He was a very positive person and I suppose we were both a bit like this; it is a weakness being single-minded, you can go like hell. Take the John Pitura swap. We got so single-minded about

Ian Wilson (centre) surrounded himself with a strong Tiger coterie ... to his right, greatly respected club patron David Mandie; to his left, Federal Treasurer Phillip Lynch.

that, it obsessed us. We just had to get him. I was president and make no excuses, it was the worst mistake I have ever made. We traded the Whale (Brian Roberts), Graham Teasdale and Francis Jackson and – what most people don't know – plus $40,000. And it took us hundreds of bloody hours, six months to do the whole thing. We both became obsessed with getting this fellow, we weren't going to be beaten and we got him and he played one good game.

Tommy (Hafey) was obsessed in getting him. Tommy was the bloke who drove us. Tommy coached the state side with John Pitura in it and he said, 'Hey, get this fellow and we can win the next 10 premierships,' or something like that ... a slight exaggeration. We put the executive time in, and money, and three great players. We were a successful club and we kept winning games and premierships, so people think about the good things we did, but I admit it was the biggest mistake I ever made. No excuses for that.

Graeme had retired as secretary, and Alan Schwab had come in. 'Schwabby' was actually assistant secretary at St Kilda and I was vice-president (at RFC). I remember Schwabby coming to Graeme and said, 'Look, there's no question I can set up a swap with Stewart for Barrot,' and I remember Graeme saying, 'They are not going to fall for that,' and Schwab said, 'They will, they will.' Schwab achieved it; it was done before the club's AGM and Ray Dunn was president. It had been announced in the paper, and they booed Ray Dunn in the Town Hall for swapping Barrot and Stewart. We were sitting on the stage at the front.

Alan Schwab was passionate about everything in life. He loved sport. He had tremendous knowledge. He had tremendous recruiting ability and could pick a player. When he was with the League he rang me up one day and said, 'Listen, I just watched the Teal Cup, there's a kid in Perth called Brian Taylor. Get over there and get him signed because he is going to be everything, the best young player I have seen playing in the Teal Cup.' And I went over there the next week and signed Brian.

I was in Spain when the Windy Hill brawl took place. I was president and I rang up my office on Monday morning and spoke to my manager and asked, 'How did the Tigers go?' and he said, 'Oh, they beat Essendon. But there is a bit of problem there, your mate Graeme Richmond is in a bit of trouble. He whacked some bloke.'

At whatever cost, Wilson (left) and Graeme Richmond claimed silverware for the Tigers.

So I got the girl in the hotel I was staying at Malaga to call the Vaucluse Hotel, and she was saying, 'Mr Richmondey, Mr Richmondey, Mr Wilson calling,' and a voice said to the girl, 'Just a moment, love, I will try and find him.' So Graeme came on the phone and I said, 'Good win on Saturday. I understand you had a bit of a problem,' and he said, 'Oh, some bloke jumped the fence and I whacked him.' And I said, 'Look, you better get David Jones, our club lawyer, and they should be able to fix that.' He said, 'There's a bit of a problem ... he's got a broken jaw.'

Now, there was a rule in the League those days that if you're an official you could be defended by anybody except a person from the legal profession and you could only be defended by a co-committeeman of the club. And Graeme said, 'When are you coming back, because I don't want Charlie Callander defending me.' So I flew back.

I had to defend Graeme and the League hated us then. They absolutely hated us because we broke every rule. When Graeme was found guilty they fined him $4,000 and barred him from going to the football.

Of course, the very next week we stopped Graeme from sitting on the bench, but we made him sit next to me in the committee box and we'd get people to take photographs of us. Then the League said, 'You haven't paid the fine.' And we said 'We're not going to pay the fine.' And they said, 'Graeme Richmond is publicly photographed sitting with you together at the football' and I said, 'Yep, what you going to do about it?'

Anyway, finally (League president) Sir Maurice Nathan and (League secretary) Eric McCutcheon pulled me in and I said, 'We are not paying the fine, you can have that in writing. You take whatever action you can but I can promise you this we are not paying the fine.'

After half an hour Maurice Nathan wanted to get it over and done with and McCutcheon wanted it to go on and he said, 'We have spent $800 in getting legal opinion for the League on how we can handle this whole thing. Would you pay the 800 dollars, paying the legal cost?' and I said, 'No, but I'll go you halves and pay you $400.' And they agreed. So I came back to Richmond and Graeme said, 'How did you go?' and I said, 'As far as you going to the football, well that's over. And I refused to pay the fine but they had expended $800 with legal opinions on how to handle that and they wanted $800. I cut it in half and gave them $400.'

Graeme said, 'You weak bastard.'

We came out of Collingwood one day in my car and all of a sudden a bloke throws something at the car, then we get around the corner in Johnson St and there are a heap of Collingwood supporters booing at us. Graeme is laughing and said, 'Cocko, we made it, they fucking hate us. That's what we want.'

Because, in the lovely days of (previous secretary) Maurie Fleming, Richmond was a beautiful place to come. But to be president of the football club in those days you had to have a bit of shit in you.

"Tommy Hafey coached the state side with John Pitura in it and he said, 'Hey, get this fellow and we can win the next 10 premierships ... a slight exagerration."

We were a tremendous drawcard then. I can remember I attacked Nathan and McCutcheon about the fact that all the money for the football went out to VFL Park, and the clubs were running on nothing. I attacked them viciously through (Melbourne *Herald* football writer) Alf Brown, who was a great friend of ours. We were hauled in to face them. Eric said, 'Under rule so and so you can be both expelled from the League for actions prejudicial,' and Graeme said, 'I'll tell you what Maurice, I reckon you should do that. We won last year's premiership and we are going to win this premiership. If you sack the big fellow and I, we will go down as legends, we will put our names in lights. We will be famous for decades.'

That's why people hated us. We broke all the rules. We didn't give a stuff, what were they going to do to us? On purpose we would engineer a big row with the VFL. Of course, there is a famous photograph of me being handed a letter from McCutcheon saying 'You will desist from making detrimental comments about the League, President of the League, Executive Director, or rule so and so will be exercised.' We didn't give a stuff about that but we did this always in March, you know why? To promote membership ticket sales.

We built up a hell of a coterie of people. There were 12 people on the coterie when I became president and there finished up being 160. We got people like Rear Admiral Sir Brian Murray, (Federal Treasurer) Sir Phillip Lynch, (Federal Country Party stalwart) Peter Nixon and (Victorian Premier) Lindsay Thompson. I found out who these Richmond supporters were and they became totally involved in the club. I used to look after that side of it.

I was an innovator in those days and used to think laterally. A friend of mine was managing director of the CUB brewery, Lou Mangan. And we were having a drink in the brewery boardroom in 1973 and I said, 'How would you like to sponsor a football club?' Now, no club had ever (had sponsorship on the jumper). And he said, 'What would it mean?' and I said, 'We would make sure they train in sweaters with CUB written on them, we'd make sure they run out in tracksuits with CUB, but the league won't obviously let us put sponsorship on the uniforms.' And he said 'How much do you want?' And I said, 'Oh, $50,000.' So we sat down had a couple of more beers and eventually we got $28,000. And we were the first club ever sponsored. And it was interesting, I went to Kevin Bartlett and Tom Hafey and I said, 'You fellows don't drink or smoke but when you go on television, Tommy, you've got to wear CUB, and train in sweaters with CUB on it.' Because we were obviously often photographed at training because we were the top club.

In 1976, I knew the coach of San Diego Chargers. I sent Tom Hafey, Bill Grainger and Barry Richardson the assistant coach, to America for two weeks on the west coast and they spent time there and with the San Francisco 49ers and the Los Angeles (Raiders) gridiron team. When you are young you think laterally and you innovate. We endeavored to be innovators and be first to do anything.

KB won every (award) in 1974. I was president and a director of the League so I was sitting right at the front table (at the Brownlow Medal count). I purposely never drank at any League function. At the back, Alan Schwab and big Charlie Priestley booed and hissed. North Melbourne's Ron Joseph came up and Charlie Priestley grabbed him by the throat and there was a scuffle. I wasn't there.

Anyway, we had quite a few drinks and I got a phone call at midnight from (Melbourne *Age* journalist) Michael Sheahan, who said to me, 'What do you think of the Brownlow Medal?' and I said, 'Oh, I was disappointed that Kevin didn't win it.' He said, 'What did you think of Keith Greig?' and I said, 'Well, I only see him twice a year and Bryan Wood seems to beat him both times.' I was going to Canberra the next day on business and I'm sitting next to a bloke on the plane who is reading *The Age* ... on the front page is my photograph! I wasn't in the scuffle, but Mike Sheahan blew it up.

We signed Dick Clay at one minute after midnight. Tommy Hafey coached Shepparton and he said, 'There is a sensational player up there called Dick Clay who plays for Kyabram.' Anyway, we find out North Melbourne has signed him, so Graeme, Ron Carson and I go up there and we say, 'Listen, we will give you a car if you don't play for North,' because there was eight months of his Form Four to go. (A Form Four expired in 12 months). If he had played for the North Reserves he would have been a North player. I remember Graeme adding, '... and the car will have a radio in it.' Dick was a country boy (so maybe he didn't know that). All cars have radios in them. So eight months ran out and we were up there that night and signed him and dated the form the next day. Dick played his first game on Ted Whitten – he hadn't played a game of League football, had only been training here for a week, and Dick Clay takes a great mark at centre half-forward.

Graeme nearly jumped out of his chair and I nearly jumped out of the stands! We broke every rule in the book.

I also signed Mal Brown. In 1966 after the (National) Carnival, Graeme came back and said, 'When are you going to Perth? Jesus, there is a fellow who gave the champion half-forward flanker of Victoria the best right cross I have ever seen.' And I went over there and signed (Brown) in 1966 at an accountant's office in Mount Bay Road.

I don't think Kevin Bartlett has been told this. Graeme Richmond, (coach) Tony Jewell and I are going to the movies in February. And we are having a cup of coffee after the movies, and Graeme or Tony said, 'Hey, what about playing KB on the half forward flank? It will extend his football career by two or three years, plus won't he give those bloody half-back flankers some curry.' So there is a discussion and all of a sudden Graeme said, 'Who's going to tell the little fella?'

If Kevin had gone to Collingwood (Bartlett sought a clearance to Collingwood when Tom Hafey left to coach the Magpies in 1977), they would have found a lamp post and Graeme and I would be hanging from it. I knew we would do anything to keep him. We would have sold the Richmond Town Hall. I worried about it – I knew we were never going to let it happen.

I'd just like people at Richmond to remember that I was passionate and loved the club. I did everything possible in my body to make it successful.

Claiming Dick Clay's signature was a typical coup for the Richmond-Wilson combination.

Tony Jewell

A tough, honest competititor during his playing days in the 1960s, 'TJ' brought an honesty and humour to a team on the rise. Yet he made his most significant mark on Punt Road as a coach, being as a coach, leading the club to the 1980 Premiership. And he did it his way.

1964-70

Born
Dec 8, 1943

Played
1964-70
80 games,
16 goals

Interviewed
May 10, 2007

I was playing for Oakleigh and living in Brighton, which was St Kilda's area, as a 16-year-old. After three years at Oakleigh I trained down at St Kilda just at the time when they were moving to Moorabbin and I knew a few blokes there from school. I played one practice game, actually, against Ian Stewart in the centre. The Richmond connection was Alby Pannam, who was coaching Oakleigh and who coached the Richmond firsts for a couple of years previously (1953-55). He was in contact with Graeme Richmond at the time. So they showed an interest in me when St Kilda didn't.

I was a Richmond supporter. My father was a Geelong supporter and my brother was a Geelong supporter and for some reason I barracked for Richmond. When I was a kid, Roy Wright came down to Caulfield, where I was playing junior games, and it was probably because of that. He was a lovely man and I got to know Roy pretty well over the years. The senior coach at Caulfield when I was playing was a bloke by the name of Polly Perkins, who was a 1943 premiership player for Richmond. (Carlton forward) Harry 'Soapy' Vallance was the junior coach who I played under, but I think it was the Roy Wright-Polly Perkins connection that swung me over to Richmond.

The VFA was a pretty wild competition then and I don't think it was a game a 16-year-old should have been playing. My mother certainly didn't want me to play there. It was very much about crash and bash. I don't think I ever learnt much about football from the VFA.

This is a true story. It was my first game at Oakleigh. We had a bloke who played centre half-back, he was an albino of all things, and he was a slaughterman at the Oakleigh abattoirs. Anyway, for my first game we were playing Sandringham, who Oakleigh had played in the Grand Final the year before, and they hated each other.

I walked in and Alby Pannam, the coach, had this meat hanging from the walls and he was walking around, screaming about Sandringham and banging this meat that was hanging up, and blood was flowing everywhere. I can vividly remember seeing him hit it with his fist. When we got in at half-time it wasn't there. You can imagine a 16-year-old, my first senior game and my eyes were popping out of my head. Alby used to let everyone in the room to hear him talk; he stopped and yelled 'Get that fucking bastard out of here!' It turned out it was Scotty Palmer, who was a cadet reporter – that was my first meeting with Scot Palmer. Alby threw Scot out of the rooms because he had written something about him the year before. He was very passionate.

First thing I remember at VFL level was the speed of the game. It was a beautiful day on my first game (round 2 v Essendon, 1964), and I can remember the ball flashing around everywhere and they were two crackerjack sides. I can remember the first few minutes thinking, 'I'll never keep up with this.' I couldn't get my breath, I think a bit of nerves were involved.

In the 1967 Grand Final, Fred Swift's famous mark was at the Punt Road End. I was running in from the city side flank and I was of no doubt that he marked it inside the playing field. As soon as he marked it I took off to make myself a target for him. I was of no doubt that it wasn't marked behind the line.

Mike Patterson was a tower of strength that day for us, and I can remember Polly Farmer screaming

Tony Jewell led the triumphant Tigers to flag glory in 1980, but was gone two years later.

at him because Patto had whacked him. The other moment was with the other Geelong ruckman (Chris Mitchell). I said to Mike Patterson 'He's a bit soft that big Geelong ruckman, he came back after being on the ball and he didn't want to come near me.' Patto started laughing and I said 'What you laughing at?' He said 'Well, he came onto the ball to swap with Polly,' and Patto had given him a backhander right across the nose and he started screaming at him, telling him he was an animal. Patto said 'Well, you think I am mad, wait until you get back to the back pocket – that Jewell is twice as bad as me.' I think that accounted for the fact he was very apprehensive.

I can remember in the rooms afterwards, the light on Charlie Callander's face. Even Graeme Richmond, who never showed much emotion, was just absolutely overjoyed by it. I think it meant so much.

"I've always had a temper ... I could certainly fly off the handle pretty easily. I'm ashamed sometimes, looking back now. I've got a temper, especially if players break team rules."

I never had an ambition to coach Richmond, or anyone for that matter. When I left Richmond I was playing-coach at Caulfield and I wanted to coach because I still wanted to play; I thought if I played under a coach in a lesser competition after playing under Tommy I could see my game slipping away and losing interest altogether. So I really wanted to coach to keep my enthusiasm more than anything for the game. I coached Caulfield (in the VFA) for six years and we had a fair bit of success. Out of the blue I was invited back to coach Richmond reserves; we won a premiership in the reserves and made the finals every year for the three years that I coached them. And out of that I eventually inherited the job. It wasn't something I ever dreamt of, or really wanted to do. I just went with the flow. I was offered the job and took it.

In my first training session, while still assistant to Barry Richardson, we did some contesting work. I don't know why I took training but I remember talking to Graeme Richmond just before training and he was lamenting the fact that he thought we were soft and that we needed toughening. Anyway, I did this drill where I had two groups at either end of the ground, I put the ball in the middle of the ground and blew the whistle and players took off from either end and had to attack the ball and get the ball. And the bloke there first was the one going to get the ball and the other bloke had to tackle him.

Anyway, it turned out to be a bit of a bloodbath. Jimmy Jess and Mick Malthouse collided, noses and eyebrows were broken. One of the funny things I found out later was that apparently we had a kid up from the thirds training with us. Now Francis Bourke loved that sort of stuff, and he was in his element and it was his turn. At the corresponding end was this kid from the thirds, who had to attack the ball against Francis Bourke!

They told me later that the blokes up Bourke's end were so concerned about the health of this kid that they grabbed Francis's shorts and held him back for a few seconds before the kid took off at the other end, so the kid easily got there first. Otherwise Francis would have sent him into the next world. From memory we lost two or three players from the next week out of it.

My game style was very much based on the Tommy Hafey, Len Smith recipe with long kicking. That style didn't alter at all. I believe in it and still do.

I've always had a temper. There was a bit of Alby Pannam in me as well. I could certainly fly off the handle pretty easily. It was genuine. I'm ashamed sometimes, looking back now. I've got a temper, especially if players break team rules, or if I didn't think we were being hard enough. I think I shocked a few blokes. If you spoke to players today the way I spoke to some players, they would walk out on you. It was a different time, of course.

At the time I wouldn't have done much different. You can't pretend to be something you're not. If I was coaching today I would certainly be a lot softer in my attitude towards a lot of things. You have to, or otherwise you would only last five minutes.

We struggled for a while in my first season (1979) and I can remember I was only into my sixth game when the papers were calling for me to be sacked. Royce Hart was my assistant. I was very unfashionable. I was never a star player. I think I came out of the blue when I was given the job and there were a lot of better credentialed players. I think the press thought I was open season. But we got through it and we just missed the finals.

Jewell and Jones come to blows during quarter-time of the 1980 qualifying final. At left are Richmond's fitness advisor Peter Grant and runner Ken Hailes, while Carlton football manager Shane O'Sullivan watches on from right.

Anyone who played in the 1980 side reckons that pre-season was the hardest they had done in their lives. We just thought there was a softness that had crept into the team.

Kevin Bartlett going to half-forward flank that year was a revelation, but he hated it. With Michael Roach, David Cloke, Jim Jess, Kevin Bartlett, Barry Rowlings, Robert Wiley and Dale Weightman all up forward it just made it a dynamic forward line. It was a nightmare for sides to match up on us. It turned out Kevin had a phenomenal year, he kicked 84 goals and Michael Roach kicked 112. It was such a potent forward line.

I used to like a drink back then and I decided I wouldn't have a drink until midnight that night (after winning the premiership). Because I wanted to absorb it all, take it all in and just be able to sit back and watch and observe the young players and even the old players.

Francis Bourke and Kevin Bartlett, who never thought they were going to play in another premiership, they really savored the fact they had won another one. I think they thought after Tommy was gone they weren't going to see another one. I just sat back and enjoyed the enjoyment of all the others being involved. They are hard things to win, you put in a hell of a lot of hard work.

The fight with Percy Jones was a number of things. Graeme Landy knocked out Ken Sheldon just on quarter-time, which Percy wasn't happy about. We also had Rudi Webster sitting on the sidelines working for us all year – the year before he had been with Carlton.

As we were running down to the ground, Percy spotted Rudi and started really getting into him about being disloyal and jumping ship, which really upset Rudi. He came to me and said 'Percy is abusing me.'

I had other things on my mind because we had to address the side. Anyway, as we were breaking up from the huddle, Jones started giving Rudi a mouthful again. And, I don't know why I did it, but I just ran at Percy, and I remember I was going to go on with it, and I was going to drop him.

Ken Hailes, the runner, screamed from behind me 'Don't do it, don't do it Tony!' and in the end I sort of pushed Percy's chest and he pushed me and off we went.

I was asked about it after the game, and I was so focused about things that I couldn't even recall what the press were talking about. It took me some time to remember there was a bit of an incident. They even bought it up in Parliament. I think there was some discussion on it about the VFL and role models and all this sort of stuff.

Mal Brown

Controversial Mal Brown came to the Tigers – from East Perth in the WAFL – with a huge reputation. He played one action-packed season in 1974, but missed the premiership win due to suspension.

1974

Born
Oct 26, 1946

Played
Richmond
1974
14 games,
25 goals

Interviewed
April 11, 2007

In 1966, Ian Wilson made contact with me after the Australian Championships in Hobart and we kept in touch through Graeme Richmond and Alan Schwab. Then I signed a Form Four with Collingwood; I was a Collingwood supporter as a kid and I loved Murray Weideman.

I came over to see Collingwood, at my own cost, with a bloke called Bradley Smith from North Melbourne and we went to Collingwood to meet an official and he never turned up. So we were stuck in Collingwood and we started walking with our suitcase and ended up running into Alan Schwab. It was a complete accident. So Schwab found us some accommodation, and that is how I came to play at Richmond.

What happened in those days was if you couldn't get cleared, you had to stand out of football. That's what Polly Farmer did, when he came over to Victoria – he had to miss a year. I was captain-coach of East Perth at 23 years of age and I was going to try to finally come over to Richmond to play. Kevin Murray was ready to take my coaching spot but a couple of days later he changed his mind, so East Perth wouldn't clear me. I ended up coming over to Punt Road when I was 27.

I couldn't care less if people think I started the Windy Hill Brawl. Nothing ever worries me. It wasn't a major thing that sparked the whole lot, it was a series of little niggly things during the game.You look back and think, how the hell did that flare up to be as big a blue as it was?

It got out of hand. It just happened. Big 'Jerker' Jenkin took a mark in the middle of the ground and I was standing on the mark, with both my legs over the top of him. And it just escalated from there.

The Essendon runner, Laurie Ashley made some comments, and some say I belted him, which I don't fully subscribe to. Then I walked off, because it was half-time and John Cassin came from around the boundary and jumped in the air with a dressing gown on and landed on me and we basically fell over.

Then all hell broke loose. Jim Bradley got belted by Stephen Parsons. 'The Whale' (Brian Roberts) got hit with a can. It was amazing. Even Graeme Richmond was in there throwing a few punches. He ended up getting fined $2000. Police were talking about the incident.

It was quite scary for a lot of people. When you went up the race people were spitting on you. People were trying to hit you through the wire, and one guy put his face up against the wire and was spitting and I just hit the wire and gave him a blood nose.

I was suspended for one match. I don't think they knew what they reported me for, but I was put up by the VFL's Investigation Officer. It was pretty much a case of no one will believe it if we don't report you. You started it so we are going to give you a week.

I got hurt in the brawl. I got trodden on by the policeman's horse and had a sore knee. It ended up turning purple.

I was lucky to be a part of Richmond in 1974 but unlucky not to be there for their premiership. In the third-last game of the season (round 20) against Collingwood at Victoria Park, I took a mark while playing on Mike Delahunty and the umpire John Sutcliffe said it was difficult to actually see which one of us took the mark, so he asked for a ball-up.

Mal Brown poses with a young Richmond fan after a game in 1974. Dick Clay looks on.

Mal Brown takes a mark in front of North Melbourne's Garry Farrant during his single season with the Tigers in 1974. Richmond beat North in the Grand Final, but Brown didn't play because of suspension.

I was so disappointed, that I threw the ball back at him. It didn't hit him or anything like that, but I got reported for misconduct. I ended up getting suspended for four matches at the Tribunal. So I missed the 1974 premiership.

Let's be honest, if the umpire had caught the ball he would have ended up in Hobart! But I genuinely believe they had been waiting for me from the Windy Hill Brawl match. I think it was the 'don't get angry, get even' square-up.

Everyone was very shocked that I got a four-match penalty. I remember media personalities Michael Williamson and Lou Richards thought the punishment was completely over the top. There was never any thought that I was going to get four matches. But there is not a lot you can do.

The only thing in my life I have ever regretted is not being available for selection in the 1974 Grand Final. Tommy Hafey has told me I would have made the team.

The following week we were training somewhere, and John Sutcliffe was training nearby and I remember I picked up a ball and threw it back at him and said 'can you catch it this *$#$@$ time'.

We were brought up in a different era, where you hated other clubs and the umpires, but once the game was over you got on with your life.

I went to the 1974 Grand Final and sat with Ian Stewart in the grandstand. We were really thrilled for the team, but deep inside we were disappointed that we couldn't be a part of it. The theory that you still feel part of a premiership team, because you contributed to games during the year is bullshit. So at the end of 1974 I was appointed captain-coach of Claremont for three years, and went back to Western Australia.

Not many people know this, but I had glandular fever throughout 1974. I've ended up with an immunity to penicillin. For years and years doctors would split my blood and all that and they reckon that has contributed to my immunity. It made me so tired. It was hard to lift my legs out of bed and I think one day I slept right through and missed training. At the time it was something you just didn't talk about to others, although our doctor Bill Granger knew. The first tests right at the start of the year showed up nothing and then later in the year it was revealed; by that stage we were heading towards the finals.

"We were brought up in a different era, where you hated other clubs and the umpires, but once the game was over you got on with your life."

I sum up my time at Richmond as a privilege. I had the privilege of being with the best team, with the best group of people I think I have been involved with in my entire football career. I'm disappointed that I was stupid enough to throw the ball back too hard and miss out on the big prize.

You've got to look at the positives. I've been good friends with people from Richmond from 1974 up until now. 1974 was a funny year because it bonded a lot of very close friendships for me in just a 12-month period. It was a marvellous time to be involved with such a successful club and with successful people.

Toothless Tiger Mal Brown was always good for a laugh off the field, but he was a tough nut on it.

David Cloke, being carried off the ground by his teammates, after kicking eight goals in his final game against Carlton at the MCG in 1991.

David Cloke

David Cloke played 333 senior games across three decades and two clubs. He famously ended his career with eight goals in his last game, and three Brownlow votes from each of his last three games.

1974-82,
1990-91

I was zoned to Richmond when I lived in Oakleigh. Peter, my older brother, went to Tigerland first in 1970 and ended up playing 28 games. I came to Richmond in 1973.

My first game in 1974 was against Fitzroy at the Junction Oval, in the back pocket. I sat on the bench and came on at the 25-minute mark of the last quarter replacing Rex Hunt. If I remember rightly, I played on big Dean Farnham, about six feet, 10 inches, in what was his second game of League football.

There was an all mighty blue on the boundary line, right near the interchange bench and Robbie McGhie was involved. Some lady reached across from the crowd with her umbrella and was hitting Robbie on the back of his head and he turned around, grabbed the umbrella, bent it in half and gave it back to her.

Rex Hunt ended up going to Geelong around six weeks later and Gareth Andrews came up to Richmond. Around this stage Royce Hart was having problems with his knees and they wanted a second centre half-forward to take the pressure off him and so Tommy moved me up to the half-forward line.

My first year in the Seniors, we won the flag. I had just turned 19 and I thought to myself, 'this is easy, too easy'.

I used to be worried about having to play so many games before winning a premiership – and here I am, in my 23rd career game, playing in the 1974 premiership. I was too young to appreciate it.

A week or so after the 1974 premiership we went over and played in the Australian Championship games in Adelaide and won that.

Then we lost a lot of players. Dick Clay and Michael Green retired. Royce was finishing, his knees were packing up on him. And Brian 'Whale' Roberts, Francis Jackson, and Graham Teasdale famously went to South Melbourne for John Pitura.

There were big wraps on Pitura as a player, but they lost the character of the club in Brian Roberts. He was one that brought everyone together, always joking, he made the place light-hearted.

Royce could hardly train by this stage. It was similar to what Ian Stewart had been for two or three years earlier. We used to joke that as soon as the Nylex clock hit six o'clock, Ian Stewart went straight up the race, into the rooms, and got changed.

Tommy Hafey knew that if Stewart stayed out on the track any longer he wouldn't get the results required from him on the weekend.

My memory of the Windy Hill Brawl was that it seemed like a typical game of football. My understanding is Graeme Jenkin and Mal Brown had a few words during the quarter and as they crossed paths at half time they had a few more words, then a push, then a shove, then players and officials jumped in and away it went. And here I was watching it all from the forward pocket.

I can remember running in and grabbing Graeme Richmond and just pushing him up towards the race. I also had to make sure he wasn't going to throw one at me in the heat of brawl.

I remember seeing 'Whale' in the changing rooms, he was on one of the rub-down tables and he had been hit

Born
Jan 28, 1955

Played
Richmond
1974-82,
1990-91

Richmond
219 games,
272 goals

Collingwood
114 games,
41 goals

Interviewed
Apr 19, 2008

with a can across the bridge of his nose and it had been split and they put a huge bag of ice across his head and blood was just pouring out. I sat in there the whole half-time break thinking 'what is going to happen in the second half, is it going to erupt again?' And you know what, it was probably the quietest second half of football I have played in. The game was the catalyst for the League enclosing the races to protect the players.

A lot of my mates I worked with were Essendon supporters. A few years later we were playing out there and Tim Watson was in his early years and I was playing centre half-forward and Ron Andrews was playing on me. So I knew what sort of game I was in for. I remember Watson picked the ball up in front of the Members' Stand, had a couple of bounces, and I was coming towards him and he went to dodge and I threw my arm out to tackle him, and I copped him head high. Down he went, right there in front of the Members' Stand. So the crowd gave me a hard time about that but I didn't even get reported.

I kicked five goals that day. After the game, I went up to the social club to drink with my mates and you could hear a lot of the supporters saying 'oh that's the bloke who hit Watson'. That was the way football was played in those days. I would say 99.9 per cent of things that ever happened on the field, stayed there.

I had good ability to read the play and sum up what was around me. I was never the quickest player around – but I never claimed to be quick. I was a reasonable mark but a lot of people reckon I wasn't a reasonable kick. But that's okay, it got me to where I had to be. I thought my kicking was sufficient enough to get me through 18 years of football.

When you're six feet, five inches, and trying to drop the ball from hand to foot, it is a long way. That's why you see most good kicks are by small players, because the distance between hand and foot is a lot closer.

I had an awkward two-handed drop. It is how I had been taught to drop the ball. That meant I dropped the ball higher than what I probably should have. It was awkward but got the job done. I felt quite comfortable with the action. Over the years, different people tried to change my style but most of the time it just felt uncomfortable. After Royce retired he was involved for a few years and did some work with us sometimes with kicking. What he tried to do was refine it and introduce a routine when having set shots for goal.

I basically averaged one goal a game for someone who played a lot of games on the ball, up forward and down back.

In Tommy's early days as my coach, he was very conscious that if you were a marking type of player he wanted you to look at handballing as the first option. Towards the end of the 1980 season, I developed a foot injury. And we found out later on that I had torn the arch away from the bone. What ended up happening was that it calcified trying to heal itself, so I had healed bone on top of bone. Everytime I stood on it, it was just bone on bone, very painful. We tried everything including cutting the heels away from my boots.

In the round 22 game against South Melbourne I played in a converted pair of runners. It didn't work. I missed the Qualifying and Semi Finals. We tried different type of treatments and had cortisone injections that probably in the end, with the amount I had, made it worse.

Tony Jewell came up to me after the Preliminary Final and said 'we have three training sessions – Monday, Tuesday, Thursday. If you get through those three training sessions you will be playing in the Grand Final.'

I was nowhere near 100 per cent. Before I got injected up I was probably around 50 per cent, when I got injected I was probably up to 80 per cent.

A story which hasn't come out too much was that, Ben Weiss, our club doctor, and I had spoken on the Monday leading up to the Grand Final. He said 'we can inject you on match day – you won't feel it you will be right', and I said, 'well I have got to get through the week first'.

So I trained the Monday night without any pain killers, got through okay, woke up Tuesday morning and it was so sore I couldn't put it on the ground. I rang Ben and told him what it was like and he said 'we can inject it match day but I don't really want to inject it for you during the week to train. It's probably not really good for you.'

Wednesday I kept off it, and by Thursday it was that sore I still couldn't walk and I had one session to get through and I knew it was going to be a long session

– probably an hour. I got my foot injected again went and trained and got picked in the Grand Final side. But the hardest thing was, we had the Grand Final parade on the Friday and I had to go to that. I was trying to walk from the bus to the cars and back again without limping.

On Grand Final day I was trying to walk from my parked car to the changing room without people seeing that I had this foot injury. People were stopping me, wishing me the best of luck, asking for autographs and I wasn't even concentrating on them. I was simply trying not to limp.

Once I got in the rooms, I stayed in the rooms, got ready, and just before we ran out I went up to Ben and he injected me. He then strapped my ankles, put my boot on and out I went.

I kicked six goals and four behinds in the 1980 premiership. My first three scoring shots were all behinds. In the first quarter I missed one from 25 metres out directly in front. The second one I was running into an open goal on a bit of an angle and I tried to hook it back, but hooked it back too much.

Basically I was trying to work out how much pressure I could apply to my foot, and how much feeling I would have in it.

After the game we were in the room and as soon as I had one drink, I just vomited it all up. I was in hospital on the Monday and had my foot operated on.

There was a large chunk of that 1980 premiership side that moved on, still in the prime of their football. Bryan Wood had been captain in 1981, Geoff Raines had been Best and Fairest three times. We all didn't leave for just one reason, there were a number of things involved. Then the following year, Robert Wiley went back to Perth, Brian Taylor left soon after that. The club lost a big chunk of experience and good players at that time.

Graeme Richmond was hard, ruthless, but put in 200 per cent for the Richmond Football Club. He *WAS* the Richmond Football Club at that stage – especially during my time.

He was the powerbroker behind the place, he pulled all the strings.

I think he did most of the contract negotiations, a lot of the recruiting and player transfers. He was the one behind the John Pitura swap.

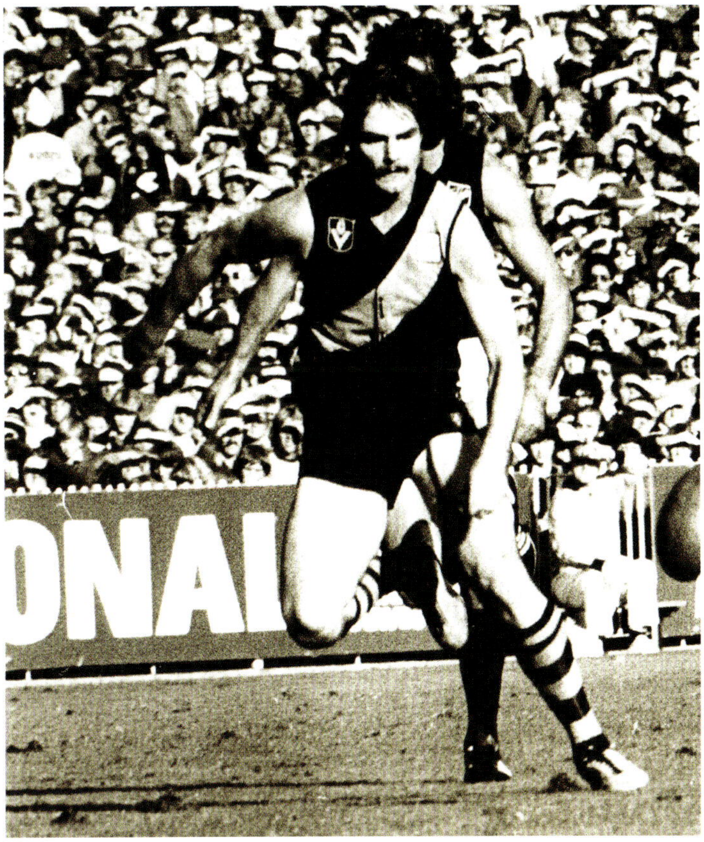

'I had good ability to read the play and sum up what was around me,' Cloke recalls.

I can remember some Friday nights before games you would get a phone call from Graeme. He would ring you up and in Graeme's way would say 'Hey Cocker, big game tomorrow son. Really important, First bounce I want you to come through the centre and take someone out.' Clunk! He'd hang up the phone. That was it. That was the whole conversation.

Then you'd get to the game and he would be walking around the rooms saying 'remember what we spoke about last night son'. So at the first bounce you would line someone up and run straight through and he'd come up to you after the game and say 'Yeah, geez well done. Hey.' And that was Graeme. He was a man of not many words, but would get to the point about things.

I think Ian Wilson and Graeme Richmond were ideal for each other. In a way they looked like the odd couple. Ian was flamboyant, always smoking little cigars, nicely dressed. Graeme was the real strong man. Ian loved the publicity. There was the standard joke that anytime a Richmond player went to the Tribunal, Ian was always there and when they took a photo, Ian had his photo in the paper.

The two of them were really good for each other. They had the heart of the RFC. Even talking to Ian today, he still bleeds for the club. He still can't understand a number of things that go on at that place.

I finished at the end of 1982 when I ended up going to Collingwood. A lot of people don't realise I nearly went to Melbourne. Dick Seddon had approached me at the same time he approached Kelvin Templeton and Peter Moore and I was going to be the third one to go across to Melbourne. We had a number of talks, again you had to be careful how you did it.

Dick Seddon would ring you and say 'we will meet you on the 15th floor at such and such room at the Hilton Hotel'. You would drive into the bottom car park, came up through the lift. All very secret.

Even Lindsay Fox, had a chat with me about coming to St Kilda, which was coached by Ian Stewart. Collingwood hadn't won a flag for so long and that was probably a driving force for me to end up going there.

However, at the end of 1989 I got a phone call to come down meet the coach and the President at the time, Alan McAllister. When you get a phone call in October to come down for a talk you really know it isn't going to be great news. I walked into the coaches room and there was a long table and three chairs. Alan and Leigh Matthews were sitting at one end of the table, and there was single chair down the other end of the table. That was mine.

They tried to convince me to retire. I was still happy with the way I was playing. I was on 290 games and had a driving ambition to play 300 games and if I had given it away, I would have kicked myself thinking I should have kept going for another year.

The club was into a youth policy and here I was going on 34 years of age. Around about Christmas time, in 1989, I was sitting around at home waiting for someone to ring. Someone did. It was the Richmond coach, Kevin Bartlett. He asked me if I would I be interested in coming back to Tigerland if they were to re-draft me.

But he added 'I have some bad news, we are in financial trouble and we really can't offer you anything.'

I thought 'shit, here we go, coming back to Richmond, getting nothing for it, busting my guts.' However, I told him to give me a couple of days to think about it as I was weighing up all the other offers, of which there were none. I think it was about 48 hours later, I rang him back and told him that I would love to.

At the end of 1990 I retired again. I had made 300 games, played every game that year and I was pretty comfortable with retirement.

Again, Kevin was ringing me, this time two or three times a week telling me, 'you should play, you had a great year'. So I told him I would come down and train for a week, to prove to him how past playing football I was and how I had had enough. I did it to try and shut him up.

I went down to train for a week and probably surprised myself how I went. I felt good, I enjoyed the team environment and helping out the new players. However, because I had resigned and therefore delisted by the club, I had to get re-drafted again.

David Cloke, back at Richmond in the twilight of his career, enjoys a post-game moment with full-forward Jeff Hogg.

So we played in a couple of practice matches and I was running around getting plenty of the ball playing really well. At a practice game out at La Trobe University, Kevin picked me in the early game, and I went out there and had 20 possessions in the first half. At half time he took me out of the game. I was confused. I told him, 'you want me to play another year, yet now your telling me to come off'. He told me there were a couple of clubs watching the practice match and there was talk one of them may attempt to draft me.

So we devised this ploy, that I would come off the ground during the practice match, strap my knee up, put a big ice pack on it, and tell those around me that it feels like I need to have a full knee reconstruction. So we did that. Sitting on the bench, I sent one of my teammates over to an ice-cream van to buy me an ice cream so I could eat it on the bench.

Scot Palmer was there and he came up to me and said 'whats the matter?' I said 'I have done my knee. Looks like it is completely stuffed. I need a reconstruction. That's it.' So Scotty wrote that all up in the paper. And the draft was the following week, so I didn't train that week and when the day came Richmond re-drafted me and I started training on the Monday and played that season again.

I played all but one game in 1991. I kicked eight goals in my last game against Carlton at the MCG. I started off in the ruck and Ty Esler, in his first game, was on the bench. Justin Madden was in the ruck for Carlton and he was giving us a hard time in the ruck. Halfway through the first quarter they moved me down to the forward pocket and put Ty Esler into the ruck.

Just before quarter time the ball came down, I took a mark and kicked a goal. I know from talking to Kevin afterwards that in the box they were telling him to get me off, and he said 'no, it is his last game, I don't care what happens, he won't be coming off even if he doesn't touch the ball'.

Just before half time I kicked a couple more and had four by the main break. In the second half, I kicked four more and had eight at the end of the day.

For my last shot for goal, I marked 45 metres out on a 45-degree angle. Craig Lambert came up to me and said, 'you have kicked floaters and mongrels all day, what are you going to kick this time' and for a joke I said 'it will be my last kick, I am going to kick a reverse torpedo.' So I've lined it up and kicked it, and it has gone straight through the middle. Peter Dean of Carlton was standing on the mark and he heard us talking about it, and when he saw it go through the goals I could hear him say, 'oh fuck'.

David Cloke, the family man, with sons Cameron (back left), Jason (back right) and Travis—all eventual AFL stars—and daughter Jodie.

I got carried off the ground by Richard Nixon and Andy Goodwin. I was asked how I felt getting carried off, and I said 'I was scared the bastards were going to drop me.'

Some people said 'why would you want to retire after that finish?' I really got everything out of my body. I had played for 18 years, it was taking a toll on me and the family were getting older so it was a very good way to finish.

I got three Brownlow votes in each of my last three games. KB got sacked at the end of that year, yet I can't help but feel if he was coaching the following year, he would have convinced me to play on.

It was such an honour to be inducted into the Richmond Hall of Fame in 2007. I never regarded myself as a brilliant player. I was the one who just persevered. To get inducted, it shows that some people thought I was a bit better than what I thought I was.

The Windy Hill brawl (above) was sparked by Essendon runner Laurie Ashley, who questioned the tactics of Richmond's Mal Brown. The infamous half-time melée is a black mark on the ground's long history, and culminated in lengthy suspensions and police charges. Young Richmond supporter, James Ferguson (wearing No. 13) had a front seat to the fight. Also pictured (from left to right): Future Essendon premiership player, then playing for Richmond, Bryan Wood (blonde hair, third from left, partly obscured), Ian Stewart (Richmond, partly obscured), Paul Sproule (Richmond, number 6 in foreground), Ken Roberts (tussling with Sproule, and who kicked four goals in what was his first game of the season), Ken Fletcher (Essendon, the second player remonstrating with Sproule), Wayne Walsh (Richmond, at back) Graeme Richmond (Richmond secretary, being restrained by Tiger official, Neil Busse), Robert McGhie (Richmond, is to the left of Graeme Richmond, in background), Mike Green (Richmond, partly obscured at back), Graeme Jenkin (Essendon, bending over and partly obscured between the two policemen), Gary Parkes (Essendon, behind Jenkin) and Laurie Moloney (Essendon, No. 34, partly obscured). Interestingly, young Ferguson appears to be wearing Essendon colours, not Richmond. One theory for this is that his local club colours may have been the same as Essendon's. Richmond's No. 13 in 1974 was Stephen Rae, while there was no No. 13 on Essendon's list in 1974. In fact, no Essendon player had worn No. 13 since Fred Gallagher in 1958!

Stephen Parsons

Stephen Parsons, aged 17 and in only his third game playing against Essendon in 1974, found himself involved in the infamous Windy Hill Brawl at half-time, which saw him charged by police for assault. He played only five games for the Tigers in that one season.

1974

My playing career was wasteful. I just wasted my opportunities. I am a coach now (North Ringwood and Ringwood junior teams). I have had a lot of success at coaching; I get a thrill out of guiding young guys through the minefield of life, because I have actually hit a lot of those mines.

Only twice in 18 years have I told them my inner-most thoughts of how it feels to miss an opportunity. Sometimes it passes you by just once and if you don't grab it, it's gone.

For the amount of games I've played (five), I've received a huge amount of publicity. I am probably better known than some 200-game players, which is ridiculous.

All the publicity came from that Essendon game, the Windy Hill Brawl. No kid my age could have got through that without getting big-headed, and I got so far ahead of myself.

Nowadays you have tutoring on how to treat the media and clubs educate you very well. But the attention I got after that incident was incredible and I believed all the publicity. I thought I was 10-foot tall, I was bulletproof and stuff the rest of the world. It was unbelievable.

Most people just want to talk about that Essendon game. You tend to get a bit sick of it. It didn't do too much for my career. What I remember is that there was an incident with (John) Cassin and (Mal) Brown and (Graeme) Jenkin, and then all of a sudden at half-time it flared up and all I saw was that Graeme Richmond had slipped to the ground and there was a bloke having a crack at him. I didn't know who it was. I thought it was a supporter because of the way he was dressed, in a dark tracksuit. That's why I hit him. It was actually Jim Bradley, Essendon's fitness advisor.

When it finally calmed down we went up the race, which wasn't very high. The abuse and the fights up that race were enormous. We had pies thrown at us, bottles thrown at us, people jumping the race to fight us. Getting into the rooms was more violent than anywhere else. It was chaotic. I don't know whether it was a figment of my imagination or not, but it looked like the windows in the room were rocking back and forth. It was out of control.

After the game I had to be kept in the rooms for an hour and a half. Essendon supporters wanted to kill me. I had to get a police escort to the car.

I had to change my phone number because we got death threats. Every day I would be on the front page of *The Sun* with Graeme Richmond. TV reporters and photographers would follow me going to school and work.

Then I got charged with assault and got trial by video. I was the first player to be charged by assault by the police and Graeme Richmond and I went to court much later over it.

I actually played against North Melbourne the following week, and the match against Collingwood. The tribunal was scheduled for the week after that because it was such a kerfuffle, there was a long investigation and many interviews to conduct. I got rubbed out for four matches.

For the next year and beyond people would taunt me. It was out of control, crazy. It was ludicrous.

My mum got crook over it because we were getting calls at three or four in the morning. For about six months after it she struggled a lot.

Born
Oct 19, 1956

Played
Richmond
1974
5 games,
1 goal

Interviewed
April 20, 2009

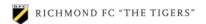

It was like something out of *The Fugitive*. If I was on a train and my photo was on the front of the paper, people in the carriage would look at me and then look at the paper. I would be at a pub having a counter meal and I would get into stoushes all the time because someone wanted to have a crack at me.

I even read in the paper where some person had mentioned they were at the Windy Hill Brawl and it had an adverse effect on their life. I thought, you're kidding aren't you!

If I could get back into a time capsule I would still do the same thing. But I would react after it in a totally different manner, only because I know what I know now. I didn't carry myself properly the year or two after it. I got so much publicity I thought I was so good. It just pulled me undone, all the reasons why I ever got to play League football seemed to go out the window.

The club got the best legal counsel they could get. They supported me well in that case, but after that I'm not quite sure how well they supported me. After it began to die down, North Melbourne was interested in me but Richmond wouldn't clear me.

Maybe it was because of the way I was carrying on, that I was a bit too big for my boots. I went through some belongings at home and I found a letter from Schwabby saying they would clear me interstate but not to another VFL club. They wouldn't let me play against them. How would that go nowadays?

On the anniversary of the Essendon game, my name always comes up and I can't stand it. It happened that a Federal Election also occurred on that day so a couple of times there has been a Federal Election on that date again and it just flairs up.

Essendon Football Club once contacted me and said 'we want to pick you up in a car and bring you out and re-enact it in the social club'. I said 'yeah you'll be re-enacting it without me', and hung up. I wasn't interesting in doing that.

I have reporters still ringing me, but I just won't talk to them. Now I don't even want to know about it. If I know who it is, I won't talk to them. I've had enough of it.

I came back for a couple of games. I got suspended again in the Reserves for two or three weeks towards the end of the year. I got reported for hitting Terry Wheeler.

I watched the 1974 premiership with our players and parents. How did I feel? Different. We'd won the Under 19s the year before, but I was coming back from suspension this year and I was rapt for the football club but at the back of your mind you always have that thought: 'what if I hadn't mucked up. I could have been out there'.

In quiet times, when I get reflective, it haunts me. What if I had dealt with it better? What could have been? Not just 1974 but beyond. Do you reckon I haven't asked myself those questions a few times. It's a nightmare.

The next year I dislocated my shoulder and was out for six months. I was told the day it happened that if I played well I would be back in the seniors the next week. And I took a grab at the MCG against Fitzroy, got up high and came down on the point of my shoulder and it popped straight out. It put me out for that year. Then I went to South Australia.

I was a hard trainer. I was in athletics before I played football and I think that's what helped me play League football. I was so fit and quick. I would like to have thought I was a fair, aggressive player, but not ridiculous. I was very creative with my hands and had ability to go when I had to go.

The junior development program they had with Ray Jordon and his crew was fabulous. The wheel has turned now, I just couldn't see the young guys of today playing under Ray Jordon now. It was different back then. Nowadays they tend to get a bit molly-coddled and question this and question that. With 'Slug' Jordon it was his way or the highway and he really toughened you up and made you really ready to go on with whatever you wanted to do. He was fantastic. I had a few run-ins with him but overall he was fantastic. He was a great coach, hard as nails but he was very fair. He groomed a lot of people. He made you train hard and made you fix your errors and if you did something good you knew about it and if you did something bad you knew about it ten-fold.

I was identified through a scholarship squad when I played at Nunawading. Then I went to training with the under 19s and 150 blokes turned up and I remember Slug taking us over the bridge to the track around the left and I can still remember my first night there and they were doing 400-metre runs and that was my cup of tea. I could blow them away and that's what pricked their attention to me and what got me through the several cuts on the way to a final list.

I followed South Melbourne, because my parents used to follow them. I can always remember going down to the Lakeside Oval and sitting on my dad's shoulders. Then going over the road to the pub and he would buy me a lemon squash and he would have a couple of beers with his mates and then take us home. They were great old days.

My first senior game, against Carlton (round three, 1974), I was to play on Bryan Quirk, at Princes Park. On the morning of the game, I walked out of my bedroom and turned around and looked at the wall and there was a big poster of Bobby Skilton. I thought 'this is crazy, I'm a kid still'. Bobby was my hero.

I received a phone call at 9pm on the Thursday before saying that I had been picked for the Senior team. I was stunned. I was only 17 years old. I didn't even have my licence. I was still living with my parents. There were some photos with Mal Brown and I at the Vaucluse Hotel being given my jumper. I went all right in that first game. I think I kicked a goal with my first kick in League football.

Ian Stewart once told me, 'Stephen, every 17-year-old has the potential to play League football. If people had the foresight to send them out to coach for two years they would come back superstars'. It is so true. Because what you learn as a coach, and I have coached for 18 years, is extraordinary compared to what you do as a player. You actually learn about the game as a coach and you have a different perspective about it.

Ian Wilson, Graeme Richmond and Alan Schwab were dynamic. I thought Graeme was a great bloke. He was hard as hooray but I tell you what, if you did the right thing and he befriended you, you were set.

"If I could get back into a time capsule I would still do the same thing. But I would react after it in a totally different manner, only because I know what I know now."

Jack Titus was an integral part of the football club. I have fond memories of Jack. He was the players' advocate at the tribunal. I got reported a few times and he'd take you up to the restaurant next to the Hilton before the hearing. You would have dinner there first, and it would blow my mind away, it was the most beautiful food and setting and here I was sitting as a kid with Jack Titus. They treated him like a god. It was out of this world. We used to sit and drink and have a laugh. I'll never forget that. It was a really special time, you're actually sitting across breaking bread with a legend.

Stephen Parsons was only 17 when he made his debut for the Tigers against Carlton in 1974.

Bruce Monteath

A talented ruck-rover, Bruce Monteath joined Richmond in 1975. He had the distinction of captaining Richmond's 1980 premiership team, while sitting on the bench as an interchange player.

1975-80

Born
Sept 20, 1955

Played
Richmond
1975-80
118 games
198 goals

Interviewed
Jul 2009

Doing this interview for your book will probably help me more than anything. I can't just sit up on the rooftops and tell everyone what really was going on with my career.

When I arrived at the club, they had won back-to-back premierships and I can remember Graeme Richmond saying to me 'Don't expect to get in the senior team straight away, we have a super team here and you're only young.' I thought to myself 'shit, that's the reason I came here!, but okay, fair enough.'

I came over as a state ruck-rover and luckily I played pretty well in all the scratch matches, most notably my opponent was the ruck rover from the 1974 Grand Final – Kevin Sheedy. As a result I was picked for the first game, and I played just about every game but was unluckily suspended for four weeks. Imagine you're trying to break into the best side in the country and you lose four weeks through a frigging suspension.

I was suspended twice in my career, both times against Collingwood. But the suspension that occurred during my first year, was at Victoria Park and I was playing half-forward flank on a guy called Doug Gott, who also played state cricket, and he and I got in a blue.

These days you have to do something pretty bad to get four weeks. Doug and I went toe to toe and he later turned up at the tribunal with a black eye. He maintained he did it playing basketball with his brother.

Maybe I did get a punch in, but I thought they'd give me a week or two, nothing more. I didn't have much time for Collingwood.

I managed to play in the 1975 final series. It was a great first year, we went within 17 points of reaching our fourth consecutive Grand Final.

North Melbourne were a great side, but we should have beaten them at Waverley, we just buggered it up in the last 10 minutes. I was 19 years old when I played my first game with Richmond.

I certainly knew what I wanted and I was pretty well driven. I won the best and fairest at my club in South Fremantle.

At the end of 1974, the first ruck and roving division of the Western Australian State Team was Mike Fitzpatrick, myself as ruck-rover and Graham Melrose was the rover. And we all came across to Melbourne.

It was a dream come true for me. I had played nearly 60 WAFL games by the time I was 18, and I had played state football against Victoria and South Australia. So I had experience under my belt by the time I got Tigerland.

I was recruited by Alan Schwab. He had seen me play state schoolboy football and I was the youngest kid playing, just 14 years of age when I made the All Australian Team. 'Schwaby' kept turning up, saying hello, sending me jumpers and said to me 'one day son you might make it and we might be interested'.

It was a boyhood dream to play for Richmond. When I was at high school I always got out books on football and read up on Royce Hart, Kevin Bartlett and Dick Clay.

I always had enough confident in my own ability. I knew if I could get in, I could cut it. In my first

'I think my time at Richmond was one of the most fulfilling in my life,' Monteath recalls.

year I won the Cazaly Award in 1975 for the best ruck-rover in the competition. Around that stage there were signs of the great side crumbling.

A lot of the stars were starting to falter. Royce Hart was having trouble with his knees, Michael Green, Barry Richardson, Gareth Andrews and Dick Clay all retired. The place nearly did fall apart.

"I desperately wanted to play football, but here I was, lying on my back for two weeks, with my eyes covered. I sometimes wonder how I ever got through it."

Alan Schwab went away. The club still had Bryan Wood, David Cloke and myself and the younger blokes like Geoff Raines, Dale Weightman and Mark Lee started to come into the side. That's why it was a wonderful effort to go from 1975 where we just missed out, down to the doldrums for a few years and then return to the top and win the 1980 premiership. It was a brilliant effort.

During my time at Richmond, there was pressure on Tommy Hafey to go. I wished he hadn't and I think it was a bad blue of Graeme Richmond to get rid of him.

I became life long friends with Tommy. When he sees me he says 'I remember when you came over with your girlfriend'. He is just great. When I came to Tigerland, he invited me down to his holiday house – what coach does that these days!

You would do anything for Tommy. I was a bit lost, I didn't know anyone here. I was living by myself. Yet he was terrific.

I was shocked he was going but I really just wanted to be successful at Richmond. I just thought about the young blokes coming into the side. If we got the right group of people and the club did it right, there was every chance that maybe we would have a chance at the premiership. It all happened.

I nearly lost sight in my eye. I got smashed in the face at training with a football. Someone did a low torpedo kick on a wet cold day and a young bloke in front of me from Tasmania thought it would be funny to duck and the ball hit me in the eye and dropped me. Blood was coming out of it onto my cheek.

Tommy was funny, he saw it and said 'whats wrong?' and I told him I couldn't see out of my eye. I didn't know at the time, but it had pushed my eyeball back into my head. Tommy just said I should go jog a lap. But Barry Richardson, our reserves coach grabbed me and said 'Bruce, just lay on the ground here' and turned to Tommy and said 'Shit Tommy, we've got to ring the ambulance mate, he is in a bad way.'

I can remember I was taken to St Vincent Hospital where I stayed for two weeks. I desperately wanted to play football, but here I was, lying on my back for two weeks, with my eyes covered. I sometimes wonder how I ever got through it.

The State of Origin was introduced in 1977 and for that very first game I was ruck-rover for Western Australia. In 1979 I made the All Australian Team and I was ruck-rover in the state carnival which Western Australia also won.

I kicked nearly 200 goals for Richmond and most of those were as a ruck rover, which wasn't a bad return for a bloke who was on the ball. I played only six seasons for Richmond but I am very proud of what I achieved. Injuries and suspensions prevented me from winning the best and fairest award during my time at the club.

It would always be Michael Tuck and myself vying for the 'Sun score' votes each week. I wasn't the flashiest player in the world but was reasonably consistent. I could read the play and I could get the ball. I was a pretty good one-grab mark and was more than confident backing back into packs. My weakness, however, was my pace.

The 1980 Richmond premiership team; back row L-R: Bryan Wood, Daryl Freame, Dale Weightman, Geoff Raines, Robert Wiley, Bruce Monteath, Paddy Guinane, Kevin Bartlett; front row L-R: Emmett Dunne, Stephen Mount, Greg Strachan, Tony Jewell, Francis Bourke, Merv Keane, Michael Roach, David Cloke.

I won the Australian kicking contest at Wagga in 1976. A guy called Des Lay had previously won the contest and was flown over to the United States. Myself and Neville Roberts drove to Wagga and along with Geoff Southby and David McKay we competed for the first prize of $1000. It was all a bit of fun and bugger me dead, I ended up winning with a torpedo that went around 70 metres.

I would love a dollar for every time I am asked about the 1980 premiership. People forget about my entire career and only ask about one thing: 'Why was I sitting on the bench in the Grand Final, as captain.'

About seven or eight years ago, Tony Jewell and I were at a function, and someone asked that question. Tony grabbed the microphone off me and said 'No, I will answer it.' What he told them was that I had been carrying injuries all year, including torn ligaments in my ankle from the first game of the season.

A celebratory cartoon by John Rogers of the Tigers' 1980 Grand Final win, featuring coach Tony Jewell.

And it's all true. From the middle of the season I hurt my back and had a giant hematoma on my spine. Ben Weiss, our club doctor, would draw the blood out of my spine on the Monday and the Friday, and sometimes Saturday morning, so I could play. I would also get injections in my leg. Today they wouldn't even let you play.

As the 1980 final series approached, I went to see Tony and withdrew from the side. I said 'I am captain of the side, but if I am really a true leader, I have got to do what is best for the side.' This sounds magnanimous now, but at the time it was the hardest decision I have ever made in my life. Yet I knew that I could be keeping out a fit player that they may need in the finals.

I have found all my life, that if you make self-sacrificing decisions you will be repaid. I made one, and within three weeks I was back in the team playing. I withdrew for the last game of the season, Round 22 against South Melbourne and we got thrashed, it was unbelievable. I missed the first Qualifying final against Carlton at Waverley Park where we won by 42 points.

I told Tony I would keep training because I was still the captain of the team. Thank Christ I did because we had a lot of injuries from that Carlton game. Barry Rowlings, David Cloke and Bryan Wood were all injured. Tony came up to me the following week and said 'Would you consider playing again?' and I said I would.

I played against Geelong in the Semi Final at Waverley Park and sat on the bench for most of the game but came on late and kicked a goal. We won by 24 points. Once I played that game, I trained my guts out the following week.

In the week of the 1980 Grand Final, Tony said 'You had withdrawn prior to the finals series, so I don't know if we should take a risk in selecting you for the Grand Final' and I said 'It is your call Tony.' And the club put me in.

It was one of those wonderful things that Richmond can do every now and again. I think the decision was made based on everything I had done, for being part of the whole club for the last six years. It was a wonderful gesture.

That whole experience is difficult to explain to people, so I just tell them I was on the bench because I was injured. But as you can see, there was a lot more to it. There would be some saying why would they take the risk. I assumed there would have been robust debate between the coach and match committee. It is a wonderful football story when you think about it.

For the 1980 Grand Final, I led the side out. I began the game on the bench, which I was more than happy to do. If you remember, Royce Hart did that in 1973 Grand Final. It was just one of those games. It was over at quarter time and no one got injured. Everyone was playing so well. So in the end I spent about 15 minutes in total on the ground.

Just before the siren sounded, I took a moment to reflect. I told myself, this is the penultimate moment in my football career, this is a great club, and I am so proud of myself. I knew that in a few seconds that siren would sound and I was going to hold the cup in the air and its ours forever. For history.

I was glad I was there. It was a childhood dream. I had come from another state, I was essentially an outsider of the club and here I was, captain of a premiership side at 24 years of age.

Even during the times I was injured, I was still the captain off the field. A leadership role is as much as what you do on the field as you do off, and that's why you find some clubs struggle because they have captains who are too quiet. You've got to have strong leadership and I believe that is the same in business. I am a pretty strong leader and by doing what I did I was trying to show strength and try not to be selfish.

There is no way known I would have swapped my jumper at the end of the Grand Final. At the end of the day that jumper has pride of place on my wall. Jesus Christ, you play for the jumper, why would I give it away. I hate Collingwood!

I was operated on eight days after the 1980 Grand Final. To even play was a miracle. But this is where the influence of Graeme Richmond came in. I went in for the operation and was recovering in hospital when Graeme came in and said, 'Will your leg come good? Maybe it might be time.' And I started thinking to myself, if I haven't got his support what happens here?

My wife and I had just had our first child, I had a lot of business opportunities offered to me in Melbourne, as well as Perth, and I came to the conclusion that I couldn't go any higher, I've had six great years at the club, am captain of the 1980 premiership side, so I will take up those business opportunities and raise my children in Perth.

We should have won the 1981 and 1982 premierships as well. But within three or four years, Bryan Wood, David Cloke, Geoff Raines and I were all gone. I can remember when I went to the club, they had all this great past success. They even said to me 'we have been such a great club since 1967 and we don't want to go back to the dark days' and I said 'what is the dark days?' and they said 'oh that's when we didn't win a premiership for 24 years!' and I thought to myself, we will never ever do that again.

"I would love a dollar for every time I am asked about the 1980 premiership."

Football teaches you a lot. It teaches you discipline, which you must have in business. It teaches you how to relate to people, but also that you can't please everyone. When you run out on the field, 50 per cent of the people hate you before you even start the game. You learn that goal-setting and hard work does pay off. It teaches you how to handle disappointment, it teaches you to be humble. Football is such a great learning curve for anyone going into business.

I think my time at Richmond was one of the most fulfilling in my life. I was going there as a young man, heading off to manhood, aiming to reach my goals in football and was surrounded by champion players and Tommy Hafey as coach. To initially nearly reach the heights with that team, then to go to the bottom and get back up again, is an experience I hold very close to my heart.

In a way I wish I played at Tigerland right through my whole football life. Looking back, my greatest regret is probably making that decision to go back and follow business. But I am still happy with what I did.

Michael Malthouse, celebrating the 1980 premiership with Jim Jess.

Michael Malthouse

In 1976, the rugged Michael Malthouse crossed from St Kilda to the Tigers, where he played with distinction on the backline, and was a member of the 1980 premiership team. He has become one of the AFL's great coaches.

1976-83

I had no intentions of going to Richmond. Three clubs – Carlton, Hawthorn and Richmond – had made contact with me about one month before I left St Kilda. I had played 50 games for the Saints to the end of 1975, after starting in 1972. In 1976 I played just three more, ending in round 12, against the Hawks. The one club I didn't want to go to was Richmond. Don't ask me why. They just didn't appeal to me whatsoever.

I was totally naive. I kept asking myself, 'why would clubs be ringing me in late May when I'm playing for St Kilda?' Then the jungle drums started beating and I realised I was on the outer. At that time I was under the impression I just wasn't good enough, because I had been given no feedback, outside of being told that I was in the seconds.

Five or six years later, Allan Jeans finally revealed to me that the club was in financial trouble and I became a victim of that. But it was too late. He needed to have said that to me at the time because I had no real understanding as to what was going on. I was totally in the dark. I got on very well with Allan Jeans. I just wish the truth had come out a lot earlier.

I certainly wasn't a highly paid player at St Kilda so I wasn't someone who was costing the club a lot of money. Yet I suddenly fell into the category of the $20,000–$30,000 transfer market. As (mid-season) clearance applications closed, I think I made it one day before the cut off.

Richmond was so professional and persistent. Paddy Guinane and Alan Schwab were like a dog with a bone. When the time came for clearances some way or another, and I can't explain how, I was with Alan signing the transfer forms. After that I went down to St Kilda, walked in to get my boots and the Reserves coach Barry Pascoe was there and he said 'what are you doing?' and I said 'I've been cleared to Richmond', and he said 'that's ridiculous, I know nothing about it'.

It was so chaotic. My first game for Richmond was against Swan Districts (From the WAFL) in the NFL Wills Cup on Tuesday 29th June 1976, in Adelaide. How do you work that out? I got cleared from St Kilda one day, and the next day I was on a plane as a Richmond footballer travelling to Adelaide with Tom Hafey sitting beside me and I was to play in the centre. Neither Richmond or Swan Districts was going to travel the full distance, so they met half way. If there were more than 20 people in the crowd in Adelaide I would have been surprised.

Four days later, I played my first official game for Richmond, against Collingwood. It was round 14 1976. I wore number 28. Just two rounds earlier, I was playing for St Kilda against Hawthorn. What's interesting about my first Richmond game is Bob Heard had come over from Collingwood, Jim Jess via Avoca through St Kilda, and myself – we all received clearances around the same time, and we're all in this match.

The biggest and marked difference for me was how friendly and warm it was. We were made very welcome at Tigerland. However, Moorabbin was rated as a newer ground, it had a new grandstand, the president's office of Graham Huggins had very plush carpet. When I got to Richmond it was like I had turned up on the last day Jack Dyer had trained. It felt as though nothing had happened at the club between 1949 and 1976. I couldn't believe it. Medicine balls would actually lose air!

Born
Aug 17, 1953

Played
Richmond
1976-1983
121 games
10 goals

St Kilda
1972-1976

Interviewed
Mar 6, 2012

Malthouse gathers the ball in front of a big crowd at the MCG against Essendon.

Allan Jeans and Tom Hafey were both outstanding men, but their methodologies were polar opposites. Allan's game was built on defence, Tom's was built on offence. One relied on challenging you all the time, while the other was focussed on pumping you up – so you had a contrasting methodology. I only had Tommy as my coach for half a year, but I still regard him as an influence.

"Allan's game was built on defence, Tom's was built on offence. One relied on challenging you all the time, while the other was focussed on pumping you up."

Barry Richardson was a man probably 10 years ahead of his time. He took over from Tom Hafey as Richmond coach the year after I arrived. Too often you see a coach take over from a former coach and the methodology is identical. You don't have to be identical. You have to identify what is still working and what *can* work. When 'Bones' took over there was no Royce Hart at full-forward, no Paddy Guinane or Michael Green. There was no Bill Barrot or Ian Stewart in the middle.

To me coaching is about getting the best out of your playing group but – first and foremost – understanding your playing group. What are their strengths? I think 'Bones' went out of his way to look at the difference between the side he had and the side he had played in (Richardson had retired after Richmond's 1974 Grand Final win). He started to introduced kick-off drills and strategies. It wasn't like everyone was gathered on one half-back flank and you kicked it as high as you could to them and they would either mark it or it roll out of bounds. It was much more structured. I really enjoyed playing under him because I thought he bought some size to it, some novelty that you only thought about and never believed would take place on the football ground. Things like structure with the kick off and players trying to play specific roles.

We needed to spend hours on these game structures and we couldn't. You went to work. Then you went to training. Then you went home. You never had enough time. If Barry had been coach 10 years later his players would have been more professional in terms of money and time and he would have been able to develop those players. He was a man before his time. I thought he was restricted by officialdom, particular by Graeme Richmond, as probably Richmond, the club, was at the time. Barry was gone after two years, which didn't seem too surprising given Richmond's 'form' at the time.

I had four coaches in the seven-and-a-half years – despite the fact we won a premiership and played off in another final. It was a bit bizarre.

Coaching was on my mind from when I was 26 or 27. I had a knee and ankle reconstruction in 1979 and even then I was thinking of coaching. I worked my bike into the grave and got back and played in 1980. Eventually I started coaching in 1984.

I got reported twice in 1980. Early in the year I got a couple of weeks for striking Grant Fowler of Essendon and then got reported in the second Semi Final when I was alleged to have hit Sam Newman. I got reported by two umpires, the central and goal umpire. It was proven they had seen the

Michael Malthouse jogging to position against the Demons.

The fitness test: coach Francis Bourke wrestles with Malthouse during the famous test of Malthouse's injured right shoulder before the 1982 Grand Final.

incident completely differently from what took place. I had a very good defence. I thought I was home when Alan Schwab remarked 'I think you're right' and I remember thinking I've got a fair chance here. I was really panic-stricken for the two or three days before the tribunal, but very relieved after beating the charge. Sam Newman was outstanding in his evidence. He was very, very forgetful.

"I was totally disappointed when my shoulder came out during the fitness test. Francis Bourke was certainly making it difficult."

I have not thought about the 1980 Grand Final for 32 years, until you asked me that question. It might seem strange but I don't remember the balloons going up, or the club colours, or even the final siren. I remember thinking one or two days after the Grand Final how I would have liked it to have been an absolute battle to the end. Don't get me wrong, I was quite happy to win, but it felt like something was missing. It's like it was built up to a big Christmas present and it turned out to be an empty box.

Grand Finals are often called the pinnacle and the hardest game of the year, but it's not always the case. That's not taking anything away from Collingwood who earned the right to be there. But sometimes you just want those gladiatorial games, where you have a great win and you lay exhausted in the field of battle. Other times you have a deflated feeling about the game because it came too easy. I was staggered at the ease at which we won. You wanted to win badly, but you wanted to win hard. So, it was bittersweet. I was going to swap my guernsey after the game, but thankfully I didn't.

I injured my shoulder in the second semi-final versus Carlton in 1982. I went to punch the ball away, but slipped, yet still got my fist to the player's back and it ripped my shoulder back, but it didn't pop out. I remember thinking it didn't feel very good. Then at my first contest in the second half it popped out and I couldn't get it back in.

I worked to get the strength in my shoulder back and my mind right for the Grand Final. And I got them both right. But I had a very negative medical and coaching staff that decided that if you have a dislocated shoulder, you are out of the Grand Final.

The fitness test probably went too long. I think by two-thirds of the way through the fitness test, the medical staff had changed their mind and felt that I was right to play. And the coaching staff probably thought the same thing. But every coach has his right to determine how you train.

God knows how long the test went for. I went through nearly every exercise a man could do. Being tackled to the ground was nothing compared to other things that took place. I was totally disappointed when my shoulder came out during the fitness test. Francis Bourke was certainly making it difficult.

I think people want me to say that I am very bitter on Francis Bourke. I wasn't bitter on anyone, especially Francis. I just think the coach at the time is in control of everything. I've coached long enough to know you only do things for the benefit of the team. Francis would have been doing everything possible for the team.

Was he excessive? It could be considered excessive. Would I have got through the game? It's academic, I don't know. Was his methodology right or wrong? In today's football it is wrong. In 1980s football it may well have been right. I don't know. I can't answer that.

Remember it was the Grand Final. It wasn't as though we had next week. That's the way it was. So I sat and watched the 1982 Grand Final from the bench. There were no rules in place, you could have had 30 on the bench if you could squeeze them all in.

I shouldn't have played football in 1983. I didn't want to play. I was finished as far as I was concerned. In my case, if I didn't have my shoulder right and didn't have my head right you don't play. But they talked me into playing and then Francis let me resign virtually half way into the year. I stayed on but it was a wasted year in many respects.

What people wouldn't know is when I came back in 1983 I actually rolled out my other shoulder in my return game (round 9). The way I played I needed all things going well and to have both shoulders vulnerable, and trusting neither of them, I knew that my time was up.

I hope supporters remember me as a team player. I played for my team and played for my mates. My prime objective was to win for the team.

Resigned not to play in the 1982 Grand Final, Malthouse has his shoulder checked by the doctor after it "popped" during a searching fitness test with coach Francis Bourke. (obscured, left)

Geoff Raines was labelled a "Rolls-Royce footballer" when in full flight.

Geoff Raines

Journeyman Geoff Raines started his career at the Tigers in 1976, and he went on to play for Collingwood, Essendon and Brisbane. The slick centreman won the Tigers' best and fairest in 1978, 1980 (premiership year) and 1981.

1976-82

I barracked for St Kilda as a kid. I lived down at Moorabbin around the time the Saints moved away from Junction Oval. I watched many games at Moorabbin and loved watching the really, really good players of the time, and St Kilda had Ian Stewart and Darrel Baldock and many others.

I remember a day down there that Richmond played and I was a lolly boy, selling drinks, lollies and potato chips, and I just sat up in the stand and watched the footy all day and sold nothing. I was engrossed in the footy. There was a guy called Royce Hart playing for the Tigers, and I remember vividly him playing that day and I just thought, 'how good is this guy'.

In 1966 St Kilda won the premiership. I was listening to it at home on the radio. But not long after that we moved to the country and went through Gippsland and Swan Hill areas. My old man was a bank manager, a runner, a good cricketer; I think he also played Under 19s for Essendon.

In those days once you were zoned, if you wanted to be 'unzoned' you had to have lived three years outside that zone. For instance, I was originally zoned to Footscray, because the Bulldogs had some of the Gippsland area. Then we moved to Swan Hill, which was a Richmond zone, and lived there for two years, so I was one year off no longer being tied to Footscray.

I had travelled down as a 16-year-old and trained with Footscray. Richmond was about to win back-to-back Premierships (1973/74) and Graeme Richmond, who was quite influential, and Alan Schwab, who was a great administrator, were instrumental in getting me across to Richmond.

So in 1975 I was going to play in Adelaide for one year, then come back and play for Richmond. I didn't want to play for Footscray. But a deal was done. A four-way round robin involving Neil Sachse, who went from North Adelaide to Footscray, Peter Cloke, who went from Richmond to North Adelaide, Laurie Fowler went from Richmond to Melbourne and I went from Footscray's zone to Richmond.

Graeme Richmond (GR) called me 'Sonna!' Around 1975 I had to front up to the committee and he said 'By Christ, Sonna, what do you want to be in life – a pisspot, a playboy or a footballer?' And I said 'Shit, it would be great to be all three.' Then I said 'only joking, I want to be a footballer.'

I turned 19 in 1975, the year I came to Richmond. I boarded in East Malvern, and I lived there for 18 months and then I moved to a flat in Lennox Street, Richmond with Cameron Clayton for 12 months – that was an experience. It was just up the road from the London Tavern where we all used to sneak in and grab a beer.

I trained with the Seniors but I went back to play Under-19s football for half a year in 1975. I thought I was actually going to play in the Reserves, but GR thought I needed a bit more grounding and felt I was a bit cocky, so he sent back to the Under 19s and made me learn my trade. I then played the last half of that year with the Seconds and we made it to the Grand Final, which we lost. Actually the Under 19s made the Grand Final as well, and that's where where all my mates were. They won.

I can remember the rugged pre-seasons we had with Tom Hafey. Obviously there

Born
Aug 10, 1956

Played
Richmond
1976-82
134 games
55 goals

Collingwood
1983-86

Essendon
1986

Brisbane Bears
1987-89

Interviewed
Nov 21, 2008

Some of Richmond's greats at the unveiling of the Jack Dyer bust at Punt Road Oval in June 2009. (L-R) Tom Allen, Mike Perry, Havel Rowe, Geoff Raines, Tom Hafey, Roger Dean, Neville Crowe, Mal Brown, Bill Clements and Matthew Richardson.

was a fair bit of influence with Tommy in the early days. The way Tommy liked to coach the game, I thrived on that – long kicking and direct.

In 1976 opportunity knocked. I think GR talked me up. I had a pretty good final series with the Reserves in 1975, in particular in the Grand Final, and GR was pretty impressed and he said 'this kid is probably going to step up and play Senior footy next year.'

My first game was against Collingwood at Victoria Park in the mud, round 4, 1976, and Barry Richardson was our coach – Tommy was coaching Victoria on that weekend. It was a great initiation although it was pretty intimidating. I played on the wing on a guy called Graeme Anderson. He had 20 disposals and I had 19.

I started with Number 40. In my first year I played three games in a row and then broke my collarbone when I ran into Bryan Wood. That pretty well ended my season. I came back in 1977 for a new pre-season under Richardson, who'd been appointed to take over from Tommy.

When Royce Hart retired he wanted me to wear his guernsey No. 4. I was pretty honoured to take that on board.

Barry Richardson was very different from Tommy. He was ahead of his time, with a lot of different strategies and set plays. I was quite impressed with 'Bones', I thought he was a very good coach.

I really stepped up in 1977. Bones started playing me on the wing then he started playing me in the middle. One of my strengths was my speed – my first 10 metres was pretty explosive. I think I also had pretty clean hands and I was pretty good over head and at ground level and was a fairly long kick.

My weakness was my endurance. I didn't have a huge tank and I had to work on that area. Kevin Bartlett and I would be in the back half of the Tan runs all the time.

In 1979 I played in a State of Origin game against WA. I was a chance for All-Australian honours (in the rep team), and Alan Schwab said to me 'this is your chance' because I had played a couple of ripper games before the match against WA. I came up against Brian Peake. He towelled me this day and I was pretty disappointed.

In 1980 we won the premiership, every boy's dream. I decided I was going to party for a month or two. However, Tommy Hafey rings me up, because he was coaching the state side in a carnival in Adelaide after the League season (October) and he said to me, 'I want you to play.' I told him I didn't really want to play. I just wanted to go out and enjoy myself, to go on a holiday and get away. I played 25 games that season and I'd had enough.

Tommy asked me to reconsider. He said these opportunities don't come along too often. So he talked me into it and I went and played and won All-Australian honours. I played on Peake and beat him in the return match in Adelaide.

I had some issues with Graeme Richmond. In 1978 I won the best and fairest and in 1979 I had a really poor start to the year for the first five games. Royce told me that Graeme had wanted to trade me to North Melbourne. I thought, I've just won a best and fairest – that's a bit rough. But that was Graeme – pretty ruthless. If the switch had eventuated, my attitude would have been, 'fuck him, if that's what he wants to do, then I will go show him who's right'.

I was always pretty confident. I think you have got to be confident in your ability, some people mistake it for cockiness, but that's their problem, not mine. You can't please everyone.

I even say to my son Andrew, there are a lot of blokes there competing for your spot, even though they are your teammates. Although it is a team game, it is also an individual game.

In 1980 I won the best and fairest in the premiership year as well as All-Australian honours. Yet I didn't get a single vote in the Brownlow Medal that year, and I was the hot favourite. It was embarrassing. The cameramen probably thought 'Beauty, he's not getting 1 votes or 2 votes, he is going to be getting all three votes'. As the night went on I knew I had no chance. I didn't get any threes and the camera kept highlighting it and I went home that night and I said to Lynne, my wife, 'that's pretty embarrassing but my target is on Saturday, the Grand Final'.

Obviously the umpires didn't like me. That's life. Some people like you and some people don't and you can't do anything about that.

We had a shocking year in 1981. I don't know why, it was like a huge premiership hangover, it was just shithouse. Then GR got rid of Tony Jewell and the favourite son, Francis Bourke, came in. It was a bad move.

In 1982 I had a fitness test on the same night as Michael Malthouse's. I tore the adductor off the bone when I kicked with my left foot, so to get back and play in a Grand Final I was full of cortisone injections and treatment for two intense weeks. Francis put me through the ringer and I got through my test and I was watching Mick's and it was pretty intense. Bourkey gave him one final shot and people reckon he would have pulled someone's good shoulder out. Mick was a leader of the backline – we had a leader for each line. He was the backline's general and was a big loss in that Grand Final.

In the 1982 Grand Final some pundits said I was nearly best on ground to half-time and then Francis, as he did most of the year, took me out of the centre and put me on the wing, because Phil Maylin was playing pretty well for the Blues. Anyway, that's history. He had done that most of my year and it was pretty frustrating for me.

"Royce told me that Graeme had wanted to trade me to North Melbourne. I thought, I've just won a best and fairest – that's a bit rough."

It was a great Grand Final. Carlton got us in the first 15 minutes in the wet and went up three goals but then we clawed our way back. In all fairness, in the last quarter or so, the injections didn't hold up and I was running out of legs.

I just feel the whole year was a funny year with Francis coaching. We had the best side easily. Francis and I have discussed this, and I think Francis is a great guy, a ripper guy, but I just don't think he coached very well.

He became all authoritarian, everything was black and white. Coming off as a former teammate and taking over as coach it was tough. A lot of confusing stuff went on. I think we were a little bit confused, the whole year was disjointed.

I would say there were multiple reasons I left Richmond. I was not happy the way 1982 worked out, I wasn't comfortable with Francis as a coach and then the Maurice Rioli issue really amazed me.

Maurice was the leading centreman in WA and I was the leading centreman in Victoria, and in those days you played in the one position. But Francis felt I could play in different spots and he put me at half-forward and the wing despite that fact I had won three best and fairests and been runner-up in five years. Maurice was to play in the centre. I felt I was playing in the wrong place, disjointed if you like.

Geoff Raines takes the mark of the year in 1982 over Fitzroy's David McMahon at the MCG.

I had no disrespect for Maurice at all. The rivalry was built up when he came over in the pre-season. We were having a game at Portsea and it was all this press build up, the two best centremen in Australia to play on one another – it didn't sit well with me. I found it strange they would go and get another centreman while they had the state's leading centreman in their team.

I was very unhappy about these issues and Collingwood were knocking on the door and I went to Graeme and told him that I can't dictate where I play but I do deserve to get rewarded accordingly, and I felt other people were getting rewarded a lot better than I was, and for what I've done at Richmond I wasn't getting recognised. So I went to Collingwood for a record sum, and I think Richmond got Neil Peart, Wally Lovett, Terry Domburg along with $200,000. At the time, I had a manager, and only two people have ever really known this – it was Roland Rocchiccioli.

In hindsight I would have loved to have worked things out with Richmond but it's not a perfect world. It was pretty bitter with the club and the supporters. The supporters were against me. You see I didn't get a clearance for about six rounds and we were going to take it to court under the Trade Practices Act because they weren't going to clear me. I believed I didn't have a contract and they said that I did have a contract.

I had made my mind up I was going to Collingwood. Behind the scenes Graeme Richmond was still trying to lure me back, because the Tigers got belted in the first three rounds of 1983 (by 60, 19 and 48 pts). Remember, they had also lost Bryan Wood and David Cloke.

GR came around at Easter in his old blue HQ Holden. I was driving home with Lynn and I said to her 'that's Graeme's car outside our house', and he wasn't even inside the car, he was inside our property. I reckon he was counting the bricks and muttering to himself, 'Collingwood have paid for these bricks'!

So he came out and told me he was visiting an old great aunt in Malvern who he hadn't seen for many years and he thought he would call in to see how I was going. Then he said 'I want you back at Richmond'. I said 'Graeme, it's over'. 'No, No, No,' he said, 'I want you back, at any cost.'

He was a very smart operator, because if he lured me back and I pulled out of the Collingwood deal, Graeme would have held me for ransom at his end. I wasn't giving him an inch. I wasn't bitter, that was just the way Graeme operated. In hindsight, Graeme probably stayed a couple years too long at Richmond.

I got over my issues with Graeme. When I was playing at Brisbane years later and my name came up for Victorian selection and Graeme endorsed it. But at the time I was 32 or 33, and they just went with youth.

I just feel that period in the 1980s, Richmond had a four- or five-year opportunity of a dynasty and that's probably a regret. But that never happened because we disintegrated and I was part of it.

My nickname was 'Pretty Boy.' Lou Richards gave me that. It annoyed me a little bit. I'd cop all the time on the field – 'pretty pretty pretty kiss kiss'.

When KB was appointed coach at Richmond, in 1988, he rang me and said 'Geoff, we need a hand, we just need some experienced blokes back.' I said 'KB, as much as I respect you there is no chance I am coming back.' I was then 31, and in my second season at Brisbane.

When I was at Collingwood, they did me over after the first two or three years. Collingwood renewed a contract with me and in the midst of that renewal, in 1986, Graeme Richmond, Tony Jewell and John Robertson approached me, trying to get me back. I said 'Collingwood have done the right thing by me, thanks for your interest but I'm going to stick with them.' Five weeks later Collingwood pulled out of the contract and asked me to take 20 per cent less.

I was lucky that Kevin Sheedy had a vacancy at Essendon, but going to Essendon was the worst thing I ever did. (Raines had played the first two games of 1986 with Collingwood, and joined Essendon from round 4.) I was contemplating retirement after the bad year at Essendon. I didn't feel welcome there, and I didn't like the place, it was terrible. Then the door opened with Brisbane forming from 1987. I was 30, and went up there and helped them out. I had some reasonable games up there.

I had some great battles against Richmond. There was one at Collingwood. I had had a broken nose and I played on David Palm and GR told him at first bounce, 're-break his nose' so I have gone to ground and David's tried to throw one in and missed, but he got reported, and I just turned to him and said 'game on'.

I was playing on Maurice Rioli, but I didn't want to punch Maurice. There was a guy called Graeme Landy and we were going for a mid-air mark and we collided and I just happened to knock Graeme out. So I got reported as well.

This shows you how bitter it was! We both front up to the tribunal and I got set up. David goes in first and says 'nothing in it, I can't even remember the incident' and it is dismissed. My turn came, and Graeme Landy comes in, in a wheelchair! I got four weeks. That's why the bitterness.

Another time was in 1987 – Richmond vs Brisbane at the MCG. it was Tony Jewell's last game as coach. It was also the battle for the wooden spoon. I had handballed over the top of Dale 'Flea' Weightman and forgotten to put my hand up to protect myself and Flea has followed through and nearly broke my cheekbone. So I told him there would be a bit of a square up and he just laughed at me.

I squared up with him about 15 minutes later. He can't remember what happened. I was that upset I was following Dale off the ground saying 'I haven't finished with you yet.'

> "It was pretty bitter with the club and the supporters. The supporters were against me."

So Richmond go in at half-time and Tony Jewell is apparently fuming. He is meant to be a mate of mine, and he sticks the whole team on me! He said 'he has hit the smallest bloke on the ground, he is a traitor, he left our club'. So the first bounce after half-time they came from everywhere. Their ruckman has tried to king hit me, their wingmen have come running in and I thought ' shit it's on here' and I look up at Brad Hardie and Jim Edmond who were pretty tough and said 'we got a battle boys, so here we go!'

In the end, Flea got reported for striking me, and Mark Lee tried to iron out one of the smallest blokes on the ground, Darren Carlson. And we beat them by nearly 10 goals. It wasn't forgotten.

My mark of year over David McMahon is a beauty. It is a classic. I just went a bit early and he took me up. I won a car for that, it was a Commodore Wagon, but it was meant to be an SS Brock, but Lynne was pregnant so I had to go for the family wagon! It was very disappointing.

I just feel that the whole affair, the bitter warfare that went on between Collingwood and Richmond really set Richmond back, and it probably hasn't recovered. I just hope there are better times for the club. Although I had to look after myself, leaving Richmond is still my biggest regret, because Richmond is a great club and my inner feelings are still with the club. I really enjoyed my formative years there and really enjoyed the premiership, they were fantastic memories.

Jim Jess lets fly with a signature monster torpedo.

Jim Jess

Jim Jess, nicknamed 'The Ghost', came to the Tigers from Avoca in 1976. A fearless key-position player with a booming kick, he became a cult figure during his 13 years at Richmond, and starred in the 1980 premiership season.

1976-88

I got my nickname, 'The Ghost' from Tommy Hafey. It was the first practice game I played in at Richmond, the light was pretty dull and I took a mark in the deepest forward pocket. My shearing shed 'tan' was pretty white and I had scruffy-looking hair and Tommy said I looked like a ghost, and the name stuck.

Tommy coached me for my first year, 1976. He was fantastic. His style of play is still the best way to play football. Kick it long, and have numbers around the contest. I was a fairly good kick and reasonable mark and I played my best football at centre half-back. If you're not having a great day down back you can play pretty negatively and try to limit your opponent. I also played at centre half-forward but I found it hard to be consistent there.

I actually belonged to St Kilda because I came from Avoca, in St Kilda's territory, however, St Kilda cleared me to Richmond. However, I played one practice game with St Kilda in the early 1970s and I played really well on 'Cowboy' Neale. I was in the best players and Allan Jeans came up after the game and he saw that I looked like a wild man from Borneo, and that I was drinking a can and he quickly lost interest in me. But he didn't know my circumstances. I had only been to Melbourne a few times in my life, I had a wife and a baby and I just couldn't pack up and leave and go to Melbourne.

Ron Carson, Alan Schwab, Graeme Richmond and Paddy Guinane all signed me to Richmond. Paddy Guinane's brother-in-law was at St Arnaud. Remember Barry Young who played at Richmond, it was Barry's father who put the Tigers on to me. He kept ringing Paddy and saying I could play so Richmond sent the recruiting guy up three times to see me play and he came back and said I would never play league football. Barry's father wouldn't have that. He told Paddy to come and have a look himself, and that's the only reason I came to Richmond really.

I thought I was quick enough but lacked real agility and I was not a great handballer. Our ruckman, Bob Heard came up to me before one of my first games and said, 'Listen Jimmy, I just want every kick-in you do today to be nice drop punts out in front of me – I'll be leading out to the pockets.' I was pretty impressionable so I went to Tommy and said 'Bob wants me to kick the ball out to him every time,' and Tommy said 'Don't take any notice of him, get back and kick a bloody torpedo straight down the guts.'

My torpedo punt kicks were pretty reliable, I didn't mess many up. I would practise it at training. Michael Roach could kick a torpedo but he had a great drop punt so he never worried about it. My drop punts were reasonable but not as accurate as I would have liked them to have been. One wet and miserable day against Footscray, I got on to a torpedo at the MCG and it was pretty good. It went up and just kept going and going and going.

I played centre half-forward in both Grand Final appearances (1980 and 1982). But during my career I enjoyed playing centre half-back, but for one reason or another, like David Cloke being injured, or the club wanting a bit more mobility up forward, I also played a fair bit of my football in the forward line. I think for my career it would have been better if I had stayed at centre half-back. But I guess as long as you are getting a game, you are happy to go where you are wanted.

Born
Jan 25, 1955

Played
Richmond
1976-88
223 games
175 goals

Interviewed
July 11, 2009

Jumping Jimmy takes a big grab against the Bulldogs.

In the 1980 Grand Final I was very nervous and I took a fairly good mark early on, got a 15-metre penalty, played on and kicked it over to Flea (Dale Weightman), who kicked the first goal of the game. I was up and away, in the play, and got all sorts of confidence from that passage of play.

All players watched Michael Malthouse's 1982 fitness test. Francis Bourke was pretty black and white. He wanted to be 110 per cent sure Mick was right, rather than just 100 per cent. I think Mick would have gotten through the 1982 Grand Final okay. It was really deflating when he did his shoulder during the test. I don't think too many of us would have passed the test ourselves. It was a bit over the top. I think it took a bit of wind out of the sails of a few blokes. Carlton jumped us early and the little fellows were doing damage and got away with a bit with Mick missing. Mick used to scare them a bit. It gave Carlton a bit of confidence knowing Mick wasn't out there.

I was right beside Bruce Doull when the streaker came on the ground during the 1982 Grand Final. I just kept backing away from her. I saw her coming from a fair way off in the distance, and so did Bruce, but I started to back off very quickly.

You would have played for nothing back then. I wasn't complaining. I had Tommy Hafey as coach, then Barry Richardson, then Tony Jewell then Francis Bourke, then Mike Patterson, then Paul Sproule and finally KB. Tommy left an influence because he was my first coach. I was a bit over-awed yet he made me feel welcomed and at home. I got on really well with Tony Jewell and he supported me and we won the flag under him. He could get absolutely ferocious, and it got scary at times. TJ didn't get on with everybody, but I thought he always coached from his heart. He would explode, go off, call you everything in the world, then he would have a beer with you after the game.

I love Francis Bourke. I reckon he is one of the best blokes you will ever meet. But as a coach he was black or white, there was no give or take. I guess he coached the way he played – uncompromising. He rubbed a few blokes up the wrong way.

Paul Sproule wanted me to play centre half-back, but also wanted me to run around and end up with 20 possessions. I was playing on some really good players at centre half-back. For me, if you play on Stephen Kernahan and he gets five kicks and I get five kicks, Richmond will win. I told Paul, if I get 20 possessions, then the bloke I am on will obviously be getting a lot more because I've got to take a few more chances, and he said 'that's the way to play.' I then told him that if the centre half-forward is getting a heap of kicks, you're not going to win many games of football. That was our basic disagreement. It came to a head when he dropped me from the side when I thought I was playing okay.

"I love Francis Bourke. I reckon he is one of the best blokes you will ever meet. But as a coach he was black or white, there was no give or take."

I was vice-captain in 1984 and Graeme Richmond said to me, 'You will be captain in 1985 because Barry Rowlings is retiring.' Then Sproule called me in before training; it was one of our first meetings and he said he had recommended I not be considered as captain, vice-captain *or* deputy vice-captain. I thought 'oh well no worries'. I took it on the chin.

Things happened and I was going to go to Collingwood in 1985. The deal was done. Bob Rose was coach, and he was going to call a special training run and I was going to be playing centre half-forward for Collingwood the following week. A lot of people at Richmond voiced their disapproval at the way things eventuated. In the end they approached me and asked me to stay and I said I would as long as I was guaranteed a senior game. So I stayed. I knew I had the support of the players, although perhaps not the coach.

I wasn't one of the great players at Richmond. The great players are Royce Hart, Kevin Bartlett and Francis Bourke. I thought I tried hard and I think I had rapport with supporters because they knew I wasn't the most skilled player out there but they knew I was having a crack at it. I think sometimes I have been a bit overrated.

"I had rapport with supporters because they knew I wasn't the most skilled player out there but they knew I was having a crack at it."

1988 was a transition time, and I didn't think I was playing badly. There were players like Michael Laffy and a couple of blokes who were younger than me, but I don't think they were better than me at the time. But KB felt I was at the end of my career and these guys were just starting. That's fair enough, it happens to us all. I got through my career without any serious injuries and I kept playing football until I was 45 years of age.

I was 21 years old when I started with Richmond, and played at Punt Road until I was 33. I had already three years of senior football at Avoca and then three years at St Arnaud before Richmond.

Jimmy Jess (No. 20) was too close to famous 1982 Grand Final streaker, Helen D'Amico, for his liking. "I just kept backing away..." A startled Geoff Raines is in the background, with Carlton's Bruce Doull in the midst of the action.

A rare recent high point: celebrations after the 2001 semi-final win. Captain Wayne Campbell and Ben Holland (left) enjoy an inspired 11-point win over Carlton. Seven days later, the Tigers fell in Brisbane by 68 points.Right: Richmond's Save our Skins fund-raising campaign attracted all ages.

1984-2011

TIGERS PAY THE PRICE

When Richmond entered the eighties, it was flush with success. Yet between the 1982 Grand Final and the 2011 season, the club tasted finals football just twice.

The 1980s began with glory but ended as a period of decline. Early in the decade, Richmond tried to lure talented footballers from other clubs but it lost some leading players itself. Collingwood was the main adversary in a period that would be remembered as the "recruiting wars".

Maurice Rioli came from South Fremantle in 1982, and finished the year with a Norm Smith Medal, the first to do so in a losing Grand Final team. Twelve months later he placed second in the Brownlow Medal count. But in 1983, David Cloke and Geoff Raines headed to Collingwood, and Bryan Wood left for Essendon. Full-forward Bryan Taylor, the club's leading goalkicker in 1982 and 1984, was signed by the Magpies in 1985. Coupled with the earlier retirement of veterans such as Bourke and Bartlett, Richmond was a shadow of its former self.

John Annear and Phillip Walsh were recruited from Collingwood in 1984 but both left three years later.

The instability of the Tigers' list was reflected off the ground. Richmond had five coaches in six years (1983-1988) In 1986, there was talk of Richmond playing 11 matches in Brisbane; Alan Bond, a West Australian businessman, was willing to underwrite it. The club carried a huge debt and even Graeme Richmond backed a failed move north. Bond was president in 1987, the same year the competition had expanded with the inclusion of the West Coast Eagles and Brisbane Bears. Much like these new clubs, Richmond virtually had to start from scratch, but with massive debt and a poor list. The Tigers still had fine players but when they met the Bears in the final round of 1987, it was a wooden spoon play-off. Brisbane defeated Richmond by 56 points, and the Tigers were to remain at the tail of the ladder for a number of years.

Brendon Gale took over as CEO in 2009. Under his direction there have been massive off-field changes at Punt Road Oval. The oval has been rebuilt, and the facilities at the club are now state of the art, for players and the administration. In the background is the Swinburne Centre, which also houses the Korin Gamadji Institute, a unique educational and training facility that works closely with Richmond to support and incubate leadership and employment pathways for Aboriginal and Torres Strait Islander people.

By 1990, the excesses and arrogance of the mid-1980s came to a head. On August 15, creditors threatened to wind up the club. The Tigers had a debt of $1.25 million and interest of $250,000 to service the overdraft. Former captain Neville Crowe was the public face of the Save Our Skins campaign that aimed to raise $1 million by October 31. Donations totalling $130-140,000 were collected on the last two days to meet the target.

Kevin Bartlett had replaced Tony Jewell as coach in 1988 but he was hampered by a young and inexperienced team. Richmond's highest finish under KB was 10th and in 1992 he was replaced by Allan Jeans – the first coach who had not played for the club since Len Smith in 1965; before Smith, you have to go back to Norman Clark in 1919. Jeans lasted only one year before being replaced by former premiership player John "Swooper" Northey. In 1993, players such as Tony Free, Matthew Knights, Wayne Campbell, Duncan Kellaway and Brendan Gale, who were blooded under Bartlett, came to the fore under Northey. In that year the club had a taste of what it had missed. Jeff Hogg led the young Tigers to the Night Grand Final against Essendon before a then-record night series attendance of 75,533. Dale Weightman retired after 274 games, yet it was also the season that Matthew Richardson, son of Alan "Bull" Richardson, made his debut.

Hogg left in a deal with Fitzroy the next year, and Michael Gale, Paul Broderick, and Matthew Dundas were cleared to Richmond in return. The Tigers finished ninth that season; they were defeated by Geelong in the last round and missed the eight narrowly, a common trait for the era.

In 1995, Richmond made the finals series for the first time since 1982. It lost its first final but the next week, courtesy of the double chance, the Tigers defeated Essendon in the second semi-final at the MCG. The Dons led by five goals well into the third quarter before the Tigers staged a comeback to win by 13 points, but were soundly defeated in the preliminary final against Geelong.

Northey decided to leave Punt Road. Robert Walls, a former Carlton player and Brisbane Bears coach, was appointed to lead the Tigers; within two years Walls was replaced by Jeff Gieschen. In 2000, Danny Frawley succeeded Gieschen and led Richmond to another preliminary final the following year, only to be defeated by Brisbane at the Gabba.

Indeed, the last three decades to 2011 Richmond has been the least successful club in the AFL. It has made just two finals series and has collected wooden spoons in 1987, 1989, 2004, and 2007. In 2005, Terry Wallace took over as coach – he played one season with Richmond in 1987.

Wallace was allowed to implement a five-year plan but he left the club without a finals birth. Having knocked on the door of finals football in 2008 and buoyed by the recruitment of former West Coast Brownlow medalist and captain Ben Cousins, much was expected of Wallace's last season in 2009 but the year was disastrous, with Richmond finishing second last with just five wins. Wallace was replaced mid-year by Jade Rawlings. Damien Hardwick has coached the club from 2010.

Allan Jeans coached the Tigers for one season in 1992 after replacing Kevin Bartlett.

Midway through 2009 Brendon Gale, a 244-game player, replaced Steven Wright as CEO, and in March 2010 he announced the *three-zero-75* plan for the club – to play finals football in three of the next five seasons and have one top four finish, to be debt free, and boast 75,000 members, almost doubling the membership base. The club would strive to add another three premierships to its tally within 10 years.

The goals were ridiculed in the press as over-ambitious. They are high and may not be attained, but striving for them is having tangible off-field outcomes. In February 2011 the club raised $2 million at the launch of the Fighting Tiger Fund to eliminate the club's debt and improve the resources of football department. In 2012, Richmond boasted a club record of 50,000 members. TREVOR RUDDELL

Michael Roach

Just the second Richmond player to kick 100 goals in a season, Michael 'Disco' Roach was a high-leaping, athletic sensation. The spearhead of the dominant 1980 premiership team, he will be long remembered for his extraordinary mark over the Hawthorn defence in 1979.

1977-89

Born
Oct 9, 1958

Played
Richmond
1977-89
200 games,
607 goals

Interviewed
Aug 3, 2007

I was a St Kilda supporter because Barry Lawrence is related to me in a distant way. Barry came from Longford, which is where I played much of my football before I came to Richmond. I came to Richmond in 1975 but I was only 15. Richmond didn't want a 15-year-old kid to sign a Form Four, so I went back home for two years and played reasonable footy in Tassie.

I came across at 17. My first year I couldn't play for a little while because I couldn't get a clearance – Longford wouldn't clear me – so I missed the first couple of games and played with the seconds. My first senior game was in round 8, 1977.

Back in Tassie you get your licence at 16, and I remember I had a car and I had an accident the first couple of weeks. I was a shocking driver and it was a bit different coming from the country roads into downtown Richmond. I stacked my car and Kevin Sheedy gave me his car. That was the sort of person he was. I was driving as a 17-year-old kid, Kevin Sheedy's car. It was just amazing how kind he was and how much he tried to help me along. Sheedy's last game was against Hawthorn, which was the day I took that mark (round 5, 1979). The next week he ran a lap of honour at Waverley against North Melbourne.

There wasn't a huge crowd (at the Hawthorn match) but to have two different people take a snapshot of that mark, one in colour and one in black and white, was amazing. I thought it felt good, I thought 'Oh, that was all right.' It felt like I was up high but I didn't know anyone had taken a snapshot of it. Mum and dad were actually over watching the game. Mum suffers from migraines, and after the game she wasn't feeling well so we went back to a flat I had in Hawthorn. And mum feels better after she has a warm cup of tea, so she went into the milk bar to get some milk and she came out with about four *Herald* newspapers. 'Look!' And I've gone 'Wow!' I thought. 'Geez, there was somebody there who took the photo.' And then on the weekend there was a colour shot of it from the *Truth*. That was only my 17th game and dad said 'If you never play another game of League football you may be remembered for something.' I wasn't very far out, about 30 metres, and I kicked the goal. Kevin Bartlett says I am hungry because in the photo I am in the perfect opportunity to handball.

I was always a reasonably long kick but had no set routine until Royce Hart got hold of me. When I started to kick goals in 1979 Royce got me to set a routine up to kick for goal. I basically kept that routine all through my football career. Royce had six points:

1. Make sure after you have taken the mark that you get back far enough from the man on the mark, because you don't want the man on the mark to interfere with your concentration.
2. Pick a spot to kick at behind the goals.
3. Have a certain number of steps when coming in. I never ever knew how many until in my routine I counted them. I took 11 steps when kicking for goal, so I knew how far to get back.
4. Keep your head down until after you kick the ball. Don't look up to see where the ball has gone.
5. Last two steps, watch the ball onto the boot.
6. Kick with enough power.

I never changed it. I had that bit of paper that Royce had written out for me and I had it in my sock before a game. If I missed a couple early, I usually knew what I would have done wrong and

Michael Roach soars into football folklore with this famous mark over the Hawks in 1979. "Kevin Bartlett says I am hungry because in the photo I am in the perfect opportunity to handball."

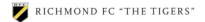

then at half-time I'd head off to the toilet and read it. I haven't got that bit of paper, I don't know where it has gotten to, but I have re-written the steps of kicking for goal.

I took Richo (Matthew Richardson) for some goalkicking when he first came to the club. We tried to go through the same routine. Since then he has probably had another 15 different routines. But he did kick 91 goals (in 1996), basically the year after he had done his knee.

"I have never been an aggressive bloke and coaches used to say a bloke my size should be hurting blokes ... Tony Jewell used to say, 'For goodness' sake, hurt somebody!'"

1980 was the most goals I kicked in a year (112), but I'd say my season before, when I kicked 90, was a better year. I was straight out from the wing and went to full-forward and kicked 90 goals in my first year at full-forward. And I made the state side, then did my ankle and missed three games. If I had maybe not missed those games I might have been able to win the League goalkicking (Kelvin Templeton, 91). If you kick 100 goals and you play in the premiership I don't think there can be any better year. In 1979 I probably played a different more exciting brand of football, because nobody knew this kid from Tassie. I was running around kicking goals and they probably hadn't worked out how to play on me.

I met Jack 'Skinny' Titus just before he died in 1978. I had come to Richmond in 1975 to do a pre-season, then came back to Richmond in 1977 and met him. I didn't realise how great 'Skinny' was until I studied the Richmond records. To be up there with the great 'Skinny' Titus was a real thrill. [Ed's Note: Titus and Roach are the only Richmond players to kick 100 goals or more in a season.]

The successful Tigers drew strong sponsorship support and were one of the competition's highest-profile clubs.

I was never an aggressive player and coaches used to say a bloke my size should be hurting blokes. It just was never in my nature but I was determined.

Tony Jewell used to say 'For goodness' sake, hurt somebody!' But I just didn't know how to do it. I never thought of elbowing or knocking a bloke over.

I was 21 years old and had been there just four years by 1980. If you look back at our side then, apart from Kevin Bartlett and Francis Bourke, you see that Mark Lee was 21, Dale Weightman was 20, Greg Strachan 21, Jim Jess 23, Stephen Mount 19 – most of us were from the under 19s and we thought this could go on for ever. When we won that Grand Final they were talking about Richmond being the team of the '80s: 'Who is going to beat this young team?'

(The Grand Final) was an amazing feeling. We started to dominate the game basically from the first few minutes. We probably should have won by more than we did (81 points). I think us young fellows were waiting for the siren to blow so the game was all over.

It was just a fantastic feeling having that siren blow and having your parents there, your brothers and sisters and all the supporters. You play Grand Finals for yourself and your teammates but you also play for the Richmond Football Club and the supporters.

One of my biggest regrets is swapping my football jumper. I have got a picture of Geoff Raines and myself running around holding the cup and Rainsey's got his Richmond jumper on and I've got a Collingwood jumper. I swapped it with Peter McCormack. I thought that's what everybody did. Now I think 'Why did I do that?!'

At the time it didn't worry me. Peter McCormack said 'Do you want to swap jumpers?' so we swapped. However, I have got my jumper back; I met with Peter and I gave him his jumper and he gave me mine, which I am rapt to have. But I look back now and I don't have any pictures of me in my premiership jumper.

I thought we would play in more premierships. 1981 was maybe a year where we got carried away. It was because we were 20 or 21 and we thought we would play again and we probably didn't work as hard. In 1982 we certainly worked hard when Francis Bourke came in as coach.

We went in as favourites but I think it went when it started to rain. We were huge, a very big side, and Mick Malthouse went out injured with his shoulder. We ran out onto the ground and it was raining and we were probably too big, we didn't have the little men. And just before half-time it stopped raining and we hit the front. We came out after half-time and it was raining again! If it hadn't had rained we may have won.

In round 21, 1980, Michael Roach kicked his 101st goal of the season, surpassing Jack Titus's 100 goals in the 1940 season. The crowd, aware of this historic moment, spill on to the ground.

It was a pretty big fitness test for Michael Malthouse (to be chosen for the 1982 Grand Final). You see players now dislocate shoulders and play the next week with all this tape on. But back in those days I don't think they knew about taping shoulders. I reckon if Malthouse had taped his shoulder and hadn't had to do that big fitness test he would have played.

The silly thing is that we watched that fitness test as players. We were hoping that Michael was going to get through. He was going to play, and it was done after training.

We were off the ground. It was a very important moment and we probably shouldn't have watched, because when Mick did his shoulder I am sure all our hearts sank a bit, because he was pretty important to us – he was a very good leader. He was being dragged along and Mick had to hold on with one arm – as he was being dragged away his shoulder popped out. I reckon we did the wrong thing by watching it. Maybe it had some effect. It was so disappointing.

I think a few mistakes were made like not recruiting well enough. Certainly Graeme Richmond and Alan Schwab went out and got players that needed to make us successful like Mark Lee, Dale Weightman, Jim Jess, Greg Strachan and Terry Smith – people that were going to be around the football club for a long time. They got Rainsey and 'Butch' Edwards, who were tied to Footscray. They really went and got the best possible ones around.

Maybe we stopped doing that. We got Maurice Rioli but we probably didn't get other recruits as well. The ones we recruited weren't as good as what we had. We lost Bryan Wood, Geoff Raines, David Cloke, Terry Smith to St Kilda, Francis Bourke retired, Kevin Bartlett retired. We needed those strong guys around and we fell away a bit.

Looking back now it was really important to play 200 games. I was finished (on 199 games) but KB gave me my last game against Carlton. I said to him 'I am going to have to retire because I've had it.' But he said, which was very nice of him, 'I reckon you've deserved 199 games but I am not sure about the 200th ... what we will do is announce your retirement and get you your last (and 200th) game against Carlton at Waverley.'

Then the club was really struggling for players and they had a lot of injuries – the seconds could hardly field a side. There were kids who weren't even good enough for under 19s playing seconds football. So (after the Carlton game) I played the last three games with the seconds, even though I had retired, to help the club out. We got beaten by 200 points down at Geelong. I was captain and I got chaired off the ground with the Richmond seconds. It was my final game.

I couldn't walk, I had rucked all day, I couldn't get off the ground. Then KB asked me 'Would you like to lead the senior team out? It would be an honour for you to lead us out onto the ground.' So I broke through the banner down at Geelong for the seniors, even though I wasn't going to play.

And it is amazing how they talk about adrenaline. I was buggered, had rucked the whole day – there was nobody else.

And I ran out on the ground like I was a spring chicken again, and I was thinking 'I could play again.' I burst through the banner and when the adrenaline stopped I basically had to be carried off again.

A star for club and state, Weightman was his era's most consistent Tiger.

Dale Weightman

There have been few more loyal servants to the Tigers than the man simply known as 'Flea'. From the day he arrived from Mildura as a 17-year-old, the brilliant rover exuded a class and consistency that marks him as a contemporary great.

1978-93

David Cloke gave me the nickname, just out of the blue. We were mucking around in the showers like boys do and he nicknamed me 'The Flea'. It's more the size of me I think. Everyone calls me Flea, no-one used to call me Dale, even around here (Punt Road) it is just 'Flea'.

I was about five-six and a half (168cm). I was playing under 17s up in Mildura at the time, and Matthew Knights' dad was coaching the under 17s Imperials and he said 'Would you mind playing centre half-forward?'

So that's what Richmond recruited me for. It just happened that the late, great Alan Schwab came down looking at some players in 1976, because it was our zone. He went back to Richmond in 1976 and said, 'We've got this young kid who can play centre half-forward.' Of course Graeme Richmond was rubbing his hands together: 'You beauty, we've got another Royce Hart!' Hart's knee had just about given way. Then Alan said, 'He is five-foot-six and weighs nothing.'

But they invited me down anyway. I think I was probably recruited as a rover, but when they saw me play I was playing centre half-forward. I had a big year at centre half-forward, kicked 100 goals. The guy who was coach of the seniors didn't want to play me, he thought I was too small. But I got one game, only 15 minutes over against Wentworth, and I kicked three goals in the 15 minutes I was on. I then won the best and fairest in the league with 51 votes. There were 18 games, so I was best on ground every game except the one I missed.

I barracked for the Saints. The old man got on the list at St Kilda in 1949 but decided not to come down as he was just getting married.

He played over 300 games up at the bush for Imperials and played until he was 47. I followed them all the way through until I came to Richmond.

The old man Reg coached me all through the juniors. He was a champion footballer and played cricket against the West Indies as wicketkeeper when they toured the country.

When I was asked to come down he said 'You've got to make sure you don't fumble, get the ball, get it on.' I suppose he was one of those dads who realised when you're small you've got to be very good with the footy, so when you have it, you've got to use the ball.

Mark Lee came down the year before from Mildura. We lived with a family in Sandringham, and I joined them in 1977. We both went to Melbourne High School – he failed the year before and they asked him to come back because Melbourne High had won the Herald Shield championship.

I had only been to the city once. It is fairly daunting, moving away from your family and friends and I suppose the hardest thing was trying to do your last year at school in a completely different environment. I was at a co-ed school at home, then I came down to Melbourne High and it's all boys and I'm thinking, 'Where are the girls?'

It was hard to settle in but Richmond did it pretty well. I was pretty keen on the hotel industry and I was pretty lucky – I worked at Parliament House for a few years, serving grog, and I worked for five years at the VFL as a development officer going around to schools working at clinics.

In 1978, my first year here, we would have a little bit of a meeting at 11 o'clock and we'd have a barbecue and they'd have steak and chops. I saw one day Ian Scrimshaw was playing on the wing and he had eaten three steaks by 11 o'clock before a game.

Born
Oct 3, 1959

Played
Richmond
1978-1993
274 games,
344 goals

Interviewed
Apr 30, 2007

A young Weightman shared a house with teammate Mark Lee.

As coach I had Barry Richardson, then Tony Jewell, then Francis Bourke, then Mike Patterson, then Paul Sproule then Tony Jewell again. Then Kevin Bartlett, then Allan Jeans for a year, and then John Northey. Tony Jewell wasn't eloquent, he would just say it how it was. But you knew where he was coming from. He was a very good tactician and I still remember the first pre-season when he took over. It was just amazing.

Barry Richardson had gotten the flick, so we started training a week or two weeks after the 1978 season. It was about 40 degrees and Tony and Peter Grant, who was his fitness advisor, got together and said 'I think we have a few weak blokes here, we just want to make them hard.'

So the first training run there was 50 of us. We went over to the Botanic Gardens and he said 'I don't want any whingers!' So we started off with a warm up lap around the Botanic Gardens ... 3.8kms! Then he said 'Now we are going to do a time trial, you are going to run it twice, as fast as you can.' So we went around it twice. And in all this time, no water. It was a sign of weakness to have water.

Then we went to the Myer Music Bowl and we were scooting up and down and we had to piggy back each other – of course everyone wanted to take me. Then we had to swap over and then we finished up with 1000 situps and 1000 pushups. No water. Not one bit of water. We started at five o'clock and at 8.45pm we were trudging back over here trying to find water, anywhere there was sprinklers going, or we were jumping in puddles.

So we got back, we were all knackered and a few of us got together and said 'Stuff this whinging, let's start the moaners club.' And half a dozen of us went to the Greyhound Hotel that Royce Hart and Craig McKellar had, and after two beers we were blind. The married ones got home after 10pm and their wives said 'What have you been doing?' 'I've been training all night,' and they would say 'Bullshit, you've been on the piss all night.' They wouldn't believe us.

It was hard yakka. It was also the first time we actually got the big heavy weights. The thing was, we were probably the fittest, strongest side in the competition in 1979 but we didn't use the football. The skills were terrible.

Halfway through 1979 Sheeds (Kevin Sheedy) retired so he became our skills coach. He made the club buy everyone a second-hand football; you had to bring them with you the whole time. Now if you didn't bring it to training they would fine you, and if you lost it you had to buy another one.

In Tony Jewell's first game as coach in 1979 we were playing at South Melbourne. There was a huge gale at one end and we had blitzed them at quarter-time. At half-time it was about even and we were all around in the little rooms there. I looked around and I saw Sheeds, KB (Kevin Bartlett) and Bourkey (Francis Bourke), where the lockers were, they were virtually in them.

And Tony has come in and said 'You (expletive deleted)s!' and got the trestle table and kicked the shit out of it and had a clipboard and threw it and nearly decapitated someone. Now I know why they were hiding. They were smart.

The quarter-time fight (1980 finals series) between Jewell and Carlton coach Percy Jones was a classic. They both wouldn't bruise a grape. I'm watching it and I'm pissing myself, thinking 'Look at these two idiots.' I still remember it because Rudi Webster, he was fantastic for us with positive things, and Jones had a dip at him and TJ, the eyes just rolled back and it was like a big haymaker. Peter Grant was there and they broke it up.

In 1980 we had a combination of older guys like Bartlett, Bourke, (David) Cloke and (Bryan) Wood, who had played in premierships, and you had these young kids coming through. We won the under 19s premiership in 1977 and six of those guys played in the 1980 premiership. We were fit and strong and had Sheeds on board for the two hours he used to have us on a Monday. It wasn't just going through the motions, it was actual game drills, so you were also picking up your skills.

Leading up to the Grand Final, we were in the meeting room at Punt Road. Bruce Tempany did his knee and couldn't play. So on the Thursday night, before the meeting started, Tony Jewell said 'Can you say a few words, Bruce?' Well, all the blokes were nearly in tears, it was really emotional. And Tony's gone 'Well if you blokes don't (expletive deleted) beat these (expletive deleted)s, you can all go get rooted', and he walked out.

I kicked the first goal (of the Grand Final). That was one of those ones where Jim Jess got a free kick from Stan Magro, who was my man. As he turned around he saw me and I got the ball and I kicked it straight.

We dominated the game but every time we came in at quarter-time, half-time, our thinking was the scores were level, let's just keep going, that was all. 19th and 20th man were Daryl Freame and Bruce Monteath. TJ made his first move at the 15-minute mark of the last quarter and the second move at the 20-minute mark. No-one wanted to come off. I didn't know what the score was until I sat down. I actually came off to give Bruce Monteath a run. 'Grub', who was the runner, came out to me and said 'Flea, no-one wants to come off, can you give the captain a run?'

"It was about 40 degrees and Tony Jewell and Peter Grant, who was his fitness advisor, got together and said 'I think we have a few weak blokes here, we just want to make them hard'."

All I remember of KB is his arms going out. For the last one he kicked (Bartlett kicked seven) I was sitting on the bench and Daryl Freame had just got on, (he) got the ball and kicked it and it kept running and running, and he shepherded Magro out of the way as well.

It's funny about Kevin. He kicked over 700 goals and I reckon I had given him a fair few of those with handballs. I remember when Jack Dyer wrote for the *Truth*: 'No good playing tennis with Kevin Bartlett because he wouldn't hit the ball back.'

I still remember him coaching us one day and we were doing a handball drill and we weren't doing it right and he said 'Stop training and I'll show you how to do it.' He took the handball drill. The sprockets were going everywhere.

I thought Francis (Bourke) was one of the best footballers I ever played with. I don't think it was his time to coach. Graeme Richmond wanted him to coach. You've got to have a pretty good rapport with players, and Francis just communicated completely differently from anyone I have ever met. That was probably his downfall in the end. It was either black or white. I still remember the first player interview and we were going through the questions; he asked me one question and I thought I gave a pretty good answer. He sat there for five minutes, his mind ticking over, and then he said 'No, I don't agree with that.'

He was just a different cat, but one of the best players I have ever played with. He said I wasn't playing our game. I used to kill them in the first half and for the third quarter he would take me off for the whole quarter! That was just Francis.

At the end of 1983 I was diagnosed as a diabetic. I probably had it five or six months earlier. I had to manage myself a lot better, the eating, the diet,

Siren time at the 1980 Grand Final. Weightman – jumping in the air alongside teammate Stephen Mount, to his left, and coach Tony Jewell to his right – headed to the bench in the dying minutes, allowing his captain, Bruce Monteath, onto the ground.

the insulin and getting through a game. Insulin is a banned drug, but I actually need it to live. We had to make the VFL aware I was a diabetic and that I needed the insulin. But they were right across that.

My older brother got it five years earlier, the same age as I did, but he was living away and I didn't know what it was. He played football in the country and he gave me a few tips.

There was no-one else I could go to, so it was really trial and error for me. When I was first diagnosed I tried to actually eat all my tucker before a game on Saturday morning, that was very hard – try and get all the carbos in your body. Then I'd get these lollies (jubes) around the ground to all the trainers, so if I felt I was a bit low in sugar I would put up my hand and they would come out. Some of the times, the trainers would say 'Oh, sorry mate, I've eaten them all.' Half-way through 1983, I worked out I needed to be able to build up continually to get to the game, so what I did was adjust. I would start eating a lot of carbs on Thursday and Friday and on the Saturday morning I wouldn't have to have too much, but I would have to adjust my insulin. If I didn't I would be as high as a kite.

Then I got John Baldry, our assistant boot studder, and told him I needed him to come out every two or three minutes to see if I needed a top-up of cordial or Gatorade. He was the fittest boot studder of all time. He had to give up smoking and did it for 10 years while I was playing. He was fantastic.

After the game, because you burnt up what you stored, you'd have to decrease your insulin for a couple of days so your body would get back to normal. The first couple of times I gave myself insulin I ended up with the 'hypos' at three o'clock in the morning.

I made sure the doctors at the time let the players know what I had. If you saw me going a bit ga-ga make sure you get some sugar into me. It was all about education. I had a talk to them a few times and they all took it on board. When you're having a hypo you look like you're pissed, that's where you have got to be careful where you're drinking and you have a hypo because people think 'Oh well, he is only drunk.'

I reckon on occasions I suffered from white line fever. I was just very competitive. I just didn't take any shit. When you're out there you're out there to do a job and do it the best you could, and I didn't really suffer fools. In an era where we were very successful early on, we had some really good players. Then for a long period of time we had blokes who probably weren't good enough to play.

We had that big changeover where we got rid of superstars like Cloke, Raines and Wood and replaced them with blokes not of the same quality.

It was frustrating. On a lot of occasions I did the wrong thing and when KB was coaching he said 'Look mate, we need you out on the ground.' He was good, Kevin, and he used to smack the crap out of them in his playing days, but he did it smart when no one was watching. He should have got reported a lot more times than once.

Alan Bond was made president in 1987 and they were doing the best and fairest up in the social club. He is presenting the Jack Dyer Medal to me and he said 'We'd like to announce that Dale Wineman has won,' and the blokes were giggling. You could see all the board members saying 'Weightman!' and that's when he lost a fair few supporters. So I just said thanks and I hung shit on his boat, saying it was leaking. The year before, I with nine other mates went up to the Whitsundays for 10 days on one of his yachts he sailed in the America's Cup. It was magnificent, the best trip I have been on. We got kicked off every island and they closed one island down until we got off.

In 1987, Carlton was going to give me a five-year deal and I wasn't going to be taxed and I was going to earn $100,000 clear. I was on about $30-40,000 here at Richmond. The money wasn't the thing because I never played for money. The thing I missed about it was that the next year they won a premiership. I always thought 'We are going to get better, it's just going to turn around.' I turned 21 the weekend after the 1980 premiership, played another losing one in 1982, and did not play in the finals for the next 11 years. And that was the hardest thing because that's all you wanted to play, get out there in September.

"I always thought 'It's just going to turn around.' I turned 21 after the 1980 premiership, played another losing one in 1982, and did not play in the finals for the next 11 years."

I reckon my best year would have been 1980. In 1978 I was just finding my feet, in 1979 you're getting there and 1980 it all came together – I suppose it is a lot easier to play when you have blokes who can play. That's why I did all right in the state games. During the mid-1980s I used to handball and hit teammates in the back of the head. Some of the players I played with just didn't know what was going on and I thought, 'This could be a struggle.'

We didn't know we were playing for free (during Save Our Skins). Don't forget, in those days I still remember the salary cap was $1.1 million and I think we were paying $400,000. It was hard because KB couldn't go out and buy anyone, that's why we had a lot of players who weren't footballers but got games.

We used to go out in the country and promote it and you'd bring the young kids along; they couldn't believe the support Richmond had when you have little kids with their 20 cent pieces coming.

They just couldn't believe the support they got. They got a feel that this club is not just about playing a game of football. This is their life, this is what they come for.

I was captain in 1991 and the next minute it was Allan Jeans as coach and I'm thinking 'Okay.' The players were the last people to know. It was just done. That's how it worked and that's the way it was. KB had a pretty good run – four years – because I was used to one every two years.

I suppose I was a bloke every week who turned up and had a go. I reckon I was probably a very good team person – it wasn't about Dale Weightman, it was about how we can be better every time we went out there. One person cannot be the whole focus of a game of football.

I was just a little bloke, five-seven when I had long stops in, who had a dip every time I went out there.

Brian Taylor

Brian Taylor was the first Richmond player to kick 10 goals in a match at the MCG. He left Richmond at the end of the 1984 season to play for Collingwood where he kicked 100 goals in 1986. Post-retirement he has forged a career as a leading football commentator.

1980-84

Born
Apr 10, 1962

Played
Richmond
1980-84
43 games
156 goals

Collingwood
1985-90

Interviewed
Feb 22, 2012

I remember vaguely the day I kicked 10 goals for Richmond at the MCG (Rd 17 1982). I played on a guy called Chris Hansen, No. 16 for Fitzroy. I was only a young guy and it was the first time I kicked a bag of goals and I was pretty happy to do so even though it was against one of the weaker teams.

I was a teenager when I came to Richmond, just 17 years. I came from a little country town called Mandurah in Western Australia, south of Perth. In my wildest dreams I would never have imagined someone was watching me, from a VFL point of view, all the way over there in Mandurah. I couldn't comprehend that they would even know of me.

All of a sudden, Ian Wilson and Gareth Andrews landed on my doorstep, almost unannounced. I took them marron-hunting up the river and it was the first time any of them were out of their shiny black shoes.

I was signed on a Form Four. I think they worked in a way that each club was only allowed to sign one interstate young player per year. So they spent something very special on me. However, there were complications. The club I was tied to in the WAFL – East Fremantle, where I only played one game in the Under 19s – wouldn't allow me to go.

It ended up in the Supreme Court. Brian Ward, Richmond's solicitor back then took it all the way as a 'restriction of trade' case and I was the first player through the Supreme Court to win a 'restriction of trade' case. That path was later taken by Silvio Foschini (South Melbourne/Sydney 1981-82, St Kilda 1983-86, 1988) and many many others. That's how I got to Richmond.

I remember arriving in Melbourne on a Friday with my family. I was billeted out in South Yarra with a lady called Mrs Reid. Richmond had found a job for me as an apprentice plumber by the next Monday. For a guy who hadn't been out of WA, that was a pretty big deal.

I remember my very first job. 7am on the Monday morning and my boss said 'you are off to the Blue Moon' and I had no idea what that was – I was only 17 and a new boy in town. We went to a block of massage parlours on St Kilda Road to fix a sewerage blockage. I remember we arrived there at 7.30am, they sent me down this 12 foot shaft. The boss said ram this thing up the pipe and that should get it out, and all of a sudden I heard gurgle, gurgle and I was covered in the night's takings. I was hosed off and sent back to the workshop in a taxi. I trained with Richmond for the first time later that evening. That was my introduction to Melbourne!

Richmond gave me a choice of what job I could do. I was a kid coming from the country. Had I stayed I was about to be a mechanical fitter for Alcoa in the Bauxite mines. I didn't have any great aspirations as a kid. So I chose to be an apprentice plumber because I thought the plumber was the next best thing to being a mechanical fitter. I always wanted to do a trade, but I should have become an electrician. Richmond was prepared to send me to university, they were going to look after me.

I think clubs should do more of this, but they don't. When I came to Richmond for the first time I was greeted at the airport by a guy that I had only ever seen on the TV – it was Kevin Sheedy. To have Kevin arrive in his R.M. Williams get up and his high boots at the airport was absolutely amazing. Here I was, watching this guy on *The Winners*

Brian Taylor training at Punt Road Oval. He went on to kick 156 goal in his 43 games for the Tigers.

Brian Taylor, marking over Hawks champion Kelvin Moore, was disappointed when he missed out on playing in the Tigers' 1982 Grand Final Premiership team.

(on ABC-TV), an absolute superstar, and here he was meeting me at the airport in 1979.

I barracked for St Kilda. Mainly because of the WA connection with Ross Smith (St Kilda 1961-1972, 1975), Bruce Duperouzel (St Kilda 1974-1982), George Young (St Kilda 1973-78) and the jumper got me as well. You've got to understand that in Western Australia all we saw was *The Winners* at 6.30pm on a Sunday night – that's how we chose our VFL team.

My father had no interest in sports. He still knows nothing about sports. He came and supported me as a junior, while I did football, basketball and motorbike racing, but he wasn't interested in any of it himself.

I think I was recruited as a forward. I kicked a lot of goals in junior football as a key forward, however, because of my lack of size in those early years at Richmond I was played at half-forward and forward pocket. Plus we had Michael Roach playing full-forward, Mark Jackson was in the Seconds, and Peter Lane in the Thirds.

In my first game of Under 19s, I did my knee and damaged my cartilage and was out for about seven weeks. I always had knee problems. But I never had any other injuries – never had soft tissue or concussion injuries, it was just knee problems – on my right knee – all through my career.

It was awkward trying to find a passage of games to prove myself. Being up against the great Michael Roach at the time meant it was never going to be easy to unseat him.

Richmond sent me to orthopedic surgeons who ripped my cartilage out. They would never do it nowadays, but it was to get you back as soon as possible. In those days, it was a full plaster cast for about six weeks then a couple of weeks of training. The medical staff at that time were fantastic.

Paddy Guinane was my Under 19s coach. I enjoyed Paddy's soft nature, in the way he handled people. He's the guy I'd love to speak with to find more about the Richmond club history and in particular my situation in 1982. Paddy was someone I leaned on right through my career at Richmond. He is a great Richmond person and I love him for that. Royce Hart was my coach in the occasional seconds games I played. He was a little more gruff, aggressive, flamboyant and flighty.

In my first game, round 19 1980, I had a very special opportunity that could have turned into gold. At the time it didn't occur to me that I could have played in the 1980 Premiership if I played well in my first game that year.

I lined up on Bruce Doull. Doull was the best half-back in the competition. I got one handball and two kicks that day and got taken off around the third quarter. I had a shocking day. If I had played well that day it would have been hard to drop me leading into the finals, because I had also played well on several senior players in my Reserves games that year.

I don't mind talking about 1982. Here I was, having arrived in 1979, and the club wins the 1980 Premiership with a side most people claim will last for a decade. All of a sudden 1982 comes along and we play in another Grand Final and I remember thinking 'it doesn't matter if I miss out, this club has played in four Grand Finals in the last 11 seasons, so I am a certainty to get my shot down the track somewhere, if I keep playing good footy.' You should never think that – it doesn't work like that.

That year I kicked 71 goals up to round 21 and both Stephen Pirrie (Richmond 1982-84, St Kilda 1984, Essendon 1985) and myself did our knees in the last game at Arden Street. I was playing full-forward and he was playing full-back. And that was the end of Stephen's career really; he didn't play many games after that.

I missed out on the Grand Final even though I had proved my fitness in a test and in a practice game. I'm not bitter about it at all, I'd just like to know for my own sake what went on behind closed doors, what was their thinking, because I never really got told.

The week between the second semi-final and the Grand Final we played a practice match against ourselves. I kicked 4 goals playing on Alan Martello. And we only played a half, and I thought that was enough to prove I was okay. I just don't think they believed I was fit.

I had not been told in the week leading up to the 1982 Grand Final that I wasn't playing. So my family made the trip over from Perth, expecting to see me playing. I expected to play. They had to play me.

Then I was told on the Thursday night that I wasn't playing. It was pretty devastating. My memories were not of a happy time. I think I went out on the Friday night to the Richmond disco for a short while.

I should have asked 'what more do you want me to do?' I should have taken someone aside on Monday or Tuesday and said 'give me a test now!' I should have sold myself more rather than sit back and let people decide my future for me on that particular game. That is a great regret.

I ran out on the ground at the start of the 1982 Grand Final. Francis Bourke had asked me to run out on the ground with the players in a 'tactical' type move, and then remove myself from the ground when our warm up was over. I guess when you are young, you go back to the thinking 'I will get another opportunity and do the team thing here'. I stayed and watched the game from up in the Northern Stand.

Mick Malthouse's fitness test was on the Thursday night before that Grand Final. I remember standing in the race at Punt Road and watching it. At the very last tackle of the night he went to move away and Francis grabbed him by the arm and pulled the shoulder out of the socket.

Mick had worked so hard in the gym to get himself right. Time may have dented my memory, but I reckon about three days after he did the injury, I saw him and Eric Leech in the gym doing bench presses. He looked like a guy who was certain to play, he was so committed.

"Paddy was someone I leaned on right through my career at Richmond. He is a great Richmond person and I love him for that."

I seem to remember that fitness test went for 30 minutes. It probably only went for 10. If you put a modern day player through the fitness test that Malthouse went through, he wouldn't be able to play on the weekend. There was deathly silence when we realised he had done his shoulder.

Perhaps I didn't see it as clearly as the senior players, but I think Francis was a good coach. But I think he may have over-analysed the game. There seemed to be a lot of meetings for the sake of meetings and a lot of video going on at the time.

Two weeks after the 1982 Grand Final, we played an exhibition game at the Brisbane Commonwealth Games. It was against Carlton. I hurt my knee again in that game. So the start of 1983 was a hangover from the end of 1982, where I had a cyst in the back of my knee, and so that was the reason for my quiet 1983 season of just six games.

It was my third knee issue. I always thought it was going to come good. It was a very stiff feeling and the flexibility I had in the knee was really restricted and that was due to the cyst in the back of the knee. The cyst was later removed.

I began thinking there was this tandem thing possible where Roach would play full-forward and I would play in the forward pocket. Or vice-versa. That had been going on for a two- to three-year period. It had its moments of success but I don't think ultimately, fundamentally, it was successful for the team.

I felt the club had lost a bit of confidence in me. I had lost a bit of confidence in the club, as well. I really didn't know where I stood at the end of 1983 and 1984. Roach was still playing although he had a really bad back. I wondered when they were going to make a decision on him. And was it was going to be me or him? They never made the call.

"The fact is, I went to play for Collingwood for significantly less than what I was being paid at Richmond."

An opportunity arose at Collingwood. I didn't seek it out, they approached me. They didn't have a full-forward, they were a great club, so that's what happened.

I think I am mentally tough. It was a rough ride, but you know what, I enjoyed Richmond, it was my family, because I had left my family behind in Western Australia. Other people would go to a friend's place for social activities, but I'd go to the Richmond Football Club to talk to people. That's all I had.

Despite all the medical obstacles, I never saw my time at Richmond as a negative period at all. I enjoyed my time immensely and I always felt that in terms of togetherness, Richmond was a lot more together than Collingwood ever was.

I think the supporters were perhaps a little bit confused. I think a couple of senior players had received some wrong information about what had transpired regarding money. The fact is, I went to play for Collingwood for significantly less than what I was being paid at Richmond. It was about opportunity for me. Some of the senior players at Richmond painted it as a money opportunity, and that couldn't be anything further from the truth.

Coming out of that successful period Richmond was too hasty moving on their premiership players, and the guys who played in the 1982 Grand Final. They got rid of too much of the heart and soul of the club too quickly. Natural attrition would have gotten those guys anyway. They wanted to move players on too quickly and that tore a lot of the guts out of the club in 1983 and 1984.

It was a really delicate period. The Graeme Richmond period of 'I rule with an iron fist and with aggression and scare people into success' was passing. I think that worked in the '70s and early '80s but I think there was a period where the modern footballer no longer reacted to that sort of tactic.

It was always a strange feeling with Graeme Richmond. As a young player hearing his name all the time I thought, What is he? Is he a great player of the club? You never saw him. He was one of these unassuming modest guys who occasionally turned up to training, but I got a feeling most of his work was done over the phone or down at Ron Carson's garage.

Yet you had this really strong sense he was actually the one picking the team. I was always amazed to find that when a young player was about to play his first game, there were photographers down there taking a picture of the young player before the player was told even he was in the team! Someone was telling the press and I am sure it was Graeme. He was doing a lot of work in the media in terms of motivating players, like telling a journalist to write an article on a player pushing him to perform better.

In 1990 at Collingwood, I wrote a diary about my football year. It wasn't released until the Grand Final was run and won, but that cost me an opportunity to play in a premiership. The club got wind of the fact I was writing this diary and were very much against it. The politics of the club again! But, I have realised that that was the wrong thing to be doing, so I don't blame anyone except myself for that.

I was always aggressive on the field. I had watched the great full-forwards be marvellous at their craft but it always annoyed me that they got knocked around like teddy bears and treated unfairly, like being belted behind the ear. Peter McKenna, Doug Wade, Peter Hudson were great players but 'soft' in responding. I got annoyed how they got treated.

Right from the start I said to myself, I am going to be different. I am going to set the mould for aggressive full-forwards. I'm going to be the one punching the full-back. I'm not going to let him punch me. That was the attitude I deliberately took through my career.

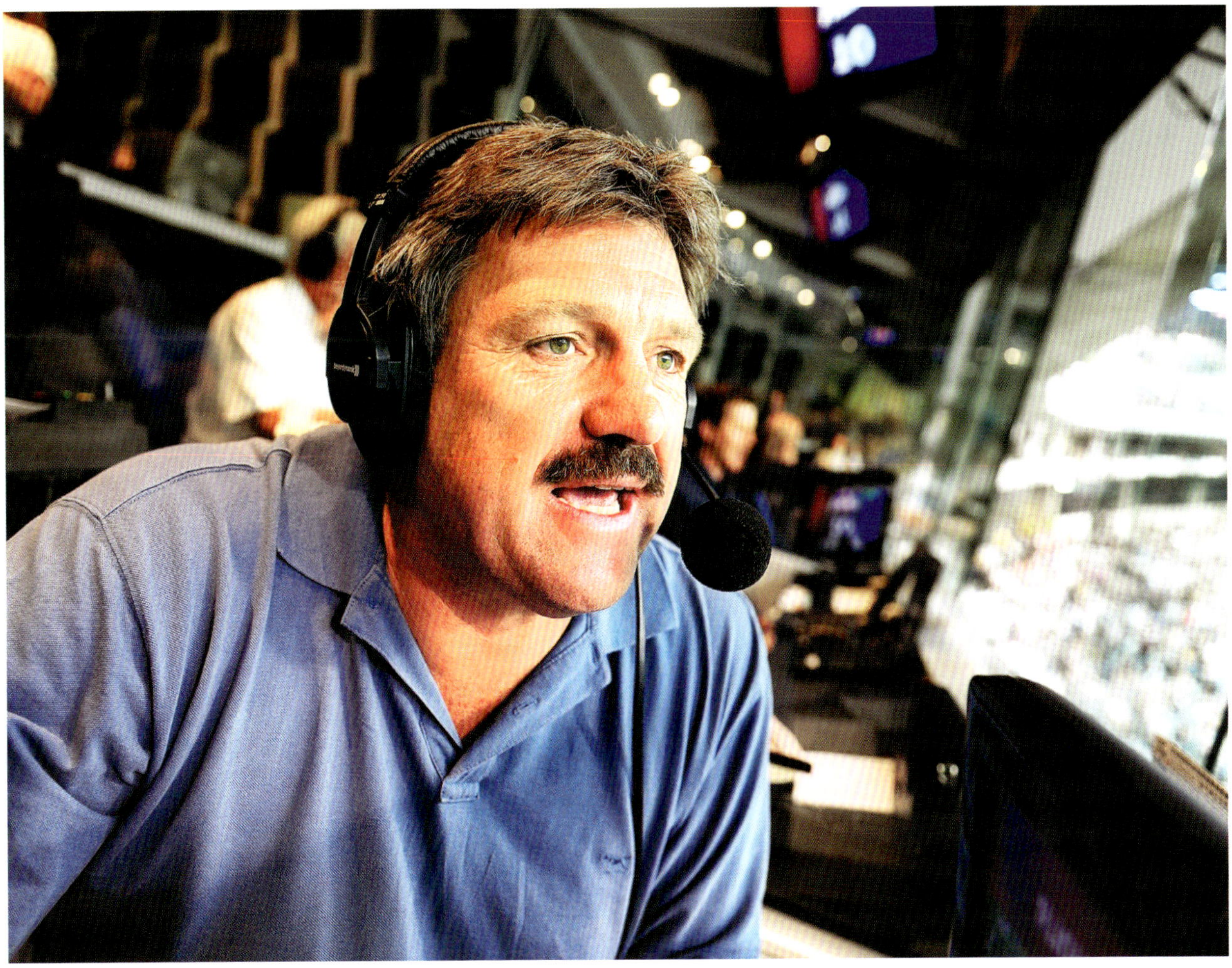

Brian Taylor has emerged as one of the AFL's leading commentators, known for his knockabout style and wit.

I always felt I needed to be in that heightened sense of aggression to play well. I never played well as a placid player. I was reported once for abusive language and another time I threw an opponent's boot over the fence at the MCG.

I wasn't a long kick. I could kick 45 metres, or 50 metres if everything worked comfortably. I always tried to mark within a radius that gave me an opportunity to score. I knew as I was running in whether I was in that comfort zone and whether everything felt like it should. It wasn't until I moved to Collingwood that I really refined my kicking and understood the technical aspects a lot more.

I've had my moustache since about 1980. I can remember a Scanlen's card of a young photo of me. We all wore moustaches at that time – Ian Scrimshaw, Mick Malthouse, Emmett Dunne, Robert Wiley – in fact it was the trend. I just haven't realised it has ended.

I was told an interesting stat one day. I was only three years old when KB played his first game of League Football. Later I went on to play in games with him! How unbelievable is that.

How do I think Richmond fans will remember me? I'm not even sure if Richmond supporters will remember me. Perhaps as a young kid who had some potential but never quite reached the place he could have and should have. I certainly remember my time at Richmond fondly. They were a family to me.

You've got to be very careful as a modern commentator not to harp back on yesteryear. You've got to go with the game and be in the moment. I can honestly say I adopt an attitude in my commentary now almost as if I never played the game. I try not to mention that I played the game, but I call with the same passion and aggression that I played the game.

I want to be known as a commentator now, not as a past player. I just want to enjoy and describe the game as it is now. I love the modern game. I think back to my day and it was great, but right now is better than it ever was.

Maurice Rioli

Maurice Rioli came to Richmond from the Melville Islands, via South Fremantle, in 1982. His ball-handling skills, pace and silky disposal made him an immediate sensation, and he won the best and fairest in his first two VFL seasons. Rioli died in December 2010.

1982-87

I went to Richmond in 1982 because of Mal Brown. I had had discussions with many clubs – including Essendon, Carlton, Footscray and Geelong. But I put a lot of trust in Mal Brown, my coach at South Fremantle.

There were lots of calls, and lots of offers. Leading into the 1981 season Mal was getting rather tired of all these calls and he said 'look, stuff ya, if anyone else rings me, I will tell them to forget about talking to you – you're going to Richmond.'

Carlton was the team I had an interest in, through the great name of Alex Jesaulenko. I can remember growing up listening to the radio, and Jezza was one player I had great respect for.

When I came over to Melbourne, I compared myself with players I had played against in Perth. I can remember considering Tony Buhagiar – he played for East Fremantle and I used to flog the arse off him! And he was a top player for the Bombers!

I know I came to Richmond with a fairly big reputation. I thought I handled it fairly well. The fact was I wanted to perform at the highest level, that's what drove me.

Opposition players used racist words to try and slow me down – to put me off my game. I would simply use that in my favour.

There weren't too many indigenous players around at that time. Phil Egan was a young kid starting out that year – he was just 19, an up-and-comer.

I was one of many indigenous players who had set the trend for others. Before me, I recognise Syd Jackson, Polly Farmer and later on Barry Cable. I was proud of the fact that being indigenous was one of the things that helped me perform at my best.

I wore No. 17, Jack Dyer's famous number. I wasn't full aware of Jack's history. It wasn't until I got to the club, that the pressure built up, and I discovered the breadth of his achievements and what he meant to the club.

It wasn't easy, as I came over with a lot of hamstring injuries. The previous year I spent half the year out of football through hamstring problems. To tell you the truth, back in the territory I had never been told how to prepare myself in the area of prevention of injuries and treatment of injuries. I was never taught that you had to stretch before a game. I just ran out and did my best. When I first went to Perth I wondered why these people were doing these stretching exercises. I had no idea there were exercises to prevent injuries. For me, one hamstring would go, and then the next. I had so many problems.

When I went to Richmond I knew I had to do something about the constant injuries. Consequently I worked harder than I had in my life. I really had to work hard to keep my hamstrings working. I then hardly missed any games, apart from one or two through knee injuries.

I was lucky to play in a Grand Final in my first season in the VFL. It is every kid's dream to play in a VFL Grand Final. I had a bit of experience behind me, playing in a couple of Grand Finals in the west and playing State football. I had plenty of support – my dad, my brothers and in-laws came down from the territory and across from Perth.

Born
Sept 1, 1957

Died
Dec 25, 2010

Played
Richmond
1982-87
118 games
80 goals

Interviewed
Feb 20, 2010

Magnificent Maurice Rioli won the best and fairest in his first two years at Tigerland. He became the first player to win a Norm Smith Medal in a losing side.

Maurice Rioli said that when he came to Richmond, he had to work harder than ever to overcome constant injuries. "I then hardly missed any games, except for one or two through knee injuries." In 2018, Rioli was made a Life Member of the Tigers, recognising his great contribution to the club. Rioli won the Norm Smith Medal as best player on the ground in the 1982 Grand Final, and is one of just four players to win the Medal in a losing side.

I had sort of tasted defeat in a Grand Final before, the previous year with South Fremantle when we lost to Claremont.

It meant a lot to me to play in the 1982 Grand Final. The fact I was an indigenous player, the fact I had a huge following back in the territory and islands where I am from, and back in the west where I had come from. There was a lot of interest and obviously the pressure was a memorable part of it all.

We were favourites against Carlton. We beat them in the second semi-final at VFL Park (Waverley) by 23 points. We went into the Grand Final as favourites. It was a strange feeling, we were playing well, we were in front (by 11 points) at half-time; the next minute they went bang, took the lead and the game was over.

I was in the centre when the streaker turned up. I did see her running onto the field and I didn't know where to look. I made sure I didn't catch her eye so she didn't come near me.

It was obviously a terribly disappointing feeling losing that Grand Final. However, I felt good in the fact that I did my best.

I was more numb than anything; I had no feeling, other than the feeling for my fellow players. But in this game I was happy with my performance. I played on Rod Ashman in the centre – he played close to me for most of the day.

In many ways it was a bitter pill to swallow when I won the Norm Smith Medal. To me, I felt a little ashamed to have received it, among the disappointment that surrounded the Richmond team.

It was just a numb feeling I had. I can remember immediately walking off the dais after receiving the medal, and I took the medallion off and tried to hide it within my hands. At the time it wasn't something to be happy about.

Now people talk about me being a Norm Smith medallist. I guess it probably means more now because it is in the record books – the fact that Maurice Rioli is a Norm Smith medallist.

In 1993, the AFL had an indigenous focus surrounding the Grand Final. They invited me down to present the Norm Smith Medal and Polly Farmer presented the Premiership Cup. I was delighted to hand over the medal to Michael Long.

Maurice Rioli returns to the MCG, the scene of many of his greatest moments in football, to present the winner's trophy to Joel Bowden after the Tigers' win over Essendon in the first Dreamtime game in 2005.

Richmond had a disappointing year in 1983 – we didn't even make the finals, winning just seven games. We finished tenth in the 12-team competition of those days. Francis Bourke, who had coached us to the Grand Final in his first year (1982) was sacked. I thought we still had a really good side. Bartlett retired in 1983 and Bryan Wood, David Cloke and Geoff Raines had all left at the end of 1982 – all had played in the 1980 premiership.

When we lost that calibre of those players, we really struggled. We haven't recovered since.

Then you had coaches coming and going, you had presidents cheering from the other side of the country, like Alan Bond from Perth. I can remember a coach going on a holiday, coming back, and he didn't have a job!

The politics affected the players of the club. You can imagine how upsetting it would have been for the club and its stability, and what effect it had on the playing group at that time. In the six seasons I was there, I had four coaches – from Bourke to Mike Patterson to Paul Sproule, and then Tony Jewell came back!

My strengths were being able to pick up plenty of possessions, read the play and get to the contest. I think my tackling was a strength and my use of the ball. I just loved football. I just ran out to play the game. I loved it.

Kevin Bartlett (The Coach)

After a supreme playing career, Kevin Bartlett agreed to coach the Tigers from season 1988. He stayed four years before being tumultuously sacked, during which time the team finished no higher than 10th. Bartlett's coaching stint, and departure, exposed the perilous state of the club's finances.

In 1987 I received a phone call from Richard Doggett, who was then general manager of the Tigers. He sounded me out whether or not I would be interested in coaching the Tigers. And I said, 'You have Tony Jewell as the coach,' and he said, 'Tony has indicated he wants to move away from coaching.' I didn't feel comfortable talking to them about coaching the Tigers, because Tony had been a teammate of mine. But Richard assured me that Tony had said to them that he wanted to give the coaching away. So I said, 'If that's the case, I will have a chat to you.'

I met with the committee and re-iterated that I didn't want to be going for a job that was already held by Tony, and even said 'Who knows, the second half of the season the Tigers may play well and Tony may want to continue, so the club should be putting its efforts in to finishing off as good as they can.' As things turned out, they came back and said 'Tony definitely wants to move on,' and they would offer me the job if I wanted to take it.

Coaching was something I was always keen to do so I accepted the job. I remember saying to them 'There will be a lot of work required to get the Richmond Football Club up. The club would need far better players than it had. Tony Jewell has already proved himself to be a premiership coach, so if Tony is sitting on the bottom of the ladder it's not because of the coaching, it's because the club has a lot of deficiencies in a lot of other areas. So we have to make certain we are in position where we are financial enough to go out and recruit and get players who can help us.'

I took on the job because I loved the club dearly and I had knocked back two other coaching offers. I just felt this immense loyalty to the club that if I was going to coach I would rather do it with the club my heart was absolutely in.

Coached
Richmond
1988-91
88 matches
27 wins
61 losses

I realised the club was in a sorry state when I first took over the job. I was the only full-time coach. Bruce Seymour was Football Operations manager, and he was tremendous. He was hard-working, nothing was too much for Bruce. But it seemed to me that Bruce was everything and therefore I realised the club was in a pretty sorry state. The rooms themselves hadn't changed from when I was playing – the conditions were as bad as in 1965 when I played my first game. Bruce actually repainted the rooms himself during the Christmas break, and he re-laid the carpet. So you can see it was very unprofessional in terms of support that people had down at the club.

I sat around and looked at the gym before we had training. Half the weights were missing, there was a punching bag hook but no punching bag. There were fittings for speed balls but there were no speed balls and half the mechanics holding the speedballs were broken or gone. I remember going down to one of the sporting companies and bought four or five speed balls myself and came back with the fittings and put them up myself.

We had a terrific bloke who was helping out the club, Phil Grant. He was running his own sporting business, he was just fantastic. Out of the goodness of his heart he produced the mitts so you could hit the speedballs; he produced weights that were missing, boxing gloves and any little bits he could help out with. You had a number of terrific people with terrific hearts wanting to do things to help the Richmond Football Club.

Michael Green was absolutely superb as chairman of selectors. He was fantastic with his wisdom. Frank Dimattina came down as team manager, somehow he found time from his restaurant, but he just wanted to help out the club. He used to bring down pizzas every Thursday night to feed an entire

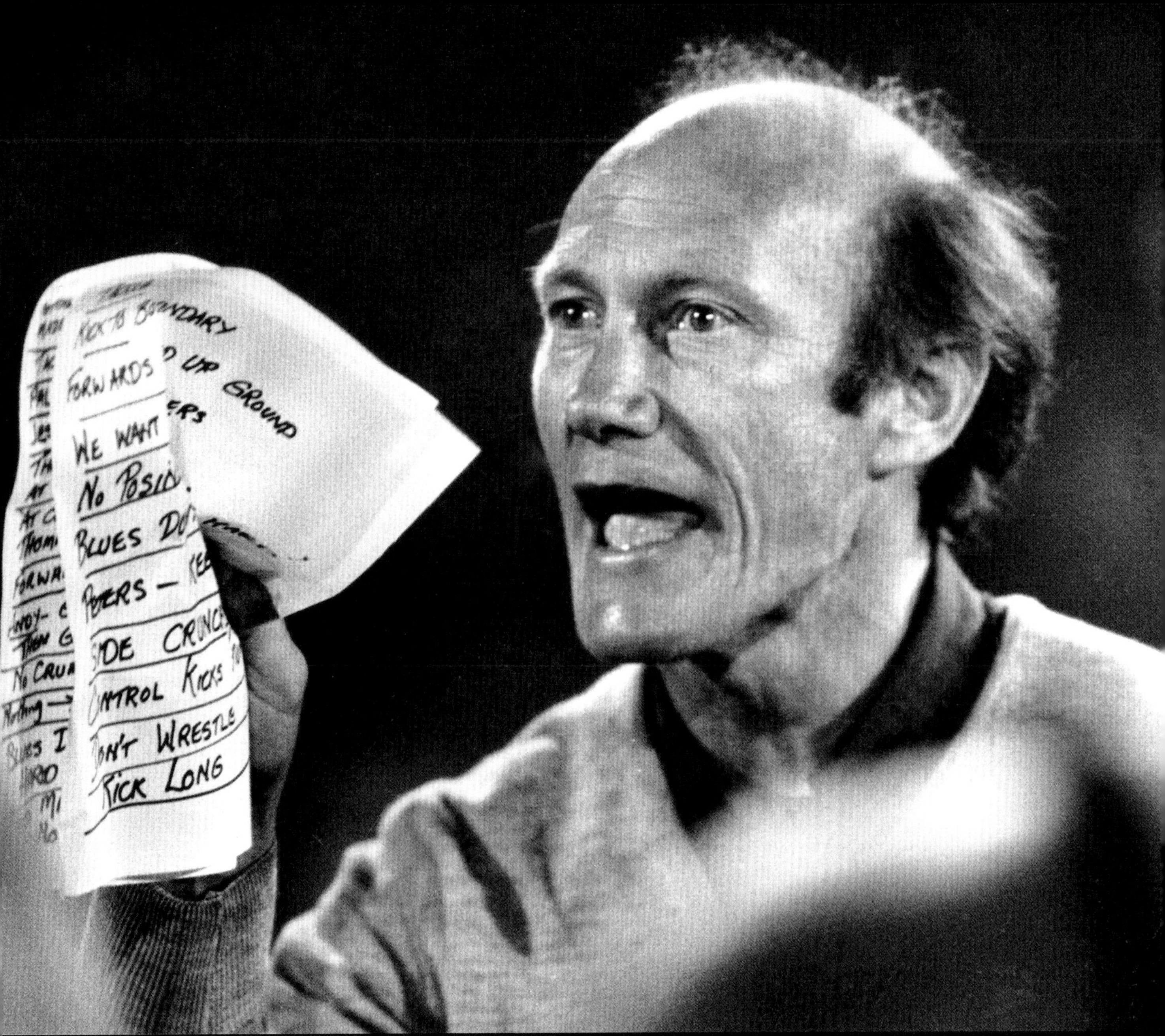

Kevin Bartlett, notes in
hand, addresses
the Tigers during his
coaching stint.

football team at no cost. Paul Callery is a great mate of mine, he came down and he was our runner and fitness adviser and was absolutely fantastic.

Ken Stonehouse, a selector, was one of a bunch of blokes who gave so much to the club over those four years that I was coach. So did Emmett Dunne, who was my assistant coach and coach of the reserves.

I didn't even really have an office. There was a players' room with a bit of carpet and some steps on it and a blackboard and I had a desk sitting in there.

I didn't know the Richmond Football Club was in debt until several months after I accepted the job. It came as a bit of surprise to me before the annual general meeting at the Richmond Social Club. We finished training and the board asked me to come up. It then told me they were going to make an announcement the club was $1.5 million in debt, at that time an enormous sum of money. That was disappointing. What that told us was that we certainly weren't going to be in a position to go out and buy any players to help the club fast-track itself from the bottom of the ladder.

"I was expecting to remain coach because I honestly believed those close to the club knew the difficulties that the Richmond Football Club was facing."

Richmond had no money. You couldn't buy players. I can remember going across with Bruce Seymour to South Australia to draft a few players, and staying with friends because the club didn't have money to put you in a hotel ... money was very hard to get.

In one of the earlier days, it was so wet, the ground was in such bad condition that we decided to train indoors at the Royal Park Netball Centre. Barry Rowlings, another fantastic person, was doing the skills work and he tried to run around all day trying to find someone from the club to give him $50 to hire the courts.

It sounds ridiculous, but if you've got no money, you've got no money. I can still recall Barry saying, 'I can't find anybody.' Anyway, he got $50 from someone and I can remember, while training was taking place indoors, Barry coming up to me, ashen-faced. I said, 'What's wrong?' and he said, 'You won't believe what's happened.' I thought, 'Don't tell me I've lost one of the young kids.' And he said, 'Someone has just broken a window.' I said, 'Well, what can we do about that?'

He said, 'How are we going to pay for it?'

We went on a training camp up near Moe. We could only take a certain number of players because we couldn't afford to take the whole group. The idea was that half would stay back in Melbourne and the other half would go and we would make up some reason why they all couldn't go. In the end I said, 'We can't do that, that's ridiculous.' So we all went on the training camp and I spent about $300 hiring some motivational sporting films. It was a difficult time for coaching staff and the board as well, because they had the responsibility of trying to keep the club afloat and trying to keep it viable.

We had some early picks in the mid-season draft and could have picked up players like Derek Kickett and Tim Pekin. But we were told under no

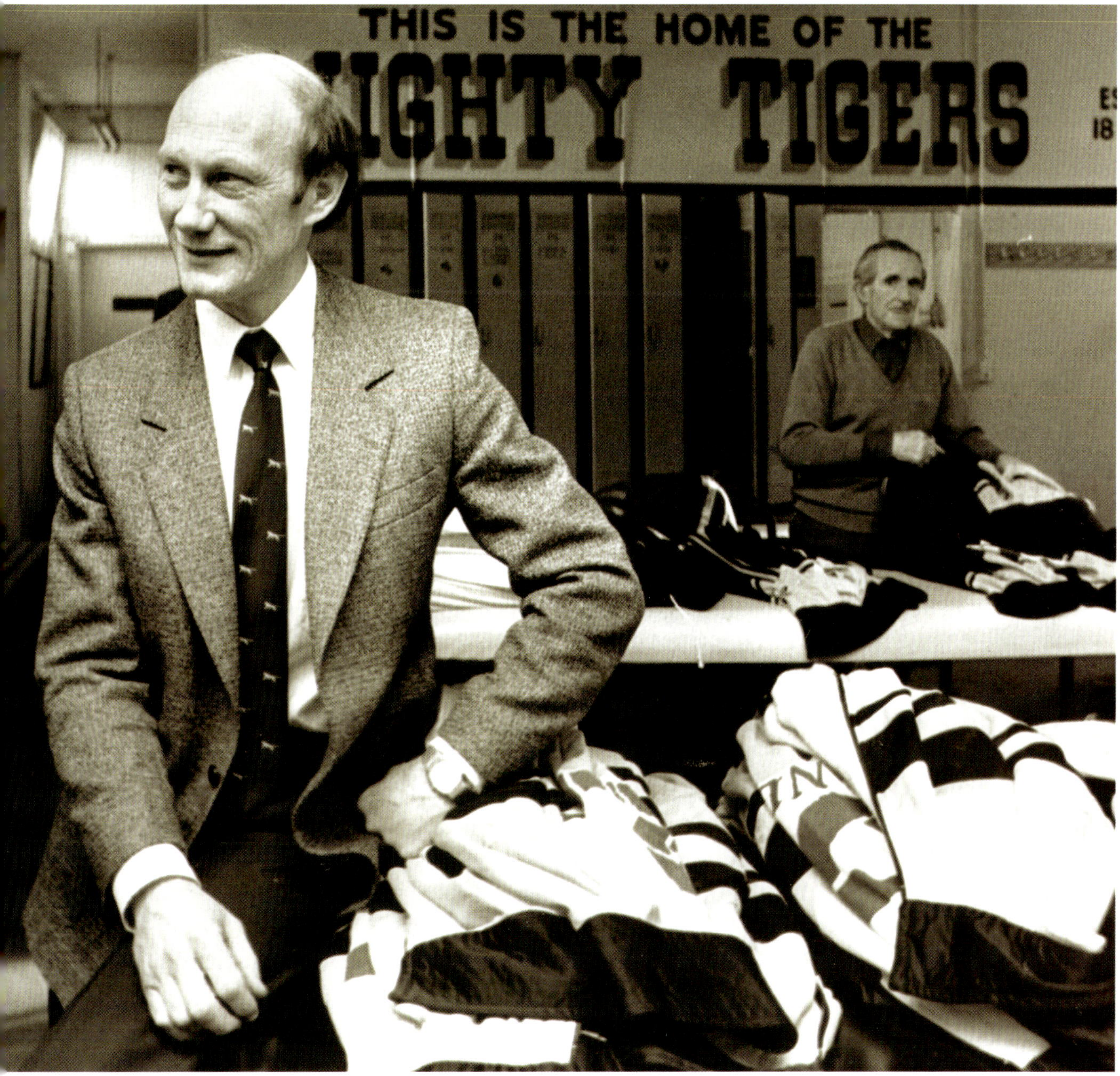

circumstances could we draft those players because we just didn't have any money to pay what they wanted. So we could only stick with the policy of drafting young kids out of school – sometimes still going to school – and maybe drafting someone from the country who hadn't made it before. Russell Morris, who grew up loving the Tigers and was a terrific player with Hawthorn and St Kilda, wanted to come to Richmond, but we were only offering half as much money as St Kilda ... and St Kilda wasn't setting the world on fire in those days.

I was desperate to get some experience, strength and agility into the team, so much so that I even rang Geoff Raines after he finished with the Brisbane Bears to come back and play. But Geoff was setting himself up in business in Brisbane and said it was not feasible to make the move.

David Cloke was coming to the end of his tether as a player at Collingwood but to me he was still good enough to get a game at Richmond. He would walk into our side and be great for our young kids because David was a very, very hard trainer and he was a fabulous player and former captain of the club. So I rang David, 'I know you're coming to the end of your career but I need some help. I need someone in the club who can lead, a bit of size. Would you be interested?'

And he said, 'Yeah, I would be interested. I think I still can play.' I said, 'We've got one problem,

Long-time property steward Dusty O'Brien (right) sees in another coaching change: Kevin Bartlett on the day of his appointment, as predecessor Tony Jewell escapes the scene (left).

David, we haven't got any money at all so we can't offer you any big contracts, any signing-on fees, you'll have to come back just out of the goodness of your heart, virtually.' And David said, 'Look, football has been good to me. I have done well, I'll just play for match payments.' And that's what he did.

David came back and had two fantastic seasons (1990-91) with us. He retired after the first season and then I talked him into coming back again and it was just great. We may not have had too many happy days when I was coach of the Tigers but my last game, even though it was sad for me, probably was still the highlight when David – in his last game – kicked eight goals against Carlton.

"Tom's first game as coach was against Carlton and I sat beside him as the 19th man, and on this afternoon, at the function, I sat beside him, too."

I didn't know it was my last game, the board hadn't told me that. There had been speculation, but I did ask to talk to the board before the end of the season at one stage and I was told that wasn't necessary. There wasn't very much communication. I was always trying to be upbeat for the club and I felt that the board obviously knew the difficulties I was coaching under, and the difficulties they were working under as a board. So I felt we were in tune right until the absolute very end. I didn't take any notice of any of the negatives, because I knew people on the board and I just knew they understood our situation better than anyone.

And I was fronting the press all the time trying to give a positive face. I can remember at different stages members of the board saying 'All you have to do is keep going with the young kids, that's all we can do.' I asked them once, 'Did we ever have a recruiting budget?' The answer was, 'No.'

I was expecting to remain coach of the club because I honestly believed that those close to the club knew the difficulties that the Richmond Football Club was facing. It was no easy fix and it was going to be a long, hard road. But you needed people who had spirit and courage and people who believed in Richmond. The first time that I knew I wasn't the coach was when Neville Crowe and Cameron Schwab, the general manager, turned up at my home and told me. I may have asked, 'Who is going to be the coach?' and they said, 'Allan Jeans.' I was fairly short and sharp once I was told. Neville and Cameron left soon after.

Cartoonist Mark Knight's 'veiled' reference to the Richmond Football Club eating its own.

No one from the club had spoken to me from the last game of the season until I saw Neville and Cameron. No-one asked me to come in and meet the board. I had been to watch the under 19s in the finals and was down in the rooms, but no-one had spoken to me about coaching. It was disappointing that the club didn't ask me to come down and speak with the board, to get my feelings on the previous four years, or where the club was at, or where we were going, what our strengths were, what our weaknesses were and what had been a very, very tough journey.

So that was always very, very disappointing, that there wasn't even a meeting. I was disappointed because I had been at the club as a player since I was 15 years of age, I had been there something like 27 years – more than half my lifetime – and I felt disappointed someone could be involved for that long yet the club couldn't find the time to speak to its coach and talk about one, his future, or two, the club's future.

So I never had a chance to defend the previous seasons ... people didn't have the courtesy or the professionalism to actually speak to the coach.

If I had had the opportunity I would have outlined the fact that I thought we achieved a lot with very little, and kept the club buoyant, and the spirit and hopes of the players up. I expected they would have realised the difficulties I had been working under, as I realised the difficulties they had been working under. Maybe they didn't want to hear what I had to say about the club, maybe some home truths may not have sat nicely. And I was disappointed most of all because I just felt that the board lost its courage and its heart.

Allan Jeans took over from me. He lasted only one year and could only win half the number of games that I won the previous season. John Northey came in the following year; he was a Grand Final coach at Melbourne and he was only able to win half the number of games, so between Allan and John they would have found how difficult it was.

I was away for a long, long time. For about 16 years

Brian Leys, Andy Goodwin, Kevin Bartlett, Michael Mitchell, and Allister Scott celebrate knocking off finals contender Essendon, at Windy Hill, in Round 17 1991.

I had no official contact with the club. I felt at the time, that if a person could be at the club for 27 years of his life – and I like to think gave a good contribution – and that amounted to nothing in terms of even been spoken to at the end of the 1991 season, then I had to do one of two things.

I either had to completely forget about that and then turn up to the very first club function I was invited to, and someone gives you a big wrap and you walk up on stage and give a smile and all is forgiven. Or walk away.

And I felt it was best to walk away. And that's what I did. I always attended Grand Final reunions every year, and I attended Christmas parties, but I never attended anything that was official by the club. I would still barrack for the club, and love the club and still see my old teammates and friends, but I would do it from afar.

In that time I was approached by a number of people to do things at the club. I was approached to be on the board, I was approached by people to try and oust somebody, I had been approached to join a group to challenge the board, I had been approached to support people running for the board. And every time someone approached me I dismissed it out of hand. I didn't want to be seen as a person who was trying to get back at people, or run people out of office, I just decided that I wanted to make a clean break and let everyone else work out everything for themselves. I said at the time when I walked away, I didn't know whether it would be five, 10 or 15 years, but at some stage I would come back.

I will go to some selected things. Tom Hafey has been a great inspiration to me and great friend of the family. He has the Tommy Hafey Club and I thought on a couple of occasions of going along. Sometimes I haven't been able to because things have been on. But I thought in 2007 I would go. I thought to celebrate my 60th birthday I would go to a Tommy Hafey Club function. I always said I will go back to attend functions when I feel comfortable to go back.

The theme was the rivalry between Richmond and Carlton and I thought those clashes have always been very dear to me. When I played, that was the big game, it was bigger than playing Collingwood, it was bigger than playing Essendon. I always enjoyed playing against them and always admired their players. My last game also as coach was against Carlton. So I thought that was a nice mix, turning 60, attending a Tommy Hafey Club function and celebrating a great rivalry with Carlton. And Tom's first game as coach was against Carlton and I sat beside him as the 19th man, and on this afternoon, at the function, I sat beside him, too.

Save our Skins

Only Richmond insiders understand how close to extinction the Tigers were before the memorable Save our Skins campaign. President of the time, Neville Crowe, and star midfielder Matthew Knights reflect on the saving of a football club as Richmond embarked on a grass roots fund-raising drive.

NEVILLE CROWE

A lot of people have said that (I saved the club). I'm very proud in the part that I played. But I've always put it in the right perspective – this was a job done by thousands of people, not just one person. The things that happened at that time were just mind-boggling.

It was just a magnificent thing when kids came in with money boxes and tipped it out on the table and said, 'Please let me save the club.' Little old ladies of 80 years of age, buying 10-year memberships like Elsie McGraw, bless her cotton socks. All those real people and grass roots people ... unfortunately these days, even in this club, there's an almighty push for the dollar at all times. I reckon that the time we ever take off our eyes those people that helped us at that time, that was just the greatest team game I ever played in.

I made so many friends. To raise a million dollars in 10 weeks, one hundred thousand dollars in one day, was just unbelievable. Perhaps in my quiet moments I thought, 'Shit, how we ever going to do this?' But on the last day, when the last dollar rolled in, it was just the most incredible feeling I have ever experienced. Maybe that's my Grand Final.

Ed's Note: Crowe missed the 1967 Grand Final through suspension.

Once I got wound up in it, I played a very big part in the theme of Save our Skins. To get the Tigers in a position, and talk with the advertising people and say, the Tiger is virtually dead and it's got to come to life in the last minute ... they picked that up particularly well, and that was something that will stay with me for a long while. It was an endangered species. A lot of people thought it was a gimmick. They said it's all a con. But we were actually trading while insolvent. Everybody on the board at that stage could have have had their life wrecked. And I must confess, the business I was involved in suffered considerably. I probably lost a lot of money coming out of that. Things I should have been doing I wasn't doing.

Michael Humphris (the finance director) went through the financial aspects of the club. It turned out ... We had our players in there valued as assets and all this sort of silly nonsense. So once Michael got all the skeletons out of the cupboard and we sat on the table and we said, 'Here's the picture, whether we like it or not, and it's a gruesome one.' You will recall Footscray had done it earlier. We planned it, and got the endangered species and the TV ads and we were ready to go and once we started, we just motored along from there.

The biggest single individual donation was from Craig Kimberley of Just Jeans. He gave us $10,000. The Former Players & Officials Association gave us $20,000. From there on, it was genuinely rattling cans, having the Family Day and putting coins right around the boundary line. The Legends game out at Windy Hill, with Rex Hunt as a commentator, there were 20,000 people there and I think only 10,000 people went to the VFA Grand Final that year!

When the job was done, it wasn't like kicking the final goal, it was just a relief more than anything else. There were lots of hugs and kisses. It was just a remarkable time in the history of the club. Some remarkable people did some remarkable things and it just shows what people can do when they put their mind to it.

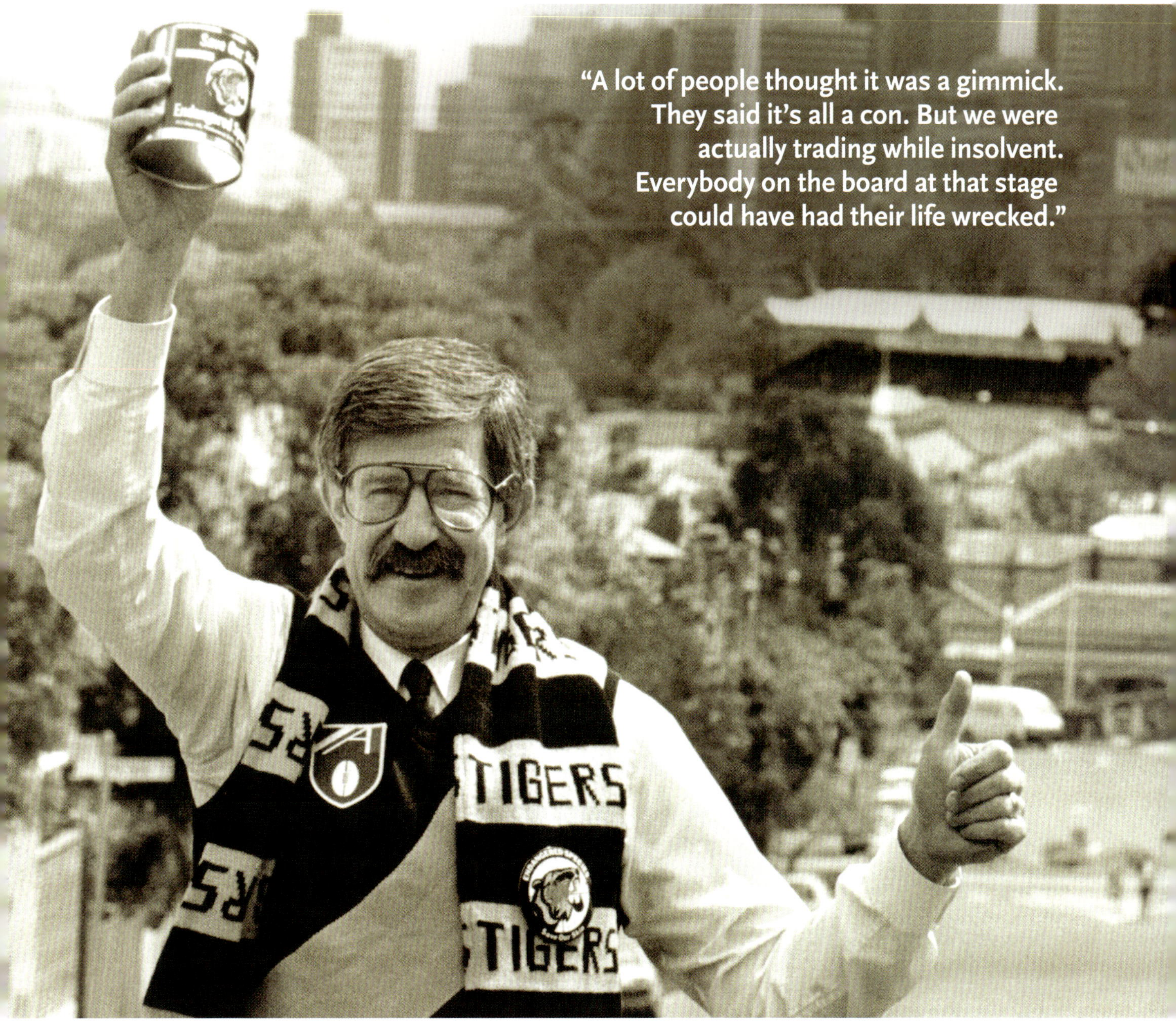

"A lot of people thought it was a gimmick. They said it's all a con. But we were actually trading while insolvent. Everybody on the board at that stage could have had their life wrecked."
TIGERS
TIGERS

Matthew Knights

The players were shielded from the financial difficulties the club had. I had an inkling it was really dire but by no means knew the extent of it. I guess Neville Crowe and Kevin Bartlett had the ability to do that. It was never burdened on the players. The players always felt like it was a good place to be around and a positive place where you can develop to get better as a player and a person. That was the most outstanding attribute from my point of view of the Richmond Football Club. From the outside they seemed like really dark times but on the inside it was a fairly united football club with a lot of good people feeling pretty good about the club coming through this time at some stage.

When I first arrived in 1988 the club was facing extinction. The willpower of the president, coach, board and people behind the scenes worked towards keeping the club alive. It made you feel that it would be very special if you came through the other side and experienced the high of pulling off the big one one day, and winning the Grand Final.

The rally was really the first time it hit home. The stark reality really hit that day at the MCG that it might be finished, it might be over. Trying to envisage life without the Richmond Football Club I just couldn't comprehend that as a young player. An achievement in itself was as a player to be a part of that struggle and come through the other side.

Crowe became the public face of a campaign that raised a million dollars, and saved a football club.

Matthew Knights

He arrived a skinny teenager with silky skills, deft hands and an unerring left foot. He departed a celebrated figure in club history, a rare bright light in a largely bleak on-field generation. Without doubt, RFC fans took to heart the gifted midfielder from Merbein.

1988-
2002

Born
Oct 5, 1970

Played
Richmond
1988-2002
279 games,
141 goals

Interviewed
Jun 7, 2006

Richmond got an opportunity to pick up five players from their zone before the National Draft came into place. It was the last dip, so to speak, for all the clubs in their zones. With me were Andrew Lindsay, a Merbein boy, Chris Wescombe from Wentworth, Dallas Kalms from Wentworth, and Julian Moloney from Imperials. They all started in the same era as I did in the under 19s and we stayed at a little place called Tiger House near Chadstone. When I first came down we started at Burnley Oval because the under 19s didn't train at the same place as the Seniors. The reserves and the seniors trained at Punt Road and the under 19s were at Burnley under Doug Searl. Ian Owen (1969 premiership player) was the runner.

I was signed up as a 16-year-old from the Sunraysia area. It was a big Richmond area, with Dale Weightman coming from there and Mark Lee. Actually, my father coached Dale in the Under 17s in Mildura. Brian Weightman was very much a huge focus in the area for developing young footballers.

I barracked for Hawthorn because of the name, Knights – blond hair and the great number 24 for Hawthorn. The first thing I remember was the name (Peter) Knights in football and I barracked for Hawthorn because of that.

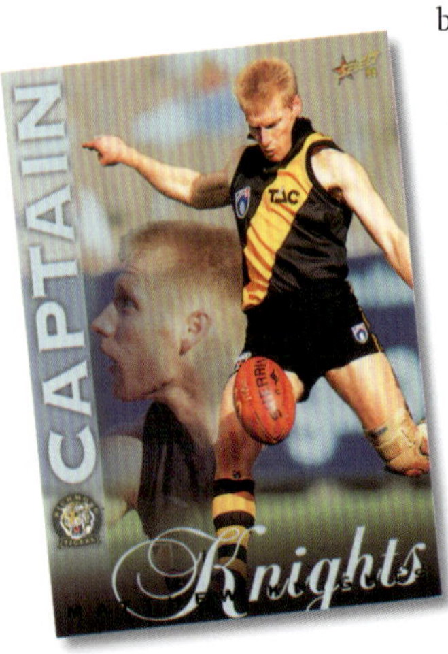

My dad, Barry, was a St Kilda supporter, he was born and bred in St Kilda. I still have vivid memories of standing on coke cans at Moorabbin watching Silvio Foschini, Greg Burns, Robert Elphinstone and 'Joffa' Cunningham. My first real recollection of watching AFL football was watching St Kilda at Moorabbin.

I wouldn't have said I always wanted to play football. Basketball was probably my first love as a sport. The traditions were basically you play basketball in the summer and football in the winter.

Once I got the bug of football I always wanted to play, I didn't necessarily think that AFL was going to be the end result because it seemed being from a little town called Merbein, of 2,500 people, you'd often watch the TV and see the VFL and it was sort of an unreal pipedream. It existed but you didn't know whether you could get there. Once Richmond chose to include me as one of those five, and sign me up, then it became a more realistic expectation.

When you first come down you're not sure of the standard. You're coming 500km and playing Under 19s footy against the most talented players in Victoria. I quickly picked up the tempo of Under 19s football and my first four weeks were pretty consistent. I won a lot of the ball so it was probably one of the keys to having a long career, my initial success in the under 19s. People started to take notice at a higher level from the senior end. I only played four games in the under 19s before KB and Emmett Dunne decided it was time to move me up into the reserves. I basically played as a ruck-rover and centre, right in the midfield. I played reserves in round 5 in the midfield, so I got wonderful opportunities straight away to play in a key area.

I played 13 consecutive games in the Reserves and then I played my first senior game against North Melbourne at the MCG, then went back and played the last game of the year against Fitzroy. That sort of springboarded my career from there.

I came third in the best and fairest in the under 19s after playing only four games. I think I polled four best on grounds. I won the reserves best and fairest that same year. From a development point of view it seemed like a natural progression, under 19s to reserves to seniors. But really I was probably very

When Matthew Knights ended his playing career, he left an enduring reputation of class and effort.

The Tigers celebrate a 2001 semi-final win over Carlton. From left: Andrew Kellaway, Darren Gaspar, coach Danny Frawley, Knights, runner Dale Weightman and Wayne Campbell.

fortunate. The club at that time was looking for young players to come through pretty quickly. I guess KB thought we will give these young players showing promise an opportunity. Maybe at other clubs I may not have got that chance. Playing those four games in the seniors late in the year gave me a real taste of AFL football and from that point I thought I am going to crunch my training standards and dedicate my life to football.

I physically wasn't ready. I was the emergency for the seniors eight times and I think KB was actually concerned about putting me out there from a safety point of view because I was about 71 kgs. I think KB had a fair bit of sympathy for my size. Eventually he bit the bullet.

He may have worked out the way I played, I relied on having great vision. If the knocks and heavy hits were going to come I was able to ride them and absorb them. I am forever grateful for the opportunities KB gave me.

I started on the bench. I had a shot at goal with my first kick and kicked a point, I was 35 metres out on the run. All I can remember was I had an enormous amount of family next to the player race. Because we weren't travelling well there wasn't a huge crowd there, only about 12,000 people.

The early part of my career was difficult so you really cherished the wins. But I think the place was always very bubbly. Myself, Tony Free and Craig Lambert always talked about this, we always felt there was light at the end of the tunnel and that's probably due to the coaching staff being fairly bubbly.

I was always proud to be a Richmond player, no matter what the situation. Maybe it was because my first two years I had a good run of form and felt like I was heading in the right direction. That's why I was always keen to be a one-club player. I never once intended to leave Richmond and play for another club.

I would like to think my greatest strength was that I made people better around me. My creativity. I took enormous pride that I put players into space and position and they could move pretty quickly off that and execute themselves. I took a lot of pride in making it easier for my teammates by hitting the body with disposals. What I mean by that, if I can hit the body with either foot disposal or hand disposal it allows them to take off straight away, or gives them more time. I felt pretty good about that.

My other asset was evasive skills. I felt I was always reasonably difficult to tackle at the best of times. Maybe later in my career when I lost half a yard, although I was never blessed with huge pace. I had to rely on my evasive skills and my subtle ball fakes to cause opposition problems. The skill component was partly natural but I worked pretty hard on my skills. The evasion and the ball fakes were instinctive. I felt I could absorb pressure; in fact a metre or half a metre in a game seemed like 10 or 15 to me. I felt if I had half a metre of space I had plenty of time. I felt good about absorbing people around me.

I never lacked confidence as a player from the moment I stepped into the club in the under 19s. I guess that stemmed from the fact that the people who were giving me feedback and advice, I kept to pretty much a minimum. Kevin Bartlett was the one to give me feedback and that's predominately the only person I would take feedback from.

I played on Tony Liberatore a lot. He was always a difficult player to play against and we had pretty even duels. He would scrag and he would hold. All I can remember of the 2001 'incident' was that I was cruising through the corridor at the MCG, about half to three-quarter pace, and the next thing I remember I was picking myself up from the deck and feeling a touch groggy. Tony was the only one in the area at the time, so I assumed it was him. I got up and looked back about 30 or 40 metres away. I had blood in the eye and I took off towards that area – at that stage he was in a scuffle with Wayne Campbell and a couple of others so I sort of started remonstrating, the arms started flying but I couldn't see much. Cambo was trying to get a piece of him.

I left the ground and I can remember giving a bit of verbal to (Jose) Romero and (Paul) Dimattina, who were on the bench at the time – they just happened to be in the area. So they patched me up and I came back on later in the game. The result of that was Tony went to the tribunal; his penalty was five weeks. I was there to give evidence but the last thing I remember of the incident was running through the corridor. I think Wayne Campbell saw the incident and he gave evidence. I haven't had a lot to do with Tony since then. It is part of football. It was quite ironic, we retired at the same time.

People still today approach me and they speak about the 1995 final. [Ed's Note: Richmond defeated Essendon in the second semi-final by 13 points; Knights is credited with keeping the Tigers in touch in the first half]. There were nearly 90,000 people there that day and it was hot. To come from behind and beat one of our archrivals, it sticks in the memories of the Richmond people. It just turned out that I kicked the three best goals of my whole career in the one half.

When I played Essendon I would either get Chris Daniher or Sean Denham, and they would run a pretty close and heavy tag, but on this day the philosophy of Denham was more to go head-to-head. And in that first half I felt like I was untouchable. I was so at ease. When you feel untouchable through the game, you exude confidence and your risk-taking becomes high risk, high reward. Early in the first half of that game I felt I was right at the top of my game, in the second half I was quieter, and Nick Daffy, Chris Naish and Matthew Rogers started to really cause some havoc. We had a super victory.

"I sort of relied on having great vision and if the knocks and heavy hits were going to come then I probably had good vision to ride them and absorb them."

I think out of the three goals there were something like 12 bounces. The second goal out of the middle, Ryan O'Connor was chasing me out of the centre bounce and I actually heard his hamstring snap while he was chasing me. In the vision you can actually see it. It is an eerie sensation. It was a day I look back on and think, 'That was great to be a part of.' I guess that was the pinnacle for me, and getting to the preliminary final in 2001.

The 1997 appointment of captain came at an interesting period. Tony Free, who was the captain at the time, would have been one of the greatest captains our club would have ever had. I just think his strength of mind and his onfield leadership was just superb, the way he attacked the ball, and his willingness to want to win every contest. Off the field he had strong values and a strong nature. When Tony Free spoke, people listened and people followed. I had no doubt Tony would have led the club as long as he wanted to. When his knee got to a stage he could no longer play it was devastating. I wasn't overly close to him, but I had an enormous amount of respect for him.

John Northey came to me and said, 'We think you are the right person to lead the club, the way you train, play and present yourself in a public arena is all excellent and we'd like to reward you with the captaincy of the Richmond Football Club.' I just relished it from that point onwards. I didn't change a lot after I was appointed captain – to make a huge change would not be natural.

My relationship with Northey was outstanding, he understood my game was probably nearly at its height in 1994 and 1995, that he would very much let my own game flow and let my leadership develop at its own speed. He had a good chemistry with the group at that time. The environment felt very natural. We had Leon Daphne and Jim Malone, who were really outstanding, assertive leaders, they were very good with people, very good with mixing with players, parents, players, friends and sponsors, they were very good at adapting.

I captained for five years, over the 100-game mark (101). That was something when you finish your career, and I have not been one big on stats, but it's something I look back on and I'm pretty proud of that achievement.

I always knew at some stage I would hand over the captaincy. But I thought it was probably a year early and that the process should have been better.

Knights cherished his time playing under John Northey more so than his other coaches.

Again, that was a decision coach Danny Frawley made at the time and that's his prerogative as senior coach to make that decision. Initially I was really disappointed, but after the initial month or two I went away and trained very hard for the 2001 season and got myself in really good physical shape. I think there was a little bit of an added incentive. I was always fairly driven to have myself in peak condition come the start of the year, but I must admit I had a very good pre-season.In 2001 I played the role of a high half-forward, as an extra midfielder, and we had a good year.

The only time I lacked confidence was in my last year of football. That's possibly due to the relationship between myself and Danny fragmenting. Maybe the last year of that relationship wasn't great because Danny was thinking it was time I moved on. Probably I could sense that to a degree as well. I thought I had one or two years left. We really had a tough year in 2002 as a football team after making the preliminary in 2001. Brendon Gale and Paul Broderick departed at the end of 2001, which I felt was an average decision to let those two players go, because they were so good for the team ethos.

As the year went on it became a little bit more difficult. I think the decision had already been made that this was going to be my last year from the coach's point of view. I played reserves one game against Geelong at the MCG. Alan Richardson was coaching the reserves at the time and I played well and they put me back up the following week. It was interesting, milestone games were a great achievement but from my point of view it was all about quality performance for the team. But I didn't realise the week I had been left out was going to be my 100th consecutive game for the second time around.

It probably wasn't a scenario that I looked heavily into but for the people and supporters of the Richmond Football Club, who had followed my career from day dot, maybe they thought that was a terrific achievement.

You've got to try and put yourself in the senior coach's shoes. Stop and think, 'Well, we have had a bad year, who are the veterans and senior players?' and sometimes that is reality in football. Danny and I certainly didn't agree on the decision. Being a fairly honest and upfront person, in my press conference I still remember saying at the press conference that I am retiring but it certainly wasn't my decision. Danny thought it was time for me to move on.

I know that at the time it may have caused some grief for Richmond but my take on the issue was I played a long career and I had an unbelievable relationship with the people and supporters. I seemed to click with most of them and I think they appreciated the way I played – I felt they deserved to know the real story, that I wasn't retiring through my own volition. When you're walking up the streets three years after you finish you don't want people coming up saying to you 'Why did you hang them up?'

My last game was against Essendon in Round 17 at the MCG. Danny and I had lunch at a café – I felt he wanted to say this a month before, but didn't get to it – and he basically said 'We think you should retire at the end of the year. It's not only my decision, it's a match committee decision.' I said to Danny 'I disagree with you, I think I have another year or two left in me.'

I knew that the team was going through a tough period but the way the game was heading, with rotations and bits and pieces, that I could play an impact role maybe 60-80 minutes a match and help guide the young players coming through at the time. I had a terrific relationship with Chris Hyde and a few of those boys at the time.

And Danny said 'No, that's our decision.' I was out of contract and I said, 'Well, let me think about it.' I got back to Danny a couple of days later and said 'Well, if I am not going to be here next year I would rather a young player fill that spot for the next five or six weeks and I'll retire after the Essendon game.' I picked Essendon at the MCG as I thought it was a very traditional clash. I had some great clashes with Essendon as a team and a player, there was a fair bit of rivalry built up there; I suppose it extended a bit from 1995.

My mum tossed the coin and mum, dad and my relatives were there at the end when I was doing a lap of honour. It was pretty decent to have all the people around who played a significant part in my career and had been there through difficult times and good times.

It wasn't a rushed lap of honour and I still have fond memories of getting to the Punt Road end in front of the Richmond faithful – that was a very special time. I stopped there and acknowledged the people who had been so good to me over time.

Wayne Campbell steps between Tony Liberatore and a bloodied Knights during the infamous 2001 MCG brawl. 'Libba' received five weeks' suspension.

And I went back to the social club after and spoke to everyone at the social club. Because it was such a big night, you're going through the scenario of retiring, everything happens pretty naturally, you don't really prepare speeches, so I think the main theme of it was that I was always proud, particularly being captain, to lead Richmond onto the MCG. Going through that race is something that is quite unbelievable.

And also I acknowledged the support the supporters had given me over an extended period because I must admit whenever I was playing and I got the ball, I felt the Richmond people ... there was a real buzz and excitement about what was going to happen and that was exhilarating.

What I regret out of my whole career was not winning the whole thing, winning a flag. From day dot, when I first got to the club in 1988 when the club was in a little bit of strife, there was always that dream that we would hold the cup one day on the MCG in front of 100,000 people. In saying that, as a player I did virtually everything in my power to try and achieve that. The fact we didn't win one still at times still irks me.

Brendon Gale had expected to join his brother, Michael, at Fitzroy but the Tigers struck first in the 1987 draft. Gale's grandfather played three games for Richmond in 1924.

Brendon Gale

Big man Brendon Gale, a magnificent servant of the Richmond Football Club on and off the field, played the first of his 244 games in 1990. He is a former CEO of the AFL Players' Association and became the Tigers' CEO in 2009.

1990-2001

I was drafted in the November 1987 draft, pick 27. That was the 'Richard Lounder' draft. (Lounder was Richmond's number 1 pick – he played just four senior games for the Tigers.) Tony Jewell had been down to Tasmania, while he was still Richmond coach, to see me play a couple of times. I had spoken with David Parkin (Fitzroy Coach) and Arthur Wilson (Fitzroy Committee) on the eve of the draft and they indicated that they were going to take me as a third-round pick, because my brother Michael was playing there. But Richmond had an earlier pick in the third round and called out my name.

I remember my old man rang me to say I had been drafted by Richmond. To be honest I was a bit shocked and disappointed at first because I was expecting to join my brother at Fitzroy, however, I remember my old man saying, 'Go to the Tigers, they are a great club and you're probably more likely to get the opportunity to play in a Grand Final or a premiership.' Gee, how prophetic that was!

Richmond has always had a strong connection with Tasmania. Our next-door neighbour in Tasmania was the great Ray Stokes, he is like Tasmanian sporting royalty in football and cricket (93 games for the Tigers from 1946-51; he represented Tasmania in cricket, and is a member of the Tasmanian football Hall Of Fame).

Kevin Bartlett had just taken over as coach of Richmond. After the draft, he flew down to Tasmania, with football manager Bruce Seymour, to see me. It was an exciting but at the same time sombre morning for me. I had learnt that morning that a friend from university had been killed in a car crash the night before.

I duly signed my life to Richmond. A month or so later I flew to Melbourne and KB picked me up at the airport. I'd been given a farewell from some mates the night before in Tasmania and was still a bit shabby upon arrival in Melbourne. I remember it was a stifling hot Melbourne November day with a hot northerly blowing. Coming from Tasmania I had never experienced heat like it. We drove to Punt Road and I recall there was a one-day international cricket match on at the MCG.

I lived at Tiger House for a few months. This was a residence where young recruits would stay, including Trent Nicholls and Barry Young. Then I trained with Richmond and returned home for Christmas, then packed up the HQ Holden and put it on the ferry and came back over.

Sadly, I don't know as much about my father's (Don) football career as I would like. My parents separated when I was about 13. There were eight kids. At that age you have a bit of yearning for knowledge but the old man wasn't around that much. I think you mark your parents a bit hard – the old man had left home and I guess I felt a bit let down. As you become older, you become wiser and you understand human nature and how things work. He gave all of us a great start in life and I'll be forever grateful.

When I retired from Richmond I looked forward to spending more time with my father and to developing a much closer relationship with him particularly as I looked forward to starting my own family. However he was diagnosed with prostate cancer and died within 12 months. He was in palliative care but I could have sworn that he was going to walk back out, he was just there for so long

Born
Jul 18, 1968

Played
Richmond
1990-2001
244 games
209 goals

Interviewed
Mar 6, 2012

Brendon Gale (centre) celebrating after a game with teammates Andrew Kellaway (left) and Joel Bowden.

and he seemed to be improving. During that time I had the opportunity to speak to him about his life and say the things you've always wanted to say I guess. This was at the end of my football career, so I had the time to do this. We spoke about his career and I took a lot of notes. That's why I reckon this stuff you do to document the past is great because it captures all this club and personal history.

Dad was a fine Tasmanian footballer. Back in those days (the fifties) Tasmanian football was very strong and we'd regularly knock off the other states in the old carnival series. He was recruited by South Melbourne but he was stopped from transferring to the VFL by the Tasmanian League. He lived with Fred Goldsmith (1955 Brownlow medallist) for a while and trained with South. But back then you had to have three completed seasons in the Tasmania Football League before you could be cleared. Often they made exceptions in special circumstances. I seem to recall that there was some sort of clearance wrangle between South Melbourne and Ron Clegg's clearance to Tassie and Dad was caught up in it. He ended up playing 180 games in Tasmanian footy (Wynyard, Hobart, Burnie). His career highlight was to play for Tasmania in that legendary match in which Tassie beat Victoria in 1960 at Launceston, the first time the state had beaten the mighty Vics. He was also the first player from the NWFU to be selected in an All-Australian team (1958).

While waiting for the clearance issue to be resolved he played in the Federal League for a few months under an alias. Dad worked in the Fire Brigade with Goldsmith but the clearance never came through and he told them that he had to get back to the farm to work with his father, Jack (my grandfather). So he went back to Tassie.

My grandfather, Jack, had played three games for Richmond in the 1924 season. I was in grade two when he died but I remember him being a very quiet and gentle man who liked a little punt. I remember him being around the farm and helping milk the cows in the morning and afternoon. He was a farmer, horse breaker and I understand that he was a reasonable local boxer.

He wore the No. 25. I was quite haunted when I discovered from Bill Meaklim (Richmond historian) that I was wearing the same guernsey number for Richmond that he had worn. I was given the number because that was what I wore with Burnie prior to arriving at Tigerland.

I remember being told that No. 25 is the 'curse' number. Evidently, Eric Leech broke his leg walking down the race one day, and Ian Satori only played 18 games for the Tigers.

It seemed like the club couldn't get a 'No. 25' player out on the ground. I had two groin operations and an appendectomy in my first two years – so it wasn't looking good.

I remember the AGM where the club announced it was $1.7 million in debt. I remember thinking, 'what does that all mean in the scheme of things'? I think the collective effort of people to get the club back into shape really resonated. I'll never forget the big day at the MCG and old Jack Dyer spoke.

I look back and realise how unprofessional things were at that time. I was a 19-year-old kid, and after the reserves you'd have a couple of cans of drink and a meat pie and people would complain that the meat pies weren't hot. I thought that was a little bit odd.

Then the players headed up to a bar, yet I always thought that you would go and watch the firsts play. VFL back then wasn't as consuming as it is today. However, I guess it was the same at all clubs.

I remember I always had really bad groin injuries. I didn't know what was wrong, yet I kept ploughing through the muddy Punt Road ground. Keep in mind, the Under 19s, the Reserves and the Seniors all trained on that ground, and occasionally games were played on it so you can imagine how bad the surface became.

I don't think I trained as hard in my life than I did in those first few years, and there wasn't any science to it. Coming from Tassie I wasn't used to heat, but we'd often train on 35 degree days with a hot northerly wind. I remember you would start at 5pm, you'd do your hour and a half of skills, then you'd do your running, then your weights and you'd be back at Tiger House at 10pm. These days in pre-season training they do 20-25 sessions a week but they are precise, very focused – everything complements something.

We used to do two Tan Track time trials. I remember crossing the footbridge on one occasion and looking over to the Nylex clock and it said 41 degrees. It was a very confronting environment to come from Tasmania to here and my body gave way. Looking back, I had OP (Osteitis Pubis), and I didn't have any core strength. My first two years were injury interrupted and required two bouts of surgery. Yet I just found a way to keep persevering and thought that if I kept the work up, my luck would turn. Importantly the club was patient and showed great faith in me.

I can remember KB brought in Jack Dyer one night after training to speak to us. We were going to play Collingwood at Victoria Park that weekend. It was the first time I had ever seen Jack Dyer in the flesh. He was god-like. He came in, and I was waiting for some profound speech. However, it just turned into a 20-minute routine of 'I Hate Collingwood' jokes. You know like, 'I hate Collingwood so much I don't read black-and-white newspapers'. But it was still funny. It was a sportsmen night's speech. I remember later on Lindsay Gaze (basketball legend) spoke to us as well. I was most impressed with him.

> "I think the collective effort of people to get the club back into shape really resonated. I'll never forget the big day at the MCG and old Jack Dyer spoke."

On one Sunday morning, KB bought in the ventriloquist Ron Blaskett with his Gerry Gee doll. Obviously KB was trying to lighten up the occasion, do something a little bit different. Ron and his doll had a 'blue' type routine. I remember the puppet sprang up out of the suitcase and turned around to Ron and said 'Where am I?' and Ron said 'Today, Gerry, you are at the home of the mighty Richmond Football Club, the magnificent Punt Road Oval, home of some of the greatest names in football, home of the mighty Tigers' and the doll turned his head back around a few times and looked at the

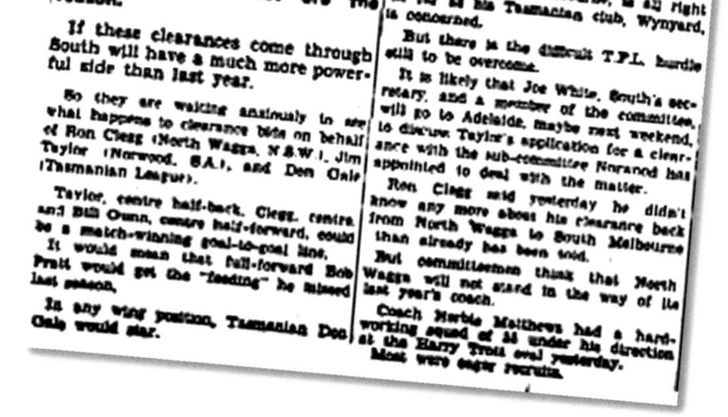

SOUTH HAS THOSE CLEARANCE 'BLUES'

OFFICIALS at South Melbourne are on tenterhooks these days — and clearances are the reason.

If these clearances come through South will have a much more powerful side than last year.

So they are waiting anxiously to see what happens to clearance bids on behalf of Ron Clegg (North Wagga, N.S.W.), Jim Taylor (Norwood, S.A.), and Don Gale (Tasmanian League).

Taylor, centre half-back, Clegg, centre, and Bill Gunn, centre half-forward, could be a match-winning goal-to-goal line.

It would mean that full-forward Bob Pratt would get the "feeding" he missed last season.

In any wing position, Tasmanian Don Gale would star.

Gale now a member of the Metropolitan Fire Brigade, Melbourne, is all right as far as his Tasmanian club, Wynyard, is concerned.

But there is the difficult T.F.L. hurdle still to be overcome.

It is likely that Joe White, South's secretary, and a member of the committee, will go to Adelaide, maybe next weekend, to discuss Taylor's application for a clearance with the sub-committee Norwood has appointed to deal with the matter.

Ron Clegg said yesterday he didn't know any more about his clearance back from North Wagga to South Melbourne than already has been told.

But committeemen think that North Wagga will not stand in the way of its last year's coach.

Coach Herbie Matthews had a hard-working squad of 34 under his direction at the Harry Trott oval yesterday. Most were eager recruits.

Brendon's father Don had clearance problems when attempting to play VFL football, as this newspaper excerpt from March 7, 1956 reports.

decrepit, possum-ridden, third-world facilities, then looked at the players and said, 'fuck, get me out of here!' It cracked the boys up.

During the 2011 season, I sat next to KB when Richmond played Carlton and Carlton smacked us! And I had never really spoken to KB about the times when he was coach and the club was financially

"The ruck allowed me to use my athleticism. It was a good opportunity to stay in play, follow the ball, influence outcomes and I reckon it added a couple of years to my career."

in trouble. Now I have perspective and now I can understand how difficult it can be for a coach and club in such circumstances. He was sharing some amusing stories with me of his times as coach and I was pissing myself laughing. I just hoped the TV cameras weren't on me, because while all this was going on, the Tigers were getting thrashed.

When we played down at Kardinia Park, I would drive down and David Honybun would lay down in the back of the car. He had terrible back injuries, and found sitting for long periods really difficult. He is a bit eccentric, but that's why we all loved him. On these trips, he wouldn't stop talking! By the time we got to the Arts Centre, not far from Punt Road, he was already hanging over the old bench seat yapping in my year, and didn't stop for the whole trip.

I'm embarrassed at my hair when I played. It wasn't a perm as Richo has often suggested and it wasn't a mullet. It was one length, but it used to be square at the top and go flat and flow at the back. It was early '90s – it was the Kurt Cobain, Seattle grunge, Eddie Vedder era. It looks stupid now, but I thought it was pretty cool at the time.

I made my debut against the Brisbane Bears at Carrara on the Gold Coast in round 1, 1990. Three other players – Chris Naish, Sean Bowden and Stephen Ryan – also started off that day. There was a big brawl. Roger Merrett was involved and about five minutes into the second quarter Jeff Hogg came off, because Merrett had opened him up. The call came down from the coach's box, 'You are on!' and that was it. I went to centre half-forward and took some marks and kicked a couple of goals but I was so nervous. We were beaten by ten goals. That is where I played for most of my first season.

In my first year I played 22 games straight. I was still getting sore, but still building strength. I didn't deserve to play 22 but KB just kept playing the kids.

It was around about 1994 that we started to emerge as a team. We would get the ball, kick long, mark it or bring it to the ground, then crumb and goal. Pretty simple stuff. We had some hard players.

I was pretty much centre half-forward until Justin Charles got himself in strife (in 1998). Then I was moved to the ruck and that probably came at a good time for me. I was very much a mark and kick forward. People bagged my kicking but I wasn't too bad. Although I missed a shot at the top of the goal square at Princes Park one day. In my last year I think I kicked 87 per-cent accuracy – mind you, they were all from the goal square.

I didn't have too many strings to my bow once the opposition started to flood. That was basically invented against us. Rodney Eade rolled out the flood in 1996 during a game at Waverley to combat our big guys.

Once they started flooding I didn't have the speed or power to get off my man and find other ways to find the footy. The ruck allowed me to use my athleticism, which, compared to other ruckman, was pretty good. It was a good opportunity to stay in play, follow the ball, influence outcomes and I reckon it added a couple of years to my career. I was lucky to get to 244 career games.

I was blessed to be part of Richmond and I'm really grateful for what the club has given me. I think it is important that I was able to establish my own career, away from my brother Michael, who was playing at Fitzroy. KB tried to get him across to Tigerland to join me early on, but it didn't eventuate until 1994, after he'd played 105 games for the Lions (he would play another 91 at Richmond, retiring in 1998).

I remember being really saddened with Fitzroy's last game in Melbourne. We smashed them (by 151 points). You could see they had given up – they had lost the will to compete. We gave them a guard of honour off the ground and I found that quite moving. It was the end of the football club, really.

Brendon Gale, in typical selfless fashion, acknowledges the fans as he leaves the ground after a round 11 match at the MCG in 2001.

The thing I remember about KB as coach was how positive he was. It is important that if you are being challenged, no matter what you do, always carry yourself in a positive way, especially in a leadership position. I didn't dwell on things too much back then, but I imagined he would have. They were bloody tough, awful times. Particular when you come from a background where success was almost assured.

He came up with this phrase – 'moral victors'. I remember on a few occasions, we'd get the videotape out and go through the game from the weekend. And we'd be beaten by 50 points or something, yet KB would say 'if you had have done this, or if you had got this free kick ... gee we were stiff there' and he'd come up with 10 different explanations as to why we had lost. I remember him saying on one particular day, 'We were stiff not to win. You might even say we were moral victors'. He had turned a regulation 50-point loss into an opportunity lost. And you would believe it. So what do you do, you get back on the bike and think to yourself 'we are going to get them next time.'

Allan Jeans was very organised and he had his philosophies. He was a commanding figure but you could see that coaching increasingly weighed heavily upon him. I remember Chris Bradshaw said to him 'I don't think you should subject yourself to this.' He coached just the one year, and called it quits after the 1992 season.

John Northey was all about 'team'. He'd never praise individuals, it was always about the team. I think we played a bit like that. Under John we were committed to each other.

It was important for me to play for the coach. I think that my old man leaving home may have had something to do with. There was a part of me that yearned for that close connection and guidance.

I also had Robert Walls, Jeff Gieschen and Danny Frawley as coaches. I had a lot of respect for Robert, he was hard but honest. He was never wrong. He was always right. He would speak and never leave a word out of place. Those words had maximum effect and impact.

A happy crew of old and new at the 2011 Edwin Flack lunch: Richmond CEO Brendon Gale (left), coach Damien Hardwick (centre) and former coach Danny Frawley (right).

Robert was under incredible pressure as coach. We had finished third the year before, yet in a bizarre set of circumstances, John Northey left the club – for Brisbane, in a direct swap with Robert – and of all sudden we had a new coach. I think Robert wore a huge amount of pressure and vitriol. But I remember the dignified way he carried himself under that pressure.

I played the night the scoreboard caught fire at the MCG – round 22, 1999. We went out for the warmup and the scoreboard was on fire! I was a delegate for the Players' Association at the time and someone asked me 'what do we do here?' and I said 'I don't know, just keep away from it'. And then there were these fumes and I remember thinking, well maybe this is pretty serious. So someone sent us all back inside. The game was delayed for 25 minutes.

I clearly remember the 1995 final series. We had finished third (behind Carlton and Geelong) with 15 wins and a draw. The qualifying final was a night game against North Melbourne and Wayne Carey got a hold on us for about 10 minutes, and we ended up losing by 20 points. Then we played Essendon in the cut-throat semi-final. I played poorly, but to win that was amazing. Chris Naish, Nick Daffy and Matthew Knights kept us in the game. I remember the deafening noise when we hit the front. I still get goosebumps thinking of it. We ended up winning by 13 points, but then in the preliminary final we got thrashed by Geelong (by 89 points).

I always saw myself as a leader. It was something I felt comfortable being. It's not something I coveted, it just sort of happened that way. I think in the early '90s, a core group had come through – Tony Free, Matthew Knights, Wayne Campbell, Craig Lambert – and I just think we had a gutful of being also-rans. We hadn't been blessed with leadership. It was like there was a whole generation that was lost. When I arrived players like Michael Roach, David Cloke and Mark Lee were on their last legs. We just felt it was our turn to put our imprint on the club. There was a real strong emergence through 1994 and 1995, but we didn't hang onto it post-1995. They were wasted years post-1995.

I was proud of the fact when I left the club in 2001, we had made the finals. When I arrived we were stone motherless last, in debt, and shaking cans. I was proud of the very small role I played in getting the club to where it was when I retired.

In my wildest dreams I didn't believe I would come back and be the CEO of the club. In fact, when I retired from football and went into the law, I worked in a particular part of the law that almost required me, as a matter of the firm's policy, to go away from Melbourne.

I was looking forward to going overseas to perhaps Hong Kong, and having a life away from football and to work in another culture and bring up a family. I did that for a few years but I found the life of a commercial lawyer increasingly unsatisfying. After a few years I ended up back at the Players' Association as CEO. Even when I was at the Players' Association, I never saw myself being back involved in the club scene. Having said that, it's terrific to back. I never had the opportunity

to play in a premiership so there's a part of me that feels unfulfilled and empty.

It is a privilege really to be in this job. I feel quite fortunate to be in a position to help get this club to where it should be, and satisfy that void, that hunger. We want it so badly.

I feel that at various stages we've suffered from a type of messiah complex here at Richmond. It's almost like we want to invest all our hopes and aspirations in one person to come in and impose their will upon the club and for that person to singlehandedly take the club to the promised land. We then tend to throw that person the keys to the kingdom and then say go and get the job done.

When the job inevitably doesn't get done they get torn apart. I don't subscribe to this view. The messiah ain't coming. Success comes from getting good people to work together for a common cause. You need to plan for success and make consistently good decisions. It sounds very boring and it's certainly not as easy as it sounds, but if we stick to it there is a proven formula.

The system allows for clubs to get better, yet, until the last few years we just haven't been able to achieve that on a sustained basis. In fact we should have received a gold medal for the manner in which we have gone against what the system has intended. If we plan well and allocate our resources efficiently and make good decisions consistently we *will* get better. It is about having the courage to hold our course.

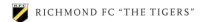

I felt I guess in the first four or five years [a premiership] wasn't in our planning. We didn't think we had the whole club capability, and the 3-0-75 plan (three flags, zero debt and 75,000 members by 2020) was about getting ourselves focussed, aligned and becoming more competitive on and off the field.

"I got into trouble because I said it's the greatest moment of my life"

When we launched the Fighting Tiger Fund in 2011 we were selling a business case to investors. We were asking people to invest in us and the first step was to get the off-field right and build capability and strength.

What we did with the Fighting Tiger Fund was we got 200 guys to pay $3000 a head and we presented the business case to them. We presented a futuristic call of the last two minutes of the 2016 Grand Final. We were playing Carlton and we got Brian Taylor to commentate and Robert Walls did special comments, and they were all terrific. The crowd was canned noise: it was all theatre.

We were trying to get people to imagine the future. In the "call" we were down two points down with 30 seconds to go and David Astbury marked the ball in the goal square and kicked the winning goal. It was a year later that we actually won, and Astbury was at the other end!

When we did the Punt Road redevelopment the then CEO Steven Wright did a lot of the heavy lifting. I thought then this balcony they had made (outside the Board room) could be turned into a stage for presenting the cup! And we always used to say to Dimma, *that's where I'm taking the cup,* and he'd say, *No I'm taking the cup*!

Over time—say once a year or when I'm tired, or driving—I'd drift off and envision that we were in the Grand Final. My wife and family are with me and at that moment we win, I cry. I just weep. It comes from nowhere.

So, I remember walking into this office on Grand Final day with Jane and the kids. And out on the balcony, overnight, they had built the stage! And I thought, *God it's that close* and I started crying then and there and my kids said, *Dad are you all right?* I'm getting emotional now thinking about it.

Three of the key players in Richmond's rise to the 2017 Premiership feature in this photo: Dustin Martin, the 2017 Brownlow Medallist, Norm Smith Medallist and MVP, Peggy O'Neal, club president (in background with Tiger scarf), and CEO Brendon Gale. O'Neal and Gale were drivers of the club's plan for the decade—three flags, zero debt and 75,000 members. At the end of the 2018 season, the outcome was one flag, no debt and 100,000+ members.

In life and sport, the discipline of being an athlete is staying in the moment contest by contest, play by play, quarter by quarter. And so, at three-quarter-time I'm thinking, *gee this is pretty good.* But you say to yourself, *it's the next play, it's the first bounce, it's the first five minutes.*

All of a sudden, it's that wonderful play Lambert to Prestia. I remember thinking at the time, *we're bloody 40 pts up now! We're gunna be hard to beat.* But you still feel the weight. The moment when Butler kicked that goal is the moment you tell yourself *we won*. And the weight lifts.

I occasionally ask myself, *god wouldn't it be good to*

be CEO at another club where I'm not as personally and emotionally invested. Because it wouldn't hurt as much. Those low moments are just devastating. Because when you are doing something you really care about you just do what you can, and the low moments are low, but the great moments are intoxicating.

What made the day special was my mother was there. She raised eight of us after my parents were divorced when I was young and she was there with my brother and the kids and Jane, and Peggy (O'Neill), and Ken Grenda.

That's the stuff I love hearing. I hear it so much, about grandparents and parents and kids *who shared the win together*. It's just wonderful.

I got into trouble because I said it's the greatest moment of my life. And people say, but how about your wife and or your kids?

And I say the reason is when babies are born it's wonderful, but they're barely conscious. And there are milestones and marriages later on. But on Grand Final day you are able to share with all of them, conscious and aware, this journey, through all the harrowing moments and kicks in the arse. It is fleeting, but you want to go do it again.

Matthew Richardson won modern Tiger hearts for more than a decade.

Matthew Richardson

An exciting forward who wore his Tiger heart on his sleeve, Richardson finished his career second only to Jack Titus on the club's goalkicking tally. His supreme athletic talent and loyalty to the club made him a Richmond fan favourite.

1993-
2009

Dad's last year of competitive football was the year I was born, 1975, down in Tassie. So I was never around the club when he was playing. He has good scrapbooks that his mum kept and I religiously used to read through those when I was younger. I really enjoyed looking at them – I looked at them all the time. Being at Richmond the last 15 years, you speak to a lot of his old teammates, so I know a fair bit. My nickname is not as good as his (Bull). It started off as 'Richo', which is pretty unspectacular. And now at the club the boys call me 'Ricky' or 'Rick.' I actually started that myself. I think it was at the end of the year and we were having a few beers and I said 'I am actually getting sick of Richo,' because strangers would come up and call you 'Richo'. And I said 'I want to be called Ricky from now on. It was just a joke but a few of the blokes started calling me Ricky and it has stuck.

I would have been five when the 1980 Grand Final happened and that's probably the first time I can actively remember following Richmond. I remember Dad had mates around at home in East Devonport, and I remember Richmond having a good day; Dad and his mates were having a good day as well. I thought 'This is the team!' And I think that was about the time I started putting things together, Dad had played there and this is the team I am barracking for.

I've obviously watched the 1967 Grand Final numerous times, but I didn't get a lot of genes from dad. He was a handballer and I don't think you would say I am handballer. I don't think he was a great kick and I'm probably not regarded as a great kick either, but I think I am a better mark than he was. I think today if you are kicking like a lot of the guys kicked back then you'd be turning the ball over regularly. Although there are obviously parts of the game back then that are probably better than our lot, like pack marking. Whereas the foot skills have gotten a lot better.

I was playing for Devonport in 1992 and (former Hawthorn champion) Peter Knights was my coach. Back then it was a statewide competition down in Tasmania, the TFL. I know Dad had been in contact with Richmond throughout my under age career. Richmond were having a bit of look at me, but that year in 1992 I played senior football for Devonport, and played in the under 17s carnival over here in Victoria, the Teal Cup. And that was the year they started to send letters and have regular contact with me.

At the end of that year, Collingwood showed a fair bit of interest. In fact, I had a call from Leigh Matthews one Thursday night at home and he was trying to convince me not to sign with Richmond under the father and son rule. He said 'Don't sign with Richmond ... go into the draft and we will make sure we get you.' And I said 'How you going to do that?' Because they didn't have the number one pick.

I thought that will be a big risk to go in the draft – Drew Banfield was Number 1 that year in 1992. I could have ended up anywhere. I really only had thoughts of playing for Richmond – couldn't have imagined going anywhere else. Though Collingwood dangled a bit of a carrot. I reckon Peter Knights got Richmond to hurry up a little bit. Because all this stuff was sort of going on and we had finals coming up with Devonport, I was being distracted by this AFL talk. So I think Knights rang the club and said 'If you're going to sign him up, get it out the way.'

Born
Mar 19, 1975

Played
Richmond
1993-2009
282 games,
800 goals

Interviewed
May 2, 2007

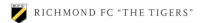

I flew over here for the round 20 game against Adelaide in 1992 and the club got thumped at the MCG. I remember going back after the game into (General Manager) Cameron Schwab's office and signing up then and there. I had Brian Leys showing me around for the day, because he wasn't playing that day. I enjoyed the day, even though we got beaten, and I was pumped I was coming over.

My first game was in 1993, against St Kilda at the MCG. We had a win, which was rare that year, as we only won four. I played on Danny Frawley, who ended up being my coach, and also Jamie Shanahan, and those two guys were pretty good defenders in their day. We had a win and I kicked a goal and took nine or 10 marks. I have spoken to Danny a couple of times about that and he remembered it. Back then I was a lot lighter and used to run around a bit more than what I do now. I remember 'Spud' was coming to the end of his career and he was sick of the way I was running around. He told me that if I kept running like that he was going to belt me. I think I ran more.

The first year we didn't win many games but it was John Northey's first year and you could just sense that he was trying everyone out that year. He probably played the whole list and at the end of that year they culled a lot of players; there were about 17 new players for 1994 – the next two years after that were just fantastic.

In 1995 we won 15 and a half games, and I did my knee in round 9. The first few years had a lot of highs and enjoyment – a big low in 1995 was having to sit out and watch, which was probably the best footy we played while I have been at Richmond.

I was having a pretty good year. It was my third year and I was really just starting to feel like a consistent senior player and for that to happen while we were playing good football was really disappointing. I injured my knee at Sydney, an incident which forced the League to change the boundary line position. The next week they bought the boundary line in a metre at the SCG, because I jumped right near the boundary line and I was pushed while I was in the air ... while I was in the air I thought 'I'm in trouble here, I am going to hit the fence', and as soon as I landed I was thinking 'I'm going to have to stop straight away.' That's why I did my knee. If I didn't end up coming back from that knee I would have had a pretty good case for suing. And that was spoken about at the time. I got

He was a fine contested mark, but Richardson's running ability usually got him into space.

a call from a guy who said 'Look, you should write a letter now, in case you don't come back.' It didn't end up happening that way, thank God.

I had a pretty ordinary pre-season in 1996 and remember in the practice games I couldn't get a kick. I thought 'Geez, I'm battling here.' And you have doubts when you're coming back from a knee. But then in round 1 against Essendon I think I kicked six goals and played really well and the knee was a distant memory. I never really thought I would make 100 goals (Richardson kicked 91). In the last game I kicked six and the week before I kicked seven, so I was never going to get there. Individually it was rewarding, but as a team we weren't great that year – we were average – so it wasn't a great year.

I wear my heart on my sleeve. If I am disappointed I probably look really disappointed. Most of my frustration and disappointment a lot of the time is directed at myself but people think it is directed in other areas. And that is frustrating as well, because people take it the wrong way. But if I sit back as an independent observer and look at it I would think the same thing.

It's frustrating, because in a team game I don't think you can blame one person for the losses. But I wouldn't say it doesn't wear you down a little bit. You do get disappointed ... they are the expectations when you're one of the more high profile players, so you're going to be the first one to cop it.

The only times it might get to you a bit is when you kick a few points in the row and you can just hear them going berserk, that's when it can start playing on your mind a bit I guess. You don't hear individual comments, you only hear a big sigh if you miss a goal. That's when it can get you a bit.

I'm not up there with the really accurate kicks but I'm not hopeless either. I go at about 60 per cent (conversion rate) and I think someone like a Matthew Pavlich goes at 61.5 per cent. So out of every 100 shots at goal he kicks 1.5 more goals than me. But he would be seen as a great kick whereas I'm not seen that way.

It's a fine line. I can see why I am seen like that. I guess what I have done, which highlights my issue, is I've missed some really easy ones. And I might do that once every 10 games, but that will always be the one that is remembered.

When you're about 35-40 metres out it is probably the most comfortable range, because you tend to kick through the ball more. Where I guess when you get up closer you start to think, 'Geez, I don't need to kick it that hard.'

I'm not saying I haven't missed a fair few easy shots in my time ... it could have been better. I don't look the most fluent either. So if you don't look the most fluent people can sometimes think you are not a good kick. But if you look at Warwick Capper or Mark Jackson, they had a pretty poor action but they were pretty accurate kicks.

He had his critics, but few could argue Richardson did not play his heart out for the Tigers.

I've never really got close to leaving Richmond. There were a few times there where there were other clubs sniffing around, but to be honest I never even got to a point with other clubs where I was even discussing contracts.

I actually met up with a couple of clubs for one meeting a couple of times but it never got past that. The club has always offered me another contract and it never got to the point where you're sitting out there being floated around. I don't think they have really ever tried to trade me. I think it's probably been loyalty on both sides.

My biggest strength as a player was my passion. If you're passionate and you want to be a good player then that helps. I've seen plenty of players with plenty of skill who have no passion, they never play that well, whereas they should be good players with their ability. My contested marking is also a strength, and my running, my ability to push myself and get to as many contests as possible.

In December, 2018, Rhett Bartlett interviewed 'Richo' again, to reflect on that 2017 moment.

Benny Gale told me I was selected to present the Premiership Cup. Before the Preliminary Final against GWS I was doing the podcast *Talking Tigers*, and Benny asked me into his office. I thought I might have been getting the sack or something.

"I'm pretty embarrassed now looking back on it but (for Richmond people) it *was* one of the best days of our life."

He sat me down. He told me that each club still in contention has to nominate someone to present the Cup to the Premiers and that the Board had nominated me. I couldn't believe it. Then I thought *gee, we've got to win a Prelim now, we haven't even got into the Grand Final yet.* Once we won the Prelim it was very excited. I told my Mum and my partner Genevieve but I was told to keep it quiet until it was announced during Grand Final week.

It was a bit of disbelief. But then I felt a little bit, not embarrassed, but a little bit silly. You think of the great names that could have done it including Kevin Bartlett, Royce Hart, Dale Weightman, Michael Roach, Jimmy Jess, Tony Jewell, Francis Bourke. There were so many people who could have been nominated. I must admit I felt pretty humbled when you mention those names. It was a great experience.

I was the boundary rider with Channel 7 on Grand Final day. We sat right next to the interchange. I remember Tim Watson said to me before the game; 'I don't reckon we need to say too much down here today, there's a lot of people up in the box' and it was probably one of the first times I reckon I didn't really contribute that much to the call.

The photo (below) taken by AFL Chairman Richard Goyder that 'Richo' claims is "the best photo I've seen of myself and the Cup out on the ground."

I felt a little bit torn. I didn't say too much. I think I only spoke when somebody asked me a question. So I didn't do much work that day, I was more of a cheerleader.

I think it was the Butler goal when I thought *'we've got this'*.

Matthew Richardson was Seven's 'boundary rider' for the 2017 Grand Final, but he couldn't hold back his Tiger emotion after he had the privilege of presenting the Cup to Coach Damien Hardwick and captain Trent Cotchin. "As I walked off the stage I couldn't help but give a bit of a fist pump and a bit of a 'Yeah, Go Tigers!'"

We've got a monitor on the boundary line and I looked at the monitor and they were showing pictures of Brendon Gale and Peggy O'Neal and Michael Gale up in the grandstand and when I saw them welling up that's when I lost it. I was about to lose it anyway but that was the catalyst.

Channel 7 milked it didn't they? They knew what a moment it was for Richmond people. I'm pretty embarrassed now looking back on it, but it *was* one of the best days of our life.

I did a couple of interviews after the siren. Dusty

Martin and Jack Riewoldt, but what I said I'm not sure. I don't remember. That whole after-the-siren moment, walking out on the ground is a real blur.

I remember the AFL Chairman Richard Goyder was out on the ground. He took a photo on his mobile, which he has since passed onto me, and it's probably the best photo I've seen of myself and the Cup out on the ground that day. You can just see how happy I was and how excited I was about to walk up on stage.

It was surreal holding the cup and waiting for your name to be called. I did hear the 'Richo' chant, it was a special moment.

I remember distinctly the moment of walking up and handing the cup over. I said 'Congratulations' and 'Well done guys' and I remember thinking when I was walking up *just hand it to the boys and get off, don't hang around, it's not about you*. But as I walked off the stage I couldn't help but give a bit of a fist pump and a bit of a *Yeah! Go Tiges!*

I didn't play in a Premiership. So it's probably just about the best moment of my sporting life.

Joel Bowden

The son of Michael Bowden, a 1969 premiership Tiger, Joel Bowden was a two-time best and fairest. Two of his brothers, Sean and Patrick, have played for Richmond, continuing a proud family tradition with an unconventional football upbringing.

1996 - 2009

Born
Jun 21, 1978

Played
1996-2009
235 games,
154 goals

Interviewed
May 2, 2007

I know a lot about my father's career, actually. His career spanned many decades. He finished playing football when he was 49 in the reserves for Rovers Football Club for Alice Springs. He has just turned 60. I witnessed some of his career, but I didn't see any of his VFL or VFA career.

We have watched the 1969 Premiership. For Mum and Dad's 25th wedding anniversary we hired a big screen and watched it on video. Mum and Dad were married in 1969 and Dad played in the premiership that year so it was a bit of a symbolic gesture by Mum, recognising Dad had played football. We have watched it a few times since. It is pretty ordinary football.

Dad tried to kick torpedoes and they were terrible. A lot of people say that my old man couldn't kick, but from what I have seen of him playing for Richmond he tried to kick torpedoes. You can't kick them consistently.

I got to Richmond fortuitously, in my opinion. I was in the wrong place for football, which was Alice Springs. But I was recognised because of my father. And because I was in Alice Springs, and the population of the Northern Territory was 80-100,000, I was able to get into representative sides. I played in four Northern Territory representative football teams at national carnivals, which puts you in the eyes of the recruiting agents.

Out of those I had one good one, in my opinion, and that gave them reason to think I was okay. At the time, in 1995, I had a back injury, I had stress fractures from playing cricket – bowling all day at school, then going in and sitting down, and after school going and playing cricket forever, thinking I was the fastest bowler.

I was lucky, because the father-son rule meant that the club didn't have to use (early) draft picks. So I was fortunate that Richmond said they would take a punt on me. At that stage we had seniors, reserves, supp lists. There were probably 50 guys at the club training and playing together and I was just another one. In that sense I feel like I was lucky. Because what I have seen now, so many guys have the talent or ability but they never get the opportunity.

A lot of guys – and I have seen it happen at Richmond – you don't think have got talent, and seriously have gone 'Hmm, I don't know how these guys are going to get out of the reserves.' But they get the opportunity and they become great players. Because they are given a chance and all of a sudden they just shine.

A good example was Dean Polo last year (2006). I used to watch him and I used to think, he hasn't got anything exceptional. He is not six-five, he is not lightning fast, he doesn't kick 70 metres on his right foot, and I was thinking, 'How is he going to break into the side?' Well, not only did he break into the side but he's become a permanent member of the team.

The next step for me after finishing school was to move to Melbourne, go to uni and, depending on where I was, play football. If I was at Richmond that was all well and good. It was hard to leave. Mum and Dad gave me a shove, which was nice. But when I moved down to Melbourne I moved over to North Fitzroy but I was sleeping on a mattress on the lounge room floor at my brother's place. That was the way we started. I loved every minute of it. When I first came down I thought, 'How good is this!?'

Just to go to training and run around with Matty Knights, who I knew from Mildura, where we lived before we lived in Alice Springs. I just thought this was the best thing ever.

Joel Bowden brought a unique form of leadership to the club.

Everyone is shaped by the experience they've had. And I am lucky enough to have travelled around a bit, in a sense that we lived in Mildura, then the outback of South Australia and Alice Springs. I've had different experiences from other people.

I think the main influence on my life has been my family and the strong family links that we have. Christmas is a tradition for us that we get together. Last year, 24 of us were all together. My mother and my father were very good parents and that has shaped the way I am. My hero was always my dad, because he was playing football. I watched him all the time. Initially, when I was 12, I had to play under 17s football because the competition in Alice Springs was not very well organised.

Dad, who was a teacher at my school said 'This is terrible, we need to do something.' There were five secondary schools in Alice Springs, so he organised a schools competition where you have year seven and eight, then year nine and 10, where they play on a Thursday afternoon. So basically that came in the next year and I started playing school football and competition football. So I played Thursday and Saturday mornings. I didn't care – I just wanted to play.

Our team in the under 18s wasn't very well organised in a sense that we didn't have enough players a lot of the time.

So one of the ways to organise a full team each week was to contact the boarding school for indigenous kids, and they'd bring in 10 or 15 kids. It was great.

My first game (round 17, 1996 vs Hawthorn) was a very big event for everyone, bar the game. Everyone came down, it was huge. Then I sat on the bench until about five minutes before half-time. The first ball I went for went through my legs. It was a scrubby ball. We were at Princes Park, I was just inside the centre square and I missed it.

When I first started a lot of it was still, 'Kick it long.' Robert Walls was in his first year as coach. He wrote on the board *Q.L.D.*, and said 'It's not just because I have come from Queensland, it's because I want to play Quick, Long, Direct.' Now it is more tactical. Don't give the ball back to them. Time in possession is a lot of it. If we have got it more than them, they can't score. And it's fast, a lot faster.

I started on the half-forward flank then I went to the back flank. In 1997 I started on the half-back flank and then after five rounds Wallsy said, 'We need someone just down in the forward line who can stay there, can you do that for me?' I'm 18 years old and he wants me to play centre-half forward!

So I went down there and played as a stay-at-home half-forward, because Richo was just playing everywhere across half-forward. I did it for a couple of weeks then I got injured. I broke my collarbone and I missed 10 weeks, came back later in the year and Wallsy had been sacked. Jeff Gieschen came in. For the next couple of years I was just a half-forward trying to kick a couple of goals a week.

In 2000 I started to get fit, to learn how to train, to know that my body could actually run out a game. I moved up onto the wing and stayed wing and midfield for five years. Half-way through 2004, through matchups and other reasons, I went to half-back again. I started getting a lot of the ball and I have been left there ever since.

Being thrown on to bigger blokes, I was marked by the press and coaching staff and supporters as better, because when you see someone up against a bigger person and you do all right, well that's a job well done. If they kick the ball up to me and Richo, well he's expected to mark it. If I mark it, it's like 'Wow.' I've had lots of changes.

When I was a young guy I just wanted to get a game, then just wanted to get a kick, to just being a flanker trying to kick a goal, to being a midfielder who got very fit and really worked hard, to now playing on some of the best forwards. In 2007, I had Brendan Fevola, Anthony Rocca and Brad Johnson in a five-week period.

I was dropped in my best and fairest year (2004). You'd have to ask the coach at the time (Danny Frawley) and the coaching panel because I honestly can't tell you why. I was dropped in round 6. I hadn't done that pre-season because I had Osteitis Pubis and I hadn't run until after Christmas. So I wasn't as fit as I could be and started round one on the bench; I was building into the season and against St Kilda three weeks before I was best on ground. Then we played Adelaide and, because of a couple of injuries, I was stationed at full-forward and I think Adelaide beat us by 10 goals. The ball didn't come down very much and I kicked one goal. We were under siege and, in times of adversity, things are done. My form after round 7 was very good. A few things went my way to win the best and fairest – Kane Johnson missed the last four weeks with a knee injury, Nathan Brown missed a number of weeks with a calf injury, and all in all we hadn't had a great year.

Joel Bowden's father, Mike (left), chats to Tommy Hafey during the early 1970s.

I will continue to do my best to lead in the manner that I see fit and encourage guys to be bold and brave and back their own ability. But to also do things that occupy their time off the field as well as just playing football. I've probably got a more holistic approach than some. Football is a religion and passion for so many people. But my belief has been very strong for a long time, that you need something else. If all your eggs are in one basket and that basket doesn't fulfill your dreams and expectations then what happens next? We see so many guys who don't get the opportunity that I've had to play 12 years of football, or five years, or even one year of football. So diversify.

My first game is a cherished memory – a great memory. We won and we sang the song and I knew the words all right. The 2001 final against Carlton will stick in my memory. Not the whole game, probably the first quarter. Then Koutoufides got injured and I knew we would win.

I thought 'How good is this, we are going into a preliminary final?!' The Carlton game and the buildup to the Brisbane game are my fondest memories, as is 2006. Playing with my brother, Patrick, playing my 200th game, being married the October before that, moving into a new phase of my life and then capping off the year with having a little baby girl the day after the best and fairest. The 12-month period from October 1 to September 22 will go down in my memory as almost unsurpassed.

Success in football is so fickle. Football is played on an oval with an oval ball. With some squares and some rectangles and some posts and we just think it should be simple. The aim of the game is to get the ball off your boot through those big sticks. But it's so much more.

When I think about history. I think 'Shit, we played that prelim final and we got beaten up in Brisbane.' But they are the greatest team of the last 50 years! Four Grand Finals in a row. I wish we had been playing St Kilda, or someone who is not the greatest team of the last 50 years.

Or 12 wins in 1998 and we didn't get into the finals! 12 wins after round 21, then we played Melbourne on a roll and we had to beat them to get into the finals and they beat us. If we had beaten them we could have finished third! That's absurd.

I hope they remember that I was a good player. That I was a good person and that I am a Richmond person and that I gave as much as I could to the club that gave me ten-fold in return.

Peggy O'Neal

Peggy O'Neal was born in America, but was quick to become a Tiger fan when she settled in Melbourne, not far from the Punt Road Oval. She joined the Board in 2005, and was appointed president in 2013, the first female president in the VFL/AFL's history.

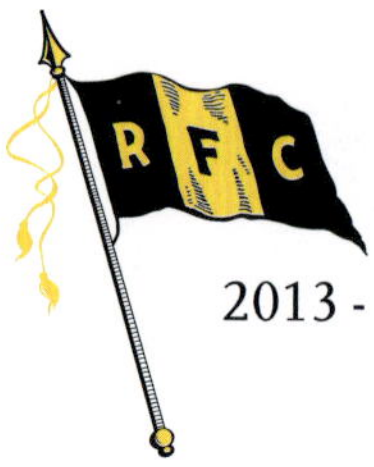

2013 -

Born
April 19, 1952

President
From 2013

Interviewed
September 11, 2018

I was always Peggy. I wasn't a Margaret. I'm Peggy Yvonne O'Neal. There was Yvonne De Carlo, an actress, and she was Peggy Yvonne De Carlo, but there was an old Irish song—"Peggy O'Neil"—and my Grandfather picked my name for that song rather than the actress.

The little town where my parents lived and where I was born is gone. It was in the coal-mining Appalachian Mountains (in West Virginia) and as the coal industry started to fail they just shut down the mines. It probably wasn't until the '70s when the oil crisis hit that coal became valuable again but the communities never came back.

The coal company also owned all the houses. It was called a camp. The miners lived there and the generation before my father's got paid in company scripts rather than dollars, so you could only spend it at a company store. You were sort of a captive to the company. It was a wild, remote area. You can imagine without the roads and communication we have today how isolated you were.

My parents tried a year in the big city—Washington D.C—but got homesick and came back. So, then I started school in a two-room school house for seven grades. There weren't many children around, so even though I was too young to officially go to school, I was allowed to start first grade.

You sort of think *that's the way everybody is.* I think you develop a sense from the people around you of great self-sufficiency. You did things yourself. People were helpful but you never really had anybody to call on—there were no services from the council.

My mother was a great volunteer. She was always helping others and I look back and think *how did she manage to do all that,* but she did. I think those kinds of values are instilled in you. I sometimes think: *how did she have an aspiration for education and an aspiration to get to the big world when your cousins and other people just stayed there.* I think it was all to the drive of my parents who wanted us to have the education they didn't have.

I lived so close to the Punt Road Oval and MCG it was easy to go to a game. I thought I'd get involved in my community club so I picked Richmond. Save Our Skins was underway so I thought that the club needed support.

Then you pick 'em and you stick with them. Little by little I got more involved and helped set up the *Tommy Hafey Club,* and became a player sponsor. I'm still in touch with most of the players I've sponsored over the years. Kamdyn Mcintosh was my player last year and this year.

This is my fifth season as Richmond President (appointed in October 2013). When I first joined the Richmond Board in 2005, Steven Wright was CEO. We had a very small management group because we couldn't afford a bigger management group. Now, we have money to hire people but no place to put them. In 2009 we had 46 employees and we have 116 now, that's not counting the players of course.

In the early days of the League, the President was more like a CEO. It was an amateur game in effect and the President was expected to make things happen. Along the way, when things became a bit more professional, you realised that chairing a board or committee, as it was called then, is one thing and being there to run the place is another

Peggy O'Neal has been on the Richmond Board since 2005, president since 2013. In that period, the Tigers have become one of the game's most powerful clubs. In 2018, Richmond's membership broke through 100,000, a League record.

thing. My role is very different from George Bennett's role (the club's longest serving President from 1887-1908).

But along the way you think *well if you hire someone to be the CEO you better let them do their job.* I think that my role is to meet with Brendon quite often, to be a liaison between the board and Brendon so I can keep the board's view in front of him. It also means he can inform me of something ahead of time so as to keep the board informed to make sure everybody gets the information they need so we can make decisions.

"I've always liked the saying, 'you aren't leading if no one's following"

And then there's a huge ambassadorial role that I didn't quite appreciate. I am invited to something every day and to speak at something every week and that's just not possible. I think if you are representing Richmond and you accept an invitation to speak, you want to do a good job, so you can't spread yourself too thin. But it's good to be able to meet our members and to hear their opinions.

I don't mind public speaking. The only time you need to be nervous is when things aren't going well. But in June 2017 it occurred to me, *gee you've got a good story now, you know, just tell it.*

Since I've became President I've saved all my speeches, all the Footy Records, all the clippings. I've been approached by a couple of people about writing a book and I say, "well it's not over yet" and if I wrote a book it would be for me. I could never tell the whole truth because you'd be surprised about what people do. But that's part of the job too.

Other people could give you a better take on my presidential style. For me, this is the way I've always worked my entire professional life. When you realise that you're really chair of a board, that your vote is the same as everybody else's—it's a committee, and if you don't like working in a committee you surely wouldn't like being on a Board. The quickest way to cause division is to make decisions on your own. And that's not the way that I've ever seen it. I've always found that good ideas are everywhere and you're not the fount of all knowledge. Just because you are the chair doesn't mean you can ignore the input from the board.

We have a good discussion at the Board before we make decisions. Everybody has bought into that decision and a great deal of unity follows that. If people aren't ready to make a decision or need more time, we just wait rather than push the point.

I've found there's very few things that can't wait another week or two, especially important decisions. I've always liked the saying, 'you aren't leading if no one's following.'

I can't think of anything that's come down to a close vote. Some people may have said, 'I can live with that' realising you win some and lose some. The nature of the board is there is one decision and you've got to stand behind it.

I was on the committee that hired Brendon Gale. Brendon and Damien Hardwick started in the same month, in August 2009. There was a lengthy process, which was rare back then, on selecting the coach. We had different filter groups and I wasn't part of that. We had a couple of board members and some external people with a large list and then there was a shortlist and then it was down to two. I met the two. In the end it was hard to split hairs. Damien did a presentation and so did Ken Hinkley.

I didn't know Damien. He was fresh and new, and you had to rely on the people who have spent a lot of their time assessing the candidates. Brendon had been hired by then. We were at the shortlist stage for the coach and we thought that it was important Brendon get involved in the selection process because he would be working with this coach.

Damien says now that there's a big difference in being an assistant than being in charge. I think every new coach goes through that—how do you manage all the people around you?

We extended Damien's contract at the end of 2015. We had won 15 games, we were in finals three times in a row but we hadn't won any of them. We still believed he was the right person and the players loved playing for him.

The Board did consider, 'what if it all goes backward next year?' Sometime fans think football is a linear process—you win 10, you win 12, you win 14; and we won 15 so next year we will win them all!

Peggy O'Neal had the pleasure of making a lap of honour with the players after the 2017 Grand Final victory. Here she shares the spoils of victory with the Norm Smith Medallist, Dustin Martin.

We were prepared to back him. Sure enough, it didn't go well in 2016. It was sort of a surprise but at the same time there was something not right that we couldn't win a final. We knew that there was work to be done and we had already started looking into that issue by the time the 2016 season was going south pretty quickly.

Brendon and I talked a lot during that period. We also met quite a bit trying to think through what to do next. Brendon conducted a gap analysis—Where are we; What are we good at; What are we not good at; Where are the best clubs; How do we bridge that gap; What resources do we need. And, do we need help with how we assess all of this? That's when we brought in a consultant to help with the methodology.

Some of the work Brendon did showed every time the club fired a coach, it got worse.

The lawyer in me kept thinking: why do we start over all the time? If you are always starting over you're never getting enough traction.

So, I also kept thinking: *why is it the coach*? So, what we needed to say was: *what do we need to change?* Well we want to change the right things, and I don't think the coach is the thing that needs to be changed, there are other things. So, Brendon and Dan Richardson, who was here at the time, did a lot of analysis for us about where Damien was at this point in the career compared with successful coaches at the same point. And he stacked up really well, and we were thinking: why would we change that?

Dan Jackson shares a winning moment with captain Trent Cotchin at Etihad Stadium in 2013. Club president Peggy O'Neal sponsored Jackson when he was playing at Punt Road (156 games, 2004-14), and he was her guest at the Grand Final in 2017.

What I've said around the board table a few times, not in a pontificating way, is this: we have more information than they (people outside the club) do, and the opinion that matters is ours. So, we listen, but they don't know what we know, and they shouldn't. We respect the external opinions but the decision and the responsibility sits with us. And so it did.

We'd also had some really good players emerging. Players like Dustin Martin Jack Riewoldt and Alex Rance and you think if you just asked them to re-sign and then we told them, 'your coach is gone', they would all be gone by now too, that's my feeling.

Yes, we *were* under attack for a while. I think it was the unity of the place that saw us through and that we all made that decision about Damien and we were all prepared to stick with him.

It's interesting now to hear people talk about the "Richmond model". What we did was right for us, but I don't know if it's right for another.

It's not always that the coach should survive but Damien should have because of the evidence that we had. Sometimes if you just get better people around the coach it works out. And then we heard that Neil Balme might be open for a change.

"When I replayed the game, I felt realty emotional. I realised the magnitude of what they had done"

The first time I met with Neil Balme he said, "I didn't realise how badly I wanted to come back to Richmond until it was a possibility". And I said to him, "well if you want to come so badly we just won't pay you anything, we will give you a job" (laughing). And he said, "Not what I meant".

Things started to fall into line. He kept saying, "I don't think you are as bad as you think you are, I think you have a lot going for you. I think if we just fix up a few things we will be okay". And he was right.

Grand Final week (2017) seems like a long time ago. It was so unique and so novel to find yourself in the middle of it. Brendon and I stepped in and did a lot of media so that the players and the coach could get on with their job.

I don't know if we thought it (the premiership) would come so quickly. But once we beat Geelong in the qualifying final I said to Brendon, "we are going to be in the Grand Final and we are going to win it". Because they were playing so well.

The Sunday before the Brownlow, the AFL Commission has lunch with the club Presidents. I just kept thinking, 'I'm here as the President of one of the clubs that are going to be in that game'. And it was like, Wow!

I remember going to the Brownlow on the Monday and we were all pretty confident Dustin would win. Neil Balme went with me. He didn't want to go because he had been to so many of them. I usually take one of the board members to the Brownlow with me, but Neil went and I remember how happy Dustin was and how happy we all were for him.

People were getting really emotional. I mean in the sense of, 'I can't believe we are here'. It was really very, very emotional. There were lots of letters and lots of people that I didn't know were emailing me. People were bringing yellow and black gifts of various descriptions for me.

So, you realise that you are a symbol of an important part of their life. Even today people are still writing me and telling me about what it meant to them. I was in Uluru recently talking at a conference about Richmond's Reconciliation Action Plan—we're regarded as one of the best in that area—and they asked me if I'd come and share it. And I'm walking around Uluru and someone goes by and says, 'Hi Peggy'. I'm thinking, 'how did you know it was me, who are you?' They were on a bicycle, so they didn't stop and I just had to smile I just thought, you never get away from it—which is a good thing.

Brendon and I almost always sit in the same row at the footy. Most of the time, Brendon sits on the aisle because he's got long legs, and then Jane his wife sits next, and then I sit third in from the aisle and then whoever is with me and then guests of various descriptions. And Jane usually lasts about 15 minutes into the game and she says, "he is too intense I have to go sit somewhere else".

On Grand Final day Dan Jackson went with me. Dan played with us, I was his player sponsor, and he happened to be in town. So the seating was a little different for some reason: it was me on the aisle then Dan, then Brendon, and then Brendon's mother and his brother, Michael. And Brendon said,"do you mind changing seats with me so I can sit on the aisle". So we moved down, so then it was Brendon, Jane had gone to get the kids, and then there was me, and then Dan and then Brendon's mother. And when When Brendon realised we were going to win he wanted to hug his mother, so he fell like a timber across us, and there's the photo of Dan Jackson and me holding on.

Kane Lambert was teasing afterwards. They asked him, when did you think you had it won? and he said, 'when we looked at the big screen and saw Brendon cry'.'

I didn't feel the same kind of emotion as did Brendon. Probably about Wednesday when all the media had died down I replayed the game for the first time and I felt really emotional towards the end of the replay because I realised the magnitude of what they had done.

The only way I knew I was on TV (during the last quarter) was a friend was watching the game in a bar in Dublin. She sent me a picture saying, "It's 6am here and there's you and Brendon on the screen". And I thought, 'so we are'.

On the Thursday night of Grand Final week, we invited back all the past CEOs, coaches and Presidents for a drink. Cameron Schwab came along and gave me his *Save Our Skins* button. He was CEO of the club at that time and said the club had a dozen of them made. I've worn that button to all the games this year along with my Richmond button. I think it is a good reminder of how far we've come.

One of the key moments of the AFL's annual season launch is the presentation of the Premiership flag to the Premiers. Left to right, CEO Brendon Gale, President Peggy O'Neal and coach Damien Hardwick.

Damien Hardwick

Damien Hardwick had learned his craft at Hawthorn under Alastair Clarkson, and was an assistant for the Hawks' 2008 Flag. He had previously enjoyed success as a player for Essendon (2000), and Port Adelaide (2004). He was appointed Richmond coach in 2010.

2010 -

Born
18 August 1972

Played
Essendon
1994-91
153 games
13 goals
1 Premiership

Port Adelaide
2002-2004
54 games
1 goal
1 Premiership

Coached
Richmond
From 2010

Interviewed
29 November 2018

I was very fortunate to play in two Premierships but the emotion is very different as a coach than it was as a player. As a coach it is more of a 'proud father' type moment. You see a group of young people that you've worked with over a long period being able to achieve something that you did and dreamt of as a boy.

As a player it's more of a sense of relief that you've won one. That was my first emotion. As a coach it's more of a sense of achievement. You're probably living your dream through others, so to speak. It meant so much more to me as a coach than it did as a player.

I remember thinking about the people that had been a part of the journey along the way. At the backend of the 2017 Grand Final—when we had the game in hand—you start to get a little emotional and realise how lucky you are to be a part of something like this.

I was 37 when I first started this job. I was always of the opinion that your first day is your worst day as a senior coach and you get better from there on in. I still look at it like that now. I consistently ask my players to improve and that I do as well.

The thing I've learned over ten years of coaching is I haven't got all the answers. When you are a young, gung-ho coach you start you feel like you have all the answers.

The greatest phrase I've learnt over the last three to four years is: "I don't know."

The growth within me as a coach has been incredible from where I started to where I am now.

It is very hard as a coach to leave a loss behind. That's a good point you make.

We've won a lot of games over the last two years but when you lose you sort of feel like *geez, for some unknown reason you can't see where your next win is coming from.* I really did struggle with the losing of games and more the stigma of being a 'loser', if that makes sense.

I am probably the same as your dad (Kevin Bartlett) was when he was coach. Straight away when I get to work, I go: *okay, how do I get it better? What do I have to do to get it better? Move the magnets, Put this player there.* And funnily enough sometimes that's the worst thing to do. You actually need the dust to settle a bit before you start making decisions.

I've been very fortunate in my career to have won a lot of footy games. Ever since I started playing as a kid to when I was an AFL player, I think I've missed finals twice as a player and four times as a coach. So, when we lost I did struggle.

That's why 2016 was so hard. I'd never been through a season like that and here I was trying to figure out a way to get out of it. As a coach you try to work your way through things, to try to understand *why it is happening* and *what we can do to make it better.*

My family found it really hard. They sit on the edge and they're getting more questions from the outside world: *what's going wrong?, are you okay?* That makes it tough on them more so than it does on me.

I'm in a protective environment here at the club. My life is basically I go to work, I get my coffee I go home. It all starts again.

In the 2017 Grand Final I was relatively confident in the third quarter after we had that burst of goals.

In 2017, Damien Hardwick became the seventh Richmond Premiership coach joining Dan Minogue (c-c, 1920-21), Frank "Checker" Hughes (1932), Perc Bentley (c-c, 1934), Jack Dyer (c-c, 1943), Tom Hafey (1967, 1969, 1973-74), and Tony Jewell (1980). At Punt Road Oval on the day after the Grand Final, Hardwick is celebrating with captain Trent Cotchin (left) and Jack Riewoldt.

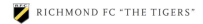

There were really good passages of play—the Grigg handball to Lambert for a goal, and then the Castagna goal. Those sorts of goals gave us real momentum, but they were pretty demoralising to the Crows as well. I felt we were then in a really strong position but as a coach you're always thinking *we need one more, one more.* Probably the moment it really sank in was the Dan Butler goal, the banana-kick on the boundary line. That was the time that I felt, *we've got it!* and started to enjoy it and laugh a little bit more.

I remember watching Butler's goal go through and that's when the emotions started to hit. Our families were sitting around that area where we were sort of looking for the ball to go through—up in that top stand and I remember trying to see if I could somehow see *my* family. For no reason in particular but just the connection I felt with them at that moment was really important to me.

"I'm very, very lucky to do what I do, and I love what I do"

I wouldn't say I can hear the Richmond supporters in the coach's box, but I can *feel* them, their energy, their vibrancy. That goal against GWS in the preliminary final—Cotchin kicks, Jack (Riewoldt) makes a good contest, Dustin (Martin) roves it and handballs to Lambert, the feel of that crowd noise coming through the box was incredible—something I'll never forget. I still get shivers down my spine thinking about it now.

Richmond's got an energy about it. I've been very fortunate to play with big clubs, but I've never felt anything like this club. It's different in a lot of ways. Everyone will say their supporters are passionate, but the Richmond supporters are always prefaced with *he's mad, he's crazy.* There's always an adjective to describe a Richmond supporter which I've found is part of a charm of this club.

People always say *who do your kids barrack for?* They're Richmond, they're done. They won't ever move, no matter if I ever go to coach somewhere else—which I hope never happens. There's something about it, it's a special place.

Allan Jeans had the great anecdote comparing coaching to cooking sausages: *you can grill them, you can fry them, you can curry them*—**and that's what coaching is.** It's trying to inspire through storytelling.

For a lot of my pre-game stories I will start with a concept. Then I'll go to someone and ask *what do you think of this?* From there there's a bit of a collaborating to see where we end up.

In the 2018 Preliminary Final I spoke about the song Bohemian Rhapsody. How the song was made by the band *Queen*, who were really a bunch of misfits. They weren't necessarily the most talented musicians going around but as a collective group they were an outstanding band. I spoke about how that summed us up. We aren't the most talented side but when we get together we become special in a way. And so that was our theme going into the Preliminary Final. It didn't work that well. But I think our players really enjoy the themes coming into a game.

I'm very, very lucky to do what I do, and I love what I do. I will forever remember the tales people told me, like *I got to share with my son, what my father shared with his dad at the 1980 Grand Final.* Many people come up and say *oh sorry to bother you....*but I love those stories.

I used to barrack for Fitzroy and I went to every game with my Dad. I say to fans, *you don't realise how lucky you are.* I never got to experience going to a Grand Final with him, and on the final siren hugging with excitement. My dad was at the 2017 Grand Final with me, but it was a different celebration again.

The day to me was so special. The senior coach gets a lot of the plaudits but it takes a whole club to win a flag and we were blessed with so many people who have been incredibly helpful to me and supported me and given me great guidance along the way. Without those people, I wouldn't be a premiership coach.

As much as I shouldn't think about it, I still think about the 2017 flag all the time.

The one great regret I had was that we won the flag but we didn't actually get to go down Swan Street. I would have loved for the bus to turn left, not right, when taking us to the Casino. We tried to get the bus driver to turn but he said, "Listen if I go in there, this bus ain't coming out". It would have been just great to spend it here with the fans.

I think it's the one downside about the Grand Final aftermath. If we could have just come back to Punt Road and got all the supporters back here and have the Premiership cup come out every 10 minutes and cheer and sing the song again. It's one of my great regrets. But we'll just have to do it again, won't we?

Premiership celebrations continued at Punt Road on the day after the night before, as the players and coach were presented to the fans. (L-R): Jacob Townsend, Daniel Rioli, Trent Cotchin, Alex Rance (obscured), Bachir Houli, David Astbury, Damien Hardwick, Shaun Grigg, Nick Vlastuin (obscured), Dustin Martin, Jack Riewoldt and Dion Prestia.

From 2012—

IT'S TIGER TIME

Trevor Ruddell celebrated with all Tiger fans when the Tigers zoomed through the 2017 finals, breaking a 32-year drought.

By 2012 Brendon Gale's three-zero-75 plan of 2010 was having great off-field effects, but Richmond's on-field results remained mediocre. Under Damien Hardwick, appointed coach in August 2009, the Tigers had finished 15th, 12th and 12th in his first three seasons. However, a nucleus of a great Richmond team was coming of age under him.

Trent Cotchin, the retrospectively anointed 2012 Brownlow Medallist, replaced Chris Newman as captain in 2013, and he was ably supported in the midfield by Dustin Martin, with full-forward Jack Riewoldt and defender Alex Rance book-ending an impressive spine. In 2013 the Tigers made the finals for the first time since 2001, and just the third time since 1982, only to be bundled out in the first week by Carlton. Richmond would also lose Elimination finals in 2014 and 2015.

That year the club released its 2015-18 strategic overview, *A Strong and Bold Premiership Club*. The document trumpeted the club's current zero debt and 73,515 members, while its very achievable on-field goal was "one or more premierships". Under Peggy O'Neal, who in October 2013 was appointed the first female president of an AFL club, Richmond continued Gary March's policy of engagement with the broader community. In 2012 the Tiger's Bachar Houli founded a multi-cultural program, and in that same year the Korin Gamadgji Institute, which conducted indigenous leadership and training programs, was officially established in a new building on the footprint of the old Ernest H. King Stand/ Social Club building.

In 2016 the club submitted an unsuccessful application for a licence to field a team in the inaugural AFLW season, the AFL's women's league. A further submission for the 2019 AFLW season was similarly unsuccessful, but the League granted the club entry from the 2020 season. In preparation for that senior debut, the club fielded a team in the VFL Women's competition from 2018.

Richmond's AFL premiership ambition received a setback in 2016 when the Tigers finished 13th. In the off-season a challenge to the current board was staged by a group of supporters and former players styled *Focus on Football*. The group recognised the club's strong management and position off the field, but criticised the club's recruiting and player development. It also placed great pressure on Hardwick. However, the club's management kept faith in him. The rebel group abandoned their challenge in September 2016, after their blue-sky proposal to recruit Collingwood Football Manager Neil Balme to a role within Richmond's football department was fulfilled by the current board.

In 2017 the Tigers under Hardwick developed a brutal game structure, based less on sublime skill or ingenious tactics, and more on a relentless pressure on opponents through speed, ball movement and aggressive tackling. The club finished the home and away season in third position behind Adelaide and Geelong. Dustin Martin, widely regarded as the best player in the competition and soon to be awarded the 2017 Brownlow Medal, re-signed with the club on the eve of the finals.

What followed was a magical finals series. All Richmond's finals matches were at the MCG, and its Preliminary Final against Greater Western Sydney was played before a crowd of 94,258, of which 95% were estimated to be Richmond supporters. Daniel Rioli's running goal in the second quarter generated a roar measured at 125 decibels.

The Tigers met premiership favourite Adelaide in the Grand Final, and after resisting pressure early, gradually wore down the Crows. The final siren would signal the end of Richmond's 37-year premiership drought. The yellow and black optimism continued after the premiership celebrations and into the following year. In 2018 Richmond was the first AFL club to boast a membership in excess of 100,000 supporters, the Tigers won the minor premiership, and the club also set a new MCG record, ultimately winning 22 consecutive matches at the home of football. Richmond was widely regarded as the best team of the 2018 season and unbeatable at the MCG until their run was upset by Collingwood in the Preliminary Final.

TREVOR RUDDELL

Jack Graham has the Premiership Cup firmly in hand as the victorious Tigers pose for photographs after the 2017 Grand Final.

The pride of Punt Road

Richmond's 2017 Premiership, the club's eleventh since joining the League in 1908, Richmond's golden eras were from 1919-34, and 1967-74, periods when the club won eight Premierships. CEO Brendon Gale's plan, put to the Board in 2011, was for the club to achieve another golden era, to have won "three more premierships by 2020, and be the team of the decade".

The 1921 premiership cap, awarded to the RFC players.

1920

Richmond 7.10 (52)
Collingwood 5.5 (35)

Goals: Don 2, Hall, Harley, H James, W James, Weatherill.

Best: Hall, Herbert, Hislop, H James, Moffatt, Smith.

Back row, from left: Artie Bettles, Wilfred Stott, Dave Moffatt, Hugh James, Barney Herbert, Frank Harley, Gerald Rush, Ern Taylor.
Middle row: Norm McIntosh, Donald Don, Max Hislop, Dan Minogue, George Ogilvie, Vic Thorp, Paddy Abbott, Jimmy Smith.
Front row: Frank Hughes, James Karthaus, Bobby Carew, Clarrie Hall, Stan Morris, Reg Hede, George Bayliss.

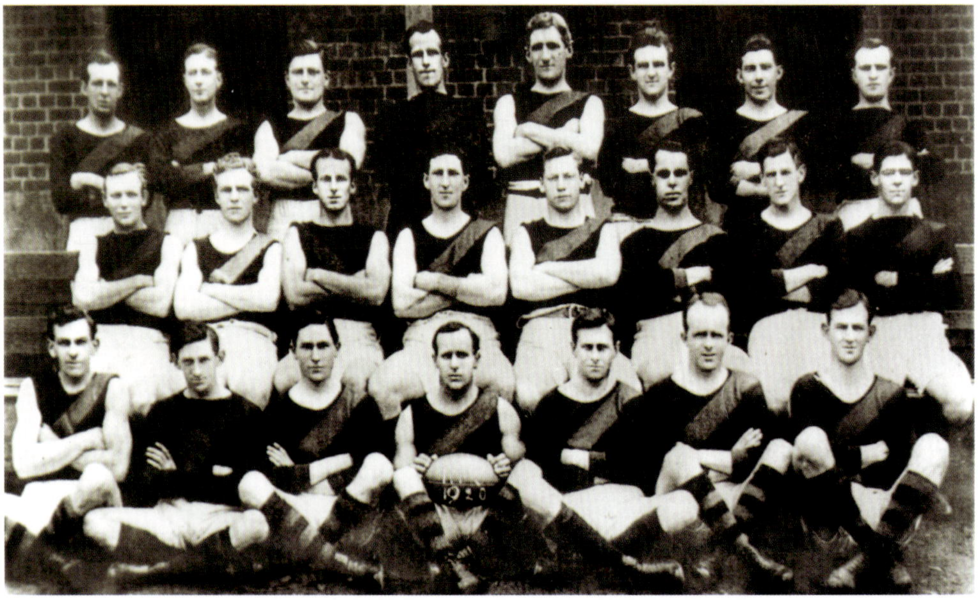

1921

Richmond 5.6 (36)
Carlton 4.8 (32)

Goals: Bayliss 2, James, Morris, Turnbull.

Best: Hislop, James, McIntosh, Minogue, Smith, Taylor.

Back row, from left: George Bayliss, Ern Taylor, Jimmy Smith, George Weatherill, Bob Weatherill, Mel Morris, Frank Harley, Vic Thorp.
Middle row: Frank Hughes, Hugh James, Max Hislop, Dan Minogue (capt-coach), Barney Herbert, Donald Don, Norm McIntosh.
Front row: Bobby Carew, Clarrie Hall, Norman Turnbull.

1932

Richmond 13.14 (92)
Carlton 12.11 (83)

Goals: D Strang 4, Titus 2, Hunter, Heifner, Martin, G Strang, Anderson, Bentley, O'Halloran.

Best: G Strang, McCormack, O'Neill, Baggott, Titus, Bolger.

Back row, from left: Doug Strang, Gordon Strang, Jack Anderson, Eric Zschech, Jack Baggott, Tom O'Halloran, Basil McCormack, Joe Murdoch, Maurie Sheahan, Fred Heifner.
Middle row: Kevin O'Neill, Jack Titus, Maurie Hunter, Perc Bentley (capt), Alan Geddes, Martin Bolger, Charlie Callander (trainer).
Front row: Jack Twyford, Stan Judkins.
Absent: Ray Martin.

1934

Richmond 19.14 (128)
Sth Melbourne 12.17 (89)

Goals: Titus 6, O'Halloran, Harris 3, Bentley, Martin 2, Baxter, Murdoch, Zschech.

Best: Titus, Bolger, Baggott, McCormack, G Strang, Martin.

Back row, from left: Dick Harris, Jack McConchie, Richie Saunders, Dave Baxter, Jack Symons, Dan Guinane, Jack Stenhouse, Dick Chirgwin.
Third row: Horrie Edmonds, Eric Zschech, Fred Heifner, Jack Dyer, Doug Strang, Gordon Strang, Joe Murdoch, Martin Bolger, Kevin O'Neill.
Second row: Bert Foster, Tom O'Halloran, Maurie Sheahan, Alan Geddes, Perc Bentley (capt-coach), Jack Baggott, Basil McCormack, Jack Titus.
Front row: Clarrie Jordon, Ray Martin, Stan Judkins, Bill Garvie.

1943

Richmond 12.14 (86)
Essendon 11.15 (81)

NB: Match played at Princess Park due to war.

Goals: Harris 7, Dyer 3, Bawden, Broadstock.

Best: Harris, Dyer, Perkins, Merrett, Bawden, Oppy.

Back row, from left: Jack Broadstock, Ron Durham, Bill Perkins, Arthur Kemp, Bob Bawden, Leo Maguire, Jack Scott, Len Ablett.
Middle row: Ray Hunt, Ray Steele, Jack Dyer (capt-coach), Dick Harris, Roy Quinn, Brian Randall, Bernie Waldron, Bert Edwards.
Front row: Max Oppy, Leo Merrett, Laurie Cahill.

1967

Richmond 16.18 (114)
Geelong 15.15 (105)

Goals: Ronaldson, Hart, Brown, Bartlett 3, Barrot, A Richardson, B Richardson, Guinane,

Best: Barrot, Hart, Brown, A Richardson, Dean, Bartlett.

Back row, from left: Kevin Sheedy, Kevin Shinners, Mick Erwin, Francis Bourke, Mike Bowden, Geoff Strang, Dick Clay, Royce Hart, Graham Burgin, John Perry.
Third row: Neil Busse, Michael Green, Mike Perry, Neville Crowe, John Ronaldson, Mike Patterson, Ross Warner, Barry Richardson, Tony Jewell.
Second row: Billy Barrot, Alan Richardson, Paddy Guinane, Ray Dunn (pres), Fred Swift (capt), Tommy Hafey (coach), Roger Dean, Graeme Richmond (sec).
Front row: Frank Dimattina, John Northey, Kevin Bartlett, Bill Brown, David Jacks, Don Davenport, Graeme Bond.

1969

Richmond 12.13 (85)
Carlton 8.12 (60)

Goals: Barrot 3, Moore, Northey 2, Bartlett, Bond, Dean, Hart, Ronaldson.

Best: Green, Bartlett, Clay, Barrot, Northey, Dean.

Back row, from left: Back row: Dick Clay, Tony Jewell, Brad Shinners, Des McKenzie, Royce Hart, Mike Bowden, Ray Ball, Eric Moore, Don Davenport.
Third row: Ron Thomas, John Ferguson, Geoff Strang, Anthony Smith, Michael Green, John Ronaldson, Barry Richardson, Rex Hunt, Ian Owen, George McInnes, Mike Perry.
Second row: Colin Beard, Graeme Burgin, Billy Barrot, Ray Dunn (pres), Roger Dean (capt), Tommy Hafey (coach), Mike Patterson, Alan Schwab (sec), Francis Bourke, Kevin Bartlett.
Front row: Brenton Miels, Graeme Bond, Bill Brown, Kevin Smythe, Graham Robbins, Derek Peardon.
Absent: John Northey, John Perry, Kevin Sheedy.

1973

Richmond 16.20 (116)
Carlton 12.14 (86)

Goals: Hart, Sheedy, Stewart 3, Balme, Sproule 2, Bartlett, Carter, Green.

Best: Bartlett, Sheedy, Green, Stewart, Hart, Sproule.

Back row, from left: Stephen Rae, Glynn Hewitt, Merv Keane, Bryan Wood, Eric Leech, Grant Allford, Francis Jackson, Dick Clay, Marty McMillan.
Third row: Graeme Teasdale, Bill Nalder, Robert McGhie, Neil Balme, Craig McKellar, Brian Roberts, Michael Green, Barry Richardson, Rex Hunt.
Second row: Kevin Morris, Roger Dean, Tommy Hafey (coach), Ian Stewart, Al Boord (pres), Royce Hart (capt), Alan Schwab (sec), Francis Bourke, Wayne Walsh, Kevin Sheedy.
Front row: Robert Lamb, Paul Sproule, Daryl Cumming, Noel Carter, Laurie Fowler, Murray Thompson.
Absent: Kevin Bartlett.

1974

Richmond 18.20 (128)
Nth Melbourne 13.9 (87)

Goals: B Richardson 5, Hart 3, Balme, Green, Sheedy 2, Cloke, Cumming, Thorpe, Walsh.

Best: Sheedy, Hart, Sproule, Green, Balme, Walsh.

Back row, from left: Michael Green, David Cloke, Robert McGhie, Brian Roberts, Neil Balme, Gareth Andrews, Barry Richardson.
Middle row: Dick Clay, Francis Bourke, Royce Hart, Tommy Hafey (coach), Kevin Bartlett, Paul Sproule, Kevin Morris.
Front row: Kevin Sheedy, Merv Keane, Cameron Clayton, Daryl Cumming, Bryan Wood, Wayne Walsh.
Inset: David Thorpe.

1980

Richmond 23.21 (159)
Collingwood 9.24 (78)

Goals: Bartlett 7, Cloke 6, Wiley 3, Roach, Keane 2, Weightman, Jess, Rowlings.

Best: Bartlett, Raines, Lee, Welsh, Bourke, Wiley.

Norm Smith Medal: Kevin Bartlett

Back row, from left: Rod Oborne, Bruce Tempany, Merv Keane, Greg Strachan, Michael Malthouse, Geoff Raines, Paddy Guinane, Shane Williams, Ian Baker, Robert Wiley, Matthew Wall, Terry Smith.
Third row: Jim Jess, Emmett Dunne, Colin Waterson, Michael Roach, David Cloke, Mark Lee, Kim Kershaw, Peter Laughlin, Francis Bourke.
Second row: Bryan Wood, Peter Welsh, Stephen Mount, Richard Doggett (gen man), Bruce Monteath (capt), Ian Wilson (pres), Tony Jewell (coach), Ian Scrimshaw, Graeme Landy, Kevin Bartlett.
Front row: Daryl Freame, Barry Rowlings, Paul Sarah, Dale Weightman, Dennis Collins, Phil Bottams.

2017

Richmond 16.12 (108)
Adelaide Crows 8.12 (60

Goals: Graham 3, Townsend 2, Martin 2, Riewoldt 2, Caddy, Houli, Grigg, Lambert, Castagna, Prestia, Butler.

Best: Martin, Houli, Rance, Astbury, Prestia, Edwards, Graham, Grimes.

Norm Smith Medal: Dustin Martin

Back row (L-R): Shane Edwards, Kane Lambert, Jason Castagna, Jacob Townsend, Nick Vlastuin, Alex Rance, Bachar Houli, David Astbury, Nathan Broad, Jack Graham, Toby Nankervis, Josh Caddy, Daniel Butler, Kamdyn McIntosh.

Front row (L-R): Dion Prestia, Dustin Martin, Dylan Grimes, Brandon Ellis, Damien Hardwick (coach), Trent Cotchin (captain), Jack Riewoldt, Shaun Grigg, Daniel Rioli.

R.F.C. Honour Board 1885-2018

Each year, the Tigers take part in the 'Dreamtime at the 'G' match against Essendon at the MCG, celebrating Indigenous culture. A new guernsey is created each season, created by Indigenous designers. Celebrating above are (L-R): Dylan Grimes, Dan Butler, David Astbury, Alex Rance, Shane Edwards, Jack Higgins, Callum Moore, Brandon Ellis.

Year	President	Secretary/CEO	Treasurer	Senior Coach	Captain	Best and Fairest	Highest Goal Kicker	Position
1885	John Charles Winn	James Charles	Clovis Mainon	George Smith	George Smith	Not Awarded	Jack Conlon (6) / William Wells (6)	8th
1886	John Charles Winn	James Charles	Clovis Mainon	Tom Graham	Tom Graham	Not Awarded	Alf Hill (10)	14th
1887	George Henry Bennett	Charles Cupit	John Egan	Jack Stewart	Jack Stewart	Not Awarded	Alf Hill (11)	7th
1888	George Henry Bennett	Charles Cupit	John Egan	George Smith	George Smith	Not Awarded	Billy Brown (53)	5th
1889	George Henry Bennett	Charles Cupit	John Egan	Pat O'Loughlin	Pat O'Loughlin	Not Awarded	Billy Brown (25)	8th
1890	George Henry Bennett	Jimmy Eastman	John Egan	Ed Burwood	Ed Burwood	Not Awarded	Alf Elder (8)	11th
1891	George Henry Bennett	Jimmy Eastman	John Egan	Tom Graham	Tom Graham	Not Awarded	Alf Elder (15)	12th
1892	George Henry Bennett	Jimmy Eastman	John Egan	Arthur Powell	Arthur Powell	Not Awarded	George Sparrow (19)	8th
1893	George Henry Bennett	Jimmy Eastman	John Egan	Charles Backhouse	Charles Backhouse	Not Awarded	George Sparrow (23)	12th
1894	George Henry Bennett	Jimmy Eastman	John Egan	George Sparrow	George Sparrow	Not Awarded	Fred Alsop (21)	11th
1895	George Henry Bennett	Jimmy Eastman	John Egan	George Sparrow	George Sparrow	Not Awarded	Fred Alsop (19)	12th
1896	George Henry Bennett	William Maybury / Dave Chessell / Jack Stewart	John Egan	Richard Kelly	Richard Kelly	Not Awarded	Richard Kelly (12)	12th
1897	George Henry Bennett	Jack Stewart	John Egan	Richard Kelly	Richard Kelly	Not Awarded	Alf Elder (28)	6th
1898	George Henry Bennett	Jack Stewart	John Egan	William Clarke	William Clarke	Not Awarded	Alf Elder (20)	4th
1899	George Henry Bennett	Robert Guthrie	Percy Sevier	William Clarke	William Clarke	Not Awarded	Hector Milne (16)	6th
1900	George Henry Bennett	Edward Sexton/ George Peckham-Beachcroft	Percy Sevier	Tom Watson	Tom Watson	Not Awarded	George Backhouse (15)	3rd
1901	George Henry Bennett	George Peckham-Beachcroft	Percy Sevier	Alec Edmond	Alec Edmond	Not Awarded	James Douglas (13)	2nd
1902	**George Henry Bennett**	**George Peckham-Beachcroft**	**Archie McNair**	**Alec Edmond**	**Alec Edmond**	**Not Awarded**	**Roland Duncan (17)**	**Premiers**
1903	George Henry Bennett	George Peckham-Beachcroft	Archie McNair	Alec Edmond	Alec Edmond	Not Awarded	Jack Main (34)	2nd (Minor Premiers)
1904	George Henry Bennett	George Peckham-Beachcroft	Archie McNair	Alec Edmond	Alec Edmond	Not Awarded	Jack Hutchison (40)	2nd (Minor Premiers)
1905	**George Henry Bennett**	**George Peckham-Beachcroft**	**Archie McNair**	**Alec Edmond**	**Alec Edmond**	Not Awarded	**Dick Knell (46)**	**Premiers**
1906	George Henry Bennett	Andrew Manzie	Archie McNair	Alec Edmond	Alec Edmond	Not Awarded	Jack Hutchison (55)	3rd
1907	George Henry Bennett	Andrew Manzie	Archie McNair	Alec Edmond	Alec Edmond	Not Awarded	Jack Hutchison (67)	3rd
1908	George Bennett	Andrew Manzie	Archie McNair	Dick Condon	Charlie Pannam	Not Awarded	Bill Bourke (24)	9th
1909	Frank Tudor	Andrew Manzie	Archie McNair	Dick Condon	Dick Condon Ivo Lawson	Not Awarded	Bill Bourke (20)	8th

Year	President	Secretary/CEO	Treasurer	Senior Coach	Captain	Best and Fairest	Highest Goal Kicker	Position
1910	Frank Tudor	Andrew Manzie	Archie McNair	Alex Hall	Bill Schmidt	Not Awarded	Mick Maguire (20)	7th
1911	Frank Tudor	Andrew Manzie	Archie McNair	Len Incigneri	Len Incigneri	Not Awarded	Mick Maguire (29)	8th
1912	Frank Tudor	George Beachcroft	James MacDermott	Charlie Pannam	Ted Ohlsen	Not Awarded	Ted Keggin (24)	9th
1913	Frank Tudor	William Lohse	Jack Archer	Ern Jenkins	Hugh James	Not Awarded	Percy Martyn (32)	7th
1914	Frank Tudor	William Lohse	Jack Archer	Charlie Ricketts	Bill Thomas	Not Awarded	Clarrie Hall (32)	8th
1915	Frank Tudor	William Lohse	Jack Archer	Charlie Ricketts	Bill Thomas	Not Awarded	Clarrie Hall (25)	6th
1916	Frank Tudor	William Lohse	Jack Archer	Charlie Ricketts	Bill Thomas	Not Awarded	Percy Martini (22)	4th
1917	Frank Tudor	Bill Maybury	Jack Archer	Percy Maybury	Percy Maybury	Not Awarded	Charlie Fehring (14)	6th
1918	Frank Tudor	Bill Maybury	Jack Archer	Bernie Nolan	Clarrie Hall	Not Awarded	Donald Don (19)	6th
1919	Alf Wood	Bill Maybury	Jack Archer	Norman Clark	Bill Thomas	Not Awarded	Donald Don (31)	Runner Up
1920	**Alf Wood**	**Bill Maybury**	**Jack Archer**	**Dan Minogue**	**Dan Minogue**	**Not Awarded**	**George Bayliss (63)**	**Premiers**
1921	**Alf Wood**	**Bill Maybury**	**Abe Aarons**	**Dan Minogue**	**Dan Minogue**	**Hugh James**	**George Bayliss (53)**	**Premiers**
1922	Alf Wood	Bill Maybury	Abe Aarons	Dan Minogue	Dan Minogue	Not Awarded	George Bayliss (32)	5th
1923	Alf Wood	Bill Maybury	Abe Aarons	Dan Minogue	Dan Minogue	Not Awarded	Don Fraser (18)	8th
1924	Jack Archer	Percy Page	Abe Aarons	Dan Minogue	Dan Minogue	Not Awarded	Mel Morris (44)	R/U
1925	Jack Archer	Percy Page	Jos Langdon	Dan Minogue	Dan Minogue	Not Awarded	Mel Morris (25)	7th
1926	Jack Archer	Percy Page	Jos Langdon	Mel Morris	Mel Morris	Not Awarded	Dave Lynch (31)	7th
1927	Jack Archer	Percy Page	Jos Langdon	Frank Hughes	Alan Geddes	Basil McCormack	Jack Baggott (37)	Runner Up
1928	Jack Archer	Percy Page	Jos Langdon	Frank Hughes	Alan Geddes	Basil McCormack	Jack Baggott (61)	R/U
1929	Jack Archer	Percy Page	Jos Langdon	Frank Hughes	Cyril Lilburne	Jack Titus	Jack Titus (54)	Runner Up
1930	Jack Archer	Percy Page	Jos Langdon	Frank Hughes	Alan Geddes	Not Awarded	Jack Titus (50)	4th
1931	Jack Archer	Percy Page	Jos Langdon	Frank Hughes	Maurie Hunter	Not Awarded	Doug Strang (68)	Runner Up
1932	**Barney Herbert**	**John Smith**	**Jos Langdon**	**Frank Hughes**	**Percy Bentley**	**Not Awarded**	**Doug Strang (49)**	**Premiers**
1933	Barney Herbert	John Smith	Jos Langdon	Bill Schmidt	Percy Bentley	Not Awarded	Doug Strang (51)	R/U
1934	**Barney Herbert**	**John Smith**	**Jos Langdon**	**Percy Bentley**	**Percy Bentley**	**Ray Martin**	**Jack Titus (80)**	**Premiers**
1935	Barney Herbert	John Smith	Jos Langdon	Percy Bentley	Percy Bentley	Ray Martin	Jack Titus (83)	3rd
1936	Lou Roberts	John Smith	Jos Langdon	Percy Bentley	Percy Bentley	Not Awarded	Jack Titus (83)	5th
1937	Lou Roberts	John Smith	George Smith	Percy Bentley	Percy Bentley	Jack Dyer	Jack Titus (65) Dick Harris (55)	4th
1938	Lou Roberts	John Smith	Charlie Turner	Percy Bentley	Percy Bentley	Jack Dyer	Jack Titus (72)	6th
1939	Barney Herbert	Maurie Sheahan	Charlie Turner	Percy Bentley	Percy Bentley	Jack Dyer	Jack Titus (48)	4th
1940	Harry Dyke	Maurie Fleming	Charlie Turner	Percy Bentley	Percy Bentley	Jack Dyer	Jack Titus (100)	Runner Up
1941	Harry Dyke	Maurie Fleming	Charlie Turner	Jack Dyer	Jack Dyer	Jack Titus	Jack Titus (87)	4th
1942	Harry Dyke	Maurie Fleming	Charlie Turner	Jack Dyer	Jack Dyer	Leo Merrett	Jack Titus (67)	Runner Up
1943	**Harry Dyke**	**Maurie Fleming**	**Charlie Turner**	**Jack Dyer**	**Jack Dyer**	**Ron Durham**	**Dick Harris (63)**	**Premiers**
1944	Harry Dyke	Maurie Fleming	Charlie Turner	Jack Dyer	Jack Dyer	Leo Merrett	Dick Harris (63)	Runner Up
1945	Harry Dyke	Maurie Fleming	Charlie Turner	Jack Dyer	Jack Dyer	Bill Morris	Fred Burge (55)	7th
1946	Harry Dyke	Maurie Fleming	Charlie Turner	Jack Dyer	Jack Dyer	Jack Dyer	Arthur Mooney (49)	5th
1947	Harry Dyke	Maurie Fleming	Jack Smith	Jack Dyer	Jack Dyer	Billy Wilson	Jack Dyer (46)	4th
1948	Harry Dyke	Maurie Fleming	Jack Smith	Jack Dyer	Jack Dyer	Billy Morris	Jack Dyer (64)	5th
1949	Harry Dyke	Maurie Fleming	Jack Smith Bill Quinn	Jack Dyer	Jack Dyer	Geoff Spring	Ray Poulter (51)	6th
1950	Harry Dyke	Maurie Fleming	Bill Quinn	JackDyer	Bill Morris	Bill Morris	Ray Poulter (56)	6th
1951	Harry Dyke	Maurie Fleming	Bill Quinn	Jack Dyer	Bill Morris	Des Rowe Roy Wright	Jack O'Rourke (58)	6th
1952	Harry Dyke	Maurie Fleming Hector Lingwood-Smith	Bill Quinn	Jack Dyer	Des Rowe	Roy Wright	Jack O'Rourke (43)	9th
1953	Harry Dyke	Maurie Fleming	Bill Quinn	Alby Pannam	Des Rowe	Havel Rowe	Ron Branton (22)	10th
1954	Harry Dyke	Maurie Fleming	Bill Quinn	Alby Pannam	Des Rowe	Roy Wright	Ron Branton (33)	5th
1955	Harry Dyke	Hector Lingwood-Smith Bill Tymms	Bill Quinn	Alby Pannam	Des Rowe	Des Rowe	Ray Poulter (49)	6th
1956	Harry Dyke	Bill Tymms	Bill Quinn	Max Oppy	Des Rowe	Laurie Sharp	Bob Dummett (32)	10th
1957	Harry Dyke	Bill Tymms	Bill Quinn	Alan McDonald	Des Rowe	Roy Wright	Bob Dummett (41)	7th
1958	Harry Dyke Maurie Fleming	Bill Tymms	Bill Quinn	Alan McDonald	Roy Wright	Dave Cuzens	Ted Langridge (28)	10th
1959	Maurie Fleming	Bill Tymms	Bill Quinn	Alan McDonald	Roy Wright	Dave Cuzens	Bob Dummett (45)	11th
1960	Maurie Fleming	Bill Tymms	Bill Tymms	Alan McDonald	Ron Branton	Ron Branton	Graeme Wilkinson (21)	12th
1961	Maurie Fleming	Bill Tymms	Bill Tymms	Des Rowe	Ron Branton	Ron Branton	Ted Langridge (29)	10th
1962	Maurie Fleming	Bill Tymms Graeme Richmond	Bill Tymms	Des Rowe	Ron Branton	Ron Branton	Ted Langridge (42)	8th
1963	Maurie Fleming	Graeme Richmond	Bill Tymms	Des Rowe	Neville Crowe	Neville Crowe	Ian Hayden (25)	10th
1964	Ray Dunn	Graeme Richmond	Garry Cameron	Len Smith	Neville Crowe	Neville Crowe	Roger Dean (23)	9th
1965	Ray Dunn	Graeme Richmond	Graeme Richmond	Len Smith Jack Titus	Neville Crowe	Billy Barrot	Mick Erwin (32)	5th

Year	President	Secretary/CEO	Treasurer	Senior Coach	Captain	Best and Fairest	Highest Goal Kicker	Position
1966	Ray Dunn	Graeme Richmond	Ron Carson	Tommy Hafey	Neville Crowe	Neville Crowe	Paddy Guinane (50)	5th
1967	**Ray Dunn**	**Graeme Richmond**	**Ron Carson**	**Tommy Hafey**	**Fred Swift**	**Kevin Bartlett**	**Royce Hart (55)**	**Premiers**
1968	Ray Dunn	Graeme Richmond Alan Schwab	Ron Carson Graeme Richmond	Tommy Hafey	Roger Dean	Kevin Bartlett	Paddy Guinane (41)	5th
1969	**Ray Dunn**	**Alan Schwab**	**Graeme Richmond**	**Tommy Hafey**	**Roger Dean**	**Royce Hart**	**Rex Hunt (55)**	**Premiers**
1970	Ray Dunn	Alan Schwab	Ron Carson	Tommy Hafey	Roger Dean	Francis Bourke	Eric Moore (39)	6th
1971	Ray Dunn Al Boord	Alan Schwab	Pat Kennelly	Tommy Hafey	Roger Dean	Ian Stewart	Royce Hart (59)	3rd
1972	Al Boord	Alan Schwab	Pat Kennelly Alan Schwab	Tommy Hafey	Royce Hart	Royce Hart	Neil Balme (55) Ricky McLean(55)	Runner Up
1973	**Al Boord**	**Alan Schwab**	**Alan Schwab**	**Tommy Hafey**	**Royce Hart**	**Kevin Bartlett**	**Neil Balme (34)**	**Premiers**
1974	**Ian Wilson**	**Alan Schwab**	**Alan Schwab**	**Tommy Hafey**	**Royce Hart**	**Kevin Bartlett**	**Kevin Bartlett (47)**	**Premiers**
1975	Ian Wilson	Alan Schwab	Alan Schwab	Tommy Hafey	Royce Hart	Kevin Morris	Kevin Bartlett (42)	3rd
1976	Ian Wilson	Alan Schwab	Alan Schwab	Tommy Hafey	Francis Bourke	Kevin Sheedy	Robert Lamb (38)	7th
1977	Ian Wilson	Max Scales (General Manager)	Max Scales	Barry Richardson	Francis Bourke	Kevin Bartlett	Kevin Bartlett (55)	4th
1978	Ian Wilson	Gareth Andrews	Gareth Andrews	Barry Richardson	Kevin Sheedy	Geoff Raines	Bruce Monteath (55)	7th
1979	Ian Wilson	Gareth Andrews Richard Doggett	Gareth Andrews Richard Doggett	Tony Jewell	Kevin Bartlett	Barry Rowlings	Michael Roach (90)	8th
1980	**Ian Wilson**	**Richard Doggett**	**Richard Doggett**	**Tony Jewell**	**Bruce Monteath**	**Geoff Raines**	**Michael Roach (112)**	**Premiers**
1981	Ian Wilson	Kevin Dixon	Ron Carson	Tony Jewell	Bryan Wood	Geoff Raines	Michael Roach (86)	7th
1982	Ian Wilson	Kevin Dixon	Ron Carson	Francis Bourke	David Cloke	Maurice Rioli	Brian Taylor (71)	Runner Up
1983	Ian Wilson	Kevin Dixon	Ron Carson	Francis Bourke	Barry Rowlings	Maurice Rioli	Michael Roach (37)	10th
1984	Ian Wilson	Kevin Dixon	Ron Carson	Mike Patterson	Barry Rowlings	Mark Lee	Brian Taylor (61)	8th
1985	Ian Wilson Barry Richardson	Kevin Dixon	John McCormack	Paul Sproule	Mark Lee	Trevor Poole	Michael Roach (86)	8th
1986	Bill Durham	Kevin Dixon Richard Doggett	John McCormack Michael Humphris	Tony Jewell	Mark Lee	Dale Weightman	Michael Roach (62)	10th
1987	Alan Bond Neville Crowe	Richard Doggett	Michael Humphris	Tony Jewell	Mark Lee	Dale Weightman	Michael Roach (43)	14th
1988	Neville Crowe	Richard Doggett Cameron Schwab	Michael Humphris	Kevin Bartlett	Dale Weightman	Michael Pickering	Jeff Hogg (57)	10th
1989	Neville Crowe	Cameron Schwab	Michael Humphris	Kevin Bartlett	Dale Weightman	Tony Free	Jeff Hogg (34)	14th
1990	Neville Crowe	Cameron Schwab	Michael Humphris	Kevin Bartlett	Dale Weightman	Matthew Knights	Stephen Ryan (28)	11th
1991	Neville Crowe	Cameron Schwab	Keith Miller	Kevin Bartlett	Dale Weightman	Craig Lambert	Jeff Hogg (68)	13th
1992	Neville Crowe	Cameron Schwab	Keith Miller	Allan Jeans	Dale Weightman	Matthe Knights	Jeff Hogg (45)	13th
1993	Neville Crowe	Cameron Schwab	Keith Miller	John Northey	Jeff Hogg	Tony Free	Jeff Hogg (57)	14th
1994	Leon Daphne	Cameron Schwab Jim Malone	Keith Miller	John Northey	Tony Free	Chris Bond	Matthew Richardson (56)	9th
1995	Leon Daphne	Jim Malone	Keith Miller	John Northey	Tony Free	Wayne Campbell	Nick Daffy (45)	4th
1996	Leon Daphne	Jim Malone	Keith Miller	Robert Walls	Tony Free	Paul Broderick	Matthew Richardson (91)	9th
1997	Leon Daphne	Jim Malone	Keith Miller	Robert Walls Jeff Gieschen	Matthew Knights	Wayne Campbell	Matthew Richardson (47)	13th
1998	Leon Daphne	Jim Malone	Keith Miller	Jeff Gieschen	Matthew Knights	Nick Daffy	Matthew Richardson (55)	9th
1999	Leon Daphne	Jim Malone	Terry Grigg	Jeff Gieschen	Matthew Knights	Wayne Campbell	Matthew Richardson (67)	12th
2000	Clinton Casey	Mark Brayshaw	Garry Cameron	Danny Frawley	Matthew Knights	Andrew Kellaway	Matthew Rogers (37)	9th
2001	Clinton Casey	Mark Brayshaw	Garry Cameron	Danny Frawley	Wayne Campbell	Darren Gaspar	Matthew Richardson (59)	3rd
2002	Clinton Casey	Mark Brayshaw	Garry Cameron	Danny Frawley	Wayne Campbell	Wayne Campbell	Matthew Richardson (36)	14th
2003	Clinton Casey	Ian Campbell	Garry Cameron	Danny Frawley	Wayne Campbell	Mark Coughlan	Matthew Richardson (33)	13th
2004	Clinton Casey	Ian Campbell Steven Wright	Garry Cameron	Danny Frawley	Wayne Cambell	Joel Bowden	Matthew Richardson (65)	16th
2005	Clinton Casey	Steven Wright	Garry Cameron	Terry Wallace	Kane Johnson	Joel Bowden	Matthew Richardson (65)	12th
2006	Gary March	Steven Wright	Garry Cameron	Terry Wallace	Kane Johnson	Kane Johnson	Matthew Richardson (45)	9th
2007	Gary March	Steven Wright	Garry Cameron	Terry Wallace	Kane Johnson	Matthew Richardson	Matthew Richardson (53)	16th
2008	Gary March	Steven Wright	Garry Cameron	Terry Wallace	Kane Johnson	Brett Deledio	Matthew Richardson (48)	9th
2009	Gary March	Steven Wright Brendon Gale	Garry Cameron	Terry Wallace/ Jade Rawlings	Chris Newman	Brett Deledio	Mitch Morton (41)	15th
2010	Gary March	Brendon Gale	Robert Dalton	Damien Hardwick	Chris Newman	Jack Riewoldt	Jack Riewoldt (78)	15th
2011	Gary March	Brendon Gale	Robert Dalton	Damien Hardwick	Chris Newman	Trent Cotchin	Jack Riewoldt (62)	12th
2012	Gary March	Brendon Gale	Robert Dalton	Damien Hardiwck	Chris Newman	Trent Cotchin	Jack Riewoldt (65)	12th
2013	Gary March	Brendon Gale	Robert Dalton	Damien Hardiwck	Trent Cotchin	Daniel Jackson	Jack Riewoldt (58)	5th
2014	Peggy O'Neal	Brendon Gale	Robert Dalton	Damien Hardiwck	Trent Cotchin	Trent Cotchin	Jack Riewoldt (61)	8th
2015	Peggy O'Neal	Brendon Gale	Robert Dalton	Damien Hardiwck	Trent Cotchin	Alex Rance	Jack Riewoldt (54)	5th
2016	Peggy O'Neal	Brendon Gale	Robert Dalton	Damien Hardiwck	Trent Cotchin	Dustin Martin	Jack Riewoldt (48)	13th
2017	**Peggy O'Neal**	**Brendon Gale**	**Robert Dalton**	**Damien Hardiwck**	**Trent Cotchin**	**Dustin Martin**	**Jack Riewoldt (54)**	**Premiers**
2018	Peggy O'Neal	Brendon Gale	Robert Dalton	Damien Hardiwck	Trent Cotchin	Jack Riewoldt	Jack Riewoldt (70)	1st

The VFA Era 1885-1907

*** Indicates playing career continued into the Victorian Football League.**

Richmond's first-ever VFA premiership team photo—in 1902. At centre is captain Alec Edmond, flanked by president George Bennett (left), and secretary George Peckham-Beachcroft (right).

Name	Played
A	
J. Ackman	1885
Adams	1885
James John Allander	1896
Frederick 'Socky' Alsop	1893-1895
Charles Alves	1901
Marty Anderson	1900
Armstrong	1886
William Henry Arnott	1893
Aspinwall	1892
B	
Charles Roger Backhouse	1891 -05
George Edward Backhouse	1897-01
William Bateman Backhouse	1891
Christopher Simon Bahen	1893, 94-02
John Bahen	1893
Baker	1891
Baker	1897-99
G. Bambrook	1899-00
Arthur Banner	1887-1890
A.Barker	1904
Albert William 'Buster' Barling	1904
Thomas Henry Barmby	1894
Barnard	1886
Barnett	1886
Walter Robert Bartholomew	1907
Bartlett	1886
William Thomas Bassell	1890
Batters	1885
J.Baylis	1907
Baxter	1894
Richard "Dicky" Beaman	1895
Alfred Beck	1907
Beckwith	1886
Bell	1899
William Edwin Bennion	1906-07
Berrigan	1897
Percy. J Beswick	1905
John Thomas Blakeley	1890-92
William Ranger Blazey	1886
Con Bourke	1894-96
William Bourke*	1906-07
Robert Emmett Bowden*	1906-07
Bownas	1896
George William Bownas	1902-07
Boyd	1885
Boyd	1887
John Thomas "Tom" Box	1886
J. Boxhall	1905
Henry "Harry" Branbrook	1896
Francis Patrick 'Bux' Bray	1893
Arthur 'Snowy' Brennan	1896-97, 04-05
Brennock	1892
Brew	1892
Brown	1899
William 'Billy' Foster Brown	1888-1889,1891
E. 'Ted' E. Brown	1905, 07
F Browne	1886
Bruce	1893
A. Bullin	1904
J. Burhop	1896
Edwin William 'Ned' Burwood	1886-1890
Herbert Alfred Burwood	1890
Byrne	1885
C	
William "Billy" J. Carroll	1886
William 'Barlow Carkeek	1899-01, 05-07
Tom Carter	1893
Jack Cathie	1900-03
Alfred Ernest Catlin	1903-05
J 'Pus'Catt/ Catte	1891, 94-95
Doug Chapman*	1907
Percy "Shakespeare" Chapman	1892
George Thomas Cheswass	1905
H Christie	1885- 1886
Clark	1890
Arthur Cleghorn	1904-06
H. 'Clinker' Clarke	1890
Jesse William "Billy" Clarke	1896-01, 05
Clements	1886
D Coleman	1888
Coles	1885
Jim Coles	1888-1893
A. Collins	1891-92
Daniel Charles 'Artillery' Collins	1891
Comport	1896
John "Jack "Conlon	1885
J Connelly	1894
James "Jim" Constable	1889
A. Cooper	1901
Cordian	1898
William Charles 'Corney' Cornigo	1893-96
G. Cornish	1900
Andrew "Andy" Creighton	1891
Cresswell	1891
Francis "Frank" Joseph Crohan	1885
Joseph Charles Crowley	1892
Cunningham	1898
Curtain	1899
Charlie Curtis	1901
D	
Daly	1897
Daley	1891
Dalton	1904
Michael Daly	1891
John "Jack". H. Davie	1903
Alfred Charles 'Chook' Davidson	1899-02

Name	Played
A. Joseph "Joe" Davis	1889-1891, 1893
Tate Davis	1894-95
Tom Deane	1890-95
F. Deathbridge	1893
Destree	1895
Harry 'Charles' Dickens	1890, 92-93
Alfred 'Peggy' Digby	1893-94
James 'Jim' Digby	1892-93
Joseph "Joe" Doble	1891
James "Jimmy" Gordon Dobson	1895-97
Docherty	1886
Donnelly	1899
James Melbourne Douglas	1901-02
James "Jimmy" Matthew George 'Tracker' Dowdall	1893-94
Downie	1897
Du Feu	1897
Duby	1892
Jas. Duff	1899
C. Duffield	1885
Ernie Dunn	1890
G. Dunne	1887-1888, 1890-93
Roland Duncan	1902-04
Dwyer	1893

E

A. Eddy	1899
Alexander 'Alec' James Edmond	1899-07
H. 'Bruce' Douglas Edmond	1904
Jack Edmonds	1900
Edwards	1890
Edwards	1899
Edwards	1906
Frederick John Ecclestone	1892, 94
Alfred "Alf" John 'Punch' Elder	1888, 1890-99
David "Dave" Elder	1885-1887
George Henry "Harry" "Jelly" Eldridge	1887-1888, 1890
William 'Billy' Ellis	1893
E. Evans	1904
L. Evans	1901

F

J. Fairbanks	1904
Ernest John 'Jack' Fayle	1904
Vincent William Fayle	1904-06
Henry Edgar "Son" Feore	1904-05
Richard Fiddes	1896
William Ernest Fildes	1906-07
Fisher	1899
J Flynn	1895
Stanley Ford	1895
Fox	1892
W. Frame	1894

G

Gardiner	1906
Tom Gault	1900-03
Stewart Drummond Geddes	1904
Edward 'Ted' Geggie	1903
Jack Geggie	1906
Gibb	1887
Percy Gibb	1902-03
Peter Gibney	1902
Alfred Gibson	1894-95
George Gibson	1907*
John Foster Gilding	1907
William 'Billy' Giles	1899-00
J. Glynn	1900
Good	1885
Percy Alfred Goode	1892-94
Benjamin James Goodwin	1892
Gorman	1886
Graham	1888
J. Graham	1885
Thomas "Tom" Graham	1885-1886, 1890-91
Grandison	1891
Grainger	1894
Gregory	1885
W. Green	1904
Grogan	1891

Name	Played
George "Snowy" Griffiths	1889-1890
Charles Guest	1905
Guthrie	1889

H

Clarrie Hall*	1907
E. "Ted" 'Joker' Hall	1903
Joseph "Joe" Hall	1889
Hanley	1891
M Hannan	1906
Hard	1897
F. Hart	1903
John "Jack" F Hardiman*	1906-07
Timothy Patrick Hardiman	1898-00, 02
K. Hardy	1902
Norman Harper	1885-1887
Harris	1890, 1892, 1897-98
J. 'Cocky' Harris	1895-97
Harrison	1886
Alf Hassett	1904
B. Hay	1901
J. Hayes	1895-98
Tom Heaney*	1906-07
Henderson	1906
William "Billy" Tulloch Hendrie	1905-06
Bert Heusker	1905
Alfred "Alf" Hill	1885-1890, 96
Herbert Hill*	1905-07
Matt Honey	1892
Hooper	1890
Hopkins	1894
Tommy Horan	1888
Sam Hore	1904-05
D. Hourigan	1895
Frank House	1888
E Howard	1894, 99
Patrick Howard	1893
Tim 'Hookey' 'Holiday' Howard	1894-97
George Howarth	1885-1888
Charles. Wyatt Hudd	1904
George "Jack" Hughes	1888-1890
W. Hughes	1901
A. Hunter	1892, 1894
Hunter	1892
Hunter	1907
John "Jack" Hutchinson	1904-07
Hynes	1897
J. Hynes	1904
Len Incigneri*	1907
Inman	1899

J

Henry 'Harry' Jackman	1885-1886
Jackson	1897
Johns	1907
George Sydney 'Mallee' Johnson	1901-04
Jones	1894-95
J. Jones	1907
Julius	1893
Henry 'Ernie' Justins	1902-04
Joseph "Joe" Justins	1901-03

K

F. Kane	1899, 1901
Jack Kearns	1900
George Keenan	1906
Kelly	1888
Richard Terence Kelly	1895-97
Sam Kelso	1885-1886
Kemp	1889-90, 1892
E. D. Kenney	1907
Edward Thomas Kenny	1903-04
Michael Kiely	1896
W. "Barber" Kight	1895-96
M. Kight	1896
J. Kilmartin	1889-1890, 94-95
Kilner	1893
Frank King	1901
Richard Joseph Knell	1905-06

L

Name	Played
William L 'Billy' Laffin	1892-93
Lane	1905
Bill Lan Franchi*	1905-07
Langdon	1889
Lawrence	1897
Layton	1891
Harry Layton	1885-1886, 1891
Charles Layton	1885
Edward "Ted" Hale Leach	1905-07
Lee	1887
W. Leaver	1890
P. Leiven	1897-98
Lempriere	1889
'Checker' Le Fevre	1893-94
Ley	1892
Austin William "Goosey" Lewis	1890
Lewis	1895-99
Lewis	1906
Leyton	1891
Robert "Bert" Joseph Lithgow	1905
George Locke	1890-92
F. Lord	1894
Jim Loriot	1896
A. 'Dodger' Lott	1900-01
Lovell	1899
Lucas	1894-95
James Luff	1905
William Luff*	1905-7
Lyons	1898
Reginald Horace "Horrie" Lyons	1903
T. "Tiger" Lyons	1889

M

Mace	1897
R MacLeod	1888
William Mahoney	1906-07*
Main	1886
Ernest Edward Main	1902
John "Jack" Alfred Main	1902-04
T. Main	1899
Manning	1902
Rupert Manzie	1903-04
John "Jack" Marmo	1892
Marsh	1906
Len Martin	1905, 07
George Martin	1891
J. Martin	1899
S. Martin	1887
Matthes	1903
McAuley	1895
J. McCall	1900
William George Greenwood McCance	1902-03
McCart	1898
McCroft	1900
Ernest McDonald*	1902, 04-07*
J.McDonald	1886
R. McDonald	1902
McEvoy	1897
McFadzen	1895
McFarlane	1895, 97
J. McGuiness	1896
M. McGuire	1899
Phillip McGuire	1898, 1901
McIntosh	1896
Denis D 'Dinny' McKay	1892-93
William 'Ollie' McKelson	1905
William Thomas McLaverty	1891-93
H. Manderson	1901
Martin	1901
C. McGeorge	1901
McLean	1896
George McLeod	1888-1889
M. F. McMeikan	1892-93
Archibald McIndoe 'Tiny' McNair	1900-04
McNamara	1905
J. McNamara	1895
McPhee	1889
P. McSweeney	1889-1890, 1892
Mead	1892
Jack Verner Alexander Megson*	1905-07*

Name	Played
Miller	1892
G. Mills	1906
Hector Norman Milne	1899 -00
J. Minnock	1887
Mitchell	1885
Mitchell	1891
Mitchell	1899
Henry Mitchell	1893-94
Rodger 'Ringer' Mitchell	1893
Moloney	1888
Moore	1890
William Arthur "Arty" Morehouse	1890
George Henry Morrison	1895-96
Herbert William Morton	1887-1889
John "Jack" Morton	1894
W. Mudge	1900-01
James Mullally	1885-1886
T.Murphy	1903
Walter Murray	1889
P. Murray	1905

N

Name	Played
William 'Bill' Thomas Newton	1895
Hector Norman	1904
Nowell	1885
Chris Nuttall	1887

O

Name	Played
O'Brien	1906
John William "Dodger" O'Connor	1892-93
O'Flaherty	1904
J. O'Grady	1895
O'Halloran	1895-96
James Patrick O'Halloran	1890-92
J. W. O'Keefe	1906-07
Patrick 'Toots' O'Laughlin	1887-1892
Jimmy O'Meara	1893-96
Edward 'Ted' James 'Janey' O'Neill	1900
John "Jack" O'Neil	1892
O'Shannassy	1899
A. O'Shannessey	1885
O'Shea	1885
Thomas O'Shea	1900
John "Jack" Orr	1889, 1894
Osborne	1895-96
Charles Edward Over	1886-1887
Fred Owen	1886
H. Owens	1905
Richard 'Dick' Owen	1885-1887

P

Name	Played
Charlie Pannam*	1907
Norman Fricand Pannam	1907
James Hewitt. 'Charcoal' Parker	1891-00
Patterson	1891
Patterson	1898
Perry	1897
Jim Paternoster	1897-99
Richard Francis Pirrie	1901-02
Franklyn Pitcher	1897
S. Pitcher	1897
Alfred Edward "Snowy" Pontin	1891, 1893, 1900
Mark Pope	1899
Porter	1894
Porter	1904
Arthur Griffiths 'Bolivar' Powell	1886, 1888, 1892, 97
J. Powell	1900
A. Power	1892,94
John Power	1896
Pratt	1896
Price	1888
Price	1899
Tom Price	1893-95
William "Billy" George Prince	1898-00
J. "Pik" Paddy Purcell	1885-1886

Q

Name	Played
Arthur Owen 'Ginger' Quinn	1898

R

Name	Played
'Tot' Reddan	1887-1889
Reid	1894
W. Read	1890
Relly	1897-98
H. Archie 'Pony' Richardson	1902-04
Charlie Ricketts*	1904-05
Claude Henry "Harry" Rigby	1905-06
G. Reilly	1896
Robertson	1894
T. Robinson	1886
Robson	1896-97
Artie. H Robson	1903
Edward 'Ted' Rodgers	1895
Rose	1885
Rose	1891
G. Rose	1895
Rowe	1887
Royal	1896
Alfred Ernest "Ernie" Henry Rudd	1896, 98-04
H. Rudd	1899
Ruddard	1898
Ernie Rudduck	1904-06
William Rushton	1885
Russell	1890
Rutherford	1886
Ryan	1885
Ryan	1889
Edward 'Ted' Ryan	1893
J. Ryan	1893
Thomas Ryan	1895-97

S

Name	Played
H. Sandilands	1900
Salmon	1886
Alexander Salton	1886-1889, 1892
Louis William "Billy" Schmidt	1907*
Scoonie	1898
Scotal	1904
Scott	1893
Alfred "Alf" Samuel Searle	1885-1890, 1893
Herbert Serle	1899
Edward "Ted" Serong	1895
Seymor	1896
Joseph Patterson Shand	1885-1886
A. Shannon	1893-94
Sheahan	1907
Sheppard	1894
James John 'Jimmy' Shore	1885, 1888, 1890-91, 1893-94
C. Sibly	1898, 1901
Fred Sigmont	1901
Simmons	1887
Jack Sinclair	1892-94
Simpson	1887
G Simpson	1894-95
John "Jack" Sinclair	1892-94
W Sinclair	1894
Slattery	1891
Denny Sloss	1900
Smale	1904
T. Smart	1885
Smith	1895
D. Smith	1886
D. P. Smith	1887
George 'Geordie' J. Smith	1885- 1888, 1890
Smith	1897
J. Smith	1887
J. Smith	1891
John "Jack" Laurence Emery Smith	1905-06
T Smith	1886
W. Smith	1886/87
Snell	1898
J. Snow	1897-98, 1901
Joseph "Joe" Henry Mason 'Soda' Soderstrom	1893, 95
Soutar	1885
George Stephen 'Sugar' Sparrow	1891-96
Rupert "Rupe" Anderson Speary	1892
Charlie Stephens	1885-1890
Stevens	1897
W. Stephenson	1896-98
John "Jack" James 'Bosco' Stewart	1885-1893, 95
William 'Ginger' 'Fatty' Stewart	1887-1893, 95, 97
Alfred Edwin Stokes	1891
Sullivan	1905
Thomas John Sweeney	1896
John Maguire Swift	1899-00
Walter "Wally" Frederick Victor Sykes	1905-06
Christopher Rees Syle	1885-1891

T

Name	Played
John "Jack" Tait	1899-00
Charles Fishy' Taylor	1894-96,98-02
John 'Jack' Taylor	1885-1886
Thomas	1904
M. Talbot	1906
Taylor	1890-91
Dudley George Tong	1906
Harry Thomson	1888-1891
S. Taylor	1901
E. Tootell	1904
Trengrove	1889
Harry Trowbridge	1888-1889
Turnbull	1896
Frederick Phipps Walter Turnbull	1907
F. Turner	1907

V

Name	Played
Ernest Robert Charles Vollugi	1901, 1900

W

Name	Played
Edward 'Ted'. Wade	1903
J. Waller	1887
Walker	1903
Walton	1885
Walton	1894
John "Jack" A Warren	1889
Watkins	1885
Watkins	1901
Watson	1886
Watson	1895-96
Dave Watson	1898-02
Joe Watson	1898-99
Thomas 'Tom' Watson	1897-01, 03
William Watson	1898
Weaver	1896
William "Billy" Wells	1885
Weston	1904
Whelan	1885
Wheeler	1896
Wilcox	1899
Wild	1891
C. Williams	1898
Charlie Williams	1902-07*
Eddie Williams	1905
Edward Hugh Williams	1892-94, 98-99
P. Williams	1898
S.Williams	1904
Thomas "Tom" James 'Tiny' Williams	1898-99, 04-06
Percy Willmott	1903
Wilson	1902
Richard "Dick" Wilson	1896
S. Wilson	1897
T. Wilson	1898-99,
William "Billy" Wilson	1891-92
Harry Windley	1894
Wiseman	1897
Frederick William Wookey	1885-1887, 1889
T. Warman	1901
Wright	1888
John Wright	1901
Wrigley	1896
Wulff	1896

Y

Name	Played
Joseph Edgar Youlden	1907
Tom Young	1904

Z

Name	Played
Zimmerman	1896

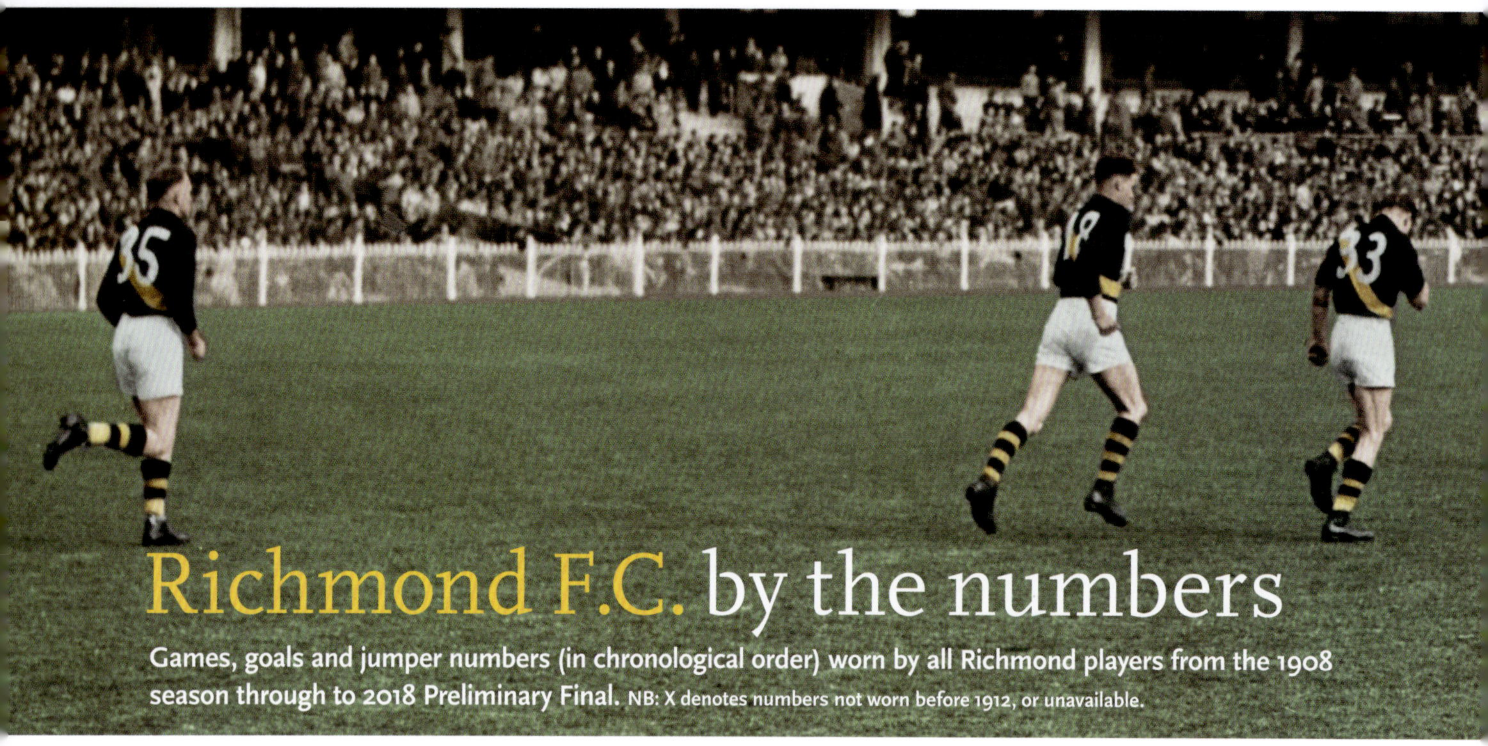

Richmond F.C. by the numbers

Games, goals and jumper numbers (in chronological order) worn by all Richmond players from the 1908 season through to 2018 Preliminary Final. NB: X denotes numbers not worn before 1912, or unavailable.

Name	Played	Games	Goals	No.
A				
Les Abbott	1910-11	31	0	x
Paddy Abbott	1919-20	18	1	5
Geoff Ablett	1983-84	16	12	4
Kevin Ablett	1984	5	0	36
Len Ablett	1939-43	70	5	3
Ken Albiston	1946-51	58	76	8
Bill Albress	1917-18	8	6	28
Fred Alder	1909	1	1	x
Harry Alessio	1915-19	38	34	24
Bert Allen	1912	2	3	20
Tom Allen	1949-52	22	8	13, 18
Grant Allford	1971-73	30	1	42
Ray Allsopp	1955-59	54	69	32
Bill Amery	1915	4	0	9
Les Amery	1956	4	2	31
Alby Anderson	1926	4	0	26
Bernie Anderson	1959-60	3	2	39
Charlie Anderson	1926	3	0	10
Jack Y. Anderson	1932-33	9	2	19
Noel Anderson	1959-60	12	0	38
Gareth Andrews	1974-75	31	1	5
Gordon Andrews	1956	1	0	36
John Annear	1984-86	65	43	5
Jack Arbrew	1913-14	10	0	23
Gary Arnold	1963-64	13	7	28
Matthew Arnot	2013-2015	9	5	44
David Astbury	2010-2018	107	8	12
Jack Atkinson	1950	3	5	20
Pat Audas	1952-54	14	7	34
Ted Aumann	1919	7	0	20
Col Austen	1950-52	51	1	16
B				
Jack Baggott	1927-35	128	140	14
Frank Bain	1979	2	0	49
Ian Baker	1980	3	0	26
Liam Baker	2018	3	1	48
Reg Baker	1928	10	7	33
Jason Baldwin	1997	2	0	32
Don Balfour	1945-46	8	1	20, 2, 4
Ray Ball	1969-70	12	0	36
Craig Balme	1983	3	0	36
Neil Balme	1970-79	159	229	21
Graham Bamford	1964	1	1	18
Anthony Banik	1990-94	49	0	45, 15
Horrie Bannister	1924	1	0	14
Syd Barker	1908	2	1	x
Tim Barling	1984-85	14	1	43, 15

Name	Played	Games	Goals	No.
Paul Barlow	1988	4	0	48
Bert Barnes	1915-16	3	4	20
Jack Barnett	1924-26	13	11	12, 2
Kevin Barnewall	1945	4	0	28
Sam Barrett	1925	3	1	6
Bill Barrot	1961-70	120	91	24
Wes Barrot	1973-74	3	0	28
Kevin Bartlett	1965-83	403	778	29
Percy Barton	1909	2	0	x
Jake Batchelor	2011-2017	84	4	31, 11
George Bates	1937-39	26	4	4
Bob Bawden	1939-45	107	107	23
Dave Baxter	1934-36	47	53	2
Ray G. Baxter	1925	2	3	30
Gavin Bayes	1985-87	5	2	33
George Bayliss	1914; 1916-23	89	217	2
Daryl Beale	1968	10	0	45
Colin Beard	1969-71	33	0	16
Gerry Beare	1924	2	0	24
Bob Beaven	1961	5	0	50
Bill Beckwith	1971-72	10	8	20
Lance Behan	1962-63	10	0	13
Edo Benetti	1961-62	9	7	9
Charlie Bennie	1912	8	5	22
Don Benson	1945	3	0	29
Percy Bentley	1925-40	263	275	1
Bill Benton	1928-32	56	41	3
Jeff Berry	1978-79	10	0	49
Kevin Betson	1952-55	42	2	5
Artie Bettles	1914-20	73	0	16
Gerald Betts	1974-75	10	0	50
Percy Bice	1944	6	0	8
Craig Biddiscombe	1999-2003	44	7	22
Arthur Birtles	1922	5	5	26
Jack Bisset	1928; 1931	38	9	7
Bruce Blainey	1960	1	0	20
Ray Bloodworth	1955-56	2	0	27
Justin Blumfield	2003-04	19	5	13
Ashley Blurton	1998-99	14	7	24
Brian Boland	1950-54	50	6	9
Martin Bolger	1930-39	185	2	21
Shai Bolton	2017-2018	9	4	29
Chris Bond	1993-97	100	32	45, 35
Graeme Bond	1967-73; 1975-77	115	61	44, 24, 45
Ian Borchard	1976; 1978	5	2	51
Bert Boromeo	1926	14	8	6
Phil Bottams	1978-81	26	4	38

Name	Played	Games	Goals	No.
Allan Bouch	1925	1	0	24
Bill John Bourke	1908-09	32	45	x
David Bourke	1995-97; 1999-2001	85	18	32, 30
Francis W.Bourke	1967-81	300	71	30
Frank M.Bourke	1943; 1946-47	16	48	23
Joe Bourke	1909	2	1	x
Paddy Bourke	1909-11	38	28	x
Ted A.Bourke	1924-26	32	15	29
Bob Bowden	1908-12	83	5	23
Joel Bowden	1996-2007	231	153	11
Michael Bowden	1967-71	59	20	11
Patrick Bowden	2006-07	25	15	16
Sean Bowden	1990-91	6	0	11
Brendan Bower	1986-91	92	19	31
Darren Bower	1987	3	2	37
Nathan Bower	1991-98	74	22	56, 22
Ray Bower	1944-45	13	8	3
Wally Bowtell	1917	1	1	x
Ray Boyanich	1970-72; 1976	66	44	19
Kevin Bradley	1954	6	10	12
Rob Brady	1922-23	2	0	30
Andy Brannan	1942-43	19	29	30
Ron Branton	1953-62	170	171	29
Todd Breman	1992-93	25	24	14
Jim Brennan	1952	2	0	27
Stan Brett	1938	9	5	34
Lloyd Brewer	1953	3	1	21
Ross Brewer	1982-83	6	8	26
Billy Briscoe	1915-18	26	6	13
Jack Bristow	1913	5	0	28
Nathan Broad	2016-2018	30	0	35
Jack Broadstock	1943-46	33	23	24
Paul Broderick	1994-2001	169	90	17
Alby Broman	1937-39	7	0	23, 33
Norm Brooker	1911	3	0	x
Keith Brooks	1941	7	0	21
Barrie Brown	1952	2	0	26
Billy Brown	1963-71	130	124	40
Mal Brown	1974	14	25	18
Nathan G.Brown	2004-06	47	86	7
Andrew L. Browne	2009-11	12	2	43, 34
Bob Brownhill	1963	4	0	52
Herbie H.Brunning	1923-24	2	0	8
Paul Bulluss	1993-98	97	20	21
Jim Burchill	1918	3	5	27
Fred Burge	1942-50	118	105	8, 10

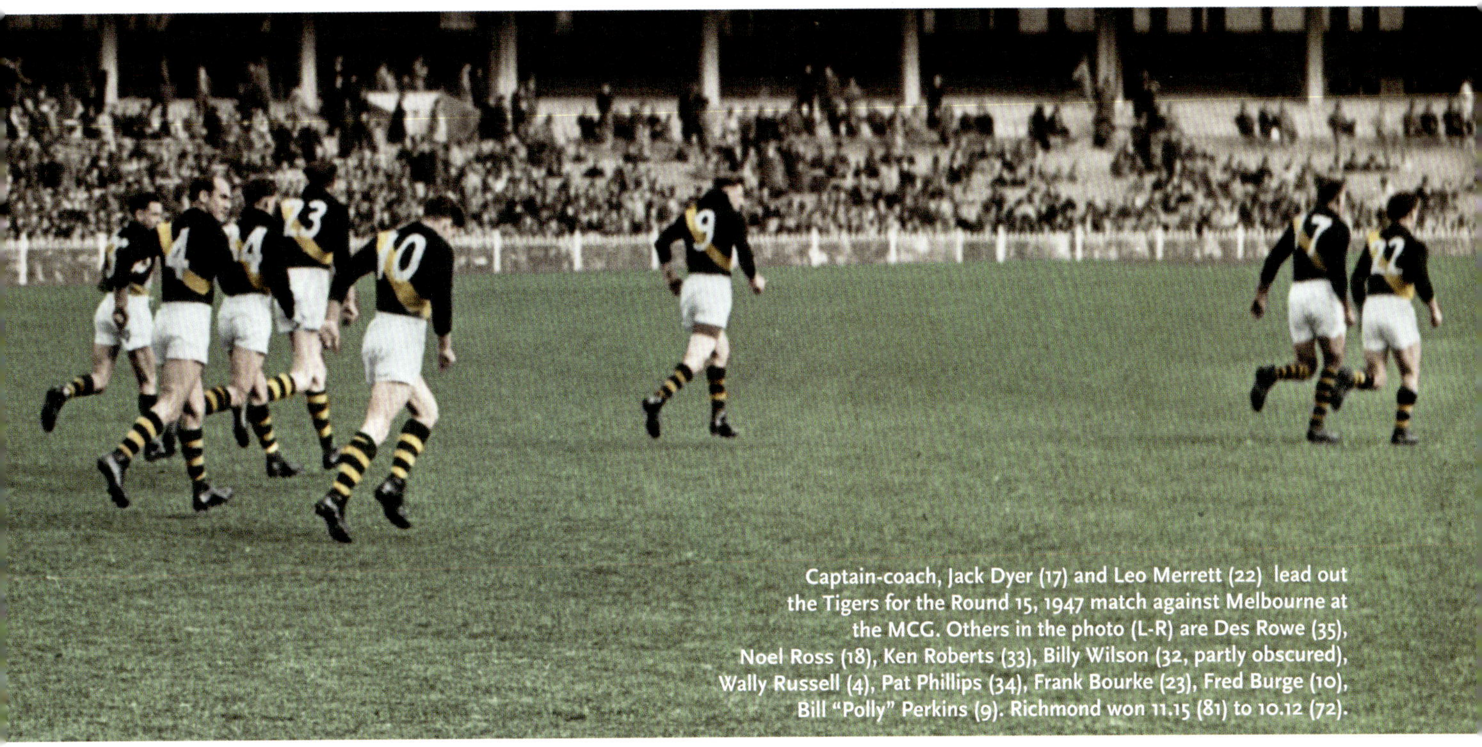

Captain-coach, Jack Dyer (17) and Leo Merrett (22) lead out the Tigers for the Round 15, 1947 match against Melbourne at the MCG. Others in the photo (L-R) are Des Rowe (35), Noel Ross (18), Ken Roberts (33), Billy Wilson (32, partly obscured), Wally Russell (4), Pat Phillips (34), Frank Bourke (23), Fred Burge (10), Bill "Polly" Perkins (9). Richmond won 11.15 (81) to 10.12 (72).

Name	Played	Games	Goals	No.
Graham Burgin	1965-71	60	0	44, 27
Jack Burgmann	1938	1	0	11
Cyril Burke	1926	2	2	28
Leo Burke	1915-19	36	0	10
Peter Burke	1987	2	0	41
Bill Burns	1908-09; 1912-13; 1916	54	10	7
Dick Burrows	1961	5	0	33
Chris Burton	1985-88	50	8	2
Harry Burton	1910	3	1	x
Neil Busse	1964-67	37	9	16
Dan Butler	2017-2018	38	48	40
David Buttifant	1987	2	0	42
C				
Josh Caddy	2017-2018	44	67	22
Laurie Cahill	1943	7	4	10
Kevin Callander	1961-62	7	1	14
Des Calverley	1946-47	18	1	19
Barry Cameron	1959-66	96	21	30
Leon Cameron	2000-03	84	40	15
Blair Campbell	1966; 1968	8	12	35
Wayne Campbell	1991-2005	297	172	46, 9, 17
Bobby Carew	1919-22	45	6	8
Bill Carrick	1956	5	5	5
Ernest Carter	1910	1	0	x
Noel Carter	1973-77	50	55	27, 7
Tristan Cartledge	2008	2	1	38
Stuart Cartwright	1945	7	0	26
Jason Castagna	2016-2018	52	54	46
Allan Cations	1952-57; 1959	104	8	33
John Caulfield	1963	9	0	53
Mark Chaffey	1997-2006	166	34	40, 6
Eric Chalmers	1924	6	4	23
Troy Chaplin	2013-2016	75	5	25
Doug Chapman	1908-09	23	5	x
Justin Charles	1995-98	55	38	15
Dick Chirgwin	1934-39	64	4	29, 13
John Chivers	1965	2	0	7
Mabior Chol	2016	1	0	41
George Clark	1922	1	0	14
Simon Clark	1986-88	27	6	42, 18
Doug Clarke	1958-59	8	7	41
Fred Clarke	1951-53	21	0	17
Leo Clarke	1949	3	0	23
John Claxton	1955-56	15	18	34
Dick Clay	1966-76	213	80	8
Cameron Clayton	1974-77	57	20	43, 26
Bill Clements	1957-59	14	2	24
Bob Clifford	1958	12	1	9
David Cloke	1974-82; 1990-91	219	272	33, 16
Peter Cloke	1970-73	28	4	41
Jack Coles	1909	3	2	x
Andrew D. Collins	2009-10	25	23	42, 24
Denis Collins	1980	17	2	28
Gerald Collins	1952-53	12	6	27
Hope Collins	1930	1	1	19
Ted Collinson	1932	4	1	10
Will Collopy	1916	1	0	17
Kevin Colls	1942; 1946-47	8	0	5, 27, 3
Reece Conca	2011-2018	104	23	30
Dick Condon	1908-09	32	26	x
Greg Conlan	1983-84	6	3	39
Daniel Connors	2007-12	29	11	39, 19
Matt Connors	1922-23	6	3	24
Craig Considine	1979	7	1	39
Fred G.Cook	1944-49	80	11	7
Keith Cook	1944-46	26	1	12
Wally Cook	1947	4	0	13
Allan Cooke	1949-58	116	54	7
Sam Cooke	1909	3	2	x
Kevin Coppock	1953	2	0	30
Joe Corfield	1926	5	0	14
Bill Cosgrove	1940	3	0	21
Trent Cotchin	2008-2018	220	123	9
Jack Cotter	1935-41	105	0	15
Mark Coughlan	2001-07	83	37	24
Darryl Cowie	1986-87	7	1	26
Graham Cox	1952-56	32	15	37, 36, 9
Lance Cox	1954-55	7	0	25, 36
Ian Craig	1970-71	5	0	54
Jack Crane	1937-42	102	25	18
Fred Crapper	1936	2	0	18
Tom Crebbin	1985	7	3	48
Kevin Crohan	1942	1	0	8
Jack Cronk	1914-17	23	11	21
Andrew Cross	1986	1	0	55
Neville Crowe	1957-67	150	84	5
Vin Crowe	1964	1	1	51
Jack Culhane	1925	1	0	12
Daryl Cumming	1971-76	88	64	1
Claude Cummings	1938	1	0	35
Tom Cunningham	1931	2	2	31
Kevin Curran	1943-45	16	28	28
Pat Curran	1968	1	0	6
Jack F.Currie	1939	6	0	25
John C.Currie	1952	3	1	10
Max Currie	1947-51	34	17	30
Ted Cusack	1930	2	0	24
Dave Cuzens	1957-61	69	3	4
Peter Czerkaski	1985-90	46	6	28
D				
Nick Daffy	1992-2001	165	181	44, 10
Arthur Danks	1912-15	48	2	23, 25, 24
John D'arcy	1959	5	1	38
Don Davenport	1964-67; 1969; 1971	56	38	41, 19, 23
Pat Davey	1935-36; 1942	10	4	3, 5
Ted Davey	1917	4	1	20
Garry Davidson	1978	10	9	18
Brian Davie	1953-59	89	36	35
Neil Davies	1955	2	1	10
Martin Davis	1956	4	1	37
Alick Davison	1910	8	1	x
Tista De Lorenzo	1958	10	0	6
Matt Dea	2010-2014	31	1	7
Kevin Deagan	1944; 1946	5	3	3, 2
Roger Dean	1957-73	245	204	41, 36, 3
Ron G.Dean	1962	2	1	50
Jim Deane	1954-55	33	17	11
Greg Dear	1994-96	53	9	14
Maurie Deery	1964-65	5	1	34
Brett Deledio	2005-2016	243	182	3
Simon Dennis	1993	2	0	54
Tom Derickx	2012	2	0	39
Ted Derrick	1916	9	6	16
Wilf Dickeson	1965-66	23	0	38
Glenn Dickson	1977-78	11	10	46, 9
Norm Dickson	1936-39	28	25	14
Kevin Dillon	1949-55	88	4	31
Frank Dimattina	1964-68	42	43	43, 32
Renato Dintinosante	1987	2	0	48
Leo Dobrigh	1923	2	0	21
Colin Dobson	1964	1	0	46
Sid Dockendorff	1932-33	13	5	32
Noel Doherty	1943; 1945	8	3	32, 16
Donald Don	1917-28	158	157	17
Daniel Donati	1997	1	0	42
Pat Dooley	1918-19	15	1	21

Name	Played	Games	Goals	No.
Marc Dragicevic	1999-2001; 2003-04	48	25	7, 42
George Driscoll	1914	2	0	27
Frank Drum	1950	2	0	34
Bob Dummett	1954-61	77	199	17, 32, 13
Nathan Drummond	2015-2016	5	2	39
Robert Duncan	1909	1	0	x
Matthew Dundas	1994-95	14	5	2
Frank Dunin	1953; 1955-59	69	30	23
Emmett Dunne	1976-84	115	56	36, 5
Jeff Dunne	1984	1	0	27
Tom Dunne	1929-31	21	1	17, 10
Ron Durham	1943-44; 1946-48	59	0	1
Harry Dwan	1942	1	0	30
Jack Dyer Junior	1960	3	0	17
Jack Dyer Senior	1931-49	312	443	30, 17

E

Name	Played	Games	Goals	No.
Cliff Eade	1954	1	0	21
Jack Eames	1946	14	1	20
Alec Eason	1916	12	8	26
Horrie Edmonds	1934-35	30	20	7
Craig Ednie	2002	7	3	43
Ray Ednie	1950; 1952-53	23	13	23
Aaron Edwards	2013-2014	12	15	27
Allan Edwards	1975-79	66	84	36, 17
Bert Edwards	1938-45	122	22	2
Bill Edwards	1959	2	1	6
Shane Edwards	2007-2018	231	154	10
Stuart Edwards	1992; 1994-96	46	52	18
Phillip Egan	1982-87	125	117	13
John Einsiedel	1978	11	1	1
Simon Eishold	1993	5	0	23
Percy Ellin	1910	1	0	x
Percy Ellingsen	1912	6	5	17
Jamie Elliott	1994-95	9	1	20
Brandon Ellis	2012-2018	153	49	5
Corey Ellis	2015-2018	27	7	32
Frank Ellis	1910	18	0	x
Graeme Ellis	1962	1	0	39
Todd Elton	2012 2015-2017	10	2	43
Ralph Empey	1924-25; 1928-30	49	29	33
Andy Ericksen	1917	1	0	15
Mick Erwin	1965-68	33	37	21
Ty Esler	1991-93	12	0	37
Mark Eustice	1985-88	62	26	4
Brett Evans	1997-2000	28	26	19
Max Evans	1947-48	7	4	6
Rodney Evans	1963-64	11	0	29
Ron J.Evans	1946; 1948-49	26	36	20
Bill Evely	1956; 1958	11	5	40

F

Name	Played	Games	Goals	No.
Horrie C.Farmer	1933	8	14	7
Mitch Farmer	2010-11	28	8	15
Ted Farrell	1911-14	41	2	9
Arthur Fehring	1919	2	0	12
Charlie Fehring	1917-19	21	24	25
Claude Fell	1918	1	0	7
Paul Feltham	1978	7	8	3
John W.Ferguson	1969	7	0	15
Artie Fewster	1919	2	0	23
Jack Fincher	1927-30	69	54	10
Bill Finlayson	1926	2	0	25
Aaron Fiora	2000-04	78	25	14
Reg Fisher	1953	4	2	20
Ted Fisher	1918	4	1	28
Kevin Fitzgerald	1961	1	0	43
Jim Fitzpatrick	1913	7	0	30
Charlie Flannagan	1955-58	26	0	25
Tim Fleming	2003-04	34	10	19
Simon Fletcher	2004	6	0	34
Les Flintoff	1950-52	17	4	29

Name	Played	Games	Goals	No.
Dan Foley	1983-85	13	9	37, 15
Nathan Foley	2005-2014	154	44	41
Bill Ford	1927	1	1	6
Eddie Ford	1942-43	4	0	7
Frank Ford	1931	16	11	24
Bert Foster	1928-36	133	65	11
Laurie Fowler	1971-74	49	7	45, 11
Brad Fox	1993	4	0	42
Arthur Fox Senior	1917-18	5	1	14, 27
Matthew Francis	1990-92; 1994	19	13	46, 13
Peter Francis	1984-86	52	22	7
Gary Frangalas	1986-89	17	2	9
Don J.Fraser	1923-25	18	25	26
Don W.Fraser	1945-52	124	125	21
Les Frauenfelder	1910	2	2	x
Daryl Freame	1977-81	17	5	58, 44
Tony Free	1987-96	133	46	49, 30
Lloyd French	1970-71	3	2	31
Robert Fuller	1984	4	1	26
Ross Funcke	1996-99	27	1	27

G

Name	Played	Games	Goals	No.
Graeme Gahan	1959-66	89	7	10
Murray Gainger	1960	3	0	9
Brendon Gale	1990-2001	244	209	25
Jack Gale	1924	3	0	25
Michael Gale	1994-98	91	20	11, 1
Les Gallagher	1926-29	62	27	23
Ian Gardner	1958-59	10	6	27
Len Gardner	1951	5	0	34
Tom Garland	1963-64	11	1	21
Ryan Garthwaite	2018	2	0	42
Bill Garvie	1934-35	9	0	10
Darren Gaspar	1996-2007	207	22	2
Graham Gaunt	1972; 1976-77	19	8	26, 32
Rex Geard	1952-53	11	0	36
Richard Geary	1985-86	18	10	51, 14
Allan Geddes	1925-35	182	14	8
Bill Gehling	1971	1	0	55
Tim Gepp	1983-85	57	3	10
Len Gibb	1914	1	0	30
Ray Gibb	1952-53	6	1	23
Rupert Gibb	1922	4	0	27
George Gibson	1908-12	70	6	6
Jack Giles	1943	1	0	34
Bob Gislingham	1933	1	1	5
Bob Gleeson	1951	1	1	10
Denis Gleeson	1917-18	22	0	9
Kevin Gleeson	1953	1	0	16
Bruce Godfrey	1910	1	1	x
Dick Godfrey	1917	4	0	30
Fred Goding	1928	9	9	31
Andy Goodwin	1987-91	56	9	43, 24
Nathan Gordon	2014-2015	21	18	39
John Gorwell	1955	9	0	27
David Gourdis	2010-11	4	0	33
Trevor Gowers	1964-66	24	5	6
Angus Graham	2007; 2009-12	48	18	44, 25
Mark Graham	2005	20	2	34
Jack Graham	2017-2018	23	11	34
Allan Granger	1914-15	11	11	25
Geoff Grant	1936-38	21	3	32
Wally Gray	1931-32	3	0	26
Bill A.Green	1953-54	10	0	10
Michael Green	1966-71; 1973-75	146	83	37
Malcolm Greenslade	1971	2	7	26
Bill J.Griffith	1930	1	0	23
Ben Grittiths	2010-2017	63	42	38, 24
Dave Griffiths	1923	10	7	12
Stuart Griffiths	1989; 1991-92	17	14	52
Shaun Grigg	2011-2018	171	86	6
Dylan Grimes	2010-2018	127	3	48, 2
Dick Grimmond	1959-64	102	6	19
Barry Grinter	1978	6	0	28

Name	Played	Games	Goals	No.
Danny Guinane	1934-39; 1942-43	102	1	22
Paddy Guinane	1958-68	146	216	1
Brad Gwilliam	1992	4	0	39

H

Name	Played	Games	Goals	No.
Tom Hafey	1953-58	67	10	18
Clarrie Hall	1912-22; 1924	150	169	22
Ray Hall	1999; 2001-07	99	28	37, 20
Reg Hall	1953-55	26	6	26
Greg Hamilton	1988-90; 1992	29	17	47, 19
Mike Hammond	1964-66	31	10	31
Shaun Hampson	2014-2016	35	6	16
Eddie Hanley	1921	1	0	24
Vin Hannaford	1908	1	0	x
Jack Hardiman	1908	15	5	x
Frank Harley	1915-17; 1919-25	114	66	20, 33, 16
Dick D.Harris	1934-44	196	548	20
Don Harris	1926-30	64	5	2
Stan Harris	1929	4	4	25
Artie C.Harrison	1911	1	0	x
Ben Harrison	1996-2000	74	39	20
Joe H.Harrison	1923-25	19	1	8, 2
Don Hart	1954	5	2	4
Royce Hart	1967-77	187	369	4
Brent Hartigan	2004-07	35	3	33
Bob A.Hay	1942	2	1	5
Ian Hayden	1962-64	30	42	20
Alan Hayes	1959-62	23	10	46, 7
Doug Hayes	1922-28	82	62	20
Gerry Hayes	1936-37	16	3	31
Ben Haynes	2000-01	5	0	38
Tom Heaney	1908-13	56	37	14, 6
Bob Heard	1976-79	54	45	15
Bill Hearn	1935	6	5	18
Arthur Heath	1913	2	1	21
Victor Heath	1917	3	0	28
Reg Hede	1914-21	85	1	6
Fred Heifner	1929-35	100	19	33
Brad Helbig	2011-2013	16	4	32
Bill Henderson	1909	5	1	x
Reg Henderson	1937-38	28	8	8
David Henry	1976	1	0	42
Barney Herbert	1909-12; 1914-21	192	90	1
Ian Herman	1992-93	14	6	36
Wayne Hernaman	1993-94	20	9	11
Glynn Hewitt	1973-74	15	15	19
Robert Hickman	1961-64	18	1	34
Robert Hicks	2010	3	1	45
Jack Higgins	2018	20	15	28
Ern Hill	1909	2	1	x
Herbert Hill	1908-09	24	4	x
Vic Hill	1947	3	1	30
Wally Hillis	1962	3	0	21
Rory Hilton	1999-2005	82	53	1
Joe Hinson	1942; 1944	8	0	1, 27
Gordon Hislop	1923-24	22	0	9
Max Hislop	1917-24; 1927	128	4	29, 6, 19
Tom Hislop	2009-11	20	10	27
Gavin Hoare	1952-53	8	3	38
Alby Hodges	1940	1	0	35
Gerald Hogan	1911-12	4	4	23
Kevin E.Hogan	1952-53	15	10	12
Peter Hogan	1963-66	40	58	23
Jeff Hogg	1986-93	144	306	48, 34
Ben Holland	1996-2003	125	124	16
Ben Hollands	1999	8	5	43
Greg Hollick	1970-72	38	19	57, 18
Colin Holt	1958-59	21	2	21
David Honybun	1988-92	55	39	42
Edmund Hood	1916-19	10	4	26
Max Hood	1949	1	0	11
Frank Horne	1925	2	0	4
Ray Horwood	1950-52	27	26	22
Bachar Houli	2011-2018	159	32	14

Name	Played	Games	Goals	No.
Adam Houlihan	2002-04	33	24	23, 44
Frank Howard	1943; 1948	8	2	10, 28
Cameron Howat	2006-08	21	10	43
John Howat	1993-96	45	2	31
Paul Hudson	2002	3	1	17
Frank Huggard	1919-20; 1922-25	33	2	10, 9, 25
Jack E.Huggard	1925-27	28	43	19, 31
Cleve Hughes	2006-08	16	23	34
Frank Hughes Jnr	1944	3	0	4
Frank Hughes Snr	1914-15; 1919-23	87	51	8, 32, 18
Ian Hull	1936-42; 1945	107	42	27
Jeremy Humm	2006	1	0	42
Jon Hummel	1977-78	9	7	23
Ray Hunt	1943	6	2	16
Rex Hunt	1968-74	113	121	43, 5
Taylor Hunt	2015-2017	42	2	28
Tony Hunt	1972	1	0	23
Maurie Hunter	1929-33	81	159	20
Cliff Hutton	1913	6	1	26
Chris Hyde	2002-08	93	39	31, 43
Steve Hywood	1972	13	0	43

I

Name	Played	Games	Goals	No.
Len Incigneri	1908-11	62	4	x
Matt Incigneri	1911	1	1	x
Ron Irvine	1949-51	14	0	12
Les Irwin	1911	6	0	x

J

Name	Played	Games	Goals	No.
David Jacks	1967	1	0	34
Daniel Jackson	2004-2014	156	61	23
Francis Jackson	1973-74	6	0	34
Stevan Jackson	1992-93	21	30	16
Graeme B.Jacobs	1959-63	50	50	16
Aaron James	1998-2000	30	19	23
Bert James	1947	3	0	6
Billy R.James	1920	1	1	11
Hughie James	1909-16; 1919-23	188	119	15, 4
Jack N.James	1926	16	19	27
Stephen James	1985-90	77	78	40
Sam Jamison	1926-29	5	0	28, 15
Billy Jenkins	1938	3	0	3
John Jenkins	1955-59	34	34	39
Noel Jenkinson	1975-79	57	0	47, 37
Jim Jess	1976-88	223	175	20
Nick Jewell	1997	1	0	39
Tony Jewell	1964-70	80	16	39, 1
Kane Johnson	2003-08	116	32	28, 17
Ron Johnson	1961-62	19	16	22
Alex Johnston	1908	1	0	x
Walter Johnston	1908	1	0	x
Les Jones	1944; 1946-49	59	23	19, 16
Bill Henry Jones Elder	1911-12	19	6	16
Clarrie Jordon	1934-36	15	6	32
Wayne Judd	1969	7	9	38
Stan Judkins	1928-36	133	5	6
Stephen Jurica	1995-97	18	25	23

K

Name	Played	Games	Goals	No.
Jim Karthaus	1920-24	26	2	25, 33, 23, 4
Merv Keane	1972-84	238	36	40, 19, 18
Jim Kearney	1916	7	0	28
Terry Keays	1991-92	25	29	2
Ted Keggin	1912-14; 1917	59	87	18
Darren Keighran	1990	2	0	14
Andrew Kellaway	1998-2006	172	30	39
Duncan Kellaway	1993-2004	180	12	48, 3
Frank John Kelly	1971	2	1	33
Arthur Kemp	1943-46	34	4	5
Vin Kenney	1912	2	0	?
Kim Kershaw	1979-80	5	0	41
Basil Kiernan	1916	2	0	24
Arthur Kight	1923	1	0	15

Name	Played	Games	Goals	No.
Frank Kight	1927-28	3	1	5
Joe Kiker	1909	1	1	x
Clinton King	2000-03	58	10	21
Jake King	2007-2014	107	79	46, 28
Kent Kingsley	2007	3	2	18
Lyster Kirkpatrick	1909	3	0	x
Chris Knights	2013; 2015	6	7	15
Matthew Knights	1988-2002	279	141	33, 29, 54
Trent Knobel	2005-07	21	4	13
Dan Knott	1947	4	0	13
Charlie Kolb	1932	3	1	15
Andrew J.Krakouer	2001-07	102	102	27

L

Name	Played	Games	Goals	No.
Jim Lacey	1910	4	2	x
Michael Laffy	1987-90	26	0	38
Robert Lamb	1973-78	58	120	22
Craig Lambert	1988-93	123	53	53, 4
Kane Lambert	2015-2018	74	43	23
Graeme Landy	1979-86	120	38	34
Bill Lang	1908-09	14	7	x
Ted Langridge	1955-62	94	149	28
Fred Larkin	1908	2	0	x
Trevor Larkins	1985	4	4	27
Peter Laughlin	1977-80	25	46	25, 35
Ivor Lawson	1908-09	32	3	x
Jeff Lawson	1963-64	10	7	51
Les Lee	1913	2	0	12
Mark Lee	1977-91	233	94	41, 1
Eric Leech	1970-79	79	0	25
Ben Lennon	2014-2017	21	10	35
Bruce Lennon	1992-93	28	7	5
Allen Lewis	1944	3	0	3
Brian Leys	1988-94	110	19	54, 26
Brian Lienert	1963-64	2	0	39, 13
Ron Lienert	1964	2	0	36
Dooley Lilburne	1926-29	74	20	16
Tim Livingstone	1992-93	8	1	43
Sam Lloyd	2014-2018	57	69	27
Bob Lockhart	1961-62	13	7	8
Michael Lockman	1983; 1986	4	0	40, 27
Sam Lonergan	2013	2	0	22
Peter Loughran	1959-63	50	6	18
Richard Lounder	1989	4	5	37
Frank Love	1910-14	49	0	4
Noel Lovell	1985-86	4	0	11
Wally Lovett	1983-84	13	6	44
Bill J.Luff	1908-10	39	0	x
Bennie Lunn	1925-26; 1928-29	28	0	4, 19
Alan Lynch	1976	2	1	6
Bill D.Lynch	1912	1	0	27
Dave Lynch	1922-23; 1926-27; 1929	20	77	30, 27, 33, 28

M

Name	Played	Games	Goals	No.
Jim Macbeth	1938	4	0	30
Johnny MacGregor	1911	4	0	x
Geoff MacIlwain	1986	2	0	45
Angus MacIsaac	1922-24; 1926-27	59	20	28, 29, 25, 24
Cedric MacLeod	1923	2	0	24
Norm Madigan	1964	2	0	44
Owen Madigan	1963-66	40	1	11
Leo Maguire	1941-48	96	4	31
Mick Maguire	1910-12	39	62	17
Bill Mahoney	1908-11; 1913-15; 1920	114	53	10
Dave Mahoney	1911	2	1	x
Brett Mahony	1989	2	0	29
Mick Malthouse	1976-83	121	10	28, 7
Matthew Manfield	1997-98	6	2	36
John Manton	1984-89	59	38	38, 11
Allan Maple	1937	3	3	3
Adam Marcon	2016	2	1	44
Addam Maric	2012	10	1	47
Ivan Maric	2012-2016	80	33	20
Oleg Markov	2016-2017	15	3	31

Name	Played	Games	Goals	No.
Ben Marsh	2004	7	1	15
Bill Marshall	1915	3	0	18
Harry Marsham	1916	7	4	27
Alan Martello	1981-83	32	3	15
Des Martin	1942	5	5	10
Dustin Martin	2010-2018	201	218	36, 4
Geoff Martin	1981; 1983	6	3	32, 16
Ray Martin	1930; 1932-40	159	135	27, 7
Percy Martini	1916	10	22	13
Percy Martyn	1913-15	21	50	29, 12
E. Herb Matthews	1915	3	0	13
Don Mattson	1976	7	0	35
Jim Maxfield	1924-25	10	2	21
Stuart Maxfield	1990-95	89	65	27
George F.May	1911	1	0	x
Percy Maybury	1910-19	128	61	3
Harry Maynard	1914	2	0	6
Liam McBean	2015-2016	5	1	34
Graeme McCartney	1957	1	0	19
Frank McCashney	1909-15	82	8	19
Bob McCaskill	1923-25	36	0	25
Jack McConchie	1932-34	16	9	31
Basil McCormack	1925-36	199	1	9
Jack McCormack	1927-29	24	74	21
Peter McCormack	1986	4	0	15
John McCormick	1923	1	0	24
Alan McCrory	1938	5	2	26
Leo McCulloch	1918	3	1	14
Alan McDonald	1939-41; 1943	49	8	10
Ernie McDonald	1908	4	0	x
Jim McDonald	1915	10	12	26
Ron McDonald	1955-60	92	84	14
Matt McDonough	2013-2015	10	1	36
Tom McEwan	1909	2	0	x
Ray McGaw	1956-58	12	0	16
Robert McGhie	1973-78	81	0	12
Ken McGown	1954-56	13	0	12
Marty McGrath	2003	4	6	30
Luke McGuane	2006-2013	105	39	38, 16
Bob McIlveen	1943	6	0	20
George McInnes	1968-70	16	6	20
Kamdyn McIntosh	2015-2018	74	19	33
Norm McIntosh	1920-24	78	3	4
Steven McKee	1998-99	20	1	38
Allan McKellar	1986-90	45	15	57, 47, 12
Craig McKellar	1971-75	96	25	9
Bob McKendry	1914	6	1	25
Michael McKenna	1985	22	10	30
Bill S.McKenzie	1958	4	0	19
Des McKenzie	1968-69	16	0	48
Joe McKenzie	1910	6	1	x
Ricky McLean	1972-74; 1976	39	103	31
George McLear	1914	3	0	21
Mark McLeod	1989	3	0	39
Jordan McMahon	2008-09	34	9	13
Brian McMillan	1962-64	22	6	17
Geoff McMillan	1978-79	11	5	42
Marty McMillan	1972-74	26	13	14
Mark McQueen	1991-94	34	14	28
Jim Meehan	1958	5	2	30
Jack Megson	1908-09	20	3	x
Connor Menadue	2015-2018	33	11	37
Todd Menegola	1991-93	19	13	29
Mark Merenda	1994-2000	75	62	39, 28, 8
Leo Merrett	1940-49	170	53	22
Danny Meyer	2005-07	17	7	22
Brenton Miels	1969-70	7	1	23
Anthony Miles	2014-2018	61	24	26
Ian Miles	1971-72	4	0	48, 35
Keith Millar	1924-27; 1930	37	38	14, 13, 28
Brad J. Miller	2011-12	24	31	13
David Miller	1977	5	7	34
Andrew Mills	2000-03	14	5	34
Dan Minogue	1920-25	94	38	12, 1
Len Mitchell	1957	6	1	21

Name	Played	Games	Goals	No.
Michael Mitchell	1987-91	81	103	7
Dave Moffatt	1912-17; 1919-20	95	25	14
Hugh Moffatt	1921-22	9	2	14
Basil Moloney	1961-63	21	3	32
Bruce Monteath	1975-80	118	198	11
Arthur Mooney	1943-48	66	94	15
Andrew Moore	2016	5	1	15
Ben Moore	1996-99	24	11	28
Eric R.Moore	1966-72	80	94	7
Callum Moore	2016; 2018	8	5	36
Kelvin W.Moore	2004-10, 2012	87	12	40
Vern Moore	1925	4	1	23
Steven Morris	2012-2017	87	12	38
Stan Morcom	1952-58	58	17	22
Fred Morgan	1913-15	31	2	16
Bill Morris	1942; 1944-51	140	98	7, 5
Kevin Morris	1971-76	110	71	38
Mel Morris	1921-26	89	148	11
Peter Morris	1955-60	89	103	38, 13
Stan Morris	1919-22	52	4	9
Steven Morris	2012	15	1	38
Paul Morrish	1986; 1989	4	0	44, 27
Brian Morrison	1960	6	0	41
Paul Morrison	1970	5	2	12
Shane Morrison	2004-05	8	3	16
Terry Morrissey	1964	5	2	42
Mitch Morton	2008-11	59	94	20
Stephen Mount	1979-82	31	9	6
John Mrakov	1991	8	0	39
Noel Mugavin	1982	2	3	35
Hugh Mulcahy	1918	1	0	7
Fred Mundy	1960	6	1	22
Frank Munro	1956-57	13	0	36
Joe Murdoch	1927-36	180	6	13
Justin Murphy	1994-95	12	9	34
Ted Murphy	1968-69	17	1	14
Tony Murphy	1960	3	1	48
Alex Murray	1909	4	1	x
Sel Murray	1945-46	13	50	6
Richard Murrie	1983	8	0	33
N				
Phil Nagle	1941; 1946	15	12	7, 3
Robin Nahas	2009-2013	83	100	38, 26
Chris Naish	1990-97	143	212	6
Vic Naismith	1956-58	31	7	10
Bill Nalder	1972-73	14	5	46
Toby Nankervis	2017-2018	47	18	25
Ben Nason	2010-11	23	17	47, 22
Greg Naylor	1977-80	18	4	43, 13
Mark Neeld	1994-96	26	16	19
Des Negri	1945	2	1	4
Harry Neil	1908-10	31	0	x
George Nelson	1946	2	0	3
Bill Nettlefold	1974-75	15	6	51
Chris Newman	2002-2015	268	56	35, 1, 17
Bill Nicholls	2003-04	10	2	26
Trent Nichols	1988-91; 1997-98	75	65	22
John Nix	1949-56	95	18	1
Richard J.Nixon	1987-90	37	3	36
Bill Nolan	1914-15	30	4	7
Alan Noonan	1977	10	14	9
John Northey	1963-70	118	192	9
Cyril Nott	1921-22	5	1	21
Dean Notting	1985-87	28	17	58
Michael Nugent	1980-81	16	2	37
Michael Nunan	1971	1	3	23
Alan Nutter	1943	1	0	26
O				
Alan Oakley	1928-31	39	24	15
Loyal Oakley	1923	2	0	14
Jarrad Oakley-Nicholls	2006-09	13	1	29, 22
Rod Oborne	1979-81	5	7	23
Cyril O'Brien	1936	9	0	5
Frank O'Brien	1926-28	23	5	25
Ron O'Brien	1961	1	0	47
Maurie O'Connell	1937; 1939-41	34	41	5
Stan O'Connell	1908	5	3	x
George O'Connor	1910-11	3	2	x
Alan O'Donoghue	1912	9	7	8
Steven O'Dwyer	1992	5	0	1
Stan Ogden	1930	1	0	?
George Ogilvie	1920	2	0	24
Tom H.O'Halloran	1925-34	142	120	18
Brett O'Hanlon	2012; 2014	9	2	45
George O'Hehir	1921	1	0	27
Ted Ohlson	1908-15	105	36	2
Les Oliver	1909-13; 1915	50	10	27
Bob O'Neill	1925; 1927-28	19	4	4
Kevin O'Neill	1930-41	209	12	16
Grant Oppy	1970	1	0	41
Max Oppy	1942-54	185	29	30, 33, 14
Ray Orchard	1966-68	8	2	46
Jamie O'Reilly	2010-11	4	0	42
Basil O'Rourke	1951	4	0	25
Jack B.O'Rourke	1949-53	44	134	4
Keith Osmond	1921; 1923-24	12	0	26, 31, 18
Laurie O'Toole	1959-60	13	8	42, 6
Brad Ottens	1998-2004	129	152	5
Roy Outram	1928	4	2	28
Ian Owen	1969-72	33	0	52, 12
P				
David Palm	1983-88	104	38	6
Alby Pannam	1947	2	6	12
Charlie Pannam	1908	14	22	x
Len Park	1962	2	0	41
Gary Parkes	1978-79	7	6	32
Roy Parkin	1926	1	0	5
George Parkinson	1919-21	12	0	23
Steve Parsons	1974	5	1	39
Tony Pastore	1987	1	0	25
Jeff Patterson	1953-54	14	4	25
Michael Patterson	1959-69	152	73	25
Adam Pattison	2005-09	61	15	26
Andy Pattison	1912	1	0	14
Les Patton	1936-37	4	3	28
Gordon Peake	1957-58	6	0	37
Derek Peardon	1968-71	20	1	50, 6
Neil Peart	1983-84; 1986-87	40	9	24
Jack Pemberton	1908	3	0	x
Bill Perkins	1940-49	148	0	9
John Perry	1964-69	26	1	33
Mike Perry	1965-69	53	6	22
Wayne Peters	1988-89	5	1	5
Ricky Petterd	2013-2015	30	17	13
Kayne Pettifer	2001-09	113	132	8, 15
Gus Petzke	1923	2	0	25
P. Len Phillips	1913	4	2	16
Pat Phillips	1947-48	15	3	34
Justin Pickering	1988-91	59	54	52, 2, 9
Michael G.Pickering	1984-91	136	160	35
Brian Pilcher	1957-58	9	2	12
Stephen Pirrie	1982; 1984	11	0	27
John Pitura	1975-77	40	24	3
Mark Pitura	1993	2	0	50
Joe Plant	1925	1	0	26
Justin Plapp	1998-99	18	22	14
Graham Polak	2007-10	38	16	6
Harry Pollock	1923-24; 1926	16	3	27, 4
Dean Polo	2006-10	56	11	14
Trevor Poole	1984-89	99	56	23
Jayden Post	2009-2012	30	6	37
Ray Potter	1945; 1947	2	3	34, 12
Ray Poulter	1946-56	170	351	30, 24
Cyril Powell	1927	6	0	7
Robert Powell	1996-2000	56	53	13
Tim Powell	1988-92	64	40	21
Ezra Poyas	2000-02	9	6	26
Ashley Prescott	1993-98	90	15	7
Dion Prestia	2017-2018	35	14	3
Andy Preston	1982-83	18	6	28
Dick Price	1912	5	0	13
Joe Price	1911	7	2	x
Syd Price	1909-10	11	7	x
Charlie Priestley	1938-47	109	12	11
Lionel Proctor	1998-2000	20	4	40
Chris Pym	1988-89	24	13	51, 10
Q				
Jack A.Quinn	1940-41	19	14	32
Roy Quinn	1940-41; 1943-44	25	25	25
R				
Keith Rae	1946	2	1	30
Stephen Rae	1973-74	20	11	13
Andrew Raines	2004-09	56	1	38, 4
Geoff Raines	1976-82	134	55	40, 4
Alex Rance	2009-2018	199	9	18
Brian Randall	1941-45	54	36	29
George Rankine	1908	2	0	x
Bob Rees	1959	6	1	34
Syd Reeves	1910-19	110	7	x
Syd Reeves	1910-19	110	7	11
Reuben Reid	1924-26	13	1	15
Ron Reiffel	1951-52	6	0	6
Joe Reilly	1940-42	17	0	34
Doug Reynolds	1958-59	15	2	8
Renato Ricci	1960	2	0	8
Alan G.Richardson	1959-69	103	30	12
Barry Richardson	1965-74	125	134	17
Howard Richardson	1915-17	19	14	8
Matthew Richardson	1993-2009	282	800	12
Ned Richardson	1913-15	28	4	20
Rodger Richardson	1964	1	0	48
John Richmond	1961-64	18	16	48, 4
Charlie Ricketts	1913-14	16	11	6
Jack Riewoldt	2007-2018	249	607	8
Frank Rigaldi	1918	2	1	31
Daniel Rioli	2016-2018	55	51	17
Maurice Rioli	1982-87	118	80	17
Bill Ripper	1935	4	0	28
John Ritchie	1951-55	40	2	35, 30
Bill Roach	1946	1	0	32
Michael Roach	1977-89	200	607	8
Stephen Roach	1978	2	0	56
Thomas Roach	2004-06	11	1	22, 8
Graham Robbins	1969-71	13	9	32
Brian Roberts	1971-74	78	34	15
Jack D.Roberts	1947-50	26	0	11
Ken E.Roberts	1947-51	58	0	33
Michael Roberts	1986	12	4	10
Neville Roberts	1975-77	48	81	15, 2
Relton Roberts	2010	2	0	50
Graeme Robertson	1976-77; 1979; 1981	51	1	24
John Robertson	1961-65	43	1	46, 2
Haydn Robins	1994	4	1	32
Arch Robinson	1911	1	0	x
George Robinson	1925-27	38	16	3
John Robson	1955	6	4	4
David Rodan	2002-04; 2006	65	43	18
Matthew Rogers	1994-2004	197	163	4
Wal Rogers	1914	1	0	27
Michael Rolfe	1983	10	4	11
John Rombotis	1998-2000	13	2	35
John Ronaldson	1965-70	59	33	2
Bradley Ross	1983	1	0	56
George Ross	1923	1	0	24
Noel Ross	1945-47; 1949	35	38	18
Ray Ross	1922	1	0	22
Des Rowe	1946-57	175	24	18, 35, 18, 15
Havel Rowe	1948-57	124	43	3
Joe Rowe	1924	2	1	14
Larry Rowe	1958-61	20	6	31

Name	Played	Games	Goals	No.
Barry Rowlings	1979-86	152	117	22
Billy Rudd	1917-18	21	8	18
George Rudolph	1922; 1924-28	80	61	27, 32
Gerald Rush	1920	15	16	19
Kevin Rush	1923-24	7	4	29
Leo Rush	1912	2	2	25
Wally Russell	1942-43; 1945-48	33	11	14, 8, 4
Damien Ryan	1996-98	30	6	37
Des Ryan	1986-92	56	29	47, 32
Emmett Ryan	1908	12	2	x
Frank Ryan	1951-57	62	4	8
Johnny Ryan	1959	2	0	7
Stan Ryan	1929	14	8	7
Stephen Ryan	1990-93	43	39	48, 8

S

Name	Played	Games	Goals	No.
Col Saddington	1956-62	102	10	26
Alex Salvado	1912	1	2	8
Clay Sampson	1999-2000	27	18	26, 24
Frank Sanguinetti	1908	1	0	x
Paul Sarah	1980-83	37	51	11
Ian Sartori	1982-83; 1985	18	7	25
Richie Saunders	1933-34	8	0	30
Herb Sawatzky	1954-55	7	0	24
Mick Schade	1911	2	1	x
Robert Schaefer	1993	11	3	24
Billy Schmidt	1908-11; 1921	75	71	18
Peter Schofield	1951-53	16	25	11
Jay Schulz	2003-09	71	58	25
Ernie Schunke	1909	6	0	x
Allister Scott	1990-93	19	10	43, 10
Bill H.Scott	1910	1	0	x
Bobby W.Scott	1910-11	12	7	x
Jack Scott	1939-45	86	43	6
Ian Scrimshaw	1976-81	40	26	36
Ray Scriven	1935-38	34	2	25
Sid Searl	1942	3	0	8
Wally Seitz	1949	1	0	35
Roy W.Selleck	1962-64	24	2	51, 22
Robert Semmens	1981	5	0	27
Ron Serich	1961-63	28	36	38
Jimmy Shand	1916-19	40	3	19
Wayne Shand	1982-84	12	1	45
Laurie Sharp	1954-57	41	14	6
John Sheahan	1962; 1965-66	17	11	4
Maurie Sheahan	1929-36	121	3	4
Kevin Sheedy	1967-79	251	91	10
Jack Sheehan	1915; 1917	14	0	28
Percy Sheehan	1912	4	0	24
Ben Sheppard	1912	1	1	?
Peter Sherman	1947	2	0	28
Brian Shinners	1969	2	0	18
Kevin Shinners	1967-68	23	0	18
Jayden Short	2016-2018	56	17	15
Gerry Sier	1950	7	0	6
Ken Sier	1948-50	38	13	25
Jarrod Silvester	2009	5	0	36
Troy Simmonds	2005-10	93	66	5
David John Simpson	1984-85	2	1	41
Tom Simpson	1956-63	126	6	11
Adam Slater	1993; 1995	3	1	49
Frank Slater	1953-55	19	0	16
Lou Sleeth	1937-38	20	22	6
Ian Slockwitch	1961	2	0	40
George Smeaton	1935-42; 1944-46	149	36	24
Anthony R.Smith	1969; 1972	4	1	39, 33
Basil Smith	1924	10	6	30
Bruce Smith	1962; 1964	11	10	27
C. Jimmy Smith	1917-26	132	40	10
Charles Smith	1921-22	3	0	22
Craig Smith	1986-87; 1989-93	72	23	39, 17
Dave Smith	1914	1	3	x
Dennis Smith	1960-61	13	1	42, 6
Harry J.Smith	1938-39	19	2	28
Jason Smith	1991	1	0	50
Kevin James Smith	1964-66	47	3	26
Laird Smith	1939-41; 1945	66	73	8
Percy Smith	1912	4	1	20
Terry Smith	1980-82; 1986	56	15	46, 10, 12
Keith Smythe	1968-70	15	8	26
Ivan Soldo	2017-2018	8	1	47
Jim Spain	1923-25; 1927	40	2	22, 11
Percy Sparks	1909	2	0	x
Percy Speakman	1908	4	4	x
Reefton Spicer	1917-18	3	1	20
Geoff Spring	1948-57	147	63	19
Paul Sproule	1972-75	86	93	6
Greg Stafford	2002-06	74	83	45, 10
Percy Stainer	1908	7	0	x
Les Stainsby	1927	2	2	27
Fred Stammers	1943	1	0	15
Horrie Stanway	1932	1	0	22
Ray Steele	1940-43	42	1	4
Stuart Steele	1993	2	0	32
Tyson Stengle	2017	2	2	44
Jack Stenhouse	1933-34	19	0	26
Orren Stephenson	2013-2014	7	0	37
Bob Stewart	1922	1	0	30
Craig Stewart	1984-86	35	3	32
Ian Stewart	1971-75	78	55	2
Ray Stewart	1915-18	31	0	30, 7
Mark Stockdale	1989; 1991	6	2	49
Jervis Stokes	1948-50	33	32	28
Ray Stokes	1946-51	93	23	27
Hamilton Stokesbury	1915	1	0	x
Ken Stonehouse	1976; 1978	12	4	27
Wilfred Stott	1919-20	9	0	31
Greg Strachan	1978-87	154	8	19
Doug Strang	1931-35	64	180	28
Geoff Strang	1965-71	88	0	28
Gordon Strang	1931-36; 1938	116	108	23
Charlie Street	1928; 1930-31	13	2	22, 5
Gordon Styles	1942-43; 1945	16	1	30, 32, 33
Chris Sullivan	1995-96	8	4	2
Jack Sullivan Elder	1941-43; 1946	31	9	26
Mark Summers	1988-89	15	4	43
Scott Sutcliffe	1986	2	0	18
Daryl Sutton	1982-83	6	0	24
Fred Swift	1958-67	146	41	15
Jack S.Symons	1934-44	111	71	19
Steven Sziller	2001-02	38	3	19

T

Name	Played	Games	Goals	No.
Richard Tambling	2005-10	108	61	30
Gerald Tanner	1941	1	0	28
Jamie Tape	1994-97	75	4	5
Steven Taubert	1974-76	15	14	47, 9
Brian Taylor	1980-84	43	156	21
Ernie Taylor	1920-26	58	2	7
Laurie W.Taylor	1944; 1947	20	48	26, 15
Roy Taylor	1916-18	33	13	12
Troy Taylor	2010	4	3	44
Barry Teague	1966-67	3	1	36
Graham Teasdale	1973	6	16	20
Bruce Tempany	1977-83	87	33	14
James Thiessen	1993	7	3	46
Bill D.Thomas	1914-16; 1918-19	62	3	28, 4
Matt Thomas	2014-2015	15	6	19
Ron Thomas	1969-70	11	0	34
Ewan Thompson	1997	4	1	34
John L.Thompson	1959-63	65	0	37
Murray Thompson	1973; 1976	14	3	23
Adam Thomson	2009-10	4	1	31
Michael Thomson	1987-90	42	15	34
Ron Thornton	1986	8	6	37
Vic Thorp	1910-25	262	7	5
Bill Thorpe	1914	2	2	26
David Thorpe	1974-76	27	24	14
George Threlfall	1919; 1923-24	8	4	7, 28, 19
Will Thursfield	2005-11	77	0	36, 2
Jack Titus	1926-43	294	970	12
Greg Tivendale	1998-2008	188	125	32
Stan Tomlins	1948	12	23	23
Jason Torney	1995-2002	118	16	29
Bill Tottey	1909	3	0	x
Jacob Townsend	2016-2018	19	28	21
Mark Trewella	1991	4	4	36
Barri Trotter	1979	2	0	51
Bruce Tschirpig	1971; 1976	10	12	35, 32
Charlie Tuck	1920	1	0	21
Shane Tuck	2004-2013	173	74	21
Russell Tully	1968	1	0	51
Norm Turnbull	1921-23	34	25	13
Brian C.Turner	1950-52	20	8	28
Jack Turner	1945-47	13	0	26, 6
Scott Turner	1991-99	144	33	41
Frank Twomey	1913-14	3	1	13
Jack Twyford	1931-33	37	14	2

U

Name	Played	Games	Goals	No.
Andrew Underwood	1991	12	4	12
Frank Uwins	1937	1	1	29
Jack Uwins	1937	6	0	9

V

Name	Played	Games	Goals	No.
George Valentine	1924-26	24	4	31
Stan Vandersluys	1953	3	0	6
Royce Vardy	2000-03	34	3	42, 41
Daryl Vernon	1981; 1985	9	3	40, 42
Tyrone Vickery	2009-2016	119	158	29
Nick Vlastuin	2013-2018	117	25	31

W

Name	Played	Games	Goals	No.
Bernie Waldron	1940-45	83	22	13
Bill Walford	1965-66	8	1	48, 13
Harry G.Walker	1912-13	9	5	8
Norman Walker	1957	1	0	27
Robert Walker	1990-92	5	0	51, 23
Matthew Wall	1980-85	60	23	43, 12
Terry Wallace	1987	11	7	16
Bob Walliker	1942	1	0	1
Gerry Walsh	1953	1	0	28
Phillip Walsh	1984-86	40	14	16
Wayne Walsh	1968; 1972-75; 1977-78	88	30	41, 7, 31
Jim Walton	1954-55	20	15	20
George E.Ward	1909	1	0	x
Ken Ward	1956-59	43	0	20
Ross Warner	1963-67	49	45	14
George Waterhouse	1926	7	2	7
Colin Waterson	1978; 1980-81	13	9	53, 12
Carl Watson	1927-31	44	3	22
Clive Watson	1948	4	1	13
Jack Watson	1947-49	18	8	29
Bob Weatherill	1917-23	72	44	15
George Weatherill	1919-23	53	5	28
Harry Weatherill	1919	6	0	19
Kevin Webb	1949	7	0	13
Jeromey Webberley	2010-12	16	3	46
Horrie Weeks	1915	2	3	9
Harry Weidner	1926-32	96	128	13, 7
Dale Weightman	1978-93	274	344	43, 3
Luke Weller	2004	7	3	30
Billy C.Wells	1936-37	23	2	10
Charlie Wells	1912	5	5	21
Peter Welsh	1980-84	46	45	31
Albert Western	1952	4	3	25
Bill White	1941	8	1	35
James White	2000	4	1	31
John J.White	1910	2	3	x
Matt White	2006-2013	105	54	35
Reg Whitehead	1921	2	2	16
Charlie Whitely	1925	1	0	28

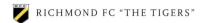

Team photo from Richmond's first-ever VFLW match. Richmond 6.5.41 def Footscray 0.3.3 (May 5 2018) at Whitten Oval.

Back Row: Tom Hunter (coach), Alice Edmonds, Jenna Colwell, Emily Findlay, Ella Ross, Jess Gardner, Trish Muller, Lisa Davie, Bethany Lynch, Kate Dixon (v/capt), Jacinta Louttit, Louise Bieniara
Front Row: Jacqueline Graham, Niamh Clarke, Emma Gunn, Courtney Musico, J Kennedy (capt), Justine Hocking , Kate Dempsey, Vittoriana Tonin, Alana Woodward, Ellie George,
Elise Hogan (v.c.), Evelyn Burry

Name	Played	Games	Goals	No.
Bob Wiggins	1944-51	68	2	3, 33, 29, 26
Stuart Wigney	1995-96	14	1	36
Robert Wiley	1979-83	95	127	2
Graeme Wilkinson	1960-61	29	32	2
Bill R.Williams	1948-49	9	3	12
Charles Williams	1908	3	0	x
Don D.Williams	1959-60	7	0	3
James Williams	1957-58	6	1	3
Peter J.Williams	1979	7	1	28
Shane Williams	1979-83	27	14	9
Gary Williamson	1961-64	42	24	23, 7
Billy P.Wilson	1944-54	185	225	32
Bob J.Wilson	1929	1	0	11
Fred Wilson	1937	7	1	33
John Wilson	1959	6	2	40
Lou Wilson	1913; 1915	4	0	23
Peter Wilson	1987-89	54	39	5, 19
Stan G.Wilson	1949	6	2	6
Trevor Wilson	1970	2	2	56
Brian Winton	1983	10	3	42
Bill Wisdom	1936	2	0	30
Bertie Wollacott	1911	3	3	x
Bryan Wood	1972-82	209	85	37, 16
Fred Wood	1925	3	0	14
Herb Woodhead	1910-12	7	0	x
Stan Wootton	1923	6	1	26
Billy Wright	1922-23	3	0	8, 27
Roy Wright	1946-59	195	127	2
Y				
Stan Yates	1925	5	0	7
Barry Young	1989-93	53	23	53, 20
Cory Young	1989-90	6	1	54, 44
Z				
Ty Zantuck	2000-04	68	20	36
Eric Zschech	1930-35	102	16	25

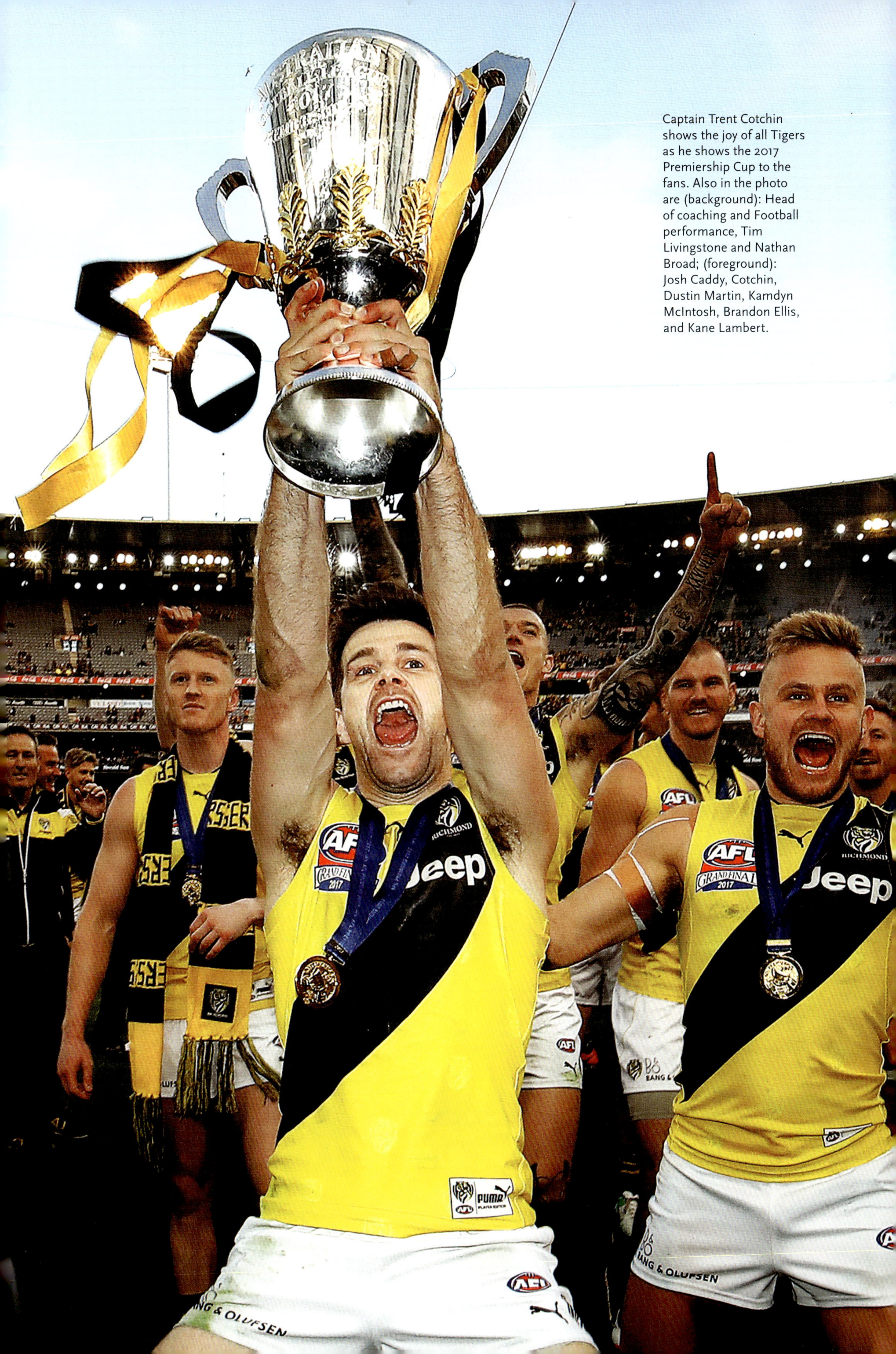

Captain Trent Cotchin shows the joy of all Tigers as he shows the 2017 Premiership Cup to the fans. Also in the photo are (background): Head of coaching and Football performance, Tim Livingstone and Nathan Broad; (foreground): Josh Caddy, Cotchin, Dustin Martin, Kamdyn McIntosh, Brandon Ellis, and Kane Lambert.

The Tiger mascot, circa 1982.

It was a natural decision for Rhett Bartlett to barrack for Richmond, given that he grew up the son of a club icon.

Rhett never saw his dad, Kevin, play; the father retired when the son was four. But when Kevin returned to coach in 1988, nine-year-old Rhett spent most nights at training, sat in on selection committee meetings and, before games, was even sent to spy in opposition dressing rooms! His passion for the Tigers was sealed. When he's not an active member of the Richmond Museum Historical Group, or of the former Players & Officials Association, Rhett is a Learning and Development Trainer. He has also been a key member of the RFC History and Traditions Committee for almost 20 years, and runs *tigerlandarchive.org*, the history of the club online. He is also the author of KB: A Life in Football, the biography of Richmond Immortal, and Australian Football Hall of Fame Legend, Kevin Bartlett.

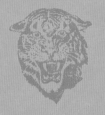

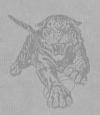

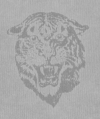

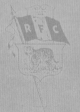

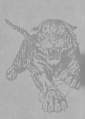

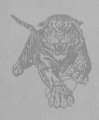